INTERNATIONAL SPORTS LAW

Second Edition

James A.R. Nafziger

Transnational Publishers, Inc.
Ardsley, New York

Published and distributed by Transnational Publishers, Inc.
Ardsley Park
Science and Technology Center
410 Saw Mill River Road
Ardsley, NY 10502

Phone: 914-693-5100
Fax: 914-693-4430
E-mail: info@transnationalpubs.com
Web: www.transnationalpubs.com

Library of Congress Cataloging-in-Publication Data

Nafziger, James A. R.
International sports law / James A.R. Nafziger.—2nd ed.
p. cm.
Includes bibliographical references and index.
ISBN 1-57105-137-6
1. Sports—Law and legislation. 2. Athletes—Legal status, laws, etc.
3. Olympics—Law and legislation. I. Title.

K3702.N34 2004
3444'.099—dc22

2004047982

Manufactured in the United States of America

To my mother,

Charlotte Monona Hamilton Nafziger,

and the memory of my father,

Ralph Otto Nafziger

CONTENTS

LIST OF ABBREVIATIONS

(Includes, *inter alia*, all Olympic Sports Federations)

AAA	American Arbitration Association
AAU	Amateur Athletic Union
ABAUSA	Amateur Basketball Association of the USA
AENOC	Association of European National Olympic Committees
AIBA	International Amateur Boxing Association
ANOC	Association of National Olympic Committees
ANOCA	Association of NOCs of Africa
CAS	Court of Arbitration for Sport
CFA	College Football Association
CGA	Commonwealth Games Association
CYO	Catholic Youth Organization
EC	European Communities
EU	European Union
FEI	International Equestrian Federation
FIBA	International Basketball Federation
FIBT	International Bobsleigh and Tobogganing Federation
FIC	International Canoeing Federation
FIE	International Fencing Federation
FIFA	International Federation of Football Associations
FIG	International Gymnastics Federation
FIH	International Hockey Federation
FIL	International Luge Federation
FILA	International Wrestling Federation
FINA	International Amateur Swimming Federation
FIS	International Ski Federation
FISA	International Rowing Federation
FITA	International Archery Federation
FIVB	International Volleyball Federation
IAAF	International Amateur Athletic Federation
IBAF	International Baseball Federation
IBF	International Badminton Federation
IBU	International Biathlon Union
ICC	International Cricket Council
ICPES	Inter-Governmental Committee for Physical Education and Sport
IF	International Federation
IIHF	International Ice Hockey Federation
IHF	International Handball Federation

IJF	International Judo Federation
ILO	International Labor Organization
IOC	International Olympic Committee
ISAF	International Sailing Federation
ISF	International Softball Federation
ISL	International Sports Leisure
ISSF	International Shooting Sport Federation
ISU	International Skating Union
ITF	International Tennis Federation
ITTF	International Table Tennis Federation
ITU	International Triathlon Union
IWF	International Weightlifting Federation
LAOOC	Los Angeles Olympic Organizing Committee
NAACP	National Association for the Advancement of Colored People
NBA	National Basketball Association
NASCAR	National Association for Stock Car Racing
NCAA	National Collegiate Athletic Association
NCGS	Non-Commonwealth Games Sport
NFL	National Football League
NFSHSA	National Federation of State High School Associations
NGB	National Governing Body
NGO	Non-governmental Organization
NHL	National Hockey League
NOC	National Olympic Committee
NZRFU	New Zealand Rugby Football Union
PCOS	President's Commission of Olympic Sports
PGA	Professional Golfers' Association
PLO	Palestinian Liberation Organization
SAF	Sports Assistance Fund (UK)
TAC	The Athletics Congress (of the USA)
TOP	The Olympic Programme
UCI	International Cycling Union
UEFA	Union of European Football Associations
UIPM	International Modern Pentathlon Federation
UNESCO	United Nations Educational, Scientific and Cultural Organization
USIA	United States Information Agency
USOC	United States Olympic Committee
USWF	United States Wrestling Federation
WADA	World Anti-Doping Agency
WCF	World Curling Federation
WD-AAU	Wrestling Division of the AAU
WFSGI	World Federation of the Sporting Goods Industry
WHO	World Health Organization
WNBA	Women's National Basketball Association
WSF	World Skating Federation
WTF	World Taekwondo Federation

PREFACE TO THE SECOND EDITION

The field of international sports law has been growing and changing rapidly. When the first edition of this book was published in 1988, at the end of the Cold War, political issues dominated the international sports arena. Etched in our recent memory were the terrorist attack at the 1972 Olympic Games in Munich, the reciprocal boycotts of the 1980 Games in Moscow and the 1984 Games in Los Angeles, the exclusion of entire national teams from international competition for reasons of both geopolitics and human rights, and on the plus side, ping-pong diplomacy.

In 1988 the issue of doping was emerging, but it, too, had a political cast. What mattered were suspicions about East German and Russian and other East bloc athletes and not a more general concern about the growing use of steroids everywhere, gene therapy, and other performance-enhancing agents in sports. In addition to political issues, the distinction between amateur and professional athletes still played a significant role in defining eligibility for competition. Open international competition was still novel. Human rights issues had emerged full-blown, but progress had been frustratingly slow, for example, in leveraging sports competition against apartheid in South Africa despite an embargo on participation by South African athletes in international competition. Nor had the process of international sports law come a very long way toward gender equality in international competition.

Growing commercialization of the sports arena had become visible in 1988, but was viewed more as a threat to the purity of competition that needed to be prohibited than as an inevitable development, and a source of support for athletic development and activity, that needed to be regulated. Then, in 1990, during the Asian Games in Beijing, a giant helium-filled balloon advertising M&M candies bobbed up and down over Workers Stadium. In a match apparently between nationalism and commercialism, members of the Chinese balloon cadre dedicated themselves to keeping the balloon lower to avoid competing for attention with the Chinese flag, to which Mars candy representatives promptly responded by hoisting the balloon up again so that it would fall within range of stadium television cameras. The metaphor was poignant. The lofty demands of nationalism and the rising surge of commercialism conspired to steal attention away from the sports event itself.

Today, five critical issues overshadow the international sports arena: doping, the rights of athletes and eligibility requirements, dispute resolution, corruption and subjectivity of judges and referees, and commercial matters such as ambush marketing, broadcast rights, and intellectual property law. Political issues still occur in the international arena, as in the controversy that followed the Baltimore Oriole's trip to Havana in 1999 for a game with the Cuban National Team. But political issues are not what they used to be. For example, a women's football (soccer) match between North Korean and American teams in the United States is hardly a cause célèbre anymore.

Happily, a distinct regime of international sports law has evolved in response to the ever-changing issues. Happily, too, the old and ultimately sterile debate about whether the term "sports law," in a fully integrated sense, or "sports and the law" better describes the relationship just does not exist in the international sports arena. Despite the complexity of the constituent institutions, the regime of international sports law, though incomplete, is coherent and fully conjoined.

Change, however, is the essence of sports. Not only have the issues and legal processes changed dramatically since the first edition of this book, but the sources of the law and the elements of legal style have also evolved. The Olympic Charter has been substantially revised and reconfigured, national legislation has been recodified, and that most puzzling of authorities, THE BLUEBOOK: A UNIFORM SYSTEM OF CITATION, has changed its rules. Because of the changed rules, readers will notice a compromise between old and new formats in order to provide efficient yet sufficient references to source material.

Mere mention of the BLUEBOOK is a reminder that this book is the product of an American pen. Although the integrity of international sports law withstands national distortion, the majority of examples and case studies in this book are those with which I am most familiar. Canadian, European, East Asian and scattered other national examples globalize the presentation, but I have rejected a surface eclecticism in favor of case studies for deeper analysis of key issues. My hope is that others will benefit from my greater focus on American jurisprudence, by way of example, just as I have appreciated commentary by writers from other legal systems that tend to emphasize football (soccer), cricket, field hockey, and other sports that are less visible in the United States. Without intending to slight the significance of the World Cup, EUFA, and other prominent institutions in the football (soccer) pantheon, for example, I gladly defer to the trenchant analysis of such topics by better-positioned scholars from other legal systems. On the other hand, I have spared readers undue attention to such American curiosities as college football, made-for-television wrestling, and surfboarding.

Several students ably assisted me in preparing this second edition: Juan Aguiar, Carlos Moncayo Castillo, Jana Drajpuch, and Mary Rooklidge. Stasinos Stavrianeas offered invaluable insights and suggestions for my revision of Chapter 8, and Li Wei was an exemplary collaborator on the study of China's Sports Law in Appendix II. I am especially grateful to Kathy Marbut for her adroit skill in processing a jumbled manuscript that, at best, reflected the complexities of the legal developments it recorded. She has set new records for speed, accuracy and endurance. Any errors are mine.

Salem, Oregon
April 2004

James A.R. Nafziger

PREFACE TO THE FIRST EDITION

The subject of this book has been a moving target for a number of years. The elements of international sports law, perhaps as in any new field of inquiry, are a bit like chips in a kaleidoscope. The law looks a little different each time. Much of the excitement, challenge, and occasional frustration of studying international law in action has therefore been mine. In writing the book I have tried to bring the evolving law into a stable focus, to cabin what George Eliot referred to as the "tempting range of relevancies called the universe."

Who knows what's next in this field of law? Despite a relatively stable framework at the moment, change abounds. Global politics, in particular, challenge the law. As this book goes to press, for example, one can only hope that the nationalism roiling around a sharply divided Korean peninsula will not defeat one of the world's most visible experiments in cross-cultural association and cooperation, the Olympic Games. In too many instances states have dominated athletes on the global playing fields, and as between states and athletes, the fields are anything but level. Perhaps that is what we should expect if we are going to refer to states as "international actors."

I am grateful to many persons for their encouragement and assistance in the preparation of this book. Professor D.H.N. Johnson of the University of Sydney has been a generous friend and colleague who bolstered my conviction that law does indeed play a role in international sports. David contributed particularly and immeasurably to my understanding of developments within the British Commonwealth. I'm not sure I understand the game of cricket any better than I did when David and I began to correspond several years ago, but that is no fault of his. Professor Oscar Schachter first put me in touch with David and encouraged me to write on the legal aspects of international sports. I am also grateful to Andrew Strenk for his framework to analyze the political uses of sport and for his collaboration and co-authorship of an article that further defined that framework, which I have used in Chapter VI. Conrad Hutterli provided invaluable assistance in preparing Chapter IX, Cindy Hogan in several phases of research and Douglas Robertson in preparing Chapter II. Katharyn Dunham has been a most insightful and congenial editor.

In reconciling inconsistencies in the primary materials of my research, I have deferred to more or less official spellings, for example, "Bye-Laws" or "By-Laws," depending on a particular organization's own preference. I have also deferred to official practices, for example, the United States Olympic Committee's reliance on the 1985 version of the Olympic Charter. This book draws upon and includes excerpts from several of my published articles, which are listed in the bibliography and for the use of which here I am most grateful to the original publishers. In completing the manuscript, perhaps I did not, with Justice Holmes, "catch an echo of the infinite," but I did catch more than a glimpse of the "unfathomable [word] process." I am indebted to Penelope Hunter, Jolie Presley, Colleen Spedale and Pam Warden for their stenographic skills and patience.

Finally, I would like to express my appreciation to the Rockefeller Foundation. As a Scholar-in-Residence at its Bellagio Study and Conference Center, where truly, "to write and read comes by nature," I found the inspiration, time and environment to do much of the book that follows.

Salem, Oregon
March 1988

James A.R. Nafziger

CHAPTER 1
INTRODUCTION

Law guides and constrains international sports activity. That should not be surprising. If there is law where there is society, the legal process can be expected to play a significant role in helping to meet people's expectations about an activity as prominent and universal as athletics. The public appreciates the need for legal intervention into the sports arena. Whenever the dream of pure competition degenerates into a nightmare of politics, doping of athletes, or spectator violence, for example, the public clamors for more effective legal controls. Today, a growing body of international sports law is on track. It is still young and growing, but capable of going the distance. What are its sources and content? What problems does it address? How does it work and how well does it work?

A. THE PROCESS OF INTERNATIONAL SPORTS LAW

1. Fundamentals; The Olympic Movement

The term "international sports law" refers to a process that comprises a more or less distinctive body of rules, principles, institutions and procedures to govern important consequences of transnational sports activity.[1] As a body of international law, it draws upon the general sources of law that are identified in the most widely accepted checklist, Article 38 of the Statute of the International Court of Justice.[2] The process of international sports law thus includes provisions of international

[1] For a discussion of the term "international sports law" see BASIC DOCUMENTS OF INTERNATIONAL SPORTS ORGANIZATIONS xi–xii (Siekmann & Soek eds., 1998).

[2] The full text of Article 38 is as follows:

1. The Court, whose function is to decide in accordance with international law such disputes as are submitted to it, shall apply:

   a. international conventions, whether general or particular, establishing rules expressly recognized by the contesting states;

   b. international custom, as evidence of a general practice accepted as law;

   c. the general principles of law recognized by civilized nations;

   d. subject to the provisions of Article 59, judicial decisions and the teachings of the most highly qualified publicists of the various nations, as subsidiary means for the determination of rules of law.

2. This provision shall not prejudice the power of the Court to decide a case *ex aequo et bono*, if the parties agree thereto. Art. 38, Statute of the International Court of Justice.

Although Article 38 was intended to define the scope of governing law in disputes before the Permanent Court of International Justice, the judicial organ of the League of Nations, it was transplanted into the Statute of the International Court of Justice in the United Nations organi-

agreements; international custom, as evidence of a general practice accepted as law; general principles (including equity and general principles articulated in the resolutions of international organizations); and, as subsidiary sources, judicial decisions (including those of both international and national tribunals) and scholarly writings.

Of particular significance is the Olympic Charter,[3] which codifies general principles, custom, and authoritative decisions applicable to international sports competition ranging far beyond the Olympic Games. The Olympic Charter thereby forms the normative foundation of international sports law.[4] Although the acceptance of its authority is not universal, and violations of its rules are all too common, the fundamental principles and operational rules of the Olympic Charter satisfy the requirements of international custom—repetition, duration and universality of practice, together with an adherence to the rules as legal authority (*opinio juris*).

Within the process of international sports law, the dominant institutional framework is the Olympic Movement, which, according to the Olympic Charter, "encompasses organizations, athletes and other persons who agree to be guided by the Olympic Charter."[5] Although the process of international sports law is more comprehensive than the Olympic Movement—incorporating judicial decisions, for example—the first two chapters will focus primarily on the institutions governed directly by the Olympic Charter. Other chapters will also confirm the central role of the Olympic Movement.

---

zation. Gradually, it became accepted more generally as a definitive list of formal sources of international law. Some experts argue that the text needs updating. For example, it does not specifically mention the resolutions and decisions of international organizations or aggregated "soft law" sources such as declarations by international organizations. Article 38 is nevertheless useful as a kind of shorthand, universally accepted restatement of the general sources of international law, regardless of the particular decision-making context.

[3] International Olympic Committee, OLYMPIC CHARTER (2003). The Charter's Fundamental Principles, Rules and Bye-laws govern a broad range of athletic objectives, activities, and initiatives under the leadership of the International Olympic Committee.

[4] CHAMPION, SPORTS LAW IN A NUTSHELL 249 (2d ed. 2000). *See* Martin v. IOC, 740 F.2d 670, 677 (9th Cir. 1984) ("The Olympic Games are organized and conducted under the terms of an international agreement—the Olympic Charter. We are extremely hesitant to undertake the application of one state's statute to alter an event that is staged with competitors from the entire world under the terms of that agreement"). One reflection of the status of the Olympic Charter in international legal relations is a provision in the Code of Ethics binding on "[t]he Olympic parties" by which they agree to help maintain harmonious relations with state authorities based on the principles of universality and political neutrality under the Olympic Charter. International Olympic Committee, CODE OF ETHICS, OLYMPIC REV., Aug.–Sept. 1999, at 15–16.

[5] OLYMPIC CHARTER, Fundamental Principle 5. "The goal of the Olympic Movement is to contribute to building a peaceful and better world by educating youth through sport practised without discrimination of any kind and in the Olympic spirit, which requires mutual understanding with a spirit of friendship, solidarity and fair play." OLYMPIC CHARTER, Fundamental Principle 6.

The Olympic Movement performs three principal functions: It provides the framework for planning and supervising association and competitions among athletes, serves as a nucleus or catalyst for the development of international sports law, and provides a foundation for managing the legal process. It is important to understand that, despite the obvious, intended identification of the term "Olympic" with the Olympic Games,[6] the role of the Movement has evolved to encompass much broader objectives that are set forth in the Olympic Charter. Together, the pertinent institutions and persons have played a dominant role in defining, implementing and enforcing a distinctive regime of authority and legitimacy. It is also important to understand that, as the institutional and legal significance of the distinction between "professional" and "amateur" competition has largely disappeared, virtually all international sports activity is in some way affected by the Olympic Movement. Of course, important aspects of competition (anti-trust) law, labor law, the law of obligations (contract and tort law), and civil rights remain within the reserved domain of national law and regulation. More and more, however, the global process of international sports law widens.

In performing the functions prescribed by its Charter, the institutions of the Olympic Movement rely on a continuous program of planning, supervising, regulating, promoting and protecting sports activity, highlighted in the global spotlight by staging the quadrennial Games. Its structure embraces the International Olympic Committee (IOC),[7] international sports federations (IFs), national Olympic committees (NOCs), the organizing committees of the Olympic Games (OCOGs), national associations, clubs, athletes, judges, referees, coaches, other sports technicians, and "other organizations and institutions as recognized by the IOC"[8] such as the International Paralympic Committee.

The "supreme authority"[9] of the Olympic Movement is the International Olympic Committee, headquartered in Lausanne, Switzerland. It is defined for

---

[6] "The Olympic Games consist of the Games of the Olympiad and the Olympic Winter Games. Both take place every four years. . . ." OLYMPIC CHARTER, Rule 9. Winter sports are defined as "[t]hose sports which are practiced on snow and ice." *Id.*

[7] OLYMPIC CHARTER, Rule 1 provides as follows:

(1) The IOC is the supreme authority of the Olympic Movement.

(2) Any person or organization belonging in any capacity whatsoever to the Olympic Movement is bound by the provisions of the Olympic Charter and shall abide by the decisions of the IOC.

Rule 2, *id.*, lists 16 principal functions of the IOC. Rule 9(2), *id.*, provides that "[t]he authority of last resort on any question concerning the Olympic Games rests in the IOC." For an example of IOC enforcement of its rules against IFs, *see* OLYMPIC REV., Sept.–Oct. 1989, at 441 (requiring, on the eve of dramatic change in South Africa, that the International Tennis Federation (ITF) comply with all rules of the Olympic Charter, so as to necessitate the ITF's suspension of its "recognition of" South Africa).

[8] OLYMPIC CHARTER, Rule 3(1).

[9] OLYMPIC CHARTER, Rule 1.

legal purposes as an "international non-governmental non-profit organization of unlimited duration, in the form of an association with the status of a legal person, recognized by the Swiss Federal Council."[10] The IOC's mission is "to lead the Olympic Movement in accordance with the Olympic Charter."[11] The charisma and high visibility of the Olympic Games help explain the IOC's unusual influence in the legal process. It is a good example of the role of some non-governmental organizations in the functional process of international integration and progressive development of international law.[12]

2. The Authority and Legitimacy of the Process

Against this distinctive institutional background, we can begin to see that international sports law, "by contrast with other fields of law, is developing under its own steam."[13] Despite its peculiar institutional and normative underpinnings, however, the process of international sports law enjoys recognition by states and intergovernmental organizations. Sometimes the recognition is judicial. As a judge of the International Court of Justice has noted, "the *sui generis* law of the Olympic Movement [is] accepted, respected and applied as a State-independent body of legal rules in a growing number of municipal court decisions."[14] Sometimes

---

[10] *Id.*, Rule 19.

[11] *Id.*

[12] Another example is the International Committee of the Red Cross, also a Swiss-chartered non-governmental organization that serves as the chosen instrument under international law to implement the humanitarian rules of the laws of war. A seminal study of this type of functionalism is HAAS, BEYOND THE NATION STATE: FUNCTIONALISM AND INTERNATIONAL ORGANIZATION (1964). The literature today on the global civic culture and the role of non-governmental organizations in the international legal process is vast.

[13] M. BELOFF, T. KERR & M. DEMETRIOU, SPORTS LAW 5 (1999). This valuable commentary continues as follows:

> [The] powerful mixture of international competition, commercial interest and public demand is fueling the development of legal doctrines particular to sport in a manner which marks sports law as inherently international in character. Its normative underpinning derives not from any treaty entered into between sovereign states, but from international agreements between bodies, many of which are constitutionally independent of their national governments—particularly the Olympic Charter and the rules of the various international governing bodies in sport. Thus sports law is not just international; it is non-governmental as well, and this differentiates it from all other forms of law.

Id. For an elaboration of the discussion that follows in this section, *see* Nafziger, *International Sports Law: A Replay of Characteristics and Trends*, 86 AM. J. INT'L L. 489 (1992).

[14] Simma, *The Court of Arbitration for Sport*, *in* VÖLKERRECHT/RECHT DER INTERNATIONALEN ORGANISATIONEN/WELT-WIRTSCHAFTSRECHT: FESTSCHRIFT FÜR IGNAZ SEIDL HOHENVELDERN 573, 580 (K.-H. Böckstiegel, H.-E. Folz, J.M. Mössmer & K. Zemanek eds., 1988). *Accord*, Silance, *Interaction of the rules in sports law and the laws and treaties made by public authorities*, OLYMPIC REV., Oct. 1977, at 619, 628 ("National jurisdictions and the highest [European] Community jurisdiction have recognized the value of sports rules laid down by the relevant International Federations and consequently admitted the existence of sports juridical orders. . . . The law of the State, whether national or Community, gives way before the law of sport in its own domain.").

the recognition is statutory. National legislation may accord monolithic control over a particular sport to a national governing body, which is then bound by rules and decisions within the Olympic Movement, including the IFs and NOCs. Under the Amateur Sports Act[15] of the United States, for example, "the organizing of competition under the auspices of the International Olympic Committee (IOC)" is "central" to the "governing structures for American involvement in international amateur competition."[16] In other countries, rules and regulations of international sports federations have supplied the norms to govern comprehensive sports activity and business as a special application of broader legislation.[17] Sometimes recognition of the process of international sports law is executive, as in the case of Kuwaiti recognition of the Olympic Council of Asia as an international organization with full diplomatic immunity.[18]

In a very real sense, then, international sports law, shaped by the Olympic Movement, is the chosen instrument of states and international organizations in the arena of sports.[19] Although the constituent non-governmental institutions and persons cannot alone compel governmental compliance,[20] their rules, regulations and decisions help determine state practice and best articulate the accepted regime of international sports law.

---

[15] Ted Stevens Olympic and Amateur Sports Act, 36 U.S.C. §§ 220501–220529 (2000) [hereinafter Amateur Sports Act].

[16] Behagen v. Amateur Basketball Ass'n of U.S., 884 F.2d 524 (10th Cir. 1989). *See also* Burrows v. Ohio High School Athletic Ass'n, 891 F.2d 122 (6th Cir. 1989); *accord*, Oldfield v. Athletic Congress, 779 F.2d 509 (9th Cir. 1985).

[17] For example, in Russia eligibility for licensing as a football player's agent must generally conform with the Players' Agents Regulations (2000) of FIFA, the international federation of football (soccer) associations. New legislation responding to post-Soviet privatization of sports agents requires cooperation among sports federations, state bodies, and insurance companies. *See* Loukine, *Legal Regulation of Sports Agents' Activity in the Russian Federation, in* INTERNATIONAL SPORTS LAW & BUSINESS IN THE 21ST CENTURY, Panel 5 (2003).

[18] *See* OLYMPIC REV., July–Aug.–Sept. 2003, at 25.

[19] *See, e.g., Recent Developments*, 25 STAN. J. INT'L L. 611, 616 (1989) ("Thus, although the IOC has neither a foundation under international law nor a membership that includes states or subjects of international law, many members of the international community have treated it as if it indeed had international personality"); Comment, *International Sports: Have States Succeeded Athletes as the Players?*, 6 DICK. J. INT'L L. 403, 424 (1988); Note, *Political Abuse of Olympic Sport: De Frantz v. United States Olympic Committee*, 14 N.Y.U. J. INT'L L. & POL. 155, 162 (1981) ("Despite its nongovernmental status, the IOC has been vested with substantial legal authority; it engages in extensive diplomatic activity and is a vital authority on intergovernmental affairs"). Silance, *supra* note 14, at 622 (Olympic sport "forms an extra-juridical order"); *accord*, Bondoux, *Law and Sport*, OLYMPIC REV., Aug.–Sept. 1978, at 494, 501; Garrigues, *The Impact of Community Law on Physical and Sports Activities*, OLYMPIC REV., June 1979, at 345. Concerning the Olympic Charter's influence on governmental decision-making, *see* Siperco, *On the Right Road to Co-operation*, OLYMPIC REV., Sept.–Oct. 1989, at 454.

[20] Effective enforcement of IOC rules requires persistent arm-twisting: "At the summit of the sports world sits the IOC. But, unlike Zeus of old, the IOC has few thunderbolts to command obedience. Instead it must negotiate, mainly with several kinds of official bodies [generally

The overall process of rule-making and enforcement "on the fringe of public international law"[21] might be classified as an "international regime,"[22] "true international law,"[23] "*droit des gens*,"[24] "transnational common law,"[25] or perhaps simply "transnational law." The label would not seem to be terribly important. What is important in understanding the structure and force of international sports law is to take account of the interdependence of public and private authority and of the emerging role of complex legal processes that blend governmental and non-governmental authority.[26] This structure reveals very clearly the "declining reliability of formal criteria of international law as guideposts to its constitution and the discrepancy between formal status and legal significance."[27] The most challenging and significant questions do not involve labeling,[28] but rather prioritiz-

---

within the Olympic Movement]." W. IRWIN, JR., THE POLITICS OF INTERNATIONAL SPORT—GAMES OF POWER 23 (1988).

21 Johnson, *Book Review*, 60 BRIT. Y.B. INT'L L. 450, 451 (1989).

22 "[T]he networks of principles, norms, rules and decision-making institutions that help stabilize state relationships in various issue areas." Farer, *Human Rights in Law's Empire: The Jurisprudence War*, 85 AM. J. INT'L L. 117, 124 (1991).

23 Vedder, *The International Olympic Committee: An Advanced Non-Governmental Organization and the International Law*, 27 GER. Y.B. INT'L L. 233, 256 (1984). ("the IOC . . . can be regarded as exercising quasi-governmental functions. Hence, an internationally autonomous legal order has been established, which, although not public international law, is true international law"). The author, a leading commentator on international sports law, provides an illuminating analysis of the status of the IOC. He notes that although the IOC cannot by itself generate public international law, states have recognized its autonomy "as an implied delegation of governmental functions in sports. [T]he crucial point is that it acts autonomously and independent [sic] of state governments and has to maintain this autonomy." *Id.* Further, "[w]hen states began discovering international sports as a matter of governmental domain, they found themselves confronted with an already existing organization, the IOC. It may very well be concluded, that governments, by not interfering with IOC matters, intend the IOC to continue operating autonomously on an international level, including having relations to states on equal terms." *Accord*, Silance, *supra* note 14, at 622, 628.

24 *See, e.g.*, Verdross, *Le Fondement du Droit des Gens*, 16 RECUEIL DES COURS 251 (1927-I). For an introduction to the seminal work of Georges Scelle on the *droit des gens*, *see* Thierry, *The Thought of Georges Scelle*, 1 EUR. J. INT'L L. 193 (1990) (followed by informative commentary on Scelle's work by Cassese, Condorelli, Dupuy and Tanca).

25 Chiba, *Sports as a Sub-Culture and Supra-Culture*, 1994 J. BEHAVIORAL & SOC. SCI., No. 3, at 225, 236, 238.

26 On these characteristic processes of modern international law, *see, e.g.*, Janis, *International Law?*, 32 HARV. INT'L L.J. 363, 370, 372 (1991).

27 Remarks by Günther Handl, 1988 PROC. AM. SOC. INT'L L. 372 (1990). On the merits and influence of soft law in the context of environmental issues, *see also* Palmer, *New Ways to Make International Environmental Law*, 86 AM. J. INT'L L. 259, 269–70 (1992) ("Considering that the system is somewhat short of means for establishing norms, it would be a great mistake to get too excited from an analytical point of view about the dangers of soft law. It has the capacity to make an important contribution and in the global environmental area it has already done so. . . . It is a vital part of the continuous process of building norms." *Id.* at 270).

28 *But see* Summerer, Book Review, 50 ZEITSCHRIFT FÜR VÖLKERRECHT 162 (1990). Defending

ing, harmonizing and enforcing pertinent rules and procedures on a more effective, pragmatic basis. It is instructive, therefore, to observe the law in action and, from that perspective, to attempt to define significant trends.

In no small measure international sports competition takes place on a grand scale and issues are routinely resolved because of this relatively stable, though incomplete, legal process. Rules and principles indisputably shape the organization and administration of global athletics. International sports law, however soft it sometimes may be, offers a well-articulated, comprehensive means of promoting and protecting the essential values of sports competition. For example, NOCs, often sanctioned by domestic law, must "preserve their autonomy and resist all pressures of any kind, including those of a political, religious or economic nature that may prevent them from complying with the Olympic Charter."[29] Rules and Principles of the Olympic Charter govern decisions of IFs and NOCs to which regional, domestic and eventually local sports authorities defer. In that way, applicable rules and procedures of international sports law eventually permeate purely domestic competition as well.

The centrality of Olympic aspirations in the commitment and training of athletes at all levels of development is an essential point in understanding the expansive role of international sports law. In today's high-tech world of sports, improved performance typically requires professional assistance and money. In response, grass-roots management and funding of training and competition are made available to aspiring athletes through local and national sports associations. These associations operate at the base of a pyramid of authority with the IFs and the IOC at the top. This structure for transmitting the authority and legitimacy of the Olympic process influences even schoolyard and sandlot activities whenever aspiring athletes receive support from sanctioned sports organizations that are even indirectly assisted and governed by organizations higher up in the pyramid of the Olympic Movement. Sometimes, funding of athletes, particularly from developing countries, comes directly from sources at the top of the pyramid such

---

an academic dissertation involving selected judicial decisions from four countries, the writer examines international sports law through a prism of either-or labels ("public" vs. "private," "intergovernmental" vs. "non-governmental," hard law vs. no law at all, and so on). This formalistic perspective on the difficult problem of validation seems unrealistic. The writer's emphasis on jurisprudential pedigree and his impatience with the subtleties of authority and legitimacy and with numerous soft elements in the regime of sports law, leave the impression that there is no regime at all. The writer identifies three pertinent ("einschlägig") decisions. Unfortunately, two of these decisions were later reexamined in the courts and the third decision was reversed well before publication of this polemic. Significantly, the appellate conclusion of one of the cases, Behagen v. Amateur Basketball Ass'n of U.S., 884 F.2d 524 (10th Cir. 1989), emphasized both the public role of a designated private association that is not a governmental actor under U.S. constitutional law and the centrality of the IOC in "governing structures for American involvement in international amateur sports." *Behagen* at 527.

[29] Olympic Charter, Rule 31(5).

as Olympic Solidarity.[30] National governments, committed to the Olympic Movement or influenced by it, often assist directly in this transmission of rules and decisions.

The agencies of transmission vary among countries. In some, the process is confined to a strictly non-governmental hierarchy, from the IOC down through IFs and NOCs to national federations and finally to local associations. In other states, national legislation, pronouncements of sports ministries or national commissions, and judicial decisions may involve governments more directly. Through these various channels, Olympic rules and decisions normally constitute either an autonomous regime to which national governments defer or international custom practiced by them.

Although international sports law crystallized around an Olympic nucleus, other institutions have also contributed to the formation of the law. These include national governments, whose foreign sports policies influence the formation of law and often aggregate into custom; political groupings, such as the (British) Commonwealth of Nations; and international organizations, such as the specialized agencies of the United Nations that have been instrumental in combating forms of discrimination such as apartheid in South Africa and in promoting education, health, and a safe environment.

The process of international sports law, though coherent, is still incomplete. Numerous sports-related problems—commercial transactions for the sale of sports equipment, anti-trust implications of sports organizations and constraints on the freedom of athletes, questionable employment practices affecting athletes, personal injuries on the playing field, and so on—remain largely the province of domestic law, under traditional headings, and therefore fit rather poorly on the map of international sports law. Sometimes other bodies of international law fill the gap. For example, the issue sometimes arises whether domestic anti-trust law and taxing authority should be applied extraterritorially to reach professional teams, athletes, and events abroad. Such issues have generally been resolved under international agreements, such as double taxation treaties, or under the normal rules of private international law that govern jurisdiction, choice of law, and enforcement of foreign judgments.

---

[30] Under OLYMPIC CHARTER, Rule 8:

1. The aim of Olympic Solidarity is to organize aid to NOCs recognized by the IOC, in particular those which have the greatest need of it. This aid takes the form of programmes elaborated jointly by the IOC and the NOCs, with the technical assistance of the IFs, if necessary.
2. All such programmes are administrated by the Olympic Solidarity Commission which is chaired by the President of the IOC.

Funding for the developmental programs is in excess of $100 million for each (quadrennial) Olympiad. *See* summary of "Olympic Solidarity Programs" in *World Conference on Education and Sport for a Culture of Peace*, OLYMPIC REV., Aug.–Sept. 1999, at 43–45.

As new kinds of problems develop, so does the legal framework. A good example involves the establishment of a comprehensive regime to govern the rampant problem of doping and drug abuse by athletes. Similarly, the law has expanded to embrace professional sports. As open competitions have become standard and the line between amateurism and professionalism has largely disappeared, commercial issues have become more prominent in the emerging process. Related issues now loom large, such as broadcasting rights, taxation of athletes, and trademark infringements.[31] Nevertheless, the main body of international sports law does not effectively address many issues, from player-contracting to anti-trust aspects of athletic activity. That may change as the law continues to develop.

B. THE IMPORTANCE OF INTERNATIONAL SPORTS LAW

1. The Stakes

The image of lawyers rushing into the international sports arena is as unappealing as watching them chase after ambulances. Nevertheless, because sports events assume heroic proportions in the public limelight, related problems may be big and complex. The stakes are huge. Resolving such problems requires the skills of lawyers and policy-makers alike.

The problems are big and complex partly because the public worships athletics. In response to the problems, sports ministries and non-governmental sports organizations alike often make important political decisions *ex cathedra*. With customary wit, a distinguished jurist, The Lord Wilberforce, referred to the "excommunication" of offending countries by today's "one true world religion," the Olympic Games.[32] At the least, sports competition could be fairly described as a leading folk religion; indeed, sportswriters often use words such as "sacrifice," "faith," "hope," and "glory."

The significance of sports in global affairs is profound. In the words of Juan Antonio Samaranch, former President of the International Olympic Committee, sports activity is "the largest social force of our time."[33] Indeed, "[n]o other modern social event makes people feel so strongly that they belong to a global village."[34] The globalization or internationalization of sports, driven substantially by market forces and profit motives, has several dimensions:

---

31 *See generally*, Ch. 7, *infra* text accompanying notes 73–102.

32 The Lord Wilberforce, *The Age of the International Lawyer*, 76 PROC. AM. SOC. INT'L L. 301, 302 (1982).

33 OLYMPIC REV., Mar. 1984, at 156. The same year another observer suggested that the Olympics are "the closest approximation to a truly global ritual system that humankind has yet generated." MacAloon, *La Pitada Olimpica: Puerto Rico International Sport and the Constitution of Politics*, in TEXT, PLAY AND STORY (Bruner ed., 1984). A scholar of sports law has emphasized the manifest and extraordinary power of organized sport ("le pouvoir manifeste et extraodinaire du sport organisé"). Will, *Les structures du sport international*, CHAPITRES CHOISIS DU DROIT DU SPORT 21 (1993).

34 Mayor, *Peace Without Victory*, UNESCO Courier, Apr. 1999, at 9.

1. an ever increasing number of international sporting events;
2. sporting events held in a country outside of the normal geographic area (home turf) of sports teams and athletes;
3. players and athletes moving from a club or team in one country to one in another country;
4. in team sports, expansion to include teams from other countries;
5. the creation of new multinational leagues;
6. teams in one country "affiliating" with teams in another country;
7. international sports marketing, in all of its various forms;
8. technical and other assistance being given by leagues or teams in one country to their counterparts in other countries;
9. sports clinics, training programs, seminars, tours, etc. conducted by organizations from one country in other countries;
10. international television and media arrangements;
11. international sports marketing of many kinds.[35]

The sheer scope of the Olympic Games, in particular, demonstrates the significance of international sports competition. Over 10,000 athletes from nearly 200 countries normally compete in the Summer Games. Some 400 events in 35 sports define The Olympics. Revenue from ticket sales alone normally exceeds $100 million. Business enterprises pay millions of dollars for official designation of their products. Rights to broadcast the Olympic Games, which first exceeded U.S. $1 billion in 1994, have soared to about U.S. $2.5 billion in 2006 and 2008.[36] In the United States alone, the NBC television network contracted to pay $793 million to broadcast the 2004 Games in Athens and $894 million for the 2008 Games in Beijing.[37] The broadcast and print media have been estimated to include half the world's population.[38] Not surprisingly, the broadcast media heavily influence scheduling of athletic events, public responses, and other aspects of international sports competition.

The 1984 Games in Los Angeles, though boycotted by several NOCs, dramatically changed the commercial stakes of major competition. To take just one example, the price tag for ABC broadcasting rights jumped nine times, from $25 million for the 1976 Games in Montreal to $225 million in Los Angeles (the 1980 Games in Moscow were not broadcast in the United States market because of the United States boycott of those Games). The 1984 Games, breaking with tradition, reaped such a huge profit that the United States Olympic Committee (USOC) had to find a way to make use of it.[39] Two years later the USOC announced that it

---

[35] A. WISE & B. MEYER, INTERNATIONAL SPORTS LAW AND BUSINESS 581 (1997).

[36] Lefort & Harvey, *What's In a Game?*, UNESCO COURIER, Apr. 1999, at 18.

[37] CHRISTIAN. SCI. MONITOR, Aug. 23, 2000, at 20.

[38] Segrave, *The (Neo) modern Olympic Games*, 35 INT'L REV. SOC. SPORT, No. 3, at 168 (2000).

[39] The Los Angeles Olympic Organizing Committee announced initially a profit of "at least

would establish a "Friendship Fund" for the distribution of some $1 million to other national committees in proportion to the number of their athletes at the 1984 Games; in addition, the USOC announced that it would disburse an additional $3.2 million for other use within the Olympic Movement.[40]

The quadrennial World Cup in football (soccer) also involves mammoth financial stakes. An estimated 33.4 billion people viewed the 1998 World Cup on television. Not surprisingly, television broadcast rights for the 2002 and 2006 World Cup spectacles, totaling U.S. $1.7 billion, increased eight times from the package deal for the previous three championships. Corporate sponsorships were reported to cost up to U.S. $45 million apiece.[41]

International competition has also had significant political dimensions and legal consequences. Several examples will illustrate this point. The terrorist kidnaping and murder of athletes at the 1972 Olympic Games in Munich led to a Convention for the Prevention and Punishment of Certain Acts of International Terrorism.[42] Boycotts of the 1980 and 1984 Olympic Games involved a flurry of diplomatic activity and a reconsideration of the efficacy of boycotts as an international sanction. Qualifying matches for the World Cup in soccer became a topic at the 1983 Conference of Nonaligned Nations.[43] In 1985 a wave of violence in the sports world led to several measures, including a European-wide treaty on spectator violence[44] that was drafted and entered into force in the record time of less than three months. The exclusion of South African nationals from international competition contributed to the end of apartheid in that country. China's aspirations to be a sports power[45] eventually led to its enactment of a new sports law[46] and prompted its successful bid to host the 2008 Olympic Games.[47]

$215 million," from which it offered retroactively to pay the expenses of some foreign participants and to make grants for sports programs. CHRISTIAN SCI. MONITOR, Dec. 21, 1984, at 2, col. 4. Final accounting revealed a $225 million profit. L.A. TIMES, Dec. 10, 1985, at 22, col. 1.

40 OLYMPIC REV., Apr.–May 1986, at 238.

41 ECONOMIST, June 1, 2002, at 4.

42 *See* J. MURPHY, THE UNITED NATIONS AND THE CONTROL OF INTERNATIONAL VIOLENCE: A LEGAL AND POLITICAL ANALYSIS 181 (1982).

43 Shaplen, *A Reporter at Large (Conference of Nonaligned Nations)*, 59 NEW YORKER, May 23, 1983, at 82, 94.

44 *European Convention on Spectator Violence and Misbehavior at Sports Events and in Particular at Football Matches*, 24 I.L.M. 1566 (1985).

45 China re-entered the Olympic arena in the 1980 Winter Games. Before the 1980 Winter Games, the Chinese Olympic Committee had last participated in the 1952 Helsinki Games. *See* 16 CHINA SPORTS, May 1984, a special issue on the Chinese reentry into the Olympic arena.

46 *See* CHINA'S SPORTS LAW, Appendix II, *infra*.

47 *See* Ch. 10, *infra* notes 26–29.

2. The Expectations

International sports law helps protect competition against a good deal of unacceptable political and commercial intervention, enhances opportunities for athletes, and ensures a measure of universality, solidarity, fairness and goodwill among athletes. Although law has its limits, it is easy to exaggerate its deficiencies and overlook its efficiencies. Too much can be expected of any body of international law, especially when it is young. If we take a good hard look at the actual practice of states, it is apparent that their actions normally accord with the prescribed rules and procedures of international sports law because the process is respected as such; in other words, they are respected as *opinio juris*.

Can international sports law transcend the competition itself to accomplish lofty goals of world order? One of the Fundamental Principles and one of the Rules of the Olympic Charter commit the Olympic Movement to participate in "actions to promote peace."[48] Generally speaking, however, regulation of international sports competition has been more concerned with the limited tasks of ensuring maximum participation and maintaining minimum order in the sports arena than with larger goals.

Despite the high profile of sports in global affairs and the existence of a corresponding legal framework, a larger role for sports in world affairs is questionable. Reliable analysis is skimpy concerning the controversial theory that sports competition inherently promotes world order. Despite an impressive literature on sports sociology and politics[49] we have few insights into the capacity of international sports events to encourage "the establishment of a peaceful society concerned with the preservation of human dignity" and "to promote peace."[50]

So far, we have little basis for concluding that sports competition contributes substantially to world order or integration. Sport is not a "miracle solution which can neutralize dangerous tension, promote greater freedom and improve human relations."[51] Instead, the contributions of sports activity to world order seem to have been more the unintended consequences of isolated decisions than the results of a deliberate promotion of organizational goals. Nevertheless, as gov-

---

48 OLYMPIC CHARTER, Fundamental Principle 3, Rule 2(4).

49 Noteworthy books on socio-political aspects of sports include R. ESPY, THE POLITICS OF THE OLYMPIC GAMES (1979); A. JOHNSON & J. FREY, GOVERNMENT AND SPORT: THE PUBLIC POLICY ISSUES (1985); K. KANIN, A POLITICAL HISTORY OF THE OLYMPIC GAMES (1981); OLYMPICS AND POLITICS (Kee, Kee, Kyu and Kee eds., 1984); R. LAPCHICK, THE POLITICS OF RACE AND INTERNATIONAL SPORT: THE CASE OF SOUTH AFRICA (1975); LORD KILLANIN, MY OLYMPIC YEARS (1983); J. LUCAS, FUTURE OF THE OLYMPIC GAMES (1992); SPORT AND INTERNATIONAL RELATIONS (B. Lowe, D. Kanin & A. Strenk eds., 1978); J. MEYNAUD, SPORT ET POLITIQUE (1966); and THE OLYMPIC GAMES IN TRANSITION (J. Segrave & D. Chu eds., 1988).

50 OLYMPIC CHARTER, Fundamental Principle 3.

51 UNESCO COURIER, Apr. 1999, at 17.

ernments and international organizations become more concerned with sports, as sports bodies grow stronger and take on more juridical functions, and as techniques develop to implement values that transcend the sports arena, the organization of international sports is becoming more oriented toward world order. This trend is, of course, consistent with the original lofty aspirations of modern sports organizations.

The institutional structure of sports competition facilitates this trend. Rules and procedures that were intended primarily to govern only specific competitions have functioned also in pursuit of larger objectives. For example, the IOC's insistence on racial and gender equality in sports has given greater resonance to global campaigns against racial discrimination. Just hosting major competition may encourage a host state to strengthen the human rights of its citizens in order to avoid foreign opprobrium. The imminence of the 1964 Games in Tokyo helps explain Japan's improvement of trade-union protection; concern about the 1988 Games in Seoul encouraged political reform, including the holding of a presidential election in 1987; and aspirations to host the 2000 (and eventually 2008) Olympic Games prompted China to enact a comprehensive sports law and relax some of its economic and political constraints on citizens. Bilateral techniques of utilizing sports competition, such as the ping-pong diplomacy conducted by the United States and China during the early 1970s and a divided Korea in the 1990s, have had broader implications. In this way, sports events may sometimes be a vital component of world order.

Legal guidance and constraints are not necessarily more important than political, economic, social or cultural ones. In a world of uncertainty it may always be unclear how these constraints relate to each other and which are more important than others in a particular case. What seems clear, however, is the need to bring together the scattered data, norms, rules, principles and procedures of law that do exist; to analyze these; to identify strengths, weaknesses, and gaps in the legal framework; and to offer some guidance to assist in codifying, reforming and progressively developing the law. The law must be dynamic. The Olympic Charter is a case in point, having more than doubled in length and elaboration in the 35 years between 1968 and 2004, for example. Ongoing revisions of the Olympic Charter will be essential in responding to new problems and the growth of international sports law.

C. THE TRACK AHEAD

The panorama of international sports competition is constantly changing, and change revitalizes. It helps to avoid "making cast-iron rituals" out of global sports or routine, laborious "hoops we must pass through."[52] The events themselves must

---

[52] "I wondered, too, about the way we treat planetary sporting occasions, making cast-iron rituals of them, hoops we must pass through. The principal sporting events are designed to show off the players at the top of the ladder formed by all who play that particular game; and, of

evolve. Consider, for example, the following sports: lawn tennis, rackets, roque, lacrosse, tug-of-war, rope climb, Indian club swinging, the 60-meter sprint, five-mile run, 200-meter hurdles, 4,000-meter steeplechase, the shot put with both hands, the javelin throw with both hands, obstacle swimming, underwater swimming, plunge for distance (from a dive, to gain the greatest distance straight forward in the water), polo, rugby, and motor boating. All used to be Olympic events, but no longer are.[53] Star athletes and nations come and go, too. The traditional distinction between amateurs and professionals now seems artificial. New problems emerge. In recent years concerns about doping of athletes and threats of terrorism have plagued the sports world as never before. What will certainly keep such constantly changing activity and problems within acceptable limits are stable institutions and law.

Chapter 2 defines the institutional legal framework of international sports competition, with particular attention to the Olympic Movement; non-Olympic organizations; European and American models of organization; and problems of organizational corruption. Chapter 3 introduces a dominant theme for legal practitioners by defining the general institutional structure of dispute resolution, including the administrative processes of international sports federations as well as the Court of Arbitration for Sport and its emerging *lex sportiva*. Chapter 4 continues this theme by examining the strengths and weaknesses of arbitration and litigation. Several in-depth case studies illustrate the analysis. Chapter 5 explores the resolution of disputes *during* competition by recourse to cameras, computers, and other technology. Chapter 6 shifts the book's focus to substantive issues, with particular attention to the human rights and duties of athletes and their eligibility for competition. Chapter 7 focuses on the problems of doping of athletes, violence, and commercialization, with attention to salient issues of marketing and intellectual property rights.

The concluding chapters of the book focus on the Olympic Games as the dominant context for considering the interrelationships among politics, policy and law in the international sports arena. Chapter 8 offers a brief offers an historical perspective, from the Ancient Games in the Greek city-states to Berlin's propaganda-ridden Games of 1936 as background for an understanding of the political issues that have beset competition. Chapter 9 addresses the topic of national politics and policy options in international sports, using United States sports policy as an example and concluding with a summary of legal constraints under the Olympic Charter. The salience of international politics becomes a premise of

---

course, the games have to be telegenic by nature. Golf has got it just right, and so have tennis, cricket, and baseball—even pool. I don't think soccer quite has. I know it is sporting sacrilege to suggest any departure from the ritual reenactment of our ancestral sports, but surely sports are meant to keep evolving, so why shouldn't they change or have sporting offspring, like all the variant racquet games, like indoor soccer?" Reid, *The Sporting Scene—Mundial Notebook: Ariel v. Caliban*, 62 THE NEW YORKER, Sept. 29, 1986, at 45, 60.

[53] *Stars in Motion* 28, No. 6 (1984).

Chapter 10, which takes a functional approach in examining the divergent political uses of sport. Chapter 11 focuses on the issues specifically related to boycotts, a political phenomenon that loomed particularly large and ominous in international sports relations during the era of the Cold War and apartheid in South Africa. Taking account of the inevitability of politics in the sports arena and the on-going need for institutional and legal reform, Chapter 12 examines the general characteristics and shared goals of competition and its management, including the need for security in the sports arena.

Appendices I and II discuss the comprehensive legislation of the United States and China, respectively, as contrasting examples of national regulation within the process of international sports law. International law typically depends on such national implementation. Whatever form the implementation of international sports law takes from country to country and from time to time, the integration of international, domestic, governmental, and non-governmental elements into a single process is essential to the emergence of a strong regime of law.

Taken together, the chapters in this book survey the distinctive, functioning framework of international sports law and identify its principal features. Although troubles abound in and around the sports arena, it is gratifying to watch a new legal process evolve and accommodate itself to changing conditions.

CHAPTER 2
THE INSTITUTIONAL FRAMEWORK OF INTERNATIONAL SPORTS LAW

A. THE ORGANIZATIONAL STRUCTURE

1. Intergovernmental Organizations

Within the United Nations system, several specialized agencies and special programs provide a framework of intergovernmental support for sports. These organizations include the Food and Agriculture Organization (FAO), establishing sports and recreational projects in poor rural communities; the International Telecommunications Union (ITU), encouraging satellite broadcasting of sports events; the United Nations Development Program (UNDP), financing sports and recreational facilities in developing countries; the United Nations Environment Program (UNEP), convening conferences that focus on proposals to promote sustainable development, ranging from green procurement in staging sporting events to design of environmentally friendly venues; the United Nations International Drug Control Program (UNIDCP), cooperating in efforts to control the use of drugs by athletes; the United Nations High Commission for Refugees (UNHCR), distributing sports equipment in refugee camps; the Universal Postal Union (UPU), encouraging issuance of sports-related postage stamps; the World Health Organization (WHO), convening a biennial Congress on sports-related health issues; the World Meteorological Union (WMO), providing forecasting assistance in staging events; and, above all, the United Nations Educational, Scientific and Cultural Organization (UNESCO).[1]

UNESCO has been particularly instrumental in seeking to promote physical education and an appreciation of the relationship among sport activity, culture, and the arts. As early as 1978 UNESCO adopted an International Charter of Physical Education and Sport[2] that puts forth a comprehensive set of rules and guidelines for national programs and international sports, based on the Olympic ideal. In 1989 the organization adopted several important resolutions that define the

---

[1] For a discussion of the cooperative agreement between these organizations and the International Olympic Committee, *see* Samaranch, *The Olympic Culture in Favour of Peace*, OLYMPIC REV., Aug.–Sept. 1999, at 35, 36.

[2] United Nations Educational, Scientific and Cultural Organization, Res. 1/5.4/2, 1 Records of the Gen. Conf., 20th Sess., at 31 (1978).

[3] United Nations Educational, Scientific and Cultural Organization, Res. 1.20, Universality of the Olympic Games, 1 Records of the Gen. Conf., 25th Sess., at 91 (1989) [hereinafter UNESCO Res.]

Olympic Movement "as proclaimed in the Olympic Charter."[3] These resolutions also encourage cooperation between UNESCO and the Olympic Movement and call for national enforcement of the Olympic Charter, "particularly the principles of non-discrimination, fair play, non-violence and the rejection of harmful substances."[4] In order to implement these provisions and encourage cooperation by states, UNESCO established the Inter-Governmental Committee for Physical Education and Sport (CIGEPS), governed by a permanent consultative committee. UNESCO has also convened International Conferences of Sports Ministers and Senior Officials Responsible for Sport. A particular emphasis of these initiatives, in cooperation with the Olympic Forum for Development and Olympic Solidarity, and the United Nations Development Program, has been the arrangement of assistance to athletics and athletes in developing countries.[5]

2. The Olympic Movement

The specific institutions of the Olympic Movement include the IOC, IFs, NOCs, and the OCOGs. Their relationship is both formally constituted by agreements and, in practice, symbiotic.[6] The constituent organizations retain their

---

[4] *Id. See also* Development of Physical Education and Sport, Res. 1.18, *noted in* UNESCO Res., *id.*, at 88; The Fight Against Doping in Sport, Res. 1.19, *noted in* UNESCO Res., *id.* at 89 (reaffirming cooperation with the Olympic Movement).

[5] *See generally, Cooperation between the IOC and UNESCO*, OLYMPIC REV., Dec. 1998–Jan. 1999, at 47; Vedder, *The International Olympic Committee: An Advanced Non-Governmental Organization and the International Law*, 27 GERMAN Y.B. INT'L L. 233, 250–51 (1984).

[6] On the central role of these organizations and their mutual relationships in the process of international sports law, *see, e.g.*, Hollis, *The United States Olympic Committee and the Suspension of Athletes: Reforming Grievance Procedures Under the Amateur Sports Act of 1978*, 71 IND. L.J. 183 (1995); Newman, *The Race Does Not Always Go to the Stronger or Faster Man . . . But to the One Who Goes to Court! An Examination of Reynolds v. International Amateur Athletic Fed'n*, 1 SPORTS L.J. 205, 207 (1994); Nelson, *Stuck Between Interlocking Rings: Efforts to Resolve the Conflicting Demands Placed on Olympic National Governing Bodies*, 26 VAND. J. TRANSNAT'L L. 895, 899, 900 (1993); Ettinger, *The Legal Status of the International Olympic Committee*, 4 PACE Y.B. INT'L LAW 97, 99 (1992).

[7] This relationship has been aptly described as follows:

> [L]a souveraineté des fédérations internationales sur leurs disciplines est non seulement préservée mais encore consolidée, notamment par le fait que les fédérations internationales olympiques participent directement â l'organisation des Jeux.
>
> S'il est certain que les principes olympiques peuvent directement influer sur le contenu de la réglementation sportive fédérale—on songe notamment aux règles relatives à l'amateurisme que les fédérations doivent intégrer à leurs propres règlements sportifs pour être reconnues par le C.I.O.—il est non moins certain que le rôle très influent des fédérations olympiques au sein du Mouvement contribue à son évolution, ce que traduisent les modifications sensibles subies par la Charte Olympique cette dernière décennie.

G. SIMON, PUISSANCE SPORTIVE ET ORDRE JURIDIQUE ÉTATIQUE 50 (1990) (footnotes omitted). A variation of this description is to view the institutionalized process of international law as pyramidal, either as a single pyramid of authority (Ch. 1, *supra* text accompanying note 30)

autonomy while participating in a mutually reinforcing process.[7] The Olympic Movement also has several partners, which include the Court of Arbitration for Sport (CAS), the International Committee for Fair Play, and the International Paralympic Committee. The Olympic Congress, which meets every eight years "in principle,"[8] consists of members of the IOC, delegates of the IFs and NOCs, representatives of other organizations recognized by the IOC, such as representatives of UNESCO, and special invitees, including athletes. The Congress can only pass resolutions following an agenda set by the IOC Executive Board; it cannot make binding decisions.

a. *The International Olympic Committee*

The 1894 Congress of Paris, which launched the modern Olympic Games, established the IOC. The latter owns the rights to the Games and, as the "supreme authority of the Olympic Movement" [binds] "any person or organization belonging in any capacity whatsoever to the Olympic Movement"[9] Specifically, the IOC, whose membership may not exceed 115,[10] has sixteen functions, the most important of which is to coordinate, organize, and develop sport and sport competitions; take measures to strengthen the unity of the Olympic Movement; and ensure the regular celebration of the Olympic Games.[11] The IOC relies heavily on the work of some 19 commissions and one working group, ranging from an Ethics Commission to a Television and Internet Rights Commission. Procedurally, the IOC is responsible for creating and applying rules and regulations, recruiting and electing its members, electing its own officers and committee chairs, and convening a general meeting at least once a year, called a "Session."[12] The IOC's most fundamental role is administrative or quasi-judicial: "to ensure the respect and interpretation of the 'Olympic Charter.'"[13]

The IOC is distinguished by its "singular composition and its peculiar recruitment."[14] Within the international legal system, the IOC is a "cosmopolitan" organization—that is, one composed of individuals rather than nation-states or

---

or as two pyramids with the IFs at the top of one pyramid and the IOC and NOCs at the top of a second. Will, *Les structures du sport international*, CHAPITRES CHOISIS DU DROIT DU SPORT 21 (1993).

[8] OLYMPIC CHARTER, Rule 7.

[9] *Id.*, Rule 1.

[10] *Id.*, Rule 20.

[11] *Id.*, Rule 2.

[12] *Id.*, Rule 22. The Session is the supreme organ of the IOC. It adopts, modifies and interprets the Olympic Charter. Its decisions are final. Upon proposal of the Executive Board, the Session elects the members of the IOC.

[13] Remarks of Juan Antonio Samaranch, President of the IOC, OLYMPIC REV., Jan. 1985, at 14 [hereinafter referred to as Remarks].

[14] *Id.* at 12.

organizational representatives.[15] It co-opts its membership on the basis of their representation to, not from, other organizations—namely, to officially recognized national federations and committees. Thus, IOC members are representatives of and not to the IOC.[16]

Recruitment to membership on the IOC is conducted by the body itself according to an elaborate set of eligibility criteria and nomination procedures set forth in Bye-laws to the Olympic Charter.[17] The IOC elects the President for an eight-year term, renewable once for four years. His duties are to preside over all activities of the IOC, represent it, and set up and supervise the work and duration of ad hoc commissions and working groups.[18] The remaining members of the Executive Board include four Vice-Presidents and ten other members, reflecting "the composition of the Session."[19] They are elected for a maximum of two successive four-year terms.[20]

Through much of its history, the IOC has been criticized for its elitism as an exclusive *club d'amis*. Several rules and regulations have encouraged a predominantly European, white-male membership. They are co-opted and must be free of governmental and private influence, and who but the rich, it is argued, can be free of such influence? Also, countries that have hosted the Olympic Games—nearly always in Europe or North America—are entitled to double membership. Moreover, members used to be elected for life. After reforms of the IOC, they are elected for eight-year terms, but they may be successively re-elected for eight-year terms until they reach the age of 70. Although these terms and age limits, as well as diverse nomination procedures, and elaborate vetting of nominations, have substantially diversified the composition of the body, the membership is still noticeably European and male. In 2001, for example, China, with three members, had the same voting strength as Liechtenstein, Luxemburg and Monaco, each represented by a member of its royalty.

Support for the IOC is provided by its administration, located in Lausanne, Switzerland. The administration is headed by a Director General and Secretary General, both appointed by the Executive Board, and several Directors of departments and services. Revenue is derived primarily from media payments and gate

---

15 *See* L. WHITE, THE STRUCTURE OF PRIVATE INTERNATIONAL ORGANIZATIONS 34, 244–48 (1933); L. WHITE, INTERNATIONAL NON-GOVERNMENTAL ORGANIZATIONS: THEIR PURPOSES, METHODS, AND ACCOMPLISHMENTS 199–200 (1951).

16 OLYMPIC CHARTER, Rule 20.

17 *Id.*, Bye-law to Rule 20.

18 *Id.*, Rule 24.

19 *Id.*, Rule 23.

20 *Id.*

receipts at the Games, but the IOC may accept gifts and bequests and all other resources that may enable it to fulfill its tasks.[21]

b. The International Federations

The 35 IFs, each of a different sport and two of which are provisional, maintain broad control over the conduct of sports competition.[22] The Olympic Charter spells out the terms by which the IOC recognition of IFs, without which they may not fully participate in authorized competitions such as the Olympic Games and otherwise achieve high public visibility.[23] In 2003 the IOC framework included some 35 Olympic IFs and another 30 Recognized IFs.[24] The IOC also recognizes associations of IFs such as the Association of International Summer Olympic Federations (ASOIF); the Association of the International Olympic Winter Sports Federations (AIOWF); the Association of the IOC Recognized International Sports Federations (ARISF); and the General Association of International Sports Federations (GAISF).[25]

Each IF exercises technical control and direction of its sport according to its own criteria of eligibility and technical rules and in conformity with the Olympic Charter.[26] Accordingly, an IF regulates the number of entrants in its sport within limits set by the IOC, equipment standards and controls, the selection of judges, and the exercise of what could be described as limited appellate jurisdiction to review administrative decisions. Each IF typically has a scope of authority to manage and develop its particular sports extending well beyond the making and enforcement of technical rules.

---

[21] OLYMPIC CHARTER, Rule 28.

[22] For a compilation of constitutions, statutes and other basic instruments of IFs and other universal sports organizations, *see* BASIC DOCUMENTS OF INTERNATIONAL SPORTS ORGANIZATIONS (Siekmann & Soek eds., 1998).

[23] THE OLYMPIC CHARTER, Rule 29, provides as follows:

> In order to promote the Olympic Movement, the IOC may recognize as IFs international non-governmental organizations administering one or several sports at world level and encompassing organizations administering such sports at national level. In order to be recognized, these organizations must adopt and implement the World Anti-Doping Code. The recognition of IFs newly recognized by the IOC shall be provisional for a period of two years or any other period fixed by the IOC Executive Board. At the end of such period, the recognition shall automatically lapse in the absence of definitive confirmation given in writing by the IOC. As far as the role of the IFs within the Olympic Movement is concerned, their statutes, practice and activities must be in conformity with the Olympic Charter. Subject to the foregoing, each IF maintains its independence and autonomy in the administration of its sport.

[24] International Olympic Committee, OLYMPIC MOVEMENT DIRECTORY 61, 71 (2000) [hereinafter Directory].

[25] OLYMPIC CHARTER, Rule 4. On the activities of the GAISF, *see The GAISF Congress and General Assembly*, OLYMPIC REV., Dec. 1998–Jan. 1999, at 53.

[26] OLYMPIC CHARTER, Rule 30.

As an example of the role of the IFs, the International Amateur Athletic Federation (IAAF) is responsible for rule-making, supervision, control and development of track-and-field competitions. Its internal legal structure, illustrative of IFs, is significant. For instance, in 1982 the IAAF adopted a new rule, which for the first time established mandatory arbitration of disputes falling within the jurisdiction of constituent national federations. As a second example, the International Federation of Association Football (FIFA) has five rather ambitious "objects." According to the FIFA Handbook, these objects are to promote the game "in every way which seems proper to FIFA or to its Executive Committee;" to foster friendly relations among the officials and players of National Associations; to control football by preventing infringements of competitive rules; to prevent discrimination against a country or an individual for reasons of race, religion, or politics; and to decide or settle "all differences that may arise between National Associations."

Disputes may arise between IFs, as, for example, one that broke out between the International Snowboard Federation, which is not recognized by the IOC, and the International Ski Federation, to which the IOC had given authority over snowboarding.[27] Disputes may also arise between the IOC and the IFs, as for example, one between the IOC and the International Rowing Federation (FISA) concerning the inclusion of lightweight shells in Olympic trials.[28] Although IOC decisions are "final,"[29] any dispute on their application or interpretation, as in the FISA dispute, may be resolved by the IOC Executive Board and, "in certain cases,"[30] the Court of Arbitration for Sports (CAS). What are these cases? Apparently, under another provision of the Olympic Charter, the CAS has competence in any dispute "arising on the occasion of, or in connection with the Olympic Games."[31] The open-ended term "in connection with" invites a broad interpretation of CAS competence.

The relationship between the IOC and the IFs is maintained through joint meetings between the IOC Executive Board and the IFs. A Draft Convention, proposed at the 1982 Congress of the IFs, attempted to further define that relationship.[32] The Draft Convention outlined the consequences incumbent upon the IFs whenever the IOC wished to discipline a National Olympic Committee (NOC) for misbehavior. The agreement was designed to protect the Olympic Movement from

---

27 *See* St. John, *I'm on the Olympic Team? Bummer!*, N.Y. TIMES MAG., Jan. 27, 2002, at 32, 34.

28 *See* Martucci, *Rowing, A Respectable Member of the Olympic Family*, OLYMPIC REV., Feb. 1986, at 117–119.

29 OLYMPIC CHARTER, Rule 19.

30 *Id.*

31 *Id.*, Rule 74.

32 OLYMPIC REV., Dec. 1982, at 764.

decisions of non-Olympic entities. If, for example, an NOC misbehaved by allowing modifications of its management or composition by a non-Olympic entity, the IOC could suspend the NOC and request the IFs to suspend their national affiliates in the offending NOC. If a particular national affiliate improperly accommodated a non-Olympic body, the appropriate IF in the particular sport would have to suspend the affiliate and notify the IOC to suspend the corresponding NOC if necessary. By providing a basis for a cooperative, protective network, the Draft Convention sought to close ranks against outside interference, including political abuse, of the Olympic Games.

c. *The National Olympic Committees*

There are some 200 NOCs. These include NOCs from most United Nations members, including each of the divisions of China and Korea, as well as from several non-sovereign territories: American Samoa, Aruba, Bermuda, British Virgin Islands, Cayman Islands, Cook Islands, Guam, Netherlands Antilles, Puerto Rico, and (American) Virgin Islands. Each of these non-sovereign territories is said to be a "country" even though the Olympic Charter's definition of a country—"an independent State recognized by the international community"[33]—patently does not apply to them. A more appropriate definition of "country," for purposes of NOC membership, might be "a dependent nation recognized by the International Olympic Committee for purposes of sustaining a single NOC."

The Olympic Charter provides that "[t]he mission of the NOCs is to develop and protect the Olympic Movement in their respective countries, in accordance with the Olympic Charter."[34] The relationship of authority between the NOCs and the IOC is comparable to that between, for example, the National Red Cross Societies in their implementation of humanitarian law and the supervisory International Committee of the Red Cross. All NOC statutes must conform to and refer expressly to the Olympic Charter.[35] Rules 31 and 32 of the Charter contain detailed requirements for the structure, procedures and programs of NOCs and prohibits governments and other public authorities from designating NOC membership so as to keep the membership as free as possible from direct political intrusion. The IOC has the power to withdraw recognition of an NOC from the Olympic Movement.[36]

The NOCs are loosely organized into an Association of National Olympic Committees (ANOC), headquartered in Paris and such regional groupings as the Association of NOCs of Africa (ANOCA), the Olympic Council of Asia (OCA),

---

[33] OLYMPIC CHARTER, Rule 34.

[34] OLYMPIC CHARTER, Rule 31.

[35] *Id.*, Bye-law to Rules 31 and 32.

[36] *E.g.*, suspension of NOC from Upper Volta (later renamed Burkina Faso), OLYMPIC REV., Nov. 1982, at 638.

the Pan American Sports Organization (PASO), the Oceania National Olympic Committees (ONOC), and the European Olympic Committees (EOC).[37] These associations of NOCs coordinate their activities and policies, but cannot act on behalf of the constituent NOCs in their relationships with the IOC.

d. *Organizing Committees of the Olympic Games*

The Olympic Charter provides for the composition of the Organizing Committees of the Olympic Games (OCOGs)[38] and for the liaison between each OCOG and its NOC.[39] Elaborate procedures for evaluating applications and electing host cities went into effect in 2003. The new procedures responded to corruption associated with the selection of sites, particularly Salt Lake City for the 2002 Winter Games.[40] An Ethics Commission and Code of Ethics,[41] guided by traditional principles of fair play,[42] strengthened this initiative.

After the IOC has selected a city to serve as host, the two parties enter into an agreement with the NOC of the host country whereby the parties become jointly and severally liable for all non-financial commitments concerning the organization and staging of a particular Olympic Games. Only the host city and its OCOG bear financial responsibilities, however.[43] The IOC President then appoints a Coordination Commission to manage and implement the working relationship among the IOC, the OCOG, the IFs and the NOCs.[44]

The IOC, its Executive Board, and particularly its President, enjoy broad discretion in supervising the administration of international sports competition by the IFs, NOCs, OCOGs and other responsible organizations. The President may take action or make a decision, subject to later ratification by the IOC, when "circumstances" do not permit such action to be taken by the Session or its Executive Board.[45] Moreover, the continuing practice of the IOC to keep its deliberations confidential, except in summary form, protects its freedom to exercise discretion in making decisions.

---

[37] *Id.*, Rule 4.

[38] OLYMPIC CHARTER, Rule 39.

[39] *Id.*, Rule 41.

[40] *See* Hasan, *Host City Selection: Reforms to the Selection Process*, 22 U.N.S.W. L.J. 829 (1999).

[41] OLYMPIC CHARTER, Rule 25.

[42] *See Fair Play*, OLYMPIC REV. 16 (1998) (special issue on sports ethics).

[43] OLYMPIC CHARTER, Rule 40.

[44] *Id.*, Rule 41. For an analysis of the type of contracts and coordination required to organize the Olympic Games, *see* Brabazon, *The Legal Structure of the Sydney Olympic Games*, 22 U.N.S.W. L.J. 662 (1999).

[45] OLYMPIC CHARTER, Rule 26.

e. *The IOC's International Legal Personality*

Even though the IOC is technically a non-governmental organization with only limited competence outside the Olympic arena, its special status under international law is well-established. States acquiesce in its decisions and conduct diplomacy with it.[46]

A federal appeals court in the United States confirmed the special status of the Olympic Charter and the Games under international law. Cautioning that "a court should be wary of applying a state statute to alter the content of the Olympic Games," the court observed as follows: "The Olympic Games are organized and conducted under the terms of an international agreement—the Olympic Charter. We are extremely hesitant to undertake the application of one state's statute to alter an event that is staged with competitors from the entire world under the terms of that agreement."[47]

The United States Supreme Court has established that although the United States Olympic Committee is non-governmental, Congress officially adopted Rule 1 of the Olympic Charter's aim "to spread the Olympic principles."[48] Four Justices of the Court described the IOC as "a highly visible and influential international body."[49] A Swiss statute accords the IOC special international status under Swiss tax and labor laws in view of its "universal vocation . . . in the world of sport."[50] A 1977 Belgian court decision, confirming a position taken by French courts, as well as the Council of Europe and the Court of Justice of the European Union, have established that the international rules of sport supersede conflicting national policies and laws in particular contexts.[51] The Second Conference of

---

[46] *See* Ch. 1, *supra* text accompanying notes 14–20. The International Court of Justice has articulated this kind of legal development as follows:

> The subjects of law in any legal system are not necessarily identical in their nature or in the extent of their rights, and their nature depends upon the needs of the community. Throughout its history, the development of international law has been influenced by the requirements of international life.

Reparation for Injuries Suffered in the Service of the United Nations, 1949 I.C.J. 174, 178–79 (Advisory Opinion of Apr. 11) [hereinafter cited as Reparation Case].

[47] Martin v. Int'l Olympic Comm., 740 F.2d 670, 677 (9th Cir. 1984).

[48] San Francisco Arts & Athletics, Inc. v. USOC & IOC, 107 S. Ct. 2971, 2981 (1987).

[49] *Id.* at 2988.

[50] Olympic Rev., Nov. 1981, at 641. The IOC, "a private entity governed by Swiss civil law, has been accorded some fiscal privileges. Furthermore the IOC is exempt to a certain extent from laws providing for limits on the issuance of working permits for foreign nationals." Letter from Jurg Leutert, Legal Adviser to the Embassy of Switzerland in the United States (Aug. 28, 1983).

[51] For background, *see* Bondoux, *Law and Sport*, Olympic Rev., Aug.–Sept. 1978, at 494, 501–02; Garrigues, *The Impact of Community Law on Physical and Sports Activities*, Olympic Rev., June 1979, at 345.

European Sports Ministers adopted a resolution that explicitly ratified the authority of the Olympic Charter.[52]

In sum, the IOC "manifests traits and actions characteristic of international organizations."[53] It meets the requirement of international legal personality. Clearly, the IOC was "intended to exercise and enjoy, and is in fact exercising and enjoying, functions and rights which can only be explained on the basis of the possession of a large measure of international personality and the capacity of operate upon an international plane."[54]

3. Other Organizations

The IOC recognizes some thirty IFs that are not officially designated as International Olympic Sports Federations. These include, for example, the International Mountaineering and Climbing Federation, the International Dance Sport Federation, the World Bridge Foundation, the International Chess Federation, the International Bowling Federation, and the World Squash Federation.[55] These IFs often have well-defined rules and procedures that mirror those of the designated Olympic federations. The code of the provisionally recognized International Federation of Motor Cyclists, for example, contains a hierarchy of sanctions for rule infractions, namely, reprimand, apology, suspension and exclusion. Similarly, the code of an unrecognized IF, the International Association of Recognized Automobile Clubs, provides for recreational safety by imposing standards on manufacturers of racing vehicles in international competition; this function is reputedly "one of the principal causes of automobile progress."[56]

---

[52] Resolution adopted by the Second Conference of European Ministers Responsible for Sport, London, Apr. 4–7, 1978, *reprinted in* Olympic Rev., June 1978, at 391. For further background, *see* Howell, *Governmental Responsibilities in Sport*, Olympic Rev., May 1978, at 209. *See also* Silance, *Interaction of the Rules in Sports Law and the Laws and Treaties Made by Public Authorities*, Olympic Rev., Oct. 1977, at 619, 622, 627.

[53] R. Espy, The Politics of the Olympic Games 9 (1979). "[T]he Olympic organization [is] a significant transnational actor . . . [Its activities] make it as much of an international actor as most of the narrow purpose IGOs." Rich, *The Legal Regime for a Permanent Olympic Site*, 15 N.Y.U. J. Int'l L. & Pol. 1 (1982). *See also* L. White, The Structure of Private International Organizations, *supra* note 15, at 34; *but see* Vedder, *supra* note 5, at 255.

[54] Reparation Case, *supra* note 46. "[T]he necessary attribute of international personality is the power to enter, directly or immediately, into relationship (by treaty or otherwise) with other international persons." Fitzmaurice, *The Law and Procedure of the International Court of Justice*, 1953 Brit. Y.B. Int'l L. 2. *See also* J. Lador-Lederer, International Non-Governmental Organizations and Economic Entities 14 (1963) ("If it was once the personality which made a function international, it is now the function which confers legal internationality to the entity which is engaged in such activity.")

[55] *See* Directory, *supra* note 24, at 71.

[56] L. White, International Non-Governmental Organizations, *supra* note 15, at 199.

Perhaps the most prominent of the recognized IFs is the International Paralympic Committee, which organizes the quadrennial Summer Paralympic Games. Coinciding with the Summer Olympic Games, they attracted 3,843 athletes from 122 countries to Sydney in 2000.[57]

The International World Games Association (IWGA) organizes and stages quadrennial competitions that deliberately involve non-Olympic sports.[58] Since the first World Games in 1980, at least six sports—badminton, baseball, taekwando, the triathlon, women's water polo, and women's weightlifting—have graduated out of that competition and into the Olympic Games. Competitors are selected on the basis of championships or other leading international events staged by their federations.

International or regional organizations that cooperate directly with the IOC include the Commonwealth Games Federation, the Pan-American Games Federation, the Bolivarian Games Organization, the Asian Games Federation, the Pan-Arab Games, the African Games, the Central African Games, the Games of the Central American and Caribbean Sports Organization, ODESUR (organizer of the South American Games), the organization of the Mediterranean Games, the organization of The Islands of the Indian Ocean Games, the organization of the Games of Small European Countries, and the Supreme Council for Sport in Africa. These organizations may involve both Olympic and non-Olympic sports and may be instrumental in implementing rules and policies of international sports law. For example, the Commonwealth Games Federation promulgated the Gleneagles Agreement, which established global principles of nondiscrimination in sport, and a code of conduct to enforce those principles. Other prominent sports organizations—for example, the America's Cup in sailing, the British Open in golf, the Tour de France in cycling, Wimbledon in tennis, and the World Cup in football (soccer)—though largely outside the formal framework of the Olympic Movement, are part of the process of international sports law.

The Council of Europe and the European Union (EU) are also developing common norms and policies to govern regional sports competition. The growing mutuality of enforcement powers between the European Commission and national courts helps ensure compliance. Ministers of Sport in member countries of the Council of Europe meet to discuss common problems, such as violence, drug usage, and Olympic boycotts. A European Sports Charter, two conventions—the

[57] *Available at* www.olympic.org.

[58] *See History of the World Games*, OLYMPIC REV., Aug.–Sept. 1999, at 67. IWGA sports include the following: air sports (parachuting), billiards (carom, pool, snooker), body building, boules sports (boule Lyonnaise, pétanque), casting, dance sport, fistball, field archery, fin swimming, flying disc (golf, ultimate), gymnastics (rhythmic gymnastics, sports acrobatics, sports aerobics, trampoline, tumbling), ju-jitsu, karate, korfball, life saving (beach, pool), netball, orienteering, powerlifting, roller skating (artistic, hockey, speed), rugby (seven-a-side), squash, tug of war for men (indoor, outdoor), and water skiing (barefoot, tournament, wakeboard).

European Convention on Spectator Violence and Misbehavior at Sports Events and an Anti-Doping Convention, and a Code of Sports Ethics—constitute the principal normative developments within the Council of Europe.[59] Sports will also be specifically included as a topic in the emerging European Constitution.

Within the EU, the policy implications of sports organizations are significant, as the Amsterdam Treaty's Declaration of Sport and the EU's role in the Olympics, for example, attest.[60] The CAS has established that the practice of sport falls within the domain of EU law, however, only insofar as it constitute an economic activity.[61]

B. TRANSNATIONAL MODELS OF SPORTS ORGANIZATION: EUROPEAN AND AMERICAN

National sports organizations may involve foreign constituents. For example, Major League Baseball (MLB), the National Basketball Association (NBA), and the National Hockey League (NHL), all of the United States, include Canadian teams. The National Football League (NFL) has established an NFL Europe league of United States-style football.

As athletic leagues expand across national boundaries, structural anomalies may result. The organizational structure of a sport in the parent country may not fit easily into that of the other country or countries. The colonization of a national sports culture by a foreign sports body such as the MLB, NBA, NHL, or NFL has led to proposals to globalize sports organizations, primarily by vesting IFs with greater control over national sports bodies.[62] Historically, two contrasting models of organization merit particular attention: those of Europe and the United States.[63]

---

[59] *See* Council of Europe, The Council of Europe and Sport (2000); Özyavuz, *Council of Europe's Work on Sport*, 2003 INT'L SPORTS L.J., No. 3, at 25. On the relations between the EU and the Olympic Movement, *see*, Rogge, *The Olympic Movement and the European Union*, OLYMPIC REV., Oct.–Nov. 1995, at 44.

[60] *See generally*, R. PARRISH, SPORTS LAW AND POLICY IN THE EUROPEAN UNION (2003); D. PANAGIOTOPOULOS, SPORTS AND EUROPEAN COMMUNITY LAW (1998).

[61] B. v. FIBA, *in* DIGEST OF CAS AWARDS 1986–1998, at 297, 301 (M. Reeb ed., 1998).

[62] *See, e.g.*, Marcano & Fidler, *The Globalization of Baseball: Major League Baseball and the Mistreatment of Latin American Baseball Talent*, 6 IND. J. GLOBAL LEGAL STUD. 511 (1999) (arguing for greater protection of second-country teams and athletes, particularly in Latin America).

[63] *See generally* Weatherill, *Resisting the Pressures of "Americanization": The Influence of European Community Law on the "European Sport Model,"* 8 WILLAMETTE J. INT'L L. & DISP. RES. 37 (2000) (arguing that the European Sports Model put forward by the European Commission may be contrasted with the United States practice of allowing professional leagues substantial autonomy in seeking to maximize wealth. European sports clubs, on the other hand, are discouraged from pursuing commercialism "without adequate respect for the nature and purpose of sport in society." *Id.* Professor Weatherill concludes by arguing for a more powerful European Union regulator that will act in the public interest but "in only a limited sense" of a

Within Europe, of course, implementation of European regional law and the European model may vary from one country to another. The well-developed law of Germany, for example, is one variation that presents illuminating comparisons with United States law.[64]

The traditional European sports model emphasizes the autonomy of sports from political and commercial manipulation. A hierarchical or pyramid system of organizations, incorporating both "amateur" and "professional" teams and athletes, tends to pool resources. Generally the federations and associations of athletic teams at the top of the pyramid own broadcasting rights and revenue. These organizations then distribute revenue among member teams, thereby depriving individual teams of the freedom to strike deals with television broadcasters. The Union of European Football Associations (UEFA) negotiates television rights and sells them as single packages to the several national leagues. The leagues then parcel out the revenue to constituent teams. Also, the European model is one of promotion and relegation of teams. Accordingly, the best team or teams in a league are promoted annually to the next higher league and the worst team or teams are relegated to the next lower league. Teams normally are not moved from city to city.

By contrast, in the United States professional sports competition is driven by commercial interests relatively less fettered by competition (anti-trust) law than in Europe. Individual teams may each own a major share of broadcast rights and revenue, as in MLB, or get an equal cut of broadcast revenue, as in the NFL. The promotion-and-relegation system does not exist. Teams are therefore more free to move from city to city in response to the market.

To be sure, the contrasts between the two models are becoming less pronounced, primarily because the European model is under stress as the sports arena becomes more and more commercial. Successful football (soccer) teams now seek independent contracting for broadcast rights and revenue. Even so, the traditional European model is still significant, as are the implications of the contrasting models.

The European promotion-and-relegation model better ensures vertical solidarity between teams at different levels of national establishment, prestige and commercial value, whereas the United States model ensures greater stability of investment. European teams more readily move in and out of prominence and

---

judge, rather than originator of decisions. Sports bodies would continue to make the primary decisions about athletes and sports competition as well as to establish the rules of the game. Consultation between private and public authorities would be essential. In Professor Weatherill's view, progress lies in a partnership among European institutions, member states, and private sports bodies).

64 The definitive comparative work is Buchberger, DIE ÜBERPRÜFBARKEIT SPORTVERBANDSRECHTLICHER ENTSCHEIDUNGEN DURCH DIE ORDENTLICHE GERICHTSBARKEIT (1999).

commercial value, whereas United States teams generally stay in place at a particular level of prominence and commercial value. This may have the negative consequence of removing an incentive for improvement.[65]

Both models can generate horizontal solidarity by redistributing revenue among teams at the same level. The European model, by investing federations and associations with authority over the distribution of television revenue, helps ensure that the rich do not get richer and the poor poorer. The United States model, by more or less locking in the composition of leagues, offers a stable basis for allocating revenue among member teams. In practice, however, both models limit financial equalization. In Europe, the promotion-and-relegation system, by limiting stability of expectations over time, discourages long-term equalization. In the United States, practices vary widely among sports. In MLB, the actual lack of salary caps defeats equalization and abets wealth maximization (the rich get richer, the poor get poorer), and distribution of broadcast revenue varies considerably among the several professional leagues. Moreover, the anomalous anti-trust exemption of MLB, though no longer absolute, discourages reform of oligopolistic practices.

C. ORGANIZATIONAL CORRUPTION

Bribery, match-fixing and other corrupt practices threaten the integrity of sports competition. Like a kind of dry rot, such practices, though often difficult to detect until it is too late, eventually eat away the structural framework.

The integrity of sports competition depends on both the principles and the public image of fairness and equality. Rules of the game, canons of ethics, and referees on the playing field help protect these fundamental principles of competition. As a result, sports competition is one of the most regulated and rule-enforced of all social activities. But such formal authority cannot overcome a corrupt framework.

Two levels of corruption are apparent: within the organizational structure and in or around particular competition. Effective rules to deter corruption at both levels are essential. This section reveals, however, that the rule structure has been inadequate at the organizational level. Chapter 5 will provide examples and discussion of corruption during competition.

Under the Olympic Charter the IOC "supports and encourages the promotion of sports ethics" [and] "dedicates its efforts to ensuring in sports the spirit of fair play."[66]

---

65 For an argument in favor of injecting a "much-needed economic Darwinism into United States football," perhaps adopting the European promotion-and-relegation system, *see* Martinez, *Along with the Super Bowl, the N.F.L. Needs a Farewell Bowl*, N.Y. TIMES, Jan. 19, 2003, § 4, at 12.

66 OLYMPIC CHARTER, Rule 2.

The very working of these provisions is more aspirational or perhaps hopeful than either descriptive or prescriptive. Clearly, the Olympic Charter by itself offers only a skimpy basis for combating corruption.

Other constituents of the Olympic Movement—principally the IFs and NOCs—have been even freer of formal ethical constraints except as provided by their own constitutions and statutes. Enforcement of such provisions is weak, however, in the absence of rules and procedures to ensure transparency of important managerial decisions.

All major sports organizations are expected to raise huge sums of money and therefore curry the favor of the very commercial interests that may fuel the engines of corruption. On the eve of the 2002 World Cup in football, a power struggle broke out that was centered on the practices of Sepp Blatter, the President of the International Football (Soccer) Federation (FIFA).[67] It became apparent that his administrative discretion extended to the purchase and sale of marketing contracts and other assets, the disbursement of millions of dollars to "needy" associations, the operation of internal audits, and the manipulation of financial officers.[68] In the end, Blatter kept his job, but reform was in the wind.[69]

Two highly visible scandals reveal the vulnerability of sports organizations to corruption and the need for a better legal mechanism to combat it.

1. The Salt Lake City Bribery Scandal

In late 1998, three years after Salt Lake City was awarded the 2002 Winter Games, a host-city bidding scandal erupted. The scandal centered on accusations that the Salt Lake City OCOG had showered IOC members and agents of IOC membership blocs with up to $1.2 million in out-right payments, gifts of goods and services, contracts, educational benefits, and employment of relatives.[70] Investigations and self-admissions disclosed an alarming extent of bribery. Bribery charges were leveled against several leading officials. For example, Jean-Claude Ganga of the Congo Republic, an IOC member who as an anti-apartheid activist had led the African boycott of the 1976 Games in Montreal, was a salient beneficiary of Salt Lake City generosity. Apparently as a sort of agent of an African regional voting bloc, investigations revealed that he had accepted "more than $300,000 in cash payments, medical treatment, travel expenses and even

---

[67] *See* Hughes, *World Cup's preopening brawl*, INT'L HERALD TRIB., May 29, 2002, at 1. For background, *see* Hughes, *Question time: FIFA's Blatter Goes on the Carpet After ISL Fiasco*, INT'L HERALD TRIB., June 13, 2001, at 19.

[68] *Id.*; Hughes, *The soccer family feuds over money*, INT'L HERALD TRIB., May 28, 2002, at 18.

[69] Hughes, *Embattled FIFA chief is re-elected*, INT'L HERALD TRIB., May 30, 2002, at 1.

[70] *See* Olson, *IOC, Steadfast, Says Indictments Won't Impede Sale Lake City Games*, INT'L HERALD TRIB., July 22–23, 2000, at 19.

doorknobs and knee-replacement surgery for his mother-in-law."[71] He was forced to resign from the IOC.

Revelations of bid irregularities extended beyond Salt Lake City, principally to Atlanta, the site of the 1996 Summer Games; Nagano, the site of the Winter Games; and Sydney, the site of the 2000 Summer Games.[72] The irregularities associated with the Atlanta OCOG appear to have been largely grease payments of uncertain consequence. Most of the evidence of bribery by Nagano officials appears to have been deliberately shredded. Sydney's promise of $35,000 apiece to IOC members, however, appears to have assured it the two-vote margin by which it received a bid in competition with Beijing.[73] Something needed to be done.

The responses included the expulsion or resignation of ten IOC members, the reprimand of several others, the establishment of an Ad Hoc Inquiry Commission by the IOC, federal government hearings, and legal action.[74] In particular, the two top architects of the successful bid for Salt Lake City were indicted on 15 felony charges[75] and other persons implicated in the scandal were convicted of tax fraud.[76]

Major reforms also ensued. The scandal intensified negotiations in the Organization for Economic Cooperation and Development (OECD) toward conclusion of a Convention on Combating Bribery of Foreign Public Officials in International Business Transactions. Modeled on the (U.S.) Foreign Corrupt Practices Act,[77] the treaty would require parties to criminalize bribery of public officials for commercial advantage. Although the Convention would not apply to OCOG and other Olympic leaders as private officials, its boost from the Salt Lake City scandal highlights the visibility and influence of issues in sports.

Within the Olympic Movement the scandal prompted major reforms of both the composition of the IOC and the terms of membership on it, as well as the

---

[71] *See* Longman, *Samaranch: Olympic Savior or Spoiler?*, N.Y. TIMES, Sept. 10, 2000, at 33, 42.

[72] Olson, *supra* note 70. After three and one-half years of legal proceedings, the court acquitted the defendants, thereby closing the book on the Salt Lake City scandal. Hemphill, *Acquittals End Scandal that Plagued Winter Games*, N.Y. TIMES, Dec. 6, 2003, at B17.

[73] Longman, *supra* note 71.

[74] Olson, *supra* note 70; USA TODAY, Nov. 6, 2003, at 8A. On the IOC inquiry, *see* OLYMPIC REV., Feb.–Mar. 1999, at 34.

[75] Olson, *supra* note 70.

[76] Foy, *Olympic scandal brings guilty plea: Businessman admits committing tax fraud in initial Utah Olympics criminal case*, DETROIT NEWS, Aug. 4, 1999, at A5; Gehrke, *Utah Olympic Scandal Has Rome Link*, ASSOCIATED PRESS, Mar. 14, 2000, *available at* 2000 WL 16859028.

[77] *See* Carter, *Wide World of Payola*, A.B.A. J., Mar. 1999, at 18.

Olympic site-selection process. The result was, first, the adoption of a Code of Ethics and establishment of a blue-ribbon Ethics Commission.[78] The IOC also approved a detailed set of amendments to the Olympic Charter that changed the bidding-and-election processes for future Olympic sites, established a separate Election Committee to select the host city, largely eliminated the direct involvement of IOC members in the site-evaluation process, and otherwise curtailed their discretion to accept gifts and other advantages related to their status and work as IOC members.[79] The scandal also encouraged the Beijing OCOG to establish an anti-corruption unit to help ensure more open bidding and market-based development in preparing for the 2008 Summer Games.[80]

2. The Cricket Scandals

A long history of suspicions about match-fixing by athletes and officials in international cricket competition came to a head with an admission to that effect by Hansie Cronjé, former captain of the South African national team, who confessed to accepting money from bookmakers in return for information.[81] It was later determined that two other international captains, from India and Pakistan, similarly had accepted money from bookmakers in return for information.[82] An Australian match-fixing scandal in 1995 also contributed to the crisis of confidence in the integrity of the sport.[83] Cricket is especially attractive to bookmakers because of the unusually broad range of statistics that can be bet upon.[84] Moreover, the growing popularity of one-day test matches provides more frequent opportunities for betting as well. Estimates of underground and illegal betting on just a single one-day international match run as high as $150 million.[85]

Each of the countries implicated in the match-fixing scandal conducted investigations. It became apparent that "[s]elf-regulation [by the cricket associations] can no longer be trusted."[86] More effective anti-gambling laws were clearly

---

78 OLYMPIC REV., Aug.–Sept. 1999, at 15–16.

79 *See* OLYMPIC CHARTER, Rules 20, 37, 39. For an excellent synopsis of the reforms, *see IOC 2000 Reforms*, OLYMPIC REV., Dec. 1999–Jan. 2000 (Supp.). *See also* Longman, *I.O.C. Displays Unity With its Reform Rules*, N.Y. TIMES, Dec. 12, 1999, at 46.

80 *See* N.Y. TIMES, Feb. 3, 2002, at Sports 9.

81 *See* Le Roux, *The Cronjé Affair*, 2002 INT'L SPORTS L.J., No. 2, at 11; INT'L HERALD TRIB., June 17, 2002, at 13.

82 *Id.*

83 *See* Gardiner, *Cricket Match-fixing: A Worldwide Update*, 3 SPORTS L. BULL., Sept.–Oct. 2000, at 18, 19.

84 INT'L HERALD TRIB., June 17, 2002, at 13.

85 *See* Gardiner, *Sports Corruption & Governance in Sport: What Is the Answer?*, *in* INTERNATIONAL SPORTS LAW & BUSINESS IN THE 21ST CENTURY, Panel 5 (2003).

86 Gardiner, *supra* note 83, at 19.

needed. The International Cricket Council (ICC) appointed an Anti-Corruption Unit to reinforce the initiatives at the national level.[87] The result was to impose lifetime bans on the eligibility for international competition of the three former national captains and to establish new enforcement procedures and penalties for match-fixing (lifetime ban on eligibility) and betting on matches in which a betting playing or sports official or country is involved (five-year ban).[88]

The battle against organizational corruption is endless. The difficulty of protecting sports from the gambling industry, in particular, is evidenced by the cricket scandals. One analysis concluded soberly that "[r]ules and regulations may superficially address the gambling problem, but the truth is that the gambling spirit is very strongly embedded in certain cricket-playing nations and rules will have very little or no impact on breaking this culture."[89] Instead, careful management of athletes, greater accountability and transparency in the supervision of sports activity, and international cooperation to combat corruption appear to be essential.

---

[87] *See* Richards, *Cricket Council to Name Investigator*, INT'L HERALD TRIB., May 4, 2000, at 18.

[88] *Id.*

[89] *See* Le Roux, *supra* note 81, at 15.

CHAPTER 3
DISPUTE RESOLUTION

A. THE PROBLEMS OF COMPLEXITY

The unique investment of competitive egos, emotions, expectations, and money in international sports almost guarantees a dividend of highly charged disputes.[1] The structure for resolving them is complex.[2] Constituent institutions include national sports organizations or governing bodies, the IOC, IFs, NOCs, mediation facilities, national arbitral tribunals and courts, the Court of Arbitration for Sport (CAS), and intergovernmental organizations such as the European Union and the (British) Commonwealth of Nations.

Unfortunately, these institutions do not play according to the same rules. Nor do they share a single captain. Concurrent authority to decide who gets to do what to whom, when and with what effect, does, of course, enhance the probability that *something* will be done to enforce *some* rules. But it also contributes to the confusion of overlapping and sometimes conflicting decisions. Although the Olympic Movement provides a basic framework for dispute resolution that extends well beyond Olympic and Paralympic competition, even its framework is complex. The challenge is therefore to find ways to consolidate the disparate authority into more coherent processes for resolving disputes. It is essential to harmonize or reconcile a welter of rules and procedures in the labyrinth of pertinent institutions, as well as to clarify their respective spheres of authority. This is not to advocate, let alone expect, instant uniformity among the numerous institutions. It is, however, to recognize the need for simplification and greater efficiency in addressing such issues as doping, intellectual property, and player transfers.

---

[1] "The stakes in the world of sport have never been higher and they seem to go on and on rising. The psychological pressures on sportsmen and women in the competitive arena grow ever greater, as the gulf between success and failure tends to widen. At the same time, technological and financial sophistication is increasing the complexity of the regulatory machinery in sport. These developments have increased the potential for conflict between those who participate in sport and those who run it. Judges confronted with the task of adjudicating upon such conflicts in national courts have to strike a balance between avoiding, where possible, the courts becoming embroiled in sporting disputes, and the need to do justice where the facts demonstrate that the regulatory or disciplinary machinery in sport is operating unfairly." M. BELOFF, T. KERR & M. DEMETRIOU, SPORTS LAW 6 (1999).

[2] The overall structure governing Olympic sports has been described as "extraordinarily complex." P. WEILER & G. ROBERTS, SPORTS AND THE LAW 907 (2d ed. 1988) (describing a "sharply heightened" tension between "external legal regulation and internal governance of sport"). *Id.* at 906–07. *Accord*, R. YASSER, J. MCCURDY, C.P. GOPLERUD, & M. WESTON, SPORTS LAW: CASES AND MATERIALS 912 (5th ed. 2003) (describing the "complex" organizational structure of the Olympics and international competition).

Often, then, the issues of international sports law are procedural. High-visibility threats to free and fair competition, from the use of steroids to the display of trademarks, challenge the legal imagination not so much because of disagreement over fundamental values or public policy but because of uncertainty and controversy about the appropriate mechanisms for expeditiously and fairly resolving disputes. Two cases illustrate a few of the problems of complexity.

1. *Foschi v. United States Swimming, Inc.*[3]

Foschi v. United States Swimming, Inc. concerned the eligibility for swimming competition of Jessica Foschi, who was subject to the authority of United States Swimming, Inc. (USS), a national governing body. Following competition in 1995, Foschi's urine samples tested positive for the anabolic steroid mesterolene. A hearing panel of the USS upheld this evidence of doping but determined that Foschi "had no knowledge of the manner in which the banned substance entered her body."[4] After lengthy administrative proceedings, the USS board of directors, acting as a final appeals body, accepted these determinations and imposed limited sanctions against Foschi. These included a two-year probation, a rescission of her times in the competition, and a warning that any subsequent determination of doping would result in a lifetime ban on her participation in amateur swimming competition. Subsequently, the USS imposed an outright ban on her eligibility for competition, but reversed itself by reinstating the original, limited sanctions. She was then allowed to participate in U.S. trials for the 1996 Olympic Games, where the question of her eligibility under IF rules became moot when she failed to qualify for the team.

Foschi then filed a demand for arbitration by the American Arbitration Association (AAA), challenging the limited sanctions that remained against her, especially the threat of a lifetime ban if she should ever be found to have engaged in doping. She proceeded under the Amateur Sports Act,[5] which governs internationally related athletic activity in the United States and of United States athletes preparing for or involved in international competition. The USS claimed that Foschi's claim was moot insofar as she was free to compete as long as she remained free of doping. The AAA panel confirmed its competence to hear the matter, however. It then heard extensive testimony and reviewed a large amount of documentation. The panel considered but did not rule on Foschi's claim that she had been denied due process because the rules of the United

---

[3] *See* In the Matter of Arbitration Between Jessica K. Foschi & United States Swimming, Inc., American Arbitration Association Arbitral Tribunal, No. 77-190-0036-96 (1996) [hereinafter Foschi arbitration]; CAS 96/156 (1976). *See also* Foschi v. U.S. Swimming, Inc. & USOC, 916 F. Supp. 232 (E.D.N.Y. 1996) (remanding Foschi's breach of contract claim from federal to state court).

[4] *Id.*

[5] Amateur Sports Act, 36 U.S.C. §§ 220501–29 (1994 and West Supp. 1998) (since 1998 known as The Ted Stevens Olympic and Amateur Sports Act) [hereinafter Amateur Sports Act].

States Olympic Committee (USOC) did not provide for alternative testing of a controverted urine sample.

The AAA panel decided to rescind all sanctions against Foschi, concluding that they violated fundamental fairness by their arbitrary and capricious nature. In doing so, the panel rejected a strict liability rule of the Fédération Internationale de Natation Amateur (FINA), the IF whose Doping Control Program and anti-doping rules govern the USS. The AAA panel noted that the USS had not contested the determination of Foschi's apparent innocence of the circumstances by which the controlled substance entered her body. It ruled that to discount her innocence would be unjust. Ignoring her innocence would only vindicate what the panel determined to be a questionable purpose of the FINA rules "to insure that not one guilty party go free, albeit that innocent parties are punished," a purpose, the AAA panel ruled, that "turns our concept of justice on its head."[6]

The arbitral panel acknowledged that its rejection of FINA's rule of strict liability left a lacuna in the penalty rules of both the USS and FINA. Nevertheless, it concluded that there was simply no authority for the penalty imposed by the USS, however admirable it might have been as a compromise. The AAA therefore sent a strong message that although it was prepared to establish certain presumptions in favor of a national governing body, it could not do so under the circumstances of the case.

This stage of *Foschi* might be viewed as just another national arbitral decision contrary to the rules of an IF—the very sort of conflict that the pluralistic regime of international sports law engenders. It is significant, however, that the AAA opinion took account of a FINA decision in a comparable doping case involving an Australian swimmer, Samantha Riley. The AAA opinion therefore gains credibility for its attention to foreign precedent, in other words, for its openness to, if not reliance on, comparative insights—an approach to dispute resolution that helps avoid unnecessary conflicts and assist in reforming the mechanisms for resolving sports-related disputes.

The AAA's decision did not end the matter, however. Instead, FINA reimposed a two-year suspension against the swimmer, retroactive in part to the date of the urine testing. Foschi appealed her suspension to the CAS. On June 17, 1997, the CAS reduced FINA's retroactive suspension to six months and ordered costs against FINA. Foschi also brought legal action for breach of contract against both USS and the USOC, leading to complicated litigation involving both state and federal courts.[7]

---

[6] Foschi arbitration, *supra* note 3.

[7] *Foschi*, 916 F. Supp. 232, *supra* note 3.

2. *Nagra v. Canadian Amateur Boxing Ass'n*[8]

A Canadian case demonstrates how pluralism can frustrate the normal resolution of even relatively simple sports disputes that do not involve such troublesome issues as the probity of evidence or *mens rea*.[9] *Nagra v. Canadian Amateur Boxing Ass'n* concerned a boxer's eligibility to compete in Canadian championship competition. As a Sikh, the boxer, Pardeep Singh Nagra, wore a beard. In order to pass a required medical examination, however, both the Canadian Amateur Boxing Association (CABA) and the International Amateur Boxing Association (IABA) require all sanctioned competitors to be clean shaven. Because he expected to be disqualified on that basis, Mr. Nagra apparently avoided the normal administrative process within the sports bodies and challenged the anti-hirsute rule in the Ontario courts. Because of the human rights implications, the courts assumed jurisdiction to review what otherwise was within the concurrent administrative review processes of the CABA and IABA. After two stages of litigation, a related delay of scheduled competition and the threat of another suit by the World Sikh Organization, the provincial court struck down the anti-hirsute prohibition as a violation of Canadian human rights law. The court further ordered CABA to allow Mr. Nagra to compete in the national championships. Although the result may have been justified, the ability of Mr. Nagra to bypass a well-established procedure of private administrative review by using precious judicial resources was questionable. It is possible, for example, that CABA and the IABA might have waived the controversial rule and thereby obviated the need for judicial review of it. In any event, the exhaustion of administrative remedies within the CABA and IABA would seem to have been a preferable approach under the circumstances.

B. THE INSTITUTIONAL STRUCTURE

The principal institutions for resolving international sports disputes are described in the following sections.

1. National Governing Bodies or Sports Organizations

National governing bodies or sports organizations have primary responsibility to avoid and resolve disputes and to apply sanctions, from playing field infractions to eligibility issues. Disagreements between athletes and their respective sports bodies are typically resolved by internal administrative review within those bodies, by independent arbitration, or by a combination of these two methods.

National governing bodies are generally subject to the rules of their respective IFs. National law may clarify the relationship between the national govern-

---

[8] Nagra v. Canadian Amateur Boxing Ass'n, No. 99-CV-180990 (Ont. Super. Ct. Jan. 12, 2000); Nagra v. Canadian Amateur Boxing Ass'n, No. 99-CV-180990 (Ont. Super. Ct. Dec. 1, 1999).

[9] *See* Haslip, *A Consideration of the Need for a National Dispute Resolution System for National Sport Organizations in Canada*, 11 MARQ. SPORTS L. REV. 245, 259–62 (2001).

ing bodies and the IFs or other international authority such as the IOC. In the United States, for example, the Amateur Sports Act provides that a national governing body for each sport shall "designate individuals and teams to represent the United States in international amateur athletic competition . . . and certify, *in accordance with applicable international rules*, the amateur eligibility of those individuals and teams."[10]

2. International Federations

International Federations (IFs) may authoritatively review decisions of constituent national bodies concerning a broad range of issues involving competitions and the status of individual athletes. Internal disciplinary rules and appellate processes are well-developed in IFs, forming what the Court of Arbitration for Sport has called "a legal régime *de privati juris*, having an international, or even global vocation."[11] What happens, however, when their decisions conflict with those of other institutions within the Olympic Movement, particularly the IOC and NOCs? Rules of the Olympic Charter are supreme, but it is somewhat unclear under what circumstances IOC decisions will trump IF decisions. What is clear is that disagreements between IFs and constituent national governing bodies that do not engage national regulation are generally resolved by arbitration.[12] Also, disagreements between IFs and NOCs are generally resolved by the IOC itself or occasionally by the Court of Arbitration for Sport (CAS). Resulting decisions have usually favored the IFs. An example is an advisory opinion of the CAS to subordinate NOC decisions on doping of athletes to the primary jurisdiction of the IFs.[13]

3. National Olympic Committees

National Olympic Committees (NOCs) may intervene in disputes involving the eligibility of athletes for participation in sanctioned competition. National laws sometimes accord NOCs exclusive jurisdiction to sanction international competition and to determine the eligibility of athletes to compete. These laws,

---

[10] AMATEUR SPORTS ACT at § 220523(a)(7), *supra* note 5 (emphasis added). This rule applies except in the instance of Olympic, Pan-American and Paralympic competition, concerning which the United States Olympic Committee has primary jurisdiction.

[11] *See, e.g.*, B. v. FIBA, CAS 92/80 (1996), *in* DIGEST OF CAS AWARDS 1986–1998, at 197, 302 (M. Reeb ed., 1998) [hereinafter DIGEST OF CAS AWARDS]. For a compilation of IF rules and processes, *see* ARBITRAL AND DISCIPLINARY RULES OF INTERNATIONAL SPORTS ORGANIZATIONS (Siekmann & Soek eds., 2001).

[12] International Amateur Athletic Federation (IAAF) Rule 21.1, for example, provides that "[a]ll disputes between Members, or between Members and the Council or Congress [of the IAAF], however arising, shall be submitted to the Arbitration Panel [of the IAAF] for determination within three months of the date upon which the disputed decision was made." International Amateur Athletic Federation, *in* BASIC DOCUMENTS OF INTERNATIONAL SPORTS ORGANISATIONS 89, 107 (Siekmann & Soek eds., 1998) [hereinafter BASIC DOCUMENTS].

[13] CAS 94/128 (1995).

however, sometimes limit the competence of NOC rulings on specific issues such as the duration of Olympic training, selection and competition.

4. The International Olympic Committee

The International Olympic Committee (IOC), on its own initiative or that of an athlete or an IF, may review a broad range of decisions by NOCs. Under Rule 31 of the Olympic Charter, the IOC recognizes the "exclusive powers" of NOCs to represent their countries or select athletes to represent them in sanctioned competition, but Rule 30 grants power to the IFs to establish criteria of eligibility and to establish and enforce rules to govern the practice of their respective sports.[14] The IOC nevertheless retains authority as a final arbiter of disputes within the Olympic Movement.

5. The Court of Arbitration for Sport

a. *Structure*

The Court of Arbitration for Sport (CAS) was created in 1983 and formally established in 1984 by the IOC for resolving disputes related to international sports.[15] Its headquarters are in Lausanne, Switzerland. The CAS also maintains offices in Sydney and New York to facilitate its work.

The purpose of the CAS is to provide a central specialized authority to decide sports-related disputes.[16] Its jurisdiction is broad, extending to "all activities pertaining to sport and whose settlement is not otherwise provided for in the Olympic

---

14 Olympic Charter, Rules 30, 31 (2003).

15 For an official summary of the CAS, *see* Court of Arbitration for Sport (CAS), II Digest of CAS Awards 1998–2000, at xxiii (2002) [hereinafter II Digest of Awards].

16 The CAS is governed by a Code of Sports-Related Arbitration, Procedural Rules, and Rules for Resolution of Disputes Arising During the Olympic Games. Court of Arbitration for Sport, Code of Sports-Related Arbitration (1995). For commentary on the CAS and its work, *see* Bitting, *Mandatory, Binding Arbitration for Olympic Athletes: Is The Process Better or Worse for "Job Security?"*, 25 Fla. St. U.L. Rev. 655 (1998); Fitzgerald, *The Court of Arbitration for Sport: Dealing with Doping and Due Process During the Olympics*, 7 Sports L.J. 213 (2000); Fumagalli, *Il Tribunal Arbitrale dello Sport: Bilancio dell'Attività e Prospettive Future*, 47 Rivista di Diritto Sportivo 715 (1995); McLaren, *The Court of Arbitration for Sport: An Independent Arena for the World's Sports Disputes*, 35 Val. U.L. Rev. 379 (2001); Nafziger, *International Sports Law: A Replay of Characteristics and Trends*, 86 Am. J. Int'l L. 489, 491 (1992); Polvino, *Arbitration as Preventative Medicine for Olympic Ailments: The International Olympic Committee's Court of Arbitration for Sport and the Future for the Settlement of International Sporting Disputes*, 8 Emory Int'l L. Rev. 347 (1994); Raber, *Dispute Resolution in Olympic Sport: The Court of Arbitration for Sport*, 8 Seton Hall J. Sport L. 75 (1998); Reeb, *The Court of Arbitration for Sport (CAS): An Institution for Settling Sports-Related Disputes by Arbitration*, *in* Sports & European Community Law 199 (D. Panagiotopoulos ed., 1998); Rochat, *The Court of Arbitration for Sport*, 26 Olympic Rev., Aug.–Sept. 1997, at 73.

Charter."[17] The Charter itself provides that "[a]ny dispute arising on the occasion of, or *in connection with*, the Olympic Games"[18] must be submitted exclusively to the CAS. According to the CAS Rules of Procedure, the applicable law to decide a dispute is that chosen by the parties or, in the absence of such a choice, Swiss law. In the instance of a dispute between an athlete and an IF where the parties have not chosen the governing law, Swiss choice-of-law rules will refer to the statutes and regulations of the IF.[19] The parties may also authorize the CAS to decide a dispute *ex aequo et bono*.[20] CAS arbitration involves both written and oral arguments.

The CAS does not resolve technical questions such as those related to the technical rules of the game, scheduling of competition, or prescribed dimensions of the playing field or ball court. Instead, it addresses such important issues as the eligibility and suspension of athletes, the adequacy of protections for individual athletes during drug testing, breaches of contract between an athlete and a sports club, the validity of contracts for the sale of sports equipment, television rights, licensing, sponsorship, and the nationality of athletes for purposes of competition.[21] Basically, the CAS hears three kinds of disputes: disciplinary, eligibility-related, and commercial.

---

[17] More fully, the CAS resolves:

> disputes of a *private* nature arising out of the practice or development of sport, and in a general way, *all* activities pertaining to sport and whose settlement is *not otherwise* provided for in the Olympic Charter. Such disputes may bear on questions of principle relating to sport or on pecuniary or other interests.

Art. 4, Statute of the Court of Arbitration for Sport (emphasis added).

[18] OLYMPIC CHARTER, Rule 74 (emphasis added). The scope of the phrase "in connection with the Olympic Games" is an open question.

[19] In B. v. FIBA, the CAS declared that "[t]he federative law adopted by the FIBA constitutes a legal régime *de privati juris*, having an international, or even global vocatioin . . . [the CAS] will interpret the provisions of this federative law in the light of general principles of law." DIGEST OF CAS AWARDS, *supra* note 11, at 302.

[20] Code of Sports-related Arbitration, Rules of Procedure, R45 (1995).

[21] As the Swiss Federal Tribunal noted, in a definitive opinion on the independence and impartiality of the CAS:

> A public-law appeal is only admissible if the arbitral tribunal concerned ruled on points of law and not solely on the application of sporting rules, which do not in principle fall under the jurisdiction of the courts. That is the case in this instance, since anti-doping rules, which deal primarily with sanctions, generally lie outside the framework of simple sporting rules. . . . Furthermore, suspension from international competitions is far more serious than simple sanctions designed to protect the smooth running of a sport and constitutes a genuine statutory punishment that affects the legal interests of the person concerned. It therefore falls within the jurisdiction of the courts.

Swiss Federal Tribunal, 1st Civil Chamber, Judgment of 27 May 2003, at § 2.1 (citation omitted).

The CAS arbitrates disputes brought by individual athletes as well as by IFs and national governing bodies. The CAS is empowered to review decisions of an IF if any of the following are at issue: the IF's constitution, its powers over an individual athlete's person or property, its adherence to the principles of good faith and general contract law, or its compliance with procedural fairness.[22] The interests of individual athletes are fundamental. On the issue of an athlete's strict liability for doping, for example, "the interests of the athlete take precedence over those of the federation."[23]

The advantages of the CAS arbitral procedures have been described as "confidentiality, specialization of the arbitrators, flexibility and simplicity of the procedure, speed, reduced costs and international effectiveness of the arbitration award."[24] CAS awards are final and binding on the parties. They can be enforced internationally by the New York Convention on the Recognition and Enforcement of Foreign Arbitral Awards.[25]

With one exception, all IFs require clauses in contracts between athletes and national governing bodies by which the contracting parties agree to submit all disputes between them to mandatory arbitration.[26] The exception is the International Federation of Football Associations (FIFA), which has its own arbitral tribunal. Athletes selected for the Olympics and other international competition must now sign a waiver form by which they agree to exclusive CAS jurisdiction over all disputes involving doping and other issues of eligibility.[27] Such waivers establish a basis for enforcing awards against individual athletes even when their future livelihood may be at issue. This has become highly significant as the distinction between "amateur" and "professional" athletes has faded and open competition has become common.

In 1993 the Swiss Federal Tribunal recognized the CAS as a true court of arbitration that had acted independently of an IF—in the case in point, the

---

22 Advisory Opinion at the request of the Australian Olympic Committee, CAS 2000/C/267 ACO (2000) (Richard M. McLaren, Sole Arbitrator).

23 A. v. XXX, CAS 2001/A/317, at 19 (2001).

24 II DIGEST OF AWARDS, *supra* note 15, at 203.

25 CONVENTION ON THE RECOGNITION AND ENFORCEMENT OF FOREIGN ARBITRAL AWARDS, *done* June 10, 1958, 330 U.N.T.S. 3 [hereinafter NEW YORK CONVENTION].

26 IAAF Rule 20.2 provides that "[e]ach Member shall incorporate in its constitution provision that all disputes between that Member and an athlete, or between an athlete and the IAAF, shall be submitted to arbitration. In the case of a dispute between a Member and an athlete and the IAAF, this dispute may, at the option of the Council, be submitted to the IAAF's Arbitration Panel." BASIC DOCUMENTS, *supra* note 12. For a detailed description of one such agreement, *see* Buti, *AOC Athletes' Agreement for Sydney 2000: The Implications for the Athletes*, 22 U.N.S.W. L.J. 746 (1999).

27 *See* OLYMPIC CHARTER, Rule 74 (2000).

International Equestrian Federation—even though both were headquartered in Lausanne and were integrated into the Olympic Movement. The court's *dictum*, however, cautioned that the close links between the CAS and the IOC might compromise the independence of the CAS in any proceedings involving the IOC as a party.

The Swiss court's observation led to reforms in 1993 that became effective in 1994. These reforms were incorporated into a two-part Code of Sports-related Arbitration (the Code). It contains Statutes of the Bodies Working for the Settlement of Sports-related Disputes (basically defining the reformed structure and operation of the CAS) and Procedural Rules. The most fundamental reform was to establish an umbrella organization, the International Council of Arbitration for Sport (ICAS), entirely independent of the IOC. Its purpose is to administer and finance the CAS. The 20 members of the ICAS must be high-level jurists who agree not to serve as either arbitrators or counsel in CAS proceedings. There are some 200 available arbitrators, all with legal training and competence to decide sports-related issues. Each arbitrator is appointed by the ICAS for a renewable four-year term.

The 1994 reforms also restructured the CAS by creating two principal arbitration divisions: an Ordinary Arbitration Division and an Appeals Arbitration Division so as to distinguish disputes of the first instance from those arising on appeal of decisions by sports bodies, including IFs. In addition to the two arbitration divisions to hear contentious cases, the Code's Procedural Rules provide for advisory opinions. Constituents of the Olympic Movement may also request consultation proceedings concerning any legal issue with respect to the practice or development of sports or any activity related to sports. Since 1999 the CAS also offers a mediation procedure, but it excludes doping and disciplinary disputes on the premise that an athlete should not be allowed to negotiate a settlement of those issues. It follows the parties' own stipulations, failing which the CAS mediator determines the appropriate procedure.

Beginning with the Atlanta Games in 1994, the CAS has maintained on-site arbitration to render expeditious decisions on issues that arise in major competition. Since 1996, the decisions from these ad hoc proceedings have arbitrated numerous issues at all of the Olympic Games, the Commonwealth Games, and the European football championships.[28] Because of the near-impossibility of achieving instant agreement on the applicable law by the parties to ad hoc arbitration, as would be necessary during competition, the special rules for the ad hoc proceedings provide for "the applicable regulations, general principles of law and the rules of law, the application of which [a CAS panel] deems appropriate."[29]

---

[28] *See* G. KAUFMANN-KOHLER, ARBITRATION AT THE OLYMPICS (2001). For an early proposal to this effect, *see* Nafziger, *On the Rules of the Games*, OLYMPIC REV., Oct. 1973, at 449, 452.

[29] *See, e.g.*, Rules for the Resolution of Disputes Arising During the XXVI Olympic Games in Athens (2004).

b. Cases

As of 2004, the CAS had received over 500 requests for arbitration and decided some 250 of them.[30] The impetus for the rapid growth of the CAS has been the agreements between it and the IFs by which the federations have acceded to the compulsory jurisdiction of the CAS. In a random survey of ten CAS cases during a four-year period of time, six were disciplinary involving charges of doping against athletes, two involved non-doping issues of eligibility for competition, one related to an endorsement contract between two private companies, and one concerned violence between two national teams in international competition.[31]

A few examples of CAS decisions are instructive.[32] Despite a general rule among IFs of strict liability for doping, CAS awards disclose an inclination by the CAS to avoid unnecessarily harsh results.[33] Second, in determining the validity of anti-doping sanctions against athletes, the CAS consistently relied on the IOC's Medical Code and Drug Formulary Guides rather than its own interpretations of doping.[34] Third, an important advisory opinion of the CAS helped resolve jurisdictional issues in doping cases by establishing the priority of IFs over NOCs in the event of conflict between them.[35] In a fourth case, *Ragheeb v. IOC*,[36] the CAS confirmed that it could review an issue of eligibility only on the basis of an arbitration agreement or a specific accreditation of an athlete for competition by the IOC. Finally, in confirming its jurisdiction, the CAS has not hesitated to deny claims based on a manipulation of rules for strategic advantage. In one case, for example, the CAS reprimanded an NOC for offending the ideal of fair play by improperly seeking disqualification of a competing team to elevate the standing

---

30 *Available at* http:/www/tas-cas.org.

31 Nagano (NAG) 4 & 5 (1998); NAG 2 (1998); Tribunal Arbitral du Sport (CAS) 96/157 (1997); CAS 96/156 (1997); CAS 96/149 (1997); CAS 96/153 (1996); CAS 95/150 (1996); CAS 95/141 (1996); CAS 94/129 (1995); CAS Award of Mar. 30, 1994.

32 Further examples of CAS jurisprudence may be found in the text at notes 69–102, *infra*.

33 A.v XXX, CAS 2001/A/317 (2001); CAS 96/156 (1997) (Foschi). *See generally* Wise, *Sports governing bodies' strict liability drug rule standards*, 14 SPORTS LAW., Sept.–Oct. 1996, at 14.

34 *See, e.g.*, the CAS award in NAG 2 (1998) (deciding the Rebagliati Case at the Nagano Games by reinstating the gold medal of the winner of the snowboarding giant slalom, Canadian Ross Rebagliati, who had tested positive for marijuana). The CAS found, under the Medical Code, that the IOC had no competency to disqualify Rebagliati in the absence of the requisite agreement between the IOC and the international skiing federation (FIS) to provide for tests for cannabinoids (marijuana and hashish). The CAS further found that marijuana was not listed as a banned substance in the Drug Formulary Guide that had been published for athletes participating in the Nagano Games.

35 CAS 94/128 (1995). *See also supra* text accompanying note 11.

36 Ragheeb v. IOC, CAS 2000/A/297 (Aug. 30, 2000).

of its team in competition even though the NOC had not been directly injured by the competing team.[37]

6. National and Regional Courts of Law

The widespread adoption of terminal arbitration clauses in licensing contracts, as well as improved methods for more informal resolution of disputes within national governing bodies and the IFs, have not inhibited litigation altogether. Courts are sometimes the best alternative. Sometimes they are the only alternative. Certain claims may not be subject to arbitration clauses and, even when they are controlling, national law may ensure a right to seek judicial review of arbitral awards. Moreover, claims may involve issues of fundamental human rights, natural justice, public order, mandatory law or *lois de police*. These issues include a professional athlete's right to work, the right to be heard in administrative proceedings, and the right to be free of bias in those proceedings.[38] In particular, the persistent problem of doping entails heavy sanctions that may raise issues of procedural and substantive fairness. Litigation is also important because of a substantial increase in the number of professional or semi-professional athletes whose income (and livelihood)-related claims may extend beyond the competence of administrative procedures and informal tribunals. The CAS has reinforced these premises for litigation by making it clear that the right to be heard (by a national governing body or IF) is a fundamental principle of due process, a violation of which will permit the tribunal to hear a case *de novo*.[39]

The judicial reviewability of decisions by sports bodies, particularly IFs, is as significant as it is controversial. The topic will be addressed at length in Chapter 4. The specific issue of whether a national court can review a decision of the CAS merits particular attention at this point, however. A highly publicized decision of the New South Wales Court of Appeal[40] crystallizes the prevailing view on that issue. There the CAS resolved a dispute just before the Sydney

---

[37] *See* award in NAG 4 & 5 (1998) (reprimanding the Czech NOC for contesting the eligibility of an United States naturalized hockey player who had played for the Swedish team. Despite its conclusion that the player had been ineligible to compete in matches already concluded in Nagano, the CAS refused to order forfeiture of the disputed matches involving the Swedish team. Forfeiture would have accrued in the standings to the advantage of the Czech team).

[38] *See* Nafziger, *International Sports Law as a Process for Resolving Disputes*, 45 INT'L & COMP. L.Q. 130, 145–48 (1996) (English cases) [hereinafter Process]; Nafziger, *International Sports Law: A Replay of Characteristics and Trends*, 86 AM. J. INT'L L. 489, 492 n.13, 505–18 (1992) (United States cases).

[39] CAS 2001/A/317A.v/XXX, at 11 (2001).

[40] Raguz v. Sullivan [2000] N.S.W. Ct. App. 240 (unpublished opinion), *reprinted in* G. KAUFMANN-KOHLER, *supra* note 28, at 51 (2001). For a helpful commentary on the case, *see* Sturzaker & Godhard, *The Olympic Legal Legacy*, 2 MELBOURNE J. INT'L L. 241 (2001).

Games in 2000 between two Australian judokas vying for a place on the Australian Olympic team. The losing competitor, Angela Raguz, challenged the CAS award in the Australian courts by bringing action against the prevailing competitor, Rebecca Sullivan, the Judo Federation of Australia, and the CAS. Sullivan and the CAS objected to the appeal on the basis of an exclusion agreement that all judokas had signed and according to which they prorogated exclusive authority over any Olympic-related dispute to the CAS.

The Australian court denied the appeal, holding that it had no jurisdiction to address the merits of the dispute because the exclusion agreement at issue applied and, further, because the agreement was "foreign" rather than "domestic." The rationale for the foreign characterization of the agreement was the court's acknowledgment that Lausanne, Switzerland was the seat of the CAS. According to the court, the parties' exclusion agreement to put their disputes to the CAS for resolution implied that Lausanne remained the appropriate venue even when the actual venue of the Ad Hoc Division of the CAS had been in Australia. The decision greatly strengthened the integrity and authority of the CAS, presenting a salient example of the reluctance of courts to interfere even with derogation provisions in an agreement under Rule 74 of the Olympic Charter.

It is apparent that international sports litigation is circumscribed. The volume and overall impact of litigation is limited. For example, by one estimate, only one-tenth of 1 percent of all decisions of football-governing bodies in Germany go to court.[41] The rate of litigation may, of course, vary according to the litigiousness of a particular national system.

Regional courts may also hear sports disputes. The prime example is the European Court of Justice, which heard the famous *Bosman* case.[42] The court has played a significant role in restructuring sports law in Europe[43] as it relates to economic integration among member states.[44]

---

[41] Klaus Vieweg, *Judicial Review of Sport Related Decisions in Germany, in* INTERNATIONAL ATHLETIC FOUNDATION, SPORT & LAW: SUPPLEMENT TO THE OFFICIAL PROCEEDINGS OF THE IAF SYMPOSIUM ON SPORT & LAW 87, 96 (1995).

[42] Union Royale Belge des Sociétés de Football Ass'n ASBL v. Bosman, Case C-415/93 [1995] 1CEC 381 (striking down football association rules limiting international transfers and foreign team membership of players, as violations of the Treaty of Rome and European Union law).

[43] European Court of Justice decisions in sports-related cases that pre-dated *Bosman* include Walrave v. Union Cycliste Internationale, Case 36/74, 1974 E.C.R. 1405, and Donà v. Mantero, Case 13/76, 1976 E.C.R. 1333. For discussion of these issues, *see* Weatherill, *Resisting the Pressures of "Americanization": The Influence of European Community Law on the "European Sports Model,"* 8 WILLAMETTE J. INT'L LAW & DISP. RESOL. 37 (2000); G. BERMANN ET AL., CASES AND MATERIALS ON EUROPEAN COMMUNITY LAW 513–14 (1993); Rogge, *The Olympic Movement and the European Union*, OLYMPIC REV., Oct.–Nov. 1995, at 44.

[44] *See, e.g.*, Lestón, *A jurisprudência do Tribunal de Justiça das Comunidades Europeias em matéria desportiva*, 1 DESPORTO & DIREITO, No. 1, at 54 (2003).

7. Alternative Dispute Resolution (ADR)

The CAS attempts to facilitate conciliation of disputes during ordinary arbitration and has established procedures for mediation.[45] The advantages of these forms of alternative dispute resolution (ADR) are greater informality, party autonomy, confidentiality, encouragement of consensus and relationship building, and cost effectiveness. The CAS mediation process is very simple. The parties must have agreed in advance to mediation, but there is no standard CAS mediation clause. The process, too, is simple, putting a premium on the parties' own initiatives. The disputes submitted for mediation have been primarily commercial or administrative (interorganizational) in nature and may not involve doping or disciplinary issues.[46]

As the regime of international sports law becomes more universal, it is likely that the role of such relatively informal methods for resolving disputes that transcend the authority of national governing bodies and IFs will increase. In East Asia, in particular, recourse to consultation, mediation or conciliation is expected. Informal procedures of dispute resolution are often prerequisites to arbitration and adjudication. Even in western industrialized countries, more informal methods of dispute resolution are increasingly important[47] and acceptable[48] to national courts.

One constraint is in disciplinary disputes involving doping or other sanctions insofar as athletes, on a theory of strict enforcement of sanctions, should not be entitled to any adjustments.[49] The CAS mediation procedure is therefore not available in either doping cases or disputes related to disciplinary matters.[50] Also, general mediators are often unable to provide the required technical expertise in some kinds of disputes, for example, involving intellectual property rights.

Another constraint to a fuller use of ADR may be a resistance by sports lawyers who view themselves primarily as litigators. A fourth constraint on the use of mediation and conciliation is the sheer intractability of disputes involving such high-stake issues as licensing, television rights, and commercial sponsorship. The interests of parties to such disputes are so differentiated and their

---

[45] *See generally* the definitive work on this subject, BLACKSHAW, MEDIATING SPORTS DISPUTES: NATIONAL AND INTERNATIONAL PERSPECTIVES (2002). For concise descriptions of the CAS mediation, *see* Rochat, *supra* note 16; Kane, *The CAS Mediation Rules*, INT'L SPORTS L.J., No. 1, at 33 (2003).

[46] Kane, *id.*, at 34.

[47] *See* Epstein, *Alternative Dispute Resolution in Sport Management and the Sport Management Curriculum*, 12 J. LEGAL ASPECTS OF SPORT 153 (2002).

[48] BLACKSHAW, *supra* note 45, at 3.

[49] BLACKSHAW, *supra* note 45, at 206.

[50] Naidoo & Sarin, *Dispute Resolution at Games Time*, 12 FORDHAM INTELL. PROP. MEDIA & ENT. L.J. 489, 517 (2002), *citing* Newmark, *Is Mediation Effective for Resolving Sports Disputes?*, INT'L SPORTS L.J., May 2001, at 37.

commitment to those interests—often stated as their "positions"—is often so hardened that attempts at mediation or conciliation of a dispute may be futile. Finally, national mandatory laws and *lois de police* may deny recourse to mediation.

8. Conclusion

It is apparent that the current institutional structure for resolving disputes within the process of international sports law is untidy. It is a process in transition, as national sports bodies and IFs gradually assume more responsibility, develop better rules, and thereby gain greater respect in dispute resolution. In this transitional period, the resolution of sports-related disputes is often complicated if not incoherent. Gradually, though, national governing bodies and IFs are becoming more skilled and sophisticated in resolving disputes. As institutions gain greater insights, their decisions will become more standardized, and arbitral tribunals and courts of law will gain greater confidence in deferring to them. Inevitably, experience is a teacher.

C. *LEX SPORTIVA*

1. Introduction

Arbitral awards are normally binding only in the cases and on the parties to which they are addressed. Unlike judicial decisions in common law systems, arbitral awards therefore have no currency as *stare decisis*. At the most, they may sometimes constitute a *lex specialis*.

In practice, however, the awards and opinions of the CAS provide guidance in later cases, strongly influence later awards, and often function as precedent. Also, by reinforcing and helping elaborate established rules and principles of international sports law, the accretion of CAS awards and opinions is gradually forming a source of that body of law. This source has been called the *lex sportiva*.

The concept of a *lex sportiva*, as a coherent and influential corpus of practice, has been identified with the *lex mercatoria* or law merchant, a venerable source of law that is said to form the foundation of international commercial practice and commercial arbitration.[51] Leaving aside the jurisprudential questions about the status of the *lex mercatoria*,[52] the association of the two terms may be

---

[51] Lord Mansfield, in a memorable statement, described the *lex mercatoria* in Latin: non erit alia lex Romae, alia Athenis; alia nunc, posthac; sed et apud omnes gentes et omni tempore, una eadem lex obtinebit. ("It will not be the law of Rome or the law of Athens; not one law now, another hereafter; but one and the same law, for all people and for all times.") Luke v. Lyde, 97 Eng. Rep. 787 (1759). For commentary on the analogy between the *lex sportiva* and the *lex mercatoria*, *see* Panagiotopoulos, Sports Law: A European Dimension 17–18 (2003).

[52] The following critique of the *lex mercatoria* argues that, unlike international sports law and the *lex sportiva*, it has developed solely on the basis of commercial practices, rather than on the basis of national and international law. The questions that the *lex mercatoria* raises, as

somewhat strained. On one hand, the *lex mercatoria*, having developed from commercial practice over hundreds of years, enjoys a cachet of custom. Also, the *lex mercatoria* extends comprehensively to international commercial activity and institutions. Moreover, the *lex mercatoria* enjoys recognition in both private and public sectors, having a claim in some legal systems to authority as public law.

On the other hand, the *lex sportiva* is the product of only a few hundred arbitral decisions within a limited range of disputes over a historically short period of time. It is still more of a *lex ferenda* than a mature *lex specialis*. Also, the concept of a *lex sportiva* is not as comprehensive of its subject as the *lex mercatoria*. Instead, it is limited to arbitral awards within the larger sphere of international sports law. Although by one interpretation the term is very broad, nearly coinciding with the term "international sports law,"[53] the present commentary adopts the normal limitation of the concept to CAS awards. Both the status and general scope of the emerging *lex sportiva* are therefore much less substantial than the *lex mercatoria* within their respective spheres of application. Still, the *lex sportiva* may eventually develop into a sort of *lex mercatoria* of sports arbitration.

2. The Scope of the Concept

Although the term *lex sportiva* is generally confined to CAS awards, its scope needs to be clarified. It will be helpful, first, to review choice-of-law rules applicable to CAS arbitration. According to the procedural rules of the CAS, the parties to ordinary arbitration proceedings may exercise autonomy by agreeing to the substantive law to be applied by the tribunal or by authorizing it to proceed *ex aequo et bono*. If the parties do not choose their own law or agree to proceedings *ex aequo et bono*, Swiss law applies.[54] Either the chosen law or Swiss law then

---

follows, are a reminder of the importance of nurturing the growth of a *lex sportiva* that generally conforms with public norms and expectations:

> The most successful case of law without a state has been *lex mercatoria*. . . . Practitioners of international commercial law are involved in a battle about fundamental questions: Should national courts recognize *lex mercatoria*'s "private justice" as a new positive law with transnational validity? Could such an ambiguous normative phenomenon which is "between and beyond" the laws of the nation-states and at the same time "between and beyond" law and society be applied by arbitration bodies according to the rules of the law of conflicts? Does it contain distinct rules and principles of its own? Obviously, a new legal practice has been established with its own substantive law and its own judge-made law that cannot be integrated in the traditional hierarchies of national and international law.

Teuber, *The King's Many Bodies: The Self-Deconstruction of Law's Hierarchy*, 31 LAW & SOC. REV. 763, 769–70 (1997).

[53] *See* Adolphsen, *Eine lex sportiva für den internationalen Sport?*, *in* JAHRBUCH JUNGER ZIVILRECHTLES 281, 282, 300 (2003) (suggesting the possibility of a *lex sportiva* free of the compulsions and requirements of national rules).

[54] Court of Arbitration for Sport, Procedural Rule R45, *in* CODE OF SPORTS RELATED ARBITRATION 58 (1995). The tribunal's procedures are not subject to party autonomy, however. Also,

provides the rules for decision, on the basis of which the *lex sportiva* may develop. It is unlikely, as yet, that the parties would choose the *lex sportiva* itself or even some blend of the *lex sportiva* with national law to govern a resolution of their dispute.

Do such issues as the arbitrability of a dispute, the validity of an arbitration agreement, or judicial remedies against awards fall comfortably within the scope of the *lex sportiva*? The Secretary General of the CAS has suggested that they do not; instead, they fall within the *lex arbitrii* of Swiss Law.[55] That is so regardless of the actual location of a CAS hearing and award because the seat of the CAS for legal purposes is always in Lausanne, Switzerland. Consequently, the Swiss Federal Act on Private International Law governs issues within its competence in all CAS arbitrations even when one of more of the parties is domiciled or has its registered office outside Switzerland.

What about arbitral pronouncements on the human rights of athletes or on labor, anti-trust (competition) and other regulatory law? They, too, would appear to fall outside the scope of the *lex sportiva*, as would any awards deviating from the requirements of mandatory (Swiss) law or public policy (*ordre public*). Also, many commercial issues bearing on sports but not directly affecting athletes do not fall comfortably within the jurisdiction of the CAS. Moreover, pronouncements about the structure and relationships among constituent federations and other institutions within the Olympic Movement would seem to be *exces de pouvoir*.

3. The Purposes of the Concept and Some Implications

An obvious purpose for developing a *lex sportiva* is to guide later awards and thereby stabilize expectations about arbitration of particular issues. Consistency of decision-making is a hallmark of any creditable method of dispute resolution. A fully developed *lex sportiva* would help apply three values that the principle of stare *decisis* serves: efficiency of the legal process, predictability or stability of expectations, and equal treatment of similarly situated parties. Thus, "[t]he lex sportiva will clearly be more beneficial than decisions taken ex aequo et bono. It would form part of the law. The law provides more predictability which is necessary for the clear determination of the rights and obligations of the parties."[56]

---

the rules for resolving disputes during Olympic competition, as distinguished from ordinary arbitration, do not provide for party autonomy, given the exigencies of prompt decisions. Instead, the applicable law ordinarily includes the Olympic Charter, applicable regulations, general principles, and rules of law the application of which the tribunal deems appropriate.

Swiss whole law, including its choice-of-law rules, would prioritize party autonomy to choose the law, and, failing that, the rules of law with which a case in question has the closest link. *See* B. v. FIBA, DIGEST OF CAS AWARDS, *supra* note 11, at 300.

55 *See* Reeb, *The Role of the Court of Arbitration for Sport, in* INTERNATIONAL LAW AND THE HAGUE'S 750TH ANNIVERSARY 233, 236 (Heere ed., 1999).

56 Oschütz, *Institutional arbitration in sport, in* SPORT ET GARANTIES FONDAMENTALES: VIO-

A broader purpose for developing a *lex sportiva* is to provide authoritative interpretations of the principles and rules of international sports law—for example, provisions of the Olympic Charter—by means of arbitral awards. Eventually, repeated interpretations may shape the development of international sports law well beyond CAS proceedings. Indeed, that is a stated purpose of the CAS,[57] and it is capable of performing this casuistic function, as its decisions on anti-doping sanctions demonstrate.

A further application of the *lex sportiva* is within the administrative review processes of sports organizations, especially the appellate panels of the international sports federations (IFs) such as the International Amateur Athletic Federation (IAAF). There is a critical need for such guidance to enhance the integrity and credibility of the IFs and to improve their image as essential elements in the regime of international sports. Otherwise, their administrative and appellate decisions tend to spark suspicions and controversy. All too often, IF decisions appear to be based on political expediency. In two leading cases, for example, the IAAF lifted anti-doping suspensions against world-class medalists Merlene Ottey of Jamaica and Javier Sotomayor of Cuba.[58] In both instances clear scientific evidence to support their suspensions seems to have been compromised by either faulty review of the evidence (Ottey) or extrinsic factors such as empathy by the IF administrative council with the particular athlete (Sotomayor) that called into question both the independence and the binding force of the arbitration. It is hard to escape the conclusion that "the IAAF panel was no more independent in its actions than the national panels whose decisions they were reviewing [and that an] international arbitration system that is not independent and for which there is a political override, no matter how well intended, will ultimately bring both itself and its sports federation into dispute."[59]

IF decisions such as in the *Ottey* and *Sotomayor* cases have important implications for the future of international sports competition and its organizational structure. Such decisions bespeak a critical need for the kind of corrective

---

LENCES—DOPAGE 507, 516 (Korcha & Pettiti eds., 2003). *But see* a listing of the advantages of more informal methods of sports-related disputes that would not ordinarily contribute to the formation of the *lex sportiva*, BLACKSHAW, *supra* note 45, at 21.

[57] *See* II DIGEST OF AWARDS, *supra* note 15, at xxx, as follows:

> The "Digest of CAS Awards 1986–1998" recorded the emergence of a *lex sportiva* through the judicial decisions of the CAS. It is true that one of the interests of this court is to develop a jurisprudence that can be used as a reference by all the actors of world sport, thereby encouraging the harmonisation of the judicial rules and principles applied within the sports world.

[58] Ottey v. IAAF, IAAF Decision, July 3, 2000 (unpublished); Sotomayor v. IAAF, IAAF Decision, July 24, 2000 (unpublished).

[59] *See* McLaren, *The Court of Arbitration for Sport: An Independent Arena for the World's Sports Disputes*, 35 VAL. U. L. REV. 379, 390 (2001).

jurisprudence that the CAS can supply in the absence of other independent and impartial tribunals with special competence to hear international sports-related disputes. Over time CAS arbitration can also lend greater coherence, rationality, uniformity, and influence to international sports law. It is in everybody's interest to pursue these objectives for the sake of greater predictability and stability of expectations.

The more the teleology of CAS is directed toward greater predictability and stability of expectations, however, the more formal the arbitral process may be viewed. That perspective would give rise to expectations of fully reasoned opinions, rules of evidence, meticulous use of precedent, and other characteristics of litigation. Fulfilling such expectations in CAS proceedings might seem to strengthen the process of international sports law in attaining greater stability and integrity, confidence in the consistency of outcomes among the cases, and growth of a reliable corpus of interpretation, a *lex specialis*.

The merits of a robust *lex sportiva* may be questioned, however. Ordinarily, arbitration represents a happy compromise between the uncertainties of more informal methods of dispute resolution, such as negotiation and mediation, and the formality and inflexibility of adjudication. The opportunity to choose specialized experts to decide a dispute is a particularly attractive feature of arbitration. What would arguably be lost by formalizing the CAS process, however, are several other advantages of arbitration: confidentiality; relatively low cost; simplified procedures; speed; mediative quality; capacity to help restore, preserve and maintain relationships between disputing parties; flexibility and customization to particular circumstances and the wishes of the parties; and international enforceability.[60] Delays and transactional costs mount as formality increases, and formalized arbitration more and more begins to resemble litigation.

Fortunately for parties to CAS arbitration, the Code of Sports-related Arbitration discourages an approximation of adjudication. The Code restricts discovery of evidence, protects confidentiality between the parties, encourages conciliation and mediation within the CAS framework, allows party autonomy in choosing the applicable law, provides for party discretion and flexibility in selecting the arbitral panel, and offers an alternative of expedited procedure. The parties' costs of arbitration are limited to relatively modest fixed rates. Appeals are free of charge. Timelines for conciliation and appeals procedures are a matter of a few months rather than years. Moreover, the Code provides that awards will not be made public (as court decisions normally are) unless an award so provides and all parties agree.

---

[60] For an acknowledgment of several of these advantages by the Secretary General of the CAS, *see*, Reeb, *The Role and Functions of the Court of Arbitration for Sport (CAS)*, 2002/2 INT'L SPORTS L.J. 21, 25.

Happily, CAS practices have conformed well to the Code. They have been sufficiently flexible, however, to enable the CAS to tailor its exercise of discretion to the circumstances of individual cases so as, for example, to strike appropriate balances between privacy and the public interest, depending on the nature of a dispute.

Despite these constraints on formalization of the CAS, the aspiration to create a *lex sportiva* may arguably give a judicial cast to its proceedings. A judgment in 2003 by the Swiss Federal Tribunal bears out this observation. At issue in *A. & B. v. IOC*[61] was a public law appeal of a CAS award in the previous year. The controverted arbitration concerned a decision by the IOC Executive Board to disqualify two cross-country skiers on the basis of positive tests for doping during three competitions in December 2001 and in February 2002 during the Salt Lake City Winter Games. The appeal also challenged the two-year suspensions that were subsequently imposed on the skiers by the International Ski Federation (FIS).

The court first established that the CAS ruling at issue involved points of law and not just sporting rules (rules of the game) on the basis that the serious sanction of suspension from competition constituted "a genuine statutory punishment that affects the legal interests of the person."[62] Much of the court's opinion thereafter addressed a claim that the FIS, IOC, and CAS lacked a requisite independence and impartiality. After examining claims of institutional and personal bias and exhaustively reviewing the history of the CAS and its decoupling from the IOC in 1994, the court concluded that the CAS was sufficiently independent of the IOC and FIS for its decisions to be considered "true awards, equivalent to the judgements of State courts."[63]

The court's litmus of verity in arbitral awards—"true" awards are equivalent to judicial decisions—bespeaks its general characterization of the CAS as a body "more akin to a judicial authority independent of the parties."[64] But how can CAS deliberations be assimilated to adjudication if the plaintiffs, according to the court, had freedom to select arbitrators and procedures? And how can CAS decisions be assimilated to judicial decisions if their publication remains within the discretion of the CAS and only with the consent of the parties? Nevertheless, the court observed that "[a] true 'supreme court of world sport' is growing rapidly and continuing to develop.[65] The court further observed that "states and all

---

61 A. & B. v. IOC, Swiss Fed. Trib., 1st Civil Chamber, Judgement of 27 May 2003.

62 *Id.*, § 2.1.

63 *Id.*, § 3.3.4.

64 *Id.*, § 3.3.3.2.

65 *Id.*, § 3.3.3.3.

parties concerned by the fight against doping . . . endorse the judicial powers [sic] of the CAS."[66]

It is hard to imagine that the court in *A. & B. v. IOC* actually meant to equate arbitral proceedings with adjudication. Perhaps the Swiss court's identification of the CAS with a court of law was only metaphorical. If not, then the Swiss court must have been prepared to vest authority in the CAS to resolve the very issues of public law, human rights, and due process (natural justice) that have been presumed to lie beyond the tribunal's competence. That may be acceptable under Swiss law, which governs the CAS, but may arouse serious apprehensions among prospective foreign parties sufficient to deter them from submitting their disputes to the CAS for arbitration.

For a prospective party not bound to CAS jurisdiction by any prorogation provisions, the idea of conceding plenary, binding, more or less judicial authority to an arbitral body that is governed, at least to the extent of the *lex arbitrii*, by national law may simply be unacceptable. Worse yet, formalized arbitral decisions on sensitive issues of public law, labor relations and human rights may invite parallel litigation in other legal systems. In any event, the Swiss court's puzzling *obiter dictum* complicates the growth of the *lex sportiva*.

The CAS would be well advised to proceed cautiously in constructing the *lex sportiva*. Nobody would deny that the tribunal needs to assume a strong enough stature to withstand extravagant interference by domestic courts[67] and expect that its awards will be recognized and enforced under the New York Convention on Arbitral Awards.[68] But the CAS runs considerable risk when it allows itself to be presented as an institution resembling a national court of law, with all of the expectations and problems associated with international recognition and enforcement of court judgments and all of a party's skepticism about the impartiality of a foreign court.

4. The Case Law

Leaving the jurisdictional questions aside, what has been the range of disputes before CAS panels?[69] What does the CAS case law teach? How well-developed is the *lex sportiva*?

---

[66] *Id.*, § 3.3.4.

[67] Even limited immunity from interference by domestic courts may generate tensions, of course. *See, e.g.*, Sturzaker & Godhard, *supra* note 40, at 248 (discussing an Australian court decision, Raguz v. Sullivan [2000] N.S.W.C.A. 240, that established the international character of CAS arbitration regardless of its physical location on the basis that its juridical seat, by prior agreement between the parties to a dispute, was Lausanne, Switzerland).

[68] NEW YORK CONVENTION, *supra* note 25.

[69] For a presentation of the decisions of the CAS ad hoc tribunals, *see* KAUFMANN-KOHLER, *supra* note 28.

From its beginning, the CAS has given advisory opinions and decided contentious cases involving two dominant themes: jurisdictional questions and eligibility of athletes for sanctioned competition. Most of the latter cases have involved athletes whose eligibility for competition had been suspended or terminated for life by national sports bodies or IFs on the basis of anti-doping sanctions imposed by their national sports bodies or international federations. In one of its first cases, which was conducted *in camera*, the CAS decided a dispute between an athletic club and a national sports body that had imposed a sanction against the club.[70] In another early case, the tribunal rendered an advisory opinion in favor of the Norwegian Olympic Committee in which it upheld the right of an NOC to exclude an athlete from sanctioned competition for life after violating the NOC's anti-doping rules within the IOC framework.[71]

Over time the CAS has fashioned specific rules and principles from its decisions with broad application. For example, equitable considerations have softened CAS review of anti-doping sanctions against athletes. Despite a prevailing rule among IFs of strict liability for doping, CAS awards generally disclose an inclination to avoid unnecessarily harsh results.[72] These awards, in turn, have helped shape the World Anti-Doping Code. Second, in determining the validity of such sanctions, the CAS has consistently relied on the authority of international sports law such as the IOC's Medical Code and Drug Formulary Guidelines, at least until their replacement by the World Anti-Doping Code, rather than its own construction of doping standards and sanctions.[73] Third, an important advisory

---

[70] The IOC's summary of the decision is as follows:

> The Court of Arbitration for Sport, based in Lausanne, has just delivered a verdict which makes a welcome development towards quicker and simpler settlement of sports conflicts. The case to be resolved started with a protest by a club against a sanction imposed on it by its federation. After exhausting all the possibilities for appeal provided for in the federation's statutes, the club brought a legal action before the civil courts. Rather than pursue a slow and expensive procedure, however,—and that is what constitutes the interest of the case—the parties decided by common assent to instruct the Court of Arbitration for Sport to look into the validity of the federation's decision. The federation agreed, it is important to note, to submit the validity of a decision issued by its highest statutory instance to evaluation by the Court of Arbitration for Sport. After consultation, the CAS delivered its verdict on 30th January 1987, confirming the validity of the decision taken by the highest instance of the national federation. However, the verdict will not be published, as the proceedings took place *in camera* in accordance with the Statute of the CAS.

OLYMPIC REV., Mar. 1987, at 96.

[71] OLYMPIC REV., May–June 1987, at 287.

[72] A.v XXX, CAS 2001, A/317 (2001); CAS 96/156 (1997). *See generally* Aaron N. Wise, *Sports governing bodies' strict liability drug rule standards*, 14 SPORTS LAW., Sept.–Oct. 1996, at 14.

[73] *See, e.g.*, CAS award in NAG 2 (1998) (reinstating the gold medal of the winner of the snowboarding giant slalom at the 1998 Winter Games in Nagano, Canadian Ross Rebagliati, who had tested positive for use of marijuana). The CAS found, under the Medical Code, that the

opinion of the CAS helped resolve jurisdictional issues in doping cases by establishing the priority of IFs over NOCs in the event of a jurisdictional conflict between them.[74] In a fourth case, *Ragheeb v. IOC*,[75] the CAS confirmed that it could review an issue of eligibility only on the basis of an arbitration agreement or a specific accreditation of an athlete for competition by the IOC. Because CAS decisions have conformed closely with trends and expectations within the larger process of international sports law, they have been playing a role in defining and refining the applicable rules in that process.

In confirming its broad jurisdiction, the CAS has not hesitated to deny claims based on a manipulation of rules for strategic advantage. In one case, for example, the CAS reprimanded an NOC for violating the principle of fair play by improperly seeking disqualification of a competing team to elevate the standing of its team in competition even though the NOC had not been directly injured by the competing team.[76]

Another important contribution of CAS jurisdictional decisions is the non-interference rule according to which the CAS will not interfere with the rules of the game or official calls in the course of competition. In drawing a line between non-reviewable rules of the game and reviewable rules that transcend the immediacy of competition, three cases of the CAS are instructive. The first arose out of an incident during the 1996 Atlanta Games.[77] In reviewing a referee's disqualification of Boxer M for landing a below-the-belt punch on his opponent, the CAS applied customary international standards, drawn particularly from practice in the United States, France, and Switzerland. The CAS concluded from the general practice that a technical decision, standard or rule during competition—in other words, a non-reviewable game rule—is shielded from arbitral or judicial scrutiny unless the rule or its application by sports officials is arbitrary, illegal, or the product of a wrong or malicious intent against an athlete. In such cases, the rule or its application is reviewable. Sanctions appearing to be excessive or unfair

---

IOC had no competency to disqualify Rebagliati in the absence of the requisite agreement between the IOC and the International Ski Federation (FIS) to provide for tests for cannabinoids (marijuana and hashish). The CAS further found that marijuana was not listed as a banned substance in the Drug Formulary Guide that had been published for athletes participating in the Nagano Games.

[74] TAS 94/128 (1995).

[75] Ragheeb v. IOC, CAS, Aug. 30, 2000 (unpublished).

[76] *See* CAS award in NAG 4 & 5 (1998) (reprimanding the Czech NOC for contesting the eligibility of a United States naturalized hockey player who had played for the Swedish team at the 1998 Winter Games in Nagano). Despite its conclusion that the player had been ineligible to compete in matches already concluded in Nagano, the CAS refused to order forfeiture of the disputed matches involving the Swedish team. Forfeiture would have accrued in the standings to the advantage of the Czech team.

[77] M. v. Ass'n Internationale de Boxe Amateur (AIBA), CAS Ad Hoc Div. (O.G. Atlanta 1996), *in* Digest of Awards, *supra* note 11, at 413.

on their face are also reviewable. The rationale for the *Boxer M* decision was two-fold: that IFs have the responsibility to enforce rules, and referees or ring judges are in a better position than arbitrators to decide technical matters.

A second application of the non-interference rule was the AOC Advisory Opinion.[78] There the CAS considered the reviewability of a decision by the international swimming federation (FINA), less than a year before the 2000 Olympic Games, to approve the use of fullbody ("long john") swimsuits. These highly elastic suits, which were first marketed by Speedo, attempted to simulate natural sharkskin. They were designed to increase a swimmer's speed and endurance, to reduce drag, and possible to enhance the buoyancy of the swimmer. The FINA Bureau, after lengthy discussion, ruled that "the use of these swimsuits does not constitute a violation of the FINA Rules.[79] In response to this ruling, the Australian Olympic Committee (AOC), concerned about possible claims of unfairness at the Sydney Games, asked the CAS for an advisory opinion. The AOC inquired whether the FINA ruling had complied with FINA's own rules and whether, in any event, use of the suits would raise contestable issues of fairness. In a thorough and thoughtful opinion, the CAS properly held that FINA had reached its decision in compliance with its own rules and that its ruling, which was tantamount to approval of bodysuits, did not raise any reviewable issues of unfair procedure, bad faith, conflict with general principles of law, or unreasonableness.[80]

In the third case regarding the non-interference rule, the CAS again applied this approach in an advisory opinion that had been requested by the Canadian Olympic Committee. Among the issues was whether the Council of the International Badminton Federation (IBF) had acted within its jurisdiction and its published rules when it made certain changes in scoring of events. The CAS ruled that it had not. The opinion by Ian Blackshaw, consistent with the *dictum* in the AOC Advisory Opinion, held that the IBF, having failed to comply with its own rules, had exceeded its powers. The IBF Council's decision to change the scoring was therefore *ultra vires*.[81]

5. The Legacy of CAS Awards

In examining the jurisprudential legacy of the emerging *lex sportiva*, two studies of CAS case law are especially instructive. In one of them,[82] a leading

---

[78] Advisory opinion at the request of the Australian Olympic Committee, CAS 2000/C/267 AOC [hereinafter AOC Advisory Opinion].

[79] *Id.* at 12.

[80] *Id.* at 19–21. *But see* Soek, *You don't win silver—you miss the gold*, INT'L SPORTS L.J., Sept. 2000, at 15 (criticizing the advisory opinion for failing to resolve the issue of fairness of the controversial bodysuits).

[81] Advisory opinion at the request of the Canadian Olympic Committee, CAS 2003, C/45.

[82] This study, by arbitrator McLaren, may be found in two sources: McLaren, *supra* note 59; McLaren, *Introducing the Court of Arbitration for Sport: The Ad Hoc Division at the Olympic Games*, 12 MARQ. SPORTS L. REV. 515 (2001) [hereinafter *Introducing the CAS*].

CAS arbitrator examined the cases heard by the Ad Hoc Division at the 2000 Games in Sydney. In the first part of his study,[83] he divided the 15 cases arising from the 2000 Games into five broad categories: doping violations, IF suspensions of athletes, commercial advertising issues, disputes with sports officials, and nationality issues as a matter of eligibility.

In one of the doping cases[84] a German athlete, Dieter Baumann, petitioned for removal of a two-year ban Baumann's eligibility that had been imposed by the IOC under a strict liability rule. The IAAF claimed that the CAS was without jurisdiction because at that time its Bylaws did not recognize CAS jurisdiction. The CAS examined Rule 29 of the Olympic Charter, which provides that "their statutes, practice and activities [of all IFs] must be in conformity with the Olympic Charter."[85] Under Rule 74 of the Olympic Charter,[86] the IAAF was therefore subject to the jurisdiction of the CAS. Also, the principle of *res judicata* did not apply to bar CAS review of the IAAF decision because neither Baumann nor the IOC had been a party to the IAAF arbitration. Acting therefore as an appeals court over the IAAF, the CAS upheld the IAAF decision to suspend Baumann's eligibility on the basis that the IAAF had properly addressed the evidence. In a similar due process or natural justice claim, the CAS upheld a suspension by the IAAF of Mihaela Melinte.[87]

The most highly publicized case decided by the Ad Hoc Division of the CAS in Sydney involved Andrea Raducan, a young Romanian gold medalist in the Women's Individual All-Round event in gymnastics.[88] After she failed a drug test, the IOC revoked the award of her gold medal. On Raducan's petition on appeal, the two issues before the CAS were whether only a *de minimis* amount of a prohibited drug (pseudoephedrine) that had been found in her system, together with the circumstances of her ingestion of the substance—in pills given to her by her team doctor as a flu remedy—were sufficient to relieve her from responsibility and a consequent revocation of her gold medal. The CAS, applying an established rule of strict liability to uphold the invalidation of Raducan's performance, found that the *de minimis* amount of the drug in her bloodstream and the circumstances of her ingestion of it were relevant only to

---

83 35 VAL. U. L. REV. 379.

84 Baumann v. IOC, CAS Ad Hoc Div. (O.G. Sydney 2000), *reprinted in* II DIGEST OF CAS AWARDS, *supra* note 15 at 65.

85 OLYMPIC CHARTER, Rule 29 (2003).

86 *Id.*, Rule 74, which provides that "[a]ny dispute arising on the occasion of, or in connection with, the Olympic Games shall be submitted exclusively to the Court of Arbitration for Sport, in accordance with the Code of Sports-Related Arbitration."

87 Melinte v. IAAF, *reprinted in* II DIGEST OF CAS AWARDS, *supra* note 15, at 111 [hereinafter Melinte Case].

88 Raducan v. IOC, CAS Ad Hoc Div. (O.G. Sydney 2000), *reprinted in* II DIGEST OF CAS AWARDS, *supra* note 15, at 665.

the discretion given to the IOC in its application of disciplinary sanctions. The IOC, however, softened its decision, simply revoking her medal without imposing any additional disciplinary measures.

Two cases involved suspensions from eligibility of weightlifters.[89] In one of the cases[90] the CAS confirmed its independence by refusing to be bound by a Samoan court order that had exonerated one weightlifter. In the other case, the CAS struck down an IOC decision. In these and other cases before and after Sydney, the CAS has made clear that the only acceptable basis for suspending the eligibility of an athlete is an explicit rule.[91]

The Ad Hoc Division in Sydney also heard a commercial case[92] involving an alleged infraction of a Bye-law to Rule 61 of the Olympic Charter that regulates the size and other aspects of commercial advertizing on clothing. What is important about the case was a determination that inconsistency in applying the Bye-law among competitors was immaterial. The CAS seemed to be saying that two wrongs do not make a right. Other cases confirmed the established presumption that CAS arbitration would not reverse in-competition decisions.[93]

Two cases involved the nationality and alleged statelessness under the Olympic Charter of Cuban-born athletes, one competing for the United States and the other for Canada.[94] In a series of decisions in those cases that were based on Rule 46 of the Olympic Charter concerning nationality of athletes,[95] the CAS addressed issues of interpretation, *res judicata*, estoppel, the balance between fairness and finality in arbitration, and third-party interests.[96]

---

89 Samoa Nat'l Olympic Comm. & Sports Fed'n v. IWF, CAS Ad Hoc Div. (O.G. Sydney 2000), *reprinted in* DIGEST OF CAS AWARDS, *supra* note 11, at 28 [hereinafter Samoa]; Tzagaev v. IWF, CAS Ad Hoc Div. (O.G. Sydney 2000), *reprinted in* II DIGEST OF CAS AWARDS, *supra* note 15, at 101.

90 Samoa, *id.*

91 *See* McLaren, *Introducing the CAS, supra* note 82, at 533.

92 FFG v. SOCOG, CAS Ad Hoc Div. (O.G. Sydney 2000), *reprinted in* II DIGEST OF CAS AWARDS, *supra* note 15, at 137.

93 *See, e.g.*, Melinte Case, *supra* note 87.

94 USA Canoe/Kayak v. IOC, CAS Ad Hoc Div. (O.G. Sydney 2000), *reprinted in* II DIGEST OF CAS AWARDS, *supra* note 15, at 13; Miranda v. IOC, *id.* at 3; Perez v. IOC, *id.* at 53; Canadian Olympic Comm. v. IOC, *id.* at 83; In the Matter of Perez, *id.* at 91.

95 Rule 46 provides in material part as follows: "Any competitor in the Olympic Games must be a national of the country of the NOC which is entering him." Bye-law 1 to Rule 46 provides that "[a] competitor who has represented one country [in designated competition] and who has changed his nationality or acquired a new nationality, may participate in the Olympic Games to represent his new country provided that at least three years have passed since the competitor last represented his former country."

96 *See* summary in McLaren, *supra* note 59, at 399–402.

In the second part of the same study of the *lex sportiva*,[97] the author expanded his enumeration of the five categories of arbitral decisions in Sydney by adding two categories that have been discussed earlier in this chapter, namely, those involving the jurisdiction of the CAS and the manipulation of sporting rules for strategic advantage.[98]

A second major study of the *lex sportiva*, which was funded by the European Union, focused sharply on the CAS appellate cases involving doping issues.[99] The investigation principally examined the extent to which the CAS cases revealed a more or less deliberate harmonization of public law and sports law to promote an effective anti-doping regime. The authors of the study came to two important conclusions.

First, the study determined that there was only a limited possibility of extracting harmonizing information from the CAS awards. Second, the authors of the study emphasized the limitations of relying on tribunals, rather than legislative reform, to accomplish any program as ambitious as a harmonization of rules. "In one sense . . . the CAS is at the 'wrong-end' of the process [of harmonization] as it only received a case [—it cannot actively seize a case—] when all other remedies have been exhausted."[100] A correlative limitation is that the CAS cannot play an active role in developing a harmonized anti-doping regime. On the other had, "if there were no CAS, or equivalent body, it is difficult to believe that the [more or less national] systems of strict liability would have survived so long without destructive domestic legal challenge."[101]

The authors of this second study of CAS awards made three suggestions to enhance the legitimacy of the CAS and, implicitly, to bolster the role of its emerging *lex sportiva*. First, the CAS, on a principle of transparency, should make its jurisprudence more freely available, presumably by releasing transcripts, recordings or other renditions of all but the most confidential discussions of issues. Second, the tribunal should distill a set of fundamental procedural rights from its case law that it will expressly guarantee (presumably extending beyond the assurances of those rights implicit in its own procedural rules). Third, the CAS should avoid the present interchange of arbitrators and legal counsel appearing before arbitrators so as to avoid even the appearance of bias that might be derived from such interchange of personnel. Ultimately, the reputation of the CAS relies on the twin pillars of independence and impartiality. Indeed, the study concludes with

---

97 *See* McLaren, *Introducing the CAS, supra* note 82, at 523.

98 *See supra* text accompanying notes 35, 37.

99 *See* Gardiner, *Extracts from E.U. funded project*, remarks at the VII Congreso Internacional de Derecho Deportivo, Nov. 28, 2001, Montevideo, Uruguay (copy on file with the author).

100 *Id.* at 8.

101 *Id.* at 9.

the observation that "[a] truly independent and distinct body of arbitrators/sports judges should have a future priority."[102]

6. The Future

The CAS deserves acclaim for two decades of high quality, productive arbitration of sports-related disputes. Among its accomplishments is the gradual development of a new and useful jurisprudence derived from its awards. This *lex sportiva*, though still incipient, is emerging as a means of resolving and potentially helping avoid a broad range of sports-related disputes. Principles and rules derived from CAS awards are becoming more clear on such issues as the jurisdiction and review powers of the CAS, eligibility of athletes, and the scope of strict liability in doping cases. The conformity of these principles and rules with the process of international sports law underscores their legitimacy. A truly effective body of jurisprudence generated by CAS awards, however, will require more development before the emerging *lex sportiva* can become a truly effective regime of authority. Much will depend on the ability of the CAS to address questions about both its impartiality and any ambiguities in its institutional status that might be provoked by greater formalization of its proceedings. Its resemblance to a judicial body, in particular, might be seen to contradict provisions in the CAS Code of Sports-Related Arbitration. It is likely, however, that the role of the *lex sportiva* in helping shape international sports law will continue to expand.

---

[102] *Id.*

CHAPTER 4
ARBITRATION AND LITIGATION

As we have seen in Chapter 3, the CAS, driven by its emerging *lex sportiva*, is becoming the paramount institution for resolving disputes in the arena of international sports. After a brief look at the general role of arbitration in sports, this chapter will turn to the alternative of litigation, with a focus on several case studies involving both arbitration and litigation. These studies indicate the limitations of litigation for resolving most sports-related disputes that do not raise serious issues of due process or human rights. There is a public consensus that international sports competition should be about time trials, not court trials.

A. ARBITRATION

Arbitration of disputes related to international sports competition is a growth industry. Certainly one of the most important developments in sports law during the past few years has been the expanded role of the Court of Arbitration for Sport (CAS).[1] Business is also brisk for the American Arbitration Association and other national arbitral bodies around the world.[2] Many of the disputes have involved the eligibility of athletes on the eve of sanctioned international competition.[3]

As recently as 1988, not a single demand for arbitration was filed during the run-up to the Olympic Games in Seoul.[4] By contrast, the docket in 2000 prior to the Sydney Games numbered some eight cases in the United States alone[5] and six times that number in Australia.[6] Arbitration of international sports disputes in Europe is also common.[7] What accounts for this "trendy Olympic event,"[8] this

[1] *See* Reeb, *The Role of the Court of Arbitration for Sport, in* INTERNATIONAL LAW AND THE HAGUE'S 750TH ANNIVERSARY 233 (W. P. Heer ed., 1999); Nafziger, *The Court of Arbitration for Sport and the General Process of International Sports Law, id.*, at 239.

[2] Newspaper headlines tell the story: *See, e.g., Ready, Set, Arbitrate!* WALL ST. J., Aug. 18, 2000, at A1; *Here is This Year's Hot New Olympic Event: Arbitration*, WALL ST. J., Aug. 18, 2000, at A6; *Roster Disputes Go Down to the Wire*, USA TODAY, Aug. 24, 2000, at 1C.

[3] *See, e.g.*, L. TARASTI, LEGAL SOLUTIONS IN INTERNATIONAL DOPING CASES: AWARDS BY THE IAAF ARBITRATION PANEL 1985–1999 (2000); DIGEST OF CAS AWARDS 1986–1998 (M. Reeb ed., 1998) [hereinafter DIGEST OF AWARDS].

[4] WALL ST. J., Aug. 18, 2000, at A1.

[5] USA TODAY, *supra* note 2, at 2C.

[6] USA TODAY, Aug. 18, 2000, at 2C.

[7] *See, e.g.*, SILANCE, LES SPORTS ET LE DROIT 406–08, 417–18 (1998) (with particular reference to Belgian and French practice).

[8] USA TODAY, *supra* note 2, at 1C.

"burgeoning Olympic sport of arbitration,"[9] as it has been called? Several explanations are immediately apparent. Video taping and electronic records of trials and final events provide better evidence to resolve disputes and thereby encourage more challenges to decisions. More obviously, perhaps, issues involving doping and the use of other performance-enhancing agents have sparked a substantial amount of arbitration. Even though the identification, testing, and sanctioning of prohibited substances and techniques are more effective today than even five years ago, the circumstances of their procurement, distribution and use are subtle and often ambiguous, giving rise to more disputes. Also, the growing role of professional agents and sports lawyers has given athletes a keener eye for infractions of their rights, procedures for implementing those rights, and alternative remedies for redressing their grievances. Today's athletes have a greater awareness of their rights and are prepared to act on them regardless of the traditional etiquette against doing so on the eve of competition. They also know that the stakes of eligibility are much higher than they used to be.

In responding to these developments, arbitration has become a preferred means for resolving sports-related disputes. Rule 74 of the Olympic Charter provides for mandatory arbitration by the CAS of all disputes arising out of or in connection with the Olympic Games. IF arbitration agreements with athletes are of even broader application. In the United States, for example, the preference for arbitration stems from of the Amateur Sports Act,[10] which mandates that method to resolve disputes in the sports arena. The law requires National Governing Bodies (NGBs) for each sport to agree to submit all disputes within the scope of the Act to binding arbitration by the American Arbitration Association (AAA). The law also entitles Olympic, Pan American and Paralympic athletes, or other parties aggrieved by decisions of the United States Olympic Committee (USOC), to a review of their grievances by the AAA.[11] Under the USOC Constitution, disputes arising out of NGB decisions are subject to arbitration by the AAA. Because of the emerging role of the CAS in resolving these kinds of disputes at the international level, one commentator has suggested that the Amateur Sports Act should be amended to substitute the International Council of Arbitration for Sport, which is the parent organization of CAS, in place of the AAA as the designated arbitral body to hear all disputes between athletes and the USOC or its designated NGBs.[12]

---

[9] Longman, *On the Olympics: Athletes Are Taking the Trials From the Arenas to the Courts*, N.Y. TIMES, Aug. 23, 2000, at C23.

[10] Ted Stevens Olympic and Amateur Sports Act, 36 U.S.C. §§ 220501–220509 (Supp. 2000) [hereinafter Amateur Sports Act].

[11] 36 U.S.C. § 220529 (2000 Supp).

[12] Hollis, *The United States Olympic Committee and the Suspension of Athletes: Reforming Grievance Procedures Under the Amateur Sports Act of 1978*, 71 IND. L.J. 183, 200 (1995).

B. LITIGATION

The growth of arbitration to resolve disputes in the sports arena has coincided with what might seem to be a contradictory trend, though still weak, toward adjudication of what formerly were non-justiciable controversies. The proliferation of terminal arbitration clauses and improved methods for more informal resolution of disputes has not inhibited litigation. Instead, athletes and their clubs have become somewhat more litigious, especially in Europe. Perhaps that is because courts have become more receptive to claims of due process, natural justice and human rights. Certainly, too, many claims transcend the competence of administrative procedures and informal tribunals. In particular, a rising number of claims against defendant sports organizations have profound implications: for example, termination of playing privileges for life, suspension from competition for unauthorized participation in foreign events, and disqualification from competition because of doping. National courts have been more willing to consider, though not always to confirm, a professional athlete's "right to work," a right to be heard in formal proceedings, and a right to be free of bias in those proceedings. Few would argue against the need for judicial review of some decisions by sports bodies that affect the rights of individual athletes. Nor, on the other hand, should sports bodies be denied judicial enforcement of their own rights, for example, those involving intellectual property.

There is also a growing appreciation of the role of courts in helping *avoid* disputes and encourage informal methods of dispute resolution by clarifying principles and rules. Although the CAS shows great promise as a preferred tribunal for resolving disputes involving international competition and eligibility of athletes, national courts will remain significant. Indeed, it is likely that the volume of sports-related litigation in national courts will continue to grow.

1. Private International Law

International litigation typically involves transactional costs related to distance, language differences, cultural complications, and different requirements of national legal systems. Lawyers must be informed of the applicable rules and procedures of all legal systems involved in a given matter. In addition, they need to know the applicable rules of private international law, generally addressed to adjudicative and subject-matter jurisdiction, choice of law, and recognition and enforcement of foreign judgments.

Although civil procedures vary from country to country, judicial complaints ordinarily must satisfy several basic requirements of private international law. These requirements include standing to sue, adequate service of process and jurisdiction over defendants, admissibility and justiciability of complaints, convenience of fora, exhaustion of any administrative or other non-judicial remedies, and taking of evidence abroad.[13] Parties to a sports contract may stipulate an

[13] The requirements are expressed here in common law terms but have civil law cognates.

appropriate choice of law to resolve disputes involving sanctions against athletes. If they fail to do so, sports authorities generally choose the proper law in conformity with accepted rules and principles of private and public international law. National legal systems ordinarily recognize and enforce foreign arbitral awards or court judgments in accordance with their own positive laws and international agreements, as well as commonly accepted principles of comity, reciprocity and judicial cooperation.

Whatever the requirements of private international law, they may raise "fiendishly complicated questions of jurisdiction, choice of law, and recognition of judgments."[14] Take for example, the often controversial issue of taking evidence abroad. The broad discovery procedures of United States law and practice—particularly open-ended depositions—are apt to come into conflict with constraints on taking evidence in other legal systems. What is considered a fixture of United States practice is often considered a fishing expedition by foreign governments and individuals.

The Hague Convention on the Taking of Evidence Abroad,[15] which stipulates acceptable evidentiary procedures in transnational litigation, resolves some of the issues, but it does not enjoy universal acceptance. Moreover, in the United States the treaty has been interpreted narrowly to serve as simply an alternative to an extraterritorial extension of normal domestic procedures, including expansive discovery.[16] Bilateral treaties for judicial cooperation and national treatment of each other's nationals may be of assistance, but they, too, are apt to be interpreted narrowly when they do not mandate specific procedures or proscribe other procedures.

National laws offer some accommodations of foreign practice. For example, United States federal courts offer a fairly expeditious procedure by which litigants in foreign courts can request discovery by deposition in the United States.[17] *In re*

---

14 Weatherwill, *Case C-415/93*, 33 COMMON MARKET L. REV. 991, 992 (1996).

15 CONVENTION ON THE TAKING OF EVIDENCE ABROAD, *opened for signature* Mar. 18, 1970, 23 U.S.T. 2355, 847 U.N.T.S. 231 [hereinafter EVIDENCE CONVENTION].

16 Société Nationale Industrielle Aérospatiale v. United States Dist. Ct., 482 U.S. 522 (1987). For commentary, *see* Nafziger, *Another Look at the Hague Evidence Convention After* Aérospatiale, 38 TEX. INT'L L.J. 103 (2003).

17 28 U.S.C. § 1782 (2000) provides, in relevant part, as follows:

> The district court of the district in which a person resides or may be found may order him to give his testimony or statement or to produce a document or other thing for use in a proceeding in a foreign or international tribunal. The order may be made pursuant to a letter rogatory issued, or request made, by a *foreign or international tribunal* or upon the application of any interested person and may direct that the testimony or statement given, or the document or other thing be produced before a person appointed by the court (emphasis added).

Application of Mats Wilander and Karel Novacek[18] tested the application of the United States federal court procedures to requests arising from proceedings within IFs. At issue was whether the Appeals Committee of the International Tennis Federation (ITF) was a "foreign or international tribunal," which alone can effectively issue a letter rogatory or make a request for discovery under the statute. The petitioners requested discovery as part of their appeal before the English High Court to lift sanctions that had been imposed by the ITF after determining that the petitioners had tested positive for the use of cocaine. A federal district court ruled against the request on the basis that the term "foreign or international *tribunal*" does not refer to a private, non-governmental tribunal even though it does refer to administrative agencies, quasi-judicial proceedings, and investigative magistrates. In arriving at this decision, the court crimped the ability of institutions with recognized status under international sports law to rely on normal evidentiary procedures for giving effect to private international law.[19] Though not without precedent outside the context of sport, the court's strained interpretation of the term "tribunal" ignored fundamental principles of private international law, especially reciprocity of evidentiary procedures and comity.

2. National Law

Courts have traditionally denied standing to plaintiffs or otherwise dismissed actions on grounds of admissibility. Typically, the result and quite often the court's explicit rationale have involved a deference to the authority of sports organizations to apply their own principles and rules or those of national federations, IFs, NOCs, or the IOC. Ordinarily, then, courts recognize and enforce rules and decisions of appropriate national governing bodies and IFs. Courts are particularly reluctant to intervene in disciplinary hearings by private bodies. Courts in the United States, for example, have been reluctant to find either express or implied rights of action in claims by individual athletes against national governing bodies and IFs. They therefore have generally deferred in the first instance to private processes for resolving disputes.[20] "The threat of claims for damages . . . seems

---

[18] *In re* Application of Mats Wilander and Karel Novacek, No. Civ. A. 96 Misc. 98, 1996 WL 421938 (E.D. Pa. 1996).

[19] *See* Reierson, *Comment: Out of Bounds? Applicability of Federal Discovery Orders under 28 U.S.C. Section 1782 by International Governing Bodies for Use in Internal Dispute Resolution Procedures*, 19 LOY. L.A. ENT. L.J. 631, 654 (1999).

[20] *See, e.g.*, R. YASSER, J. MCCURDY, C. GOPLERUD & M. WESTON, SPORTS LAW: CASES AND MATERIALS 930 (5th ed. 2003) (referring to "a strong emphasis on resolving disputes through internal administrative procedures" in the United States); Behagen v. Amateur Basketball Ass'n of U.S., 884 F.2d 524 (10th Cir. 1989). ("The Act . . . makes clear that Congress intended an NGB to exercise monolithic control over its particular amateur sport, including coordinating with the appropriate international sports federation and controlling amateur eligibility for Americans that participate in that sport."), *cert. denied*, 110 S. Ct. 1947 (1990). *See also* Walton-Floyd v. USOC, 965 S.W. 35 (Tex. Civ. App. 1998). Federal courts in the United States have therefore required athletes to exhaust available administrative remedies before filing court actions. *See* Barnes v. Int'l Amateur Athletic Fed'n, 862 F. Supp. 1537 (S.D. W.Va. 1993).

to accelerate the efforts to find solutions within the relevant international sports associations and federations."[21]

Also, domestic courts and other authorities normally enforce CAS awards and therefore refuse to conduct hearings *de novo* in matters that have already been arbitrated. But there are exceptions, for example, when an award contravenes a fundamental public interest or when issues are raised about the jurisdiction of the CAS, its competence to decide a given matter, or fundamental irregularities in administrative or arbitral procedures. What, then, are the parameters of judicial review?

a. English Cases

English courts have been particularly helpful in defining the parameters of judicial review.[22] Normally, judicial review is very limited. Judges have often refused to review the decisions of private or "domestic" tribunals, such as review panels within sports organizations. In the words of one court, the rules of approved sports organizations are said to be "more than a contract: they are a legislative code laid down to be obeyed by the members."[23] English courts do, however, accept jurisdiction whenever a plaintiff has been denied an appropriate hearing or has been confronted with bias; whenever a sports organization has exercised a monopolistic position over its members; and whenever a sports organization's administrative tribunal exercises public law functions, its decision would violate statutory law, or would have other public law consequences.

In *Gasser v. Stinson*,[24] the English High Court hinted at a restraint-of-trade exception to the normal requirement that domestic courts must recognize and enforce otherwise valid arbitral awards, at least when an athlete's livelihood is at stake. Although the High Court denied relief to an athlete who had been suspended from competition after testing positive for banned substances, the opinion suggests that if an arbitral award deprives an athlete of his or her livelihood, the reasonableness of the award may be reviewable by a court.[25]

---

21 Vieweg, *Judicial Review of Sport Related Decisions in Germany*, *in* INTERNATIONAL ATHLETIC FOUNDATION, SPORT & LAW: SUPPLEMENT TO THE OFFICIAL PROCEEDINGS OF THE IAF SYMPOSIUM ON SPORT & LAW 87, 96 (1995).

22 For further discussion of the English jurisprudence, *see* Nafziger, *International Sports Law as a Process for Resolving Disputes*, 45 INT'L & COMP. L.Q. 130, 145 (1996).

23 Breen v. AEU, [1972] 2 Q.B. 175, 190. *See also* McInnes v. Onslow-Fane, [1978] 3 All E.R. at 223 ("Courts are reluctant to review the decisions of private sports bodies even where those bodies are concerned with the means of livelihood of those who take part in those activities"); *accord*, Law v. Nat'l Greyhound Racing Club Ltd., [1983] 1 W.L.R. 1302, 1307. Thus, judicial review in the United Kingdom seems to extend at least to cases involving clearly monopolistic practices in restraint of trade or to those involving violations of the fundamental human rights of athletes.

24 Gasser v. Stinson, Q.B. (June 15, 1988), *available in* LEXIS, Intlaw Library, UK-CASE file.

25 *Id. See also* Nagle v. Feilden, [1966] 2 Q.B. 633.

Three English court opinions provide particular guidance in defining the parameters of review.[26] In the earliest of the three cases, *Greig v. Insole*,[27] the Chancery Division of the High Court of Justice assumed jurisdiction to hear a dispute brought by several professional cricketers against two sports associations, the International Cricket Conference (ICC) and its English member, the Test and County Cricket Board (TCCB). The court then held that the two associations had tortiously injured the players by unlawfully attempting to induce a breach of their lucrative contracts with a sports promotional organization, the World Series Cricket. The court also held that both associations had engaged in unreasonable, *ultra vires* restraints of trade by retroactively barring the players' eligibility for international competition. Of particular relevance to the process of international sports law was the court's conclusion that neither of the defendant sports associations was an employers' association entitled to statutory immunity. Rather, the ICC was composed of member countries, not individuals who might be deemed to be employees, and the TCCB had no power to regulate relations between employers and workers. Hence, their decisions were subject to judicial scrutiny under English law.

In *Reel v. Holder*[28] the Court of Appeal held that the International Amateur Athletic Federation (IAAF) had misinterpreted its "only one member for each country" rule in a mutually exclusive manner by allowing athletes from the People's Republic of China to compete to the exclusion of Taiwanese athletes. The Court of Appeal held that membership in the IAAF should not have been confined to teams from sovereign states recognized by the United Kingdom. Instead, the court gave a plain meaning interpretation to the governing word "country" in the IAAF rule which provides that "[t]he jurisdiction of members of the federation shall be limited to the political boundaries of the country they represent." Lord Denning wrote that "[w]e are simply concerned with the interpretation of the rules of the federation" and that "[e]very athletic association in any territory is eligible for membership provided that it is the supreme athletic association for that territory and is not subject to any control by another athletic association." Thus, "[t]he jurisdiction of the Athletic Association of Taiwan is limited to Taiwan. The jurisdiction of the Athletic Association of mainland China is limited to mainland China." In sum, a "country" is not necessarily a recognized "state," as officially defined under national law, but rather a term of art under international sports law.[29]

---

26 For a thorough discussion of issues and applicable English law, *see* GRAYSON, SPORT AND THE LAW (1988). This book fully acknowledges the role of courts in giving effect to the public interest and ensuring fairness and natural justice to individual athletes when their rights are seriously threatened.

27 Greig v. Insole, [1978] 3 All E.R. 449, [1978] 1 W.L.R. 302.

28 Reel v. Holder, [1981] 3 All E.R. 321, [1981] 1 W.L.R. 1226.

29 Unfortunately, the Olympic Charter defines "country" in formal, sovereign terms so as to call into question "sport nationality" and the common sense of Reel v. Holder. *See* discussion

Finally, in *Cowley v. Heatley*[30] the court questioned its jurisdiction to review a decision by the Commonwealth Games Federation (CGF) that had denied eligibility to a swimmer. The court nevertheless did interpret a national domicile requirement imposed on all athletes under the Commonwealth Games Constitution. The South African plaintiff, Annette Cowley, had recently begun to reside in England and had been nominated to represent England in the Games. The Federation denied her eligibility as a member of the English team on the basis that her "domicile" was not in England. The plaintiff argued that she was domiciled there under a legal definition according to which she could demonstrate current residence in England, however brief, and her intent to remain there. The court concluded, however, that an ordinary meaning of the term applied, rather than the definition provided by the common law. Under the ordinary meaning of the term, she had not resided long enough in England to be domiciled there for the purpose of establishing her eligibility to compete on the English team in the Games.

Of particular interest in *Cowley* was the court's observation "that the constitution covered a large number of different nations in the Commonwealth with members upholding many different systems of law. In those circumstances it was the court's view that the articles of the constitution could not be governed by the law of one constituent member country." The opinion concluded with a famous *dictum* that "[s]port would be better served if there was not running litigation at repeated intervals by people seeking to challenge the decisions of the regulating bodies."

Taken together, these three opinions help define the parameters of judicial review. *Greig v. Insole* affirms the judicial role in ensuring fair and proper organization and administration of competition, particularly as it involves the livelihood and contractual integrity of professional athletes. In the later case of *Reel v.*

---

in Ch. 6, *infra,* text accompanying notes 44, 47, 48. Judge Eveleigh, concurring in the decision, emphasized the lack of agreement among states concerning the sovereign status of particular entities. In his words:

> Those who formed the federation were not concerned with international politics; they were concerned to set standards for athletics throughout the world. They were concerned to collect together people who would be in a position to exercise control over athletics in various parts of the world. Unless a governing body of some kind applies for membership, the federation is not concerned to determine if a given place or area is a country. It is only in connection with an application for membership by an applicant who puts himself forward as a governing body for a particular place, district or region that it becomes necessary to consider the meaning of "country" in the rules. One thing that is clear is that there may only be one member for each country. Therefore, in entertaining an application, it has to be seen whether or not there is an existing member who has control, or a measure of control, over the same area as that for which the applicant contends. There must be no doubt who is to speak with authority as the governing body for a particular group of athletes. The word "country" has been used in the rules in order to delineate the area of authority. They do not use the word in the sense of sovereign state.

30 Cowley v. Heatley, 1986 T.L.R. 430.

Holder, the court reinterpreted an IF's "country" membership rule contrary to the organization's own interpretation. The court made clear, however, that it was relying on a plain meaning of the word "country" rather than a strict legal definition based on the dictates of national law or on sovereign recognition by the Crown. In the more recent case of *Cowley v. Heatley*, the court was faced with another nationality question, this time not involving the membership of a national group but rather the eligibility of an individual competitor. The decision continued a modest trend away from applying national law to interpret the rules of private sports associations. The court also extended another trend when it questioned its jurisdiction to hear a complaint brought by an amateur athlete against an international sports organization, the Commonwealth Games Federation.

English courts, then, have normally limited their jurisdiction to disputes requiring them to vindicate natural justice, due process, or fundamental human rights; to interpret or enforce professional contracts; or otherwise to protect a person's ability to earn a living. "Amateur" athletes, therefore, have generally lacked standing to challenge decisions by their sports organizations when they cannot show that their livelihood is at stake. Generally, the courts have refused to issue orders of *certiorari* to review the decisions of private or "domestic" tribunals, such as non-governmental review panels and other organizational mechanisms for dispute resolution. Their rules are said to be "more than a contract: they are a legislative code laid down to be obeyed by the members."

Significantly, judicial unwillingness to review the decisions of sports organizations has been overcome in several cases: where a plaintiff was denied a right to respond to objections or was confronted with bias; where a sports organization's administrative tribunal was deemed to be exercising public law functions or its decision would have had public law consequences; and where the relationship at issue between the parties was an amateur contract not governed by organizational rules. A final exception involves parties in a monopolistic position, such as international and national federations. These exceptions demonstrate a modest trend toward the judicial assumption of competence to review "public" issues or issues of procedural fairness.

Thus, the jurisprudence of English courts cautions judicial restraint in examining sports-related issues.[31] As a result, English sports organizations enjoy

[31] The English courts accept "the worthy principle that sporting bodies alone administer sport," subject to due process requirements. Temple, *Atlanta Games under threat*, TIMES (London), Dec. 6, 1992, at 11 (on British acceptance of this principle). The British Court of Appeal dismissed an action by the Aga Khan challenging the Jockey Club's disqualification of his horse, for lack of judicial powers in an essentially private dispute. "British courts appear to trust more than their American counterparts in the fairness of the disciplinary procedures of sporting organizations." TIMES (London), Dec. 5, 1992, home news. "The alternative vision, of every ill-accepted decision being followed by a trackside phone call to the athlete's lawyer, is as nightmarish as a pitchside policeman being continually asked by footballers to reverse the referee's decision." Temple, *Atlanta Games under threat*, TIMES (London), Dec. 6, 1992

substantial autonomy so long as they do not offend fundamental public interests nor unjustifiably endanger the livelihood of athletes.[32] The commendable view seems to be that competition in the courtroom is a poor substitute for competition in the sports arena.[33]

b. *United States Cases*

Courts in the United States also have been reluctant to find either express or implied rights of action in challenges by individual athletes against sports associations and have generally deferred to private processes for resolving disputes.[34] As in the United Kingdom, courts are particularly loath to intervene in disciplinary hearings by private associations or to vacate awards of arbitration prescribed by them.[35] A prominent federal judge, Richard Posner, has observed that "there

---

at 11. What ordinarily might distinguish the American concept of judicial review in such matters is the applicability of the Amateur Sports Act, which prescribes more formal dispute resolution alternatives.

[32] "[T]he principal feature of English sport law appears to be the freedom enjoyed by sporting organizations to regulate the sport concerned, provided that no right falling within an established legal category is violated. The interest of an individual in participation in sport does not so fall. To the extent that such regulation is thus protected against effective challenge in the ordinary courts, the state could be said to have been captured by such bodies. Such capture might be thought simply to reflect judicial recognition of the fact that the essence of sporting activity would be threatened by the transfer of sporting competition from the stadium to the courtroom. . . . There is no apparent reason why public interest considerations should not equally well be invoked to justify the overruling of restrictions imposed on individual participation by a sporting organization." Evans, *English Law of Sport*, *in* AUF DEM WEGE ZU EINEM EUROPÄISCHEN SPORTRECHT? 91, 95 (Will ed., 1989).

[33] McInness v. Onslow-Fane, [1978] 3 All E.R. 211, [1978] 1 W.L.R. 1520, observed that:

> the courts must be slow to allow any implied obligation to be fair to be used as a means of bringing before the court for review honest decisions of bodies exercising jurisdiction over sporting and other activities which those bodies are far better fitted to judge than the courts. . . . The concepts of natural justice and the duty to be fair must not be allowed to discredit themselves by making unreasonable requirements and imposing undue burdens.

Id. at 1535.

[34] "Unlike many domestic disputes involving sports, courts are extremely reluctant to intervene in resolving international sports disputes." R. YASSER, J. MCCURDY, C.P. GOPLERUD & J. WESTON, SPORTS LAW: CASES AND MATERIALS 930 (5th ed. 2003).

[35] "The courts should rightly hesitate before intervening in disciplinary hearings held by private associations. . . . Intervention is appropriate only in the most extraordinary circumstances, where the association has clearly breached its own rules, that breach will imminently result in *serious* and irreparable harm to the plaintiff, and the plaintiff has exhausted all internal remedies. Even then, injunctive relief is limited to correcting the breach of the rules. The court should not intervene in the merits of the underlying dispute." Harding v. U.S. Figure Skating Ass'n, 851 F. Supp. 1476 (D. Or. 1994) (*dictum*). *See also* Hollis, *supra* note 12; Gault v. U.S. Bobsled & Skeleton Fed'n, 578 N.Y.S.2d 683, 685 (S. Ct. App. Div. 1992) (refusing to vacate an arbitral award, finding "most unfortunate the increasing frequency with which sporting events are resolved in the courtroom").

can be few less suitable bodies than the courts for determining the eligibility, or the procedure for determining the eligibility, of athletes."[36] The case studies that follow in this chapter illustrate Judge Posner's wisdom about the limitations of sports-related litigation in United States courts.

Courts in the United States ordinarily refuse to overrule the decisions of sports associations because these decisions do not involve the requisite "state action" that would subject them to constitutional scrutiny and hence to judicial review in the absence of statutory direction. Neither the Amateur Sports Act nor any other federal law, however, gives athletes a right to compete or a cause of action in the courts.[37] Indeed, courts have declared that "Congress made clear choices to keep disputes regarding the eligibility of amateur athletes to compete out of the federal courts."[38]

United States courts have, however, become more willing to address claims of procedural fairness as a constitutional requirement. Courts are also bound to apply statutory law. For example, the United States Constitution explicitly provides for legislative protection of intellectual property rights. Consequently, courts normally review claims involving trademarks and other intellectual property rights, especially when these are held by Olympic or Pan-American organizations to which the Amateur Sports Act defers.

In sum, English and American courts are similarly reluctant to interfere with the decisions of sports associations. In the United States this is true despite the Amateur Sports Act's authorization of an official designation of sports bodies within the Olympic Movement. Ultimately, what may distinguish some of the specific details of the American experience from the English experience is the strong role of the United States Constitution in judicial analysis.

---

[36] Michels v. United States Olympic Comm., 741 F.2d 155, 159 (7th Cir. 1984).

[37] In the United States, for example, federal courts seldom allow private causes of action to proceed against sports bodies or federations. *See, e.g.*, San Francisco Arts & Athletics v. United States Olympic Comm., 483 U.S. 522 (1987); Behagen v. The Athletics Congress of the U.S.A., 884 F.2d 524 (10th Cir. 1989); Martinez v. United States Olympic Committee, 802 F.2d 1275, 1281 (10th Cir. 1986); Oldfield v. The Athletic Congress, 779 F.2d 505 (9th Cir. 1985); Michels v. United States Olympic Comm., 741 F.2d 155 (7th Cir. 1984); Barnes v. Int'l Amateur Athletic Fed'n, 862 F. Supp. 1537 (S.D. W. Va. 1993); Myricks v. United States Olympic Comm., CV 90-2381-WMB (C.D. Cal. June 18, 1990); Cady & Powell v. The Athletics Congress of the U.S.A., C 89-1737-SC (N.D. Cal. Oct. 24, 1989); DeFrantz v. United States Olympic Comm., 492 F. Supp. 1181 (D.D.C. 1980); Walton-Floyd v. U.S. Olympic Comm., 965 S.W.2d 35 (Tex. App.–Houston (1st Dist.) 1998). As *Walton-Floyd* notes, 965 S.W. 2d at 38 n.1, courts have been willing to hear such disputes only between organizations (United States Wrestling Fed'n v. Wrestling Division of the AAU, 545 F. Supp. 1053, 1061 (N.D. Ohio 1982), as provided by federal statutory law, or when the disputes were premised in breach of contract claims (Harding v. United States Figure Skating Ass'n, 851 F. Supp. 1476 (D. Or. 1994)); Reynolds v. International Amateur Athletic Fed'n, 841 F. Supp. 1444 (S.D. Ohio 1992)). In neither of the latter actions did the plaintiff succeed.

[38] Barnes v. Int'l Amateur Athletic Fed'n, 862 F. Supp. 1537 (S.D. W. Va. 1993).

Paradoxically, the resolution of sports-related disputes in the civil law systems of continental Europe is increasingly litigious whereas the Amateur Sports Act has been instrumental in pushing parties in the United States toward arbitration rather than litigation. These developments are counterintuitive because historically the European civil law system has been less reliant on courts than the common law.[39]

3. Case Studies

Generally, litigation has not proven to be a very satisfactory method of resolving disputes in the arena of international sports competition. The in-depth case studies that follow indicate the limitations of litigation.

a. *The* Reynolds *Case*[40]

The United States track star Butch Reynolds famously brought legal action that went on for four years and some 15 stages of litigation and arbitration. At one point, after the International Amateur Athletic Federation (IAAF) had refused to appear in the proceedings, Reynolds won a $27 million default judgment. In the end, however, his case was dismissed for lack of jurisdiction even though the real issue was not jurisdiction but choice of law, which the court completely overlooked.[41]

The significance of *Reynolds* is not so much its high visibility nor even its outcome, but the extent of judicial errors throughout the complicated proceedings

---

[39] It was ever the case apparently. For example, in 1835 the famous French sociologist Alexis de Tocqueville, after visiting the United States, published a number of observations that have endured to this day. One of these was that the United States is a litigious society: "Scarcely any political question arises in the United States which is not resolved, sooner or later, into a judicial questions." DE TOCQUEVILLE, DEMOCRACY IN AMERICA ch. 14, at 106 (Washington Square Press ed., 1964).

[40] These stages culminated in an appellate decision, Reynolds v. Int'l Amateur Athletic Fed'n., 23 F.3d 1110 (6th Cir. 1994), *cert. denied*, 115 S. Ct. 423 (1994). *See generally*, Butcher, *Reynolds row threatens Games*, EUROPEAN, Dec. 10–13, 1992, at 30; Powell, *IAAF takes on Reynolds*, Dec. 5, 1992, at 32; Bondy, *27.3 Million Award for Reynolds Will be Hard to Collect*, N.Y. TIMES, Dec. 4, 1992, at B11; Goodbody, *US court awards Reynolds record damages of £17m*, TIMES (London), Dec. 4, 1992, at 48; Janofsky, *Reynolds Loses His Last Claim to Olympic 400*, N.Y. TIMES, June 25, 1992, at 31; Janofsky, *Supporters Race to Reynolds's Side*, N.Y. TIMES, June 26, 1992, at 14; Janofsky, *Reynolds Advances Amid a Legal Rat Race*, N.Y. TIMES, June 25, 1992 at B8 [hereinafter Reynolds Advances]; Janofsky, *Reynolds Finally Focuses on the 400*, N.Y. TIMES, June 24, 1992, at B8; Janofsky, *Solution Offered in Reynolds Dispute*, N.Y. TIMES (late ed.), June 22, 1992, § 8 at 1; Janofsky, *High Court Decision Favors Reynolds*, N.Y. TIMES, June 21, 1992, at 25; Janofsky, *Appeals Court Keeps Butch Reynolds Out of Olympic Trials*, N.Y. TIMES, June 20, 1992, at 33. *See also*, Janofsky, *2d Athlete Pursues a Legal Course to the Olympic Trials*, N.Y. TIMES, June 23, 1992, at B13 (successful challenge in the West Virginia circuit court by shot-putter Randy Barnes in a situation similar to that of Butch Reynolds without favorable rulings by the USOC or TAC).

[41] *See infra* text accompanying notes 59–62.

that could have been avoided had the prescribed process of international sports law been followed.[42] As the case bounced up and down the federal court system of the United States over a period of three years, one thing seemed certain: there would be surprises regardless of which side might prevail at a particular stage of the litigation.

In 1990 Harry "Butch" Reynolds, a world-class runner, who had won a silver medal in the 1988 Olympic Games and held the world record for the 400-meter run, tested positive for the anabolic steroid nandrolone during competition in Monaco. The International Amateur Athletic Federation (IAAF), headquartered at the time of both the alleged wrong and the litigation in London, suspended Reynolds from competition for a period of two years. The suspension was to remain in effect until two days after the Barcelona Games. According to IAAF Rule 59, immediate suspension would be followed by a hearing and a final declaration on the issue of eligibility. In the United States that hearing would normally be conducted by The Athletics Congress (TAC), which was the name of the United States governing body for track and field at the time. If, after the required hearing an athlete was declared to be ineligible, the IAAF may then apply its so-called "contamination rule," rendering an athlete ineligible for sanctioned competition if he or she competes against a blacklisted athlete like Reynolds.

Reynolds responded to the IAAF's suspension by putting on his running shoes. He maintained that he had not consumed any banned substances, but that defective IAAF drug test procedures had resulted, to his legal injury, in a confusion of urine specimens. Refusing to comply with the prescribed procedure for an administrative hearing by TAC, Reynolds appealed his suspension in the United States District Court for the Southern District of Ohio. The court, however, required him to exhaust his administrative remedies. The Sixth Circuit Court of Appeals not only agreed, but vacated the judgment and, quite properly, directed that the entire case be dismissed for lack of subject-matter jurisdiction.

Reynolds next attempted to exhaust his administrative remedies before the American Arbitration Association. The arbitrator found in favor of Reynolds, but failed to apply IAAF rules. Administrative review by TAC's Doping Control Review Board produced a similar impasse with the IAAF. Under IAAF rules, the IAAF and TAC referred their conflict to independent arbitration in London. In the arbitral hearing both Reynolds and his attorneys participated fully on the merits of the dispute. The tribunal ruled against Reynolds, however, finding that there was "no doubt" about his guilt, and upheld the two-year suspension against him.[43]

---

[42] The case is also controversial because all of the district (trial) court opinions were decided by a single, 88-year-old senior judge. When the IAAF finally appeared in the proceedings, it moved (unsuccessfully) to recuse the judge, questioning his impartiality. *Reynolds*, *supra* note 40, 23 F.3d at 1114.

[43] In the Matter of An Arbitration Initiated by the International Amateur Athletic Federation (IAAF), Applicant, Under IAAF Rule 20.3(ii) On The Case of Where a Member IAAF—The

That is where the matter should have ended. Instead, Reynolds promptly revived his federal court action against the IAAF and TAC, alleging breach of contract, defamation, denial of due process, and tortious interference with business relations. He sought $12.5 million in damages and injunctive relief. Under the Amateur Sports Act, however, Reynolds could not, however, claim any right to compete.

The IAAF specially appeared before the federal court to request dismissal of the action for lack of personal jurisdiction. The court denied this motion to dismiss, confirmed its personal jurisdiction over the IAAF and TAC,[44] and issued an order[45] enjoining the TAC and IAAF from interfering with Reynolds's participation in competitions, including the 1992 United States Olympic Trials and the 1992 Summer Games. The IAAF appealed the decision but agreed not to apply its contamination rule against competitors of Reynolds at the trials.

The Court of Appeals overturned the injunction, but the United States Supreme Court eventually ruled that Reynolds should be allowed to compete at national trials for a position on the United States team in Barcelona.[46] The essence of the Court's decision was that the IAAF's sanction would cause Reynolds irreparable harm and that he would probably succeed on the merits of his case, given what the Court described as "intangible values [in the Olympic Games] for which the world's greatest athletes compete."[47] The Court therefore allowed a preliminary injunction against the IAAF, but did nothing to nullify the drug-test result nor to rule on the runner's eligibility under Olympic and IAAF Rules.

The Supreme Court's decision opened up the possibility of a serious jurisdictional dispute. The top three finishers at the trials would qualify for certification by the USOC, but under the Amateur Sports Act,[48] certification requires that an athlete must be in good standing in his or her international federation. For Reynolds, this clearly was not the case. The USOC indicated that the final authority in the case would be the IOC.[49] Fortunately, no conflict resulted between

---

Athletics Congress of the US, Respondent—Has Held A Hearing Under the IAAF Rule 59 "Disciplinary Procedures For Doping Offenses" And the IAAF Believes That In the Conduct or Conclusion of Such Hearing The Member Has Misdirected Itself Or Otherwise Reached An Erroneous Conclusion (May 11, 1992) (London arbitration); ARB. TIMES, Summer 1992, at 1 (report on earlier AAA arbitration).

[44] Reynolds v. Int'l Amateur Athletic Fed'n., No. C-2-92-452, 1992 U.S. Dist. LEXIS 8625 (E.D. Ohio, June 19, 1992).

[45] Reynolds v. Int'l Amateur Athletic Fed'n., No. C-2-92-452, 1992 U.S. Dist. LEXIS 8383 (E.D. Ohio, June 19, 1992).

[46] Reynolds v. Int'l Amateur Athletic Fed'n., 112 S. Ct. 2512 (1992).

[47] *Id.* at 2513.

[48] 36 U.S.C. §§ 371–396 (2000).

[49] Janofsky, *Reynolds Advances, supra* note 40.

Reynolds and the USOC before the Barcelona Games because Reynolds failed to qualify as an individual runner, although he remained eligible for selection as a member of the medley team.[50] Later, the IAAF extended its suspension until the end of 1992 on the basis of its rule that disqualifies any athlete "who has committed an act or made any statement . . . which . . . is considered to be insulting or improper or likely to bring the sport into disrepute."[51]

After the 1992 Games, Reynolds filed a supplemental complaint with the district court. The IAAF declined to appear so as to contest the merits of this action. The court therefore entered a default judgment against the IAAF of $27,356,008, including $6.8 million in compensatory damages and $20.5 million in punitive damages. Reynolds thereby became a record holder not only in the 400-meter run but also in the adjudicative derby. To collect on the judgment, the plaintiff initiated garnishment proceedings against four corporate creditors of the IAAF in the United States. At this stage of the protracted litigation, the IAAF finally made an appearance in order to quash the garnishment proceedings, vacate the default judgment and recuse the judge. The district court denied all motions.

Finally, however, the Sixth Circuit Court of Appeals reversed this decision and ordered the district court to dismiss the action for lack of jurisdiction. The court held that due process did not permit assertion of specific personal jurisdiction over the IAAF; that the IAAF did not waive its personal jurisdiction defense by failing to appear until after the default judgment was entered; and that the intervention by TAC in the action as a co-defendant did not waive the IAAF's objection to personal jurisdiction.

Thus, after some twelve court and arbitral proceedings over a period of nearly four years, Reynolds was left with nothing to show for his marathon exercise in adjudication. Although dismissal of the *Reynolds* action was surely the proper outcome, the case as a whole raises disturbing questions about the merits of adjudicating disputes emerging from the international sports arena.

Reynolds was time-consuming, complicated and unnecessary. Judicial handling of the case was questionable for several reasons. First, the district court does not seem to have fully appreciated the implications, under federal law, of allowing

---

[50] Janofsky, *Reynolds Loses His Last Claim to Olympic 400*, N.Y. TIMES, June 27, 1992, at 31. Writing just before Butch Reynolds failed to qualify for the Games, the writer observed as follows:

> And the prospect of further litigation only raises more questions, not the least of which is where such an action might be filed: London, where the I.A.A.F. is based? Rome, where its president, Primo Nebiolo lives? Columbus, Ohio, where a district court has ruled three times that Reynolds can compete? New Jersey, where T.A.C. is incorporated? The World Court at the Hague?

Janofsky, *Reynolds Advances*, *supra* note 40.

[51] *Quoted in* USA TODAY, Aug. 11, 1992, at C1; N.Y. TIMES, Aug. 11, 1992, at B11.

sports bodies to provide for binding arbitration of eligibility issues such as that which divided TAC and the IAAF.[52] In this case, TAC submitted to the IAAF-initiated arbitration. The district court should have enforced the London arbitral decision in favor of the IAAF and against TAC, thereby upholding the suspension of Reynolds from competition. The United Nations Convention on the Recognition and Enforcement of Foreign Arbitral Awards,[53] to which the United States is a party, would then have required enforcement of the London award in the United States.

It was immaterial that Reynolds himself had not entered into a written agreement to have his dispute with the IAAF resolved by arbitration. First, he and his attorneys fully participated on the merits of the dispute in the arbitral hearing. Second, even had Reynolds been absent from the proceedings, he would have been bound by the decision in the absence of clear and convincing evidence that he had been denied due process. Under federal law of the United States, once an athlete's governing body has agreed to arbitrate a dispute, either in advance of a dispute or by special submission after the fact, an arbitral decision may be binding both on the submitting organization and on its members through the sports organization's rules and contracts with them. In enacting the Amateur Sports Act, Congress clearly intended to avoid direct judicial regulation of sports in this way.[54]

Second, although both the rationale and the outcome of the *Reynolds* case are commendable, the appellate court's jurisdictional premise merits scrutiny, if only to clarify broader jurisdictional premises for future cases. The appellate court based its decision to order dismissal of the action on a theory of *specific* rather

---

[52] *See* 36 U.S.C. §§ 393, 395; Dolan v. U.S. Equestrian Team, 608 A.2d 434 (N.J. Super. A.D. 1992). Referring to "the Congressional determination that these types of disputes should be resolved outside the judicial processes," the opinion emphasizes that "courts are hardly suitable to determine the eligibility, or the procedures for determining the eligibility, of athletes to participate on our behalf in international competitions." *Id.* at 437.

[53] *Done* June 10, 1958, 21 U.S.T. 2517, T.I.A.S. 6997, 330 U.N.T.S. 3. The Convention provides that arbitral decisions may be refused only by a "competent authority of the country in which . . . [the] award was made" (art. V § 1(e).) Although the Convention authorizes a party to refuse to enforce a foreign arbitral award if it is contrary to the public policy of that party (art. V, § 2(b)), the public policy of the United States, as expressed in the Amateur Sports Act, would support enforcement of the award. The district court ignored this policy in its discussion of the enforceability of the arbitral award. Instead, the court relied on the lack of a written arbitration *compromis* between Reynolds and the IAAF even though Reynolds and his attorneys participated fully in the arbitration (23 F.3d 1110, 1113) and even though, as a technical matter, the arbitration was not directly between those parties but rather between TAC and the IAAF. Reynolds v. Int'l Amateur Athletic Fed'n., No. C-2-92-452 slip. op. (S.D. Ohio July 13, 1993).

[54] *See* Comment, *Butch Reynolds and the American Judicial System v. The International Amateur Athletic Federation—A Comment on the Need for Judicial Restraint*, 3 SETON HALL J. SPORTS L. 173, 182, 187, 191 (1993).

than *general* jurisdiction[55] over the London-based IAAF. The court understandably focused on *specific* jurisdiction because of the reliance put on that theory by Reynolds, to his disadvantage in clearing the jurisdictional hurdle. Accordingly, the court determined that it lacked personal jurisdiction over the IAAF because the latter did not have minimal contacts with Ohio to make such jurisdiction reasonable. Nor did the plaintiff's cause of action arise from specific activities in Ohio by which the IAAF had purposely availed itself of the privilege of acting or causing consequences there. Ordinarily, the long-arm jurisdiction of state law, as applied in diversity-of-citizenship actions by federal courts in the United States, reaches out-of-state principals, such as the IAAF, on the basis of personal jurisdiction over their agents, such as TAC. In the *Reynolds* case, however, the principal (IAAF) and the agent (TAC) had been at odds; it was their ostensible disagreement that had required the arbitration in London. Thus, although the courts consistently focused on the contractual and tortious relationship between the IAAF and the plaintiff, they could have reasonably concluded, as a matter of specific jurisdiction, that Ohio jurisdiction over the IAAF could not have been premised on the basis of the court's "alter ego" jurisdiction over TAC.

The peculiar requirements for *specific* jurisdiction, however, should not have been dispositive. The court should have also considered whether it had *general* jurisdiction over the IAAF. The IAAF was not only the principal of TAC, but, in effect, an ultimate authority over international competition involving trials, final

---

55 Under a theory of *specific* jurisdiction, a plaintiff must show that a cause of action arose out of, or was related to, the defendant's activities in the state where the federal district court is located. Most significantly the IAAF had not "purposely availed itself" very directly of the benefits of that state, Ohio, a due process requirement that was first articulated in Hanson v. Denckla, 357 U.S. 235 (1953). Under a theory of *general* jurisdiction, on the other hand, a plaintiff need only show that the defendant has had a "systematic and continuous presence" in a particular state, regardless of whether the plaintiff's cause of action arose out of, or was related to, that local presence. Two United States Supreme Court decisions establish this basis of jurisdiction: Perkins v. Benguet Consolidated Mining Co., 342 U.S. 437 (1952); Helicopteros Nacionales de Colombia, S.A. v. Hall, 104 S. Ct. 1868 (1984). *Perkins* established the jurisdiction of a court in Ohio, perhaps because of the inaccessibility of the only other alternative venue, Japanese-occupied Philippines during World War II. The "general jurisdiction" test is *obiter dicta* in the *Helicopteros* case, where the court denied jurisdiction to a Texas court in a dispute otherwise centered in Colombia and Peru.

The district court has interpreted the Ohio long-arm statute to extend "to the full limits of the Due Process Clause," which would include both specific and general jurisdiction. Int'l Pizza Co. v. C. & F. Packing Co., 858 F. Supp. 696, 697 (S.D. Ohio 1994) and authority cited therein. Also, the *Reynolds* court seems to assume that Ohio law would ordinarily accept a theory of general jurisdiction even though the court failed to apply the theory. Reynolds v. Int'l Amateur Athletic Fed'n., 23 F.3d 1110, 1116 (1994). ("Depending on the type of minimum contacts in the case, personal jurisdiction can be either general or specific [citation omitted]. Reynolds relies on specific jurisdiction because he claims that jurisdiction arose out of the IAAF's alleged wrongful acts in Ohio.") The court did analyze the applicability of Ohio's provision for jurisdiction related to a non-resident's "Transacting *any* business in this state," but limited the applicability of that provision of the Ohio long-arm statute to specific jurisdiction, 23 F.3d at 1115 (emphasis added), as seems to be consistent with Ohio common law.

competition, and athletes residing in Ohio. Thus, the IAAF ultimately governed track-and-field activity in Ohio on a systematic and continuous basis and was therefore subject to the jurisdiction of Ohio courts, even if the plaintiff's cause of action did not arise out of any specific activities of the IAAF in Ohio. To be sure, it is unclear whether state courts in Ohio would ordinarily entertain general jurisdiction over foreign parties,[56] but the court seems to have assumed so. In any event, the issue should have at least been addressed. Unfortunately, the court never properly did so because of the exclusive reliance Reynolds had placed on a theory of specific jurisdiction and the IAAF's decision not to appear in the case until its collateral attack on the default judgment.[57] At the very least, we may conclude that the jurisdictional issues were clearly more complicated than either the parties or the courts intimated. Ultimately, the litigation's focus on jurisdiction may have been misplaced. As we shall see, choice of law, which was not properly addressed, rather than jurisdiction, should have been pivotal in determining the outcome of the case.

Third, in returning to the district court proceedings, it is not at all clear that due-process analysis of Reynolds' claim should have begun with a clean slate. Instead, even in the absence of the IAAF, the district court should have begun with a presumption that the IAAF's hearings and the arbitral decision upholding the IAAF were consistent with procedural due process. The court should then have required Reynolds to carry the substantial burden of showing why the arbitration should not have been enforced. Merely showing the possibility of a mistake in testing procedures, even a serious mistake, was inadequate. Rather, the plaintiff should have had to prove that any mistake in the testing procedures was clearly determinative and, on the issue of punitive damages, that the IAAF had acted maliciously. Again, however, the technical questions were not properly addressed because of the defendant's absence in court.

Fourth, on the issue of justiciability, the district court ignored the general rule that decisions of sport bodies do not constitute "state action" subject to constitu-

---

[56] Ohio's long-arm statute is primarily concerned with specific jurisdiction, but language in it could be interpreted more broadly. *See* OHIO REV. CODE ANN. § 2307.382 (Banks-Baldwin 1994) (*e.g.*, "Transacting *any* business in this state," § (A)(1) (emphasis added); "Causing tortious injury . . . if he regularly does or solicits business . . . in this state," § (a)(4)). Both the district and appellate courts in *Reynolds* seem to have assumed that Ohio courts would ordinarily entertain general jurisdiction but found an insufficient basis for doing so in *Reynolds* itself. This was apparently because of the plaintiff's failure to seek jurisdiction on that basis.

[57] In the United States, a non-appearing defendant may preserve a right to collaterally attack a default judgment on jurisdictional grounds, typically to bar recognition or enforcement of a judgment. On July 14, 1993, the IAAF lost a motion to vacate the judgment against it. The motion was heard by the same judge who made all district court decisions in the case. *Supra* note 42. For a summary of American common law rules concerning collateral attack on the validity of judgments, *see* R. LEFLAR, L. MCDOUGAL & R. FELIX, AMERICAN CONFLICTS LAW 236 (4th ed. 1986).

tional scrutiny.[58] Neither the Amateur Sports Act nor any other federal law gives athletes a right to compete or a cause of action in the courts based on such a right.

Fifth, the district court's choice of law under private international law was badly flawed on the issues of liability and damages. The court gave no reasons whatsoever for its selection of Ohio substantive law. Although Ohio *choice-of-law* rules would clearly apply in a diversity-of-citizenship action such as this, the resulting applicability of Ohio *substantive* law is another matter. Ohio law providing for punitive damages was certainly one possibility, but only a *lex fori* rule or a presumption of *lex fori* would justify the court's complete lack of analysis, and Ohio has not adopted a rule or presumption of *lex fori*.[59] Despite the defendant's failure to appear in the case, the court had a responsibility to apply the right choice-of-law rule. Had it done so, it might have at least considered the law of Monaco (presumably the law of the place of wrong[60]) or English law (the law of the defendant's place of business and residence at the time of the alleged wrong and the litigation). After the *Reynolds* litigation, for example, another federal court of appeals, approving of the *Reynolds* decision, acknowledged the status of the IAAF as an "international organization" and that of Reynolds as an "international athlete whose professional reputation is not centered in Ohio."[61]

Sixth, had the courts engaged in even a cursory choice-of-law analysis, they would have been alerted to the existence of the prescribed organizational remedies, namely, the rules and procedures of the IAAF and binding arbitration. Instead, the district court seemed to have viewed the customary process of international sports law as little more than a prerequisite to virtually a *de novo* court action. The court's failure to consult established process deprived it of an adequate standard for testing the reasonableness of the IAAF decision. Although there is no "right to compete" in the United States, the court held that the sports federation had violated the "individual rights" of Reynolds without defining those rights under the Amateur Sports Act. The court also failed to premise eligibility for the Olympics on approval by international federations such as the IAAF, as the same federal law requires.

Worse yet, the tone of the district court opinions suggests a presumption of malice on the part of the IAAF. Although neither the IAAF's decisions nor binding

---

58 *See, e.g.*, Behagen v. Amateur Basketball Ass'n, 884 F.2d 524 (10th Cir. 1989); Oldfield v. The Athletic Congress, 779 F.2d 509 (9th Cir. 1985); Michels v. United States Olympic Comm., 741 F.2d 155 (7th Cir. 1984); DeFrantz v. United States Olympic Comm., 492 F. Supp. 1181 (D.D.C. 1980); Dolan v. U.S. Equestrian Team, 608 A.2d 434 (N.J. Super. A.D. 1992).

59 Ohio has adopted the more complicated, policy-oriented approach of the Restatement (Second) of Conflict of Laws. *See, e.g.*, Smith, *Choice of Law in the United States*, 38 HASTINGS L.J. 1041, 1121–23 (1987).

60 Historically, the *lex loci delicti* was generally dispositive, but that is no longer so in many legal systems, including Ohio.

61 Far West Capital, Inc. v. Towne, 46 F.3d 1071, 1079 (10th Cir. 1995).

arbitration could preclude constitutional review of the plaintiff's due process claim, the United States Constitution has been interpreted to establish international custom as "our law."[62] By failing to acknowledge the customary process of international sports law, the district court misunderstood what process was "due" in the absence of a strong showing that the plaintiff's rights had been violated.

Finally, and perhaps most obviously, the district court's award of over $27 million, including more than $20 million in punitive damages, was absurd. Such an extravagant amount is grossly disproportionate to any reasonable calculation of actual, projected and punitive damages. It would surely contravene the public policy of virtually any foreign state in which the plaintiff might have sought to enforce the judgment. The court's own summary of Reynolds' earnings demonstrated the injustice of the award. It was *over 50 times* the amount of the plaintiff's normal, very comfortable income from endorsements and advertising over a two-year period, which was the duration of his suspension from competition. Moreover, in assessing the reasonableness of the requested damages, the court did not take into account Reynolds' failure to qualify for the Olympics as an individual runner. Even taking generous account of possible malice by the IAAF and his lost opportunity to compete for a spot on a medley team in the 1992 Olympic Games, the award can only be described as unjust.[63] The award might itself have threatened the interests of athletes, particularly those in developing countries whose training and eligibility for competition is dependent on IAAF financing. Of course, at this stage of the litigation, the IAAF could not have justifiably complained of such injustice since it had refused to defend itself on the merits of the case.

---

[62] *See, e.g.*, Paquete Habana, 175 U.S. 677 (1900).

[63] The district court found as follows:

> Prior to his suspension, Plaintiff earned the following in appearance fees and endorsement contracts:
>
> 1987: $ 56,000
>
> 1988: $255,112
>
> 1989: $316,915
>
> 1990: $333,375

Reynolds v. Int'l Amateur Athletic Fed'n., No. C-2-92-452, slip. op., at 27 (S.D. Ohio Dec. 3, 1992). The above data would not seem to confirm the court's earlier finding that the "[p]laintiff, as an individual, has limited economic resources." Reynolds v. Int'l Amateur Athletic Fed'n., No. C-2-92-452, slip op., at 25 (S.D. Ohio July 13, 1993).

The court then speculated about projected loss of earnings, premised on a finding *after Reynolds failed to qualify in the Olympic trials except as an alternate* that "[p]laintiff was likely to win a gold medal in the 1992 Olympic Games." *Id.* Although Reynolds failed to qualify for the Olympics as an individual runner, he remained eligible for selection as a member of the United States medley team. Janofsky, *Reynolds Loses His Last Claim to Olympic 400*, N.Y. TIMES, June 27, 1992, at 31.

Although the appellate court in *Reynolds* properly dismissed the action, its jurisdictional rationale is somewhat questionable, and the district court opinions are replete with errors. In sum, *Reynolds* was a judicial steeplechase in which the courts, particularly the district court, stumbled badly and repeatedly.

b. The Harding *Case*

A vicious attack on United States figure-skating star Nancy Kerrigan shortly before the 1994 Winter Games threatened her eligibility. The complicity of her rival, Tonya Harding, became front-page news. On February 5, 1994, the United States Figure Skating Association (USFSA) concluded that there was reason to believe Harding had violated the Olympic code of fair play because of her role in the assault and its aftermath.[64]

Two days later, the USOC announced plans to convene a disciplinary hearing concerning Harding. Had it taken place, it would have been conducted by a nine-member Games Administration Board, whose decision would have been subject only to final approval by the IOC. The Board scheduled the hearing in Norway because of the imminence of the Winter Games there. It appeared, therefore, that an interesting question might be whether Harding's due process rights under the United States Constitution and the Amateur Sports Act could be satisfied by proceedings conducted on foreign territory.

What followed, however, was a sort of judicial ice follies in which Harding compelled the USOC to trace a series of complicated court maneuvers.[65] On February 9, she filed a $25 million lawsuit against the USFSA for breach of contract and asked for an injunction against the disciplinary hearing in Norway. Three days later, with the court's encouragement, the parties reached an agreement whereby Harding would compete in the Winter Games but appear at a USFSA disciplinary hearing in the United States whose date would be determined by the parties after conclusion of the Games. She then competed in the Games but did not win a medal. Afterward, in the face of a possible criminal indictment for her role in the assault, Harding pleaded guilty to a lesser felony charge of hindering the prosecution and was placed on three years' supervised probation with the following conditions: an assessment of $160,000 in fines, court costs and charitable donations; resignation from the USFSA; performance of 500 hours of community service; and her submission to psychological evaluation. This plea-bargained agreement in criminal proceedings forced her to resign from the

---

[64] "The association found that she was either involved in the assault or that she knew about the attack and failed to prevent it, that she failed to notify authorities or that she made false statements about what she knew of the attack." Janofsky, *Harding's Lawyers Prepare Strategy*, N.Y. TIMES, Feb. 9, 1994, at B7; Longman, *Official Says Harding Should Skate*, N.Y. TIMES, Feb. 5, 1994, at 34.

[65] *See generally* Longman, *Reynolds Overturned in I.A.A.F. Victory*, N.Y. TIMES, May 18, 1994, at 16 (on both the *Reynolds* and *Harding* cases).

USFSA and effectively barred her from major competition.[66] The USFSA later stripped Harding of her 1994 national title and banned her for life from sanctioned competition.[67]

Before the postponed USFSA disciplinary hearing was to take place, the federal district court vacated the injunction against the hearing but dismissed Harding's action.[68] Although the court held against the USFSA on several procedural points, it determined that the main action was moot after Harding had resigned from the USFSA and pled guilty to criminal charges. It followed that "[a]ny intervention by the courts in the internal affairs of the Figure Skating Association should be restricted to that necessary to vindicate the rights at issue."[69]

Significantly, the *Harding* court expressed frustration with the complicated and potentially unfair posture of the litigation, but acknowledged that "[t]his is one of those rare cases where judicial intervention was appropriate."[70] The court cautioned, however, as follows:

> The courts should rightly hesitate before intervening in disciplinary hearings held by private associations, including the defendant United States Figure Skating Association. Intervention is appropriate only in the most extraordinary circumstances, where the association has clearly breached its own rules, that breach will imminently result in *serious* and irreparable harm to the plaintiff, and the plaintiff has exhausted all internal remedies. Even then, injunctive relief is limited to correcting the breach of the rules. The court should not intervene in the merits of the underlying dispute.[71]

To its credit, the court orchestrated a settlement of the dispute under intense time pressures on the eve of the Winter Games. The proceedings were, however, decidedly dicey. The threat of Tony Harding's $25 million nuisance action clearly shaped the outcome. Rather than risking a rather dicey settlement, the court might have stayed judicial proceedings pending a final decision by the USOC after the scheduled hearing in Norway. Courts should avoid preempting customary international authority and thereby prejudicing the expectations of the international

---

66 The court also barred further prosecution by "any" jurisdiction for her involvement in the assault on Nancy Kerrigan. If another court initiated a prosecution contrary to the order, Harding would have the right to withdraw her plea and have her sentence set aside. State v. Harding, No. 94-0331872 (Multnomah County Cir. Or. Mar. 16, 1994). Longman, *Harding Deal Handed Something to Both Sides*, N.Y. TIMES, Mar. 20, 1994, at 21.

67 THE OREGONIAN, July 1, 1994, at A14.

68 Harding v. U.S. Figure Skating Ass'n, 851 F. Supp. 1476 (D. Or. 1994), *vacated on other grounds*, 879 F. Supp. 1053 (D. Or. 1995).

69 *Id.* at 1481.

70 *Id.* at 1479.

71 *Id.*

community. In the long run, the integrity of the process may be as important as outcome in an individual case.

The *Harding* dispute raised the issue of how to avoid or otherwise respond in a timely manner to legal action brought on the very eve of major competition when it is too late for the appropriate national governing body, NOC or IF to take effective action. Last-minute litigation of this sort invites abuse by athletes and sports organizations alike. Claimants can thereby delay or obfuscate an issue of eligibility for competition. As a result, the flurry of arbitration and litigation that typically marks the eleventh hour before Olympic and other major competitions is often more tactical than justice-seeking. Under time pressures, litigation often serves little more than an *in terrorem* or bullying function.

In response to this kind of ambush filing of litigation, the United States Congress amended the Amateur Sports Act in 1998.[72] Under the amendments, a court may generally not impose any injunction against the United States Olympic Committee within 21 days of the beginning of a major competition. The 1998 amendments thereby strengthened the law's encouragement of arbitration as a preferred means for resolving disputes in the arena of international competition. The amendments also established the office of an ombudsman who, among other powers, may seek to mediate disputes. This is a positive step even though disputes involving the eligibility of athletes are not easily mediated because the stakes are usually very high.

c. *The* Lindland *Case*

A third cause célèbre in United States courts featured two competitors for a single weight-class position on the United States Greco-Roman wresting team for the 2000 Olympics in Sydney. The loser of the match, Matt Lindland, complained that the winner, Keith Seracki, had used illegal holds. The dispute went through 13 stages of arbitration and litigation in the federal courts, including unsuccessful appeals to the United States Supreme Court, as well as the CAS.[73]

On June 24, 2000, in Bout #244 of the Greco-Roman Wrestling trials to determine the United States Olympic team, Keith Sieracki beat Matt Lindland 2-1 in a best-of-three series to gain a berth on the team in the 76-kilogram (167.5-

---

[72] Amateur Sports Act, *supra* note 10, at § 220509.

[73] *See* Lindland v. United States Wrestling Ass'n, Inc., 230 F.3d 1036, 1038 (7th Cir. 2000); Lindland v. United States Wrestling Ass'n, Inc., 228 F.3d 782, 783 (7th Cir. 2000); Lindland v. United States Wrestling Ass'n, Inc., 227 F.3d 1000 (7th Cir. 2000); Lindland v. United States Wrestling Ass'n, Inc., Am. Arb. Ass'n No. 30-190-00443-00 (Aug. 9, 2000) (Burns, Arb.); Sieracki v. United States Wrestling Ass'n, Inc., Am. Arb. Ass'n No. 30-190-00483-00 (Aug. 24, 2000) (Campbell, Arb.); Grenig, *Arbitration of Olympic Eligibility Disputes: Fair Play and the Right to be Heard*, 12 MARQ. SPORTS L. REV. 261 (2001); Nafziger, *Arbitration of Rights and Obligations in the International Sports Arena*, 35 VAL. U. L. REV. 357 (2001) (from which this case study draws);Thompson, *Olympic Team Arbitrations: The Case of Olympic Wrestler Matt Lindland*, 35 VAL. U. L. REV. 407 (2001).

pound) class. In accordance with U.S.A. Wrestling rules, the three mat officials included a referee, a judge, and a mat chairman. Lindland immediately protested the officiating of his loss, claiming that Sieracki had applied an illegal hold by using his legs and had also attempted to flee a hold in violation of the rules of both the international wrestling federation (FILA) and U.S.A. Wrestling.[74] Lindland's protest complied with the Protest Procedures of U.S.A. Wrestling and special procedures for 2000 Olympic trials. The Protest Committee, however, refused to overturn the decision against Lindland on the basis that it involved judgment calls by mat officials that were beyond the Committee's competence to review. For good reason, mat decisions are simply not subject to change on review. Lindland appealed the denial of his protest to U.S.A. Wrestling's Standing Greco-Roman Sport Committee. He argued before this body, in a telephonic hearing on July 13, 2000, that the mat officials had not simply misinterpreted U.S.A. Wrestling rules but had misapplied them. For proof of his claim, he demanded that the Committee view a videotape of the match despite an organizational rule against the use of videotaped evidence. The Committee refused this request.

Six days later, on July 19, 2000, the Standing Committee denied Lindland's appeal, 4-1, largely on the basis of the discretion vested in mat officials to make or not make penalty calls. As a result, U.S.A. Wrestling added Sieracki's name to the roster of nominations to be submitted to the USOC for the 2000 Olympic team. Lindland then brought a demand for arbitration in Chicago of his grievance against U.S.A. Wrestling,[75] as he was entitled to do under the Amateur Sports Act.[76] Such proceedings are usually referred to as Article IX arbitrations, after Article IX of the USOC Constitution.[77] In accordance with the Amateur Sports

---

[74] The Official Rules of FILA (the Fédération Internationale des Luttes Associées) (1999), are the international rules of wrestling. These rules have largely been adopted by U.S.A. Wrestling with some modifications. Article 61 of the FILA Rules provides as follows:

> A. In Greco-Roman Wrestling, it is forbidden to grasp the opponent below the hips or to squeeze him with the legs. All pushing, pressing or "lifting" by means of contact with the legs on any part of the body of the opponent also is strictly forbidden.
>
> In Greco-Roman wrestling, unlike Free Style wrestling, it is necessary to accompany the opponent to the ground.
>
> B. In Free Style wrestling, a scissor lock with the feet crossed is forbidden on the head, the neck or the body.
>
> Article 57 of the FILA Rules provides as follows:
>
>> (a) Fleeing a hold occurs when the defending wrestler openly refuses contact in order to prevent his opponent from executing or initiating a hold.

Article 59 of the FILA Rules ("Illegal Holds") establishes several duties of the referee in the event of a prohibited act by a competitor. Lindland claimed the referee failed to fulfill these duties.

[75] In the Matter of Arbitration between Matt Lindland and U.S.A. Wrestling, No. 30-190-00443-00 (Am. Arb. Ass'n, Aug. 9, 2000) [hereinafter Chicago arbitration].

[76] 36 U.S.C. § 220529 (2000 Supp.).

[77] This provision implements the provision in the Amateur Sports Act for arbitration of grievances against the USOC. Constitution of the United States Olympic Committee, art. IX.

Act, the winner of the disputed event, Keith Sieracki, was not a party to the arbitration between Lindland and U.S.A. Wrestling.

In the Chicago arbitration, Lindland argued that U.S.A. Wrestling had not provided "procedures for the prompt and equitable resolution"[78] of his grievance, as the Amateur Sports Act requires. This requirement formed the legal framework of the proceedings that followed. The gist of Lindland's arguments was that the Greco-Roman review committee had failed to follow U.S.A. Wrestling's own rules and had fashioned new ones to suit its interests, for example, by recusing four committee members who might have supported Lindland's claim. The arbitrator, Daniel Burns, agreed with Lindland and ordered a rematch between the two competitors. Sieracki participated in the rematch under protest. This time Lindland won, 8-0. U.S.A. Wrestling, however, simply added Lindland to its Olympic eligibility list as an alternate, leaving Sieracki as its nominee to the USOC for the Olympic team. Lindland responded by seeking enforcement of the arbitral award in the federal District Court for the Northern District of Illinois. The court dismissed his action, without a written opinion, apparently for lack of federal jurisdiction.[79] Now, let us return to the arbitral award.

After the Chicago award but prior to the rematch, Sieracki filed his own arbitration demand in Denver before A. Bruce Campbell,[80] seeking confirmation of his status as the sole nominee in his weight class for the Greco Roman wrestling team. Lindland counterclaimed to the opposite effect. So, the prospect arose of a rematch of dispute resolution as well as wrestling. As we shall see, however, the prospect of repetitive dispute resolution by virtue of a second round of arbitration in Denver was fuzzy because some of the issues in Denver were materially different from those in the Chicago arbitration. The Denver arbitrator first determined the arbitration was proper and allowed all evidence offered by the parties except the videotape of Bout #244. Sieracki won this second round of arbitration.

---

78 36 U.S.C. § 220522(a)(13) (2000 Supp.): "[a]n amateur sports organization is eligible . . . to continue to be recognized, as a national governing body only if it . . . provides procedures for the prompt and equitable resolution of grievances of its members." 36 U.S.C. § 220529(8) assigns the following purpose to the USOC and therefore, by delegation, to the NGBs:

> to provide swift resolution of conflicts and disputes involving amateur athletes, national governing bodies, and amateur sports organizations, and protect the opportunity of any amateur athlete, coach, trainer, manager, administrator, or official to participate in amateur competition.

79 *See* Lindland v. U.S.A. Wrestling Ass'n, 2000 U.S. App. LEXIS 21754, No. 00-3177, at 3 (7th Cir. 2000).

80 In the Matter of the Arbitration between Sieracki and U.S.A. Wrestling and Matthew Lindland, No. 30-190-00483-00 (Am. Arb. Assn, Aug. 24, 2000) [hereinafter Denver arbitration]. Since this second arbitration did not fall within the prescribed process for reviewing a grievance under the Amateur Sports Act, *supra* note 10, it had the rather odd posture of a friendly action between the like-minded Sieracki and U.S.A. Wrestling as a means to confirm the latter's decision in Sieracki's favor, to challenge the fairness of the Chicago arbitration, and to question whether the notice and circumstances of the rematch were fair.

After four conferences in which all parties in the overall dispute participated, Arbitrator Campbell determined that Sieracki was not bound by the Chicago Award because he had not been a party to it. He found no evidence that the mat officials in Bout #244 had misapplied the rules or otherwise abused their authority. He also found that U.S.A. Wrestling's procedural arrangements, including the review committee's refusal to hear the team coach's testimony or to view video tape of the match, had not prejudiced either wrestler, did not constitute an irregularity or impropriety, and did not justify setting aside the grievance process. The Denver Award concluded by ordering U.S.A. Wrestling to withdraw Lindland's name from the eligibility list for the team and to confirm Keith Sieracki as the sole nominee on the team roster to be submitted to the USOC.

Just a few hours after the Denver Award, however, the Seventh Circuit Court of Appeals reversed the lower court in its refusal to enforce the Chicago Award in Lindland's favor and issued a mandate to U.S.A. Wrestling to enforce the award by nominating Lindland to the USOC.[81] When Lindland sought to enforce this decision, however, the district court refused again on the basis that it lacked jurisdiction.[82] Lindland then obtained a writ of *mandamus* from the circuit court that ordered the lower court to enforce the Chicago Award.[83] At this point U.S.A. Wrestling and the USOC were faced with what appeared to be contradictory orders.

Since arbitration is not normally subject to issue and claim preclusion,[84] each of the wrestlers therefore was free to seek judicial confirmation of the arbitral award in his favor under Section 9 of the Federal Arbitration Act.[85] Lindland, who was therefore back in the federal courts for the second time, specifically requested a court order to compel the USOC to send his name to the IOC despite the USOC's argument that it could not do so because it had already sent Sieracki's name to the IOC. The Denver court, on the other hand, transferred the Sieracki action to the Chicago court, where the opposing federal actions were consolidated. (One might well ask what would have happened if the federal district court in Denver had not transferred the Sieracki action to the federal court in Chicago for consolidation of the two actions.) After consolidation of the two actions, the Northern District of Illinois court, in the face of the *mandamus* order issued by the Seventh Circuit, directed the USOC to substitute Lindland for Sieracki as U.S.A. Wrestling's sole nominee to the USOC and denied Sieracki's petition to

---

[81] Lindland v. U.S.A. Wrestling Ass'n, 2000 U.S. App. LEXIS 21754, No. 00-3177 (7th Cir. 2000).

[82] *See* Lindland v. U.S.A. Wrestling Ass'n, 2000 U.S. App. LEXIS 22213, No. 00-3177, at 3 (7th Cir. 2000).

[83] *Id.*

[84] Brotherhood of Maintenance of Way Employees v. Burlington Northern RR., 24 F.3d 937 (7th Cir. 1994).

[85] 9 U.S.C. § 9 (1996).

confirm the Denver Award in his favor. In compliance with the district court order, the USOC requested the IOC to replace Sieracki with Lindland as a member of the Olympic team. It also appealed the court ruling that required it to take this action. U.S.A. Wrestling appealed each of the mandated district court decisions to the Seventh Circuit, which upheld both orders.[86] In the end, less than two weeks before the beginning of the Olympic Games, United States Supreme Court Justice Stevens (also from Chicago, incidentally) denied a request by the USOC for a stay of the Seventh Circuit's *mandamus* order.[87]

From the record, it appears that the case was very ably, indeed admirably argued by counsel for the parties. In view of the time constraints, the advocacy was exemplary. Reasonable minds can certainly differ on the outcome of the case, but the process itself was flawed. Fundamentally, the Chicago Award was based on a determination that U.S.A. Wrestling's review of Lindland's protest was procedurally defective. The arbitrator found that the organization's rules were inadequate to deal with the issues that arose in the case concerning possible conflict of interest, recomposition of the review committee, and restrictions on testimony.[88] The materiality of these defects is questionable,[89] as was the advisability of ordering a rematch rather than a recomposition and reconvention of the Protest Committee.[90] Simple mathematics reveals that if Lindland's corner coach in Bout #244

---

[86] Lindland v. U.S.A. Wrestling Ass'n, 2000 U.S. App. LEXIS 22692, No. 00-3220 and No. 00-3236 (7th Cir. 2000).

[87] *See* Bravin, *High Court Ensures Wrestler's Trip to Olympics*, WALL ST. J., Sept. 7, 2000, at B19 (noting that Justice Stevens denied the request for review without comment).

[88] *See* Chicago arbitration, *supra* note 75, Findings of Fact ¶ 9.

[89] *See* Denver arbitration, *supra* note 80, at II-4 .

[90] The justification in the Conclusion and Award reads as follows:

> Changed situations of Committee participants, the question of the President of USA will attend and vote [sic], the exigencies of the present circumstances of final team selection, the fact that a crucial witness's testimony was chilled at the first hearing, the potential atmosphere of a reconvened full Committee, and the very lack of guidance in USA Wrestling by-laws and rules, when grouped together, are convincing that Lindland cannot be put back to the same position he was on July 12th, and cannot receive the prompt and equitable resolution of his grievance that he has been promised. For example, one excluded member of the Committee was a fellow wrestler with a grievance *pending* at that time. That grievance has now been finally resolved. Another mistake made in fashioning the July 13 Committee, [sic] was the erroneous belief that some members of the Greco-Roman Sports Committee had also *voted* on that Protest Committee, and they were excluded for that reason. In fact, only one member had actually *voted* at the Protest Committee and that was the president of the USA Wrestling, who testified he was an *ad hoc* member of the Committee and may have attended one Committee meeting over the past several years. As significant is the lack of guidance and advance notice on these issues to Lindland, and Committee members, as he attempted to process his protest. Unfortunately, the same lack of guidance defeats any attempt to reconvene the Committee and provide a clean slate to press his claim in the short time before final team selection.

Chicago arbitration, *supra* note 75, Conclusion and Award, ¶ 2.

had recused himself, as would surely be appropriate, and if all of the remaining three committee members who recused themselves had instead voted in Lindland's favor, the result at least would have been a tie, which would have been insufficient to reverse the original decision in favor of Sieracki.[91]

Even so, the bases for review within U.S.A. Wrestling, as the process developed, are murky. What is clear is that the by-laws and rules of U.S.A. Wrestling did not provide any real guidance on appropriate procedures for reviewing a protest of this sort.[92] As a result, simply reconvening the Protest Committee might not have overcome apprehensions about the fairness of the administrative process.

U.S.A. Wrestling's refusal to entertain videotaped evidence except for during-match viewing by mat officials and for viewing flagrant misconduct and allegations of brutality is also questionable. The rule against videotaped evidence is designed to shield judgment calls from endless challenge and dispute. The rule thus protects the integrity of officiating and avoids substituting arbitrators for referees. Nevertheless, excluding videotaped evidence clearly conflicts with the rules of FILA, the international wrestling federation.[93] Moreover, the governing law of the Amateur Sports Act seems to contemplate a freer evidentiary environment by stating that "[t]he parties may offer any evidence they desire and shall produce any additional evidence the arbitrators believe is necessary to an understanding and determination of the dispute. The arbitrators shall be the sole judges of the relevance and materiality of the evidence offered."[94]

Reasonable minds may, of course, differ on the advisability of allowing videotaped evidence. What is hard to dispute, however, is the complexity of the legal

---

[91] *See* Denver arbitration, *supra* note 80, at ¶ I(f).

[92] The Chicago award found

> [t]hat USA Wrestling has not provided any written rules, regulations, by-laws, or precedential authority justifying its actions and decisions regarding: 1) the determination of the number and identities of the Greco-Roman Sports Committee when hearing appeals such as Lindland's; 2) grounds for excluding sitting Committee members from participating and deliberating in appeals such as Lindland's; 3) limitations on the nature and extent of the testimony of witnesses; 4) who is permitted to appear and participate in the hearing;[.]

Chicago arbitration, *supra* note 75, Findings of Fact ¶ 9.

[93] In the event of a protest, Rule 63 of the Official Rules of FILA, *supra* note 74, clearly encourages the use of videotape. To the contrary, one of the few modifications of the FILA rules by U.S.A. Wrestling provides as follows: "Under no circumstances shall the use of video tapes or films of a bout be considered or shown in the evaluation of any protest. Elements of the FILA Protest procedures may be applied as determined by the protest committee." U.S.A. Modifications, Article 63, U.S.A. Wrestling Protest Procedures (1999).

The Denver Award wisely sidestepped the issue of whether U.S.A. Wrestling's rules are "less or more wise" than those of FILA. Denver arbitration, *supra* note 80, ¶ II-6.

[94] 36 U.S.C. § 220529(5) (2000 Supp.).

process which extended over a period of two-and-one-half months and involved thirteen stages of dispute resolution.[95] Surely that was an unlucky thirteen, not just for Sieracki, but for the reputation of dispute resolution related to international sports competition. In the cogent words of Matt Lindland's wife, "[t]hey're probably going to have to change the rules after this one."[96]

Although the selection of Lindland to the Olympic team may have been a reasonable outcome of the dispute, the premises of the Seventh Circuit's orders to that effect are shaky. Indeed, *Lindland* is a good example of the difficulty that federal courts have had in defining their role in disputes involving the eligibility of athletes for international competition.

At the heart of the Seventh Circuit's opinions, written by Judge Frank Easterbrook, is a conclusion that the Chicago Award was valid while the Denver Award was invalid.[97] The rationale was that because the Chicago Award had been upheld by a court of law, any later award, namely the one in Denver, could not purport to countermand it. Once the court had ordered U.S.A. Wrestling and the USOC to substitute Lindland for Sieracki on the Olympic team, that was it, period. Although the Seventh Circuit's confirmation of the Chicago Award is certainly reasonable, its negative conclusion about the Denver Award is much less compelling.

While acknowledging the lack of issue and claim preclusion in arbitration, the court's opinion enlists two principal arguments against the Denver Award, concluding therefore that it was "doubly flawed."[98] First, Judge Easterbrook concluded that the Denver Award was, in his words, *ultra vires* because, unlike the Chicago Award, it was not conceived as an appeal of a USOC or NGB decision under the Amateur Sports Act. But he failed to appreciate that, unlike the Chicago arbitration, which was premised in the Amateur Sports Act, the Denver arbitration was brought under the USOC's Grievance Procedures for Code of Conduct and Team Selection 2000 Olympic Games.

Second, Judge Easterbrook construed Rule 48 of the Commercial Arbitration Rules of the American Arbitration Association to bar the Denver Award as a redetermination of the merits of a claim already decided. But Rule 48 merely bars a redetermination of the merits in a *modification of a single award*. What makes the double arbitration in *Lindland* so interesting is that the two awards involved different parties and, to an extent, different issues. Not only did the circuit court minimize these differences, but it took Denver Arbitrator Campbell to task for

---

95 *See* the several stages of litigation in Lindland v. U.S.A. Wrestling Ass'n, *supra* notes 73, 75, 79, 80, 81, 82; USA TODAY, Sept. 14, 2000, at 1C.

96 USA TODAY, *supra* note 2, at 2C.

97 Lindland v. U.S.A. Wrestling Ass'n, 2000 U.S. App. LEXIS 22692 at 12.

98 *Id.* at 7.

deciding, in the court's words, to "ignore" Rule 48 "utterly"[99]and thereby to flout the judicial confirmation of the Chicago Award. But Campbell had reason to ignore Rule 48 because it simply did not apply!

Judge Easterbrook's opinion emphasized that the winner of a contested event is normally not a party to an Article IX proceeding. That is certainly true and appropriate under the law. But there were four material differences between the Chicago and Denver arbitrations. First, the Denver claimant, Sieracki, had been unable to appear formally in the Chicago arbitration. Although that did not in any way call into question the Chicago Award, by the same token it enabled him to demand relief in Denver from the mandatory rematch ordered by the Chicago Award. Judge Easterbrook seems to have been bothered by Sieracki's timing of this demand prior to the event itself. But what was Sieracki supposed to do to vindicate his position after the Chicago Award to which he was not a party? Perhaps he should have waited a few days until he had lost the rematch before pursuing a judicial remedy. But, under the time constraints imposed by the Amateur Sports Act, it was probably wise for him to get off the mat and get moving again. In any event, he had standing under the 2000 Protest Rules to demand arbitration. Surely, the Denver arbitrator was acting properly in hearing the demand of an athlete whose original selection to the team was in jeopardy.

Although many Article IX disputes involving allegations against an athlete of doping and other grounds for ineligibility impact only indirectly, on other identifiable competitors, an either-or eligibility issue of the sort at issue in *Lindland* is materially different. Article IX's exclusion of the disputed winner of an event in an arbitration of that dispute presents a serious issue. It is simply unfair to ignore the winner's interests on the basis that arbitration of a grievance under the Amateur Sports Act excludes the winner as a party. In the Denver arbitration, on the other hand, both of the contesting wrestlers, as well as U.S.A. Wrestling, made appearances. Ultimately, then, what makes the federal court's process so eminently unfair was its refusal to allow Sieracki to assert his own claim, independent of his sports organization.

Second, the Denver arbitration, although it considered Lindland's protest *de novo*, also heard new issues related to the rematch that occurred while the Denver arbitration was pending. It simply is not correct to conclude, as the Seventh Circuit opinion does, that "[t]he whole point of the Campbell proceeding [Denver arbitration] was to redecide issues."[100] That may have been part of the point but by no means the whole point. Judge Easterbrook's opinion itself acknowledges that Sieracki pursued the arbitration, "protesting the result of the rematch."[101] Moreover, unlike the issues raised by Lindland in the Chicago arbitration,

---

99 *Id.* at 11.

100 *Id.* at 11.

101 *Id.* at 7.

Sieracki's demand in Denver sought a determination that he should be the sole nominee to the Greco-Roman Olympic team, to the exclusion of Lindland.

Third, it is reasonable to view the Denver arbitration as a fresh proceeding, unaffected in part by the Seventh Circuit order that confirmed the Chicago Award. After all, the rematch had converted Sieracki, the original winner, into a loser. Surely, Sieracki, the "new" loser, so to speak, should have been entitled to the same right to demand the same kind of arbitration as Lindland, the "old" loser, so to speak, had enjoyed. Thus, Sieracki could claim the arbitrability of his grievance under either the Code of Conduct and Team Selection or, arguably, under a theory that the results of the rematch could be contested as a fresh action and hence that the second arbitration in Denver was proper under the same provision of the Amateur Sports Act which Lindland had legitimately invoked.

Even if one does not accept the recharacterization of the Denver arbitration as a fresh action, perhaps because Sieracki had not exhausted the internal protest and grievance procedures required by law,[102] it nevertheless seems clear that the complex of dispute resolution was more of a muddle than the Seventh Circuit seems to have appreciated. For instance, the opinions failed to appreciate the very real dilemma faced by U.S.A. Wrestling and the USOC in the face of two inconsistent awards. Instead, one of Judge Easterbrook's opinions intimates that NGBs such as U.S.A. Wrestling are "scofflaws,"[103] chastises the USOC for insisting that "it is entitled to do as it pleases—defying injunctions to its heart's content,"[104] and surmises a conspiracy between U.S.A. Wrestling and the USOC in contempt of court.[105] These observations may or may not be correct, but such fighting language by an appeals court, without adequate proof, is disconcerting.

That said, one of the Circuit Court opinions does hint at some productive new directions for resolving these kinds of disputes. In Judge Easterbrook's words, conflicting instructions may not be an "irremediable evil. Injunctions create property rights, which may be altered by private agreements. Bargaining among Sieracki, Lindland, and U.S.A. Wrestling could lead to a settlement that would relieve U.S.A. Wrestling of an incompatible obligations."[106] Judge Easterbrook caps this observation with a challenge: "Definitive resolution of the right way to handle conflicting awards, after one has been confirmed, may await another day."[107]

---

[102] *See* 36 U.S.C. § 220529 (2000 Supp.); Dolan v. U.S. Equestrian Team, Inc., 608 A.2d 434 (N.J. Super. A.D. 1992). Sieracki, on the other hand, was seeking to vindicate his initial victory under severe time constraints.

[103] Lindland v. U.S.A. Wrestling Ass'n, 2000 U.S. App. LEXIS 22692, at 22.

[104] *Id.* at 19.

[105] *Id.* at 17.

[106] *Id.* at 7.

[107] *Id.*

That day does not yet seem to have arrived. What, nevertheless, can be done, specifically, to improve the process? Both the Chicago and Denver arbitral awards in *Lindland* were creditable. Neither was spoiled by any of the defects of corruption, fraud or evident partiality for which the Arbitration Act allows an award to be set aside.[108] Even if one were to agree that a first award ordinarily should bar a second award, the two awards in this case differed substantially from each other.[109] Consequently, Judge Easterbrook's misunderstanding of the express reach of the first award,[110] his caustic appraisal of the second award, and his injudicious name-calling were simply off the mat. The problem lay not in the second arbitration itself but in the structure of dispute resolution that encourages proliferation and, worse yet, redundancy of proceedings.

d. The Mercury Bay *Case: An America's Cup Maelstrom*

> Is the game worth the playing when players must be prepared to split hairs like barristers? . . . [T]o voluntarily seek it as sport is, we think, asking a bit too much.[111]

> As litigious sporting events go, nothing tops the America's Cup.[112]

A tempestuous controversy roiling around the 1988 America's Cup race in sailing demonstrates, by negative example, the need for careful administrative planning and supervision of competition to avoid disputes, the deficiencies of litigation to resolve these kinds of disputes, the importance of articulating and applying principles of fairness, and the advisability of vesting an impartial body with the authority to perform those functions.

i. The Deed of Gift

In 1851, in a race around the Isle of Wight, the owners of the yacht America won a silver trophy cup that they later conveyed to the New York Yacht Club (NYYC). A Deed of Gift stipulated that the "America's Cup," as it came to be known, would be "a perpetual Challenge Cup for friendly competition between

---

108 *See* 9 U.S.C. § 10a (1996).

109 *See supra* text accompanying notes 78–80.

110 Despite Judge Easterbrook's argument that the Denver Award purported to rescind the Chicago Award's order to place Lindland on the Olympic team, not only does the Denver Award contain no such attempted rescission, but the Chicago Award, in the first instance, did not actually order Lindland's selection to the United States Olympic team. Chicago arbitration, *supra* note 75.

111 *See* W.M. Lawson & T. Thompson, The Lawson History of the America's Cup—A Record of Fifty Years 279 (2d ed. 1986). On the history of the Cup, see Hines, About the America's Cup (1986).

112 St. John, *America's Cup: Lawyers, Hulls and Money*, N.Y. Times, Dec. 1, 2002, § 8, at 1.

foreign countries" and would be "the property of the [winning] Club subject to the provisions of [the] deed, and not the property of the owner or owners of any vessel winning a match."[113] Successive winning clubs would accept Cup challenges, serve as trustees of the charitable trust, administer sailing races according to the Deed of Gift, and assign the Cup to successful challengers.

The 1988 version of the Deed[114] provided for competition between one-mast vessels of 44 to 90 feet "on the load water-line"[115] or two-mast vessels of 80 to 115 feet. The Deed permitted any organized yacht club "of a foreign country" to challenge the defender of the Cup to a race or series of races. The challenger must specify the load water-line and other dimensions of the racing vessel and the date of the race, and give at least ten months' notice of a challenge in advance of that date. The defending club might then select the site for the race, but need not reveal the specifications of its vessel until the race. Alternatively, as became the custom, prospective competitors might consent mutually to terms of the race not prescribed by the Deed.

ii. *Mercury Bay Boating Club v. San Diego Yacht Club*

For 126 years the New York Yacht Club remained undefeated in the America's Cup competition, after 24 consecutive victories since the Cup was formally established in 1857. The NYYC interpreted the Deed by adopting resolutions. The only two adjudications during this period[116] applied the *cy pres* doctrine of charitable

---

[113] "America's Cup Deed of Gift" [hereinafter Deed] (copy on file with author), *reprinted in* Johnson & Taylor, *Revolutionizing Judicial Interpretation of Charitable Trusts: Applying Relational Contracts and Dynamic Interpretation to Cy Pres and America's Cup Litigation*, 74 IOWA L. REV. 545, app. C (1989).

[114] The original Deed of Gift dates from 1857. Lawson & Thompson, *supra* note 111, at 45. In 1882 and 1887 the Cup was reconveyed back to George L. Schuyler, one of the original donors of the Cup, in order to modify the Deed. The modifications included the addition of clauses which (1) require the challenging club to give ten months' notice of a challenge; (2) clarify that the successive winning clubs would be the successive defenders/trustees of the Cup; and (3) establish a "mutual consent" provision, under which competing clubs could agree to ignore certain stipulations in the Deed, including the ten months' notice requirement, but must otherwise comply with the Deed. *See* ROUSMANIERE, THE GOLDEN PASTIME: A NEW HISTORY OF YACHTING 123 (1986). *See also* N.Y. TRIBUNE, *Races for the America's Cup 3* (1893) (original deed and modifications of it in 1882 and 1887). The 1988 version of the Deed incorporated these modifications as well as others made in 1956 and 1985 by the New York Supreme Court.

[115] The load water-line is the contact line where the water meets the hull. For references and further discussion, *see Recent Development, International Sports Competition: The America's Cup 1988—The Legal Battle*, 30 HARV. INT'L L.J. 264, 264, n.2 (1989) (quoting HENDERSON, SAIL AND POWER 17 (3d ed. 1979)). The challenger must specify the owner, name and rig of the challenging vessel as well as dimensions of the load water-line, water-line beam, maximum beam and draft of the challenging vessel.

[116] In the matter of the application of New York Yacht Club for an order pursuant to Section 12 of the Personal Property Law, or otherwise, amending the terms of the Deed of Gift of the America's Cup, No. 12,696/56 (N.Y. Sup. Ct. 1956) [hereinafter Application of New York Yacht

trust law, which allows a court to modify a trust instrument when provisions have become obsolete because of changed circumstances for which the original settlor did not provide. This doctrine corresponds roughly to the doctrine of *rebus sic stantibus* under international law.

More important than the NYYC's resolutions and the *cy pres* adjudications was the role of custom in interpreting the Deed under its mutual consent clause. For example, to accommodate an increasing incidence of multiple challenges, the practice developed of treating all challenges within particular dates as simultaneous. The challenger for the Cup was then determined by a series of elimination races. Other established practices, inscribed in a memorandum that the NYYC issued prior to each Cup defense, included the use exclusively of 44-foot or 12-meter yachts, a two-year notice period to change the class of a boat from the prevailing custom, and three or four-year intervals between races. Thus, by 1980 the international sailing community had largely stabilized expectations about Cup challenges and races by customary practices within the broad language of the Deed.

In July 1987 the Mercury Bay Boating Club of New Zealand (Mercury Bay) challenged the San Diego Yacht Club[117] to a race for the Cup, thereby setting in motion a fierce battle in the courts rather than at sea. These legal skirmishes began when Mercury Bay, barely within the required ten-months' notice requirement, challenged San Diego to race against its 90-foot behemoth, approximately twice the customary length of vessels since 1956. In doing so, Mercury Bay broke with tradition by failing to adhere to the three cardinal customs of racing in 44-foot or 12-meter boats, waiting three or four years between races, and entering into an agreement with the defending club under the Deed's mutual consent provision. Rather, Mercury Bay invoked the "challenge" provision of the original Deed. San Diego rejected the challenge, claiming that ten months' notice of the race was insufficient under the circumstances and that Mercury Bay's radical 11th-hour departure from the established custom of 44-foot or 12-meter yachts was contrary to practice under the Deed.

The dispute might have been resolved, and perhaps should have been resolved, by a five-member jury of experts on yacht racing from the International Yacht Racing Union (IYRU), under its rules. However, Mercury Bay chose to file

Club] (reducing the minimum load water-line length from 65 to 44 feet in order to attract more competitors and eliminating a requirement that the challenging vessel sail to a match "on its own bottom"); *In re* Royal Perth Yacht Club, Nos. 18,436/84, 4615/85 (N.Y. Sup. Ct. 1985) (permitting races to be held in the Southern Hemisphere and construing the term "arm of the sea" in the Deed to include all of the Great Lakes, so as to widen potential Canadian participation).

[117] In 1983 the Royal Perth Yacht Club of Australia (Royal Perth) defeated the NYYC's entry, thereby becoming the first non-American winner of the Cup and successive trustee of the competition. Four years later the San Diego Yacht Club (San Diego) defeated Royal Perth, obtained the cup and succeeded to the trusteeship.

a legal action in the New York Supreme Court seeking to confirm the validity of its challenge and to enjoin San Diego preliminarily from accepting other challenges before Mercury Bay's challenge was decided. San Diego responded by requesting the court to amend or interpret the Deed of Gift again under the *cy pres* doctrine, in order to confirm the customary practices of racing 44-foot or 12-meter yachts and conducting a multiple-challenge elimination series. Thus, San Diego sought the power to establish conditions for the Cup race on the basis of the custom. The New York Supreme Court granted Mercury Bay's motion for a preliminary injunction and ordered San Diego to either accept the challenge, forfeit the Cup, or negotiate agreeable terms with the challenger.[118] The race was on.

San Diego accepted Mercury Bay's challenge by itself radically departing from custom: it entered a multihulled catamaran, within the acceptable dimensions prescribed by the Deed, rather than the usual monohulled vessel. Catamarans are typically much faster. Mercury Bay, crying foul, filed a second action, in which it claimed that a catamaran would deny it a "match" under the Deed because the two boats were not like or similar to each other, that is, they were not evenly matched. Mercury Bay claimed, therefore, that San Diego was in contempt of court. The court, however, allowed the race to go on.[119]

In September 1988, after San Diego won the first two of three potential races, it claimed the Cup. When Mercury Bay revived its deferred action against San Diego, the New York Supreme Court unexpectedly upheld Mercury Bay's claim, declared Mercury Bay the winner by forfeit of the race, and directed San Diego to transfer the Cup to Mercury Bay.[120] The opinion relied on the spirit and intent of the Deed of Gift.[121] On appeal, San Diego contended that the court had improperly construed[122] an equitable condition in the Deed of Gift; that extrinsic evidence would justify the entry of multihulled vessels; and that the Deed of

---

[118] Mercury Bay Boating Club v. San Diego Yacht Club, No. 21,299/87 (N.Y. Sup. Ct. Nov. 25, 1987).

[119] Mercury Bay Boating Club v. San Diego Yacht Club, No. 21,299/87 (N.Y. Sup. Ct. July 25, 1988). The court rejected Mercury Bay's contempt of court claim, refused to give an advisory opinion regarding the validity of a multihulled defense against a monohulled challenge, and ordered the rival clubs to reserve any further legal challenges until after their race. Because San Diego could wait to select its boat until the day of the first race, the court held that a decision would be premature; it would only "countenance continued bickering, and encourage further litigation." *Id.*

[120] Mercury Bay Boating Club v. The San Diego Yacht Club, No. 21,299/87 (N.Y. Sup. Ct. Mar. 28, 1989).

[121] *Id.* Contrary to the court's previous holding based on the "letter" of the Deed, it relied this time on the "spirit" of the Deed. The court reasoned that the challenge provision of the Deed would be meaningless if it simply served the defender with notice to build a superior vessel.

[122] "[T]o sail a multihulled vessel against a monohulled yacht . . . is, in the opinion of most boating authorities, to create a gross mismatch and, therefore, is violative of the donor's primary purpose of fostering friendly competition." *Id.* at 7–8.

Gift required that disputes regarding the validity of challenges and the conduct of the clubs be decided pursuant to the defender's rules, which followed those of the IYRU.[123] The Appellate Division, reversing, declared San Diego to be the winner of the race.[124]

Ultimately, the New York Court of Appeals, refusing to entertain extrinsic evidence, upheld the decision of the Appellate Division of the Supreme Court. The court determined that nothing in the Deed prevented San Diego from entering a catamaran and that San Diego had fulfilled its fiduciary responsibilities as trustee of the charitable trust.[125] In restricting itself to the four corners of the Deed, the court found no evidence of an express intent to restrict multihulled boats from the competition and refused to consider extrinsic evidence of the settlors' intent.

iii. The Issue of Fairness

Of particular note was the court's refusal to consider the "fairness" of the strange race:[126] "Questions of sportsmanship and fairness with respect to sporting contests depend largely upon the rules of the particular sport and the expertise of those knowledgeable in that sport; they are not questions suitable for judicial resolution."[127] A dissenting opinion argued, however, that issues of fairness are fundamental to a proper interpretation of the Deed. Indeed, the settlor of the trust had emphasized that "the governing principle of America's Cup competition is fairness."[128] Although both sailing clubs may have acted in an unsports-

---

[123] The IYRU promulgates rules every four years that are then adopted by national yacht racing unions (which may add to or modify the rules by "prescription"), such as the United States Yacht Racing Union (USYRU). PERRY, UNDERSTANDING THE YACHT RACING RULES THROUGH 1992, at 23, 24, 269 (appendix d, part I) (1989).

[124] Mercury Bay Boating Club v. San Diego Yacht Club, 150 A.D.2d 82, 545 N.Y.S.2d 693 (1989) (nothing in the Deed required *evenly* matched, like or similar vessels. Moreover, after earlier controversies, trustees of the Deed had adopted a resolution that confirmed the right of defenders to design and enter any vessel that complied with the terms of the Deed).

[125] Mercury Bay Boating Club v. San Diego Yacht Club, 76 N.Y.2d 256, 557 N.E.2d 87 (1990). *See* Note, *The Litigation of the America's Cup Runneth Over with Inconsistencies: A New Approach to Interpreting Charitable Trusts*, 12 LOY. L.A. ENT. L.J. 221 (1992).

[126] "The question of whether particular conduct is 'sporting' or 'fair' in the context of a particular sporting event . . . is wholly distinct from the question of whether it is legal." *Mercury Bay, id.*, 76 N.Y.2d at 265, 557 N.E.2d at 92. Thus, the court limited its decision to the legal issue whether the original settlors intended to exclude catamarans.

[127] *Id.* Correspondingly, the court noted, the Deed contemplates that issues of fairness and sportsmanship are to be decided by the yachting community, whereas club rules or mutual consent provisions govern the terms for conducting a race.

[128] *Mercury Bay, supra* note 125, 76 N.Y.2d at 283, 557 N.E.2d at 103 (Hancock, J., dissenting). *See also* letter from George Schuyler to Commodore Bennett (Mar. 1871) (discussing the propriety of the NYYC's practice of racing a fleet of defending vessels against a sole challenger), *reprinted in part in* LAWSON & THOMPSON, *supra* note 111, at 60, as follows:

manlike manner, *in pari delicto*, that did not cancel out the issue of fairness. It surely remained a question suitable for judicial consideration. The dispute centered not on a whistle-blowing issue related to the technical conduct of the race, but on fundamental rules for "friendly competition" as a "condition" of a "match" that could only be interpreted in equitable terms. If fair play and sportsmanship are required of athletes on the field or in the water, they should be required of sports organizations as well, especially if a legal instrument, in this case the Deed, requires fairness. Trustees of the Cup have an obligation under the Deed to enforce all conditions "faithfully and fully" against contestants in a race. Thus, "the notion of a fair match on equal terms is inherent in the concepts of a `Challenge Cup' and `friendly competition between foreign countries.'"[129] This interpretation echoed a lower court judge's observation that "[t]he goal of fostering friendly competition is the condition upon which the Cup was donated."[130] The argument is persuasive.

As we have seen, a procedural right of due process and natural justice is fundamental in municipal adjudication of issues involving athletes and sports organizations, as reflected in English and United States cases. The dissenting opinions in *Mercury Bay* have sparked a consideration of extending the requirement of procedural fairness to help analyze the merits of a dispute as well. In *Mercury Bay* an issue of substantive fairness arose in the narrow context of interpreting certain words in a trust instrument, but dissenting opinions at two stages of the litigation relied on broader principles that distinguish a sporting from a market-place context.

Resolution of *Mercury Bay* by the IYRU would have been far preferable to the Dickensian experience in the courts. "Ultimately," one judge wrote, "it must be the contestants, not the courts, who define the traditions and ideals of the sport."[131] If, however, courts are involved, they should be prepared to make equitable determinations, for which clear guidelines will be necessary. The *Mercury Bay* litigation demonstrates the importance of an on-going authoritative process

---

> I think that any candid person will admit that when the owners of the America sat down to write their letter of gift to the New York Yacht Club . . . he [would not] think it very likely that any contestant for the cup, under conditions named by them, should be subjected to a trial, such as they themselves had considered unfair and unsportsmanlike.

[129] *Mercury Bay, id.*, 76 N.Y.2d at 282, 557 N.E.2d at 102 (Hancock, J., dissenting). The dissent pointed out that (1) there had been a long established custom of monohulled races, (2) the competing boats always bore "a close resemblance to each other with each vessel having a *reasonable chance to win*" and (3) the load water-line lengths of the boats almost always had been nearly identical, as a matter of custom. *Id.* (emphasis in the original).

[130] *Mercury Bay, supra* note 124, 545 N.Y.S.2d at 710 (Kassal, J., dissenting) ("The 1988 America's Cup races were manifestly unfair in every sense. True sportsmanship and the integrity of this great sport demand far more, as does the very Deed of Gift by which this competition has been sponsored for over a century." *Id.* at 711).

[131] *Mercury Bay, supra* note 125, 76 N.Y.2d at 273, 557 N.E.2d at 96.

to define the guidelines, rules and principles of competition with sufficient clarity to obviate litigation. The greater the confidence in this authoritative process, the less the litigation. In the interest of fairness, either the IYRU or another international process, perhaps within UNESCO, might take the lead in formulating basic principles and guidelines for interpretation of instruments such as the Deed of Gift.

iv. Issues of Private International Law

Reliance on New York courts to resolve all disputes arising out of America's Cup competition is troublesome for reasons of private international law. As challenges by foreign clubs become further and further removed from the NYYC and New York, reliance on the broadly worded Deed may be precarious. When neither the defender-trustee nor the challenger is a national of the United States, it is unlikely that the disputants would select a New York forum or New York law to resolve a dispute arising from the administration of America's Cup races when neither disputant has a direct connection with the state. Contractual and statutory bases, however, purport to establish New York jurisdiction over dispositions of trusts valid under New York law. Since 1987 the contractual source of New York jurisdiction and New York law has been a forum and choice-of-law provision in the Assignment and Acceptance letter by which the America's Cup has been transferred between clubs since San Diego won the Cup from Royal Perth.[132] Also, New York statutes confer jurisdiction upon New York courts over disputes regarding the administration and interpretation of charitable trusts formed by New York domiciliaries.[133] New York courts may not have exclusive jurisdiction, however, if neither the trustee/defender of the Cup nor the Cup itself, as the *res* of the trust, is any longer in the state,[134] particularly if it is transferred to the territory of a state which refuses to recognize or enforce New York law. The only possible exception may occur when a settlor has intended to establish exclusive New York jurisdiction, but it is questionable whether foreign legal systems would necessarily give effect to such an expression of intent.

---

132 Royal Perth Yacht Club of Western Australia and the San Diego Yacht Club, Assignment and Acceptance Agreement (Feb. 1987) (copy on file with the author). Each trustee, upon turning the Cup over to a successful challenger as the new trustee, is supposedly bound by the Deed to assign its rights as trustee to the new, successive trustee and agree to be bound by New York law.

133 N.Y. EST. POWERS & TRUSTS LAW § 8-1.1 (McKinney 1992) [hereinafter N.Y. TRUSTS].

134 RESTATEMENT (SECOND) OF CONFLICT OF LAWS § 267, comment d, at 137 (1971) ("[C]ourts of other states may exercise jurisdiction in proper cases if they have jurisdiction over the trustee, or if they have jurisdiction over trust assets insofar as interests in those assets are concerned"). *See also id.*, § 267, comment e, at 137–38; § 272, comment on clause a, at 181–82; clause (b), at 182–83. Jurisdiction elsewhere may be inferred from a trust's provision for successive trustees in other jurisdictions. *Id.*, § 272, comment e, at 183–84. In this case, the original settlors of the Cup specified neither an exclusive forum nor law to govern disputes, yet specifically allowed for foreign trustees. *See* BOGERT & BOGERT, THE LAW OF TRUSTS AND TRUSTEES §§ 291–92, at 391–416 (2d ed. rev. 1977) for a discussion of judicial jurisdiction and choice-of-law regarding "multistate" trusts.

Whether the America's Cup Deed of Gift established a charitable trust[135] in the first place is a troublesome issue of characterization that also bears on the capacity of the modified Deed to impose New York jurisdiction and law as a means of resolving all future issues. New York law did not recognize charitable trusts when the Deed was created.[136] Administration of the trust fails to yield clear evidence of a charitable purpose.[137] Ordinarily, a trust set up solely to promote a sports competition would not be "charitable" unless the public, broadly defined, receives a benefit,[138] and the lucrative effect of the America's Cup calls into question its charitable character.[139] Even if the America's Cup competition was intended to benefit the public[140] by promoting international friendly relations, the actual races have not always been "friendly" in any genuine sense.[141] Moreover,

---

135 To create a charitable trust, the settlor must intend to create a trust for a charitable purpose. *See* RESTATEMENT (SECOND) OF TRUSTS § 351 (1959). N.Y. TRUSTS, *supra* note 133. It is not surprising that the charitable nature of the trust was never questioned by parties to the America's Cup litigation, for if the trust were not charitable, it might have been voided under the Rule against Perpetuities. *See* Johnson & Taylor, *supra* note 113, at 548, n.8, *citing* Wilson v. Flowers, 58 N.J. 250, 277 A.2d 199 (1971); MCGOVERN, KURTZ & REIN, WILLS, TRUSTS, AND ESTATES § 13.7, at 548 (1988).

136 At that time, only charitable gifts and *not* charitable trusts were legal in the state of New York. *See* Westmore v. Parker, 52 N.Y. 450, 458 (1873) (charitable corporation may receive personal property provided that the gift of the principle is "immediate and vested"); Holmes v. Mead, 52 N.Y. 332, 339 (1873) ("[t]he trusts retained are four in number, and . . . do not include perpetual trusts for charity, or for the benefit of classes or of corporations"). It was not until 1893, with the passage of the Tilden Act, 1893 N.Y. Laws ch. 701, that charitable trust law in New York was revived. BOGERT & BOGERT, *supra* note 134, § 322, 521–22, at n.46; *see also* practice commentaries to N.Y. TRUSTS, *supra* note 133.

137 In 1956, when applying for an amendment to the Deed under the *cy pres* doctrine, the NYYC defined its "charitable" purpose as the advancement of yachting, naval architecture, and "international good will and understanding." Application of New York Yacht Club, *supra* note 116.

138 *See generally* N.Y. TRUSTS, *supra* note 133; RESTATEMENT (SECOND) OF TRUSTS § 374 comment n ("A trust *merely* for the promotion of sports is not charitable") (emphasis added). BOGERT & BOGERT, *supra* note 134, § 323 at 207. The charitable purpose of trusts set up for the creation of prizes or awards, such as the America's Cup, must appear from either the trust instrument itself or extrinsic evidence to resolve any ambiguity in the trust instrument. 15 AM. JUR. 2D *Charities* § 66 (1976). *In re* Harmon's Will, 80 N.Y.S.2d 903, 910–11 (1948), held that a trust under which trophies for a competition were to be awarded, was charitable, inasmuch as the donor had clearly intended to promote peace. *See also In re* Judd's Estate, 274 N.Y.S. 902 (1934), *aff'd*, 270 N.Y. 516 (1936) (court found a charitable trust in the award of a prize).

139 While charitable trusts may be favored by law, the effect of the trust may be relevant in questioning a "charitable purpose." BOGERT & BOGERT, *supra* note 134, § 364, at 36–37 ("there must be no element of profit-making for individuals or non-charitable organizations").

140 The Deed of Gift does not explicitly identify the beneficiaries of the trust. At the time the Deed was executed, a failure to specify beneficiaries of a charitable trust might have been fatal. Under current New York law, however, a trust will not fail for lack of designated beneficiaries. N.Y. TRUSTS, *supra* note 133, *unless the public benefit is not evident. See, e.g.*, Matter of Shattuck, 193 N.Y. 446, 451, 454 (1908).

141 *See* Riggs, KEELHAULED—THE HISTORY OF UNSPORTSMANLIKE CONDUCT AND THE AMER-

the NYYC's reconveyances of the Cup to Schuyler so that he could fine-tune the Deed may have been inadequate bases for the resulting amendments.[142]

v. Reform in the Wake of the *Mercury Bay* Litigation

The *Mercury Bay* litigation and lingering uncertainties about the legal basis and efficacy of the Deed of Gift recall scathing assessments of it throughout its history.[143] The Deed has been an unreliable rudder for the America's Cup. The *Mercury Bay* episode demonstrates, once again, the advisability of a more stable institutional basis for organizing sailing's premier competition, for ensuring that principles of fairness govern it, and for resolving any disputes in a less adversarial and time-consuming manner. Although the outcome of the litigation may have been reasonable, the process was dubious. It involved too many appeals and reversals, delays, expense, and uncertainty about its precedential value in future cases and foreign courts.

It is not surprising that the America's Cup maelstrom led to a more institutionalized process for administration of the America's Cup, based on a revival of the mutual consent provision of the Deed of Gift. In lieu of the IYRU, the Board of Directors of the San Diego Yacht Club adopted several interpretive resolutions which, as a gloss on the Deed, were designed to establish a new class of boat for all competitions, to regulate the acceptance of Cup challenges, and to resolve disputes prior to the 1992 America's Cup races.[144] One of these resolutions, the San Diego Protocol,[145] provided for a Trustees Committee comprised of three mem-

---

ICA'S CUP (1986). Dennis Conner, captain of San Diego's crew against Mercury Bay, declared that "[s]portsman-ship is nonexistent [in the America's Cup competition]. This isn't tiddlywinks; it's business . . . [t]here has never been any sportsmanship in the America's Cup. Anyone who thinks so is kidding himself." LIFE, Sept. 1988, at 85, *quoted in* 76 N.Y.2d 256, 290, 557 N.E.2d 87, 107 (1990) (Hancock, J., dissenting).

142 While legal title vests in the trustee, *see* N.Y. TRUSTS, *supra* note 133, "the [inter vivos] settlor has the power to revoke the trust or to modify it *only* if he has reserved such a power, or if the omission to reserve such a power is due to a mistake." 4A A. SCOTT, THE LAW OF TRUSTS § 367 (W. Fratcher 4th ed. 1989) (citations omitted) (emphasis added). *See also id.*, § 367.2 (modification ineffective even with the consent of the settlor and trustees); RESTATEMENT (SECOND) OF TRUSTS § 367 (1959).

143 *See, e.g.*, the following appraisal from 1901: "The new deed is a mixture of bad sportsmanship, bad law and bad English, made in a hurry by a little clique, and never yet ratified by the New York Yacht Club. It is encumbered by meaningless legal verbiage, and its provisions are obscure and contradictory." LAWSON & THOMPSON, *supra* note 111, at 271.

144 This system was implemented for the first time during "World Championships" (now known as the Vuitton Cup), which serve as a "wet-run" for the America's Cup races. The World Championships involve "fleet racing" as opposed to a one-on-one "match." The May 1991 World Championships were won by an Italian entry. Telephone interviews with Tom Wilson, Public Information Officer, SDYC (Sept. 26, 1991); Terry Harper, General Counsel, America's Cup Organizing Committee (June 6, 1991).

145 SDYC Interpretive Resolution of Sept. 8, 1988 [hereinafter San Diego Protocol] implemented changes in the administration of the races, including the method by which a club may

bers, one each from the New York Yacht Club, Royal Perth and San Diego.[146] It resolved disputes between potential challengers and defenders that did not involve technical or whistle-blowing rules of conducting a race.[147] Disputing clubs must first attempt to resolve their differences by negotiation. Failing that, the Trustees Committee was charged with resolving a dispute under rules established by the disputing parties.

Subsequently, the arbitral process of the Trustees Committee was regularized. As a result, competitors for the America's Cup had to agree to submit their disputes to a five-person arbitration panel rather than a court. Ironically, the availability of arbitration may have encouraged the submission of claims. Ultimately, the America's Cup has been severely handicapped by the lack of an on-going, effective governing body or disinterested commissioner.[148]

vi. Conclusion

Sports activity often initiates a spectacle of issues that are largely played out beyond the television cameras that have transformed sports into a microcosm of society. The evolving process of international sports law and dispute resolution responds to these issues. As the *Mercury Bay* litigation demonstrates by negative example, no sports competition can outpace the problems it generates without teamwork between private and public sectors, stable institutions, clear rules, and an abiding commitment to principles of procedural and substantive fairness in resolving disputes. Principles of sportsmanship and fairness that apply on the field should also apply off the field to govern the organization of sports. The shared task for international and comparative lawyers is to refine, prioritize,

---

challenge the holder of the Cup. First, multiple challenges received within 60 days after a successful defense of the Cup are treated as if they had been received simultaneously. This is a return, in effect, to the practice of both the NYYC and Royal Perth. Second, challenging yacht clubs select a "Challenger of Record" within 30 days after the close of the 60-day period during which challenges are timely received. *Id.* The selection of a Challenger of Record is meant to facilitate the negotiation of race terms under the "mutual consent" clause of the Deed of Gift. If the challenging clubs fail to select a Challenger of Record, the Trustees Committee does so. *Id.* Third, the challenger not only proposes the dates, number of races, and type of course for them, but the "class of vessel . . . to be used by both the challengers and the defender" in the race. *Id.* Finally, elimination races between all challengers determine the single challenger in the final race. *Id.*

146 The Committee's membership was questionable insofar as a current trustee and defender of the Cup was represented. Without a system of recusal, a challenger might have had to bring a dispute against a defender before a triumvirate on which the defender has one of three votes and on which the challenger was not assured of any representation.

147 The first rulings were that (1) the challenging Club was required, without the defender's approval, to name its boat ten months prior to the Cup races, and (2) that an Italian club could not conduct tank testing of its vessel in another country. LOS ANGELES TIMES, March 5, 1991, at 6, col. 4.

148 St. John, *supra* note 112, at 15.

harmonize, and seek better means to enforce this dynamic new body of law and to improve the institutional structure for administering it and resolving disputes within it.

e. *The* Swiss Equestrian *Case*

By contrast to the other litigation, the *Swiss Equestrian* case,[149] decided by the Swiss Federal Tribunal, was a model of dispute resolution. There, a doping test at an international competition revealed the presence of a banned substance in the urine of a horse. The International Equestrian Federation (FEI) disqualified both the horse and its rider and suspended the rider for three months from international competition. The rider appealed this decision to the Court of Arbitration for Sport (CAS),[150] which the FEI had selected to resolve eligibility and disciplinary disputes of this sort. The CAS upheld the disqualification but reduced the suspension and imposed a fine against the rider. On the rider's appeal of this decision, the Swiss Federal Tribunal ruled that the CAS award was binding. The court cautioned, however, that the financial, legal and administrative links between the CAS and the IOC were so strong as would call into question the impartiality and independence of the CAS in any CAS action to which the IOC might be party.[151]

Unlike *Reynolds*, the issue of personal jurisdiction was not before the Swiss court, and the court enforced the arbitral award despite a few procedural issues in the arbitration. Also, the FEI testing procedures do not seem to have been sharply at issue. More importantly, however, the *Reynolds* and *Swiss Equestrian* cases are in stark contrast on the fundamental issue of the weight that a national court should give to a customary process of organizational and arbitral review. This contrast is only partially explained by the status and prestige of the Olympic Movement and international sports federations headquartered in the court's venue of Switzerland. A fuller explanation would take account of the failure of the *Reynolds* courts to view their role within an established international legal process. Another court in the United States is perhaps more typical in finding "most unfortunate the increasing frequency with which sporting events are resolved in the courtroom."[152]

---

[149] Gundel v. FEI/CAS, I Civil Court, Swiss Fed. Trib. (Mar. 15, 1993).

[150] On the CAS, *see* Ch. 3, *supra* text accompanying notes 15–37, 54–102.

[151] "In a judgement notified to the parties on 18th June 1993, the 1st Civil Court of the Federal Tribunal dismissed the appeal lodged against the FEI and the CAS, and ordered the rider to pay SFr. 9,000.—in judicial costs. The federal judges confirmed in their judgement that the CAS is a real arbitral court whose decisions properly constitute arbitral awards at an international level. The CAS therefore represents an alternative to state justice while, of course, respecting certain inalienable fundamental rights. This neutral and independent institution is therefore in a position to pronounce final and enforceable awards which have the force of a judgement. Thus, through recourse to the CAS, sports organizations, athletes and their partners can avoid referring any disputes they might have to ordinary state courts for settlement." OLYMPIC REV., July–Aug. 1993, at 305.

[152] *In re* Gault, 578 N.Y.S.2d 683, 685 (A.D. 3d Dept. 1992).

A comparison of the *Reynolds* and *Swiss Equestrian* cases, both decided by national courts, demonstrates the efficacy of international sports law. It can be instrumental in blending national and international institutions into a single process of justice that avoids judicial complexity. Although courts can be expected to address the most serious issues of due process and public interest, judicial abstention is advisable in most disputes between individual athletes, on the one hand, and designated sports bodies and organizations, on the other. Unless injunctive relief is absolutely necessary to prevent gross injustice to individual athletes or the public, adjudication is especially doubtful under the kind of time constraints that made the *Reynolds* and *Harding* cases so exciting but perilous on the eve of major competition. The excitement of sports competition is best left to the sports arena, not the courtroom.

Decisions of English courts, particularly *Greig v. Insole, Reel v. Holder*, and *Cowley v. Heatley*, suggest the parameters of judicial review. Despite the willingness of national courts to review issues of procedural fairness and fundamental public interest, they properly view adjudication as only a last resort for resolving international disputes. Normative trends thus confirm a growing commitment of national legal systems to the special processes of international sports law.

C. IMPROVEMENTS IN THE STRUCTURE OF DISPUTE RESOLUTION

Several steps could be taken to improve the structure for resolving disputes by arbitration and litigation. First, in reviewing arbitrations, the courts should proceed cautiously. Judicial relief from the decisions of sports bodies should be reserved for cases where due process violations are patent, and the violations dispositive, as they were not in *Lindland*. The financial stakes for athletes, absent such public law issues as those of labor law,[153] do not alone provide a compelling basis for judicial intervention.

Second, repetitious proceedings and the complexity they entail, particularly in eligibility cases, could be avoided by amending the Amateur Sports Act and the USOC Constitution to enable an individual winner of a disputed competition to participate in a single arbitration alongside the individual claimant, NGB and, as appropriate, the USOC. It is simply unfair to presume that a contested winner's interests are fully represented by an NGB.[154] A unified arbitration would then bar

---

153 *Cf.* the timely observation that

> U.S. courts and international federations must begin viewing amateur athletics in a more employment-related light, as substantial sums of money are at stake when suspensions of Olympic athletes occur. In the United States, amateur athletes have traditionally not been viewed as "employees" due to the strict NCAA regulations prohibiting college athletes from receiving financial rewards for their talents.

FitzGerald, *The Court of Arbitration for Sport; Dealing with Doping and Due Process During the Olympics*, 7 SPORTS L.J. 213, 236 (2000).

154 The USOC CONSTITUTION, art. IX § 2 provides that a demand for arbitration must des-

subsequent arbitration. In team sports, the problem of standing to appear is considerably more complicated. Even so, as a starter, team members of a class potentially affected by an eligibility decision might simply elect one of their number to represent their common interests.

Third, the non-interference rule should apply to all claims for arbitral or judicial review of all technical infractions during competition. The Amateur Sports Act should be interpreted or, if necessary, amended to avoid arbitration of a referee's decision so long as a claimant has had the benefit of a full and fair review by the appropriate NGB, unless that body would itself permit such a review.[155] In *Lindland*, the Chicago Award steered clear of scrutinizing judgment calls. The Denver Award, on the other hand, seemed to comment fairly directly on the judgment of the mat officials. A procedural rule barring review of such judgment calls in all but the most egregious cases would help avoid understandable suspicions by the media and the public that arbitrators can make second calls. In the Lindland-Sieracki match, there were three mat officials, all of whom appear to have satisfied U.S.A. Wrestling's requirement that they understood the rules and avoided wrongful, dishonest, intentionally improper, or bad faith conduct.[156] Even if they failed to take account of illegal wrestling maneuvers in violation of the rules of the game, such bad judgment calls or inaction should not be subject to arbitration or litigation in the absence of evidence that they had simply failed to understand the rules or that they abused their authority.

Fourth, it should be made clear, therefore, that the merits not only of judgment calls but of the rules of the game are generally beyond the competence of arbitration or litigation. After all, technical rules are constantly under review and reform by the IOC, IFs and NGBs themselves. One commentator has therefore proposed that the Amateur Sports Act be amended to provide that the jurisdiction of courts under the Act should be limited to determinations of whether responsible sports organizations have complied with their own rules, presumably within an acceptable margin of discretion. This proposal would bar courts from evaluating the merits of a technical dispute, confining their review to an evaluation of procedural due process.[157]

Fifth, NGBs and other sports associations, under the supervision of IFs, should draft more explicit and uniform rules of eligibility and remedies for relief

---

ignate "such USOC member" (normally an NGB) as an adverse party. As Judge Easterbrook's opinion points out, this is in keeping with the arrangement in labor arbitration that an employee who is discharged from employment may arbitrate a grievance with his employer but need not designate as an additional party a replacement who may be dischargeable by an award in favor of the grievant. 2000 U.S. App. LEXIS 21754, at 7.

[155] "There is no quicker way to kill spectator interest than to have a game played and the outcome decided a month later by lawyers." Longman, *supra* note 9.

[156] Denver arbitration, *supra* note 80, at II-1, 2.

[157] Hollis, *supra* note 12, at 200.

of legitimate grievances by athletes. Sheer chaos reigns today, and that is grossly unfair to athletes. For example, NGBs should clarify the precise weight that they are prepared to give to career records and recent international performance in determining eligibility when team tryouts are not alone determinative. Such clarification would have avoided arbitrations such as ones to determine the composition of the U.S. women's softball team and the U.S. women's cycling team at the Sydney Olympic Games.[158] The demand by Tammy Thomas, winner of the 500-meter women's trial for the 2000 Olympics, against Christine Witty, whom the United States cycling federation selected on the basis of her superior two-year performance profile, was a variation on the *Lindland* case. Although an arbitrator ordered a ride-off to settle the controversy, much like the *Lindland* wrestling rematch, Witty, unlike Sieracki, simply refused to show up and promptly filed her own arbitration action.

It will be essential, for reasons of fairness, to harmonize rules and remedies to make them as uniform and predictable as possible, across the range of sports. Serious questions of equity and due process arise whenever a track-and-field athlete is barred for life for ingesting a substance that is permitted in baseball. Similarly, the Amateur Sports Act should make it clear that ad hoc measures, such as rematches, should be only a last resort when reconstitution of a defective eligibility review process would be grossly unfair or impossible.

Finally, judicial decisions and arbitral awards should take account of obligations or duties as well as rights of athletes.[159] To do so would be in the best interests of sports. Although the ideal of athletes as role models is often romanticized and exaggerated, they unquestionably influence young people.[160] In reviewing claims, therefore, arbitrators should consider the special obligations or duties that athletes owe to society as well as their rights. In reviewing disputes involving the status of athletes, the issue ought to be what is in the best public interest, not just what is in the best interest of particular sports.[161] In that light, it is difficult to justify the outcome, for example, of the arbitration in the United States involving suspension of Latrell Sprewell by the National Basketball Association (NBA). Sprewell's physical, indeed nearly homicidal, assault on Head Coach Peter Carlesimo and the Golden State Warriors' team trainer, followed by his angry return from the locker room to reiterate his threats and repeat his assaults, surely warranted the most severe penalty. Accordingly, in consultation with the Warriors, the NBA imposed a one-year, 82-game suspension from play without pay—the most severe sanction that the NBA had ever imposed on a player. The Warriors

---

158 WALL ST. J., Aug 18, 2000, at A1.

159 On the obligations or duties of athletes, *see* Ch. 6, *supra* text accompanying notes 34–40.

160 *See, e.g.*, Lefort & Harvey, *What's in a game?*, UNESCO COURIER, Apr. 1999, at 18.

161 See P. WEILER & G. ROBERTS, SPORTS AND THE LAW: TEXT, CASES, PROBLEMS 86 (#3) (2d ed. 1998).

also terminated the remaining year's in Sprewell's Uniform Player Contract with the Golden State Warriors.[162] But then the matter went to arbitration.

The arbitrator hearing Sprewell's demand for relief mitigated the suspension to the remaining 68 games of the season and reinstated Sprewell's contract with the Warriors.[163] The Grievance Arbitrator's generous treatment of Latrell Sprewell unfortunately minimized the social consequences of his decision. In all fairness, the Grievance Arbitrator was fundamentally concerned about the issue of due process insofar as there had been no precedent for the severe penalty of a one-year suspension and termination of Sprewell's guaranteed contract. Perhaps, though, precedent, like consistency, can be a hobgoblin. It would seem that serious physical assault in the sports arena and sports arbitration should be treated with the same contempt as it is on the streets. The arbitrator's generosity to Sprewell would not seem to have been in the best interests of sports. Indeed, Sprewell's chronic temper tantrums continued years later,[164] bespeaking the need for strict application of disciplinary sanctions.

By the same token, sports organizations have ethical obligations to society, too. This expectation underlies an arbitral decision that upheld the most severe penalty ever imposed by the National Basketball Association (NBA).[165] The Minnesota Timberwolves had received this sanction for secretly conspiring with an athlete to avoid the NBA's salary cap, a requirement that is further elaborated in the league's collective bargaining agreement with the players' association. Ethical issues of this sort are particularly serious when, as in this case, an athlete and a sports association conspire to violate fundamental organizational rules.

Sports are special and so are athletes. But their special status means a higher standard of conduct. In the words of one observer, "players are highly visible in the community, and that carries a public obligation."[166] Sport, too, is highly visible in the community. In all litigation and arbitration of sports-related disputes, the public interest, including the best interests of sports, should be paramount.

---

[162] *See Latrell Sprewell Reinstatement Ruling, in* CHAMPION, FUNDAMENTALS OF SPORTS LAW 442 (Cum. Supp. 1999).

[163] Sprewell later brought action in the federal district court against the National Basketball Association and the Golden State Warriors, claiming $30 million damages on the basis that the arbitral award against him was racially discriminatory. *See* Sprewell v. Golden State Warriors, No. C-98-2053-VRW (N.D. Cal. 1998). Sprewell's action and a revised version of it were both dismissed as meritless suits in 1998 and 1999, respectively. On review, the Ninth Circuit Court of Appeals upheld the lower court. N.Y. TIMES, Nov. 8, 2000, at C22.

[164] *See Sprewell fined $25,000 for tempter tantrum*, STATESMAN-JOURNAL (Salem, Or.), Dec. 25, 2003, at 2B.

[165] *See* DuPree & Michaelis, *Smith cap ruling upheld*, USA TODAY, Nov. 10, 2000, at 1C (summarizing the arbitrator's approval of a penalty that denied the Timberwolves first-round draft picks during the next five NBA drafts and fined them $3.5 million).

[166] Gibeaut, *When Pros Turn Cons*, A.B.A. J., July 2000, at 108.

CHAPTER 5
RESOLUTION OF DISPUTES DURING COMPETITION

A. INTRODUCTION

A neglected aspect of dispute resolution in the international sports arena involves disputes involving the technical rules of the game and their application by judges and officials. The contrived or artificial nature of conflict in the sports arena presents unusual, if not unique, issues of dispute resolution. Although some sports provide for the resolution of disputes during competition—one example is the America's Cup race jury in sailing—the rules of the game, or simply rule of competition, are generally immune from legal challenge. The CAS has articulated a rule of non-interference in rules of the game and their application.[1] Consequently, in the waning moments of a football (soccer) game, players cannot seek to enjoin further play until the constitutionality of a penalty is reviewed. A yellow warning card or a red ejection is generally final. Nor may a basketball player, on a theory of proximate cause or scope of liability, challenge a basket resulting from a freak series of ricochets. Although rules of the game bear some similarity to rules and regulations in other administrative systems, their dual functions—first to provide for conflict and then to regulate it—set them apart. Rules of the game constitute a closed system that understandably is relatively free of external challenge.

This is not to say that disputes arising out of competition are non-justiciable. Quite the contrary: such issues as intentional infliction of physical injury, use of banned substances by athletes, and corruption of officials, not to mention spectator violence in the stands, generate business for the legal profession. Even when available remedies are limited to administrative challenges within sports associations, lawyers may be instrumental. High stakes, complicated rules, infrequent championships, and weak governing bodies increase the likelihood that the application of technical rules of the game may be at issue. The America's Cup in sailing is perhaps the foremost illustration of this tendency. With multi-million dollar hulls, infrequent races, more than 600 pages of regulations, and the lack of a governing body, the disputes over hull design and racing infractions are legion.[2] But the America's Cup is a special case, and even so, the rules themselves escape

---

1 *See generally* Ch. 3, *supra* text accompanying notes 77–81.

2 *See* St. John, *America's Cup: Lawyers, Hulls and Money*, N.Y. TIMES, Dec. 1, 2002, § 8, at 1, 15. On the *Mercury Bay* litigation, *see* Ch. 4, *supra* text accompanying notes 117–31.

challenge during competition. Generally in the sporting world, then, technical rules are supreme with the possible exceptions of grossly unfair sanctions[3] and, at least in theory, of unnecessarily risky rules.[4]

A more difficult question is the reviewability of judgment calls and decisions by officials, who are often called upon to make split-second decisions. It is clear that their judgment calls generally must be protected if the game is to go on. Official discretion in the sports arena is primarily kept in check by the rules of the game, the standards of officiating, and the principle of good faith.[5] Officials are therefore liable in tort law only for acts of gross negligence and bad faith.[6] The Court of Arbitration for Sport (CAS) has ruled that officiating should be shielded from arbitral or judicial scrutiny unless it is conducted in bad faith or is the product of wrong circumstances.[7] The rationale for this con-

---

[3] *See, e.g.*, the *dictum* to this effect in M. v. Ass'n Internationale de Boxe Amateur, 1996/006 CAS Ad Hoc Div. (O.G. Atlanta 1996) [hereinafter *M. v. A.I.B.A.*], *in* DIGEST OF CAS AWARDS 1986–1998, at 413 (M. Reeb ed., 1998) [hereinafter CAS AWARDS]. In *M. v. A.I.B.A.*, a boxer was disqualified at the Olympic Games in Atlanta for punching below the belt. The Court of Arbitration for Sport (CAS), while refusing to review a video tape of the match on the basis that technical rules of sport were not within its jurisdiction, nevertheless agreed to review the sanction of disqualification. After doing so, the CAS concluded that the sanction was appropriate, and the boxer's petition was dismissed.

[4] *But see* Agar v. Hyde, 173 A.L.R. 665, 74 A.L.J.R. 1219 (2000), a leading case on the issue of institutional liability for failing to amend rules of play and thereby avoid unnecessary risks on the playing field. The High Court of Australia ruled in *Agar* that the International Rugby Football Board (IRFB), in establishing the rules of the game, had no duty of care to avoid serious spinal injury to a player participating in a more or less freewheeling scrum. Afterward, however, the IRFB amended its rules to provide for a precautionary crouch-touch-pause-engage sequence for scrum formation. For analyses of *Agar* and its significance, *see* Opie, *The Sports Administrator's Charter:* Agar v. Hyde, 9 TORTS L.J. 131 (2001); Opie, *Medico-Legal Issues in Sport: The View from the Grandstand*, 23 SYDNEY L. REV. 375, 378 (2001).

[5] *See* Crouch v. Nat'l Ass'n for Stock Car Auto Racing, 845 F.2d 397, 403 (1988) (in reviewing a penalty decision, a court must defer to the authority of NASCAR decisions and interpretations of its own rules, absent an allegation of bad faith or violation of the law).

[6] *See* Cornelius, *How final is the final whistle? Review of and liability for decisions taken by officials at sports events*, 2002–4 TYDSKRIF VIR DIE SUID-AFRIKAANSE REG: J. S. AFR. L. 628, 636, 646–47.

[7] "CAS arbitrators do not review the determinations made on the playing field by judges, referees, umpires, or other officials who are charged with applying what is sometimes called "rules of the game" (one exception among others would be if such rules have been applied in bad faith, e.g. as a consequence of corruption)." Segura v. Int'l Amateur Athletic Fed'n, 2000/013 CAS Ad Hoc Div. (O.G. Sydney 2000), II DIGEST OF CAS AWARDS, at 680 (M. Reeb ed., 2002) [hereinafter II CAS AWARDS]; *see also M. v. A.I.B.A., in* CAS AWARDS, *supra* note 3, at 414 (traditionally, doctrine and judicial practice have always deemed that game rules, in the strict sense of the term, should not be subject to the control of judges, based on the idea that "*the game must not be constantly interrupted by appeals to the judge*"). *In M. v. AIBA, id.*, the CAS acknowledged in dicta, however, that "the distinction between what can be submitted to a court or arbitral panel—the rule of law—and what cannot—the game rule—is vague. . . . A new approach tending to abolish this distinction is being seen which consists of holding the view

clusion[8] is, first, that technical issues are best left to trained officials,[9] and, second, that sports federations should bear the ultimate responsibility to enforce rules of the game.[10]

Fairness must always be a litmus of quality in sports. Maintaining a level playing field is, after all, the principal rationale for the relentless war on doping of athletes. But applying even the best rules is subject to human error. Subjectivity inheres in judging and scoring, especially in sports that put a premium on style, aesthetics, or general presentation, such as figure skating, gymnastics, synchronized swimming, and free-style skiing. How, then, can there be any full assurance of fair play and objectivity in judging? The answer is that, although such assurance is impossible, much can be done to increase the transparency and on-the-spot reviewability of decisions to the extent practicable.

In particular, technological advances offer a significant corrective to error and unfairness. Ball-tracking technology, for example, uses super slow-motion cameras to determine whether a power serve in tennis has landed a millimeter inside or outside a service box. It is apparent that computerized scoring and timing systems as well as video replays can help eliminate some of the subjectivity and opportunities for abuse by officials in both their initial decisions and in any review process that might follow. Accuracy may be particularly critical as the professional stakes in sport increase. Mistakes can be extremely costly to players and teams. A measure of justice may therefore be at issue.

The *Lindland* controversy[11] on the eve of the 2000 Summer Olympic Games

---

that, in high level sport, applying the game rules very often has consequences in terms of property and financially, or may affect rights relating to personality, and is thus open to examination by the courts." The CAS did not, however, apply the suggested approach nor does it seem to have been generally adopted by sports bodies.

8 *Id.*

9 In the words of one leading commentator:

> Do we really want to settle matches months later in court or some other forum, or should they be settled on the playing field? Will the public accept results that are obtained in the court-room or other forum rather than the playing field? Would it be possible for a judicial officer or other adjudicator to accurately determine the outcome of an event if a certain decision is overturned? . . . One has to question whether interested parties could have some remedy at their disposal to undo the wrongs caused as a result of decisions that are incorrectly taken or not taken at all. One also has to question whether it would be possible for a judicial officer or other adjudicator to accurately determine the outcome of a race if such a decision, or lack of decision, is overturned.

Cornelius, *supra* note 6, at 629–30.

10 *See* SILANCE, LES SPORTS ET LE DROIT 83 (1998) (noting the unique niche filled by the rules of the game ("règles du jeu") in the complicated juridical order of international sports competition).

11 *See* Ch. 4, *supra* text accompanying notes 73–110, from Nafziger, *Arbitration of Rights*

in Sydney is a case in point. A controversial wrestling match between two competitors for a place on the United States Olympic team resulted in an acrimonious, time-consuming, and ultimately questionable series of arbitration and litigation. One can say that both wrestlers went to the mat of formal dispute resolution. The underlying controversy involved judgment calls. When the loser of the match, Matt Lindland, appealed the decision, an administrative ruling by USA Wrestling's Standing Greco-Roman Sport Committee upheld it in deference to the discretion of mat officials. Lindland then brought legal action, claiming procedural irregularities in the process of reviewing his grievance about the judgment calls.

A video tape of the match was available that might have settled the matter. Unfortunately, in the interest of shielding mat calls from routine review, the protest committee refused to accept videotaped evidence[12] even though the official rules of the international wrestling federation (FILA) encourage its use in such circumstances.[13] In so doing, the protest committee not only failed to avoid a legal battle but violated at least the spirit, if not the letter, of the Amateur Sports Act.[14]

Reliance on technology is not the last word in officiating and judging, however. It is far from an unmixed blessing. The necessary technology may be unavailable or prohibitively expensive, especially in developing countries. Often the technology is beyond the means of sports organizations wherever they are located. Also, use of technology, particularly video replays, can be intrusive; indeed it can be intolerably disruptive of competition. Sometimes technology may be a poor substitute for human perception, vigilance and decision on the field of action. Judgment calls generally depend on a fine balance between perceptions and second evaluations. Reliance on technology, as a routine arbiter of activity, may even be disastrous if it breaks down or fails in the course of competition. Moreover, technology-based reversals of official calls and decisions may undermine the authority and legitimacy of the officials based on the principle that "the referee is always right—even when he is wrong."[15]

As a legal consideration, the procedures for video filming, review and access to video tapes require not only substantial resources but effective regulation. The

---

and Obligations in the International Sports Arena, 35 VAL. U. L. REV. 357 (2001), *citing* Lindland v. United States Wrestling Ass'n, 230 F.3d 1036 (7th Cir. 2000) and other stages of the dispute resolution.

[12] Nafziger, *id.* at 362, 366.

[13] *See* Rule 63, FILA Rules (on file with the author).

[14] The Ted Stevens Olympic and Amateur Sports Act, 36 U.S.C. §§ 220501–220529 (2000) [hereinafter Amateur Sports Act] provides as follows: "The parties may offer any evidence they desire and shall produce any additional evidence the arbitrators believe is necessary to an understanding and determination of the dispute. The arbitrators shall be the sole judges of the relevance and materiality of the evidence offered." *Id.*, § 220529(b)(5).

[15] Gardiner, *The Third Eye: Video Adjudication in Sport*, 7 SPORT & L.J., No. 1, at 26, 27 (1999).

review process requires skill and great care. In *Jones v. Welsh Rugby Union*, an English court imposed a temporary injunction against suspension of a player who had neither access to nor an opportunity to comment on the video film upon which the suspension was based in part.[16] Such are some of the pitfalls of technology as a means of dispute resolution.

Despite these disadvantages, the use of technology to help resolve disputes and ensure greater fairness is becoming commonplace in sports. Two examples highlight this trend: the recent computerization of scoring in figure skating after a judging scandal during the 2002 Olympic Winter Games, and expanded use of video replays in both domestic and international competition.

B. CORRUPTION OF OFFICIALS DURING COMPETITION: SKATEGATE AND THE NEW JUDGING SYSTEM

The integrity of international figure skating was compromised by a judging controversy at the 2002 Winter Olympics Games in Salt Lake City concerning allegations of score-fixing by judges. When Russians Elena Berezhnaya and Anton Sikharuldze were declared the winners of the pairs event in figure skating, their victory surprised many who believed that Canadians Jamie Sale and David Pelletier had outperformed the Russians. A French judge, Marie Reine Le Gougne, promptly informed International Skating Union (ISU) members that she had agreed to give high marks to the Russians in exchange for a Russian judge's support of the French ice dancing team, which won a gold medal in their competition.

The ISU responded to the "Skategate" scandal by suspending Le Gougne and the President of the French skating body for three years and the 2006 Olympics. Later Le Gougne retracted her statements and denied that she had been pressured by superiors to vote for the Russians.[17] A brief investigation by the ISU revealed no evidence of Russian complicity in the alleged conspiracy. The Executive Board of the International Olympic Committee (IOC) ratified the ISU council's decision to throw out the French judge's score and award gold medals to both the Russian and Canadian teams.[18] It was the first time in Olympic history that a decision by a skating judge had been overturned, controversial as judging in that sport had been. The IOC President, emphasizing the cooperative spirit between the ISU and the IOC, described the double award of gold medals as "a matter of fundamental justice."[19]

---

[16] *See* Naidoo & Sarin, *Dispute Resolution at Games Time*, 12 FORDHAM INT'L PROP. MEDIA & ENT. L.J. 489, 499 (2002).

[17] Clarey, *As Championships Begin, Skating Elite Tries To Keep Focus on Ice*, N.Y. TIMES, Mar. 23, 2003, at SP10.

[18] Roberts, *Canadian Skaters Awarded Share of Olympic Gold; French Judge Suspended, Her Scoring Thrown Out*, N.Y. TIMES, Feb. 16, 2002, at 1 (somewhat confounding the respective roles of the ISU and IOC, however).

[19] Clarey, *IOC Chief Keeps Links to Nations Balanced*, N.Y. TIMES, July 28, 2002, at SP9.

Despite the ISU and IOC's prompt response to Skategate, it remained a cause célèbre. During the 2002 World Figure Skating Championships, demonstration marchers chanted "Hey, hey, ho, ho, secret judging has got to go," and a poster dubbed the ISU the "Axel of Evil."[20] Skategate, however, was not the first incidence of questionable collusion among figure skating judges. Earlier instances of unethical collusion among judges, often linked with politics, had already tainted the legitimacy of the sport. At the 1999 World Championships in Helsinki, for example, it was evident that Russian and Ukrainian judges were communicating with each other by tapping their feet. This impropriety, revealed on video tape, resulted in a brief suspension of the judges, but not a reversal of results, which included the award of a gold medal to the same Russians who were to share the gold medal in Salt Lake City.

Skategate was really the last straw. With the strong encouragement of the IOC, officials of the ISU, meeting in March of 2002, decided to reform its judging system. Two general approaches to the problems were introduced on an experimental basis: electronic scoring and more random, anonymous judging. The first alternative is an "anonymous" or "interim" system of judging that employs 14 judges, all of whose scoring is to be reported and displayed anonymously. The scores of nine of the 14 judges are then randomly chosen by a computer. Only those nine scores count. In contrast to the traditional scoring system, the judges are barred from discussing their marks.

As a second alternative to the existing system of scoring, ISU President Ottavio Cinquanta introduced a "New Judging System" of scoring[21] to deter bloc voting by judges and to overcome the subjectivity and confusion of the existing system.[22] Under the New Judging System, the existing 6.0-based scoring system is to be replaced by exacting criteria for judging every aspect of performance. This system contrasts with the traditional, highly discretionary 6.0-based system that relies on each judge's determination of all scoring elements. The new system uses computers and video to aid the judges in determining scores.[23] Each judge has a flat touch screen depicting the skater's performance as it is taking place. Bordering the image of the skater is an L-shaped frame. The name of the particular jump element, spin, or other sequence[24] that a skater is executing appears on the left side of this frame. Each specific element is assigned a value. For example, a triple lutz is worth 6.1 points. By touching the bottom portion of the screen,

---

20 Vecsey, *To the Barricades! Yes, Even in Figure Skating*, N.Y. Times, Mar. 30, 2003, at SP1.

21 Communication No. 1207, International Skating Union, New Judging System Figure Skating/Ice Dancing, (Apr. 16, 2003) [hereinafter ISU Communication 1207].

22 Leonhardt, *Who's in First*, N.Y. Times, Feb. 24, 2002, at WK4.

23 Press Release, International Skating Union, Year-end Update—Figure Skating Judging for the 2002–03 Season and Beyond, Dec. 27, 2002.

24 All of these maneuvers will be referred to as "elements" hereinafter.

each judge may then subtract points for errors in execution and also edit any mistakes as a particular performance progresses.

The New Judging System provides not only a more accurate evaluation of the technical aspects of performance, but also a method for assessing artistic factors. Five factors—skating skills, transition, performance, choreography and interpretation—are scored on a 10-point scale. An explanation of each factor appears on the judges' touch screens to assist them in their evaluations.

This reform requires several new administrators.[25] Two "technical specialists," experienced in figure skating, sit at their own computers. One specialist identifies each particular element and its degree of difficulty as it is being executed and sends that information to the judges' computers. The second specialist's function is to monitor the work of the first specialist. The two specialists, working together, may then review video film and make any necessary corrections. Another new administrator, the "technical controller," ensures that the information the technical specialists send to the judges is accurate. The controller also moderates an apparently mandatory Event Review Meeting to provide feedback among the judges regarding the application of regulations during a particular event. A "judge coordinator," formerly known as a referee, provides organizational support for the judges and also performs some of the duties of a referee, for example, by identifying overtime or undertime performances as well as vocal music violations and costume or prop deficiencies. Finally, an "event referee" coordinates the panels of judges to ensure that events function within the existing rules.

The New Judging System also includes a process for randomly selecting judges' scores in order to minimize the effect of any cheating or sharp deviations from the norm by judges. With eight judges on a panel, for example, only five scores are to be used; with ten judges, seven scores, and with 12 to 14 judges, nine scores. Computers help identify any anomalies that may require further investigation. The new system also allows officials to identify suspicious patterns in scoring, although the identity of individual judges remains confidential. ISU President Cinquanta remarked that individual judges' scores would be reviewed three times per year rather than just once per year, as has been the practice.

Reaction to the proposed reforms was mixed. Ron Pfenning resigned from his position on the ISU's technical committee, after his dismissal from refereeing the World Figure Skating Championships in 2003.[26] The ISU claimed that Pfenning was planning a breakaway group while still working with the ISU technical committee. The ISU also feared that Pfenning would not comply with the anonymous or interim judging system that had been adopted for that

---

25 ISU Communication 1207, *supra* note 21.

26 Clarey, *supra* note 17.

competition.[27] In response to the more general criticism of the new system, several skating luminaries, including Ron Pfenning, organized a World Skating Federation (WSF)[28] to replace the ISU. Scott Hamilton, a 1984 Olympic gold medalist, joined the new organization. The IOC, however, pledged to support the ISU. In March 2003, Hungarian judge Judit Fuerst-Tombor, after endorsing the WSF, was withdrawn from judging the women's competition at the World Figure Skating Championships.

C. THE USE OF CAMERAS IN DOMESTIC AND INTERNATIONAL COMPETITION

1. Domestic Competition

The use of video cameras to facilitate review of calls by officials has become an integral part of many sports competitions. The Professional Golfers' Association (PGA), for example, uses video for important decisions.[29] In the 2000 Honda Classic, golfer Brian Gay attempted a putt for a birdie. The ball wavered on the edge of the cup as Gay approached the hole. When he reached the cup, he made a motion to indicate that the ball was still moving before it fell into the cup. The rule that came into question establishes that a ball is in play from the time the player reaches the hole, without reasonable delay, plus ten seconds. Afterward, the ball, whether it is actually moving or not, is considered at rest. When NBC officials decided incorrectly that the putt was good, Gay believed that he was tied for first place. After the tournament, however, a PGA tour official reviewed a video of the putt and determined that 16 seconds had passed from the time of Gay's arrival at the hole before the ball dropped into it. The violation of this rule cost Gay one stroke and moved him into a tie for fourth place.

In England, the use of film and video dates back to at least 1947 in recording photo finishes in racing, but its use to assist officials is a recent development. Since 1993 video replays have been used in football (soccer) and are also used in rugby and cricket. Video recordings have also been accepted as evidence by courts in personal injury actions and other challenges of incidents and calls on the playing field.[30]

---

[27] Media Release, International Skating Union, Apr. 1, 2003. *See also* Vecsey, *supra* note 20 at SP5.

[28] The WSF is skeptical of the system of anonymous judging, questions the qualifications of ISU President Cinquanta because he is a speed skater, not a figure skater, and limits its memberships to figure skaters, as opposed to the ISU's representation of both figure and speed-skaters. The WSF promotes a system of checks and balances based on the traditional (6.0-point scale) scoring system, which is now 70 years old. The new organization is averse to the use of technology, preferring to establish an ethics committee to handle any allegations of impropriety among judges. By contrast, the New Judging System's emphasizes technology to solve the judging problem.

[29] Maisel, *Down But Not Out: You Didn't Have to be Dudley Hart to Feel Like a Winner in the Honda Classic*, SPORTS ILLUS., Mar. 20, 2000, at G7.

[30] Gardiner, *supra* note 15, at 28.

Video replay systems are expanding in both professional and collegiate football in the United States. Under a Referee Replay Review system, both the use of video replay by the National Football League (NFL) and its significance have increased. In 1999 there were 195 reviews of plays, 29 percent of which resulted in reversals, whereas in 2001 there were 258 reviews of which 34.5 percent resulted in reversals.[31] In January 2002 a video replay during a playoff game between the New England Patriots and the Oakland Raiders overturned what was initially ruled to be a costly fumble by the Patriots' quarterback Tom Brady. Two weeks later, Brady was hailed as the most valuable player at the Super Bowl.

Officials use video replay in both National Hockey League (NHL) and National Collegiate Athletic Association (NCAA) competitions.[32] In the NCAA semifinal championship game in 2003 between New Hampshire and Cornell, a goal was reversed when video replay revealed that the puck had been redirected with a high stick in violation of NCAA rules. Often, however, instant replay in hockey is ineffective because of the exigencies of competition. The NHL's commendable practice of resuming play as quickly as possible after an interruption may inhibit use of video replay to correct referee errors. For example, in one match the New Jersey Devils were denied a goal because the replay process was too slow.[33] Although a video film revealed a goal that officials had failed to see, it was too late because the puck had already dropped and play had resumed. The rules prevented any adjustment of the score.[34] Referees are instructed to take extra time if they think a play might be reviewed, but communication with the on-ice officials and those "upstairs" is often impaired.

Video replay is used by National Association for Stock Car Racing (NASCAR) competitions as well.[35] Although cameras are not as common as in football or hockey, a driver complaining about another driver's actions may request an immediate review of video tape.

The National Basketball Association (NBA) adopted the use of instant video replay, beginning with the 2002–03 season, in four situations: if a basket is made

---

[31] Tuck, *High-tech Replays Score in Sports*, GLOBE AND MAIL (Toronto), Feb. 14, 2002, at B16. For 25 years (1966–91) an instant-replay official was available to review a limited number of challenges from each team, but the pilot program is substantially more intrusive.

[32] The NCAA Ice Hockey Video Replay Protocol provides as follows: "The use of instant replay is permissible in tournament competition. A replay must be conclusive for an instant-replay official to overturn an on-ice official's call." The official determines whether the video replay is conclusive.

[33] *NHL Admits Officials Missed Devils' Goal*, USA TODAY, May 16, 2003.

[34] NHL rules provide as follows: "No goal may be awarded (or disallowed) as the result of video review once the puck has been dropped and play has resumed following the first stoppage of play after the potential goal."

[35] Jenkins, *Controversy Envelops Earnhardt's Record Victory*, USA TODAY, Apr. 7, 2003, at 10C.

at the end of the first, second or third quarters with no time remaining; if a basket is made at the end of the fourth quarter with no time remaining and the result will affect the outcome of the game; if a foul is called at the end of the first, second or third quarters with no time remaining; or if a foul is called at the end of the fourth quarter or overtime with no time remaining and a free throw may affect the outcome of the game.[36] The Women's National Basketball Association (WNBA) later adopted similar rules for video review of last-second plays beginning with the 2003–04 season.[37] Referees can use the video to determine whether a shot was worth two or three points, a boundary violation has occurred, or a shot-clock or backcourt violation has occurred.

At least one study has shown that errors by officials are surprisingly uncommon. In the 2003 season of collegiate football in the United States, the Big Ten Conference of the NCAA introduced a behind-the-scenes system of video replays, with no effect on games, simply to help the league evaluate findings which had revealed that 15–20 percent of some 13,000 plays would have been overturned if video challenges had been available. The pilot program revealed, however, that only 50 of 11,000 plays were determined to be reviewable, of which about one-half (less that one-quarter of 1 percent) would have been overturned. In 2004 the Big Ten decided, therefore, to permit designated observers to monitor play on the field and challenge calls. The observers have the discretion to halt play for a review of the call and to reverse it in the event that a replay would clearly show "conclusive evidence" of error.[38] Coaches, however, are unable to challenge calls under this system.

2. International Competition

Technology is somewhat less common in international competition. One problem is the divergence among different sports cultures concerning expectations about the role of referees and the margin of appreciation for errors and infractions. In international competition, it is apparent that judges or referees from different countries behave differently. Scientific precision in officiating is therefore more controversial. Moreover, because discrepancies between national and international rules may confuse players in international competition, somewhat greater tolerance, especially in team sports, may be expected.[39] Also, the principle of equality among all athletes, whether they are nationals of technology-

---

[36] NBA rules state as follows: "Instant replay reviews will be conducted and processed in two minutes or less by the game officials. The call made during play will only be reversed when the replay provides the officials with a clear and conclusive basis to do so."

[37] Women's National Basketball Association, *WNBA Approves Use of Instant Replay*, Press Release, May 22, 2003.

[38] STATESMAN-JOURNAL (Salem, Or.), Feb. 26, 2004, at B1; Wieberg, *Big Ten is a review [sic] from instant replay*, USA TODAY, Feb. 12, 2004, at C1.

[39] Yu, *The Harmonization Game: What Basketball Can Teach About Intellectual Property and International Trade*, 26 FORDHAM INT'L L.J. 218, 224–25, 232 (2003).

endowed or technology-poor countries, helps account for this lesser reliance on sophisticated cameras, computers and timing systems. In the World Cup for Soccer, for example, the Fédération Internationale de Football Association (FIFA) has placed extra assistant referees behind goal lines, but has ruled out the use of video replays because of a determination that their use is unsuitable in fast-moving, non-stop sports like football (soccer).[40] The International Tennis Federation (ITF) also relies on the human eye to make and correct calls.[41]

Technology is nevertheless becoming more common. The International Amateur Athletic Federation (IAAF), which governs track-and-field competition, has established protest procedures whereby referees have recourse to video film.[42] Similarly, FILA, the international wrestling federation, encourages video replay of controversial mat calls.[43] In 2002 the International Cricket Council (ICC) approved the use of video replay in its matches.[44] A third umpire may review video film after being consulted by one of the first two umpires.

Rowing competition is a prime example of reliance on cameras and sophisticated timing systems not only to review outcomes but also to determine outcomes in frequently close races.[45] Several cameras and cables are placed along a course to allow officials to note when shells pass points marked every 500 meters. Three different cameras are placed at the finish line to record the exact times that shells cross the finish line. Although four judges sit at the finish line to determine the winner, photo-finish cameras, taking 1,000 photos per second, provide assistance when a race is close.

In *Neykova v. Int'l Rowing Fed'n (F.I.S.A.) & Int'l Olympic Comm. (IOC)*,[46] the CAS arbitrated a dispute between two NOCs resulting from a photo-finish in the women's single sculls event during the 2000 Olympic Games in Sydney. According to an official Swatch camera-and-timing system, only 12 one-thousandths of a second separated the first two sculls at the finish line. The NOC of the losing rower challenged the accuracy of the technical equipment[47] in recording a

---

[40] *Spotlight*, MILWAUKEE JOURNAL SENTINEL, Oct. 3, 2002, *at* 2C; Gardiner, *supra* note 15, at 27.

[41] International Tennis Federation, Rules of Tennis 2003, Rule 29: Role of Court Officials.

[42] For a good summary of the IAAF protest procedures, as found in Rule 146 of the IAAF Handbook, *see* Cornelius, *supra* note 6, at 633.

[43] *See* text accompanying notes 12–14.

[44] Press Release, International Cricket Council, ICC Champions Trophy to Experiment with Technology Trial, Mar. 18, 2002.

[45] *At the Core of Timing—Inside the Finish Tower*, June 26, 2003, *at* http://www.worldrowing.com/news.

[46] Neykova v. Int'l Rowing Fed'n (F.I.S.A.) & Int'l Olympic Comm. (IOC), 200/012 CAS Ad Hoc Div. (O.G. Sydney 2000) [hereinafter *Neykova*] *in* II CAS Awards, *supra* note 7, at 674.

[47] *Neykova, id.* at 677.

split-second finish despite somewhat conflicting evidence from an unofficial television video. The CAS, citing its earlier award in *M. v. A.I.B.A.*,[48] confirmed the integrity of the official system whatever the margin of error might have been in the photo finish. Most importantly, *Neykova* emphasized that race judges, after interpreting video film, must ultimately make the decisions. The CAS will not disturb the decision of judges when endorsed by recognized sports bodies, although this deference seems to be subject to the exceptions in *M. v. A.I.B.A.* that have been cited in later CAS awards.

D. CONCLUSION

As technology improves, international sports federations and their constituent national organizations are relying increasingly on computers and cameras for judging, determining results and reviewing controversial decisions. Disparities among countries in the availability of technology and resources to pay for it constrain wiring of the global sports arena. Other issues of fairness and practicality constrain reliance on technology. The human element of judging, however prone to error and subjectivity, often seems preferable to the expense, intrusion, and disruption of electronic referees.

Figure skating and other sports of aesthetic merit and athletic style have presented particularly troublesome issues because of the subjectivity of judging and complexity of scoring. Apparent corruption of officials at the 2002 Winter Games in Salt Lake City prompted reforms that rely heavily on computerization of scoring.

Video replays are becoming a more common arbiter of sports competition. Reliance on video cameras has several disadvantages that merit continuing concern, and reliance on split-second timing systems, as in rowing, has also sparked disputes. Despite the controversies and the economic constraints, however, it is likely that the sporting world will welcome limited and carefully managed use of cameras and computers to overcome the vicissitudes of the human eye and conscience.

---

[48] *Id., citing M. v. A.I.B.A.*, in II CAS AWARDS, *supra* note 7, at 677.

CHAPTER 6
RIGHTS, DUTIES, AND ELIGIBILITY OF ATHLETES

Having examined the process of international sports law and its institutions for avoiding and resolving disputes, the book will focus on the major issues within that process.

A. RIGHTS OF ATHLETES

1. The Olympic Charter Provisions

Fundamental Principle 8 of the Olympic Charter establishes that "[t]he practice of sport is a human right. Every individual must have the possibility of practicing sport in accordance with his or her needs." What does this mean? Is the right to practice sport incorporated into international human rights law? What are its sources and what are its consequences?

The meaning of the stated human right is clarified by subsequent provisions in the Olympic Charter, particularly in Rule 2, on the Role of the IOC, and Rule 3, on Belonging to the Olympic Movement. Rule 2(5), which "strongly encourages" the promotion of women in sport, is rooted in "the principle of equality of men and women." Rule 2(9) requires measures "to prevent endangering the health of athletes." Rule 2(11) "encourages sports and organizations and public authorities to use their best efforts to provide for the social and professional future of athletes." Rule 2(12) of the Olympic Charter wipes away the last cobwebs of the elitism upon which the modern Olympic Games were founded by democratically encouraging "the development of sport for all." Rule 3(2), long a cornerstone of the Olympic Movement, declares that "[a]ny form of discrimination with regard to a country or a person on grounds of race, religion, politics, sex or otherwise is incompatible with belonging to the Olympic Movement."

These provisions for protecting and promoting human rights resonate in IF statutes and constitutions.[1] The International Charter of Physical Education and Sport of 1978,[2] though only aspirational, establishes that "[e]very human being

[1] *See* BASIC DOCUMENTS OF INTERNATIONAL SPORTS ORGANISATIONS (Siekmann & Soek eds., 1998) for three examples: the International Tennis Federation art. 50, *id.* at 435, 449; the International Canoe Federation, art. 2, *id.* at 179, 180; and the International Handball Federation, art. 6, *id.* at 317, 318.

[2] *Available at* www.unesco.org/human rights/hrbe.htm.

has a fundamental right of access to physical education and sport. The freedom to develop physical, intellectual and moral powers through physical education and sport must be guaranteed both within the educational system and in other aspects of social life."[3]

If, however, there are no rights without a remedy, what has been the record of implementation within the Olympic Movement of the right to practice sport? Certainly institutions within the Olympic Movement, such as Olympic Solidarity, have been on the forefront of implementing such social and economic rights as "sport for all," with particular attention to providing financial assistance to budding athletes from developing countries and protecting the health of athletes. But what about the requirements of equality and non-discrimination? Chapters 10 and 11 depict the long struggle for racial and political equality in international sports. In particular, the crusade within the Olympic Movement against sports apartheid in Rhodesia and South Africa and the sorry phenomenon during the Cold War of sports boycotts for political purposes highlight the struggle for equality. After the end of apartheid and the Cold War, gender equality has been a particularly prominent issue.

a. *Gender Equality*

The Convention on the Elimination of All Forms of Discrimination Against Women,[4] which binds its parties to work toward an abolition of gender discrimination, has been a formal source of efforts to encourage full participation by women in the sports arena.[5] The Convention, however, is not very specific, does not provide a timetable of specific measures to be taken by states, and lacks effective enforcement machinery.

Women were initially barred from international competition, including the Olympics. Even after this barrier was lifted in 1928, progress toward gender equality was slow. It will be instructive to trace the recent history of this progress. Until 1988, when only 25 percent of Olympic athletes were women, their participation was governed by Rule 28 of the Olympic Charter (since replaced), an embarrassing anachronism with no corresponding provision for men. Under Rule 28, "[w]omen are allowed to compete according to the rules of the IFs and after approval of the IOC." Questions arose: Wouldn't singling out women in this way violate the shared goals of international sports competition and the human rights

---

[3] *Id.*, art. 1.

[4] The Convention on the Elimination of All Forms of Discrimination Against Women, Dec. 18, 1979, U.N.G.A. Res. 34/180 (XXXIV), 34 U.N. GAOR, Supp. 46, at 193, U.N. Doc. A/RES/34/180 (1980).

[5] *See, e.g.*, New Zealand Herald, Jan. 26, 1985, at 1, col. 3, concerning a protest by a New Zealand group against Pakistani sports authorities for allegedly discriminating against women.

of athletes? Suppose the governing rules of an IF were discriminatory? Because of such questions, the IOC repealed Rule 28 in 1988.

After 1988 one unresolved issue involved a suspicion that women were overdosing on testosterone to enhance their performances in sports competition. In response, the Olympic Charter's "Medical Code" in Rule 29(d) required that "[f]emale competitors must comply with the prescribed tests for femininity," a patently discriminatory provision. Another issue concerned equality of opportunity. Specifically, a question arose whether the events scheduled for men and women, respectively, must be identical in type and number. Just as the ancient Hera Festival offered women athletes fewer events than the Olympic Festival offered men, so more events have been scheduled for men than for women in modern international competition. To challenge this differentiation before the 1984 Olympic Games in Los Angeles, two track-and-field organizations and 82 female distance runners from 27 countries brought legal action against the IOC, the International Amateur Athletic Federation (IAAF), the USOC, and the LAOOC.[6]

---

[6] According to the women runners, the process used to select new Olympic events resulted in the continuation of a historical pattern of discrimination against women participants in the Olympic Games. The district court's opinion extensively reviewed the history of women's participation in the Games and concluded that the women runners had made a strong showing that the early history of the modern Olympic Games was marred by blatant discrimination against women. The district court also found that women's participation in the Olympics had increased markedly during the previous 36 years. Although there was no parity between men and women in either the number of competitors or the number of events, the district court found that women were progressing in both these areas. For example, three new women's track-and-field events—the 3,000 meters, the 400 meter hurdles, and the marathon—would be included for the first time in the 1984 Games.

Although the pertinent background extended to the beginning of this century, the critical occurrence for the lawsuit occurred in 1949 when the IOC adopted rules to slow the rapid growth in the number of Olympic events within recognized sports.

The successor rule of that effort, which was at issue in this litigation, was Rule 32 of the 1970 Olympic Charter. It provided as follows:

> [International Federations] concerned shall decide the events which shall be included in each sport, in bearing with the global aspect of the Olympic programme and statistical data referring to the number of participating countries in each event of the Olympic programme, of the world championships, of Regional Games and all other competitions under the patronage of the I.O.C. and the patronage of the IFs for a period of one Olympiad (four years).

Under this rule, an event had to be recognized internationally through national championships and international competition during the four years before the time it was first considered for inclusion, and the decision on whether to include an event was made four years before the games in which it would first appear. Thus, the critical qualifying time period for races to be run for the first time in 1984 was from 1976 to 1980. Martin v. IOC, 740 F.2d 670, 673–74 (9th Cir. 1984). *See also* Note, *Is the International Olympic Committee Amenable to Suit in a United States Court?*, 7 FORDHAM INT'L L.J. 61 (1983–84).

In *Martin v. IOC*, the plaintiffs sought a court order to require the addition of 5,000 and 10,000-meter races for women at the Games, just as these events had been scheduled on the men's program. The women attached the rules that governed the adoption of new Olympic events. Rule 32 of the then applicable version of the Olympic Charter required an event to be included in international competition for four years before it could be in the Olympics.[7] The IAAF, which recommends new track-and-field events for inclusion in Olympic competition, recognized world records for women in the two events in 1980, but had not included them in world championship competition. Because the races were not yet sanctioned for international competition in 1980, when decisions were being made about the 1984 Games, the 5,000 and 10,000-meter women's races were not eligible for inclusion in the 1984 Games. The IOC therefore rejected them as Olympic events. (It might be noted that women have been treated more favorably in at least one respect: in order to qualify for Olympic competition, only those sports widely practiced by men in at least 50 countries are eligible whereas sports widely practiced by women in only 35 or more countries are eligible.)

The *Martin* plaintiffs argued that the Olympic Rules unjustly deprived them of equal protection under United States law and had to be viewed against a historical background of gender-based discrimination.[8]

---

[7] The applicable (1980) version of the Olympic Charter provided that "[s]ports are admitted to the Olympic programme six years before the next Olympic Games," that all events have "an established international standing, numerically and geographically to be included at least twice in world, continental and/or regional games to be admitted to the Olympic programme," and that "[e]vents are adopted four years before the next Olympic Games. No change is permitted thereafter."

[8] Their allegation was summarized in a dissenting opinion as follows:

> Baron Pierre de Coubertin, founder of the modern Olympic Games, described the Olympics as "the solemn and periodic exaltation of male athleticism with internationalism as a base, loyalty as a means, art for its setting, and female applause as reward." As late as 1954, the International Olympic Committee (IOC) voted to limit women's participation to those events "particularly appropriate to the female sex." This attitude toward women has resulted in a continuing disparity between male and female opportunities to compete in the Olympic Games.
>
> From the beginning, women athletes have challenged the IOC's policy of discriminating against them in track and field. Women were not permitted to participate in track and field events until the 1928 Games, when the IOC included eight events for women. That year, women from the British team boycotted the Games to protest the IOC's failure to include a full program of events for women athletes. After the 1928 Games, in which several women athletes collapsed after the 800 meter race, the IOC voted to further limit women's races to 200 meters (1/2 lap around the track). This restrictive policy continued for 32 years until the IOC reinstated the 800 meter race for the 1960 Games.
>
> Until quite recently, the IOC and its track-and-field affiliates refused to sanction any distance races for women. When officials of the Amateur Athletic Union discovered that Katherine Switzer had run the 1967 Boston Marathon, they suspended her from the AAU. The longest race for women at the 1980 Games was only 1500 meters.

Martin, *supra* note 6, 740 F.2d at 681 (Pregerson, J., dissenting) (footnotes omitted).

Both the trial and appellate courts rejected the suit. The appellate court held that even if there had been intentional discrimination, which had not been proven, neither federal nor state law in the United States requires "separate but equal" treatment of women. Of particular significance, the court wrote that it was

> wary of applying a state statute to alter the content of the Olympic Games. The Olympic Games are organized and conducted under the terms of an international agreement—the Olympic Charter. We are extremely hesitant to undertake the application of one state's statute to alter an event that is staged with competitors from the entire world under the terms of that agreement.[9]

Clearly, issues of gender discrimination, having become internationalized, require international resolution.

Since 1984, many women's events have been added to the Olympic program and other competition. For example, at the 2000 Games in Sydney, women for the first time could participate in weightlifting, triathlon, taekwondo, modern pentathlon, water polo, the hammer throw, and pole vault. The phenomenal popularity of women's basketball and football (soccer) attests to the popular acceptance of greater gender equality in sports.[10] The IFs also have gradually provided more opportunities for women athletes. In 1991, after 78 years of males-only competition, the Federation of International Association Football (FIFA) established the first Women's World Cup. By 2004 about half of the total number of athletes in major international competition (44 percent in the 2004 Olympic Games) were women, and almost all Olympic sports except for boxing had women's events. Although women are also gradually gaining opportunities in athletic leadership, the first woman was named to the IOC only in 1981 and women are still vastly underrepresented in most governing councils of sport.

Parts of the Islamic World remain bastions of gender suppression in the sports arena. Gradually, though, women are gaining a foothold. Ironically, the separation of the sexes, as in Iran, has often led to greater participation in sports, precisely because women can at least compete substantially in their own separate athletic events. Several Islamic Women's Games have been convened.[11] In 2003, in the world track and field championships, Lima Azimi became the first Afghan woman ever to compete in a major international event in any sport. This breakthrough betokens the effect that progressive measures in international competition can have on larger social agendas.

---

[9] *Id.* at 677.

[10] For a graphic commentary on these developments, *see* Longman, *Women Move Closer to Olympic Equality*, N.Y. TIMES, Aug. 20, 2000, at 1.

[11] Ghazi, *Iranian women put on their running shoes*, UNESCO COURIER, Apr. 1999, at 20, 21.

b. Rights of the Disabled

The rights of the disabled have also commanded attention within the process of international sports law. Although not specifically identified in the anti-discrimination provision of the Olympic Charter's Rule 3, except within the catch-all category of discrimination "otherwise,"[12] the rights of the disabled have been advanced, primarily through developmental programs such as Olympic Solidarity and the institution of the Paralympic Games and organization.[13] Also, the Winter Olympic Games have featured exhibition events for disabled athletes since the 1984 Winter Games in Sarajevo and Summer Games in Los Angeles. In a few sports, such as shooting, suitable arrangements can be readily made to permit physically disabled athletes to compete on equal terms with non-disabled athletes. The handicapped do not, however, enjoy any special international privilege to compete against non-disabled athletes. Health and safety factors, particularly related to the hazards of physical impairment, are cited to justify the effective exclusion of those who cannot achieve the "fastest, highest, strongest." The extent to which that purpose is adjusted to open up opportunities for the physically disadvantaged is of emerging concern.

c. Other Suspect Classifications

Religious discrimination has not been a significant issue in international sports. As to age discrimination, the Olympic Charter prohibits age limits for Olympic competitors "other than as prescribed for health reasons in the competition rules of an IF."[14]

2. International Human Rights Law

General international law does not articulate a human right to practice sport, as enshrined in the Olympic Charter. None of the principal global instruments, including the Universal Declaration of Human Rights,[15] the two United Nations Covenants on Human Rights,[16] and the specialized human rights conventions

---

[12] OLYMPIC CHARTER, Rule 3(2) (2003).

[13] The Paralympic Games take place immediately after the Olympic Games in the same venue. For a report on the 2002 Paralympic Games in Salt Lake City, *see* Reiff, *Outstanding Performances at the VIII Paralympic Games*, OLYMPIC REV., June–July 2002, at 14.

[14] OLYMPIC CHARTER, Rule 47.

[15] UNIVERSAL DECLARATION OF HUMAN RIGHTS, G.A. Res. 217A, U.N. GAOR, 3d Sess. Pt. 1, Resolutions at 71, U.N. Doc. A/810 (1948); *see* Keba Mbaye, *Sport and human rights*, OLYMPIC REV., Dec. 1998–Jan. 1999, at 8–12.

[16] INTERNATIONAL COVENANT ON CIVIL AND POLITICAL RIGHTS, G.A. Res. 2200 (XXI), 21 U.N. GAOR, Supp. (No. 16) 52, U.N. Doc. A/6316 (1966), 999 U.N.T.S. 171, *reproduced in* 6 I.L.M. 368 (1967), *entered into force* Mar. 23, 1976; INTERNATIONAL COVENANT ON ECONOMIC, SOCIAL AND CULTURAL RIGHTS, G.A. Res. 2200, 21 U.N. GAOR, Supp. (No. 16), U.N. Doc. A/6316 (1966), 999 U.N.T.S. 3, *reprinted in* 6 I.L.M. 360 (1967), *entered into force* Jan. 3, 1976.

provide specifically for sports. For example, the Convention on the Rights of the Child[17] emphasizes the rights to healthy development, but does not specify a right to athletic activity. Similarly, the international labor convention regarding the minimum age for employment[18] calls into question intensive sports training programs for children as, in effect, a questionable form of child labor, but is not specific on that characterization.

One exception to the silence of international human rights agreements on the specific rights of athletes is the International Convention Against Apartheid in Sports,[19] to be discussed in Chapter 10. Another exception is the Fourth Geneva Convention on the Treatment of Prisoners of War,[20] which has been a focus of attention in the military incarceration at Guantánamo Bay of suspected terrorists in Afghanistan. Article 38 of that agreement provides that "[p]risoners shall have opportunities for taking physical exercise, including sports and games."[21]

Despite the lack of specificity about sports in human rights instruments, they do provide a foundation for the protections prescribed by the Olympic Charter. A specific example is the Convention on the Elimination of All Forms of Discrimination Against Women,[22] which has served as textual authority for expanding the profile of women in sports and in leadership of sports organizations. More generally, the "first generation" rights (political and civil) of free speech, association, and non-discriminatory treatment, the "second generation" rights (economic, social and cultural) to enjoyment of culture and employment, and the "third generation" rights (collective) of peoples to heritage, a clean environment, good health, peace, and development provide an essential vocabulary for the good of sports and individual athletes.

3. European Law

Both the Council of Europe, on the basis of its Convention for the Protection of Human Rights and Fundamental Freedoms,[23] and the European Union, under

---

17 Convention on the Rights of the Child, G.A. Res. 44/25 (Annex), U.N. GAOR, 44th Sess., Supp. (No. 49), at 166, U.N. Doc. A/RES/44/49 (1990), 1577 U.N.T.S. 3, *reprinted in* 30 I.L.M. 1448 (1989), *entered into force* Sept. 2, 1990. *See* David, *Children's rights and sport*, Olympic Rev., Dec. 1998–Jan. 1999, at 36.

18 International Labor Convention, Convention Concerning Minimum Age for Admission to Employment, No. 138 (1973).

19 Convention Against Apartheid in Sports, G.A. Res. 40/64 (1985).

20 Convention Relative to the Treatment of Prisoners of War, 6 U.S.T. 3316, 75 U.N.T.S. 135, *entered into force* Oct. 21, 1950.

21 *Id.*, art. 38.

22 Convention on the Elimination of All Forms of Discrimination Against Women, G.A. Res. 180 (XXIV 1979), 1249 U.N.T.S. 13, *reprinted in* 19 I.L.M. 33 (1980).

23 European Convention for the Protection of Human Rights and Individual Freedoms, 213 U.N.T.S. 221, E.T.S. No. 155, *entered into force* Sept. 3, 1953.

the Rome Treaty,[24] seek to promote and protect human rights in sports. The European Human Rights Convention is specifically applicable to define and protect a limited range of athletes' rights. Article 6, for example, requires member states to ensure the right to a fair trial. Arguably, that protection extends to sports disciplinary proceedings, but whether they engage in the requisite "determination of [an athlete's] civil rights and obligations"[25] is subject to interpretation. Other provisions of the Convention, principally Article 8, which proscribes interference by member states in personal matters, protect athletes' personality assets, privacy, and employment rights within a burgeoning sports industry.[26]

The most significant judicial vindication of athletes' rights, by far, was made not by the European Court of Human Rights under the European Convention on Human Rights, however, but by the European Court of Justice in its landmark *Bosman* decision.[27] In order to understand this decision, it will be helpful to summarize a few long-standing practices in European football (soccer).

Player movement in European football (soccer) was long governed by a transfer system that had a number of components similar to those in major American sports. First, the rules governing the transfer system only came into play at the expiration of a player's contract. Second, a player's current club had the advantage in signing the player over any other club because the current club had the power to determine whether to offer the player a new contract, if he was any good, or to let him go, if he was washed up and no longer a good player.

Similar to the old "Rozelle Rule" in the National Football League (NFL) of the United States, a European football (soccer) club would have to pay a sum of money to the former team that was calculated by taking the player's gross annual income and multiplying it by a specified factor based on the player's age. This transfer fee was justified as compensation for the former team's training of the player. For a star player, in particular, this transfer fee could cost the new team a great deal of money. In addition, the new team still had to pay the player's new salary. The effect of this transfer system was that very few big name "free agents" were signed by new teams because their price tags were too high. Even a quick

---

24 TREATY ESTABLISHING THE EUROPEAN ECONOMIC COMMUNITY, O.J.C. 340/173 (consolidated version), *entered into force* Mar. 25, 1957.

25 *Id.*, art. 6. *See* M. BELOFF, T. KERR AND M. DEMETRIOU, SPORTS LAW 203 (1999).

26 *Id.*, art. 8 states as follows: "everyone has the right to respect for his private and family life, his home and his correspondence." *See* King, *Human Rights Protection in Sports Industry*, 2003 INT'L SPORTS L.J., No. 2, at 35.

27 Union Royale Belge des Sociétés de Football Association ASBL v. Bosman, Case C-415/93, Judgment of Dec. 15, 1995, E.C.R. 4837 (1995). *Bosman* builds upon decisions of the European Court of Justice that had struck down a limited range of nationality restrictions as violations of the Treaty of Rome. The two principal cases are Walrave v. Union Cycliste Internationale, Case 36/64, E.C.R. 1405 (1974) and Donà v. Mantero, Case 13/76, E.C.R. 1333 (1976).

look at the European transfer system confirms that the clubs had virtually all of the power to diminish the marketability and mobility of players.

In 1990, the contract of a Belgian football (soccer) star, Jean-Marc Bosman, with RC Liege expired. The team offered him a new contract at the league's minimum wage, a salary which was about one-quarter of that which he had made the previous year. After Bosman refused to sign the new contract, he was placed on RC Liege's transfer list, carrying a high price tag that no other team was willing to pay during the compulsory transfer period. He eventually contracted with a French club, US Dunkerque, which had reached an agreement with RC Liege for Bosman's transfer. The required approval certificate from the Belgian Football Association was never issued, however, because RC Liege had never requested it in the belief that US Dunkerque would not be able to pay the required transfer fee. Subsequently, RC Liege suspended Bosman and prevented him from playing during the next season. Bosman brought a civil action, claiming that the Belgian Football Association's transfer system violated the 1957 Treaty of Rome that established the integrative mechanism that became the European Union.

The European Court of Justice's decision in *Bosman* was a landmark in the development of international mobility and eligibility of athletes. The court barred the Union of European Football Associations (UEFA) from requiring US Dunkerque to pay a transfer fee to RC Liege. The court also struck down nationality restrictions that had imposed a limit of three non-nationals on teams engaged in inter-club matches within the member states of the European Union.[28] The decision, based on a freedom of movement enshrined in Article 48 of the Treaty of Rome, extended to players and competition in the member states of the European Union. Later, in *Deutscher Handballbund v. Kolpak*,[29] the European Court of Justice extended *Bosman* to protect athletes from Candidate States for membership in the European Union and to Member States of the European Economic Area (EFA) (Iceland, Liechtenstein and Norway).

Bosman highlighted the expanded scope of international sports law to govern professional as well as amateur athletes in Europe. To what extent, then, is the European Court of Justice, focused as it is on economic integration, inclined to favor new controls over sports associations? On one hand, the European Court of Justice's decision in *Bosman* and the European Union's Declaration of Sport, attached to the Treaty of Amsterdam,[30] acknowledge that sport is "different" from normal market behavior. For example, clubs do not have the aim of driving each other from the market; they need credible rivals. A variety of historical and

---

28 On the implications for third country nationals, *see* Van der Mei, *The* Bosman Case *and the Legal Status of Third Country Nationals Under European Community Law*, ASICL Pro. 8, at 144 (1996).

29 E.C.R. C-438/00/2003.

30 *See* Hargreaves, *Brussels to rule on soccer transfer costs*, FIN. TIMES, May 21, 2000, at 2.

practical reasons explains the unusual degree of autonomy that sports bodies enjoy in working out their differences. Therefore, even though the economic stakes may have become high in the sports arena, the incidence of economic regulation is low. On the other hand, there may be a need for further regulation to protect and equalize opportunities for athletes.

In disputes arising out of decisions by private sports bodies that affect fundamental rights of athletes, particularly their economic rights, the European Commission and Court of Justice, as community institutions, are likely to assume a prominent role in limiting the margin of appreciation that is accorded to private rules to the detriment of athletes. For example, the European Commission has addressed these kinds of cases under Article 81 of the Rome Treaty, which prohibits concerted practices that restrict competition. "Game rules" are still within the reserved domain of sports bodies and thereby insulated from court review, but contracts rather than cartels increasingly govern the status and entitlements of players.

4. General Practice of States

Finally, to what extent does the general practice of states, reflected in national laws, establish athletes' rights as international custom? Is there a customary right to compete?

Several national constitutions provide for the promotion and protection of sports for all.[31] The Brazilian constitution establishes a state duty "to foster the practice of formal and informal sports, *as each individual's right*."[32] Many national laws also provide for the promotion and regulation of sport to the benefit of athletes, but generally do not rely on a fundamental right to practice sport. In other countries, primarily of the common law tradition, the courts have established that there is no right to compete in organized sports competition.[33] In sum,

---

[31] *See, e.g.*, the ECUADOR CONSTITUTION (1998), C.P.E., art. 82, which provides that "[t]he state will protect, promote and coordinate physical activities, sports, and recreation, as activities for the [development] of people. It will provide resources and infrastructure to allow masses to reach these activities. It will sponsor the preparation and participation of high-performance athletes in national and international competitions and it will foster the participation of people with disabilities."

[32] C.F., art. 217 (Braz.).

[33] In the United States case law, *see* Seamons v. Snow, 84 F.3d 1226, 1235 (10th Cir. 1996) (no constitutional right to participate in sports); Spath v. NCAA, 728 F.2d 25, 28 (1st Cir. 1984) ("There being no fundamental right to education, there could hardly be thought to be a fundamental right to play intercollegiate ice hockey."); Herbert v. Venetetuolo, 638 F.2d 5 (1st Cir. 1981) (high school students have no right to play interscholastic sports under state law); Rutledge v. Ariz. Bd. of Regents, 660 F.2d 1345, 1352–53 (9th Cir. 1981); Walsh v. La. High Sch. Athletic Ass'n, 616 F.2d 152–160 (5th Cir. 1980) ("The privilege of participating in interscholastic athletics must be deemed to fall . . . outside the protection of due process." *quoting* Mitchell v. La. High Sch. Athletic Ass'n, 430 F.2d 1155, 1158 (5th Cir. 1970)); Albach v. Odle,

there does not seem to be a general practice, as a matter of *opinio juris* binding on states, that establishes a right to practice sport or to compete in it outside the programs of the Olympic Movement. Nevertheless, as we have seen, international human rights law generally supports or reinforces the implementation of the right to practice sport that is articulated in the Olympic Charter.

B. DUTIES OF ATHLETES

Rights arise out of reciprocal relations within a community. They are confirmed by social contract. Duties are therefore also a part of the equation of human dignity. Article 29 of the Universal Declaration of Human Rights specifically confirms that "[e]veryone has duties to the community in which alone the free and full development of his personality is possible."[34] Similarly, the African Charter on Human and Peoples' Rights of the African Union[35] acknowledges obligations and duties of individuals toward society,[36] and the American Declaration of the Rights and Duties of Man[37] establishes ten specific duties.[38]

To be sure, this broad authority only reflects the reciprocal nature, in very general terms, of the social contract that puts human rights into play. None of the human rights instruments identifies any specific duties of athletes or provides any specific legal basis for imposing duties on them. Still, the general authority provides a normative foundation for more specific requirements. Several decisions of the CAS have elaborated on the obligation of athletes to serve a broader community interest in ensuring fairness and a level playing field for all. For example, in several equestrian doping cases, the CAS established a duty of responsible parties to disclose information coming to their attention about doping to the detriment of competition.[39] At the very least, state practice discloses that, under

531 F.2d 983 (10th Cir. 1976); Tiffany v. Ariz. Interscholastic Ass'n, Inc., 726 P.2d 231 (Ariz. Ct. App. 1986) (no constitutional right to play interscholastic sports); Hawkins v. Nat'l Collegiate Athletic Ass'n, 652 F.Supp. 602, 610–11 (C.D. Ill. 1987) (no constitutional right to compete in intercollegiate athletics); Robinson v. Kan. State High Sch. Activities Ass'n, 917 P.2d 836, 840 (Kan. 1996) ("Participation in extracurricular school activities is not a fundamental right.").

The same doctrine seems to apply in Canadian judicial opinion. *See* Tassopoulos v. Ontario Ministry of Educ. (1991) (unreported).

34 *Supra* note 15, art. 29.

35 AFRICAN CHARTER ON HUMAN AND PEOPLES' RIGHTS, A.U. (formerly O.A.U.) Doc. CAB/LEG/67/3 Rev. 5 (1981).

36 *Id.*, arts. 27–29.

37 AMERICAN DECLARATION OF THE RIGHTS AND DUTIES OF MAN, O.A.S. Res. XXX, O.A.S. Off. Rec. OEA/Ser. L/V/I.4 Rev. (1965).

38 *Id.*, arts. 29–38.

39 DIGEST OF CAS AWARDS 1986–1998, at 142, 143, 158 (M. Reeb ed., 1998).

national law, the right or opportunity to compete in international competition is conditional.[40]

C. ELIGIBILITY

The eligibility of athletes for international competition is, of course, strengthened by the right to practice sport within the Olympic Movement. Outside that institutional framework, however, the absence of a general right to practice sport removes a pillar of eligibility. Even within the Olympic Movement, however, the two concepts are not the same. A right to practice sport does not imply a right to engage in any means to enhance performance, including the use of drugs. Nor did a right to practice sport allow amateur and professional athletes, until recently, to compete with each other. Historically, such open competition was rare.

This section will trace the radical change of thinking and reformation of rules that has made open competition the norm today. The first subsection provides an overview of the applicable rules today. The second subsection will trace the remarkable history of the dichotomy and, later, merger between amateurism and professionalism.

1. Open Competition Rules Today

Long-dominant issues of athlete eligibility centered historically on futile attempts to define and give effect to the hallowed but increasingly archaic concept of the "amateur" so as to exclude its antithesis and perceived threat, the "professional," from major sanctioned competition. This dichotomy arose in the 19th century on the bases of European elitism and a fairly widespread revulsion to betting, monetary rewards and other commercialization of sports activity.[41] Today, however, athletes in most sports may enter into lucrative commercial identifications in advertising and public relations so long as they comply with regulations established by their IFs in conformity with the Olympic Charter. This concept of eligibility has expanded to govern not just athletes, but coaches, officials, trainers, managers, administrators and all participants in sport.

The Olympic Charter's Eligibility Code today is very simple. It provides as follows:

> To be eligible for participation in the Olympic Games a competitor, coach, trainer or official must comply with the Olympic Charter as well as with the

---

[40] Davis, *Rights and Obligations of Athletes*, *in* SPORTS & EUROPEAN COMMUNITY LAW 154, 161 (D. Panagiotopoulos ed., 1998).

[41] *See, e.g.*, Camp, *Track Athletics in America*, 40 THE CENTURY 203 (1890) ("[t]he professional side offers but little of interest to us beyond the records. The reason for this is that, in America at least, [professional sports are] under a heavy cloud of questionable practices in the way of buying and selling races.") *See also* Shropshire, *Legislation for the Glory of Sport: Amateurism and Compensation*, 1 SETON HALL J. SPORT L. 7, 9 (1991).

> rules of the IF concerned as approved by the IOC, and the competitor, coach or trainer must be entered by his NOC. The above-noted persons must notably:
> — respect the spirit of fair play and non violence, and behave accordingly on the sportsfield; and
> — respect and comply in all aspects with the World Anti-Doping Code.[42]

Bye-laws to the Eligibility Code establish that the IFs must establish eligibility criteria in accordance with the Olympic Charter and subject to IOC approval.[43] Application of the criteria lies with the IFs, affiliated national federations, and NOCs. Another provision of the Bye-laws to Article 45 requires approval by the IOC Executive Board of all advertising during the Olympic Games by competitors, coaches, trainers, and officials. Finally, the Bye-laws prohibit the conditioning of the entry or participation of a competitor on any financial consideration.

As additional qualifications on eligibility, the Olympic Charter also contains a rule of nationality,[44] an age limit "for health reasons,"[45] and an incorporation by reference of the World Anti-Doping Code.[46] Issues of nationality have been particularly vexing. Some IFs attempt to avoid the nationality questions by requiring athletes to establish a minimum duration of residence before nationality accrues to redefine eligibility. Despite such provisions, the "genuine link" of nationality[47] has been subject to widespread manipulation and abuse. An emerging issue is the growing practice of states to grant "quickie" citizenship to star foreign athletes. "Quickie" citizenship states, such as the Sudan and Qatar, are willing to forego any genuine link with a prize athlete in return for the prospect of basking in the glory of a newly acquired "citizen's" athletic prowess. If the country of origin agrees to a newly acquired nationality, the durational residence requirement is simply ignored or minimized. If, however, the country of origin does not accept the newly acquired nationality of an athlete, then the durational residence requirement applies, and the question becomes whether it is sufficient to establish a

---

42 OLYMPIC CHARTER, Rule 45.

43 Chriss, *Remarks*, International Athletic Foundation International Symposium on Sport and Law, Monte Carlo, Monaco (Jan. 1991) (copy on file with author) [hereinafter IAF Symposium]. Within the rules of the Olympic Charter the primacy of the IFs means, for example, that a breach of IF eligibility criteria that are consistent with Olympic rules, as extended to a national federation, may disqualify an athlete from Olympic and other competition. *See, e.g.*, Feinstein, *Seles's Ban from the Olympics is Milestone for Tennis*, N.Y. TIMES, Aug. 18, 1991, at 22, col. 1.

44 OLYMPIC CHARTER, Rule 46 ("Any competitor in the Olympic Games must be a national of the country of the NOC which is entering him."). On the problems of applying this rule, *see also* N.Y. TIMES, Feb. 15, 2004, at SP6.

45 *Id.*, Rule 47. *See supra*, text accompanying note 14.

46 *Id.*, Rule 48. *See* Ch. 7, *infra*, text accompanying notes 56–59.

47 In *The Nottebohm Case* (Liechtenstein v. Guatemala), 1955 I.C.J. 4, 1955 WL 1, the International Court of Justice, in denying standing to the applicant to complain against the respondent, established a "genuine link" test to determine the international legal validity of a sovereign grant of nationality.

"sports nationality" under pertinent IF rules. In making a distinction between "legal nationality" and "sports nationality," the CAS defined the "two different notions [of legal nationality], deriving "personal status from citizenship of one or more states" [and sports nationality], "a uniquely sporting concept, defining the eligibility rules of players with a view to their participation in international competition."[48]

To the extent that IFs and other sports organizations cling to the traditional amateur/professional dichotomy, "amateurism" is no longer antithetical to *commercialization* of an athlete's or club's name, likeness or reputation, but only to *professionalism*, by which sustaining payments are expected for athletic performance, and even that distinction has faded. Some organizational rules distinguish, for example, between the taboo of direct compensation for performance and the acceptability of status-related income that athletes may receive from advertising or promotional appearances.

Explanations of this change in the concept of eligibility include a growing recognition of the hypocrisy of "shamateurism" which turns a blind eye toward rampant employment, subsidy, and training of athletes by governments and academic institutions. The ideology of amateurism has also suffered from its identification with Victorian-Edwardian elitism; an erosion of public hostility to commercial exploitation of athletes; perceived inequities in denying remuneration to one class of athletes (amateurs) as salaries skyrocketed for others (professionals); and expanded coverage by the media of sports competition, with all of its financial enticements to promoters and athletes. Within the Olympic framework, therefore, strict rules of amateurism have given way to flexible rules of eligibility that accept open as well as regulated compensation. In the few IFs that are still limited to amateurs, the definition of an amateur is left to bye-laws or rules of competition.[49] Only the International Tennis Federation appears to maintain a definition of an amateur in its constitution.[50]

These rules have become institutionalized, essentially as standards for licensing sports participants to engage in regulated activity, and have influenced the management and regulation of strictly domestic competition.[51] Issues of strict "amateurism" having faded, the dominant issues of eligibility now involve compliance by individual athletes with specific rules of IFs and national sports associations, commercialization, and doping. As the IOC, IFs, affiliated associations, and NOCs consolidate immense resources from sponsorships, advertising and broad-

---

[48] *See also* N.Y. TIMES, Feb. 15, 2004, at SP6.

[49] *See, e.g.*, International Amateur Boxing Association (AIBA), Article of Association, art. II, *in* BASIC DOCUMENTS OF INTERNATIONAL SPORTS ORGANISATIONS (Siekman and Soek, eds. 1998); International Rowing Federation (FISA), STATUTES, art. 2(4), *id.*, at 111.

[50] International Tennis Federation (ITF), CONSTITUTION, art. 62, *id.*, at 435, 461.

[51] *See* Shropshire, *supra* note 41, at 18, 27; Chriss, *supra* note 43.

casting rights, and as sponsors, advertisers and broadcasters assume greater leverage over athletes, the force of eligibility rules in their lives cannot be exaggerated.

The rules and institutions of international sports law that historically governed only "amateur" competition are of heightened relevance today to "professional" athletes and events with the erosion of the amateur/professional distinction. "Amateur" sports associations are taking their places as cartels alongside professional sports leagues. The extension of professional sports leagues into international markets[52] has highlighted the need for international agreements and more uniform third-party machinery to resolve issues of player contracting, anti-trust implications of mergers and acquisitions, labor rights of athletes, and taxation of income. Efforts to extend international sports law to professional activity face formidable hurdles, however, ranging from sharply divergent anti-doping standards and procedures to the central role of collective bargaining agreements and employment laws to the very idea of regulating income from individual sports activity. As open competition, income management, and cartelization of sports grow, however, the common ground of all athletic activity becomes apparent.

2. History of Amateurism

One of the hoariest and most controversial sets of issues in international sports law involved the definition and requirements of amateurism. "Amateur" sports organizations long had to struggle with a self-definition that was complicated by creeping professionalism within their ranks.[53] The rather easily skirted line between amateurs and professionals seemed hypocritical, if not an historical hoax. Amateurism, it was said, was just a snooty Victorian-era conceit promoted by Baron de Coubertin and others to insulate the aristocracy from working-class competitors. Accordingly, it is argued that the modern concept of amateurism is little more than the product of the times and personal philosophy of de Coubertin and his circle. Arising when organized sports were thought of principally as activities for "gentlemen," the concept of amateurism continued to appeal not only to those genuinely committed to mass participation in athletics, but also to devotees of elitism. To the latter, professionalism is "entertainment;" only amateurism is "sport."

The ancient Greeks did not distinguish between "amateurs" and "professionals." Indeed, the Greek Games encouraged athletic activity by independently wealthy or subsidized males who could afford to undertake the requisite commitments of time and money for training and performance. The competition itself

---

[52] *See* Shropshire, *Thoughts on International Professional Sports Leagues and the Application of United States Antitrust Laws*, 67 DEN. U. L. REV. 193, 211 (1990); Eskenazi, *Pro Leagues in America Eye the Globe*, N.Y. TIMES, Apr. 9, 1989, at 19, col. 1.

[53] For a discussion of the concept of "amateurism" and some of the problems of defining it, *see* J. WEISTART & C. LOWELL, THE LAW OF SPORTS 5–8 (1979). On the ambiguities in the concept of amateurism, from a philosophical viewpoint, *see* P. WEISS, SPORT: A PHILOSOPHIC INQUIRY (1969).

and, to an extent, the competitors, were supported by the city-states. Although the ancient Greeks did not contribute the word or the modern concept of "amateurism," they did develop a sports culture that, during its Golden Age, generally relied on religious and other values besides money. Greek athletes could be fairly described as non-professionals inasmuch as they could not generally rely on competition for a living. By the Hellenistic period, however, the merchant class had become more predominant. City-states began to offer subsidies to prize athletes of money, food, homes, tax exemptions, and military deferments. Indeed, the word "athlete" is itself derived from the Greek "athlos," one who competes for a prize.

The term "amateur" is derived from the Latin "amator." Hence, the classic amateur is one who engages in an activity (sport) for the love of it alone. The term "professional" seems to have been first applied in the modern era to English jockeys who rode horses for a fee. Nobles had begun racing for awards around 1512, but hired hands soon competed instead. In 1788 the term "amateur" crept into modern usage to separate "Gentleman Jack" Jackson, an aristocratic English boxer, from the riffraff who competed for small purses or side bets. By the 19th century an amateur was viewed as a cultivated, sporting man of leisure, whereas the professional was viewed as an uncultivated money-grubber. It was said that in the United States, a professional might instruct a gentleman's son, but he left by the servant's door.

The first time the issue of amateurism seems to have arisen in a modern sense was in 1872, nearly 25 years before the first Modern Olympic Games in Athens. At a rowing contest on the Schuylkill River in Philadelphia, half of the oarsmen were barred from participating because they were deemed not to be "amateurs." In the next year representatives at a meeting of rowing clubs formally adopted the distinction between amateurism and professionalism. Seen in this light, Baron de Coubertin's concept of a completely amateur athletic structure in the modern Olympic Games was in keeping with the times.

Even by the time of the first modern Games, however, the requirement that amateurs should accept no money at all for their sports activity had begun to erode. In the 1890s the idea of "broken time pay"—compensation of athletes for pay lost at the workplace during periods of training—led to the withdrawal of the Rugby Football League from the Rugby Football Union in Great Britain. Since then, state subsidization, military or border-guard employment, university "scholarships," commercialization of the world of sports, foreign bank accounts, and sports agents or sharks, all helped blur the distinction between amateurs and professionals. Athletic status often goes hand-in-hand with related professional activities such as teaching of physical education. Tempting advertising revenue has grown in proportion to the expansion of television and the sports equipment industry. Spectators demand higher and higher levels of performance that have required amateurs to devote greater amounts of time to training and dry-runs.

Moreover, varying definitions of "amateur" have made the rule hypocritical. For example, in Africa a good "amateur" athlete is often a police inspector or an army lieutenant who may spend most of his time in training. In Scandinavia, an Olympic-bound cross-country skier is often a customs official who can devote much of his time to training. In many countries today, athletes are state-supported, and in the United States, top "amateur" college athletes typically receive compensation in the form of all-inclusive scholarships. State support or Coca Cola endorsements: it's all the same to athletes.

The general elimination of the distinction between amateur and professional status within the Olympic Movement was a product of historical development. The history of the Eligibility Code in the Olympic Charter provides a rich commentary on the trend away from a strict interpretation of the concept of amateurism. For lawyers, athletes and sports officials alike, this experience offers numerous insights.

3. Development of the Olympic Movement's Eligibility Code

Rule 1 of the Olympic Charter used to read that "[t]he aims of the Olympic Movement are to promote the development of those fine physical and moral qualities which are the basis of *amateur* sport."[54] Thus, all participants clearly had to be "amateur," as defined, in strict terms, by Rule 26, which until 1971 read as follows:

> To be eligible for the Olympic Games a competitor must always have participated in sports as an avocation without material gain of any kind. He can avail himself of this qualification: a) if he has a basic occupation designed to ensure his present and future livelihood; b) if he does not receive or has never received any remuneration for participation in sport; 3) if he complies with the rules of the International Federation concerned, and the official interpretations of this rule (see Eligibility Code).[55]

A separate Eligibility Code was designed to interpret this Rule. In general, the rather complex Code barred eligible amateurs from accepting any compensation, other than limited expense money, which might be attributable to their athletic activity or status.[56] This prohibition extended to receiving compensation for

---

54 OLYMPIC CHARTER, Rule 1 (1970) [emphasis added]. The word "amateur" was later deleted.

55 OLYMPIC CHARTER, Rule 26 (1970).

56 Any athlete was disqualified who, without permission of the appropriate sports federation, accepted any prize worth $50 or more; had capitalized on or secured employment promotion on the basis of athletic fame or success; became a professional in any sport or had decided to become one or played in a professional team with a view to become a professional; had been paid for teaching or coaching others for competition in sport; had been awarded a scholarship mainly for his athletic ability; had demanded payment or expense money for a manager, coach,

playing, teaching, or coaching competitive sports and to making promotional endorsements or appearances. The athlete could neither use his fame to obtain a job nor interrupt his job or studies for more than four weeks of training in a camp per year. Eligibility "decisions" by the IOC interpreted these rules strictly. For instance, athletes who had been subsidized by governments, institutions or business concerns were not "amateurs."[57]

By 1971, in the face of a growing number of difficult cases, Rule 26 in the Eligibility Code proved to be inadequate. Ranging from overly detailed provisions to ball-park-size "thou shalt nots," the eligibility regime no longer reflected the true nature of contemporary sport competition. The Olympic Charter therefore offered little juridical or normative support for the principle of amateurism. Worse yet, the Eligibility Code was unevenly applied and enforced. Some violators were caught; most were not.

In 1971 the IOC adopted a new Rule 26 that was more realistic, better focused, and binding. An Eligibility Code remained but was more clearly subordinated to Rule 26 and was substantively limited to provisions on the use of dope, the participation of women, penalties in the case of fraud, and the status of "non-amateurs" and "semi-professionals." The strengthening of Rule 26 represented another step in the gradual transformation of the IOC into a rule-creating and rule-enforcing organization.

The 1971 changes in Rule 26 and the Eligibility Code were substantive as well as formal. The subjective "intent to become a professional" and "neglect of usual employment" elements in the definition of a "non-amateur" were elimi-

---

relative or friend; had received payment of expenses in excess of the actual outlay, although he might receive clothing and equipment in addition to reimbursement of expenses or "pocket money to cover petty daily expenses during the Games;" had interrupted his occupation, studies or employment for special training in a camp for more than four weeks in any one calendar year; had received expense money for more than 30 days exclusive of the time spent in traveling in any one calendar year; had neglected his usual vocation or employment for competitive sport whether at home or abroad; or was paid for the use of his name or picture or for a radio or television appearance. OLYMPIC ELIGIBILITY CODE, at 44–46 (1971).

[57] The rules specifically barred financially supported athletes from participating in "amateur" competition. For example, business and industrial concerns sometimes employ athletes for their advertising value. The athletes are given paid employment with little work to do and are free to practice and compete at all times. For national aggrandizement, governments occasionally adopt the same methods and give athletes positions in the Army, on the police force or in a government office. They also operate training camps for extended periods. Some colleges and universities offer outstanding athletes scholarships and inducements of various kinds. Recipients of these special favors, which were granted only because of athletic ability, were not eligible to compete in the Olympic Games. However, "[a]n athlete paid for teaching elementary sport (beginners or school children) on a temporary basis without abandoning his usual occupation remains eligible. An athlete may be a full-time professional journalist, radio or television reporter, or a full-time manager of or worker in an athletic facility without forfeiting his amateur status." *Id.* at 47.

nated. Physical education teachers of beginners became eligible as amateurs, whatever the extent of their professional teaching or the existence of another occupation. The definition of acceptable expense money or other assistance was broadened to include prizes without dollar limit, insurance related to training, medical care, and sports equipment. Athletic scholarships awarded on the basis of "academic and technical" standards became acceptable, and the acceptable period for full-time training was extended from 30 to 60 days in one calendar year. In general, the new Rule 26 adopted in 1971, though still quite strict, responded to changing conditions and greater tolerance of compensation for athletes.

Most importantly, new Bye-Laws to Rule 26 established three "directives." First, the prohibition against compensation from advertisements was limited to those cases where an athlete permitted his name, photograph, or sports performance to be used "individually" for advertising purposes. A second directive permitted athletes to associate themselves or their names with the mass media during the Olympic Games, subject to the approval of their *chefs de mission*. A third directive provided that, subject to certain controls, advertising would be permitted which resulted from equipment contracts entered into by responsible national organizations.[58]

The 1971 reforms also included a flexible enforcement mechanism, in the form of an Eligibility Commission, to "consult and cooperate" with IFs and NOCs.[59] This replaced an earlier provision for a more formal investigatory committee that had proven to be weak because it did not directly involve the IFs and NOCs in the enforcement process. Most importantly, Rule 26 was further amended in 1980 to allow the IFs for each sport to set their own rules. A case study illustrates the need for these reforms.

a. *The 1972 Olympic Skiing Crisis*

The need for the 1971 reforms of the Olympic Eligibility Code became apparent in a crisis that erupted under the old Eligibility Code of the Olympic Charter over the wisdom and legality of permitting Olympic participants in the 1972 Winter Games to receive money for releasing their image or name for advertising purposes. To be sure, Rule 34, as it then read, provided that "no commercial advertising is permitted on equipment used in the Games nor on the uniforms or numbers worn by contestants or officials." Enforcement was provided as follows:

---

[58] For current versions of these, *see* OLYMPIC CHARTER (2003), Bye-Laws to Rules 6 and 53, and Rule 26.

[59] The Commission was appointed on November 23, 1971 to serve primarily as a watchdog over the NOCs. N.Y. TIMES, Nov. 24, 1971, § C, at 42, col. 2.

> The display of any clothing or equipment such as shoes, skis[,] handbags, hats, etc. marked conspicuously for advertising purposes in any Olympic venue (training grounds, Olympic Village, or fields of competition), by participants[,] either competitors, coaches, trainers, or anyone else associated with an Olympic team in [an] official capacity, will normally result in immediate disqualification or withdrawal of credentials.[60]

Athletes and their corporate patrons, however, easily and consistently flouted this provision. Indeed, a victorious skier, for example, customarily showed off his or her equipment before international television cameras. These "eligibility" provisions, moreover, covered the athletes during the Games only.[61] Rule 26 and the Eligibility Code therefore had to be invoked to determine initial eligibility of competitors for the Olympic competition. The enforcement machinery was clearly limited.

The 1972 Olympic skiing crisis began in 1971, on the eve of the Winter Games, when the President of the IOC took the highly unusual step of proposing to eliminate alpine skiing from the 1972 Winter Games because of numerous incidents involving the remuneration of alpine skiers by ski equipment manufacturers. Acting primarily in response to the President's threat, the IOC Executive Board unanimously revised and approved the text of the new Rule 26, which was then formally adopted by the IOC. As noted earlier, the new rule considerably relaxed restraints on monetary inducements, while retaining a qualified distinction between amateurs and professionals, however those terms might be defined more precisely by different authorities. The IFs were given greater authority and encouragement to define these and other terms of eligibility. The revised rule was intended to govern the eligibility of all athletes, but more particularly to resolve the alpine skiing crisis. The IOC issued a directive that barred from competition any athlete who had "directly or indirectly allowed his name, his photograph or his sports performance to be used individually for advertising purposes."[62]

The new mechanism was very soon put to a severe test in the skiing crisis because of the lack of any investigatory machinery; the importance to the Winter Games of alpine skiing, then representing about one-half of all events in the Winter Games; the threat of a boycott of *all* skiing events by the International Ski Federation (FIS); and the Japanese investment of an estimated $20 million in preparation of the 1972 site in Sapporo.

Fortunately, the new regime for eligibility worked because of the cooperation of constituent organizations. One NOC implemented Rule 26 by expelling several top skiers although the reaction to Rule 26 was mixed and the threat of a boy-

---

60 OLYMPIC CHARTER, Rule 54 (1970).

61 *Id.*

62 WASH. POST, Mar. 27, 1971, § E, at 3, col. 3.

cott persisted.[63] The IOC warned the NOCs that they risked the disqualification of entire teams if they failed to exclude violators of the new, more accommodating Rule 26.[64] Shortly before the 1972 Winter Games the FIS dropped its threat to boycott the Games, declaring, however, that if the IOC did not accept its "good faith" interpretation of the new rules, it would not recognize the Olympics as a world championship that year.

Just before the Winter Games, a new, four-member Eligibility Commission, chaired by Hugh Weir of Australia, began to review evidence of violations of the new Rule 26 that had been submitted to it from several quarters, primarily from the President of the IOC himself.[65] The evidence presented to the Weir Commission included the testimony of several athletes, including an East German refugee who charged his government with encouraging "state amateurism" in violation of Rule 26 by providing successful athletes with handsome bonuses, higher salaries, priority in military promotions and special housing and automobile allocations.[66] Aside from such testimony, the evidence apparently was limited to anecdotes, advertisements and other material from newspapers and periodicals. This evidence was rejected, however, by both the Weir Commission and the IOC's Executive Board, especially as it pertained to the period before April 2, 1971.[67] The Weir Commission recommended to the IOC that only one athlete, Karl Schranz of Austria, should be disqualified for violating Rule 26. The IOC adopted the Weir Commission's report after a two-hour debate. Unfortunately, in resolving the dispute, which had challenged the integrity of the IOC, neither it nor the Eligibility Commission granted a hearing to either Mr. Schranz or any of the others accused of violating Rule 26; nor could they appeal the decision. To be sure, the IOC was handicapped by its lack of policing authority and capacity to gather evidence, a lack of cooperation from some of the NOCs, and a consensus that a lawsuit for perjury in sports would be inappropriate. Even so, the new Rule 26 was an improvement.

b. Developments and Problems During the 1980s

By the time of the highly commercial Los Angeles Olympic Games in 1984, the integrity of amateurism had become "just a play on words."[68] It had become somewhat passé as a legal consideration of any significance. Nevertheless the

---

63 WASH. POST, Nov. 30, 1971, § D, at 5, col. 3.

64 WASH. POST, Jan. 1, 1972, § C, at 3, col. 4.

65 WASH. POST, Jan. 28, 1972, § F, at 4, col. 5.

66 *Id.* at 4, col. 6.

67 WASH. POST, Jan. 29, 1972, § E, at 1, col. 4; *id.*, Jan. 30, 1972, § K, at 8, col. 1.

68 Testimony of Edwin Moses, Olympic Gold Medalist in the 400-meter hurdles, *quoted in* 124 TIME, Aug. 20, 1984, at 31. Moses admitted to earning $457,000 in 1983 alone. Gold Medalist Phil Mahre filed an affidavit stating that he made more than $1 million in the last two years of his amateur skiing career. 124 TIME, Apr. 3, 1984, at 81.

concept labored on, influencing decisions as much as it perplexed thoughtful decision-makers. International sport was clearly facing serious challenges as it attempted to reconcile 19th century ideals of amateurism with 20th century realities.

On the eve of the 1984 Winter Games in Sarajevo, the International Ski Federation (FIS) declared two of the world's top skiers, Ingemar Stenmark of Sweden and Hanni Wenzel of Liechtenstein, to be ineligible because they were deemed to be professionals. The Executive Board of the IOC upheld the decision, thereby barring the two athletes from competing in the Winter Games. The rationale reveals a slippery slope of eligibility rules. The FIS, like other IFs, allowed a member athlete to accept prize money by transferring it into a special fund held in trust by the athlete's national sports federation. Stenmark and Wenzel, however, held "B licenses" under a system, abandoned in 1983, which had allowed skiers to enter into commercial contracts and keep their earnings confidential. Under this system, though the two skiers had been eligible for World Cup competition, they did not comply with requirements for Olympic competition.[69] The anomalies of the system were becoming glaringly apparent.

Also in 1984, the IOC declared five hockey players to be ineligible because they had played in the professional National Hockey League (NHL) in North America. The decision was particularly controversial because players in professional leagues other than the NHL were allowed to compete. The IOC said that it was following the guidelines of the International Ice Hockey Federation (IIHF), which labeled as professional only competitors in the NHL.[70] This capricious distinction reflected the instability of "amateur" eligibility rules and standards.

In the runup to the 1984 Games in Los Angeles, two professional players of a non-Olympic sport—American-style football—lost lawsuits challenging rulings of ineligibility against them by The Athletic Congress (TAC), the International Amateur Athletic Federation (IAAF), and in one case, the IOC. The plaintiffs argued unsuccessfully that they were entitled to enjoin the defendants from enforcing eligibility rules against them merely because they had played professional football. They claimed that their professional football status was irrelevant in determining their eligibility to compete in track-and-field events. In 1985 the IAAF formally denied their petitions for amateur status but reversed itself in 1986.[71] The world-class shot-putter, Brian Oldfield, was also disqualified for having earned money as a professional.

---

[69] Olympic Rev., Dec. 1983, at 809; Christian Sci. Monitor, Jan. 30, 1984, at 16, col. 1.

[70] Christian Sci. Monitor, Feb. 9, 1984, at 24, col. 1.

[71] *See* Nehemiah v. The Athletic Congress of the U.S.A., 765 F.2d 42 (3d Cir. 1985); Gault v. IOC, Civil No. 84-2353, (C.D. Cal., May 29, 1984). *See generally* Comment, *Antitrust Policy and Olympic Athletes: The United States Ski Team Goes for the Gold*, 1985 Utah L. Rev. 831, 855–56, n.146. In the *Nehemiah* opinion, District Court Judge Fisher wrote as follows:

> As a former participant and an avid follower of the sport of Track and Field I cannot help but comment on the pervasive hypocrisy of the so-called rules governing the amateur

These incidents illustrate the type of problems that the evolving definition of eligible "amateurs" had to address. By 1988, the Olympic Charter made no mention of an "amateur" but retained some of the idea. Compensation for living and training expenses was permissible, and, as of 1982, athletes could retain endorsement and prize income so long as it was deposited in a trust fund administered by the athlete's national sports federation. To participate in the Olympic Games under Rule 7 ("Only persons who are eligible within the definition laid down in these Rules may take part in the Olympic Games"), Rule 26 required competitors to

— observe and abide by the Rules of the IOC and in addition the rules of his or her IF, as approved by the IOC, even if the federation's rules are more strict that those of the IOC:
— not have received any financial awards or material benefit in connection with his or her sports participation except as permitted in the bye-laws to this Rule.[72]

Under the Bye-Laws to Rule 26 each IF was responsible for drafting its own eligibility code for use according to IOC guidelines and for determining a competitor's eligibility. The IOC guidelines began with the principle that "an athlete's health must not suffer nor must he or she be placed at a social or material disadvantage as a result of his or her preparation for and participation in the Olympic Games and international sports competitions." This principle replaced a rather cumbersome list of awards, scholarships and employment explicitly permitted to potential competitors. Six specific guidelines followed, concluding with an injunction against anyone who "manifestly contravened the spirit of fair play in the exercise of sport, particularly by the use of doping or violence."

These provisions offered greater flexibility in enforcing Rule 26 and reflected an awareness of the dilemma non-professional athletes face in having to support themselves while trying to meet the demands and expenses of training. Thus, approved programs in which the NOCs supplied funds and facilities for qualified athletes became acceptable. That still left the status of state-supported athletes in doubt, but such support appeared to be permissible with the approval of the

---

> standing of participating athletes. Athletes are the recipients of all kinds of expense accounts and equipment endorsement income in this country and overseas. It is well known that at least the eastern block [sic] countries, if not others, are entering athletes in these meets as pure professionals. But his knowledge is of little consolation and no legal weight with respect to the current disputes. If plaintiff desires to play in fantasy land, he must abide by their [sic] rules.

Civil No. 84-1133, D.N.J., Mar. 30, 1984.

Later, the IAAF refused to reinstate the amateur track status of both Renaldo Nehemiah and Willie Gault. INT'L HERALD TRIBUNE, July 15, 1985, at 14, col. 2, but reversed that decision unanimously in early 1986.

[72] OLYMPIC CHARTER (1983), Rule 26.

appropriate IF and NOC. Under the circumstances, such approval was generally easy to obtain.

In the event of conflict with IF eligibility provisions and decisions, Olympic rules and decisions took precedence. The skiing crisis shows, however, that the real efficacy of Rule 26 depended on cooperation between the IOC and the IFs. The initial conflict between the FIS and the IOC was noteworthy because it arose out of a direct clash between the new Rule 26 and a more liberal rule of the FIS. Ironically, the FIS rule might have been given some force by a provision in the 1971 Code that "[a] competitor must observe and abide by the Rules of the International Federation that controls the sport in which he participates, *even if* these Rules should be stricter than those imposed by the International Olympic Committee (emphasis added)." This rather poorly drafted provision seems, mistakenly, to have given priority to IF rules "even if," not "only if," the federation's rules were stricter than those of the IOC. Although the intent of the provision was no doubt to combat creeping professionalism, a literal (but erroneous) reading could have easily upset the customary precedence of the Olympic Rules. Byelaws to Rule 26 corrected the faulty drafting of the earlier version by requiring the IOC's Executive Board to approve an IF's code of eligibility and, inferentially, by giving priority to the stricter of the two sets of rules.[73]

To participate in the Olympic Games, competitors therefore had to conform with the rules of the IOC and the recognized IF for their sport. Infringements were punished by disqualification and loss of any medals the competitor may have won in a disputed event. Under Rule 31 of the Olympic Charter, NOCs and NGBs were also subject to sanctions for complicity in an infringement. Once an IF or NOC reported an infringement, the IOC's Eligibility Commission took it into consideration along with the IF's recommendation. The accused competitor might request a hearing before the Executive Board whose decision was then final.

The freedom of the IFs to draw up strict eligibility rules was made clear when the FIS recommended that Ingemar Stenmark and Hanni Wenzel be declared ineligible to compete in the 1984 Sarajevo Winter Games. Although both skiers requested a waiver, the IOC Executive Board confirmed the decision of the FIS. Speaking for the Executive Board, Monique Berlioux, Director of the IOC, stated that "[t]he IOC feels it must support the international federation which is governing that sport."[74] As a practical matter, this called into question a review on the merits by the Executive Board, although formally it still had that power. The Olympic rules, by emphasizing consultation and conciliation rather than more

---

73 An example of such a process was briefly reported in OLYMPIC REV., June 1983, at 356–57. At the annual meeting of the Executive Board and the Presidents and Secretary-Generals of the IFs, an alignment of the IF eligibility codes and the Olympic rules was undertaken.

74 THE (PORTLAND) OREGONIAN, Nov. 26, 1983, § E, at 3, col. 5.

formal procedures of dispute settlement, offered a more satisfactory means for resolving conflicts between the IFs and the IOC over the issue of amateurism. Problems resulting from different standards for different IFs and uneven enforcement of eligibility rules remained, however.

4. Reforms of the Late 1980s

By 1985 a sweeping response to the dilemma, if not hypocrisy, of maintaining an amateur-professional distinction in global sports led to its gradual disappearance from the Eligibility Code. The new Code would simply emphasize good sports behavior based on the Charter's Rules and principles, including requirements of fair play and honor and a rejection of drugs and violence. Binding on all athletes, the Code adopted the idea of eliminating the amateur-professional distinction but obligated athletes to cooperate in other respects in order to be eligible for international competition.

The eligibility and athletes commissions of the IOC therefore unanimously recommended replacing Rule 26 of the Olympic Charter with The Athlete's Code. It opened up Olympic competition to all eligible athletes so long as they took part in the Games in a spirit of fair play and without direct compensation, including remuneration received as a result of their victories. Under the Code, athletes were bound to follow the rules of their respective IFs and agree to submit themselves to anti-doping tests and other measures imposed in both competition and training. The new approach went into effect after the 1988 Olympic Games. "Amateurism was a lovely theory that crashed on the shores of reality."[75]

Although the new version of Rule 26 proved capable of resolving important crises, the Olympic rules regarding amateur standing continued to be abused. Faced with growing professionalism and the blurring of the dichotomy between "amateur" and "professional" status, the IOC had begun as early as 1986 to permit open competition between amateurs and professionals, over the opposition particularly of Eastern bloc countries and their NOCs for whom the distinction between "amateurs" and "professionals" had always accrued to their advantage insofar as socialism helped blur the distinction.. New eligibility provisions for five sports, effective in the 1988 Olympic Games, brought the rules for eligibility in the Games into conformity with those of the IFs and their World Championships.[76] Thus, to give a few examples, track-and-field events in the Games were opened to professionals in other sports. In equestrian events professional riders could then compete in their discipline, subject to the approval and regulations of their respective NOCs and the International Equestrian Federation (FEI). In football (soccer) professional players became eligible for the Games, initially excluding those from Europe and South America who had taken part in World Cup

---

[75] OLYMPIC REV., Nov.–Dec. 1985, at 684; *id.*, Feb. 1986, at 80; *id.*, Nov.–Dec. 1986, at 663–64.

[76] OLYMPIC REV., Nov.–Dec. 1986, at 651.

matches. In ice hockey all players, including those who had played professionally for the National Hockey League (NHL), could participate in open competition, subject to the final approval of the IF.

In early 1988 the governing board of the International Amateur Basketball Federation (FIBA) recommended open competition in that sport. As a result, further acceptance of compensation for athletes and the creation of "dream teams" of professionals in open competition, including the Olympic Games, seemed likely. Aside from the establishment of a costly monitoring system, the only alternative to completely reshaping Rule 26 in order to accept a measure of professionalism appeared to be the creation of two levels of competition, one for professionals and one for amateurs. Instead, the IFs and the IOC, on the model of the Davis Cup Competition in tennis, seemed ready to amend their rules to regulate, but not prohibit, commercialization of sports competition and to allow open competition between amateurs and professionals.

To some critics, eliminating the distinction entirely between amateurs and professionals provided an undesirable result: professionals were apt to be viewed as entertainers rather than true competitors. The ideal amateur, by contrast, was more apt to be seen, rightly or wrongly, to embody ideals of purity, integrity, and wholesomeness. Image, however, gave way to more important considerations. Consequently, revised eligibility rules refocused attention not on the financial status of athletes but on the more functional premise of protecting and supporting individual athletes and ensuring fair play in competition.

CHAPTER 7
DOPING, VIOLENCE AND COMMERCIALIZATION

UNESCO's Intergovernmental Committee for Physical Education and Sport has warned against three threats to the implementation of the Olympic Charter: "inappropriate" commercialization, drugs and violence.[1] These threats dominate the attention of international sports lawyers today.

A. DOPING

Whilst that for which all virtue now is sold
And almost every vice, almighty gold;

—Ben Jonson (1616)[2]

I got caught in Seoul and lost my gold medal. I'm here to try to tell people . . . it's wrong to cheat, not to take drugs, they're bad for your health.

—Ben Johnson (1989)[3]

1. Introduction

In 2002 the President of the IOC, Jacques Rogge, declared that "[d]efinitely the No. 1 issue [for the Olympic Movement] is doping."[4] In 2004 United States President Bush, during his annual State of the Union message, took the unusual step of singling out the dangers of performance-enhancing drugs, particularly steroids, and their negative influence on youth.[5] It is hard to argue with those observations, in view of almost daily revelations about doping in sports and the plethora of litigation and arbitration involving the issue. Doping issues have overshadowed such sports as track and field, swimming, cycling and baseball,[6] but

---

1 UNESCO SOURCES, Dec. 1990, at 23.

2 Jonson, *Epistle to Elizabeth, Countess of Rutland, in* THE FOREST, in BEN JONSON 198 (I. Donaldson, Oxford ed., 1985).

3 N.Y. TIMES, Oct. 6, 1989, at D23, col. 4.

4 *See* Clarey, *I.O.C. Chief Keeps Links to Nations Balanced*, N.Y. TIMES, July 28, 2002, at SP9.

5 *See State of the Union: The President's Address*, N.Y. TIMES, Jan. 21, 2004, at A14, A15.

6 On drugs in cycling, for example, *see* Barnes, *The Hardest Test: Drugs and the Tour de*

virtually no sport has been spared. Even table tennis, badminton, and synchronized swimming have been tainted by doping of athletes in those sports.[7] Some 65 percent of all CAS cases are disciplinary, of which the vast majority are appeals of doping-related suspensions from competition, disqualifications from events in competition, and sanctions for doping.

There is general agreement that doping is simply cheating. It creates an uneven playing field for athletes who do not take performance-enhancing agents. A related concern is to avoid turning athletes, especially young, impressionable athletes, into chemical stockpiles. The problem seems so pervasive, however, that any semblance of a level playing field seems either Utopian or, given the extent of the problem in some sports, unnecessary if the playing field is evenly distorted for all competitors. Moreover, the doping controversy foreshadows a brave new world of genetic therapy and comprehensive regimens of high-tech performance enhancement. What was once only science fiction is becoming reality.

The framework for anti-doping measures has been the Olympic Charter. Under Rule 2(8), the IOC "leads the fight against doping in sport and participates in the international fight against drugs" (Rules of the Olympic Charter often appear to be descriptive when they were intended to be prescriptive). The Bye-law to Rule 45 (the Eligibility Code) requires competitors, coaches, trainers and officials to respect and comply in all aspects with the World Anti-Doping Code. Rule 48 incorporates the World Anti-Doping Code after first providing for a Medical Commission to implement it and to "elaborate guidelines relating to the medical care and health of the athletes." A system of IOC-accredited laboratories conducts both routine and unannounced tests.[8] Within that framework, the

---

France, NEW YORKER, Aug. 21 and 28, 2000, at 94. On the problems in swimming, *see, e.g., infra*, note 33, and baseball, *infra* note 35.

[7] Longman, *Samaranch: Olympic Savior or Spoiler?*, N.Y. TIMES, Sept. 10, 2000, at 33, 42.

[8] In an early report, the IOC Medical Commission summarized anti-doping samples analyzed in 1988 by IOC-accredited laboratories, revealed the following statistics:

> Out of 47,069 samples analyzed, 1,153 were found to be positive, or 2.45% of the total. In 1987, there were 854 positive cases out of 37,882 samples analyzed, or 2.25%, and in 1986 the figure was 623 cases out of 32,982, or 1.89%. It is naturally at major international meetings that the highest percentage of positive samples is recorded, with a figure of 2.84%. Before major championships the figure is 2.70%. National competitions produce a figure of 2.53%, while samples from unannounced out-of-competition tests produce 2.18% positive cases.

OLYMPIC REV., May 1989, at 198. In 1990 IOC-accredited laboratories administered 61,000 tests, a 36 percent increase over the previous year. The percentage of positive tests dropped to below 1 percent for the first time. Olympic Rev., July 1991, at 322. The 1984 Los Angeles Games produced the following statistics:

> Within 15 days, 1510 different urine specimens underwent 9440 screening analyses by a combination of gas chromatography-mass spectrometry, "high performance" liquid chromatography, and radioimmunoassay. These tests covered more than 200 different

Olympic Movement has struggled to find an effective mechanism for formulating the right rules, uniformly applying them, imposing sanctions under them, and resolving disputes involving anti-doping measures against athletes.

2. Listing of Prohibited Substances

Any anti-doping system must proceed from an agreed upon list of prohibited substances. In 1998 a case testing the IOC's list made headlines during the 1998 Olympic Winter Games in Nagano.[9] Ross Rebagliati of Canada won the first-ever gold medal in the new event of snow-boarding. Immediately after his victory, however, the IOC rescinded his medal after he tested positive for marijuana in a blood sample. Rebagliati petitioned for a review of the decision by the Ad Hoc Division of the CAS. He argued that he had not smoked marijuana but had inhaled second-hand smoke at a party in Canada before the Games. (His defense was the reverse of United States President Clinton's admission that in his younger days he had smoked but not inhaled marijuana). That fine distinction was, however, immaterial to the CAS. What mattered was that marijuana was not on the prohibited list. Rebagliati was therefore allowed to keep his medal, and marijuana was added to the prohibited list of substances.

The questions about listing prohibited substances are legion. First and foremost, what substances should be banned? Generally nine categories of substances are used to enhance performance: stimulants (to increase heart rate, blood pressure, and alertness); beta-blockers (to slow heart rate and steady the hand of target shooters, for example); anabolic steroids and related substances (to build muscle mass, reduce fatigue and increase aggressiveness); cannabinoids such as marijuana (to ease pain and produce a comfortable feeling); narcotics (to ease pain and produce a sense of euphoria); diuretics (to purge or mask drugs and to reach lower weight limits, primarily by urination); peptide hormones and mimetics such as insulin (to control sugar and its effects in the bloodstream); human growth hormone (to help build muscle mass and decrease body fat); and erythropoietin (EPO) (to increase red blood cells and improve endurance).

Despite a general consensus on this general range of categories, the inclusion of particular agents is difficult. Why are particular agents banned when natural techniques to accomplish the same objectives in training or competition are not?[10]

> drugs and metabolites, including psychomotor stimulants, sympathomimetic amines, central nervous system stimulants, narcotic analgesics, and anabolic steroids.

Catlin, Kammerer, Hatton, Sekera & Merdink, *Analytical Chemistry at the Games of the XXIIIrd Olympiad in Los Angeles, 1984, in* 33 Clinical Chemistry 319 (1987).

[9] Rebagliati v. International Olympic Committee, CAS Arb. NAG2 (1998).

[10] One critic of anti-doping efforts points out that there are three ways to raise the hemoglobin level of blood: train at high altitudes or in chambers with low oxygen levels, use erythropoietin (EPO), or store and later use one's own blood cells. The rationale for allowing only the first method is that only it is natural. But, in the critic's view, this rationale for distinguish-

Should otherwise prohibited agents that are found in medications be exempted? Should otherwise prohibited agents that are found in food or other nutritive supplements be exempted?[11] Should all of the agents be prohibited for all athletes, regardless of their value for particular sports? What about otherwise prohibited agents that in certain sports are performance neutral or even performance-detracting? What about gene therapy?

A particularly complicated issue relates to agents that are difficult to detect, such as the designer steroid tetryahydrogestrinone (THG) that was deliberately modified to escape detection in standard testing.[12] Other common agents, such as erythropoietin (EPO) and human growth hormone, have also frustrated reliable detection.[13] "The basic problem with drug testing is that testers are always one step behind athletes. It can take years for sports authorities to figure out what drugs athletes are using and even longer to devise effective means of detecting them."[14]

3. Testing Procedures

Ethical issues of urine or blood sampling are also troublesome. Acceptable testing must be scientifically valid, carefully handled, and well-documented in the chain of handling substances. Certification of laboratories that comply with the highest scientific standards is often difficult. The handling of sample is essential. Normally, two samples are taken in each testing. If sample "A" is positive, the athlete involved may appeal the finding, at which time sample "B" is analyzed. Thus, if the initial finding is appealed by the athlete, both samples "A" and "B" must be positive in order to suspend the athlete from competition. The collection and storage of the two samples involves very careful procedures. If not analyzed on appeal of a positive "A" test, the "B" sample must be sealed and retained for later review if necessary. Careful storage of the second or "B" specimen for later review is essential.

---

ing among the three methods may be questioned in view of the acceptability of "unnatural" assists throughout sports, from high-tech running shoes to fiberglass poles for pole vaults. Kolata, *Slippery Slope on the Playing Field*, N.Y. TIMES, July 11, 1999, WK18.

[11] *See* Sandomir, *I.O.C. Finds Banned Substances in Many Food Supplements*, N.Y. TIMES, Oct. 12, 2001, at C15; *Sports-supplement dangers*, CONSUMER REP., June 2001, at 40.

[12] *See* Sappenfield, *How far sports steroid scandal might spread*, CHRISTIAN SCI. MONITOR, Feb. 10, 2004, at 2; Sokolove, *The Lab Animal*, N.Y. TIMES MAGAZINE, Jan. 18, 2004, at 28, 30 (concerning the production and distribution of difficult-to-detect steroids by the Bay Area Laboratory Co-Operative (BALCO)). *See also, 2 in World Championships Tested Positive for Drug*, THE OREGONIAN, Nov. 23, 2003, at SP 7 (reporting on the issue of reviewing 402 (stored) "B" samples from testing during competition three months earlier after science acquired the ability to detect and test for the elusive substances). On December 4, 2003, the IOC Executive Board decided to retest for THG the "B" samples collected during the 2002 Winter Games in Salt Lake City.

[13] *See* Zorpette, *All Doped Up—and Going for the Gold*, SCI. AM., May 2000, at 20.

[14] Gladwell, *Drugstore Athlete*, NEW YORKER, Sept. 10, 2001, at 52, 54.

Before summarizing legal issues that arise in the process of enforcing and reviewing anti-doping measures, it will be useful to trace the history of the doping problem in the sports arena and the development of anti-doping measures, primarily by institutions within the Olympic Movement.

4. Brief History of the Doping Problem and Anti-Doping Measures

Since the IOC first instituted rules against the use of stimulants and tranquilizers in 1967, urinalysis, blood tests and more sophisticated methods have been used to deter drug violations and enforce prohibitions on their use. Spot checks, computerized testing and the use of a such technology as gas chromatographic mass spectrometers have made it possible to detect prohibited substances in concentrations as minute as one part per billion and traces of compounds taken many months earlier.

During the 1970s, in order to enforce a ban on certain drugs,[15] the IOC required that each competition site have adequate testing facilities and that each competitor agree to submit to medical control at the risk of exclusion. Thus, any competitor who refused to submit to medical control or examination or who was found guilty of doping was excludable from competition. If the individual was a team member, the competition or event at which the infringement occurred was forfeited by that team. If the pertinent NOC lodged a protest, the Medical Commission heard the team's explanation and discussed the case with the appropriate IF. The IOC then decided whether to exclude the team from competition. The identity of violators was reported to that athlete's IF for possible additional sanctions by them.[16] Thus, in preparation for competition at the Olympic Games or other sanctioned competition such as the Pan-American Games, the IOC would submit the names of competitors who had failed a drug test to their NOCs. The NOCs, in turn, were obligated to ban them from participating in forthcoming sanctioned competition. During the 1980s the new CAS upheld the right of an NOC to impose even a *lifetime* ban on competition by athletes who used drugs contrary to international standards.

In 1987, as a way of encouraging uniform standards among IFs, the IOC's Medical Commission recommended to them a two-tiered plan of sanctions to be applied against athletes who used banned substances. The plan therefore distinguished between drugs used exclusively to enhance performance, such as steroids, and those typically taken for medical purposes. Penalties varied according to whether the use was deliberate or accidental and also whether the use constituted a first, second, or third offense. An offense effective during competition would

---

15 *See* Howald, *Medical and Pharmacological Means of Influencing Performance in Top Competition Sport*, OLYMPIC REV., May 1978, at 297; de Mérode, *Doping Tests at the Olympic Games in 1976*, OLYMPIC REV., Jan. 1979, at 10; *id.*, May–June 1987, at 245; *id.*, Mar. 1988, at 86.

16 *See* OLYMPIC CHARTER, Rule 29 (1976).

lead minimally to suspension from the competition and forfeiture of all medals won during it. In support of its anti-doping efforts, the IOC cooperated with the International Narcotics Board in Vienna.[17]

Drug testing was, however, notoriously haphazard. National sports bodies often failed to cooperate in effectively administering the tests. For example, as recently as 1983 The Athletics Congress of the USA (TAC) refused to conduct extensive tests at its three-day track-and-field trials prior to the 1983 Pan American Games. The chair of the TAC women's track-and-field committee protested and warned that the reluctance to test for drugs amounted to an admission that the use of illegal drugs had been condoned. The women's committee voted twice to conduct doping tests at the meet "to protect the innocent as much as to punish the guilty,"[18] but its requests to do so were denied.

Worse yet was growing evidence that sports administrators—those in charge of enforcing the rules and promoting the ideals of sports competition—actively or passively encouraged the use of prohibited substances. During the Cold War era, massive sports programs, particularly in Eastern Europe and the Soviet Union,[19] relied on doping to enhance performance in virtually all types of international competition. During the 1990s, China became a particular focus of concern when its burgeoning program of sports development was corrupted by doping. Such exposés of government-sponsored steroid usage have alarmed, though perhaps not surprised, the public.[20]

State-administered doping continued to plague the sports arena, but fortunately, many NOCs began to assume greater leadership in drug testing and control. A $2.5 million testing program at the 1984 Games in Los Angeles was designed to deter and detect the use of drugs. The improved testing was designed to encourage sports associations and their members to remember "the moral qualities which are the basis of sport" and "the spirit of fair play" that they have undertaken to foster. Eleven athletes were expelled from competition after failing drug testing. The testing procedures were effective even though they had to comply with strict legal standards under the United States Constitution. Such standards precluded the involuntary use of blood or saliva tests and evidentiary

---

17 Olympic Rev., May–June 1987, at 245. *See also id.*, Mar. 1988, at 86.

18 Wisconsin St. J. (Madison), Aug. 25, 1983, § 2, at 1.

19 *See, e.g.*, Fisher, *E. German Sports: Ruled by Steroids*, Wash. Post, Sept. 7, 1991, at 1, col. 1.

20 *See, e.g.*, Longman, *Just Following Orders, Doctors' Orders*, N.Y. Times, Apr. 22, 2001; Int'l Herald Trib., July 19, 2000, at 18; Kim, *Tarnished legacy of Olympic gold*, Christian Sci. Monitor, May 10, 2000, at 6 (all three stories focusing on more than 400 indictments against East German defendants who had allegedly injured athletes in the course of East Germany's drug-ridden sports program). On China's problems and response to them, *see* China's Sports Law, *infra*, Appendix II.

presumptions of responsibility attributable to trainers or coaches of athletes found to have used drugs.

In 1985 the USOC announced plans for semi-random urinalysis of athletes in all major competitions, even in non-Olympic years. Essentially, the testing program involved urinalysis of the top three seeded competitors in each event, plus randomly selected other competitors. If an athlete failed a test, the duration of his or her suspension varied according to individual drug-taking records.[21]

Despite such measures, however, the problem of drug abuse by athletes only grew. It had been dramatized at the 1983 and was to recur at the 1987 Pan-American Games. During the 1983 Games, in the biggest drug scandal and expulsion of athletes in the history of amateur sports at that point, 14 athletes, including nine medalists, were disqualified for having used drugs banned by the IOC. At the 1987 Games six athletes were disqualified.[22] A rule in the Olympic Charter required disqualified athletes to return their medals. National federations and sports organizations responded by suspending members found to have used drugs.[23]

An emerging problem related to drugs but not involving them was the practice of blood-packing or blood-doping. Blood-packing is a technique aimed at increasing an athlete's red blood cell count and oxygen level by administering transfusions of the athlete's own blood whereas blood-doping involves a transfusion of someone else's blood. Some athletes believe that blood transfusions increase their stamina. Despite the advantages that are attributed, correctly or not, to transfusions, they are banned by international rules. In 1985, the Executive Board of the IOC, after hearing a report of the Medical Commission, specifically banned them (as well as beta-blockers). Prohibiting blood-packing or blood-doping is, however, very difficult to enforce. It is almost impossible to detect the procedure in the absence of a self-confession. In one of the earliest anti-doping actions in 1988, the International Ski Federation (FIS) took action against Kerry Lynch, a leading member of the United States skiing team, for having engaged in blood-doping. Rejecting light penalties that had been imposed by the U.S. Ski Team and the United States Skiing Association, the ISF, relying on Lynch's confession, banned him from the 1988 Winter Games and stripped him of a silver medal he had won in 1987 at the Nordic Combined World Championships, for which he had admittedly doctored his blood.[24]

---

21 INT'L HERALD TRIB., Mar. 25, 1985, at 12, col. 4.

22 *See, e.g., The Big Caracas Drug Bust*, 122 TIME, Sept. 5, 1983, at 70; CHRISTIAN SCI. MONITOR, Aug. 29, 1987, at 1, col. 1.

23 *See generally* THE AUSTRALIAN (SYDNEY), Aug. 25, 1983, at 16, col. 5.

24 For discussions of the problem, *see* OLYMPIC REV., July 1985, at 383; *id.*, Mar. 1987, at 92, 93. For an account of the action taken against Kerry Lynch, *see* CHRISTIAN SCI. MONITOR, Jan. 22, 1988, at 18, col. 1.

Also, it was becoming apparent that the use of ephedrine stimulants and anabolic steroids, in particular, was becoming widespread among athletes. Often prescribed to promote weight gain among surgical patients, burn victims and others, steroids have long been particularly popular with body builders, football players and weight lifters. Many athletes and their coaches believe that anabolic steroids, derived from the male hormone testosterone and taken as pills, speed muscle development, increase aggressiveness and promote strength. Medical evidence suggests, however, that the steroids can cause irreversible damage to health, including kidney, liver and heart failure, and changes in sexual desires and characteristics. Adolescent users can suffer a stunting of bone and sexual development. Other drugs were also becoming rampant on the playing field.[25]

At the 1988 Games in Seoul, the problems came shockingly to a head. The IOC retracted Canadian Ben Johnson's gold medal in the 100-meter sprint after tests revealed the presence of an anabolic steroid in his urine.[26] Johnson's stature as an erstwhile world record-holder served to rivet global attention on the problem of substance abuse by athletes and accelerated efforts to establish a uniform, effective anti-doping mechanism. The Canadian government responded to the Johnson incident and the suspension of four Canadian weightlifters for substance abuse, by appointing a blue-ribbon Commission of Inquiry headed by Ontario's Chief Justice Charles L. Dubin. The resulting Dubin Report highlighted the enormity of drug abuse in the international sports arena and the need for improved supervision and enforcement by the IOC and the IFs.[27]

The IOC promptly adopted stiff sanctions against drug trafficking and a comprehensive International Olympic Charter Against Doping in Sport, and entered into an agreement with the association of IFs to harmonize and mutually enforce rules, procedures and sanctions under the IOC's Medical Code.[28] The Johnson

---

[25] During the 1980s, the IOC's Medical Commission established an extensive list of banned substances and procedures. These include (1) classes: stimulants, narcotics, anabolic steroids, beta-blockers, and diuretics; and (2) methods: blood-doping and packing (enhancing red blood cell counts by transfusion of oxygen-rich blood to improve stamina) and deliberate masking of urine content. Restricted, but not banned, substances include alcohol, local anesthetics, corticosteroids, and human chorionic gonadotrophin.

A report by the Commission revealed the leading substances detected by IOC-accredited laboratories in 1988, as follows, in order of frequency of positive tests: anabolic steroids (791 cases, of which nandrolene accounted for 304); testosterone (155); stimulants (420, of which pseudoephedrine accounted for 140 and phenylpropanolamine for 109); narcotics (58, of which codeine accounted for 35); diuretics (57); probenicide, a masking agent, (19); and beta blockers (8). OLYMPIC REV., May 1989, at 198.

[26] Altman, *New 'Breakfast of Champions': A Recipe for Victory or Disaster?*, N.Y. TIMES, Nov. 20, 1988, at 1, 34, col. 1.

[27] Armstrong, *The Lessons Learned From Canada's Dubin Inquiry, in* International Athletic Foundation, IAF SYMPOSIUM ON SPORT AND LAW (1991) (copy on file with the author).

[28] OLYMPIC REV., Nov. 1988, at 628, 631; *Id.*, May 1989, at 198.

incident inspired other accords as well. These included a U.S.-Soviet Mutual Doping Control Agreement providing for mutual testing of athletes and other anti-doping cooperation;[29] a trilateral agreement between Australia, Canada, and the United Kingdom for information-sharing and cooperation in drug testing;[30] a multilateral agreement based on the U.S.-Soviet pact, supervised by the IOC's Medical Commission;[31] and the Council of Europe's Anti-Doping Convention.[32] These instruments helped in some measure to universalize standards and broaden the jurisdiction of testing bodies, though troublesome inconsistencies and spotty enforcement continued to pose a threat to the integrity of the testing and hence of international competition.

5. Development of Uniform Rules: The *Lex Sportiva* of the CAS

During the 1990s, as the doping problem began to spin out of control,[33] it was apparent that the regulatory framework was collapsing. Ironically, the doping crisis began to seem acute just at the collapse of the East European and Soviet regimes whose state-sponsored, drug-ridden sports programs were notorious. During the 1990s particular sports, such as baseball, track and field, cycling, and swimming were at the vortex of controversy. Major League Baseball (MLB) and such national governing bodies as USA Track and Field were, at best, slow off the starting blocks in the race to keep ahead of cheaters.

---

[29] USOC FACT BOOK 39 (1990); *Recent Developments*, 25 STAN. J. INT'L L. 611 (1989).

[30] Armstrong, *supra* note 27, at 29.

[31] WASH. POST, Dec. 14, 1989, at D9, col. 4.

[32] *Infra* note 54. The parties agreed to adopt the IOC list of doping agents and methods. They also agreed to harmonize domestic anti-doping regulations, such as those restricting availability and use of substances, funding and conducting of tests, and premising support of athletes on tests. The Convention committed parties to help establish and provide access to control laboratories, institute educational programs, and cooperate with national and international sports organizations. A Monitoring Group oversees application of the Convention.

[33] *See* Sokolove, *supra* note 12, at 33. Chinese swimmers were a prime example, as follows:

> The most graphic illustration in the 1990s involved Chinese swimmers. After the Chinese team hired an East German coach in the mid-1980s, its swimming performance suddenly blossomed: China garnered a substantial number of gold medals at the 1988 and 1992 Olympic Games, and 12 of the 16 golds at the 1994 World Championship in Rome. But only a few months later, tests administered without warning to the Chinese team at the Asian Games in Hiroshima disclosed a host of drug users: by 1998, 27 of the team's top swimmers had been banned from international competition.

P. WEILER, LEVELING THE PLAYING FIELD: HOW THE LAW CAN MAKE SPORTS BETTER FOR FANS 78 (2000). *See also*, Longman, *Chinese Coach and 6 Distance Runners Out of the Games*, N.Y. TIMES, Sept. 7, 2000, at C29; *40 Chinese Out of Olympics: 7 Tied to Drugs*, N.Y. TIMES, Sept. 6, 2000, at C25.

The black eye the Chinese received from its bad record of doping, coupled with its aspiration to become a sports power and host major international competition, including the Olympic Games, led to a comprehensive new sports law. *See* CHINA'S SPORTS LAW, *infra* Appendix II.

A particularly serious issue has been the lack of uniformity in virtually every aspect of doping controls among IFs.[34] Harmonization of a welter of disparate rules and procedures has been clearly needed. A related problem has involved a lack of cooperation in the anti-doping campaign from professional sports leagues governed by their own collective bargaining agreements, lack of disciplinary rules, general tolerance of doping, and imperviousness to measures by the IFs governing their sports. MLB in North America has stood out as a particularly bad example.[35]

The emerging *lex sportiva* of the CAS, in its decisions on appeal of anti-doping sanctions by IFs,[36] contributed to the establishment of uniform standards for testing, applying rules and sanctions, and review of them.[37] In *Lazutina v. IOC*,[38] the CAS confirmed that the IOC must bear the burden of proving three elements: that a sample at issue was properly taken, that there had been a complete chain of custody of the sample from the location of a controverted testing to the laboratory, and that the test used was reliable for discovering the presence of the prohibited substance. Carrying this burden of proof established a rebuttable presumption that the testing and custodial procedures had been conducted in accordance with prevailing and acceptable standards.

The *Lazutina* case illustrates another emerging issue. Ms. Lazutina, a Russian cross-country skier, was disqualified from the 30-kilometer race at the 2002 Olympic Winter Games in Salt Lake City. She was also asked to return two silver

---

[34] *See generally*, DOPING RULES OF INTERNATIONAL SPORTS ORGANISATIONS (Siekmann & Soek eds., 1999). Useful summaries appear in Engelbrecht, *Adoption, Recognition and Harmonization of Doping Sanctions Between World Sports Organisations*, 2000 INT'L SPORTS L.J., Special Edition Olympic Games Sydney 2000, at 3, 4. On the general problems confronting a pluralistic system of international control, *see generally* DOPING—SANKTIONEN, BEWEISE, ANSPRÜCHE (Fritzweiler ed., 2000).

[35] *See, e.g.*, Sokolove, *supra* note 12, at 33–34; Mihoces, *Questions of substance*, USA TODAY, Feb. 21, 2003 (focusing on the refusal of Major League Baseball (MLB), unlike many sports federations and associations, to ban the use of ephedrine, a weight-loss aid and energy booster. The report followed the death of a baseball pitcher who had used the drug). *See also* Araton, *Players' Steroid Proposal Totally Lacking in Muscle*, N.Y. TIMES, Aug. 11, 2002, § 8, at 1 (pointing out the difficulty in MLB to gain any agreement for effective anti-doping measures in baseball's collective bargaining agreement); Regan, *Rising clash over drugs in sports*, CHRISTIAN SCI. MONITOR, Aug. 12, 1999 (discussing gap between strict amateurs and lax pros).

[36] For a comprehensive study of pertinent IAAF arbitral awards, *see* TARASTI, LEGAL SOLUTIONS IN INTERNATIONAL DOPING CASES: AWARDS BY THE IAAF ARBITRATION PANEL 1985–1999 (2000).

[37] *See generally*, Oschütz, *Harmonization of Anti-Doping Code Through Arbitration: The Case Law of the Court of Arbitration for Sport*, 12 MARQ. SPORTS L. REV. 675 (2002); Reeb, Die CAS—*Rechtsprechung in Doping—Fällen, in* DOPING FORUM: AKTUELLE RECHTLICHE UND MEDIZINISCHE ASPEKTE 63 (Röhricht & Vieweg eds., 2000); Kavanagh, *The Doping Cases and the Need for the International Court of Arbitration for Sport (CAS)*, 22 U.N.S.W. L.J. 721 (1999).

[38] Lazutina v. IOC, CAS 2002/A/370.

medals that she had won in other events. She then lost an appeal before the CAS of the decision of the IOC Executive Board. After the federal court upheld the CAS decision against her, the IOC Executive Board annulled all results Ms. Lazutina had obtained at the Games and requested the Russian Olympic Committee to effect the return of the corresponding medals and diplomas to the IOC. The Executive Board then awarded the silver medals to the bronze medal winners and awarded their bronze medals to the next-place finishers in the two events.[39]

The revocation and re-awarding of medals after competition raises interesting questions of repose. Should such attempts be made to rewrite sports history? Should the process continue indefinitely? Should medals be reassigned years, even decades, later after revised awards? Can medals be revoked and re-awarded posthumously?

In a definitive set of opinions, the CAS developed a rule of strict liability for the presence of a prohibited substance in a urine or blood sample whenever it has been detected by approved scientific testing procedures.[40] This rule may seem harsh for individuals in some circumstances, but it is justified on the basis of fairness to competitors. Negligence is no excuse.[41] According to the principle of *prima facie* proof, discovery of a prohibited substance in an athlete's body fluids entails a double presumption: the use of the substance and the athlete's culpability for its use.[42] After a positive determination, the CAS shifts the burden to the athlete to rebut the evidence by showing either a lack of knowledge about ingestion of the agent or innocence in doing so.[43] Carrying this burden of proof mitigates the sanction

---

39 OLYMPIC REV., July–Aug.–Sept. 2003, at 17.

40 *See* Straubel, *Doping Due Process: A Critique of the Doping Control Process in International Sport*, 106 DICKINSON L. REV. 523, 543 (2002) ("The CAS has stood firmly behind the strict liability doctrine for positive doping results regardless of the cause of the doping."). The presumption of guilt, subject to an athlete's rebuttal, has been followed in a long line of CAS decisions. *See, e.g.*, S. v/FEI, CAS 91/56, II DIGEST OF CAS AWARDS 1998–2000, at 93 (M. Reeb ed. 2002), 95; G. v/FEI, CAS 92/63, CAS DIGEST, *id.* at 115, 120; N. v/FEI, CAS 92/73, CAS DIGEST, *id.* at 153, 157; W. v/FEI, CAS 92/86, CAS DIGEST, *id.* at 161,163; R. v/FEI, CAS 98/204, CAS DIGEST, *id.* at 8; G. v/FEI, CAS 91/53, CAS DIGEST, *id.* at 79, 87; C. v/FINA, CAS 95/141, CAS DIGEST, *id.* at 215, 220; F. v. FINA, CAS 96/156, CAS DIGEST, *id.* at 40; B. v/FIJ, CAS 98/214, CAS DIGEST, *id.* at 17; FCLP v/IWF CAS 99/A/252, CAS DIGEST, *id.* at 22; CAS 2000/A/309, R. v/RLVB, CAS DIGEST, *id.* at 5.

41 *Gundel*, CAS 92/71.

42 *See* Vieweg, *The Definition of Doping and The Proof of a Doping Offence*, 2002 INT'L SPORTS L.J. 2, 5.

43 CAS 2001/A/317, A v/XXX, interpreting a "cocktail" of definitions and legal principles in the applicable IF's regulation. Under Swiss law, the CAS established the following rules for allocating the burden of proof:

> The so-called "strict liability" rule, i.e. a rule as advocated by the Respondent according to which the mere presence of a prohibited substance in an athlete's body justifies his suspension, does not, in the Panel's opinion, sufficiently respect the athlete's right of personality (*"Persönlichkeitsrecht"*) as established in Article 20 and 27 et seq. of the Swiss

to be applied except in the instance of in-competition disqualification for an event where the need for a quick decision and the integrity of the event are at issue. Disqualification in itself does not determine the imposition or not of additional sanctions such as a fine or suspension or termination for life of an athlete's eligibility to compete. These are two different, though factually related issues.

> Civil Code which CAS panels are required to apply (Art. 58 of the Code of Sports-related Arbitration). . . .
>
> In recent times the fight against doping has become sport's most burning problem. At times, public attention and, in particular, that of the media is focused more on whether the athletes are under the influence of doping substances than on the sporting event itself and its results. This development is a very serious threat to the entire sporting movement and, indirectly, to an industry which accounts for an important percentage of the world economy. . . .
>
> When weighing up the interests of both sides the Panel is of the view that the interests of the athlete take precedence over those of the federation to enforce a rule of "strict liability." The contrary view would only be acceptable if a strict liability rule were the only meaningful weapon in the fight against doping. . . . As will be shown below, there are other means, in particular when allocating the burden of proof, to ensure an effective fight against doping without accepting the risk of sanctioning an athlete who is not guilty of an offence or whose level of guilt does not justify the full extent of the sanction.
>
> Having established the principle that the suspension of an athlete for a doping offence requires fault on his/her part, this does not, in the Panel's view, mean that it is for the federation to provide full proof of every element of the offence, as is necessary in respect of a criminal act for which a presumption of innocence operates in favour of the accused. There is no doubt that the federation has to establish and—if contested—to prove the objective elements of the offence, in particular, for example, that the sample was taken properly, that there was a complete chain of custody of the sample on its way to the laboratory and that the analysis of the sample was state-of-the-art. This follows from the general rule that a person who alleges a fact has the burden of proof. . . .
>
> However, it would put a definite end to any meaningful fight against doping if the federations were required to *prove* the necessary subjective elements of the offence, i.e. intent or negligence on the part of the athlete. . . .
>
> For this reason the Panel believes that, with regard to the subjective elements of a doping offence, when weighing the interests of the federation to combat doping and those of the athlete not to be punished without fault, the scales tip in favour of the fight against doping. In fact, doping only happens in the sphere of the athlete: he/she is in control of his/her body, of what he/she eats and drinks, of who has access to his/her nutrition, of what medication he/she takes, etc. In these circumstances it is appropriate to presume that the athlete has knowingly or at least negligently consumed the substance which has lead [sic] to the positive doping test. . . .
>
> Therefore, if the federation is able to establish the objective elements of a doping offence, there is a presumption of guilt against the athlete.
>
> The principle of presumed fault on the part of the athlete does not, however, leave him without protection because he/she has the right to rebut the presumption, i.e. to establish that the presence of the prohibited substance in his/her body was not due to any intent or negligence on his/her part. The athlete may for example provide evidence that the presence of the forbidden substance is the result of an act of malicious intent by a third party.

Id. at V. 2-1 (citations omitted).

The principle of strict liability does not apply to sanctions other than the remedial measure of disqualification, for the sake of an expeditious decision and fairness to competing athletes. Instead, proof of culpability is required for further sanctions.[44] The application of such sanctions must therefore take account of mitigating circumstances. In assessing the weight to be given to circumstances, the German principle of proportionality has been influential. Accordingly, in the normal context of a disciplinary dispute, the athlete's interest, particularly his right of personality, must be weighed against those of the sanctioning federation.[45] The fundamental principle is to strike a reasonable balance between enforcement of strict liability and exceptional circumstances.

Over time, sanctions upheld by the CAS became more uniform. A two-year suspension of eligibility for unmitigated violations and termination for recidivism became standard. Other anti-doping rules and principles, despite wide variations among IFs and other sports bodies, became standardized. For example, thresholds of doping concentration became more uniform, on the basis of scientific determinations of the normal amounts of a substance in the body, everyday food, or the natural environment.[46]

6. National Jurisprudence

The opinions of national courts have also been influential. German courts, in particular, have developed a sophisticated jurisprudence in conformity with the *lex sportiva*.[47] United States courts have been reluctant to review decisions of the IFs and other private bodies, in the absence of state action, or to grant athletes a private cause of action.[48] In certain procedural contexts, however, United States courts have established important doctrine.

In *Slaney v. The Int'l Amateur Athletic Fed'n*,[49] the issue was the enforceability of an IAAF arbitral award against a track-and-field athlete, Mary Slaney, whose urine test had disclosed the presence in her body of a prohibited level of testosterone. In holding that the arbitral award was enforceable under the New York Convention on the Recognition and Enforcement of Arbitral Awards, a federal appeals court confirmed several important principles: the finality of arbitration, even by private associations, in resolving sports disputes; the (fairly substantial) latitude of an arbitrator's procedural discretion; the exclusivity of USOC determinations of eligibility; and the unavailability of judicial intervention

---

44 *Id.*

45 *See* Baddeley, L'Association Sportive Face au Droit 239 (1994).

46 *See* Vieweg, *supra* note 42, at 5.

47 *See generally* Doping-Forum, *supra* note 37.

48 *See, e.g.*, Barnes v. Int'l Amateur Athletic Fed'n, 862 F. Supp. 1537 (S.D. W. Va. 1993).

49 Slaney v. The Int'l Athletic Fed'n, 244 F.3d 580 (7th Cir. 2001).

in disciplinary hearings of sports associations except in the most extraordinary circumstances.

Even given these constraints on review, the court addressed Slaney's argument that the basis for the arbitral award was contrary to public policy and would therefore fall within a public policy exception to the New York Convention. Essentially, Slaney challenged the burden-shifting test used by the IAAF, under which a specified presence of exogenous testosterone in urine creates a presumption that the athlete used the testosterone, and that presumption is rebuttable only by clear and convincing evidence. The court decided that the burden-shifting test was not contrary to public policy, leaving intact a determination by the district (trial) court that Slaney had failed to sustain the burden of proving her innocence.

The *Slaney* decision is particularly interesting because of the difficulty of determining whether a particular level of testosterone is natural or not. In fairness to athletes, the critical ratio of testosterone to epitestosterone that is used in order to calculate the presence of exogenous testosterone is set at a threshold amount of six times the normal level in females in order to take account of such factors as birth control pills, age, menstrual cycle, bacterial contamination of the urine sample, and presence of alcohol in the bloodstream. Slaney's samples tested at ratios that were 50 percent–93 percent higher than even the threshold. The court held that the ratio itself was scientifically valid, and that the sampling procedures complied with scientific standards.[50]

7. Codification and Institutionalization of Uniform Rules and Procedures

Support for harmonization of rules has been strong,[51] but codification of the *lex sportiva*, national jurisprudence, and scattered other guidance on anti-doping

---

[50] The related issues, identified as follows, are vexing:

> USA Track & Field's controversial four-year suspensions in 1997 of star U.S. runners Mary Decker Slaney and Sandra Farmer-Patrick, on the grounds that their testosterone-to-epitestosterone (t/e) rations exceeded the 6:1 female guideline, underscored the complexity and difficulty of regulating this type of "drug" use. Should sports authorities even be concerned with such a substance which emerges naturally in everyone's body? Since natural levels of these substances can vary depending on several medical circumstances personal to the individual (such as menstrual patterns or birth control methods), is regulating and testing for testosterone a greater intrusion upon an athlete's privacy than testing for objectively measurable artificial drugs? If so, should the justification for such action have to be more compelling? And what t/e ratio should be required to support a finding of banned artificial introduction—a ratio that cannot possibly be attained by natural production, or one that in a small percentage of cases could be purely natural? In either case, would banning only those female athletes who tested at or above the set ratio solve the problem?

P. Weiler & G. Roberts, Sports and The Law: Text, Cases, Problems (2d ed. 1998).

[51] *See, e.g.*, general statements of commitment by the European Olympic Committees and the Supreme Council for Sport in Africa, Olympic Rev., Feb.–Mar. 1999, at 20.

issues has required considerable acumen. Even the definition of "doping" is problematic. There are essentially two options.[52] The term can be reduced to an abstract generalization or expressed simply in terms of specific types of violations of the prohibited use of the listed agents, however complete or incomplete the list might be.

One example of the abstract type of definition is that of the International Shooting Union (UIT), as follows: "the use of one or more of the [listed] substances *with the aim* of attaining an increase in performance by injection, oral or other means, arid [sic] whether the drug is administered by the competitor himself or the substance is transmitted to the competitor's body by another person."[53] Given the complexities of such generalized definitions and related issues such as intent, it is not surprising that the definitional approach based on violations of specified agents proved to be definitive. Thus, violations are expressed in terms of "use," "second use," "trafficking," "administration of," and so on. The preferred approach takes account of the possible incompleteness of the list by including the catch-all category of "related substances," a term that arguably suffers from uncertainty.

In 1989 the European Anti-Doping Convention[54] provided a system of regional cooperation to restrict the availability and use of doping agents and methods and to assist sports organizations in harmonizing doping controls and disciplinary procedures. The 1989 Convention defined "doping in sport" as "the administration to sportsmen or sportswomen, or the use by them, of pharmacological classes of doping agents or doping methods."[55] A 2002 Protocol to the European Anti-Doping Convention provides for evaluation of member-state compliance.

In 2000 the Olympic Movement Anti-Doping Code came into force.[56] Essentially, it crystallized the *lex ferenda* of IF rules and procedures, CAS awards, and domestic judicial decisions. With some modifications, the Olympic Code led to the approval of the World Anti-Doping Code by some 73 states and 65 sports organizations.[57] As such, the Code is applicable beyond the Olympic Movement and mandatorily enforceable by all states parties to the Code. The Code is to be administered by the World Anti-Doping Agency, which was established at Lausanne, Switzerland in 1999 but has its headquarters in Montreal, Canada. National agencies, for example, the United States Anti-Doping Agency, have since

---

52 *See* Vieweg, *supra* note 42, at 2.

53 *See* USA Shooting & Quigley v. Int'l Shooting Union (UIT) ¶ 8, CAS 94/129 (1995).

54 Anti-Doping Convention, ETS 135 (1989).

55 *Id.*, art. 2(1)(a).

56 *See* Vieweg, *supra* note 42, at 2; Soek & Vrijman, *The Shepherd's Courage—The Olympic Movement Anti-Doping Code*, 2002/1 INT'L SPORTS L.J. 6.

57 Abrahamson, *Worldwide Anti-Doping Code is Given Approval*, L.A. TIMES, Mar. 6, 2003, at SP9; Shipley, *Nations Agree to Uniform Drug Code*, WASH. POST, Mar. 6, 2003, at D8.

been formed to help carry out the work of WADA and, as of 2003, to implement the World Anti-Doping Code. "In theory [WADA] is the ultimate authority on matters of drugs and sport—looming over national Olympic committees and the national and international federations of all the individual sports and making it more difficult for those parochial interests to protect athletes against doping."[58]

Declaring that "[d]oping is fundamentally contrary to the spirit of sport," the Code seeks to protect the athletes' fundamental right to participate on an even playing field of doping-free sport; to promote health, fairness and equality for athletes worldwide; and to ensure harmonized, coordinated and effective anti-doping programs at the international and national levels in terms of detection, deterrence and prevention of doping. The Code seeks to accomplish all three objectives by providing a single set of requirements to replace the national variations and by thwarting subjectivity in applying sanctions. Sports bodies generally were required to adopt the Code by the time of the 2004 Olympic Games in Athens but could make modifications to some of its provisions.

The Code is one of three elements in the strategic Program of WADA. The two other elements are international standards and models of best practice. The Code's standards are implementary so that adherence to them is mandatory for full compliance with the Code. Technical experts can make timely changes to the international standards without amending the Code or specific rules and regulations under it. The models of best practice are the recommended methods for giving effect to the Code and related international standards. WADA provides training assistance in implementing the models, tailored to the needs of each of the major groups of signatories. "Stakeholders," as signatories of the Code are called, may modify the models or develop their own models, subject to review and approval by WADA.

On an annual or more frequent basis WADA is assigned the task of publishing a "prohibited list" of doping and doping-related agents, including masking agents. The signatories have the responsibility of distributing the list to members and constituents. The Code lists three criteria for prohibiting a substance or method: evidence that it has the potential to enhance or does enhance sport performance; evidence that its use has an actual or potential health risk to the athlete; and a determination by WADA that its use would violate the spirit of sport. If a substance or method meets any two of the three criteria, it is included on the prohibited list. The health-related criterion is particularly instrumental. Of course, the criteria are ambiguous, requiring interpretation, but they are just that—criteria, not detailed rules.[59] WADA's use of this scheme involves not just the sanctioning process but additional WADA programs. One example is a blood test

---

[58] Sokolove, *supra* note 12, at 48.

[59] *Id.*

funded by WADA to detect hemoglobin-based oxygen carriers (HBOCs) such as erythropoietin (EPO) that raise the level of oxygen in the blood, thus enhancing stamina. The two criteria of performance-enhancement and violation of the spirit of sport qualify EPO for inclusion on the list.

Anti-doping rule violations include the presence of a prohibited substance or its metabolites or markers in an athlete's bodily specimen; use or attempted use of a prohibited substance or prohibited method; a refusal or other unjustified failure to provide a sample of body fluid after notification as authorized in applicable anti-doping rules or otherwise evading sample collection; a failure to provide required whereabouts information and missed tests in connection with out-of-competition testing; tampering, or attempting to tamper, with any part of doping control; possession of prohibited substances and methods; trafficking in any prohibited substance or method; and administration or attempted administration of a prohibited substance or method to any athlete by assisting, encouraging, aiding, abetting, covering up or otherwise being in complicity with that athlete in violation of the Code.

All athletes who are candidates for national Olympic teams are subject to random, out-of-competition testing. This includes selected professional players in such leagues as the NBA, the NFL, MLB and the NHL, for example. Exemptions from use of prohibited agents for therapeutic purposes are subject to WADA review and approval. Without such an exemption, any person alleged to have used a listed agent may be subject to prescribed sanctions by a sports body or federation. During the sanction process each tested athlete is entitled to a timely hearing in front of a fair and impartial hearing body. He or she has the right to be represented by counsel, at his own expense; the right to be fairly and timely informed of the asserted anti-doping violation; the right to respond to the asserted violation and resulting consequences; the right to present evidence and call and question witnesses; the right to an interpreter at the hearing; and a timely, reasoned decision in writing.

WADA must carry the burden of establishing that an anti-doping rule has been violated. The standard of proof is whether a violation has been established to the "comfortable satisfaction of the hearing body bearing in mind the seriousness of the allegation which is made." This standard is higher than a mere balance of probability but lower than proof beyond a reasonable doubt.

A violation of the Code during competition disqualifies an athlete, compels retraction of any medals already won during the competition, and subjects them to additional consequences.[60] A first-time violation of a prohibited substance or

[60] "An anti-doping rule violation in connection with an in-competition test automatically leads to disqualification of the individual result obtained in that competition with all resulting consequences, including forfeiture of any medals, points, and prizes." World Anti-Doping Agency, World Anti-Doping Code, art. 9.

prohibited method regulation results in two years' ineligibility. A second violation results in lifetime ineligibility. A showing of no fault or negligence may alter the sanction imposed, however. When more than one member of a team has been notified of a possible anti-doping rule violation, the team is subject to target testing for the event. If more than one member of the team is found to have violated an anti-doping rule, the team may be subject to disqualification.

The Code includes provisions for appealing decisions, at both the international and national levels. Action commenced against an athlete or person must be brought within eight years of the alleged violation.

On October 16, 2003, the UNESCO General Conference in Paris voted to create an international convention against doping in sport.[61] This convention is intended to serve as a means for governments to accept and employ the regulations set forth in the WADA Code. Whether the emerging regime for controlling the use of performance-enhancing agents and methods will work, particularly in view of advances in genetic therapy, remains to be seen. What is clear is the necessity of international cooperation among sports organizations and governments.

B. VIOLENCE

1. Spectator Violence

Spectator violence has been an unfortunate by-product of the mob sociology that may well up before, during and after major international competition. When conflict erupts, typically, the sports competition itself is not the underlying cause in any true sense and governments are not the instigators. For example, in 2001 several violent post-game outbreaks in Tehran erupted during a two-week period as an expression of frustration by spectators with the political and religious establishment in Iran. At least one of these disturbances occurred during a celebration, namely, of the Iranian national team's playoff victory over the national team of the United Arab Ermirates.[62] An infamous tragedy at a Brussels soccer stadium in 1985, caused by visiting English fans, demonstrated that even if violence takes place *during* competition, the latter may be only incidental. Even so, a rash of bloody hooliganism during soccer games throughout the year-and-a-half preceding the 1985 incident, and even after it, evidenced an unfortunate link between sports and violence.[63]

---

[61] World Anti-Doping Agency, Press Release, *WADA Praises UNESCO Decision for International Convention Against Doping in Sport* (Oct. 17, 2003).

[62] Fathi, *Soccer Melees Keep Erupting in Iran, With a Political Message*, N.Y. TIMES, Oct. 26, 2001, at A7.

[63] Scores of spectators were killed and several hundred were injured during the brawl in Brussels, which was instigated by English fans at a match—the Cup of Champions—between teams from Turin, Italy, and Liverpool, England. N.Y. TIMES, May 30, 1985, at 1, col. 1. *See also* (1) a report on the riot after a soccer match between Hong Kong and China, CHRISTIAN SCI. MONITOR, May 22, 1985, at 10, col. 1; (2) reports in a single week of two separate melees after

When such violence erupts in the sports arena, international cooperation may be required to avoid greater conflict. European and international sports organizations responded to the 1985 violence in the Brussels soccer stadium by imposing a temporary, worldwide ban on participation by English teams in international competition. Thus, athletes initially paid for the sins of the spectators.

The Brussels tragedy quickly led to a European treaty to cooperate in measures to prevent and respond to violence related to sports.[64] The European Convention on Spectator Violence relies on regional cooperation in transferring proceedings to countries of residence of apprehended persons, extraditing persons suspected of violence or other criminal activity at sports events, and transferring convicted persons to "the relevant country." Other provisions in the treaty provide for enforcement of security measures at stadia; consultations in advance of potentially troublesome matches; control of ticket sales and (non) availability of alcoholic beverages; and information sharing, particularly among police. The

---

soccer matches, INT'L HERALD TRIB., Mar. 15, 1985, at 17, col. 16 (rioting among English spectators); *id.*, Mar 22, 1985, at 19, col. 7 (attack by Italian spectators on visiting Germans after an international match in Rome).

The year-and-a-half period preceding the 1985 crisis in Brussels witnessed no fewer than seven serious acts of violence related to soccer. The incidents, mostly provoked by English spectators, were as follows:

1984

Feb. 18—British fans caused nearly $1 million damage in and around the Parc de Princes Stadium in Paris after a non-league international game in which France beat England, 2-0.

May 8—A fan of the English club team, Tottenham Hotspur, was shot dead and 200 of the team's supporters arrested in a rampage through the streets of Brussels before and after a match against Anderlecht.

Sept. 30—A man who waved the opposing team's flag was fatally stabbed in Milan, Italy.

1985

March 15—Twenty-three people were injured and 10 arrested during fights after a domestic English League game at Chelsea, West London.

March 15—Forty-seven people were injured in fights at a match at Luton, 25 miles north of London, started by fans of the visiting Millwall team.

May 10—At least ten foreigners and police officers were injured in riots in Beijing after China was eliminated from the World Cup competition by Hong Kong.

May 27—Eight people were killed and more than 50 injured in a stampede of fans trying to get into a Mexico City stadium for a championship game.

Also, 53 spectators were killed on May 11 when a fire, possibly set by an arsonist, engulfed the main stand during a soccer match in Bradford, England. N.Y. TIMES, May 30, 1985, at 6, col. 1. For an account of continuing British soccer violence in 1986 and the foreign reaction to it, *see* 128 TIME, Aug. 25, 1986, at 15.

64 EUROPEAN CONVENTION ON SPECTATOR VIOLENCE AND MISBEHAVIOUR AT SPORTS EVENTS AND IN PARTICULAR AT FOOTBALL MATCHES, ETS 120, *reproduced in* 24 I.L.M. 1566 (1985). For key provisions of the Convention, *see* Ch. 10 *infra* n. 8

Convention also establishes a standing committee to monitor the implementation of the Convention and related issues such as racism, racial intolerance and xenophobia in sports.

Two years after the treaty entered into force, in 1987, the British House of Lords granted extradition of 26 English soccer fans to stand trial in Belgium for their alleged incitement of the Brussels tragedy.[65] The willingness of the British to extradite their own nationals was a measure of the significance to sovereigns of international sports competition.

Spectator violence remains a serious problem despite the European Convention on Spectator Violence and other efforts to improve national and international legal controls. Although events have overtaken the observation that the post-Cold War era began "with less violence than we have come to fear from a single soccer game,"[66] hooliganism in the stadium continues. The European Convention on Spectator Violence provides one model of judicial cooperation and extradition, but it has its limitations. It applies only to international competitions, it is regional, and even in the European region it has failed to deter bloodshed in the bleachers, often instigated by British soccer fans.[67] Rule 2(7) of The Olympic Charter requires the IOC, and by delegation, the IFs, to dedicate efforts to ensuring that "violence is banned," but no universal implementing mechanism exists.

2. Player Violence

Violence on the playing field or hockey rink, even in international competition, is normally regulated by domestic criminal and tort law, which lies outside the scope of this book. Administrative sanctions against violent conduct, involving fines and suspensions, are often criticized for their leniency, but have nevertheless generated a cottage industry of arbitration, as the Sprewell controversy attests.[68] Arbitration within the IFs or before the CAS is possible but not likely in professional sports because of the exclusive role of other arbitral bodies stipulated in collective bargaining agreements. When the underlying conduct at issue has

---

65 On the extradition decisions, *see* INT'L HERALD TRIB., July 14, 1987, at 2, col. 7.

66 Bundy, *From Cold War Toward Trusting Peace*, 69 FOR. AFF. 198 (1990).

67 *See* Blackshaw, *The Ugly Side of the Beautiful Game*, 2002 INT'L SPORTS L.J., No. 3 at 28; Haberman, *English Fans Tangle With Police Before Game*, N.Y. TIMES, June 17, 1990, at 27; MacLeod, *British Government to Pass New Laws to Clean up Soccer*, CHRISTIAN SCI. MONITOR, Feb. 1, 1990, at 5; Hazleton, *British Soccer: The Deadly Game*, N.Y. TIMES MAGAZINE, May 7, 1989, at 40; Baum, *British Soccer: On the Line*, CHRISTIAN SCI. MONITOR, Apr. 19, 1989, at 4.

68 In the violence-prone National Hockey League (NHL), for example, Todd Bertuzzi of the Vancouver (Canada) Canucks brutally attacked Steve Moore of the Colorado (U.S.) Avalanche, breaking the latter's neck. The sanction imposed against Bertuzzi—suspension from the remaining weeks of the NHL season and from any championship playoffs—was criticized for its leniency. *See* Bossy, *N.H.L. Was Too Tolerant of Bertuzzi's Brutal Act*, N.Y. Times, Mar. 2004, at SP9, and accompanying commentary and letters to the editor. On the *Sprewell* controversy, *see* Ch. 4, *supra*, text accompanying notes 162–64.

occurred off the playing field, the abiding principle at stake is the public image and reputation of sport and the status of athletes as role models.[69]

3. Terrorism and Security

The "Black September" action at the Munich Games in 1972 was an attempt to further the objectives of militant Palestinians, particularly to gain diplomatic recognition, by staging a stunning propaganda coup at a major sporting event. Arab terrorists sneaked into the Olympic village at night and seized nine Israeli hostages, killing two others. The terrorists demanded the release of 200 Palestinian prisoners held in Israeli jails. After a rescue attempt by West German police failed, all nine Israelis and five terrorists died in a shoot-out.[70] The sports arena was never the same again. At the Montreal Games four years later, extraordinary security precautions were taken to prevent a recurrence of similar terrorist attacks. Soldiers and police officers outnumbered athletes; more than 16,000 troops were mobilized in Canada's largest military operation since World War II.[71] Subsequently, security precautions have been elaborate at virtually all major world competitions. Even then, incidents continue to occur. For example, at the 1996 Olympic Games in Atlanta, an explosion at the central Olympic Park, which killed one person, tarnished the image of that competition.

In the face of global terrorism, extraordinary measures must be taken to protect the international sports arena. The 2002 Winter Games in Salt Lake City featured "an unprecedented security operation that transformed the area into a veritable fishbowl,"[72] surveilled by a complex digital video system. The price tag rose to about $800 million for security at the 2004 Olympic Games in Athens, with a security force of about 20,000 personnel, including 16,000 soldiers and other standby NATO troops. This figure was almost four times that for security at the 2000 Games in Sydney ($210 million).[73]

C. COMMERCIALIZATION

Organized athletic activity is big business. The sports arena has become commodified. Victorious skiers flash prominently displayed trademarks on their equipment before television cameras. Medal winners receive prizes from their NOCs. Cities compete to host high-stakes competition, commercial enterprises vie for exclusive rights to use the Olympic emblem in advertising or otherwise in

---

69 *But see* Gibeaut, *When Pros Turn Cons*, AM. BAR ASS'N J., July 2000, at 38, 41, 108 (questioning the significance of image, reputation and role modeling).

70 D. SCHAAP, AN ILLUSTRATED HISTORY OF THE OLYMPICS 356 (1976).

71 Shirley, *Olympic Village is an Armed Camp*, L.A. TIMES, July 14, 1976, § 3, at 1, col. 2.

72 *Watching You*, NAT'L GEOGRAPHIC, Nov. 2003, at 23.

73 STATESMAN-JOURNAL (Salem, Or.), Nov. 30, 2003, at 10B; Shipley, *Greece Playing It Safe With Olympics*, WASH. POST, Jan. 14, 2003, at 1.

marketing their products, and media networks bid in astronomical figures for the right to cover major competitions. The coming of age of the media is reflected in the figures paid for exclusive broadcasting rights, which are about U.S. $2.5 billion for the 2006 and 2008 Winter and Summer Olympic Games.

A comparison of dollar figures in just a little over a half century between the 1932 and 1984 Games, both in Los Angeles, illustrates this trend. In 1932 a ticket to the opening ceremonies cost U.S. $3 and a season ticket $22; in 1984, the prices were, respectively, $200 and $1,008. Ticket-sale revenue in 1932 was $1.5 million; in 1984, $90 million. Even taking account of depression-era deflation and subsequent inflation, the contrast between 1932 and 1984 figures is dramatic. The contrast between figures for 1932 and the 21st century are even more dramatic.

The IOC, IFs, NOCs, OCOGs and other sports bodies have come to rely on revenues from business interests. For example, over U.S. $1 billion or 60 percent of the operating budget for the 2004 Games in Athens came from the sale of broadcast rights and world-wide corporate sponsorships.[74] Many observers therefore contend that commercial considerations dominate the organization and conduct of international sport. Although the Games themselves are theoretically "non-commercial" and the IOC prohibits venue advertising, sponsorships of athletes now play a substantial role in sports. The IOC has therefore developed extensive rules, bye-laws and programs to contain the surrounding commercialism. The IOC's recognition of the inevitability and benefits of commercialization, however, has important implications for the development of international sports law.

These developments are on the whole beneficial to the development of sports, but commercialization of the sports arena also creates new problems. In particular, the role of sports bodies, federations and leagues in the financial management of athletes raises significant legal issues. These issues relate to sponsorship of athletes, labor contracts, agreements with anti-trust implications, broadcasting contracts, and intellectual property rights. In particular, the dominance of broadcasting interests and commercial sponsorship has generated controversy and disputes.

It is important to understand, of course, that most of these issues lie outside the process of international sports law. Ordinarily, they are the province of national or regional, especially European, regulation. Thus, for example, protection of sport-related trademarks, labor contracts, broadcast ventures, and agreements among sports associations are all subject primarily to normal regulatory legislation.

Even though issues of commercialization primarily fall within the domain of domestic legislation, a few issues are specific to the sports arena. Within the

---

[74] *Available at* http://www.olympic.org/uk/organisation/facts/future/index_uk.asp.

Olympic Movement the process of international sports law has had to address four sets of issues in particular: funding of international competition, sports development and licensing of related intellectual property rights, ambush marketing, and the impact of commercialization on athletes.

1. Olympic Funding and Licensing

Licensing and merchandising within the burgeoning sports industry raise complicated issues of national law that largely lie beyond the process of international sports law. Grants of trademark rights and other provisions in commercial agreements may, however, convey applicable rules of the Olympic Charter and other international authority. Also, drafting of international licensing and merchandising agreements requires careful attention to choice of forum, choice of law, and other aspects of private international law.[75]

The IOC has been deeply involved in licensing and merchandising as a source of revenue. The stakes are enormous. Historically, however, the IOC was hostile to commercialization of sports, lest it taint the purity of "amateurism" or corrupt the integrity of athletes, coaches, and officials. Today, of course, sports competition is thoroughly commercialized. It is not surprising, therefore, that in recent years the IOC has devoted more and more attention to raising funds to support an ambitious agenda of sports development around the world. Consequently, the IOC has become a leader, along with major sports leagues, in a trend toward commercializing sports. Its marketing programs (the percentages refer to total IOC revenue, 2001–2004) include television broadcast partnerships (50 percent), corporate sponsorships (40 percent), ticketing (8 percent), and licensing (2 percent).[76]

The Olympic Charter provides that "[t]he IOC may accept gifts and bequests and seek all other resources enabling it to fulfil its tasks. It collects revenues from the exploitation of rights, including television rights, as well as from the celebration of the Olympic Games."[77] The huge sources of revenue on which the

---

[75] *See* Blackshaw, *Sports Licensing and Merchandising—The Legal and Practical Aspects*, 2002 INT'L SPORTS L.J., No. 1, at 22.

[76] *Available at* http://www.olympic.org/uk/organisation/facts/revenue/index-uk.asp.

[77] OLYMPIC CHARTER, Rule 28. *See* broadcast revenue data in Chapter I. For radio or television rights, the IOC grants the rights to a company or network to broadcast the Games only for its national territory or region. The price of exclusive rights to televise the Olympic Games within a single country or region has risen dramatically. Recently, for example, the National Broadcasting Company (NBC) successfully bid a record $1.27 billion for exclusive rights in the United States to broadcast the 2000 Summer Olympics in Sydney and the 2002 Winter Games in Salt Lake City. According to IOC rules, this fee will be divided by the IOC, the national Olympic committees and the local organizing committees. Richard Sandomir, *For $1.27 Billion, NBC Accomplishes An Olympic Sweep*, N.Y. TIMES, Aug. 8, 1995, at A-1. *See also Broadcast Olympics: Lillehammer Success*, OLYMPIC REV., Dec. 1994, at 587; *Sports Eurovision*, OLYMPIC REV., Sept. 1994, at 354. On Eurosport, *see* Stephen Townley, *Some Current International Issues on Rights to Sporting Events and Trademarks*, SPORTS LAW., July/Aug. 1994, at 6.

Olympic Movement depends include broadcasting contracts and The Olympic Partners Program (TOP) of multinational commercial sponsorships.[78] In the waning years of its first century, the IOC launched an initiative called the New Sources of Finance Commission, whose purpose was "to increase Olympic marketing revenues and balance the resources of the Olympic Movement so that it is not entirely dependent on television rights."[79]

The basis for TOP is the IOC's control over the licensing of its extraordinarily valuable intellectual property rights. The Olympic Charter provides, quite simply, that "[a]ll rights to the Olympic symbol, the Olympic flag, the Olympic motto, and the Olympic anthem belong exclusively to the IOC."[80] An elaborate set of Bye-laws sets forth in detail descriptions of the Olympic attributes, the terms for their approved use within the Olympic Movement, direct and delegated licensing authority, the general terms of licensing agreements, and the formulas for derivative revenue-sharing among organizations within the Olympic Movement.

Accordingly, for use of the Olympic emblems, the IOC must approve any contract between a commercial organization and an OGOC or an NOC outside the OCOG territory. If approved, the commercial organization is required to respect both the terms of the contract and the Olympic spirit in its promotions. In return for the rights which it grants an OCOG or NOC, the IOC is entitled to claim a portion of the resulting revenue. The IOC distributes royalties by allocating portions of the money to the Olympic Solidarity Program of sports development, the OCOG, IFs and NOCs.

Until 1985 business enterprises needed to negotiate for exclusive licensing not only with the IOC but with each NOC and OCOG in whose territory the enterprise wished to have an exclusive franchise to use any Olympic emblem. Only then could an enterprise properly use an emblem in advertising or other marketing. For the most part, marketing was therefore geographical rather than global; it was piecemeal. It became apparent that this process was extremely time-consuming and inefficient. Quite likely, the requirement of local approval in each market deterred potential commercial sponsorship of the Olympic Games and thereby eliminated potential sources of revenue.

In response to this problem, the IOC established its TOP program in 1985.[81] The IOC's presumption was that, within specified product and service categories, major sponsors would be willing to contribute more generously to the Olympic

---

78 *See generally, Working toward greater independence*, OLYMPIC REV., Jan.–Feb. 1994, at 36.

79 *See* D. Echard, *104th Session: Work Accomplished*, OLYMPIC REV., Aug.–Sept. 1995, at 7, 9.

80 OLYMPIC CHARTER, Rule 17 (2003).

81 OLYMPIC REV., July 1985, at 384; *id.*, Feb. 1986, at 84–86; *id.*, Nov.–Dec. 1986, at 663–64.

Movement in return for exclusive, worldwide rights. The service-product categories include, for example, automobiles, soft drinks, computers, sports equipment, and chronometers. This marketing effort, which was ambitiously called The Olympic Programme and later renamed The Olympic Partner Program, is a major success, involving nearly all the NOCs. The IOC manages and negotiates corporate sponsorship commitments, each of which extends through an entire Olympiad of four years. Contracting sponsors contribute substantial fees, 92 percent of which are then transferred by the IOC to the OCOG, the IFs, the NOCs, and, through the NOCs, to individual athletes to pay their expenses to participate in designated competition. Provisions for payments to individual athletes were designed to deter them from seeking compensation elsewhere, whether above or below the table, and also to assist athletes from developing countries.

The Bye-laws to Rule 17 provide that an NOC is entitled to half of all net income from exploitation by the IOC of licensing agreements within the territory of the NOC, less taxes and related-out-of-pocket costs. Also, an NOC's participation in the Games entitles it to a slice of the pie. NOCs receive a substantial percentage of the total revenue, which is divided between a fixed dividend plus another fixed amount, to be administered by each participating NOC, for each participating athlete. Before TOP, the majority of NOCs did not have marketing programs or even the capacity to obtain revenue from major sponsors, often because the NOCs are of developing countries with only limited capacity to generate consumer purchases or hard currency to pay for a sponsor's product or service. These NOCs benefit greatly from their share in the revenue from the global marketing scheme. OCOGs, which also share in TOP revenue, benefit particularly from not having to negotiate separate agreements with each business in order to gain revenue from the use of the Olympic emblems in their territory.

Finally, in preparation for major competition, the Bye-laws to Rule 17 of the Olympic Charter require that the NOC and the local OCOG must approve all commercial use of Olympic emblems within their territory. Rule 17 also prioritizes IOC approval above any protection that national law might otherwise provide for use of the Olympic symbol. IOC approval, in practice, has been contingent on a determination that the Olympic Movement would not be seriously damaged thereby.

The NOC's commercial interest in preserving its Olympic rights is apparent in a line of judicial decisions.[82] In *San Francisco Arts & Athletics, Inc. v. USOC*

---

[82] *See, e.g.*, the decision of United States courts in San Francisco Arts & Athletics, Inc. v. USOC & IOC, 483 U.S. 522 (1987); USOC v. Intelicense, 737 F.2d 263 (1984); Int'l Sports Mktg, Inc., v. IOC & USOC, No. 83–44 (D. Vt. 1983); USOC v. Union Sport Apparel, 220 U.S.P.Q. 526 (E.D. Va. 1983); USOC v. Int'l Fed. of Body Builders, 219 U.S.P.Q. 353 (D.D.C. 1982); USOC v. David Shoe Co., Inc., No. C-1-82-596 (S.D. Ohio 1982); Stop the Olympic Prison v. USOC, 489 F. Supp. 1112, 1120 (S.D.N.Y. 1980).

& IOC,[83] the United States Supreme Court enjoined an organization from applying the name "Olympic" in sports competition without the consent of the United States Olympic Committee (USOC). In another of the cases, *USOC v. Intelicense*,[84] the court enjoined a Swiss corporation from marketing the five-ring Olympic emblem in the United States without the USOC's consent, after the IOC had required the corporation to obtain that consent. The court interpreted the Amateur Sports Act to provide the USOC with remedies under the Trademark Act.[85] A fundamental policy consideration in support of the injunction was the importance of marketing revenue to the USOC, which, unlike other NOCs, no longer receives direct governmental contributions. It must rely to some extent, instead, on royalties from intellectual property rights in order to carry out its responsibility of financing the participation of United States athletes in the Olympic Movement. The court noted that the United States, in view of the Act, had "cast the lone dissenting vote against a treaty that was to give the IOC worldwide control over the use of the Olympic symbol."[86]

On the other hand, in *Stop the Olympic Prison v. USOC*,[87] a federal district court upheld the use of Olympic designations as part of a protest against the conversion of the Winter Olympic facilities in Lake Placid. The court reasoned that the use of the Olympic designation was neither commercial nor apt to be interpreted as an endorsement by the Olympic Movement of the protest.

Issues involving intellectual property rights and other commercial interests are becoming highly visible as sports competition relies increasingly on revenue generated by valuable Olympic symbols and other attributes. Although many of the issues, unlike those in *Intelicense*, are not technically in the sphere of international law, they clearly bear on persons affected by developments in the international system.

2. Ambush Marketing

Ambush marketing, also known as parallel or parasite marketing, refers to advertising that enables an advertiser to associate itself with activity for whose sponsorship it has paid no fees. The advertiser's parasitic objective is to project an appearance of official sponsorship without any commercial entitlement to that status.[88] Of course, piracy of symbols, emblems and other trademarks identified

---

[83] San Francisco Arts & Athletics, Inc. v. USOC & IOC, 483 U.S. 522 (1987).

[84] USOC v. Intelicense, 737 F.2d 263 (1984).

[85] 15 U.S.C. §§ 1116–1118. *See generally* Comment, *Guarding the Olympic Gold: Protecting the Marketability of Olympic Trademarks through Section 110 of the Amateur Sports Act of 1978*, 16 Sw. U.L. Rev. 461 (1987).

[86] *USOC v. Intelicense, supra* note 84, 737 F.2d at 268.

[87] *Stop the Olympic Prison, supra* note 82, 489 F. Supp. 1111 (S.D.N.Y. 1980).

[88] *See generaly*, Davis, *Ambushing the Olympic Games*, 3 Vill. Sports & Ent. L.J. 423

with the sports event would illegally infringe intellectual property rights. Ambush marketing, however, is not ordinarily illegal insofar as it does not involve trademark piracy. For example, a billboard or broadcast advertisement might feature an athlete hoisting a beverage against the apparent background of an otherwise fee-sponsored event.

As host to the 1996 Olympic Games in Atlanta, the 2002 Winter Olympic Games in Salt Lake City and other international competition, the USOC has been active in designing measures to combat ambush marketing. Under the Amateur Sports Act, which vests the USOC with exclusive rights to control the use of Olympic marks, symbols, and technology within United States territory, the USOC has organized licensing authority that extends to the problem of ambush marketing.[89] In preparation for the 1996 Games in Atlanta, for example, the USOC created Atlanta Centennial Olympic Properties (ACOP) as the licensing arm of the Atlanta Committee for the Olympic Games (ACOG). Three incidents exemplify their work to combat ambush marketing related to the 1996 Games.[90]

When the United States Postal Service (USPS) announced plans to license Olympic-themed stamps to merchandisers, the ACOG and USOC sent a cease-and-desist letter to the USPS. After denying any infringement, the USPS nevertheless agreed to grant the Olympic authority exclusive licensing rights to the stamps' designs.

Another incident involved marketing of athletic shoes. Although Reebok was an official sponsor of the 1996 Olympic Games, Adidas aired a television commercial linking the latter's shoes with the Olympics. The advertisement included images of past Olympic Games and implied an association between Adidas and Olympic events. The USOC, accusing Adidas of misleading customers, threatened a lawsuit. Adidas responded by terminating its campaign.

In the third incident Eastman Kodak Company also faced an ambush marketing problem when Fuji undermined its sponsorship with plans to display photos honoring Olympic track and field athletes. Despite the confusion that such an exhibit might create, however, the ACOG and USOC took no action to prevent Fuji from usurping Kodak's rights as an official corporate sponsor.

(1996); McKelvey, *Atlanta '96: Olympic Countdown to Ambush Armageddon?*, Seton Hall J. Sports L. 397 (1994); Wall, *The Game Behind the Games*, 12 Marq. Sports L. Rev. 557 (2002).

89 Nish, *How Far Have We Come? A Look at the Olympic and Amateur Sports Act of 1998, The United States Olympic Committee, and the Winter Olympic Games of 2002*, 13 Seton Hall J. Sports L. 53, 56 (2003).

90 *See* Batcha, *Who are the Real Competitors in the Olympic Games? Dual Olympic Battles: Trademark Infringement and Ambush Marketing Harm Corporate Sponsors—Violations Against the USOC and its Corporate Sponsors*, 8 Seton Hall J. Sports L. 229, 232 (1998).

In preparation for the Winter Games of 2002, the USOC again took precautions to combat ambush marketing, this time in cooperation with the Salt Lake Organizing Committee (SLOC) by forming the Olympic Properties of the United States (OPUS). OPUS, a limited liability corporation, was granted a right to license Olympic and Paralympic symbols, marks and images to sponsors, suppliers, and financers of the games. In one of several incidents related to the 2002 Winter Games,[91] the Nabisco Company advertised its products in several sport publications. Conflict arose when PowerBar, Inc., an official Olympic sponsor, protested Nabisco's advertisements of Fig Newton cookies, which depicted an ancient Olympic athlete throwing a discus. The caption read as follows: "The ancient Olympians worshiped the fig and used it for energy during training." Another marketing ploy boasted that Nabisco's Fig Newton was the Official Energy Food of USA Cycling.[92] After the USOC sued Nabisco, the two parties reached a confidential agreement that terminated Nabisco's advertising campaign.

USOC and SLOC efforts to combat ambush marketing also included the purchase of billboard space in Salt Lake City for resale to official sponsors. Despite such efforts, ambush marketing nevertheless was highly visible in Salt Lake City. For example, although Nike was not an official sponsor of the 2002 Winter Games, the equipment of hockey players was marked by the identifiable Nike swoosh. Similarly, the NBC network announcers wore Columbia Sportswear when broadcasting even though it was not an official sponsor.

The 2002 World Cup in football was beset with ambush marketing incidents.[93] The IF for football (soccer), FIFA, relies for revenue on exclusive sponsorships. Coca Cola was one of the sponsors of the World Cup. A television commercial by its non-sponsoring competition, PepsiCo, featured leading football (soccer) players playing against a World Cup backdrop featuring a cohort of sumo wrestlers. Also, Nike, another non-sponsor, ran an advertisement in 30 countries featuring leading soccer players decked out in Nike shoes. Chase De Vere Investments PLC, a unit of the Bank of Ireland, offered "World Cup" mortgages with rates tied for two years to English victories in the competition. Even the government of a host state got into the act when the Korean state tobacco monopoly produced ten million packages of "World Cup" cigarettes.

National legislation specifically addressed to the problem of ambush marketing is typically inspired by a need to protect local sponsors of major international competition. Australian legislation applicable to the 2000 Olympic Games in Sydney transferred ownership of Olympic words and related images to the Australian Olympic Committee (AOC). On that basis, the Sydney Organizing

---

[91] *See* Nish, *supra* note 89, at 67, 70.

[92] United States Olympic Comm. v. Nabisco, Inc., No. 3-00-3086 (N.D. Cal. Aug. 25, 2000).

[93] *See generally* INT'L HERALD TRIB., June 1–2, 2002, at 9.

Committee for the Olympic Games (SOCOG) pushed for stronger legislation designed to extend the Olympic Insignia Protection Act of 1987 (OIPA) so as to protect Olympic Symbols against ambush marketing.[94] The subsequently enacted Sydney 2000 Games Protection Act 1996 provided a balance between marketing rights and protection of Olympic symbols, but problems of ambush marketing nevertheless arose during the 2000 Games. In response, Australia amended its OIPA in 2001. In an effort to combat ambush marketing, players have since been prohibited from displaying advertising logos on their uniforms in the matches, at press conferences, or during travel.

In 2003, Australia confronted ambush marketing as host to the Rugby World Cup. Special efforts were made to assure Rugby World Cup, Ltd. (RWC), which controls the securing of sponsors on behalf of the International Rugby Board (IRB), and its sponsors that unauthorized advertisers would not be allowed to infringe the sponsor's trademark rights.[95]

The South African parliament amended its trade practices legislation to respond to the anticipated problem of ambush marketing.[96] The resulting law prohibits commercial statements that suggest or imply a contractual or other connection with a sponsored sports events or a person sponsoring an event. The parliament also amended merchandise marks legislation specifically to prohibit infringement of intellectual property rights in connection with (before, during and after) officially protected events. Sanctions for violation of either law include stiff fines and imprisonment of offenders.

Similarly, in preparation for the 2008 Olympic Games in Beijing, The Peoples Republic of China promulgated anti-ambush marketing regulations that are integrated with special protections for Olympic-related intellectual property rights. The regulations include civil and criminal penalties.[97]

It is apparent, then, that laws are beginning to address the highly visible phenomenon of ambush marketing. Despite the efforts to combat the ability of non-official sponsors to profit from the Olympic Games and other international sporting events, however, clever marketers find ways around applicable legislation. Without broad reassurance to sponsors of sports events that the billions of dollars they have invested will secure sole advertising privileges, international sporting competition could face a decline in financial support. Combating ambush marketing is therefore essential to the future of international competition.

---

94 *See* Misener, *Safeguarding the Olympic Insignia: Protecting the Commercial Integrity of the Canadian Olympic Association*, 13 J. LEGAL ASPECTS OF SPORT 79, 87, 88 (2003).

95 Lloyd & Howarth, *Sponsorship Scrum*, BUS. REV. WKLY., July 17, 2003.

96 *See* Cornelius, *Marketing in Sport*, 2003/1 INT'L SPORTS L.J. 38.

97 *See* Blackshaw, *Beijing Introduces "Ambush Marketing" Law for 2008 Olympics*, 2003/1 INT'L SPORTS L.J. 29.

3. Impact of Commercialization on Athletes

Greatly enhanced financial opportunities for athletes, from support of their training and competition to compensation for their use of commercial clothing and equipment and player endorsements have accrued not only to the benefit of individual athletes but to the quality of competition. Even athletes who in the past would have been rigidly defined as "amateur" now have substantial leverage in gaining corporate sponsorships and endorsements. It is important to keep in mind, however, that virtually all athletes with aspirations to compete in major international competition should be made aware of the constraints on commercial practices that are imposed by IFs and national associations or governing bodies. In some measure those constraints bind even "professional" athletes, whose contracts are otherwise subject to labor, anti-trust and other national regulation. Sponsorship contracts are therefore a critical aspect of the daily lives of marketable athletes.

Despite the advantages of commercialization to many athletes, its impact raises important issues. Athletes complain about being the pawns in the commodification of the sports arena.[98] For example, the dominance of the broadcast media in the sports arena has been somewhat of a mixed blessing for the athletes. On one hand, the heightened public exposure improves their visibility and enables them thereby to gain additional financial support from commercial advertising on their clothing and equipment. On the other hand, athletes and their sports associations may lose control over scheduling of events. For example, athletes challenge decisions by executives of their national governing bodies and IFs to enter into broadcasting contracts that require a rescheduling of events to the detriment of the athletes. The United States Figure Skating Association, for example, has struggled to reconcile its need for broadcasting revenue with the interests of individual skaters.[99]

Sometimes commercialization forces athletes to make significant choices between competition and income. For example, Belgian tennis star Kim Clijsters withdrew from participation in the 2004 Olympic Games because her exclusive contract to wear FILA clothing precluded her from complying with a requirement by the Belgian Olympic Committee to wear Adidas apparel exclusively.[100]

---

98 For a post-modern interpretation of the Olympic Games, *see* Segrave, *The (Neo) Modern Olympic Games*, 35 INT'L REV. SOC. SPORT 268 (2000).

99 Telephone interview with Jonathan Fishbein, sports law consultant (Mar. 30, 1995). On other problems related to the relationship between the United States Figure Skating Association, the International Skating Union and the Amateur Sports, *see* Fishbein, *When Sovereigns Collide: Why America's Figure Skating Competitions are the Ultimate Losers Under the Amateur Sports Act of 1978*, 9 CARDOZO ARTS & ENT. L.J. 231 (1990).

100 *See* STATESMAN-JOURNAL (Salem, Or.), Dec. 2, 2003, at 1B.

The expanded financial support of athletes has magnified problems of taxation. Athletes are mobile. Teams are multinational Competition is transient. The size of a winner's purse is often substantial. These considerations pose complex and important questions such as whether an athlete can be taxed by the governments both of his citizenship or nationality and of the source of his income or prize.[101]

National laws vary widely. As one example, the Internal Revenue Code of the United States (IRC) governs all citizens and residents of the United States for tax purposes, as well as others earning income within United States territory.[102] Specifically, citizen and resident athletes are subject to (1) income tax on United States income; (2) income tax on all foreign-source income; (3) tax on shares in a foreign corporation on their pro-rata shares of the corporation's earnings if the corporation is either a foreign personal holding company or a controlled foreign corporation; (4) income tax on all capital gains derived from both United States and foreign sources; (5) gift tax on all gifts of United States or foreign property; (6) tax on transfers of appreciated securities or property to a foreign company; and (7) tax upon death of estates based on all property owned whether it is located in the United States or anywhere else in the world.

United States citizens and resident aliens are subject to tax on their worldwide income according to a general, graduated tax rate scheme. Income which is effectively connected with a United States trade or business is taxed, after allowable deductions, at the graduated rates applicable to United States citizens and resident aliens. An athlete's federal taxable income would be calculated by taking the athlete's gross income and subtracting allowable deductions. Income from United States sources which is not effectively connected with a trade or business in the United States is taxed without an allowance for deductions at a flat rate unless that rate is reduced by a tax treaty.

Many taxable athletes have income from both within and outside the United States. The IRC provides that compensation for labor or personal services, including athletic activity, that is performed in the United States is to be treated as income from sources within the United States. Compensation for labor or personal services performed outside the United States, on the other hand, is to be treated as income from a source outside the United States.

---

[101] *See generally* International Bureau of Fiscal Documentation, THE INTERNATIONAL GUIDE TO THE TAXATION OF SPORTSMEN AND SPORTSWOMEN (R. Betten ed., 2002–03).

[102] *See* Adams, *Why come to training camp out of shape when you can work out in the off-season and lower your taxes: the taxation of professional athletes?*, 10 IND. INT'L & COMP. L. REV.79 (1999); Baker, *Tax Considerations for Australian Athletes Joining Professional Teams in the United States*, 6 VILL. SPORTS & ENT. L.J. 1 (1999); Berry, *Taxation of U.S. Athletes Playing in Foreign Countries*, 13 MARQ. SPORTS L. REV. 1 (2002).

This brief summary of just one national system of taxation bespeaks the need for international agreements to allocate transnational income and avoid double taxation. Although older double taxation treaties often did not address the issue, modern treaties often specify relief for athletes and entertainers.[103] Some of these treaties provide a per diem or per annum ceiling on income exempt from taxation, while others establish both a ceiling and a limit on the period of time an athlete may be present in the country without being subject to normal income taxation.

Whenever income generated by an athlete's activities accrues to the benefit of others, the more recent treaty models allow taxation of that income in the jurisdiction where the athlete performs services. The treaties thereby seek to discourage tax avoidance by the use of corporations. These anti-abuse provisions confirm state practice. For example, in *Johansson v. U.S.*, a United States court refused to allow the Swedish boxer Ingemar Johansson to use a Swiss corporation to avoid federal taxation of the purse he had received in his heavyweight fight against Floyd Patterson on United States territory.[104]

---

[103] For a discussion of the treaty background, *see* Zagaris, *Personal Service Income, in* American Law Institute—American Bar Association (ALI-ABA), INCOME TAX TREATIES: COURSE OF STUDY MATERIALS 105, 130–34 (1982). *See also* Dobray, *A Survey of Legal Issues Facing the Foreign Athlete*, 4 ENT. & SPORTS L.J. 1, 16 (1987).

[104] Johansson v. U.S., 336 F.2d 809 (5th Cir. 1964).

CHAPTER 8
HISTORY OF ORGANIZED INTERNATIONAL SPORTS COMPETITION

Organized sports competition dates back at least to the ancient Egyptians. As early as 1829 B.C. the Lugnasad and the later Tailteann Games hosted Irish track-and-field events. Organized international competition has its most direct roots, however, in the Panhellenic Games of ancient Greece. Although these Games were not truly international in the modern sense, they did bring together athletes from several city-states, and later, from elsewhere in the Roman Empire. The ancient Olympic Games, in particular, were based on religious traditions and flourished for over a millennium in a relatively stable political environment jarred by periodic conflict.[1] By contrast, the modern Games have relied not on religious principles but on a secular belief in such Olympic ideals as universality and fraternity, and have taken place over little more than a century in the volatile political environment of two world wars, a depression, a cold war, and nearly constant civil wars and regional conflicts. Despite these differences between the ancient and modern Games, a brief history of "international" sports competition discloses a continuity of issues.

A. THE ANCIENT GAMES

Before the first Panhellenic Games, religious festivals had been held in the Greek city-states in honor of fertility gods. In Homeric times these festivals, which may or may not have included athletic competition, came to provide a popular forum for worship, burial, and political rites. By the end of the sixth century B.C., festivals in honor of the dead included four regularly scheduled athletic competitions that together constituted a cycle (*periodos*) of events: the Olympic, Nemean, Pythian, and Isthmian Games. The four Panhellenic festivals, as the

[1] For details on the ancient Games, upon which this chapter relies, *see* two classical commentaries: PAUSANIAS, DESCRIPTION OF GREECE (J.G. Frazer trans., 1913), particularly *id.*, vol. III, Book Fifth at 465–652 and vol. IV, Book Sixth, at 1–114; THUCYDIDES, THE PELOPONNESIAN WAR, *passim* (S. Lattimore trans., 1998). Modern commentaries include L. DREES, OLYMPIA: GODS, ARTISTS AND ATHLETES (1968); M. FINLEY & H. PLEKETT, THE OLYMPIC GAMES: THE FIRST THOUSAND YEARS (1976); N. GARDINER, GREEK ATHLETIC SPORTS AND FESTIVALS (1910); H. HARRIS, GREEK ATHLETES AND ATHLETICS (1964); and V. OLIVOVÁ, SPORTS AND GAMES IN THE ANCIENT WORLD 111 *et seq.* (1984) (also provides information about earlier and concurrent competition elsewhere in the ancient world). Two very readable introductions are Kyle, *Winning at Olympia*, ARCHAEOLOGY, July/Aug. 1996, at 26, and Casson, *The way things were at the first Olympics*, SMITHSONIAN, June 1984, at 64. A good summary of the ancient and modern Olympic Games may also be found at 25 ENC. BRIT. 197 (1990).

most important athletic competitions, attracted the best athletes from throughout the Greek territories. Although ancient Greek sports competition is often identified exclusively with these four festivals, other competition—private, local and municipal contests—formed the foundation of the athletic culture in numerous cities of the ancient world.[2]

The Olympiad, honoring the winner of the one-stadium foot race at Olympia, was a single-venue cycle that served as a basis for reckoning time throughout much of the classical world. During the first 50 Olympiads (200 years) participants traveled to Olympia from 12 or more Greek cities. In the next three centuries, some 100 city-states participated, and by the last 100 years, under Roman domination, athletes came from as far as Antioch, Alexandria, and Sidon. Generally, however, women, slaves, foreigners, and dishonored persons were not allowed to compete in the ancient Games nor, except for the priestesses of Demeter and unmarried minor women, even to attend them. Under the laws of Elis, which hosted the Olympic Games, adult women other than the priestesses of Demeter could be put to death for even entering the Olympic venue. Greek women did, however, have their own quadrennial festival in honor of Hera, which continued for centuries until the Roman conquest of Greece.[3]

Although scholars debate the precise origin of the Olympic Games, it is clear that some local cult activities were held in Olympia, a site on the Alpheios River controlled by the Eleans. More precisely, these activities took place at the Altis, which was a beautiful grove of trees sacred to the Olympian cult and interspersed with its monuments. The first recorded, regularly scheduled Olympic Games were held on this site in 776 B.C. King Iphitus of Elis is often credited with transforming traditional funeral rites in honor of several deities and the legendary hero, Pelops, into a quadrennial festival in honor of Zeus.

The Olympic Games in the first century or two were rudimentary, involving mostly foot races. The Games held in 776 B.C. involved only one athletic event, a 200-meter *stade* or foot race. Coroebus of Elis, a cook, won the event. The development of other events was slow; during the first 15 Olympiads additional foot races alone were added. Other events, such as the pentathlon, wrestling, boxing, stallion races, chariot racing, and the ever-popular free-for-all called the pankration were added over the next ten Olympiads. There were, however, no water, ball, winter, or team events. Until 472 B.C. all events took place on a single day; after that, the duration of the Games expanded to five days.

1. The Political Role of the Olympic Games

The quadrennial Olympic festival was seen as a way to promote goodwill and unity among the disparate city-states of ancient Greece. Rivalries among the city

---

[2] *See* W. DURANT, THE LIFE OF GREECE 211 (1939).

[3] Scanlon, *Games for Girls*, ARCHAEOLOGY, July/Aug. 1996, at 32.

states promoted participation and intensified competition.[4] Indeed, although religion may have failed to unify Greece, "athletics—periodically—succeeded [as an] ecumenical assemblage of varied Greeks sharing a common culture."[5] To the same purpose, the several Panhellenic festivals included not only athletics but "Greek" poetry and music in various mixes.

In order to accomplish the ecumenical purpose of the Games, Elis entered into a compact with Pisa and Sparta. This compact, called the *ekecheiria* or Sacred Truce, provided that for at least three months before, during, and after the Games, all hostilities were suspended among the city-states whose athletes were invited to compete in the Games. *Spondophorai*, or nobles from Elis, traveled among the city-states to proclaim each approaching *ekecheiria*. The rules of the Games required that all competitors and their escorts arrive and remain in Olympia one month beforehand in order to train under the supervision of the Elean judges. As time went on, the duration of the Truce expanded to accommodate athletes having to travel from distance colonies. During the Truce no one was permitted to bear arms, legal disputes were suspended, and all competitors, emissaries and spectators traveling to Olympia for the Games were to be brought under the protection of Zeus. Any violation of the Truce was punishable by heavy fines to be paid into the treasury of the Olympian Zeus. Sparta, for example, received a huge fine, and its athletes were disqualified from competition for violating the Truce.[6]

Thucydides and Pausanias both emphasize the important role of the Truce in bringing disputing, sometimes warring parties together to negotiate with each other, enter into political agreements, and even form alliances. The ancient Games thereby may have provided the first politically neutral ground in western history, and the Eleans may have been among the first established purveyors of good offices for settling disputes. The Olympic ideal of honor was particularly instrumental in generating trust among the city-state representatives (*amphictyonies*) and promoting alliances among them.[7] The agreements, often based on mutual

---

[4] Kyle, *supra* note 1, at 28.

[5] DURANT, *supra* note 2, at 211.

[6] THUCYDIDES, *supra* note 1, at 279, 280.

[7] For example, Thucydides wrote as follows:

> Since the Lacedaemonians told the Mytilenean envoys sent out on the first ship to be at Olympia so that the rest of the allies as well could hear them and decide, they came to Olympia . . . and when they were brought forward to speak after the festival they said the following:
>
> > "We know, Lacedaemonians and allies, the convention prevailing among the Hellenes: when men revolt in wartime and desert their previous alliance, those who receive them view them favorably to the extent that they are of service but think less of them for being traitors to their former friends. And this assessment is not unjust, as long as those who revolt and those they defect from are alike in their policies and loyalties and evenly matched in preparation and strength, and no rea-

oaths, were inscribed in stone or bronze pillars set up at the sites of the Olympic and other Panhellenic Games.[8]

The agreements worked out in the Panhellenic, particularly Olympic, venues inspired on-going mediation and arbitration of disputes. The Council at Delphi, for example, became a sort of early multi-door dispute resolution center. Several scholars have argued that the religious basis of the Olympic Games was critical to its success. The extent of religious influence is controversial, but religion certainly played a role in bringing the city-states together for Olympic Games under the banner of Zeus, the universally accepted ruler of the gods. Since the Peloponnese was dominated by worshipers of Zeus, the dedication of the Olympic Games to that god strengthened their significance.

Although the religious significance of the Games eventually all but disappeared, the early Games became a truly cherished forum because of the combined stature of Olympia and its patron state, Elis. The relationship between Olympia and Elis was mutually beneficial. Olympia became a well-governed center of Zeus worship and Elis, because it had to remain politically and militarily neutral, avoided entanglement in conflict among the Greek city-states. Olympia's position of religious prominence enabled Elis to obtain guarantees of nonaggression and military protection of its neutrality from other city-states. Thus, Olympia, as part of Elis, provided a stable environment in which the Games were able to develop and expand. The symbiotic relationship between Olympia and Elis helps explain why the Games enjoyed unusually widespread participation and popularity. In a larger sense, the political relationships among the city-states, the status of the Games not only promoted cooperation and greater unification among them but, as Herodotus notes,[9] an actual basis for formal recognition of its participants, perhaps "the most enduring of Greek institutions."[10]

2. Governance of the Ancient Games

The respect accorded the rules and judging of the Games, including the Sacred Truce, helped elevate the larger festival to a lofty status. In order to main-

---

> sonable excuse for revolt exists. This was not the case with us and the Athenians, and let no one think worse of us if we were honored by them during peace and revolted in dangerous times. Especially since we are requesting an alliance, we will speak first about justice and honor, knowing that friendship between individuals and associations between states can in no way be permanent unless they are formed by those who recognize one another as honorable and have similar principles in general; for through discord in thinking, differences in conduct also come about."

THUCYDIDES, *supra* note 1, at 134–35. *See also, e.g.*, PAUSANIAS, *supra* note 1, at 620.

[8] *Id.* at 264, 266, 278, 279.

[9] HERODOTUS, THE HISTORIES 311 (R. Waterfield trans., 1998).

[10] Kyle, *supra* note 1, at 27.

tain that status in the ancient world, the integrity of governance at the Games was essential. The governance of early Olympic festivals seems to have been shared between the Eleans and the Pisans.[11] While Elis governed the Olympic site, control over the conduct of the Games was vested in a joint council composed of representatives, some of whom came from surrounding communities. This body appointed ten judges, who were usually wealthy financial contributors to the Games. These judges organized, officiated and awarded prizes at the Games. The council was charged with the responsibility of ensuring that the requisite ceremonies were properly performed and that the rules of the game were observed.[12] It also appears that in later years this council was a final court of appeals for disputes arising out of the games. A council house, or *Bouleuterion*, consisted of two Doric buildings between which there was a rectangular court. There, before a statue of Zeus, athletes took an oath to compete honorably during the Games.

The judges were the administrators and officials of the Games.[13] They issued invitations to the Games, determined the eligibility of the athletes, supervised their training, umpired the contests, and heard complaints. To ensure compliance with the rules, the judges possessed considerable powers of enforcement. Wearing purple robes, brandishing whips and followed by whip-carrying servants, they imposed fines and penalties in order to discourage or punish infractions of the Truce and the rules of each contest, as well as such behavior as bribing opponents. Bribes usually were initiated not by gamblers but by competitors anxious to buy off their opponents. In the first recorded case of corruption, a certain Eupolis of Thessaly was convicted of bribing three boxing opponents, and both he and his opponents were fined accordingly. Because the judges were Elean, they provoked persistent suspicion that they were biased toward local athletes.[14]

The judges could fine violators, whip them in public, disqualify them, banish them, or even impose sanctions against the city-state that was directly involved in the infraction or, especially after the Peloponnesian War, the city-state that the athlete represented. A decision by the judges could be appealed to the council. It is unclear whether all decisions could be appealed, or just those involving underlying accusation of referee bias. In any event, appeals were probably rare since Olympia's judges gained a reputation for conscientious and unbiased performance of their duties.

---

[11] GARDINER, *supra* note 1, at 30. This dual control did not prove to be successful as conflict developed between the city-states. Generally, with one interruption, the Eleans controlled Olympia and its Games after the Peloponnesian War (431–404 B.C.). By then, however, the influence of Elis had weakened.

[12] PAUSANIAS, *supra* note 1, vol. IV, at 9.

[13] DREES, *supra* note 1, at 54. Originally there was only one judge, King Iphitus. In later years, the number of judges increased significantly to respond to the increase in the number of events and participants.

[14] *See* PAUSANIAS, *supra* note 1, vol. IV, at 9.

Some of the contests were brutal by modern standards. Athletes were immune from sanctions for unintentional homicide such as strangling a wrestling opponent, but no athlete was allowed willfully to kill his opponent. When this occurred, the judges took action to recompense the violation. In 564 B.C., Arrhichion of Phigalia was competing for his third title in the *pankration* (an event that combined boxing and wrestling) when he died during the bout. His opponent was thereby disqualified and forced to relinquish his olive wreath to the deceased. In a later incident a boxer, having killed his opponent in the Games, was not only disqualified, but also expelled from Olympia, a punishment which disgraced the violator.[15]

A rather sensational penalty was imposed in 420 B.C. when Elis banned Sparta from participating in the Olympic Games because the latter had occupied a fortress and a town in violation of the Sacred Truce.[16] The Spartans were also required to pay a very large fine. Several thousand troops protected the ensuing Games because of fears that the Spartans might retaliate by invading sacred Olympia itself.

Revenue from the fines imposed on athletes and city-states was used to build statutes dedicated to Zeus. Called *zanes*, these were placed near the entrance to the stadium to remind athletes of the oaths they had taken. The first six *zanes* were financed by fines that had been imposed upon the boxer Eupolis and those of his opponents who had accepted bribes from him. Later, the city of Athens was asked to pay for six more statues but requested relief from that burden. When the Eleans denied this request and the Athenians refused to pay, they were expelled from the Games. They finally agreed to pay when the Delphic god, no less, threatened to deny them more oracles.

At first there were few infringements. Recorded violations, including bribery, were more frequent as the Games became more secularized and important to the individual competitors and city-states. The secularization of the Games had another consequence. Originally, the imposition of fines, banishment, and other sanctions had been respected by athletes and city-states alike because of the religious significance of the athletic events: The Olympic festival as a whole honored the omnipotent Zeus. The threat of his wrath and the more mundane prospect of banishment from their city-states helped keep the athletes honest. In later years, as the Games became more secular and the religious underpinnings collapsed, participants became less respectful toward the judges and their rules. Individual competitors still adhered to the judges' decisions because of the threat of individual banishment, but the enforcement powers of the council and the judges against city-states decreased. The reduced strength of Zeus worship and a loss of respect for the sanctity of Olympia seem to have undermined the sanctioning process.

---

15 *Id.* at 52.

16 THUCYDIDES, *supra* note 1, at 279–80.

3. Characteristics of the Ancient Games

Because of the religious origins and nature of the Olympic Games and the celebration there of Zeus, the ancient Greeks and their city-states respected them more than other festivals. At least that was true for many Olympiads before the character of the Games changed into a more secular affair. Athletes participated for reasons of both athletic achievement and respect from and for the gods. The concept of sportsmanship was, at best, inchoate. Losers were often jeered. Winning was everything (there was only a first prize). Victors were usually granted only an olive wreath of leaves (*kotinos*) cut from trees in the sacred grove of the Altis.

Why, then, was winning so important? Although there is considerable evidence of compensation of athletes by their native city-states and a degree of professionalism among them, the greatest reward for victory may have been the prestige attached to it. Pausanias tells of the extraordinary success of one family, three generations of which—a man named Diagoras, his two sons, and two grandsons—won Olympic events. When his two sons were victorious on the same day, Diagoras was reminded that there was no greater happiness.[17] Aside from the moral satisfaction, a winner became eligible for a higher status in both his community and (more speculatively) in the realm of Zeus. The performance of an athlete would likely enhance the reputation of his city-state, for the gods were believed to favor the homes of Olympic prowess. Thus, city-states identified closely with athletes and were financially supportive of them. Politics and sports became teammates.

There was, however, a moral cast to the competition. The religious dimension of the Games may help explain why they were originally limited to men of pure Greek descent. The organizers wanted to ensure that all competitors participated with what they regarded to be the same more or less pure and honorable spirit. Eligible athletes were free citizens of the Greek city-states who presumably did not practice a sport for its own sake, but as a means of pursuing physical perfection, military proficiency and, of course, religious homage.

Abiding values were the purity of the athletic ideal of competing according to the rules for a moral victory, the humble submission of the body to the physical environment, and the apotheosis of the human physique.[18] Prestige was a paramount reward although compensation, even professionalism, doubtlessly played

---

[17] PAUSANIAS, *supra* note 1, vol. IV, at 25, 28.

[18] It is said that the vaunted environment of the Games

> gave birth to yet another Greek idea, a whole attitude to life—the attitude of a free man competing with his peers, naked, unfettered by any element foreign to his own body, conforming only to the rules of the game, with the sole aim of winning for himself an olive crown—in other words a purely moral victory—and the praise of his fellow-men.

M. ANDRONICOS, OLYMPIA 12 (1982).

a role in the ancient Games. The prospect of victory in competition inspired young men to train hard under the supervision of coaches in the *gymnasterion*. This practice is the foundation of modern organized sports and the characterization of sports, integrated with music, philosophy and poetry in the Greek tradition, as a cultural phenomenon.

Individual training for the Games, which averaged ten months, preceded a final month of special dieting (mostly cheese) and more organized training in Olympia under the watchful eye of judges. Aspiring athletes did not have to go through trial competition; they simply traveled to the Games on their own and agreed to go through a month of closely supervised on-site final training that might lead to their disqualification from competition. They also had to take an oath that they had faithfully trained for the Games.

Although some athletes were compensated by their native city-states, others had to bear the costs of individual training, travel expenses and lost job time. Thus, time and money requirements, in light of the marginal level of existence for much of the society, encouraged participation originally by the relatively affluent. In later years, when the Games had become increasingly secular, this changed. Victors were often of the lower class, often professionals who traveled among different festivals to compete for a living. This discouraged the traditional, religious-based participation by the elite, thereby eroding an original foundation of the Games. Bribery and other violations began to occur with greater frequency.

4. The Decline and Fall of the Ancient Games

For many Olympiads, the religious significance of Olympia and the neutrality of Elis were the cornerstones of the ancient Games. These factors ensured the necessary sanctity and respect for the Games and provided a strong basis for the enforcement of rules to govern the contests and agreements among the city-states. These cornerstones began to crumble as the cult of Zeus weakened and as secularization and commercialization of the Games developed.

The Peloponnesian War, in particular, damaged the Games. During the Golden Age of Pericles in the fifth century B.C., the spell of the Olympia cult had begun to deteriorate. The introduction of alternative religious practices weakened the supreme sanctity of Olympia and Elis. With the onslaught of the Peloponnesian war, Elis, recognizing its lost position of religious status and authority, abandoned its neutrality and entered the conflict.

This decision led Elis to become embroiled in Greek political and military battles. Sparta retaliated against Elis for its previously hostile attitude, which had led to the exclusion of Sparta from the Games. The Spartans took cattle and slaves and annexed border territory. The Spartan pillage clearly violated the Sacred Truce and seriously weakened the Olympic tradition. In 365 B.C. Elis turned control of Olympia and the Games over to Pisa after losing a war. Although Elis regained control a few years later, it had, for the first time, failed to preserve the sanctity of Olympia and to share control over the Games. From then on, the Games were less stable. Elis was no longer respected as a protector of Zeus, its control over the Games became tenuous, the sanctity of Olympia was tarnished, and enforcing the rules of the Games became more difficult. The Games had become squabbling, secular affairs.

The Roman conquest of Greece further changed the character of the Olympics, making them more truly cosmopolitan and somewhat more professional. The Romans viewed the Games more as public entertainment than as contests for more sublime purposes in the Greek tradition. Generally, though, the Romans appear to have respected Olympia and to have been respected for their handling of the Games. The major exceptions involved the Emperor Sulla's attempt to move the Olympics to Rome and Nero's reported intimidation of opponents and bribing of officials. The English historian Gibbon writes that, in extending the Olympic concept during Roman times, imitation Games were initiated at Antioch's sacred grove of Daphne in a stadium built by a special privilege purchased from Elis and maintained at considerable expense to the local inhabitants.[19]

In 261 A.D. the Games in Olympia were interrupted in the face of a threatened invasion by the Herulians. In 391 A.D. the Christian Emperor Theodosius I banned all pagan cults, including that of Zeus. After what proved to be the last Games in 393 A.D., Theodosius decreed their termination and returned the chryselephantine statue of Zeus to Constantinople.[20] In 426 A.D. the Emperor Theodosius II decreed that the Temple of Zeus be burned to the ground. The religious underpinnings of the ancient Games meant that brief lapses into paganism led to revivals of Olympic competition, but it was never the same. In later years the Olympic temples were pillaged by invaders and eventually ruined by earthquakes and floods. The site of the ancient Games lay buried in sand until it was rediscovered in 1766. In 1829 a French scientific team excavated the site and shipped their finds to the Louvre in Paris.

B. THE PERIOD BETWEEN THE ANCIENT AND MODERN GAMES

Although the history of sport between 393 and 1800 A.D. is thinly documented, it appears that there was little sports competition among participants from different polities—what we might very loosely describe as international competition.[21] In the Middle Ages the organization of sports competition was very

---

[19] E. GIBBON, II THE HISTORY OF THE DECLINE AND FALL OF THE ROMAN EMPIRE 166 (J. Bury ed., 1908).

[20] J. BURY, I HISTORY OF THE LATER ROMAN EMPIRE 370 (Dover ed., 1958).

[21] One expert noted that no international athletic competition occurred between 394 and 1896 that could be compared with the ancient Olympic Games. Telephone interview with John A. Lucas, Nov. 6, 1984 (hereinafter cited as Interview).

limited.[22] Later, in the 14th century, perhaps to make sure they did not survive in England, King Edward III banned all sports competitions because he claimed they interfered with the noble pursuit of archery. Occasionally, regional contests were organized as a part of fairs and festivals, and there were more ambitious competitions such as Robert Dover's "Olympick" Games, held on the Cotswold Hills in Gloucestershire beginning in 1612, a similar festival which appears to have been initiated in 1604 by one Captain R. Stower, and yet another near Cambridge as early as 1620. The program of the latter was reported to include wrestling, leaping, running, bowls, shooting, and bull-baiting. These Games were later terminated by the Puritans, but were revived by Charles II. It appears that "Saxon Olympicks" were held every four or five years during the last 50 years of the 18th century.[23] Neither these Games nor similar efforts elsewhere and at other times appear, however, to have achieved the level of performance nor the prominence of the ancient Games.

During the 18th century sports competition developed between teams from different city-states, duchies, and other sovereign entities in a much-fragmented Europe. The first major transatlantic cricket match, between London and New York teams, took place in 1751. The territorial extension of sport competition began to raise legal issues that required litigation. An 18th-century case from Tuscany is illustrative. During the summer of 1778, the Fabronis, a noble family living in Tuscany, requested their Community Magistrate to prohibit ball games that had been held "since time immemorial"[24] in the public square in front of their house. The Community Magistrate refused to do so.[25] The ball games therefore took place on schedule. In subsequent proceedings,[26] the Fabronis requested dam-

---

22 28 ENC. BRIT. 115 (1990).

23 The English festivals are discussed in Burns, *Robert Dover's Cotswold Olympick Games*, OLYMPIC REV., Apr. 1985, at 231, and Goulstone, *The 'Saxon Olympick Games' in 1738*, OLYMPIC REV., Sept. 1985, at 560 (the 1738 date refers to a proposal of the Games which, however, did not commence until later in the 18th century).

24 Gino Gorla, *A Decision of the* Rota Fiorentina *of 1780 on Liability for Damages Caused by the "Ball Game,"* 49 TULANE L. REV. 346, 349 (1975). Another version of this case appears in Nafziger, *Globalizing Sports Law*, 9 MARQ. SPORTS L.J. 225 (1999).

25 The Community Magistrate was apparently an administrative body that, having denied the Fabronis' request for an injunction against the ball games, had no jurisdiction to address their request for damages. *Id.* at 350. On the same date, the Community Magistrate, acting on the request of the Auditore Fiscale, one of the highest agents of the Grandduke of Tuscany, determined that the ball game, as usual, could be conveniently played only in the public square in front of the Fabronis' house. *Id.* at 350–51. The Fabronis filed no appeal of either decision.

26 Before the commencement of the ball games, the Fabronis had filed a second action in the *Vicario*, the ordinary local court. They requested damages for any injury to their property that might result and a *cautio de damno infecto* (a kind of warranty or suretyship to cover estimated damages). When a private citizen provided a personal suretyship (*cautio*) to the Fabronis, the games proceeded as scheduled without prejudice to later consideration of the claim for damages. *Id.* at 351. After the alleged injury to the Fabronis' property, the Vicario ordered partial payment of damages. Both parties appealed this decision to the Magistrato Supremo in Florence. The Magistrato Supremo commissioned the Rota Florentina to hear the appeals.

ages from the responsible team for injury allegedly caused by stray balls that hit their house during the games.[27] Ultimately, one of the highest courts in Tuscany, the Rota Fiorentina, denied relief to the Fabronis.[28] The court ruled, in effect, that they had come to the nuisance. Because there was nothing new or unusual about the annual ball games, the court found that any harm the Fabronis might have suffered was "merely intrinsic and natural"[29] to the games. The legal rationale for this vindication of sports over torts seems to have been that well-established public amusements create a legal servitude on neighboring property.[30] Today, the Italian Civil Code would probably reach the opposite result and award damages to the Fabronis, on a theory of strict liability.[31]

With the birth of sports organizations in the 18th century—the Jockey Club, for example, was founded in 1750—sports competition became more durable. In the 1800s attempts were made to revive the ancient Olympic Games. Greek independence from Turkey in 1830 prompted suggestions to stage a national sports festival every four years in the town of Pyrgos. Greek sport festivals, called "Olympic Games" were held in 1859, 1870, 1875 and 1888, but were limited to Greeks. In Sweden and Great Britain similar contests were held. In Ramlösa, Sweden, "Olympic Games" held in 1834 and 1836 involved a variety of athletic events.[32] "Olympic Games" were held in Much Wenlock in Shropshire during the early 19th century and elsewhere in England from 1825 to 1885. All these efforts, although they were bold steps toward the modern Olympic Games, were too localized to be considered immediate precursors of the Games. International sports encounters were, indeed, uncommon. They usually involved professionals, such as the exhibitions by an English cricket team in the United States (1859) and Australia (1861), a boxing match between Tom Sayers of England and John Heenan of the United States (1860), and the running exhibition on an English

---

27 Anyone who has witnessed a traditional game of *gioco del pallone*, at issue in the Fabronis' action, or *gioco del calcio*, as played in Florence and Lucca, will appreciate the risk to life and limb, if not the Fabronis' property. The medieval game of *calcio* I attended in 1997 on the Piazza di Santa Croce in Florence was the longest sustained free-for-all I have ever witnessed. Stray balls seemed far less threatening, however, than stray fists, strangleholds and kicks administered by the players.

28 MARRADIENSIS PRAETENSAE REFECTIONIS DAMNORUM, 2 COLLEZIONE COMPLETA DELLE DECISIONI DELL'AUDITORE GIUSEPPI VERNACCINI 279 (1824), *cited in* Gorla, *supra* note 24, at 347 n.5.

29 Gorla, *supra* note 24, at 355.

30 *Id.* at 356.

31 Article 2050 of the Italian Code, which is apparently the most specific provision on point, reads as follows: "*Liability arising from exercise of dangerous activities.* Whoever causes injury to another in the performance of an activity dangerous by its nature or by reason of the instrumentalities employed, is liable for damages, unless he proves that he has taken all suitable measures to avoid the injury." Italian Civil Code 504 (Mario Beltramo, Giovanno Longo & John Henry Merryman trans., 1969).

32 Svahn, *'The Olympic Games' at Ramlösa in 1834 and 1836*, OLYMPIC REV., Oct. 1984, at 753–58.

track by an American Indian named Deerfoot (1860).[33] In 1886 a lacrosse team from the Iroquois nation beat an English team in England, but was promptly outlawed from further international play for having accepted modest reimbursement of travel expenses.[34]

C. BIRTH AND FIRST 40 YEARS OF THE MODERN GAMES

The revival of the Games was due primarily to one individual, Baron Pierre de Coubertin.[35] He believed that physical education and competition among elite amateurs could make a vital contribution to world society, with a ripple effect of promoting global harmony. De Coubertin's *idée fixe* depended on a commitment by states not to intervene in the sports arena. After 1889, when he formulated the modern Games more precisely, he traveled around Europe and the United States to promote the idea and curry the support of influential persons. In 1894 these efforts bore fruit when the Congress of Paris, of which he was the organizer, created the International Olympic Committee (IOC), which is today one of the world's oldest international non-governmental organizations. The IOC was established as a non-profit corporate body with the purpose of encouraging international athletic competition and ensuring a regular celebration of the Olympic Games in different locations.

However controversial de Coubertin's ideas on amateurism and non-intervention in the sports arena by national polities and politics might become, it is an example of the man's genius that he established the ambulatory nature of the Modern Games. Moving the Games every four years would in the long run minimize the burden of travel on any one nationality and maximize the opportunities for spectators and host countries. The first Games of April 1896 were held, appropriately enough, in Athens under the patronage of the King of Greece. Thirteen nations were represented by 300 athletes in ten different sports and 200 different events. The Games grew rapidly in participation, global recognition, and scope of events. Women first competed in international sports competition at the 1900 Games in Paris. Under the tight control of de Coubertin, the IOC established the Olympic Movement as a prominent arena of international cultural relations.

Problems emerged, the first of which involved the autonomy of the Olympic Games. After the initial Games in Athens (1896), the Paris (1900) and St. Louis (1904) Games were staged as side shows of larger expositions. These tended to swallow up the Games, which thereby gave local organizers more control than they had previously enjoyed. Additionally, the cost of European travel to St. Louis for the 1904 Games precluded broad participation. Overall organization was hap-

---

33 2 Enc. Brit. 275 (1974).

34 Alden, *Living Iroquois Confederacy*, 172 Nat'l Geog. 370, 375 (1987).

35 For his memoirs on the establishment of the modern Games, *See* P. de Coubertin, Une Campagne de Vingt-et-un Ans (1887–1908) (1908).

hazard. The unofficial 1906 "Games" in Athens, however, provided a much needed boost to the Olympic Movement. Global support even by the Turks, traditionally hostile to Greek initiatives, as well as expanded press coverage, spread Olympic enthusiasm throughout Europe and confirmed the Olympic revival.

At the London Games in 1908, publicity was ample, but questions about the quality of the officiating arose, and for the first time the policy of allowing the host country to select the judges was questioned. Battles over opening ceremonies, staging of the preliminary heats, officiating in many events, bowing before the king, and a controversial finish in the marathon demonstrated the arrival of the Games in the public conscience and perhaps, inevitably, their exposure and elaboration under the political limelight. Indeed, Britain deliberately used the Olympics to illustrate and publicize a change in its diplomatic orientation and thereby to put itself in a more positive light in the international arena. Another development at the 1908 Games was the entrustment of much of the organization of individual events to sports bodies other than the IOC. The Games were coming of age.

Similarly, the Swedish government used the Stockholm Olympics (1912) to its diplomatic advantage. The policy of "home control" over the Games, as an incentive to host them, still existed, but did not prove to be troublesome even though some had claimed that the policy had resulted in biased judging and unfair advantage to participants from the host country. Instead, the biggest issue related to the definition of an "amateur," as illustrated by the penalties imposed on the American runner Jim Thorpe because he had earlier accepted money for playing baseball.

The incident concerning Thorpe reflected an interesting official response to his acknowledgment that he had received a modest "professional" payment. Having been stripped of his Olympic medals for victories in the decathlon and pentathlon and of his amateur status, he was obliged under the rules to return his medals to the Olympic host, the Swedish Olympic Committee. At first, its head refused to accept Thorpe's medals back, believing the latter's loss of his amateur status was enough. The (U.S.) Amateur Athletic Union (AAU), however, pressured the Swedes reluctantly to accept the medals. In 1983 the President of the IOC posthumously presented substitute medals to Thorpe's surviving children.

The early Olympics experienced growing pains as the new rules began to require durable interpretations. For example, issues of amateurism were addressed frequently, but remained difficult if not intractable to resolve. The issue of possible bias in judging because of the "home rule" that vested the selection of judges in the local committee was addressed by the IOC at its Congress in 1914. The IOC scrapped the "home rule" by assigning jurisdiction for judging and rule making to the international sport federations, where those responsibilities generally remain today.

After a wartime cancellation of the Games in 1916, they were resumed in 1920 in Antwerp, a city devastated by the war. While the postwar conditions there were less than ideal, the Games contributed to a rejuvenation of the Olympic spirit after an eight-year absence, despite an unfortunate exclusion of teams from the Soviet Union and the recently defeated states. The Belgian local organizing committee was at liberty to prepare its own invitation list.

The first Winter Games took place in Chamonix, France, in 1924. The strong showing of the Norwegian Sonja Henie, who emerged as world figure skating champion, encouraged the further participation by women in the Olympics. Few issues of consequence arose in the 1928 and 1932 Olympics, although the organizers again had to wrestle with the definition of an "amateur" and alternative responses to political issues, primarily Japan's invasion and occupation of Manchuria.

The 1936 Games in Berlin were very controversial.[36] From 1920 to 1932 Germany had been trying to reenter the mainstream of international relations. The Locarno Treaties of 1925 and the admission of Germany into the League of Nations in 1926 formally reintroduced the Weimar Republic into world councils, such as they were. German representation in the International Fencing Foundation followed in 1925, and soccer and track-and-field exchanges with France and Great Britain were resumed in 1926. In 1932 the award of the 1936 Games to Berlin helped confirm the Weimar Republic's reentry into the mainstream of international relations. Then Hitler took power, taking Germany far outside the mainstream and bringing the 1936 Games under his shadow, and thereby initiating the use of international sport as mass spectacle to generate propaganda.

The controversy about the Berlin Games was two-fold. First, both before and during the Games strident criticism of Hitler's racial and religious bias prompted the American Jewish Committee and the National Association for the Advancement of Colored People (NAACP) to advocate a boycott of the Games. Initially, the AAU decided to withhold its athletes from the Games unless Germany changed its racial and religious attitudes, but was persuaded by its new president, Avery Brundage, to separate athletics from politics. Second, the Hitler regime unabashedly used the Games for propaganda purposes, to the understandable displeasure of numerous teams and governments, most especially the French Socialists under Léon Blum. Of all the national teams that threatened boycotts, however, the Irish alone declined to participate in Berlin.

The Games were disrupted by World War II in 1940 and 1944. Postwar Games were held in London (1948), Helsinki (1952), Melbourne (1956), Rome (1960), Tokyo (1964), Mexico City (1968), Munich (1972), Montreal (1976), Moscow (1980), Los Angeles (1984), Seoul (1988), Barcelona (1992), Atlanta

---

[36] *See* J. HOLMES, OLYMPIAD 1936 (1971); R.D. MANDELL, THE NAZI OLYMPICS (1971).

(1996), Sydney (2000), and Athens (2004). The Winter Games have convened in Chamonix (1924), St. Moritz (1928), Lake Placid (1932), Garmisch-Partenkirchen (1936), St. Moritz (1948), Oslo (1952), Cortina D'Ampezzo (1956), Squaw Valley (1960), Innsbruck (1964), Grenoble (1968), Sapporo (1972), Innsbruck (1976), Lake Placid (1980), Sarajevo (1984), Calgary (1988), Albertville (1992), Lillehammer (1994), Nagano (1998), and Salt Lake City (2002). In 1986 the IOC decided to convene the Olympic Winter Games half-way through each four-year Olympiad, in four-year cycles, rather than in the same year as the Summer Games.[37] This change became effective after the 1992 Winter Games. Thus, the 17th Winter Games were in 1994, the 18th in 1998, and so on, in the middle of each Olympiad. The change was made primarily for reasons of administrative convenience and efficacy in fund-raising by the National Olympic Committees. Major political issues arising in the Olympiads since 1936, including the Winter Games, are addressed in the chapters that follow.

D. COMPARISONS AND CONTRASTS BETWEEN THE ANCIENT AND MODERN GAMES

The ancient and modern Games have struggled with many of the same kinds of issues: political intervention, individual cheating, limits on professionalism, waves of cynicism, and so on. *Plus ça change, plus c'est la même chose*. Even so, it is instructive to reflect upon some obvious contrasts in order to gain a deeper understanding of the role and future of the Olympic Movement in international relations.

One contrast between the ancient and modern Games was the role, or at least original significance, of religion in the ancient Games before they, too, became secular. The religious dimension generated public appeal and helped secure adherence to the rules and agreements that structured the conduct of the quadrennial sports festival. Other important contrasts between the ancient and modern Games were the commitment in the former to a significant Sacred Truce, the single site for the ancient Games, and the political neutrality and religious dominance of the perpetual host, Elis.

Although a more or less symbolic Truce was established for the modern Games, beginning in 1992, it is of short duration. The Sacred Truce of the ancient Games not only was much longer, but generated rapprochement, armistice agreements, cooperative alliances, and an ongoing process of dispute resolution among the Greek city-states. To this extent, the ancient Games helped shape political events whereas the modern Games have more characteristically been shaped by them. Finally, the range of issues that beset the modern Games, including doping and commercialization, distinguish them from the classical model, although the ancient Games and its participants were far from pure.

---

[37] OLYMPIC REV., Nov.–Dec. 1986, at 651. Rule 2 of the Olympic Charter provides that "the expression 'Games' means the Games of the Olympiad [that is the (Summer) Games] and the expression 'Winter Games' means the Olympic Winter Games."

E. NON-OLYMPIC COMPETITIONS

In addition to the Olympic Games, other regional and transcontinental competition has included the Far East Games (established in 1913 and disbanded in 1934), Central American and Caribbean Games (1926), the Maccabiah (Jewish) Games (1929), the Commonwealth Games (established as the British Empire Games in 1930), the Bolivarian Games (1938), and the following competitions that have all been established since World War II: the Pan-American Games, the Mediterranean Games, the Asian Games, the Pan-Arab Games, the African Games, the South American Games, the World Games of Non-Olympic Sports, the Central African Games, the Islands of the Indian Ocean Games, the Games of Small European Countries, and the Goodwill Games.

CHAPTER 9

NATIONAL POLITICS AND POLICY OPTIONS IN INTERNATIONAL SPORTS

A. INTRODUCTION

The father of the modern Olympic Games, Baron Pierre de Coubertin, envisaged international athletic exchange as the "free trade of the future."[1] No nation would regulate this trade to its political advantage. The Olympic Games, as well as other international sports events, would be undisturbed by political currents. To a remarkable extent, considering the course of 20th century history, these aspirations have been met. Sovereign states and other international actors have conformed their behavior to a general practice of respect for the integrity of the sports world. Nevertheless, sports and politics are linked like Olympic rings.

Simply stated, the international sports arena is also a political arena. The ancient Greeks, Hitler, terrorists, Canadian wheat lobbyists, anti-apartheid forces, United States Presidents Carter and Clinton, Soviet President Chernenko, Chinese President Jiang Zemin, and Cuban President Fidel Castro all have known and sought to take advantage of the link between politics and sports. The status of national cricket matches between two adversaries, India and Pakistan, rises and falls according to political developments.[2] This is nothing new. In Shakespeare's King Henry V, the French Dauphin's insulting gift of tennis balls to the English monarch served as a pretext for war and the game of tennis as a metaphor for war.[3] Governments use sport as an instrument of foreign policy. It might be

---

[1] P. DE COUBERTIN, UNE CAMPAGNE DE VINGT-ET-UN ANS 1887–1908, at 90 (1908). De Coubertin's statement, made during the Sorbonne Conference of November 25, 1892, was met by indifference and misunderstanding. *See* Lucas, *Olympic Genesis: The Sorbonne Conferences of 1892 and 1894*, OLYMPIC REV., Nov.–Dec. 1974, at 607.

[2] *See* Guha, *Batting for the nation*, UNESCO COURIER, Apr. 1999, at 30.

[3] The king's memorable lines are as follows:

We are glad the Dauphin is so pleasant with us.

His present and your pains we thank you for.

When we have matched our rackets to these balls

We will in France, by God's grace, play a set

Shall strike his father's crown into the hazard.

Tell him he hath made a match with such a wrangler

That all the courts of France will be disturbed

thought that sovereigns race and wrestle with each other only metaphorically and not vicariously in the sports arena, but athletes and spectators know better. "Once you have a government, there will be policy, and this policy will cover sport. . . . [P]olitics has never been separated from sport."[4] The sports arena "may well be the world's most visible forum for nationalism."[5] Realistically, therefore, the question is how to manage rather than eliminate sovereign intervention and how to encourage the use of sport as a positive rather than negative force in international relations.

Even when governments are not directly involved, political skirmishes may be highly visible in the sports arena. For example, a television broadcaster's remarks about Team China in the 1996 Summer Olympic Games led to vigorous protests and heated debate.[6]

Governmental intervention in sports raises several issues of particular concern to policy-makers, each of which will be addressed in this chapter: the identification of national political objectives and limitations on political options; the assessment of power to effect results; and the legal constraints, domestic and international. Chapter 10 will examine the nature and efficacy of policy options and international legal constraints in greater detail, and Chapter 11 will focus on political boycotts of competition.

The historical sketch of Olympic competition in Chapter 8 identified the principal political issues in the ancient and modern Games through 1936. In the Berlin Games that year, Germany's strident nationalism and brutal Nazism left an indelible stain on international sports history and introduced the deliberate manipulation of sports competition for ideological and nationalistic purposes. In a much milder form, politics survived the wartime postponement of the quadrennial festival of sport from 1936 until 1948, when the first postwar Games were held in London. During the war, NOCs from the Axis powers, Germany and Japan, were

---

With chaces (King Henry V, 1, ii, 258–268) . . .

And tell the pleasant Prince this mock of his

Hath turned his balls into gunstones. (*Id*., 1, ii, 281–82.)

See Segrave, *The Sports Metaphors in American Cultural Discourse*, 8 CULTURE, SPORT, SOCIETY 48, 49 (2000).

[4] Kidane, *Sport and Politics: Diplomacy of an Olympic Truce*, OLYMPIC REV., Aug.–Sept. 1999, at 48, 49.

[5] Wong, *Olympic Cheer: Put Out More Flags*, N.Y. TIMES, Feb. 10, 2002, § 4, at 4 (referring specifically to the Olympics).

[6] *See* Suping Lu, *Nationalistic Feelings and Sports: The Incident of the Overseas Chinese Protest Against NBC's Coverage of the Centennial Olympic Games*, 8 J. CONTEMP. CHINA 517 (1999); Friedman, *Comment on "Nationalistic Feelings and Sports,"* 8 J. CONTEMP. CHINA 535 (1999); Suping Lu, *A Response to Friedman's Comment*, 8 J. CONTEMP. CHINA 539 (1999); Friedman, *Rejoinder*, 8 J. CONTEMPORARY CHINA 543 (1999).

barred from an active role in the Olympic Movement, as later was the Israeli NOC because of the Palestinian imbroglio. In 1952 the East German NOC declined to participate in the Helsinki Games because of the IOC's refusal to accord formal recognition to East Germany in a diplomatic sense. Several NOCs boycotted the 1956 Games in Melbourne to protest the Soviet invasion of Hungary, the British-French seizure of the Suez Canal, and, as far as China was concerned, the participation by a Taiwanese team in the Games. In 1968 two American sprinters raised their gloved fists to publicize Black Power, and in 1972 organized political expression resulted in the nightmare of terrorism against Israeli athletes at the Munich Games.

From 1964 until 1994, South African teams were barred from competition because of their government's apartheid regime. In 1976, many African teams boycotted the Montreal Games because New Zealand, whose athletes were entered in the Games, had allowed one of its rugby teams to compete the previous year against a South African team. The exclusion of Taiwanese teams at the 1976 Summer and Winter Games and 1980 Winter Games and the multinational boycott of the 1980 Games in Moscow initiated by the Carter Administration further evidence political intrusion into sports. The boycott of the 1984 Olympic Games in Los Angeles by the Soviet Union and its allies acknowledged a well-forged link between politics and sports.

These are front-page matters, but foreign sports policies may be limited to more modest measures, such as financial support of training and athletic exchange programs. The norm for governmental intervention seems to involve a moderate supervision of amateur athletic competition and financial support of nationals engaged in international competition. Financial support may include direct subsidization of promising athletes, prizes for medal winners, provision of training facilities, programs of compensation of athletes during extended periods of training, encouragement of nationals to train and study abroad, support of national sport festivals, and military employment for full-time training of world-class athletes. Examples from the Soviet Union, Cuba and East Germany have been legion in Olympic history, but almost all governments support national athletes in one way or another. For example, most European athletes have received income from private sources free of governmental restraint, while in Canada, under the Fitness and Amateur Sport Act of 1961, the federal government directly remunerates athletes for their expenses in international competition.[7]

Even indirect governmental involvement in sports may have international consequences. Support which complies with pertinent norms and rules within the Olympic framework is entirely acceptable, and may even be encouraged, but international disputes may result. For example, in 1984 the Canadian government

[7] Sack & Kidd, *The Amateur Athlete as Employee*, *in* A. JOHNSON & J. FREY, GOVERNMENT AND SPORT: THE PUBLIC POLICY ISSUES 41, 52 (1985). The authors provide an excellent summary of the Canadian legislation at pages 52–57, *id*.

began a controversial sports betting pool to help finance the 1988 Winter Olympic Games in Calgary. The pool elicited legal action by all ten provinces, United States-based baseball teams, and the Commissioner of Major League Baseball (MLB), which is headquartered in the United States. Canada's provinces claimed that the federally run pool violated a 1979 agreement that gave them control over lottery prizes. The provinces were joined by United States-based baseball teams and the baseball Commissioner who argued that the pool would tarnish the game's image and impair its integrity. Despite these arguments, Canadian courts ruled that the plaintiffs had no standing to challenge the sports betting pool.[8]

There are, roughly speaking, three levels of possible intervention by governments in sports:

> Level I—simple governmental financial assistance, either by direct appropriations, use of revenue from governmental lotteries, or similar means. Such assistance is not only acceptable but encouraged as an international practice;
>
> Level II—indirect or direct governmental authorization, supervision, or control over the administration of sport, widespread practices that in some countries may be conducted directly by a Ministry of Sports and in others, such as the United States, more indirectly under the national sports legislation;
>
> Level III—exploitation of sports in the external affairs of a government by such means as boycotts, sports propaganda, refusal of visas, and covert activities.

To sharpen the focus, this chapter will draw heavily on the United States experience, but the analytical principles apply more generally. United States foreign policy has operated on all three levels of the above paradigm, but, as will be shown, it usually operates only on the first two levels.

1. Sport as an Instrument of Foreign Policy: The United States Example

a. *Traditionally Modest Role*

Until 1978, the United States had virtually no national sports policy,[9] but one could discern a limited pattern of involvement at Levels I and II that included oligopolistic protection from anti-trust laws for professional baseball (but generally not for other sports); simple congressional chartering of the United States

---

[8] CHRISTIAN SCI. MONITOR, Apr. 30, 1984, at 2, col. 4; CHRISTIAN SCI. MONITOR, May 3, 1984, at 2, col. 4.

[9] *See, e.g.*, Lowell, *Federal Administrative Intervention in Amateur Athletics*, 43 GEO. WASH. L. REV. 729 (1975); Weistart, *Athletics*, 38 LAW & CONTEMP. PROB. (1973); Koppett, *Sports and the Law: An Overview*, 18 N.Y.L.F. 815 (1973); Hochberg, *Second and Goal to Go: The Legislative Attack in the 92nd Congress on Sports Broadcasting Practices*, 18 N.Y.L.F. 841 (1973); Samuels, *Legalization of Gambling in Sports Events*, 18 N.Y.L.F. 897 (1973); Carolson, *The Business of Professional Sports: A Reexamination in Progress*, 18 N.Y.L.F. 915 (1973).

Olympic Committee (with indirect transnational implications); congressional authorization of financial support for the 1980 Winter Games in Lake Placid; laws and regulations governing the broadcasting and televising of sports; allocations of military security appropriations for sports in the armed services; support of sports programs within the Peace Corps and domestic action programs; state and local governmental support of physical education and individual athletes; and a limited presidential role. United States Presidents have chaired such advisory groups as the Council on Physical Fitness and the Commission on Olympic Sports, and tossed out a baseball on the opening day of the professional season.

b. *The Growth of Foreign Sports Policy*

The internationalization of domestic sports has contributed to the growth of foreign sports policy. For example, the exemption of professional baseball from United States anti-trust laws has implications in Canada, where two of the major league teams have been located. Federal courts have extraterritorially applied regulatory laws and policy that were established principally for domestic purposes. In *San Francisco Seals, Ltd. v. National Hockey League (NHL)*,[10] a federal court considered the anti-trust implication of the NHL refusal to grant the plaintiff a franchise in Vancouver, British Columbia. The court noted in *dicta* that major league professional hockey extending from a United States-based league to Canada was subject to federal anti-trust laws. The court ruled, however, that the relevant geographical market for professional hockey before live audiences, under Sections 1 and 2 of the Sherman Act, was international—it encompassed the United States and Canada. In that larger market, the territorialism imposed by the NHL did not sufficiently restrain trade or commerce within the language of the Sherman Act.

State or provincial governments have also helped shape foreign sports policy, especially in federal systems such as those of Canada, Australia, Germany, and the United States. Local governments flex their muscles too. For example, in 1976 Colorado voters, apparently for environmental reasons, rescinded an invitation conveyed by the USOC to the City of Denver to host the 1976 Winter Games there. In 1978 Los Angeles voters refused to pledge unreimbursable tax revenue to finance the 1984 Games there.

These examples do not, however, reflect a deliberate use of sport as an instrument of foreign policy. In the United States, a more deliberate, coherent foreign sports policy did emerge, however, in the 1970s. Since then, sports has become a part, though only a minor part, of the complex of United States foreign policy.

---

[10] San Francisco Seals, Ltd. v. National Hockey League (NHL), 379 F. Supp. 966 (C.D. Cal. 1974). A lengthy list of judicial decisions and law review commentary on the application of United States antitrust law to professional sports activity may be found in N.C.A.A. v. Bd. of Regents of Univ. of Ok., 104 S. Ct. 2948, 2961 n. 24 (1984).

The sources of the new attention to sport during the 1970s were a gradually accepted awareness that governmental involvement in sports may help promote the national interest; that political adversaries abroad score points in the sports arena, particularly in the absence of official United States involvement; that the erosion of pure amateurism cherished by Pierre de Coubertin, the father of the modern Olympics, would occur with or without governmental assistance; and that governmental intervention could actually promote and protect basic values of sports competition including the encouragement of amateur athletes.

The more immediate motivations for the initiation of United States foreign sports policy included public disenchantment with the management and quality of participation by the United States team in the 1972 (Munich) Olympic Games and the public's shock of witnessing terrorism there (always an impetus for governmental intervention). The spectacular expansion of media coverage of international athletic competitions brought all the excitement, glory, humanity, administrative bungles, and ultimate horror of the 1972 Games into living rooms. Graphic coverage confirmed the important role of sports in global affairs. The involvement of this country's athletes in global competition, always of interest to the public, became a matter of concern. The terrorist nightmare in Munich prompted the State Department to introduce a Draft Convention for the Prevention and Punishment of Certain Acts of International Terrorism[11] and generated legislative proposals to govern internationally related aspects of amateur athletics. These proposals eventually led to the enactment in 1978 of the Amateur Sports Act. It also became apparent after the Munich Games that responses to political problems in sports could not arise strictly from the private sector.

The early 1970s introduced a foreign policy interest "in furthering mutual understanding and communication through sports."[12] Accordingly, the federal government strengthened its role in sports by committing further resources to facilitate people-to-people communication and public diplomacy conducted by private individuals and groups.[13] A mundane illustration was the production by the United States Information Agency (USIA) of a film entitled "Summer Fever" about little league baseball, and Congressional authorization to Little League Baseball, Inc. for inclusive U.S. distribution of the film. Like other governments, Washington became more involved in supporting technical athletic assistance

---

11 J. Murphy, The United Nations and the Control of International Violence: A Legal and Political Analysis 181 (1982).

12 *See* transcript of the speech delivered by Alan A. Reich, Deputy Assistant Secretary of State for Educational and Cultural Affairs, before the General Assembly of International Sports Federations, in 119 Cong. Rec. 95 (daily ed. June 19, 1973); remarks of Walter Boehm, *in* R. Singer, Multidisciplinary Symposium on Sport and the Means of Furthering Mutual International Understanding (U.S. Dep't of State, Bureau of Educational Cultural Affairs, Dec. 4, 1973) (1974).

13 *See* Reich, *New Role for Associations in Promoting World Understanding*, Ass'n Mgmt., Feb. 1973, at 32.

abroad and in helping procure athletic equipment for programs in developing countries. The federal government recognized that transnational athletic exchange could help improve international relations. Even limited athletic exchange might serve to make foreign policy more "humane."

A study undertaken for the Department of State in 1971 observed that sports had largely been ignored in diplomacy and suggested two policy options that were more ambitious than the existing role of the Department as a mere *facilitator* of international athletic exchange and competition. The study proposed that:

> (1) As an *active promoter* the Department would work to increase the stature of United States participation in international sports programs as a primary means of achieving the objectives of the Fulbright-Hays Act;
> (2) Alternatively, the Department could become a *programmer* of United States participation in international sports, viewing sports as a foreign affairs resource which, when balanced with other such resources, might be important to the achievement of foreign policy objective.[14]

The study recommended that the government's choice of options should be made by balancing the attendant risks and benefits. As to risks, the facilitative role seemed the safest; the promoter role was sightly riskier because it would depend on the vagaries of congressional funding; the programmer role seemed even riskier still, as foreign affairs officials might not know how to employ sports skillfully as a diplomatic tool; moreover, athletes and a sports-minded public might dislike the political implications. As to benefits, the promoter and programmer roles offered greater assurance of effective and more visible participation in international competition; the programmer role would recharacterize the government as a partner rather than a handmaiden of sports activities, and would, therefore, tend to encourage a more positive role for sports and physical fitness in public life. In considering which option to pursue, the study concluded that the Department should first formulate its objectives in the area of sports and then develop a plan for achieving the objectives before very strong feelings, either way, could emerge.

Criteria for judging the efficacy of a foreign sports policy may vary according to the objectives and the intensity of governmental involvement. A government's sports program may combine elements of domestic and foreign policy, and its objectives may change over time. For example, East Germany's pervasive, highly successful, and ultimately drug-ridden program began as an inward-looking effort to implement postwar reconstruction on the basis of Marxism, with its

---

[14] Harris/Ragan Management Corporation, *International Sports Policies for the Department of State: A Presentation of Options* 25 (unpublished, Sept. 24, 1971) [hereinafter cited as *Harris/Ragan Report*].

heavy dose of social welfare ideology. Although two objectives of the program have been simply to promote healthy lives and to enable workers to have fun, East Germany's revised Constitution provided that "the state and society encourage the participation of citizens in . . . physical culture and sport, for the complete expression of the socialist personality." Eventually, this prescription of social engineering became controlling as a fundamental tool to achieve socialism and to assert national prowess abroad, more or less reciprocally. The East Germans acknowledged that "[w]e don't overlook that good results abroad stimulate people back home. Great performances will be seen in connection with the social system."[15] Consequently, East Germany's heavily funded, bureaucratic programs favored precocious starts in the cradle-to-grave firmament of state paternalism.

The United States program, on the other hand, has always been modest. Low-level policies have been concerned with more or less immediate returns on each dollar invested. For example: What works at an educational clinic in a particular country? What doesn't? Should the government send a basketball coach to Mauritania after his visit in Dakar? If the government sees itself merely as a facilitator, the exposure which it receives and the contacts which the activity generates will be critical at Level I of governmental involvement. If, however, the government's role extends to that of a promoter or programmer, other factors may be important: the success of its athletes in competition abroad, the degree to which a foreign country adopts a newly introduced sport, or the accomplishment of some other major objective.

On Level I of governmental intervention—simple governmental financial assistance—the State Department's former Bureau of Educational and Cultural Affairs, which was absorbed into the United States Information Agency in 1978, established three objectives that still shape official programs of athletic exchange: (1) to enlarge the circle of those able to serve as influential interpreters between the United States and other nations; (2) to stimulate institutional development in directions which favorably affect cross-cultural comprehension; and (3) to reduce structural and technical impediments to the exchange of ideas and information. Within this framework, the government has conducted programs of athletic exchange, while often eschewing direct sponsorship.

Troublesome questions emerged as pressures developed during the 1970s for the federal government to expand its role in sports, beyond limited financial support for sports exchanges and the 1980 Winter Games in Lake Placid.[16] For

---

[15] TIMES (London), Apr. 19, 1985, at 29, cols. 1–2.

[16] The Olympic Winter Games Authorization Act of 1976 provided support for the Lake Placid Games. 90 Stat. 1336 (1976). Earlier in the decade, public and professional pressures had been somewhat ambiguous. A 1971 sampling of 44 sports administrators, government administrators, sports commentators, government observers, and sports participants revealed mixed attitudes toward expansions of the government's role in sports including federal financial support for sports and questions about the efficacy of a sports policy; most of those surveyed did,

instance, in the context of events during the 1970s and 1980s, when teams from State X were boycotted by States Y and Z in order to implement human rights, how should the United States government have responded? Should national teams have been discouraged from competing against teams from national states or liberation movements that the government did not recognize? Clearly, rules and principles were necessary to guide decisions effectively. The Kheel Commission, which attempted unsuccessfully in the early 1970s to resolve the internecine dispute between the Amateur Athletic Union and the National Collegiate Athletic Association,[17] urged that the conduct of national sports policies ought to conform to international rules, particularly those of the Olympic Movement.

After years of discussion, Congress committed the country to a comprehensive sports policy and to the supremacy of the Olympic Movement by passing the Amateur Sports Act of 1978.[18] The intensity of United States foreign sports policy peaked at Level III (full governmental intervention) in 1980 when the Carter Administration compelled a boycott of the 1980 (Moscow) Olympic Games. The Reagan Administration and subsequent Administrations have generally maintained a low profile, limiting its actions to Levels I and II. For example, in 1990, during the Administration of President George H.W. Bush, the U.S. Treasury Department denied a specific license that would have permitted the American Broadcasting Company (ABC) to engage in generally unrestricted broadcasting of the 1991 Pan-American Games in Havana.[19]

2. The Amateur Sports Act (An Overview)

The relationships between "nationalism and sports" and "politics and sports," respectively, have often been viewed as disjunctive or antagonistic. Until recently, for example, any acknowledgment of an official United States intervention in sports was shunned. Now, however, there is explicit recognition of the inevitability of athletic Realpolitik and of governmental involvement in sports.

---

however, agree on what they then saw as a need to separate "politics" from sports and to improve the program administered by the Department of State. *Harris/Ragan Report, supra* note 14. This survey was taken prior to the Munich Olympic Games and the demise of plans for the Denver Winter Games. A Harris Sports Survey taken after the Munich Games disclosed a considerable public disenchantment with both the administration and particularly the enforcement of rules, and indicated considerable public support for official protection by the government of U.S. interests in the Games. *Sports Fans Assess '72 Olympics*, *in* THE HARRIS SURVEY (Oct. 5, 1972).

[17] For 75 years the fratricidal feuding between the Amateur Athletic Union (AAU) and the National Collegiate Athletic Association (NCAA) jeopardized both individual athletes and the representation of the United States in international competition. For a succinct history of this dispute, *see* 120 CONG. REC. 58,780 (daily ed. May 21, 1974) (remarks of Senator Pearson). *Cf.* Koch, *A Troubled Cartel: The NCAA*, 38 L. & CONTEMP. PROB. 135 (1973).

[18] 36 U.S.C. §§ 371–396 (Supp. III 1979). *See supra* Appendix I.

[19] *See* Capital Cities/ABC, Inc. v. Brady, 740 F. Supp. 1007 (S.D.N.Y. 1990); Note, *Another Inning in Cuban-United States Relations*, 1 IND. INT'L & COMP. L. REV. 281 (1991).

The Amateur Sports Act largely defines the scope and nature of involvement by the federal government in sports. The Act establishes the United States Olympic Committee (USOC) as a chosen instrument to "promote and support amateur athletic activities involving the United States and foreign nations," and to "establish national goals for amateur athletic activities and encourage the attainment of those goals." Among other provisions, the Act instructs the USOC to "coordinate and develop amateur athletic activity in the United States directly relating to international amateur athletic competition, so as to foster productive working relationships among sport-related organizations." With specific references to the Olympic and Pan-American Games, the Amateur Sports Act expresses a public determination to "obtain for the United States, either directly or by delegation to the appropriate national governing body, the most competent amateur representation possible in each competition and event."

A jurisdictional provision in the Amateur Sports Act is particularly significant in defining options for using sport as an instrument of foreign policy. The provision states that the USOC shall:

> exercise *exclusive jurisdiction*, directly or through constituent members or committees, over (A) all matters pertaining to United States participation in the Olympic Games, the Paralymic Games, and the Pan-American Games, including representation of the United States in the games; and (B) the organization of the Olympic Games, the Paralympic Games, and the Pan-American Games when held in the United States. (36 USC § 220503(3)) (emphasis added).

Although this provision cannot in itself constrain federal action which is otherwise legitimate, it nevertheless does establish an expectation that the decisions of the USOC, within a larger international framework, will alone shape the implementation of foreign sports policy in the Olympic and Pan-American Games.

B. IDENTIFICATION OF OBJECTIVES AND LIMITATIONS ON POLITICAL OPTIONS

Political events have nurtured the growth of foreign sports policy in many countries.[20] Ping-pong diplomacy between the United States and China in the

---

[20] During a formative period in 1974–75, for example, the press frequently reported on international politics in sports. *E.g.*, N.Y. TIMES, Oct. 25, 1974, at 49, col. 4; WASH. POST, Oct. 30, 1974, § F, at 1, col. 8 (refusal of India to participate against South Africa in Davis Cup competition); WASH. POST, Feb. 7, 1975, § A, at 14, col. 1; and 42 SPORTS ILLUS., Feb. 24, 1975, at 18 (refusal of India, contrary to its prior commitment, to allow participation by South Africa and Israel in world table tennis championships held in Calcutta, together with a simultaneous invitation to the Palestinian Liberation Organization). Indian teams in particular appeared to be "guided by the rules and regulations of the State." WASH. POST, Feb. 7, 1975, § A, at 14, cols. 1, 5; WASH. POST, Mar. 20, 1975, § E, at 4, col. 5 (refusal of the Mexican government to grant visas to a South African Davis Cup tennis team to play in Mexico and a directive to Mexicans not to compete with South Africans elsewhere); 42 SPORTS ILLUS., May 12, 1975, at 15 (same,

1970s and "tennis diplomacy" between South Korea and China in 1984[21] were early symbols of rapprochement through sports. High-level security planning for both Summer and Winter Games to combat the terrorist threat that marred the 1972 Games underscored the political vitality of international sports competition. Quite often, sports activity has mitigated international tension, but sometimes it has generated it, as illustrated by the 1969 Soccer War between Honduras and El Salvador and the international tensions following the 1985 soccer riots in Belgium. Sport has also encouraged mutual recognition of governments, for example, between the United States and both East Germany and China. Sport has also encouraged some social and political progress, if only gradually and spasmodically in South Africa and the Middle East. During the Cold War, governments as diametrically different as those of the Soviet Union and the United States supported efforts by their national committees to host major competitions. It is evident that sports competition has various political dimensions.[22]

What should be the objectives of a foreign sports policy? At what level of involvement should it operate? Perhaps a government should look upon sport simply as a diplomatic tool to serve immediate purposes or perhaps it should view sport more ambitiously as a tool to promote world order. If a government acts unilaterally, either perspective may be dim because of the degree of ambiguity, complexity, and ultimate uncertainty inherent in unilateral decisions and policy. A government is therefore ill-advised to "go it alone." Rather, governments are well advised to develop comprehensive and coherent foreign sports policies consistent with international sports law.

Good policy can mean an end to bad politics. What is important is not separating politics from sports, but conforming sports politics with acceptable rules and principles of global order. Optimally, governments should be encouraged to construct policy, not on the basis of bureaucratic interplay, political expediency, ideological constraints and pluralistic pressures, but on the basis of accepted international practice. Foreign sports policy consistent with even a soft body of international sports law seems the best means of protecting individual athletes from political injury and promoting athletic values in global society.

The policy options include seven political uses of international sports competition, to be discussed in Chapter 10: international cooperation, enhancement of human rights, national ideology and propaganda, official prestige, diplomatic

---

with respect to World Championship Tennis Competition in Mexico); WASH. POST, May 7, 1975, § D, at 2, col. 3 (French exclusion of the Rhodesian tennis team). On the politicization of the International Chess Federation, *see* THE OREGONIAN, Mar. 20, 1975, § A, at 10, col. 1 (on rule-changing proposals by the United States Chess Federation: "The voting Wednesday went generally by blocs, with East and West European and Arab federations siding with the Russians, and Asian and Latin American federations lining up with the United States.")

21 CHRISTIAN SCI. MONITOR, Mar. 5, 1984, at 2, col. 4.

22 On the ambitious East German program, *see supra* text accompanying note 15.

recognition and non-recognition, protest, and conflict.[23] Of these, only diplomatic non-recognition and conflict are patently improper uses of sports competition by governments, although variations on the other uses may either be unfriendly or improper.

Within the acceptable margins of discretion, a government's capacity to articulate clear objectives may be critical. The Carter Administration's compulsion of a boycott by the USOC of the Moscow Games[24] was questionable from the start because of unclear, often contradictory policy statements. The Administration variously argued principles of diplomatic protection of its nationals, deterrence and retribution. The President first justified the boycott on the grounds of a presumed danger to United States athletes and spectators,[25] which was the rationale parroted by the Soviet Union to justify its boycott of the 1984 Games. After having advanced this rationale for the compelled boycott, the White House later changed its mind by asserting that the real reason for the boycott was to deter future aggression and to send the Soviets a "signal of world outrage."[26] To add to the confusion, the Secretary of State appeared to disagree by viewing the boycott as retribution for the Soviet violation of what he thought was a principle against contemporaneous involvement by a sovereign host in open warfare.[27] Apparently he had in mind the Sacred Truce of the ancient Games. It became clear that the Carter Administration's rationale for the compelled boycott lacked coherence.

In 1984 the Reagan Administration's quiet handling of the Soviet retaliatory boycott of the Los Angeles Games implicitly acknowledged the futility of distinguishing between the 1980 and 1984 cases. President Reagan observed quite correctly that there was no "prudent" action within his discretion, and pledged to work through "citizens groups and our people" to encourage the Soviet Union and its allies to reverse their decision not to compete in the Los Angeles Games.[28] By responding carefully within the ambit of his authority under the Amateur Sports Act, President Reagan limited the federal government's response to a deference at Level II to the authority of the Olympic Movement. This low-key policy worked to ensure successful sports competition and a favorable image for the United States government outside of sports.

In the United States, foreign policy objectives are limited not only by specific law—in particular, the Amateur Sports Act and international law—but also by the United States Constitution. The federal government could do nothing to

---

23 *See* Ch. 10, *passim.*

24 *See* Ch. 11, text at notes 56–98, *infra.*

25 80 Dep't St. Bull., Jan. 1980, at Special-B.

26 80 Dept. St. Bull., Mar. 1980, at 51.

27 *Id.* at 50.

28 Int'l Herald Trib., May 15, 1984, at 1, col. 1.

override a decision by the people of Colorado not to host the 1976 Winter Games. Similarly, the financial structure of the 1984 Games in Los Angeles was beyond direct federal supervision. In 1978 the citizens of Los Angeles overwhelmingly approved an amendment to the city charter that prohibited the city from spending any tax revenue on the Games that would not be reimbursed by binding, legal contract. This meant that the Los Angeles Olympic Organizing Committee (LAOOC) had to break with Olympic tradition and ostensibly violate the Olympic Charter. It provided, contrary to the LAOOC arrangements, that the NOC—that is, the USOC—"*and the city chosen* shall be jointly and severally responsible for all commitments entered into and shall assume complete financial responsibility for the organization of the Olympic Games." While previous organizing committees had been integrated with the municipal government of the host city, the LAOOC was formed as a private, non-profit corporation under California laws.

Aside from these limitations on policy options, policy failures and embarrassments sometimes result from ineffective implementation. For example, when the Australian government compensated those athletes and sports bodies that had stayed home from the 1980 Games, it did so for the express purpose of financing their involvement in alternative sports events. Later, to the chagrin of the public and the delight of the media, it was determined that Canberra had failed to supervise or at least monitor the use of the payments to ensure that they were not simply being pocketed by the recipients. Hence, to the embarrassment of the policy-makers, the public came to view the compensation payments as a questionable use of tax revenue.[29]

C. ASSESSMENT OF POWER TO EFFECT RESULTS

A foreign sports policy will be unproductive if it is not realistic. Power is a driving force of policy. Thus, the Carter Administration's failure to assess its power to compel a boycott of the 1980 Games by athletes from allied countries led to diplomatic embarrassment and unnecessary harm to individuals. The boycott divided athletes, threatened to destabilize the Olympic Movement, aggravated a global public, worried business with a stake in the Moscow Games, and threatened to isolate the United States from some of its most important allies.[30] "The boycott policy was long on risks and short on assurances."[31]

Although the deficiencies of the 1980 boycott policy were numerous, the "power failure" was prominent. The IOC President emphasized that factor.[32] The

---

[29] SYDNEY MORNING HERALD, Nov. 29, 1983, at 3, col. 5; SYDNEY MORNING HERALD, Nov. 28, 1983, at 4, col. 1–4.

[30] OLYMPISM 377 (J. Segrave & D. Chu eds., 1981).

[31] Goldstein, *The 1980 Olympic Boycott: The Role of National Olympic Committees and of the International Olympic Committee* 86 (May 19, 1981) (Unpublished manuscript).

[32] N.Y. TIMES, July 19, 1980, at A-3; *id.*, July 21, 1980, at C-7. Goldstein, *supra* note 31, at 84, observed as follows:

Administration would have had the power to compel a more widespread boycott if the latter had conformed to international norms, but it did not. The Administration failed to understand that unilateral boycotts, by and large, are of doubtful legality, do not work well, and are almost guaranteed not to work in a geopolitical context. In the words of IOC President Samaranch, "the boycott, even if it may be a useful weapon in certain cases, is particularly negative and counterproductive when attempts are made to apply it to sport and in particular to the Olympic Movement.[33]

Sports boycotts differ very little from economic boycotts, and examples of the futility of boycotts outside the sports arena are legion. They failed against Italy in the 1930s (after that country's occupation of Ethiopia), Rhodesia in the 1960s (after the marshaling of global opinion against the segregationist regime of Ian Smith), and Cuba from 1960 into the 21st century. A major study of economic sanctions, cautioning governments to "look before you leap," offered these sobering conclusions to boycott-inclined government officials during the 1980s:

> The sender government should think through its means and objectives *before* taking a final decision to deploy sanctions. Leaders in the sender country should be confident that their goals are within their grasp, that they can impose sufficient economic pain to command the attention of the target country, that their efforts will not simply prompt offsetting policies by other major powers, and that the sanctions chosen will not impose insupportable costs on their domestic constituents and foreign allies. These conditions will arise on only infrequent occasions, and even then the odds of success are not great. The prudent leader will weigh carefully the costs and benefits of economic sanctions before resorting to their use in foreign policy ventures.[34]

Whether governments are engaged in Level III measures or less ambitious sports programs, they must be well equipped to deal with international sports organizations and other governments if they choose to make sports competition an instrument of national policy. If a foreign sports policy is to work, the imple-

---

> In the final analysis, the policy posed too stern a test for the Western alliance over a noncrucial matter. While sports can certainly be used as a political weapon, the Administration was ill-equipped to employ it effectively as a sanction of the Afghanistan invasion. Participation in Moscow would have been less harmful to U.S. interests than the boycott. . . . The Administration gave very little thought to the Olympics prior to Afghanistan. . . . Possibly, some Administration members were familiar with amateur sports, but only one or two had had personal contact with amateur sports officials. This lack of knowledge caused the government to underestimate the USOC's independence and to overestimate the USOC's status in international amateur sports.

[33] OLYMPIC REV., Nov.–Dec. 1985, at 681.

[34] G. HUFBAUER & J. SCHOTT, ECONOMIC SANCTIONS RECONSIDERED: HISTORY AND CURRENT POLICY 91 (1985). *See also* Newsom, *For all their huff, sanctions don't work*, CHRISTIAN SCI. MONITOR, May 13, 1988, at 14, col. 2.

menting government must have sufficient power and resources, including expertise and supervisory personnel, and must gain acceptance of its policy by pertinent international bodies within the process of international law.

D. LEGAL CONSTRAINTS

Policy decisions affecting international sports competition must also have integrity. Sheer power cannot alone achieve policy objectives. Instead, foreign policy draws strength from an adherence to principles and shared expectations of the global community. In an international legal system driven by comity and reciprocity, a government risks rebuke and isolation if it bases decisions on "whose running-shoes are pinched."[35] Of course, a government's perception of the strength of international norms and institutions may influence its decisions. For example, rightly or wrongly, the Dutch government compelled a boycott of the 1980 Games in Moscow, but shortly afterward drew only passing attention to human rights problems in Uruguay when the issue arose of whether to disallow participation by the Royal Dutch Football Federation in a Uruguayan tournament: "It is not for the Government to say in a case like this: you may not go."[36] Football not having been an Olympic sport, the Minister of Foreign Affairs justified the distinction between the two situations largely on the basis of the strength and transcendental purposes of the Olympics, "unlike a series of football matches."[37] The distinction is questionable.

E. THE *HU NA* CASE: THE PROBLEM IN MINIATURE

An immigration case illustrates well the close relationship between sports, international politics and legal options. Until the defection of Chinese tennis star Hu Na to the United States in 1983, she had been China's top-seeded woman tennis player and its Female Athlete of the Year in 1981.[38] After competing in a tournament in Santa Clara, California during July 1982, Hu Na applied for political asylum. She claimed that she would face persecution on her return to China if she refused to join the Communist Party. After a lengthy review, the Department of Justice granted her request for asylum despite high-level warnings from Beijing that it might respond by suspending bilateral cultural relations. It was therefore no surprise when the Chinese responded to the grant of asylum to Hu Na by temporarily suspending all government-to-government cultural exchange programs and calling the asylum illegal, immoral, and a "grave incident harming the

---

[35] N.Y. TIMES, Jan 8, 1980, § A, at 18, col. 1.

[36] *Netherlands participation in the mini world football championship in Uruguay*, 13 NETH. Y.B. INT'L L. 268 (1982).

[37] Id.

[38] The data on this case are from the following sources: N.Y. TIMES, Apr. 5, 1983, at A1, col. 4; N.Y. TIMES, Apr. 7, 1983, at A4, col. 2; N.Y. TIMES, Apr. 8, 1983, at A1, col. 4; N.Y. TIMES Apr. 10, 1983, at A41, col. 4; N.Y. TIMES, Apr. 10, 1983, at E2, col. 1; CHRISTIAN SCI. MONITOR, Apr. 6, 1983, at 3, col. 1; CHRISTIAN SCI. MONITOR, Apr. 8, 1983, at 3, cols. 1, 3.

relations between the two countries."[39] The Chinese response affected some 19 sports and cultural exchanges and ten distinct programs. Thus, for example, the Julliard String Quartet, Brooklyn Art Museum, and Hollywood studios had to cancel forthcoming activities in China, and the Chinese cancelled art and film exhibitions and participation in some ten sports tournaments scheduled in the United States. The suspension did not affect tourism or student exchange programs. The result of the essentially political processing of Hu Na's petition was a decision neither state (nor Hu Na's parents) wanted. In the candid words of a Chinese observer, "[i]t is unfortunate that the United States and China have botched the Hu Na case."[40]

Hu Na was not the first Chinese national to be granted asylum since normalization of relations between the United States and China. By 1983, the United States government had quietly granted asylum to some ten of 300–400 applicant Chinese, particularly students, most of whom apparently applied from temporary residence in Taiwan or Hong Kong. One applicant was rejected only a few days after the decision to grant asylum to Hu Na.[41]

Even so, the Chinese vigorously fought asylum for Hu Na. Although the reasons are not absolutely clear, it is reported that Deng Xiaoping personally demanded her return when he met Secretary of States Shultz during their February meeting.[42] Hu Na's problem was that she was famous, she had been no less than the doubles partner of Deputy Prime Minister Wan Li, publicity in her case had begun to get out of control, and China wanted to discourage other athletes and artists from seeking asylum abroad. Also, Hu Na apparently evoked concern for her situation by comparing her future to that of Zhuang Zedong, a world champion tennis player who became Sports Minister only to be disgraced in a labor camp when Beijing's leadership changed.[43]

The Justice Department apparently based its decision to grant political asylum on Section 201 of the Refugee Act of 1980[44] that implements Article 1 of the Protocol to the Convention Relating to the Status of Refugees.[45] This definition

---

[39] N.Y. TIMES, Apr. 5, 1983, at A1, col. 4.

[40] Zhao Jinglun, *The Hu Na Case—some lessons to be learned*, CHRISTIAN SCI. MONITOR, May 10, 1983, at 23, col. 1.

[41] N.Y. TIMES, Apr. 10, 1983, at 13, col. 5.

[42] N.Y. TIMES, Apr. 10, 1983, at E2, col. 1.

[43] *Id.* at col. 2.

[44] Refugee Act of 1980, Pub. L. No. 96–212, 94 Stat. 102 (1980).

[45] That provision defines a refugee, essentially, as "any person who owing to well-founded fear of being persecuted for reasons of race, religion, nationality, membership of a particular social group or political opinion, is outside the country of his nationality and is unable or, owing to such fear, is unwilling to avail himself of the protection of that country; or who, not having a nationality and being outside the country of his former habitual residence as a result of such

of a refugee was originally designed to respond to the plight of World War II refugees in Europe, not to present circumstances. In today's world it is a very inadequate means of determining eligibility for asylum. The definition of a "refugee" is so vague that almost any decision, within certain guidelines, is supportable. China evidently objected vigorously on behalf of Hu Na's parents and to save face. The Chinese did not want the stigma of having one of their best athletes become an asylee. The United States government, on the other hand, evidently wanted to gain some publicity in the matter by taking a hard line against the Chinese position.

The Justice Department had better legal options. The government could have returned her, as her parents wanted, without violating refugee law. Better yet, at the time of its decision the Justice Department could have allowed her to remain without offending the Chinese by simply extending her J-1 non-immigrant classification, maintaining her status to that of a non-immigrant or adjusting her status to that of a lawful permanent resident. Ling Jian-wei, a Chinese ballet dancer, had been given permanent residence in the United States, based on his occupation as a dancer. Even though a petitioner for formal refugee status is entitled to have a petition reviewed, the government may reject it but quietly grant another status to entitle the petitioner to remain in the United States. Although a Chinese position on any extension of time under the J-1 category would have been influential, the Justice Department nevertheless could have simply granted her the new status without provoking the tensions it did by granting her asylum as a refugee. Foreign diplomats argued this persuasively.[46]

The lesson is clear: sports relations mirror political relations. Both require adept diplomacy. Just as ping-pong diplomacy signaled a rapprochement between the United States and China, so the suspension of government-to-government sports exchanges in the wake of the Hu Na case signaled troubled relations. In retrospect, the case might have been a tempest in a teapot, but it must be seen in the context at that time of Chinese unhappiness over arms sales to Taiwan, quotas on Chinese textile imports, a United States federal court decision against China on a railway bonds claim, and restrictions on the sale or other transfer of American technology to China.

F. CONCLUSION

Politics is in the international sports arena to stay. It can, however, be effectively regulated. Playing politics at the expense of athletes and competition can turn out to be futile. The Olympic boycotts of the 1970s and 1980s generally did not work and may even have redounded against the boycotters. Governments are

---

events, is unable or, owing to such fear, is unwilling to return to it." Protocol Relating to the Status of Refugees, *done* Jan. 31, 1967, 19 U.S.T. 6223, T.I.A.S. No. 6577, 606 U.N.T.S. 267, art. 1.

[46] N.Y. TIMES, Apr. 8, 1983, at A8, col. 1.

well-advised to tailor their foreign sports policies not to geopolitics but to accepted norms and rules of law, within the Olympic framework of custom. Good policy can mean an end to bad politics. Internationally acceptable policies will help keep athletes and governments running on the same track.

CHAPTER 10
INTERNATIONAL LEGAL REGULATION OF POLITICS IN SPORTS

The games that nation-states play, like those that people play, need rules. National policies need to be regulated or harmonized in what has been described as a "dialectic between the national and international."[1] Within the general framework of international sports law, an evolving body of rules, principles, and practices addresses seven national uses or policy objectives of sports policies: to provoke conflict, to promote international cooperation, to acquire prestige, to enhance human rights, to confirm or manifest diplomatic recognition or nonrecognition of states, to provide propaganda, and to register protest. This chapter, adopting a functional approach to international legal regulation, will discuss each of these national policy objectives and corresponding efforts to regulate or harmonize them.

A. CONFLICT

The sovereign use of sports to provoke conflict is generally illegal.[2] That, however, is seldom a problem. Although sports competition may cause blood to boil and spectators to fight, instances of deliberately provoked international conflict by means of sports are fortunately rare, though sometimes dramatic.

Infrequently, state sponsorship of sports competition may contribute directly or indirectly to domestic conflict. For example, the Mexican government's large

---

[1] *See* Wong, *Olympic Cheer: Put Out More Flags*, N.Y. TIMES, Feb. 10, 2002, § 4, at 4, *quoting* Olympics expert Jeffrey O. Segrave, as follows: "Every couple of years, these sports reflect the dialectic between the national and the international. . . . It's a way of taking stock of ourselves, of what we've made of this planet, which is a sense of increasing global identity on the one hand, and on the other hand you have this sense of national identity." *Id.*

[2] Article 2 of the United Nations Charter provides that:

> (3) All Members shall settle their international disputes by peaceful means in such a manner that international peace and security, and justice, are not endangered.
>
> (4) All Members shall refrain in their international relations from the threat or use of force against the territorial integrity or political independence of any state, or in any other manner inconsistent with the purposes of the United Nations.

UNITED NATIONS CHARTER, June 26, 1945, 59 Stat. 1031, T.S. 993, art. 2, paras. 3 & 4.

expenditures on preparations for the 1968 Games, the first in a developing country, rather than on welfare and other economic programs, helped spark student unrest and rioting just before those Games. Even so, the underlying cause of the disturbances was not so much the government commitment to the sports competition itself, but rather widespread public disenchantment with the authoritarianism of the Diaz Ordaz government of Mexico.[3] The sports competition was only indirectly a cause of conflict.

The "soccer war" between Honduras and El Salvador in 1969[4] was a notorious example of underlying international conflict brought to a dramatic head in the sports arena. Although tension between the two countries had been gathering for some time, the catalyst for violence was a three-game qualifying match in both countries and Mexico for the World Cup finals. Each game was followed by rioting. Fans of the home team attacked players of the visiting team and several people were killed. When the Honduras team won the series, El Salvador protested. Military forces were mobilized, followed by border violations in disputed territorial areas, and an armed conflict was soon underway.

The "Black September" action at the Munich Games in 1972 was an attempt to further Palestinian objectives, particularly to gain diplomatic recognition, by staging a stunning propaganda coup at a major sporting event. Arab terrorists sneaked into the Olympic village at night and seized nine Israeli hostages, killing two others. The terrorists demanded the release of 200 Palestinian prisoners held in Israeli jails. After a rescue attempt by West German police failed, all nine Israelis and five terrorists died in a shoot-out.[5] The sports arena was never the same again. At the Montreal Games four years later, extraordinary security precautions were taken to prevent a recurrence of similar terrorist attacks. Soldiers and police officers outnumbered athletes; more than 16,000 troops were mobilized in Canada's largest military operation since World War II.[6] Subsequently, security precautions have been elaborate at virtually all major world competitions.

Usually when violence occurs in the sports arena, neither the competition itself nor a government is to blame. In order to prevent such violence from festering into international conflict, however, governments need to cooperate with each other. In response to the notorious 1985 brawl in the Brussels football (soccer) stadium and earlier instances of football (soccer)-related hooliganism,[7] the European Convention on Spectator Violence[8] established a cooperative regime,

---

[3] A. RIDING, DISTANT NEIGHBORS: A PORTRAIT OF THE MEXICANS 59 (1985).

[4] N.Y. TIMES, June 29, 1969, § 5, at 15, col. 5; *id.*, June 28, 1969, at 1, col. 1. *See also* N.Y. TIMES, June 30, 1983, at 8, col. 5, for an account of serious conflict stemming from a sports event.

[5] D. SCHAAP, AN ILLUSTRATED HISTORY OF THE OLYMPICS 356 (1976).

[6] Shirley, *Olympic Village is an Armed Camp*, L.A. TIMES, July 14, 1976, § 3, at 1, col. 2.

[7] *See* Ch. 6, *supra* text accompanying notes 63–65.

[8] *European Convention on Spectator Violence and Misbehaviour at Sports Events and in*

premised on the principle of state responsibility under international law, to control such conflict. Beginning in 1987, this agreement has led to international extradition of many persons suspected of violence or other criminal behavior at sports events.[9]

Particular Football Matches, ETS 120, *reproduced in* 24 I.L.M. 1566 n.362 (1985). Several provisions, in particular, underscore this responsibility:

Preamble

> . . . Considering that both public authorities and the independent sports organisations have separate but complementary responsibilities to combat violence and misbehavior by spectators, bearing in mind that the sports organisations also have responsibilities in matters of safety and that more generally they should ensure the orderly conduct of the events they organise; considering moreover that these authorities and organisations should work together for this purpose at all appropriate levels;
>
> Considering that violence is a current social phenomenon with wide repercussions, whose origins lie mainly outside sport, and that sport is often the scene for outbreaks of violence; . . .
>
> Article 3
> *Measures*
>
> 1. The parties undertake to ensure the formulation and implementation of measures designed to prevent and control violence and misbehaviour by spectators, including in particular . . .
>
> a. to secure that adequate public order resources are employed to counter outbreaks of violence and misbehaviour, both within the immediate vicinity of and inside stadia and along the transit routes used by spectators;
>
> b. to facilitate close co-operation and exchange of appropriate information between the police forces of the different localities involved or likely to be involved;
>
> c. to apply or, if need be, to adopt legislation which provides for those found guilty of offences related to violence or misbehaviour by spectators to receive appropriate penalties or, as the case may be, appropriate administrative measures. . .
>
> 4. The parties shall seek to ensure, where necessary by introducing appropriate legislation which contains sanctions for non-compliance or by any other appropriate means, that, where outbreaks of violence and misbehaviour by spectators are to be feared, sports organisations and clubs, together with, where appropriate, stadium owners and public authorities, in accordance with responsibilities defined in domestic law, take practical measures at and within stadia to prevent or control such violence or misbehaviour, including [eight listed measures]. . .
>
> Article 5
> *Identification and Treatment of Offenders*
>
> 1. The Parties, respecting existing legal procedures and the principle of the independence of the judiciary, shall seek to ensure that spectators committing acts of violence or other criminal behaviour are identified and prosecuted in accordance with the due process of the law. . .
>
> *Id.*

[9] *See* Ch.6, *supra* text accompanying note 65.

B. COOPERATION

Cooperation is the antithesis of conflict. International sports law, evidenced by international custom, encourages the sovereign use of sports to open up new relations, to foster international harmony, and to develop national sports programs.

1. Ping-Pong Diplomacy: Opening Up New Relations

A good example of the use of sport to open up new relations was the "ping-pong diplomacy" conducted in the early 1970s between the United States and China, whose relations had been frozen by over 20 years of Cold War. Ping-pong, with its onomatopoeic sound and its symbolism of initiative and response, was an especially appropriate metaphor for the process of rapprochement between the two countries. Similar initiatives involved a tennis match in 1984 between South Korea and China, joint participation by North and South Korean table-tennis players on a single squad in international competition, soccer competition between Albania and the United Kingdom, a baseball competition between Cuban and United States teams.[10] Sometimes such nods at rapprochement have legal consequences. For example, when North Korea agreed to participate in the 2002 Asian Games in South Korea, the host government, as a gesture to its long-lost cousin, agreed to abandon a law prohibiting the flying of the North Korean flag. Sometimes, however, new relations in the sports arena lead nowhere, as with baseball diplomacy between Cuba and the United States.[11]

The story of the ping-pong diplomacy conducted by the United States and China is illuminating. In April 1971, during the 31st World Table Tennis Championships in Nagoya, Japan, the government of the People's Republic of China (PRC) invited the United States table tennis team to visit China immediately following the Nagoya matches. Although similar invitations were extended to teams from the United Kingdom, Canada, Colombia and Nigeria, China's initiative was prompted by a particular desire for better relations with the United States. The United States government appeared ready for the initiative: For example, just three weeks earlier the United States government had validated United States passports for travel to China.

The invitation to play ping-pong was the first officially extended by the PRC to a group of United States citizens. United States table tennis representatives quickly accepted. During the visit media accounts consistently emphasized the warmth of both the reception and the interaction between hosts and guests.[12]

---

[10] Respectively, STATESMAN JOURNAL (Salem, Or.), Feb. 26, 1984, at 4F, col. 2; INT'L HERALD TRIB., Aug. 7, 1986, at 15; CHRISTIAN SCI. MONITOR, Jan. 28, 1988, at 9, col. 1; CHRISTIAN SCI. MONITOR, Mar. 30, 1999, at 9.

[11] For a commentary on Cuban-United States baseball diplomacy and its repercussions, *see* Schneider, *Baseball Diplomacy*, 12 MARQ. SPORTS L. REV. 473 (2001).

[12] *See* 14 PEKING REV., 10–12 (1971); N.Y. TIMES, Apr. 23, 1971, at 7, col. 1 (city ed.).

The Chinese succeeded in generating an immense amount of favorable global opinion in a manner that helped both countries. Later, the United States government officially proposed a reciprocal visit by Chinese players. Broader diplomatic initiatives, including President Nixon's acceptance of an invitation to visit China, the Shanghai Communiqué, and eventual exchange of diplomatic relations followed. Rarely has cultural exchange been employed so effectively as a tool of rapprochement. It was international sports diplomacy at its finest.

The timing and location of the Chinese invitation was propitious. It occurred in the year of China's return to world table tennis competition after a six-year absence during the first half of the Cultural Revolution. At the same time, the United States, apparently committed to a gradual renewal of friendly ties with China, had already begun to explore new avenues of cultural exchange and limited trade. It was also significant that the United States had begun a vigorous military withdrawal from China's backyard in Southeast Asia.

So as to avoid any political embarrassment, the Chinese seem to have taken pains to de-emphasize any political underpinnings of their hospitality, ostensibly inviting the Americans so that each side could learn athletic skills from the other and thereby elevate its standards of performance. This represented a significant change from the stridently political International Table Tennis Tournament that Beijing had hosted as recently as 1966, at the beginning of the Cultural Revolution. There, almost all of the invitees came from countries friendly with China. The Nixon Doctrine in Asia and growing disillusion about the Cultural Revolution encouraged rapprochement. The Chinese wisely selected a posture which stressed the merits of conducting "people's diplomacy." Two incidental aspects of the Chinese approach are noteworthy. First, the hosts chose a sport—not widely followed in the United States—in which any competitive tension would be minimized and the visiting team's national prestige least tied to athletic success. Second, the almost simultaneous withdrawal of the Chinese from the International Lawn Tennis Association to protest the admission of Taiwan as a member indicated that to conduct successful sports diplomacy, the Chinese wished to be free of such externalities as the "two Chinas" controversy.

Ping-pong diplomacy illustrates the continuing interplay of law and politics in sports. The successful use of sports as an instrument of rapprochement seems to follow a sequence of sovereign initiatives: first, to provide an orderly, ritualized, but politically harmless setting for initiating friendly interaction among adversaries; second to prepare for diplomatic contacts by means of interpersonal contacts and public diplomacy; third, to encourage popular approval of forthcoming diplomatic initiatives; and, fourth, to permit the host some assurance of victory without significant loss-of-face to guest nationals.

Diplomacy is often as much of a challenge for international non-governmental organizations such as the IOC as it is for sovereign states. China's ping-pong diplomacy presented a challenge to the skill of IOC decision-makers. At a time when the IOC's one-China policy still favored exclusive recognition of the Taipei government, the IOC responded within its Rules to the challenge of Beijing's initiatives.[13] The IOC thereby moved from a distinctly hostile position toward the PRC to one of gradual inclusiveness.[14] The IOC's leadership engendered a pattern of invitation and response throughout the international sports world.[15]

2. Fostering International Harmony

Although athletic exchanges generate goodwill, the efficacy of sports as an inherent instrument of world order is questionable. Considered globally, the cultural contexts and the athletic activities themselves are apparently too diverse to support extravagant claims of world ordering; international sport simply represents a microcosm of human society. To recall Baron de Coubertin's metaphor, it would seem that trade in sports, like material goods, will neither save the world nor, by itself, threaten world order. Sports exchanges do, however, involve states in the process of harmo-

---

[13] Under the revised OLYMPIC CHARTER, Rule 34 (2003), a "country" is "an independent State recognized by the international community," but this would not seem to square with the admission to membership of NOCs from several entities falling short of statehood and recognition of that status under international law. In practice the term "country" is liberally construed.

[14] *See* Closing Speech of Lord Killanin, 1973 Olympic Congress in Varna, Bulgaria, in OLYMPIC REV., Nov.–Dec. 1973, at 471, 473.

[15] *See, e.g.*, WASH. POST, Feb.15, 1974, § D at 8 (initial exclusion of the People's Republic of China by the International Amateur Athletic Federation (IAAF) from track-and-field participation in the 1974 Asian Games), *but see* discussion below; WASH. POST, June 12, 1974, § D at 6, col. 1 (vote by the International Football Federation (FIFA) against Chinese membership); 41 SPORTS ILLUS., Oct. 21, 1974, at 18 (membership vote by the International Volleyball Federation to replace Taiwanese representation by representation from the PRC). The evolution of the PRC's readmission into the global sports arena is fascinating. In 1958, the PRC withdrew from all international athletic federations. With the exception of a few exhibition tours, principally of its table tennis team, China was isolated from transnational competition until 1974. The 1974 Asian Games provided a major boost to renewed involvement by teams from the PRC in international competition. A good account of the politics involved in the invitation to the PRC appears in Putnam, *A Great Plunge Forward for China*, 41 SPORTS ILLUS., Sept. 16, 1974, at 33:

> [w]hen the Iranians were awarded the Asian Games for 1974, they made it clear that they wanted the People's Republic, not Taiwan, to represent China. By an overwhelming margin, the Asian Games Federation agreed, [by throwing out the Taiwanese and inviting] the mainlanders to replace them. The International Olympic Committee, which has a long history of supporting Chiang Kai-Shek at the expense of all the Chinese athletes who do not live on his island, threatened to withdraw its sanction for the Asian Games. Numerous federations said they would boycott the Games and the generalissimo sulked.
>
> Undaunted by the threats, the Iranians began quiet negotiations with IOC members, who finally agreed to approve the Games if the federations of the various sports would go along with the new China policy. After more negotiations, the federations slowly began unloading Taiwan to make room for the People's Republic. FINA, the federation that controls swimming, diving and water polo, proved the toughest group to crack. The mainland Chinese applied for membership, but stipulated that if Taiwan was not ousted from FINA, the federation could forget their application. By a two-vote margin, the 30 members of FINA's executive committee voted to forget it. Following 11th-hour negotiations

nizing cultural and other differences. The use of sports in this way promotes a spirit and sometimes a lasting pattern of international cooperation.

National sports cultures differ. In some societies, such as the early Christian Roman Empire, Puritan England and Afghanistan during the Taliban era, sports, or at least some sports, have been discouraged altogether. Elsewhere or at other times, individuals have been culturally conditioned to participate actively or passively for a variety of reasons: for aesthetic pleasure related to the beauty of controlled body movement, for dramatic effect, for the sheer excitement of competition, for the thrill of physical exertion, or for the experience of learning. Each national approach may depend on the particular sport, age, gender and other characteristics of the participants; the level and intensity of competition; and most importantly, national norms, cultural characteristics, and policies.

A few examples of this last factor may be useful. Until recently, the Chinese appeared to be interested primarily in developing cross-cultural friendships and in learning new and better techniques. The exquisite manner in which Chinese athletes conducted themselves in sports competitions, often involving a careful selection of team members on a par with foreign visitors but capable of rewarding competition with friendship and new skills, testified to this distinctive approach. Now, however, the Chinese are pursuing a more aggressive, nation-building and public relations-minded policy toward international competition.[16] The Chinese Sports Law attests to a more determined approach. The notorious East German program during the Cold War era emphasized physical and mental well-being as well as the exigencies of preparation for socialist mobilization. In Cuba "massive sport" has been seen as "one of the fundamental objectives of the revolution."[17] In the Moslem World, participation in sports has been largely limited to men and quite frequently to the military, the affluent, and the professional elite. The Islamic Republic of Iran has discouraged forms of organized sports altogether, prohibited men and women from swimming together, and required women swimmers to wear a special swimming chador.[18] A medal won by a Moroccan woman at the 1984 Olympic Games was therefore extraordinary.

> with FINA President Dr. Harold Henning of the United States, the Chinese dropped the offending clause from their application, and the day before the Asian Games opened approval was granted for them to participate in the water-sports events as nonmembers.

The IOC formally "deplore[d] the fact that the Asian Games Federation ha[d] decided not to invite one of the recognized NOC's, which was a member of the Asian Games Federation." Nevertheless, noting precedent, and "[i]n view of these facts, it has been decided unanimously that in the interests of the development of sport in Asia, the IOC should continue to give its recognition and patronage to the Asian Games Federation, which automatically goes to the Games." OLYMPIC REV., Mar.–Apr. 1974, at 103.

16 *See* 16 CHINA SPORTS, May 1984, at 3 *et seq*; Gabriel, *China Strains for Olympic Glory*, N.Y. TIMES MAG., Apr. 24, 1988, at 30.

17 CHRISTIAN SCI. MONITOR, Aug. 7, 1987, at 1, 9, col. 2.

18 CHRISTIAN SCI. MONITOR, Aug. 6, 1985, at 21, col. 3.

Despite such differences, states routinely use sports to promote international harmony. Indeed, cultural diffusion and differences of opinion about the nature and role of sports require states to fashion ways to harmonize their differences in a spirit of cooperation, often with broader consequences. Within the legal framework of the Olympic Movement, bilateral agreements and less formal understandings help ensure that the Games go on and stimulate more general patterns of cooperation as well. A good example was the memorandum signed in September 1985 between representatives of the NOCs of the Soviet Union and the United States after two successive boycotts of competition on each other's territory.[19]

3. International Sports Development

Sports programs are a significant contributor to economic development, national health, modernization, social progress and political transformation. Football (soccer), in particular, has played a role in the reconstruction and nation-building of such countries as war-torn, demoralized Rwanda,[20] Afghanistan,[21] and Iraq.[22] In less dramatic circumstances, football (soccer) is a proven means for developing countries to gain respect that is otherwise difficult to elicit from the global community.[23]

Athletic activity has become an important aspect of national development and of foreign aid programs. On a bilateral level, a number of developed states offer assistance for developing programs in developing countries often by providing credits, equipment, training programs and facilities in either the developing or donor countries.[24] Olympic Solidarity has taken a lead in coordinating and financing this effort. It allocates funds to the NOCs and IFs for clinics, seminars, hundreds of courses each year and training manuals. Olympic Solidarity has grown rapidly, thanks to heightened awareness by the NOCs and to increased funding derived heavily from television royalty agreements. NOCs sometimes play an active role. For example, the USOC's multimillion dollar Friendship Fund, derived from profits of the 1984 Games, was reserved for the IOC and for those NOCs that had participated in the Los Angeles Games.

---

[19] *See* OLYMPIC REV., Oct. 1985, at 608. This memorandum responds to the problem of Olympic boycotts, discussed in the next chapter, but extends beyond that problem. The memorandum offers a broad basis for international sports cooperation.

[20] *See, e.g.*, Casert, *Soccer helps Rwanda heal wounds*, STATESMAN J. (Salem, Or.), Jan. 25, 2004, at 8B.

[21] *See* ECONOMIST, Nov. 8, 2003, at 40.

[22] *See* Murphy, *From tortured past, Iraqi team gets kick out of soccer again*, CHRISTIAN SCI. MONITOR, Nov. 20, 2003, at 1.

[23] *See* ECONOMIST, June 1, 2002, at 7.

[24] Anthony, *The North-South Dialogue in International Sports*, OLYMPIC REV., Jan. 1983, at 27, 31–33 (a good summary of these programs of assistance).

In an early example of technical assistance in sports, the IOC concluded an agreement in 1986 with the World Federation of the Sporting Goods Industry (WFSGI) to help provide sports equipment for Third World athletes from developing countries.[25] The agreement provided that the WFSGI, working with the IOC, would have exclusive rights to respond to the requests of NOCs in developing countries for the supply of sports equipment. All the equipment was provided entirely free of charge, with transportation costs borne by the donor. The IOC, in cooperation with its Solidarity Program and the NOCs, arranged for duty-free treatment by recipient countries of the donated equipment. Several countries have committed themselves to providing favorable tax concessions to encourage donations. In the United States, for example, a company that donated appreciated inventory could deduct the original value plus half the appreciation.

The distribution of equipment has posed the problem of misappropriation. The IOC labors to ensure that distributions are carried out through correct channels and under correct supervision, so as to avoid misappropriation of donated items.

C. PRESTIGE

A country takes pride in the success of its athletes in international competition. Even more prestigious is the award of a major international sports event to a country, which "is seen as a validation of the host's nationhood."[26] For example, the selection of Valencia, Spain to host the 2007 World Cup in sailing was greeted as a huge boost in the city's campaign to raise its reputation, not to mention the anticipated largess of some U.S. $1.55 billion for the city.[27] The IOC's announcement of Beijing's selection to host the 2008 Olympic Games led to nation-wide celebrations.[28] A jubilant crowd of 30,000 in Tiananmen Square[29] was a poignant reminder of China's long campaign to improve its international reputation after the tragic massacre of civilians 12 years earlier in the same location.[30] The prestige value of the IOC's decision was extraordinary.[31]

---

25 Olympic Rev., Feb. 1986, at 82–83; *id.*, Jan.–Feb. 1987, at 22.

26 Wong, *supra* note 1, at 4.

27 Clarey, *A Spanish City Look to the Cup for a Lift*, N.Y. Times, Nov. 30, 2003, at SP3.

28 *See* Clarey, *Beijing is Awarded 2008 Summer Olympics*, Int'l Herald Trib., July 14–15, 2001, at 1; Longman, *Beijing Wins Bid for 2008 Olympic Games*, N.Y. Times, July 14, 2001, at 1.

29 Smith, *Joyous Vindication and a Sleepless Night*, N.Y. Times, July 14, 2001, at 1.

30 *See* Hessler, *Great Sprint Forward*, New Yorker, May 7, 2001, at 38.

31 "While an Olympics is a boon for any nation, it is particularly important for China. The country has long equated sports and nationalism, and it has been hungry for international respect ever since it began opening to the world in the late 1970s. . . . Since winning the bid to host, China has made it clear that the Olympics are not merely a symbol of national prestige but a repository of the government's national ambitions to be a world player." Ang, *China's Olympic promise*, The Standard (Austl.), July 13, 2002, at 30.

The 1936 Games in Berlin were the most prominent and controversial example of the sovereign use of sports to gain prestige. Fifty years later, North Korea, concerned about the prestige that would accrue to its peninsula rival, South Korea, as the prospective host of the 1988 Olympic Games, decided to take some action. The Pyongyang leaders persuaded the Cuban Head of State, Fidel Castro, to urge that the Games should be held in North Korea. The President of the IOC initially replied to this suggesting by pointing out that "[t]he IOC is not ready to conduct a meeting of the two Koreas on the subject, for the simple reason that it has not been asked to do so."[32] When the North Korean government became resigned to the probability that the NOCs of allied socialist countries would send teams to the 1988 Games, it undertook two efforts. First, it expressed its willingness to pursue talks with South Korea about a joint team, and second, it sought to be named by the IOC as a co-host for some of the events of the 1988 Games.[33] Such co-hosting has been rare. Although the World Cup in football was split between Japan and South Korea, the Olympics were split only once—in 1956, when equestrian events of the Melbourne Games were held in Sweden because of Australia's strict quarantine laws—but never for political reasons.

The IOC organized and mediated meetings between representatives of the two Koreas to discuss the possibilities for cooperation in the 1988 Games. The two delegations met in October 1985, January 1986, June 1986 and July 1987. At first, the North Korean delegation proposed that a third of the 23 Olympic sports take place in the North. Following the third and fourth meetings, the two NOCs agreed to study a proposal by the IOC to hold several events in the North: table tennis, archery, women's volleyball, the first part of the 100 km. cycling road race and some of the elimination rounds in the football competition. A positive reply would have prompted the IOC to convene another meeting between representatives of the two NOCs in order to discuss such organizational questions as circulation between the two states and issues of television broadcasting. The two Korean delegations further confirmed "that free access of all members of the Olympic Family to the relevant venues in the North and South would be ensured." Although the NOC of the Republic of Korea later approved the proposal, the NOC of the Democratic People's Republic of Korea did not. South Korea became the sole host of the 1988 Games. By 2002, however, the still separate teams of athletes from the two political divisions of Korea marched together at the Sydney Games under a single, Olympic flag[34] and would do so again at the 2004 Games. In 2004, also, the two Korean NOCs agreed to form a unified team for the 2008 Games.

---

[32] OLYMPIC REV., Jan. 1985, at 20.

[33] For capsule histories of ensuing negotiations and mediation by the IOC, *see* OLYMPIC REV., Feb. 1986, at 87; *id.*, July 1986, at 368; *id.*, Aug. 1986, at 442; *id.*, Nov.–Dec. 1986 at 664; *id.*, Sept. 1987, at 446.

[34] INT'L HERALD TRIB., July 29–30, 2000, at 18.

The prestige value of national achievements in the international sports arena can have positive effects not only on the conduct of foreign affairs but in domestic society. For example, "Cuban muscle serves the ideals of the revolution. Sport is a jewel that is proudly shown to the outside world and acts as an incentive within the country."[35]

In order to discourage disruptive chauvinism in sports, however, it is the general practice of states and sports organizations to maintain a balance between a tolerance for national identity, with its capacity to generate mass interest in physical education, and protection of individual athletes, requiring a dampening of potentially disruptive nationalism. The Olympic Charter encourages such a balance by allowing the display of national symbols at appropriate times, while advancing overarching ideals by means of such well-known symbols as the Olympic torch runner and the familiar emblem of interlocking rings, and by denying official acknowledgment of national standings based on the composite scores of individual participants. In sum, the sovereign use of sports to enhance national prestige is acceptable so long as it does not result in discrimination or a triumph of nationalism over the shared goals of international competition.

D. ENHANCEMENT OF HUMAN RIGHTS

Rule 3 of the Olympic Charter prohibits discrimination in the Games against any country or person on grounds of race, religion, politics or otherwise, and Rule 31 requires NOCs to "commit themselves to taking action against any form of discrimination . . . in sport." These provisions provide a legal framework for defining the relationships between sports and human rights.

In practice, however, this framework needs further elaboration. There is often a dilemma whether to abide by the customary Rules of the Olympic Charter in a strict sense or to implement human rights by a more liberal interpretation of those Rules. For example, during the 1987 Pan-American Games, the United States reportedly refused to issue a visa to a Chilean athlete who was deemed to have committed human rights violations. This incident posed a clear conflict between an obligation to promote and protect human rights, which is clearly an aspiration of the Olympic Movement, and the customary rule against exclusion of athletes for political reasons.

Another troublesome question is whether it is best to pursue human rights objectives by excluding racist individuals or nationals of racist countries from sports competition or to use the IOC framework to work from within sports to change abhorrent policies. The IOC has generally chosen to isolate racist governments and thereby to exclude their nationals from international competition. To be sure, the Olympic Rules, in barring the IOC from discriminating against

---

35 Bustillo, *A Cuban mix of muscle and ideology*, UNESCO COURIER, Apr. 1999, at 32.

participants and their parent states might therefore be interpreted to bar it from "discriminating" against countries which pursue politically racist policies. The IOC must, however, comply with peremptory norms of human rights law and supervise the obligations of the national committees, which are responsible for ensuring that no one has been left out of competition for racial reasons. The IOC's practice has been to apply the Olympic Charter's provision against discrimination to bar participation in the Games by nationals of several (but not all) racist states, on the ground that admitting athletes from those states would put the IOC in a position of sanctioning de facto segregation. In adopting this principle, the IOC targeted the governments of South Africa and Rhodesia (today's Zimbabwe). Each present an illuminating case history.

1. South Africa

During the era of apartheid in South Africa, pressures exerted through sports competition were significant because of the importance traditionally attached to athletics in South Africa. The Pretoria government includes a Minister of Sport. Thus, the application of legal sanctions by the IOC and affiliated international sports federations gradually contributed to more liberal policies and practices in South African sports competition. Opposition to the use of sports to implement general human rights centered on the harm to athletes deprived of competition, both from South Africa and from boycotting countries—many black South Africans were deprived of international competition because of boycotts against athletes from that country—the inefficacy of boycotts as an instrument of foreign policy, and the questionability of singling out South African sports within a more comprehensive tragedy of human rights throughout the African continent.

In 1964 South African athletes were barred from participating in the 1964 Olympic Games because of opposition to a strict apartheid policy that limited eligibility for the South African Olympic team to whites. Between the 1964 and 1968 Games, the South African government agreed to adopt a non-discriminatory policy of training, selecting and lodging its Olympic participants. The Pretoria government nevertheless continued to enforce its policy against the holding of multiracial competition within the country and insisted on segregated trials. In 1968 the IOC decided that the South African NOC was in fact complying with the Olympic Charter and could therefore participate in the Mexico City Games. Thirty-two national teams, however, were so incensed by South Africa's practice of segregated trials that they threatened to boycott the Games unless the IOC excluded South African nationals.

The President of the IOC, apparently adhering to a strict interpretation of the Charter, maintained that the South Africa NOC had satisfied the literal requirements, and that exclusion of South African athletes would harm South Africa's black athletes more than anyone else. His basic premise was that "[w]e can't change the politics of any country—that's not our business . . . if participation in sport is to be stopped every time the laws of humanity are violated, there will never be any international contests."[36] The goals of promoting world athletic participation and of implementing global standards of human rights were at odds.

Pressure quickly mounted in favor of rescinding the IOC's invitation to the South Africans. The host of the Games, Mexico City, was justifiably nervous about the probable effect of a massive boycott and an incipient black-power movement threatening the composition and quality of the United States team. On the request of the Supreme Council for Sports in Africa, representing 33 African states[37] and supported by a South African black pressure group, the IOC President exercised an "urgency" provision of the Olympic Charter by submitting a proposed resolution to IOC members, the effect of which was designed to bar South African participation in the 1968 Games.

The IOC voted to rescind the invitation to the South African NOC. Its decision was supported and amplified after the Games by the U.N. General Assembly,[38] which requested all states and organizations to suspend domestic sports competition with South Africa and with any organizations and institutions in that country that practiced apartheid. Later, the U.N. Committee on the Elimination of Racial Discrimination, which was established in January 1970, called for strict implementation of the resolution. The Committee promptly publicized the identity of states that had either violated or adhered to the resolution.[39] Five months later the IOC voted to exclude not only South African competitors from the 1972 Games, but also their NOC from the Olympic Movement.

In 1975 the United Nations General Assembly adopted Resolution 3411(E), which urged all nations to boycott New Zealand's teams in the 1976 Olympics because of a New Zealand rugby team's participation in competition against a South African team. This resolution "[c]ommended all Governments, sports bodies and other organizations which have taken action for the boycott of racially

---

36 Furlong, *A Bad Week for Mr. B.*, SPORTS ILLUS., Mar. 11, 1968, at 18.

37 Lobbying for the banishment of South African nationals was skillfully led by a Congolese, Jean-Claude Ganga, who became a member of the IOC but in 2004 was expelled for alleged corruption. In addition to what was reported to be a well-argued brief in support of his position, Mr. Ganga was substantially aided by current fears of a retaliatory boycott by United States black athletes. Moreover, the Congolese government had created a receptive atmosphere by presenting the President of the IOC with the Insignia of the Commander of the Republic of the Congo.

38 The dimension of gross human rights violations took the General Assembly's action outside the scope of the nonintervention provision of the U.N. Charter art. 2, para. 7 ("Nothing contained in the present Charter shall authorize the United Nations to intervene in matters which are essentially within the domestic jurisdiction of any state or shall require the Members to submit such matters to settlement under the present Charter.").

39 G.A. Res. 2396, 23 U.N. GAOR Supp. 18, at 19, U.N. Doc. A/7348 (1968).

selected South African sports bodies or teams" and "[called upon them] to refrain from all contacts with sports bodies established on the basis of apartheid or racially selected sports teams in South Africa."[40] Since such resolutions are not ordinarily binding in themselves,[41] Resolution 3411(E) was exhortatory.[42]

The U.N. Special Committee Against Apartheid continued to pressure states to require national teams to boycott competition with South African athletes,[43] and justified boycotts against New Zealand athletes by criticizing that country's failure "to exert its influence" against cooperation between New Zealand sports unions and South African teams.[44] In 1976 the U.N. General Assembly adopted Resolution 6(F),[45] which proposed an International Convention Against Apartheid in Sports, and established an ad hoc organizational committee. The General Assembly urged all states to implement the Special Committee's recommendations, which included reducing official sponsorship of, or assistance to, sports competition with South African athletes, and refusing visas to South African sports bodies. In 1977 the General Assembly adopted an International Declaration Against Apartheid in Sports.[46] Similar measures followed repeatedly.

In 1981 the Special Committee submitted to the Secretary General[47] the draft International Convention Against Apartheid in Sports. This document called for an end to all sports exchanges with South Africa and requested states parties to take appropriate action against any organization or individual that engages in sports exchanges with South Africa. The Draft Convention proposed to establish an International Commission against Apartheid in Sports that would first receive reports from states parties on measures taken to fulfill the Convention and then make recommendations to the General Assembly based on these reports. It would also examine complaints about breaches of the Convention. In 1983, the Special Committee announced revisions; these took into account potential constitutional difficulties that might have arisen in the state's efforts to comply with the original wording of the Draft Convention. Parties to it would pledge to take "all pos-

---

40 G.A. Res. 3411(E), 30 U.N. GAOR, Supp. (No. 34) 37, U.N. Doc. A/10034 (1975).

41 *See* R. Higgins, The Development of International Law Through the Political Organs of the United Nations 5 (1963).

42 *See, e.g.*, U.N. Monthly Chron., Feb. 1976, at 29; *id.*, Dec. 1975, at 25.

43 *See* U.N. Monthly Chron., Oct. 1976, at 43; *id.*, Aug–Sept. 1976, at 28; *id.*, May 1976, at 18; *id.*, Feb. 1976 at 29, 30; *id.*, Jan. 1978, at 19, 122.

44 U.N. Monthly Chron., Aug.–Sept. 1976, at 28.

45 G.A. Res. 6(F), 31 U.N. GAOR, Supp. (No. 39) 12, U.N. Doc. A/31/39 (1976).

46 U.N. Monthly Chron., Jan. 1978, at 122; G.A. Res. 105(M) and Annex, 32 U.N. GAOR.

47 Report of the *Ad Hoc* Committee on the Drafting of an International Convention against *Apartheid* in Sports, U.N. Doc. A/36/36 (1981).

sible measures to prevent sports contact with a country practising apartheid."[48]

Also in 1981 the Special Committee published the first annual register of sports contacts with South Africa.[49] The register listed sports exchanges that had occurred and individual athletes who had competed in South Africa. Its purpose was to implement the U.N. resolutions against apartheid in sports by extending a boycott to blacklisted organizations and individuals in the hope that they would be disqualified from further international competition. This individualized blacklisting was controversial. In particular, the U.N.'s competence to ostracize particular individuals, even in the name of human rights, was questioned.

The report of the Special Committee to the 1982 Session of the General Assembly proposed to intensify publicity for sports boycotts and to continue publicizing the names of athletes who have visited South African.[50] The Chairman of the Committee stated that until social, economic and political equality was achieved in South Africa, there could be no equality in its sports. The Chairman argued that the sports boycott should continue until apartheid was totally abolished, not just until equality in sports had been established. This conformed with the Declaration that had been adopted in 1983 by the International Conference on Sanctions against *Apartheid* in Sport.[51] It endorsed both the Olympic principle of non-discrimination and the Gleneagles Agreement among members of the (British) Commonwealth. The Declaration specifically acknowledged the leadership of the Commonwealth in urging the IOC to emulate the Commonwealth Games Federation by taking action against national teams that maintained contact with South African teams.

In addition to these actions by the United Nations and the IOC, pressure from various other sources was leveled against the South African government to modify its racial restrictions in sports competition. Objections and threats were voiced by the otherwise conservative South African Cricket Association, particularly when the Pretoria government refused to allow two non-white cricketers to accompany a domestic team on a tour of Australia. The International Amateur Athletic Federation and the International Lawn Tennis Association, among several organizations, took stands against the South African policy. Nationally and internationally, prominent athletes demanded reform.

---

[48] United Nations Press Release 6A/AP/1477, Aug. 29, 1983. *See* Report of *Ad Hoc* Committee on the Drafting of an International Convention against *Apartheid* in Sports for 1983, U.N. Doc. A/38/36 (1983).

[49] Report of the Special Committee against *Apartheid*, U.N. Doc. A/36/22 (1982), at 16–17 and 18. *See* Letter dated 15 July, 1983 from the acting Chairman of the Special Committee against *Apartheid* to the Secretary General. U.N. Doc. A/38/310.

[50] Report of the Special Committee against *Apartheid, id.* at 16.

[51] Declaration of the International Conference on Sanctions against *Apartheid* in Sport, held in London from June 27–29, 1983, U.N. Doc. A/38/310.

Such publicity, boycotting and legal sanctions curtailed substantial sporting contact with South Africa. Many African, Asian and Eastern bloc nations extended no invitations to athletes listed on the register.[52]

Sports exchanges with South African teams nevertheless continued to occur. Examples were the tours of the United States and New Zealand by the South African Springbok rugby team in 1982, British cricket matches in South Africa, and an English rugby tour of South Africa in 1984.[53] In 1985, the Board of the International Rugby Union agreed unanimously to go ahead with plans for an international tournament in 1987 that, had it materialized, as planned, would have included South African representation.[54] Also, there was vigorous opposition at least in the United Kingdom, to what was perceived as political interference in the name of human rights. In the words of the Chairman of England's Sports Council, "[a]ll sportsmen are against apartheid. But the tragedy is it is not sport making the decisions any longer, it is the politicians."[55]

In 1993 apartheid ended in South Africa with the establishment of a democratic constitutional system and, in 1994, a new, multiracial government. In retrospect, what role did the anti-apartheid process of international sports law play in the political transformation? Certainly, apartheid in sports itself diminished as time went on, but it is unclear to what extent this progress can be attributed directly to specific, sports-centered international efforts. Perhaps the erosion of apartheid in sports was simply part of a more general, gradual erosion of apartheid in all sectors of South African society and the growing militancy and effectiveness of opposition to apartheid, at home and abroad. In any event, one can trace a steady erosion of apartheid in sports, as follows.

The South African government initially eased apartheid in several of the most important and internationally visible sports, principally lawn tennis and sports of medal-winning capacity to South Africa in the Olympic Games, if ever or whenever the prohibition against participation by South African teams might be lifted by the IOC.[56] In 1971 the South African Amateur Athletic Union took a first step

---

[52] THE INTER-DEPENDENT, May–June 1983, at 1.

[53] Issues Before the 37th General Assembly of the United Nations 1982–1983, at 33 (1982). In Selfridge v. Carey, 522 F. Supp. 693 (N.D.N.Y. 1981), *aff'd per curiam*, 660 F.2d 516 (2d Cir. 1982), the court declared that an attempted cancellation by the Governor of New York of a rugby match between South African and American teams, in order to avoid a threatened protest, was unconstitutional because it violated the plaintiffs' rights to freedom of expression under the First Amendment. *See* Comment, Selfridge v. Carey: *The First Amendment's Applicability to Sporting Events*, 46 ALB. L. REV. 937 (1982).

[54] INT'L HERALD TRIB., Mar. 23–24, 1985, at 15, col. 3.

[55] SYDNEY MORNING HERALD, Mar. 1, 1983.

[56] For accounts of initial steps in the early 1970s, *see* WASH. POST, Apr. 20, 1971, § D, at

by organizing and holding a completely integrated individual meet.[57] In 1976 the Minister of Sport allowed sporting bodies of various racial groups to meet in "inter-group" competition or leagues.[58] The new policy was, however, very limited, for it required members of different races to belong to separate clubs. There was no provision for mixed teams nor for a free flow of players among the separate clubs.[59] In 1978 the Minister of Sport announced a further modification of South African sports policy: legal permission would no longer be necessary for mixed clubs or games.[60] In 1981 a senior cabinet minister urged South Africans to ignore race laws in sports.[61] The same year one observer provided a summary of the situation that rang true until the end of apartheid: "Sport, in the forefront of change due to foreign pressures, continues to be a sensitive subject. The government lifted all legal restrictions against multiracial sport, and blacks began playing on some South African international teams, but at the club level integration remains discretionary."[62]

Despite these developments and strong indications since the 1970s of public support for integrated sports,[63] desegregation of the sports arena remained incomplete until the end of apartheid and the installation of the government of Nelson Mandela. The problem was fundamentally one of South African racism, enshrined in the notorious Separate Amenities Act and Influx Control Regulations, but perhaps governments and sports organizations alike might have encouraged a more rapid pace of social change by accepting the half-loaf of considerable sports integration rather than settling only for the elimination of apartheid throughout South African society before dealing with South Africans in the sports arena.

Nevertheless, sanctions against South African athletes and teams were effective as part of a gradual transformation within South African society. This trans-

---

3, col. 3; *id.*, Apr. 23, 1971, § D, at 4, col. 2. The Davis Cup organization responded by lifting a controversial two-year ban on South African participation, while at the same time maintaining a ban on Rhodesian participation in view of U.N. sanctions against Rhodesia. WASH. POST, Jan. 15, 1972, § C, at 3, col. 4. The WASH. POST, June 20, 1971, § C, at 6, col. 5, carries an account of the first competition between white and non-white South African athletes, which took place in Salisbury, Rhodesia. Because of the participation of athletes from Malawi and Rhodesia, the competition was "international" under the new South African definition.

57 Announcement of the South African Amateur Athletic Union, May 16, 1971.

58 Shaw & Shaw, *Sport as Transnational Politics: A Preliminary Analysis of Africa*, *in* LOWE, KANIN & STRENK, SPORT AND INTERNATIONAL RELATIONS 386, 394 (1978).

59 GUARDIAN (Manchester), Oct. 3, 1976, at 24, col. 5.

60 O. ÖZGUR, APARTHEID: THE UNITED NATIONS AND PEACEFUL CHANGE IN SOUTH AFRICA, 139 (1982).

61 CHRISTIAN SCI. MONITOR, Oct. 16, 1981, at 13, col. 3.

62 de St. Jorre, *South Africa: Is Change Coming?*, 60 FOREIGN AFF. 87, 108 (1981).

63 CHRISTIAN SCI. MONITOR, June 7, 1979, at 7, col. 2.

formation was attributable to a combination of governmental and non-governmental pressures and to the special importance of international sports competition to the South African public. The exclusion of South African teams from such an important global stage as sports competition at least provided a strong symbol of human rights and a viable, though frustratingly slow, technique for gradually implementing the objective of racial equality. The modest conversion of major international sports competition into a politically involved instrument of human rights may prove to be one of its most significant contributions to world order.

2. Rhodesia

The apartheid policies of the Rhodesian government were less severe than in South Africa.[64] Multiracial competitions of foreign teams were permitted in the country, and multiracial teams representing Rhodesia competed outside the country after July 1971. An investigatory mission dispatched by the IOC reported favorably on conditions in Rhodesia and recommended that country's continued involvement in the Games. Accordingly, the Rhodesian NOC, which had not been invited to participate in the 1968 Games, was invited in 1972. In response to this invitation, 20 of the 24 members of the U.N. Special Committee on Decolonization adopted a resolution that urged the IOC to take steps to "suspend the so-called 'National Olympic Committee of Rhodesia' from its membership and to ask the Organizing Committee of the 20th Olympic Games to annul forthwith its invitation for the Olympic Games in Munich."[65]

The response of the IOC to the resolution of the U.N. Special Committee struck a sensible compromise that served to accommodate the relatively favorable situation for black athletes in Rhodesia, to distinguish Rhodesia from South Africa in this respect, to permit Rhodesian nationals to complete in 1972, and yet to avoid any identification with an independent, white-supremist government in Salisbury. In 1971, during a joint meeting in Luxembourg between the IOC executive Board and representatives of the NOCs, the President of the IOC, referring to his recent meetings with African delegates, proposed that a Rhodesian team compete with the same flag and anthem, namely the Union Jack and British anthem, under which they had competed in the "pre-independence" 1964 Games while still a member of the British Commonwealth, and that the matter be reviewed following the 1972 Games. The Luxembourg Compromise, though unusual, had precedent. For example, Finns and Irishmen competed under the imperial flags of Russia and Great Britain, respectively, during the 1908 Olympics. The compromise, moreover, seemed acceptable under the Olympic Charter and United Nations Resolutions.

---

[64] Separative practices were, however, encouraged by the laws and policies of Rhodesia. *See, e.g.*, Zimmerli, *Human Rights and the Rule of Law in Southern Rhodesia*, 20 INT'L & COMP. L.Q. 239 (1971).

[65] *Decolonization Committee Deplores Olympic Invitation to Rhodesian Team*, UN Press Release WS/501, May 7, 1971, at 4.

The proposal, which was drafted by a special commission consisting of an Australian, a Nigerian, and a Swiss national, already had been accepted by both the Rhodesian delegation, participating as an observer, and its adversaries. It had also been endorsed by the Permanent General Assembly of the NOCs (70 affirmative votes to six abstentions). The IOC's executive Board concurred. Despite this compromise, the plenary IOC excluded the Rhodesian team from the 1972 Games, contrary to the Luxembourg Compromise.

The Luxembourg Compromise is perhaps most noteworthy because it explicitly took account of the "uncertain international position" of Rhodesia. The implications for Taiwanese and Palestinian teams, for example, became obvious. Accordingly, although the Rhodesian team was to be identified by colonial symbols it had rejected, and might therefore have declined to compete in the 1972 Games, no official political significance was to be attributed to the symbols. At the same time, no recognition would have been given to the rump, "post-independence" regime of Ian Smith. Thus, the IOC's executive Board seemed prepared to meet the threat of politicization and at the same time to apply basic standards of participation in a highly charged political context. The purpose was to encourage Rhodesian participation in one of the only spheres of human interaction, sports competition, in which Rhodesia had, for whatever reason, committed itself to global standards of racial integration.

Three years after the exclusion of Rhodesian athletes from the 1972 Games, the IOC issued the report of a Commission, consisting of a Brazilian, a Canadian and a Pakistani, which determined that the Rhodesian NOC (RBOC) represented a distinct geographical and political entity that was competent to confer citizenship and issue passports.[66] The Commission appeared to be troubled with de facto discrimination in Rhodesia, particularly in the schools, but concluded that the constitution, rules and practices of the RBOC were neither racially discriminatory nor violative of the IOC Rules;[67] the RBOC was deemed to be independent of the Rhodesian government. The report of the Commission suggested that the IOC, whenever feasible, would support social change through inclusion, rather than exclusion, South Africa being the salient exception.[68] But such was not to be. Although the 1972 decision to exclude Rhodesia, taken under pressure as it was, seemed exceptional, the IOC nevertheless decided to extend its decision to bar Rhodesian participation again in the 1976 Games.

The legal framework to govern the relationship between sports and human rights is imprecise. There is a need to develop clearer rules. Still, diplomatic efforts and decisions of international bodies to employ sports competition as a

---

66 EXCELSIOR (Mexico City), Feb. 12, 1975, at 7, col. 1.

67 OLYMPIC CHARTER, Rule 24 (1971) (on the autonomy of NOCs).

68 N.Y. TIMES, Oct. 22, 1974, at 51, col. 1.

means of eliminating state-sanctioned racial cleavage in Rhodesia and South Africa seem to have worked somewhat better than other techniques.[69] Such efforts can be made to work without injuring the competition itself so long as political pressures are expressed in accordance with well-articulated rules and principles. Regrettably, they were not in the instance of the IOC decisions to bar Rhodesian participation in the Munich and Montreal Games.[70] These decisions were particularly ironic because Rhodesian teams were racially mixed. Moreover, in the instance of the decision to bar Rhodesia from the 1976 Games, the IOC declined to follow the recommendations of its own investigatory commission on the status of the RBOC. On the whole, however, the actions within the Olympic Movement struck a blow for self-determination by the Rhodesian majority and, generally, for the use of sports to advance human rights.

E. DIPLOMATIC RECOGNITION AND NON-RECOGNITION

Although international sports law encourages the peaceful use of sport to help establish diplomatic relations or recognize states, it does not condone the unilateral use of sport to manifest non-recognition of states. Although, as we have seen, international sports law encourages states to deny recognition of teams from states that clearly violate human rights, this differs materially from a state's use of the sports arena as a public setting in which to manifest its non-recognition of other states. The customary law of the Olympic Charter expressly prohibits discrimination by those bound by it, including states, by international custom. The anti-discrimination rule extends to "a country or a person on grounds of race, religion, politics, sex, or otherwise."[71] The only exceptions are those prescribed by international law, such as discrimination against South African athletes as a means of combating apartheid.

Because key participants in international sports competition—athletes, sports bodies, and the IOC—are non-governmental, it should be possible, with the cooperation of sovereign states, to free the sports world of disputes involving issues of

---

[69] For a detailed history and analysis of the interrelationship between sport and apartheid in South Africa, *see* Lapchick, "South Africa's Use of Sport in Foreign Policy and the International Response," Mar. 23, 1974 (unpublished paper presented at the 15th Annual Convention, International Studies Association). Note the author's quotation of the following editorial in the JOHANNESBURG SUNDAY TIMES (May 31, 1970):

> South Africa's critics have simply discovered that sport is the most useful weapon they have yet found with which to beat us and while it is the sportsmen who are the sacrificial victims—they are being ostracized and deprived of the right to participate in world sport—the main target of attack is the racial policy of South Africa, or, to put it more precisely, the racial policy of the Nationalist Party.

[70] *E.g.*, an early instance of this problem occurred when India refused to allow teams from Israel and South Africa to compete in the 1975 World Table Tennis Championships even though, ironically, the South African team was racially mixed. WASH. POST, Feb. 7, 1975, § A, at 14, col. 1.

[71] OLYMPIC CHARTER, Rule 3.

recognition and non-recognition. The only issue should be whether a particular team has the authority and control to represent a population of athletes. Hence, a team need not represent a fully sovereign state, as defined by international law. The IOC has extended membership in the Olympic Movement to several NOCs from non-sovereign territories. They are anomalies because each NOC must represent a "country," and Rule 34 of the Olympic Charter defines a "country" as a fully sovereign state.

Two decisions of British courts[72] reached sensible conclusions on sports-related issues of recognition because of the judges' apparent determination to avoid an identification or confusion of sovereign recognition of another state with recognition under international sports law of a national team and its member athletes. In these cases the issue was whether an exclusion of Taiwanese teams could be legally justified on the basis that the rules of particular international sports federations precluded a team from representing a nonsovereign country.

In *Reel v. Holder* the Court of Appeal held that the International Amateur Athletic Federation (IAAF) could not expel Taiwan on the basis that its rules allowed "only one member for each country," which the IAAF had decided should be the People's Republic of China. Instead, the Court of Appeal held that membership was not confined to athletes or teams representing sovereign states, so that the term "country" could embrace colonies and other entities such as Taiwan, which the court acknowledged was not generally recognized as fully sovereign under international law. In making it clear that nationality-based criteria for membership in IFs do not imply diplomatic recognition on a political level, the Court of Appeal established that the geographical description "country" is a term of art under international sports law. For purposes of sports competition, Taiwan is one "country," another is the People's Republic of China. Thus, the jurisdiction of Taiwanese sports organizations is effectively limited to Taiwan, and the jurisdiction of Chinese sports organizations to mainland China.

Judge Eveleigh, concurring in *Reel*, pointed out that it would be unwise for a court to rely on state recognition to define membership status because of the frequent lack of agreement among states concerning the sovereign status of particular polities. Instead, the essential criteria for recognition are de facto control over territory and capacity to speak with authority for a particular group of athletes. In his words:

> Those who formed the federation were not concerned with international politics; they were concerned to set standards for athletics throughout the world. They were concerned to collect together people who would be in a position

---

72 Reel v. Holder, [1981] 3 All E.R. 321, [1981] 1 W.L.R. 1226, *summarized in* Ch.4, *supra* text accompanying notes 28–29; Shen Fu v. Stellan Mohilin (Goff, J., unreported). The following discussion in the text is drawn from the opinions in Reel v. Holder, *id.*

> to exercise control over athletics in various parts of the world. Unless a governing body of some kind applies for membership, the federation is not concerned to determine if a given place or area is a country. It is only in connection with an application for membership by an applicant who puts himself forward as a governing body for a particular place, district or region that it becomes necessary to consider the meaning of "country" in the rules. One thing that is clear is that there may only be one member for each country. Therefore, in entertaining an application, it has to be seen whether or not there is an existing member who has control, or a measure of control, over the same area as that for which the applicant contends. There must be no doubt who is to speak with authority as the governing body for a particular group of athletes. The word "country" has been used in the rules in order to delineate the area of authority. They do not use the word in the sense of sovereign state.

Despite this well-advised approach to dispute resolution, issues of sovereign recognition and non-recognition related to international sports competition have loomed large. A flagrant example of the denial of recognition for political purposes, at the expense of athletes, has been Spain's campaign to prohibit the Gibralter Football Association from joining the Union of European Football Associations (UEFA).[73] Without membership in the UEFA, Gibralter athletes are barred from participation in either European or World Cup qualifying matches. Spain has therefore held Gibralter athletes hostage in the long-standing controversy with the United Kingdom about the sovereign status of the Rock.

The IOC has been particularly embroiled in recognition controversies. What are the governing rules? The Olympic Charter used to provide very explicitly that "[r]ecognition of . . . a country['s National Olympic Committee] does not imply political recognition of that country. Recognition of [a National Olympic Committee] is dependent upon [its] country having enjoyed a stable government for a reasonable period of time."[74] NOCs and host countries have been expected to respect the decisions of the IOC concerning the admission of a national team: "All NOCs recognized by the IOC are entitled to send participants . . . to the Olympic Games to which they shall be admitted without discrimination on grounds of religion, race or political affiliation."[75]

Fortunately, disparities between the Charter and individual state policies of recognition have usually been resolved in favor of the Charter. States have acqui-

---

73 Johnson, *Blackballed Gibralter: World Cup Wannabe is Thwarted by Spain*, WALL ST. J., Apr. 8, 2002, at 1.

74 OLYMPIC CHARTER, Rule 25 (1976).

75 *Id.* at 83, *Organization of the Games, § I Conditions Laid Down for Candidate Cities*, #1 Participants (1983) [hereinafter cited as Participants].

esced in the IOC's determination and have themselves been willing to subordinate their own law and policies to the Olympic Rules. The general practice therefore supports international sports law. Thus, although Australia did not recognize the Soviet Union in 1956, it was obliged, against its initial objection after the Soviet invasion of Hungary, to permit the participation of Soviet athletes in the Melbourne Games that year. Similarly, France, a member of the North Atlantic Treaty Organization (NATO), permitted East Germans to participate in the 1968 Winter Olympics, although the issuance of visas to them ordinarily would have violated NATO regulations at that time. Also, contrary to a resolution of the United Nations General Assembly, the government of West Germany, which was not then a U.N. member, drew upon Olympic precedents to clear the way for participation (later aborted) of Rhodesian athletes in the 1972 Games in Munich. In each of these cases, a potential conflict was avoided by the waiver of municipal visa requirements and the issuance of special clearance papers, contrary to local law. In 1987 the United States issued visas to a large delegation of athletes from Cuba, with which the United States did not maintain diplomatic relations, to enable them to participate in the Pan-American Games in Indianapolis.

There have been exceptions to this general practice. Canada's refusal to admit Taiwanese athletes into the country to compete in the 1976 Montreal Games[76] was a particularly flagrant violation of the international custom. First, since the NOC of the Republic of China had been recognized by the IOC under that name, Canada violated its express commitment to the IOC "that all parties representing the National Olympic Committees and International Sports Federations recognized by the IOC will be free to enter Canada pursuant to the normal regulations."[77] Also, by denying Taiwanese athletes permission to enter, whatever the designation of their team by the IOC, the government of Canada made it impossible for the Canadian NOC to fulfill its international responsibilities by "guarantee[ing] that the Games shall be organized to the satisfaction of and in

---

[76] WASH. POST, July 6, 1976, § D, at 1, col. 1. Canada's Secretary of State for External Affairs, Allan J. MacEachen, stated at a press conference on July 16, 1976: "We have not accepted [the People's Republic's] views, which asked us to prohibit totally the admission of Taiwanese athletes under any circumstances. That we are not prepared to do. We were prepared to admit athletes if they accepted a designation that was compatible with our national policy on China." Canadian Embassy, Public Affairs Division, CANADA REP., July 27, 1976, at 3. Several days before MacEachen's news conference, Canada's motive for its action against Taiwan on the even of the Games was disclosed: the People's Republic was Canada's largest overseas purchaser of wheat. Canada's wheat exporting deals with Beijing had brought a new prosperity to farmers in Western Canada. Deford, *More Dark Clouds Over Montreal*, SPORTS ILLUS., July 19, 1976, at 32: N.Y. TIMES, July 17, 1976, at 1, col. 6; *id.*, July 16, 1976, § 1, at 1, col. 1; *id.*, July 16, 1976, § 1, at 1, col. 1; *id.*, July 15, 1976, at 43, col. 1; *id.*, July 14, 1976, at 29, col. 1. WASH. POST, July 17, 1976, § B, at 5; *id.*, July 16, 1976, § D, at 1, col. 4; *id.*, July 15, 1976, § D, at 1, col. 4; *id.*, July 10, 1976, § E, at 1, col. 2; *id.*, July 7, 1976, § A, at 14, col. 1; *id.*, July 6, 1976, § D, at 1, col. 1; *id.*, July 5, 1976, § D, at 7, col. 1; *id.*, July 4, 1976, § C, at 1, col. 6; *id.*, July 3, 1976, § E, at 1, col. 1.

[77] Deford, *More Dark Clouds Over Montreal*, SPORTS ILLUS., July 19, 1976, at 33.

accordance with the requirements of the IOC."[78] Canada could not justify the exclusion of the Taiwanese by contending that "normal regulations" within the Olympic Rules included a denial of travel papers; indeed, such action is impermissible according to the Olympic Rules that regulate recognition procedures for international competition.[79] Moreover, Canada had not informed the IOC that "normal regulations" would be construed as a political reservation before it denied travel papers to members of the Taiwanese team.[80]

Second, the government of Canada violated international custom by refusing to abide by the provision of the Olympic Charter that explicitly prohibited discrimination against any country or person on political grounds.[81] The 1976 version of the Charter provided that "[t]he expression 'country' wherever used in these Rules shall mean any country, state or territory which *in its absolute discretion* is accepted by the IOC as constituting the area of jurisdiction of a recognized NOC."[82]

Canada also refused to give effect to a related provision that:

> [A]ll NOCs recognized by the IOC are entitled to send participants . . . to the Olympic Games to which they shall be admitted without discrimination on grounds of . . . political affiliation.
>
> It is desirable that such persons shall be allowed to enter the host country simply on presentation of the Olympic [identity card].[83]

Taiwanese athletes had already received Olympic identity cards when Canada announced its decision not to admit them.[84] Technically, although the use of an identity card has resolved problems of recognition in other host countries, the Olympic Charter did not require Canada to accept the identity cards. Nevertheless, once it had rejected their use, Canada was obligated to devise an alternative procedure to admit the IOC-recognized team from Taiwan.

Third, Canada violated the Olympic provision that "[n]o legal condition or regulation may be valid in opposition to [the IOC] Rules."[85] The Canadian government

---

78 OLYMPIC CHARTER, Rule 4 (1975).

79 *See especially id.*, Rule 8, and Participants, *supra* note 75.

80 *See* Killanin, *Clarification by the IOC*, OLYMPIC REV., Sept.–Oct. 1976, at 460 [hereinafter cited as Killanin].

81 OLYMPIC CHARTER, Rule 3 (1975).

82 *Id.*, Rule 8 (emphasis added).

83 *Id.*, Participants, *supra* note 75.

84 *See* Killanin, *supra* note 80.

85 OLYMPIC CHARTER, Organization of the Games, § I *Conditions Laid Down for Candidate Cities*, #1 IOC Rules (1983).

asserted that requiring the Taiwanese team to use the designation "Taiwan" simply adhered to a precedent established in the 1960 Rome Games. That, however, was incorrect. Although "Republic of China" had not been the official IOC designation in 1960, it was in the 1964, 1968, and 1972 Olympic Games.[86]

Finally, IOC records reveal that although the Canadians had had an opportunity to voice objections to a Republic of China team by that name in April 1976, they failed to do so, apparently preferring the strategy of last-minute surprise that would foreclose the possibility that the IOC might transfer the Games out of Montreal.[87] As a result, Canada violated its own policies to encourage universal participation in international events and to oppose the diplomatic bullying of small countries, apparently in an effort to further the economic objectives of its wheat-growing and exporting interests by purposely misconstruing both the facts and the Olympic Charter.

Four years later, the Taiwanese question again arose. The team that had been selected to represent the Taiwanese people in the 1980 Winter Olympics in Lake Placid sought to do so again under the designation of the "Republic of China." This time the problem was that although the IOC had decided in 1979 to allow both China and the Taiwanese people to compete independently in 1980, it had since 1960 prohibited the Taiwanese from using the symbols and designations of the Taipei government although the Taiwanese were invited to submit alternative, unofficial designations for approval by the IOC.

Having failed to propose alternative designations and therefore to gain credentials for a national team from the "Republic of China," the Taiwanese NOC brought two civil actions. One of these actions was brought against the IOC in the courts of Switzerland,[88] where the IOC is chartered, and the other action was brought against the Lake Placid Organizing Committee in the courts of New York,[89] where the Winter Games were about to take place. In both actions the plaintiffs sought judicial assistance to entitle them to use the flag, emblem, name, and anthem of the Republic of China when the team participated in the Winter Games.

The Swiss action was somewhat cryptically dismissed on the grounds that the plaintiff had failed to evidence possible damages and that the Republic of China Olympic Committee lacked standing to bring the particular action.[90] In the New York action, the trial court partially granted the plaintiff's motion for a pre-

---

86 CANADA REP., *supra* note 76.

87 *See* Killanin, *supra* note 80; CANADA REP., *supra* note 76, at 2, 3.

88 Petition of Maître Wurzburger, summarized in *The IOC in Court*, OLYMPIC REV., Jan.–Feb., 1980, at 66 [hereinafter Petition].

89 Liang Ren-Guey v. Lake Placid 1980 Olympic Games, Inc., 49 N.Y.2d 771, 403 N.E.2d 178 (1980).

90 Petition, *supra* note 88.

liminary injunction to enable the Taiwanese team to use political designations of the Taipei government. On appeal, the Appellate Division of the New York Supreme Court granted the motion of the United States Attorney General to file a Statement of Interest of the United States, and reversed the order of the lower court on the ground that the Department of State's visa-denying deference to the authority of the IOC was beyond the court's review powers because the underlying issues were "political."[91] Finally, the Court of Appeals of New York affirmed the decision in a *per curiam* opinion.[92]

The Taiwanese thus did not participate in the Lake Placid Games nor, for that matter, in the Summer Games in Moscow.[93] The Taiwanese epic quickly brightened, however. In March 1981 the island's Olympic Committee and the IOC agreed on the designation of a "Chinese Taipei Olympic Committee," in addition to a special, non-sovereign flag and emblem. In return for these concessions, Taiwanese athletes were able to participate fully and independently in Olympic Games beginning in 1984 and in other international sports activities over which the IOC has authority.[94] A heartwarming feature of the 1984 Games was the association and even fleeting fraternity between athletes from opposite sides of the Taiwan Strait.

The Taiwanese saga demonstrates both the fragility and the efficacy of international custom, as expressed in the authority of the Olympic rules and decisions. Although the IOC is technically a non-governmental organization, national authorities defer to decisions by it and the IFs. They are willing to accept its decisions as binding, even on sensitive issues concerning the recognition of "countries."[95] In the case of Taiwanese athletes, deferring to the authority of IOC decisions is consistent with, though not specifically addressed by, Section 4(d) of the (United States) Taiwan Relations Act,[96] which provides as follows: "Nothing in this chapter may be construed as a basis for supporting the exclusion or expulsion of Taiwan from continued membership in any . . . international organization." Therefore, when issues of sports competition threaten the tightrope diplomacy over the Beijing-Taipei chasm, national authorities can avoid disaster by deferring to international sports law's regime of recognition.

---

91 Liang Ren-Guey v. Lake Placid 1980 Olympic Games, Inc., 72 A.D. 439, 424 N.Y.S.2d 535 (1980).

92 *Id.*

93 The Taiwanese did not petition for entry in the Moscow Games after it became apparent that the USOC would boycott them.

94 Olympic Rev., Apr. 1981, at 211.

95 Reel v. Holder, [1979] 1 W.L.R. 1252.

96 Taiwan Relations Act, Pub. L. No. 96-8, 93 Stat. 14 (1979) (codified at 22 U.S.C. §§ 3301–16 (Supp. V. 2000).

Issues of diplomatic recognition and non-recognition continued after 1980. The most serious issue of recognition prior to the 1984 Olympic Games involved the unsuccessful application of the Palestinian Liberation Organization (PLO) to enter a team.[97] In 1987 the United States government refused to grant visas to North Korean athletes to enable them to attend a short-track speed skating event in St. Louis. The problem of the two Koreas, discussed earlier,[98] loomed large in planning for the 1988 Games in Seoul. Ultimately, a record 161 out of 167 NOCs chose to participate in the 1988 Games.[99] After 1988 recognition issues proved to be of less significance. In 1992 the IOC allowed athletes of the former Republic of Yugoslavia, then in the throes of civil war, to participate individually in the Barcelona Games. In 2000 the two Korean delegations to the Sydney Games paraded together under a common flag of the Korean peninsula.

F. PROPAGANDA

The use of sports by governments to spread propaganda against other countries is discouraged by the Olympic Charter's provisions that "[t]he Olympic Games are competitions between athletes in individual or team events and not between countries,"[100] that "NOCs shall preserve their autonomy and resist all pressures of any kind, including those of a political, religious or economic nature,"[101] and that "no kind of demonstration or political, religious or racial propaganda is permitted in the Olympic areas."[102] These prohibitions emphasize the apolitical nature of the Olympic Rules. In addition, the Rules anchor the national committees and federations as much as possible within the private sector to discourage the governmental use of sport for political propaganda. At one time the Charter also warned specifically that the ideals of the Olympic Movement are endangered by "certain tendencies . . . which aim primarily at a national exaltation of the results gained instead of the realization that the sharing of friendly effort and rivalry is the essential aim of the Olympic Games."[103]

Aside from these provisions, which primarily forbid propaganda on the Olympic sites, there are no restraints on propaganda as a legitimate use of sport. Indeed, propaganda and the desire to gain prestige may foster a national public's identification with sports competition in a manner that may enhance global peace and understanding, an essential goal of the Olympic Movement. For example,

---

97 CHRISTIAN SCI. MONITOR, Apr. 11, 1984, at 23, col. 3.

98 *See supra* text accompanying notes 32–33.

99 OLYMPIC REV., Jan. 1988, at 20 (1988). The non-participating NOCs were from North Korea, Cuba, Nicaragua, Ethiopia, Albania and the Seychelles.

100 OLYMPIC CHARTER, Rule 9 (2003).

101 *Id.*, Rule 31.

102 *Id.*, Rule 61.

103 OLYMPIC CHARTER, Instructions, § I Political Use of Sport (1983).

China promotes its National Games of Traditional Ethnic Sports,[104] which engage the participation of its national minorities for both domestic and international admiration. It is apparent that a case-by-case, contextual analysis alone can determine the validity of using sports for purposes of propaganda.

G. PROTEST

1. Individual Protest

Protest may be individual or official. The 1968 Games highlighted an act of individual protest. During the Mexico City Games, the demeanor of two United States athletes was controversial when they refused to face the American flag as it was raised at an award ceremony but instead raised their fists in a black power salute as a protest. The Olympic Charter then required that during the playing of the National Anthem at awards ceremonies, "the three competitors and the spectators shall face the flag."[105] The Executive Board of the IOC *sua sponte* decided that "[a]fter the insulting display of the two American athletes given in the stadium on 7th September, when they were awarded their gold and silver medals for the 400 meter event . . . these two athletes had broken Rule 26, paragraph 1, in respect of the traditional Olympic spirit and ethic and would, therefore, be eliminated from taking part in any future Olympic competition."

There were at least three serious defects in this decision. First, it represented an IOC intervention to rectify a political insult to the United States by its own nationals. Ironically, it was primarily the U.S. team that was harmed by the IOC decision. Second, the decision did not comply with minimum standards of procedural due process: There were no procedural safeguards, hearings, prior standards, or appeal available. Finally, the decision was based on the application of the wrong rule. Rather than invoking the then applicable Rule 57 requiring the three victorious competitors to "face the flag," the IOC improperly invoked Rule 26: "a competitor must observe the traditional Olympic spirit and ethic."[106] This is an important requirement of eligibility, to be sure, but had nothing to do with the decorum of athletes; rather, it addressed problems of so-called professionalism in sports. By every canon of reasonable construction, it is clear that Rule 26 was not pertinent.

In response to the black power incident, the Olympic Charter was revised to provide that "[e]very kind of *demonstration or* propaganda, whether political, religious or racial, is forbidden in the Olympic areas."[107] It was then possible to inter-

---

[104] RENMIN RIBAO (Beijing), Sept. 30, 1999, at 3.

[105] OLYMPIC CHARTER, Rule 57 (1968), which became OLYMPIC CHARTER, Bye-Law to Rule 65 (1985).

[106] OLYMPIC CHARTER, Rule 26 (1968).

[107] *Id.*, Rule 53 (emphasis added).

pret this provision to proscribe both individual political demonstrations against one's own culture, such as that in the 1968 Games, as well as official, organized political demonstrations or propaganda.

2. Official Protest

Although official protest may be perfectly acceptable in sports, it sometimes becomes a matter of legal concern when it provokes international conflict or when it is illegal per se. Protest is often associated with other uses of sports. An earlier section dealt with its use, among other techniques, to enhance human rights. As the South African and Rhodesian cases demonstrate, the usual form of official, sovereign protest is a compelled boycott of competition or of a particular national team. Because of the complexity and special importance of boycotts, the next chapter is specifically devoted to a discussion of that subject.

H. CONCLUSION

The official use of sports to provoke *conflict* is generally illegal, whereas its use to promote international *cooperation* is commendable. The official use of sport to acquire *prestige* is permissible so long as a government does not violate such specific rules as those pertaining to non-discrimination against individual athletes, the authorized use of Olympic emblems and symbols, and a host country's acceptance of the emblems and symbols of other countries. General practice encourages the use of sports to enhance *human rights* within the United Nations framework, with certain exceptions. Although the use of sport to convey or confirm diplomatic *non-recognition* generally violates international sports law, its peaceful use as a basis for *diplomatic recognition* is highly acceptable. Whether the use of sports for purposes of *protest* or *propaganda* is legal or illegal depends on case-by-case, contextual analysis.

CHAPTER 11
BOYCOTTS

Boycotts used to be a serious problem in international sports. To paraphrase the famous statement of General Karl von Clausewitz: sports boycotts, like war, represent an extension of politics by other means. Although Baron Pierre de Coubertin envisaged international athletic exchange as the free trade of the future, which no nation would regulate to its political advantage,[1] boycotts have too often disrupted athletic competition and harmed athletes in the past. Politics in the sports arena is inevitable and can even provide a healthy outlet for international tension, but boycotts have often been harmful and seldom, if ever, productive.

Not all boycotts are political. For example, Russian and Korean threats to boycott the remainder of the 2002 Winter Games in Salt Lake City[2] because of what they considered to be unfair judging and drug testing are examples of non-political boycotts. Far more important, however, have been boycotts for political purposes. Accordingly, teams from the Soviet Union stayed away from the Olympic Games between 1920 and 1952 and Chinese teams between 1956 and 1980. Since 1948, boycotts and embargoes[3] have plagued the Olympics. At the 1948 Games in London, German and Japanese athletes were barred because their governments had been Axis powers, and Israeli athletes were excluded in order to dissuade Arab athletes from a boycott. The East Germans boycotted the 1952 Games because the IOC refused to recognize East Germany as a separate country entitled to its own national committee—that is, separate from the West Germans. In 1956 seven nations withdrew teams from the Melbourne Games: Egypt, Iraq and Lebanon to protest the Suez invasion by the United Kingdom; France, Spain, Holland and Switzerland to protest the Soviet invasion of Hungary; and China to protest participation by a Taiwanese team.

Several African teams, mostly under governmental direction, boycotted the 1976 Games in Montreal to protest the participation of a team from New Zealand, whose government had earlier allowed a national rugby team to meet South

---

[1] P. de Coubertin, Une campagne de vingt-et-un ans 1887–1908, at 90 (1908).

[2] Dodd, *Russians, Koreans threaten to leave Games*, USA Today, Feb. 22, 2002, § D, at 1.

[3] A state may impose measures to prohibit either participation by its nationals in foreign competition (loosely, a "boycott") or access by foreign athletes to competition on its territory (loosely, an "embargo"). Whether a prohibition attaches to the outflow or the inflow of athletes does not, however, usually determine its legitimacy under international sports law. The threshold question is the *purpose, not the nature*, of a particular measure. For convenience, therefore, the term "boycott" generally will be used to refer to either of the two means of restricting athletes or competition.

African athletes in that non-Olympic sport. United States athletes did not participate in the 1980 Games in Moscow, in response to which the Soviet Union boycotted the 1984 Games in Los Angeles. In 1986 more than a score of national teams boycotted the Commonwealth Games in Edinburgh to protest the refusal of the British Prime Minister to apply sanctions against South Africa. Soviet teams have also avoided competition with teams from Chile, South Korea (until 1988), and other countries. To protest racism, boycotts have been directed against teams, even integrated ones, from South Africa and Rhodesia (today's Zimbabwe). Since 1988, however, political boycotts of sports competition have been uncommon. They nevertheless present a continuing threat to athletes and athletic competition.

A. THE LAW

1. The General Rules of Retorsion and Reprisal

When are boycotts of international sports competition legal? They are clearly illegal when their purpose is to induce conflict or to engage in measures of coercion in violation of the United Nations Charter.[4] They are also illegal when their purpose is to manifest diplomatic non-recognition in violation of the governing rules of international sports competition. Canada's refusal to issue visas to members of the Taiwanese Olympic team in 1976—a kind of embargo—is a salient example. The most important and difficult issues relate, however, to the use of sport for official protest.

At best, boycotts are unfriendly acts. If, however, they are within a legally protected range of retaliatory sanctions, they may be acceptable measures of *retorsion*.[5] To be acceptable, they must not violate provisions of the United Nations Charter or other binding instruments, they must conform to state practice, and they must not violate general principles of law. Ordinary trade embargoes that do not violate multilateral treaties, friendship, navigation and commerce treaties, bilateral treaties of establishment, or other international obligations are generally regarded as acceptable measures of retorsion.

Neither the letter nor the history of Article 2(4) of the United Nations Charter indicates clearly whether its provisions were intended to prohibit the threat or use of political "force," or just military force.[6] Even if Article 2(4) prohibits only the latter, general principles of peaceful non-intervention are found in the United Nations General Assembly Declaration on the Inadmissibility of Intervention in

---

[4] "All Members shall refrain in their international relations from the threat or use of force against the territorial integrity or political independence of any state, or in any other manner inconsistent with the Purposes of the United Nations." Art. 2(4), UNITED NATIONS CHARTER, June 26, 1945, 59 Stat. 1031, T.S. 993.

[5] A retorsion is defined as "an unfriendly act or acts whereby one State answers *objectionable* (though not necessarily illegal) conduct of another State in a retaliatory manner." J. STONE, LEGAL CONTROLS OF INTERNATIONAL CONFLICT 288–89 (1959).

[6] *See* Maw, *Historical Aspects and the U.S. Involvement in Boycotts*, 71 PROC. OF THE AM. SOC. INT'L L. 170, 173 (1977).

the Domestic Affairs of States and the Protection of their Independence and Sovereignty,[7] and in the Declaration on Friendly Relations.[8] The 1970 Declaration on Friendly Relations confirms "the duty of the states to refrain in their international relations from military, political, economic or any other form of coercion aimed against the political independence or territorial integrity of any state [and] the threat or use of force . . . in any manner inconsistent with the purposes of the United Nations." The Pan-African boycott of competition involving the participation of South African teams during the apartheid era arguably threatened the political independence of South Africa, but only as a product of internal self-determination and the advancement of human rights. Nevertheless, it might seem at first that resolutions of the Organization for African Unity (OAU) calling for boycotts may have contravened one of the "purposes" of the United Nations: "to practice tolerance and live together in peace with one another as good neighbors."[9] To the contrary, however, the emerging law of human rights, especially when it is clearly expressed by international consent or consensus, legitimates such political protest in sports.

Questionable boycotts also may be acceptable, in some circumstances, as *reprisal* measures against illegal acts of another state. The *Naulilaa Incident Arbitration*[10] enumerates three conditions of legitimacy for such countermeasures: (1) that the state against which reprisals are taken must have itself violated international law; (2) that prior to the reprisal measure, the state must have attempted without success to obtain redress from the first state for the consequences of its illegal conduct; and (3) that reprisals should not be excessive. A reprisal must be necessary and not out of proportion with the act that motivated it. Thus, boycotts or embargoes may be acceptable as reprisals

> after an unsatisfied demand to an act contrary to international law on the part of the offending state. They have the effect of suspending momentarily in the relations of the two states the observance of this or that rule of international law. They are limited by the experience of humanity and the rules of good faith, applicable in the relations of state with state. They would be illegal if a previous act contrary to international law had not furnished the reason for them. They aim to impose on the offending state reparation for the offense or the return to legality in avoidance of new offenses.[11]

---

[7] Dec. 21, 1965, G.A. Res. 2131 (XX), 20 U.N. GAOR, Supp. 14, at 11, U.N. Doc. A/6014 (1966).

[8] Declaration on Principles of International Law concerning Friendly Relations and Co-operation among States in Accordance with the Charter of the United Nations, Oct. 24, 1970, G.A. Res. 2625 (XXV), 25 U.N. GAOR, Supp. 28, at 121, U.N. Doc. A/8028 (1971).

[9] Preamble, UNITED NATIONS CHARTER, *supra* note 4.

[10] (Portugal v. Germany), [1928] 2 R.I.A.A. 1012 (1949); *see also* Case Concerning the Air Services Agreement of 27 March 1946 (France v. U.S.), 18 R.I.A.A. 417 (1978).

[11] *Id. See generally* A. DE GUTTRY, LA RAPPRESAGLIE NON COMPORTANTI LA COERCIZIONE MILITARE NEL DIRITTO INTERNAZIONALE (1985).

In view of these requirements, states typically justify self-help measures in terms of reparation, deterrence, or both. For example, after the United States' rather garbled decision to compel a boycott by the USOC of the Moscow Games, the Carter Administration argued principles of diplomatic protection of nationals, deterrence and retribution. The President's first justification of the boycott was a presumed danger to United States athletes and spectators,[12] but he apparently changed his mind. The purpose of the boycott, according to his new thinking was to deter future aggression, to send the Soviets a "signal of world outrage."[13] The Secretary of State, however, viewed the boycott as retribution for the Soviet violation of what he suggested was a principle against contemporaneous involvement in armed combat by a sovereign host.[14]

2. The Olympic Legal Framework

To appraise the validity of sports boycotts, it is essential to go beyond the customary law governing retaliation by reexamining the special regime of international sports law. In this analysis, the Olympic Charter best evidences custom—itself a source of international law—pertaining to international sports competition.

3. Applicable Rules of International Sports Law

The principal safeguards against unwarranted intrusion by governments into international sports are found in the Olympic Charter, even for non-Olympic competition. One of the cornerstones of international sports law thus provides that "any form of discrimination with regard to a country or a person on grounds of

---

12 80 DEP'T STATE BULL., Jan 1980, at Special-B.

13 80 DEP'T STATE BULL., Mar. 1980, at 51.

14 *Id.* at 50. The following dialogue took place at a presidential news conference on February 13, 1980:

> Q. You have said that the Soviets have to be made to pay a price for invading Afghanistan, and your counsel has said that our boycott of the Olympics is not intended to be punitive. How do you explain the seeming difference between these two positions?
>
> A. We have no desire to use the Olympics to punish, except the Soviets attach a major degree of importance to the holding of the Olympics in the Soviet Union. In their own propaganda material, they claim that the willingness of the International Olympic Committee to let the games be held in Moscow is an endorsement of the foreign policy and the peace-loving nature of the Soviet Union.
>
> To me it's unconscionable for any nation to send athletes to the capital of a nation under the aegis of the Olympics when that nation—that host nation—is actively involved in the invasion of and the subjugation of innocent people. And so, for that reason, I don't believe that we are at all obligated to send our athletes to Moscow.
>
> And I would like to repeat, if the Soviet Union does not withdraw its troops from Afghanistan by the 20th of this month, then neither I nor the American people nor the Congress will support the sending of an Olympic team to Moscow this summer.

80 DEP'T STATE BULL., Mar. 1980, at Special-D.

race, religion, *politics*, sex or otherwise is incompatible with belonging to the Olympic Movement."[15] Also, "[t]he Games are competitions between athletes in individual and team events and not between countries."[16] NOCs must remain autonomous, resist all political pressures, and enforce the Rules and Bye-Laws of the IOC.[17] "NOCs shall be the sole authorities responsible for the representation of their respective countries at the Olympic Games."[18] The Bye-Laws to the Olympic Rules define the term "representation" in part as the decision to participate. Violations of these Rules, such as yielding to political pressures, expose NOCs to withdrawal of their status.[19] Governmental intrusion into these rules of international custom is abusive.

The Helsinki Accords,[20] although non-binding in themselves, articulate normative support for this rule structure. The Accords, signed by the Soviet Union, the United States, Canada, and all European countries except Albania (and acceded to by Albania at the end of the Cold War), provide that: "In order to expand existing links and cooperation in the field of sport, the participating States will encourage contacts and exchanges of this kind, including sports meetings and competitions of all sorts, on the basis of the established international rules, regulations and practice."[21] The rules to which the Helsinki Accords apparently refer are not simply the technical "rules of the game," such as the length of the playing field, but also the more comprehensive rules of international sports law within the framework of the Olympic Movement.[22]

---

15 OLYMPIC CHARTER, Rule 3 (emphasis added).

16 *Id.*, Rule 9.

17 *Id.*, Rule 31.

18 *Id.*

19 *Id.*, Bye-laws to Rule 31, No. 7.

20 Conference on Security and Cooperation in Europe [hereinafter cited as CSCE], Final Act, Aug. 1, 1975, *reprinted in* 73 DEP'T STATE BULL. 323 (1975), 14 I.L.M. 1292 (1975) [hereinafter cited as Accords]. The original European signatories were: Austria, Belgium, Bulgaria, Cyprus, Czechoslovakia (now the Czech Republic and Slovakia), Denmark, Finland, France, the German Democratic Republic, the Federal Republic of Germany (now simply Germany after merger of the two Germanies at the end of the Cold War), Greece, the Holy See, Hungary, Iceland, Ireland, Italy, Liechtenstein, Luxembourg, Malta, Monaco, the Netherlands, Norway, Poland, Portugal, Rumania, San Marino, Spain, Sweden, Switzerland, Turkey, the Union of Soviet Socialist Republics (now Russia and other constituent republics of the former U.S.S.R.), the United Kingdom, and Yugoslavia (now divided among five independent republics). Canada and the United States also signed the Accords. Even though the Accords technically are not legally binding, they have provided at least a morally compelling, comprehensive expression of norms to guide the behavior of the signatory states.

21 CSCE, *id.* at 341, 1315.

22 The qualifying adjective "international" in a code or agreement such as the Helsinki Accords is properly construed to refer to the relations among nations at the more or less governmental level.

B. APPLICATIONS OF THE LAW

States have usually imposed political boycotts for one of two purposes: to combat apartheid and official racism or to implement geopolitical strategy. Sports boycotts for the first purpose are generally legitimate whereas boycotts for the second purpose may or may not be, depending on a particular case.

1. Boycotts to Combat Apartheid and Racial Discrimination

a. *Olympic Rules*

Although the Olympic Charter prohibits discrimination against "any country or person on grounds of . . . politics," discrimination by states against South African athletes, for example, may be regarded as a legitimate response to racial discrimination by the South African government, against which a range of international sanctions have been imposed. The easiest justification of a sports boycott is specific discrimination in the training, team selection, and integration of amateur athletes rather than a more general pattern of discrimination by a racist government. One possible problem, however, is posed by Rule 9, which provides that the Olympic Games are "competitions between athletes in individual and team events and not between countries." Broadly interpreted, Rule 9 would see to prohibit any sovereign use of sports competition as a contest against another country. Rule 9 may be interpreted in this context, however, to apply only to the *mode* of physical competition in the sports arena. That is, Rule 9 may bar only overtly political activity and displays *at the time of* the competition. Even under a broader preferred reading, Rule 9 may not be interpreted in a manner inconsistent with international human rights law, as discussed below.

b. *Rules of Affiliated Sports Organizations*

The Olympic Charter's prohibitions against discrimination are reflected in, and strengthened by, rules and practices of the NOCs and IFs of both Olympic and non-Olympic sports. For example, in its 1984 (Mexico City) Declaration the NOCs requested the Association of National Olympic Committees to "make representations to the relevant International Federations urging them to exclude South Africa from membership in line with the policy of the IOC, until that country renounces its policy of apartheid which is in contravention with the Olympic Charter."[23]

Several IFs took the Mexico City Declaration very seriously. For example, in 1988 the International Amateur Athletic Federation threatened to suspend the British Track Association from membership, effectively barring British track-and-field athletes from international competition, unless the Association suspended the British, née South African runner, Zola Budd, for a year. Budd's infraction was

---

[23] OLYMPIC REV., Dec. 1984, at 966–969 [hereinafter cited as Mexico Declaration].

to "take part" in South African sports, not by competing but by observing and training near competition and by fraternizing with South African athletes.[24]

One of the objects of the International Federation of Association Football (FIFA) is to prevent discrimination in football (soccer) competition, as expressed in the FIFA Handbook. For enforcement, the national associations are charged with the responsibility to prevent any racial discrimination in football (soccer) in leagues and clubs under their jurisdiction. FIFA itself has a duty to ensure than no discrimination is practiced. A national association, when applying to take a part in a competition or deciding to organize one, shall give assurances to the Federation, that its provisions will be respected. Also, without the special consent of FIFA's Executive Committee, affiliated associations and their clubs may compete only against other member associations and clubs. Thus, membership in the FIFA is limited to sports organizations which are themselves free of discrimination, are from countries free of sports discrimination, and do not allow clubs within their jurisdiction to meet unapproved clubs.

c. *International Human Rights Law*

International sports law must, of course, conform to more general rules and principles. Apartheid and official racism violate fundamental human rights at one or another level of custom and positive law. Arguably, under the *jus cogens*, apartheid and official racism may conflict with peremptory norms of human rights from which no derogation is permitted, at least with the protection of an international agreement, such as one which might formalize competition by South African athletes in another country. Apartheid and official racism are also condemned by hundreds of international resolutions and declarations, the Universal Declaration of Human Rights,[25] the Advisory Opinion on Namibia,[26] and the norms of the International Convention on the Elimination of All Forms of Racial Discrimination.[27] The latter agreement provides in part, as follows:

Article 2(1)

(b) Each State Party undertakes not to sponsor, defend or support racial discrimination by any persons or organizations;

---

[24] N.Y. TIMES, Apr. 24, 1988, at S10; CHRISTIAN SCI. MONITOR, Apr. 13, 1988, at 18. This crisis ended when Ms. Budd returned to South Africa. Neff, "A Runner Runs Home," 68 SPORTS ILLUS., May 23, 1988, at 26; CHRISTIAN SCI. MONITOR, May 11, 1988, at 10, col. 3.

[25] UNIVERSAL DECLARATION OF HUMAN RIGHTS, Dec. 10, 1948, G.A. Res. 217A(III), U.N. Doc. A/810, at 71 (1948) (as interpreted and applied).

[26] [1971] I.C.J. 16.

[27] INTERNATIONAL CONVENTION ON THE ELIMINATION OF ALL FORMS OF RACIAL DISCRIMINATION, *opened for signature* Mar. 7, 1966, 660 U.N.T.S. 195 [hereinafter Convention Against Racial Discrimination].

(c) Each State Party shall take effective measures to review governmental, national and local policies, and to amend, rescind or nullify any laws and regulations which have the effect of creating or perpetuating racial discrimination wherever it exists;

Article 3

States Parties particularly condemn racial segregation and apartheid and undertake to prevent, prohibit and eradicate all practices of this nature in territories under their jurisdiction.[28]

The Supervisory Committee created under the Convention established that states parties have a duty under Article 3 to eliminate racial segregation and apartheid.[29] Also, by 1981, 92 of the 107 states parties had taken steps to prohibit South African athletes from entering their territories; of the remaining 15 states, only eight continued to allow South African athletes to compete in their territory.[30] This general practice of states provided evidence of *opinio juris*, that is, the subjective element of custom—whether a state considers itself bound as a matter of law by a particular practice.

In 1985 the Secretary-General of the United Nations declared that there had not been enough progress in South Africa to justify a termination of U.N. boycotts. He nevertheless added that it was for each nation to decide for itself whether to maintain sports contacts with South Africa.[31] In view of the latter statements, it would seem that the general practice of states under human rights law and the special rules of international sports law have particular significance.

United Nations General Assembly Declarations against Apartheid in Sports reach both parties and non-parties to the Convention Against Racial Discrimination. They provide specifically as follows: "States shall deny visas and/or entry to representatives of sports bodies, members of teams or individual sportsmen from any country practising apartheid."[32]

In the New Zealand case of *Ashby v. Minister of Immigration*,[33] the plaintiffs asked the court to enjoin the defendant from granting temporary permits that

---

[28] *Id.* On legal provisions against racism, *see, e.g.*, B. WESTON, R. FALK & A. D'AMATO, INTERNATIONAL LAW AND WORLD ORDER 615–16 (1980).

[29] Ashby v. Minister of Immigration, [1981] 1 N.Z.L.R. 222, 227–28, (1981) (hereinafter cited as Ashby).

[30] *Id.* at 228.

[31] NEW ZEALAND HERALD, Feb. 12, 1985, at 4, col. 6.

[32] U.N. MONTHLY CHRON., Jan. 1978, at 122; G.A. Res. 105(M) and Annex, 32 U.N. GAOR (1978).

[33] [1981] 1 N.Z.L.R. 222.

would enable the Springboks, a South African rugby team, to enter the country for the purpose of competition with local teams. Their case rested on two grounds: that the Convention prevented the Minister of Immigration from issuing entry permits, and that, at the very least, the Minister should have explicitly taken the Convention into account, as he had failed to do. The court, however, upheld the orthodox view of British Commonwealth countries that in the absence of a specific Act of Parliament, a treaty does not become a part of municipal law. The court also expressed the opinion that in allowing the Springboks to enter, the immigration authorities would be properly exercising their discretion within the flexibly language of the Convention. One judge suggested, however, that the government's actions ought to have been subject to the Gleneagles Agreement, an important British Commonwealth measure against apartheid in sports. Besides the Commonwealth of Nations, regional organizations, particularly the Organization of African Unity, have been active in pressuring even nonmember states to implement a boycott of South African athletes.[34]

d. Commonwealth Law: The Gleneagles Agreement and Code of Conduct

The Gleneagles Agreement, in the form of a communiqué of the 1977 meeting of the Heads of Government of the (British) Commonwealth of Nations, sought to prevent all sporting contact with South Africa or any other country that allowed apartheid in sports.[35] More specifically, it stated that apartheid in sports ran counter to certain Principles adopted by the Heads of Government of the British Commonwealth in Singapore in 1971, and that sports contact with athletes from states that practice apartheid encourages a misperception that the Commonwealth is unwilling to take measures against apartheid. Under the Agreement, the Heads of Government reaffirmed their support for the international campaign against apartheid and welcomed U.N. efforts to devise effective ways of fighting apartheid in sports.[36]

Members of the Commonwealth accepted the urgent duty to combat apartheid "by withholding any form of support for, and by taking every practical step to discourage contact or competition by their nationals with sporting organizations, teams, or sportsmen from South Africa or from any other country where sports are organized on the basis of race, colour, or ethnic origin."[37] The Agreement left each government "to determine in accordance with its laws" the method by

---

[34] *See, e.g.*, Freeman & Marsden, *South Africa: is this the crunch?*, SUNDAY TIMES (London), Apr. 21, 1985, at 29, col. 1.

[35] The Gleneagles Agreement, *as reported in* 23 KEESING'S CONTEMPORARY ARCHIVES 28507 (1977). [hereinafter cited as *Keesing's*.]

[36] This is a reference to the International Declaration against Apartheid in Sports, U.N. Doc. A/32/105M, adopted by the General Assembly in December of 1977 upon the recommendation of the Ad Hoc Committee on the Drafting of an International Convention against Apartheid in Sports.

[37] *Keesing's, supra* note 35, at 28507.

which it might discharge these commitments. The Agreement ended by expressing the belief that there was "unlikely to be future sporting contacts of any significance between Commonwealth countries or their nationals and South Africa while that country continues to pursue the detestable policy of apartheid."[38]

The Gleneagles Agreement clearly endorsed the use of boycotts to combat apartheid in sports. It expanded the range of sports beyond the Olympics to include non-Olympic sports that are included in the Commonwealth Games.

The Agreement discouraged contact or competition with teams, individuals, or organizations from any country that organized sports on the basis of race. It did not, however, define prohibited "contact" or "competition." Thus, for example, it is unclear whether athletes from a Commonwealth state were to be subject to censure for merely associating at a competition with South African athletes, though not competing against them. The definition of "contact" might also have been limited by a provision for discharge of the Gleneagles commitment in accordance with the laws of member states. This allowed "contact" between spectators or news reporters and South African athletes. Presumably, the definition of "contacts" was intended to be limited to "sporting contacts" (on the playing field), a term found in the last paragraph of the Agreement.

Enforcement of the Agreement presented some problems. It did not provide guidelines for appropriate sanctions or other response when a member state neglected to fulfill its duties or is so accused. Disagreement on the appropriate response by member states led to the Nigerian boycott of the Commonwealth Games in 1978, a threatened African boycott in 1982, and the threatened exclusion of the United Kingdom from the 1986 Commonwealth Games in Edinburgh. It was an open question, under the Agreement standing alone, whether a member state was subject to sanctions if it failed to prevent a national team from competing in South Africa in a private, non-representative capacity. The provision that each state should determine in accordance with its laws how to fulfill its commitments left room for wide variation in enforcement among the member states. One state might allow its nationals a freedom of travel to compete in South Africa and another might not. Such variation in enforcement gave rise to claims of bad faith by certain member states. This highlighted another problem: there was no permanent, specialized body for monitoring compliance with the Agreement nor to which disputes could be taken for effective and prompt resolution. The Agreement seemed to recognize some of these problems when it called for cooperation by nationals of all member states.

New Zealand rugby was a particular focus of controversy. Teams belonging to the New Zealand Rugby Football Union (NZRFU) met the South African

---

[38] 24 *Keesing's, supra* note 35 at 29215, 31268–70 (1978); SYDNEY MORNING HERALD, Apr. 7, 1982, at 2; *id.*, Apr. 29, 1982, at 28; *id.*, May 15, 1982, at 3; *id.*, June 26, 1982, at 3.

Springboks on several occasions. The New Zealand government repeatedly requested the NZRFU to retract such invitations.[39] The Springboks' 1981 tour of New Zealand was particularly controversial, leading to riots during which nearly 2,000 demonstrators were arrested and which the New Zealand government spent about $U.S. 3.5 million to control.[40] When the NZRFU refused to retract its invitation to the Springboks, the New Zealand government took no further action, such as ordering a cancellation of the tour or denying visas for the South African team. In response, the Commonwealth Secretary-General, Mr. Ramphal, moved the scheduled meeting of Commonwealth Finance Ministers from New Zealand. A disagreement ensued over the extent of the obligations that the Gleneagles Agreement required. Mr. Muldoon, the Prime Minister of New Zealand, citing the history of the adoption of the Agreement, maintained that it simply created an obligation to *discourage* sporting contacts with South Africa, rather than to *prohibit* them, and therefore New Zealand had not breached its duty. As with the Nigerian boycott in 1979 and the threatened African boycott of the Commonwealth Games in 1982, no new initiatives to resolve the New Zealand dispute were taken at the 1981 Heads of Government Meeting in Melbourne, despite the major controversy it caused.

Controversy flared up again in 1985 when the best New Zealand rugby team, ironically called the All Blacks, received an invitation to tour South Africa. Governmental opposition to the tour delayed a decision by the Council of the NZRFU on the issue of whether the All Blacks should have been allowed to accept the invitation. The government informed the NZRFU that it would take measures to prevent the tour unless the Union overwhelmingly supported it.[41] The position of pro-tour spokesmen emphasized the disadvantages of a boycott for athletes, the futility of boycotts as an instrument of foreign policy, and, in the words of former Prime Minister Muldoon, the "pity" of singling out sports and apartheid "from all the other problems and tragedies of Africa."[42] In an apparent tradeoff, the NZRFU voted in favor of the tour in return for South African support of a proposed World Cup, to be inaugurated in New Zealand and Australia.

---

[39] 24 *Keesing's, supra* note 35, at 29207 (1978); 25 *Keesing's, id.*, at 29901–8 (1979); 28 *Keesing's, id.*, at 31268–70; NEW ZEALAND HERALD, Feb. 9, 1985, at 1, col. 1; *id.*, Feb. 12, 1985, at 1, col. 4.

[40] *See* Hamlin, *The 1981 Springbok Tour of New Zealand*, 4 AUCKLAND U. L. REV. 313 (1982); G. CHAPPLE, 1981: THE TOUR (1984).

[41] NEW ZEALAND HERALD, Feb. 12, 1985, at 1, col. 4.

[42] NEW ZEALAND TIMES, Jan. 27, 1985, at 8, col. 3. In addition to Mr. Muldoon's observation, other comments, *id.*, are of interest:

> It is a myth to state that sporting contacts with South Africa lessen our external reputation when so many countries, some signatories to the Gleneagles agreement and others outside the ambit of contact with New Zealand have such abysmal human rights records. In a year again of political interference in the Olympics it is galling that sportsmen have to bear the brunt of political interference or, in the South African situation, selective morality.

The New Zealand government, under domestic pressure and international pressures such as those of the Organization of African Unity, declared that the decision marked rugby's days of shame.

On July 15, 1985, the High Court of New Zealand granted a temporary injunction against the proposed tour. Several dissident members of the NZRFU had filed the action, arguing that the proposed tour was *ultra vires* the Union's constitution and that it would violate the Union's constitutional purposes of promoting, fostering, and developing rugby in New Zealand, essentially in accordance with the Gleneagles Agreement. The High Court issued the injunction on the basis of the potential damage to the NZRFU and the public interest. The NZRFU responded to the decision by formally cancelling the tour.[43]

Since the 1981 crisis in New Zealand, several interpretative problems in implementing the Gleneagles Agreement have apparently been resolved by the Commonwealth Games Federation. To ensure that the Commonwealth Games would not be endangered by disparate actions of individual states, the Federation adopted a Code of Conduct in 1982.[44] The Code prohibited Commonwealth athletes from participating in any "sports event" at which athletes from a state practicing apartheid might be present. The term "sports event" was undefined, but apparently referred to a competition in which athletes specifically represent their countries. Otherwise, the Code attempted to clarify the vagueness of the Agreement by defining what action constituted a breach of it by individual athletes, by teams and by sporting organizations. It specified what actions the Commonwealth Games Association (CGA) of each member country must take against anyone within its jurisdiction who breached the Code, even against competitors in non-Commonwealth Games sports (NCGS). If the CGA breached this duty, the Commonwealth Games Federation was empowered "by due process and for good cause" to suspend the right of the CGA and nationals of the same country to participate in the Commonwealth Games.

In order to comply with the Code of Conduct and thereby ensure national participation in the Commonwealth Games, a CGA had to notify the Commonwealth Games Federation of any violations which the CGA had the responsibility to prevent. It also had to notify the Federation of any violations by participants not only of Commonwealth Games sports but of NCGSs. Finally, CGAs had to disqualify all violators of the Code from membership on a Commonwealth Games team. This sanction applied to all athletes, officials, or teams within its national supervision, including NCGSs.

---

[43] Sunday Times (London), Apr. 21, 1985, at 2, col. 2; *id.* at 29, col. 1 (the government's declaration); Int'l Herald Trib., July 15, 1985, at 15, col. 1 (High Court case and decision).

[44] Revised Draft Code of Conduct for the Commonwealth Games Federation, Oct. 5, 1982 (adopted without amendment Oct. 6, 1982).

The question arose whether a CGA, or an umbrella organization including a CGA among its constituent sports organizations, should dissociate itself juridically, that is, in a formal organizational sense, from NCGSs over whose activities it had no real control but for which it might bear some responsibility under the Code of Conduct. The answer to the question was a tentative "no" because the CGA's responsibility over NCGSs extends only to notification requirements and exclusion of non-complying athletes from Commonwealth teams. This answer, however, had to remain tentative because of the ambiguity of such undefined terms in the Code as "Commonwealth sportsmen," "sports event," and "representative capacity."

Thus, a CGA had obligations only to notify and declare a competitor or administrator ineligible for the Commonwealth Games in any instance where that person had breached the "no contact with" provision of the Gleneagles Agreement. For example, auto racing is not a Commonwealth sport and could not claim a "National Governing Body" in a particular Commonwealth country. If an auto racer from a Commonwealth country were to have competed in a sports event in South Africa or against South Africans elsewhere, the respective CGA of the auto racer's country, as a corporate entity, would have had the responsibility of ensuring that NGBs of CGA sports declared the auto racer ineligible to participate in other sports in the Commonwealth Games. Thus, each CGA was delegated to enforce the Gleneagles Agreement and its Code of Conduct even against NCGSs, but its NCGS-related responsibilities were restricted.

If a CGA did nothing to prevent the auto racer from competing against South African drivers and ordinarily cooperated with the hypothetical, non-complying NGB in auto racing, this alone did not jeopardize participation in the Commonwealth Games by athletes and teams of the CGA nationality. Despite some ambiguity in the meaning of such pertinent terms as "sportsmen" and "sports administrator," there was nothing to suggest that a Commonwealth government must, or the Commonwealth Games Federation could, declare complying athletes, teams or administrators ineligible so long as the CGA observed the notification and disqualification requirements.

Fundamentally, then, the Code of Conduct attempted to prevent the kind of international disputes that imperiled the Commonwealth Games on several occasions since the Gleneagles Agreement was put in effect. The Agreement and the Code differed somewhat in their objectives and in the scope of their applicability. The approach taken by the Agreement was to discourage member states from permitting sporting contacts with athletes from South Africa, whereas the Code sought to prohibit such contacts by imposing sanctions against non-complying organizations in each member state. The Code and the Agreement thus fit together, hand-in-glove.

In implementing the Code of Conduct, the government of Australia, as an example, strengthened its policy of support for the Gleneagles Agreement. Unlike the experience in New Zealand, no Australian rugby side went against a South African side since 1971, when the South African Springboks won all 13 games, including three tests, against Australian sides. Despite its good record of implementing the Gleneagles Agreement, Australia had to weather a storm over scheduled participation in the 1982 Commonwealth Games in Brisbane by teams from countries whose nationals had met South African teams. The Brisbane Games also provided a stage and publicity for demonstrations by Australian Aborigines who claimed confiscation of their land rights. The Commonwealth (or "Brisbane") Code of Conduct was concluded during this period of time. Despite the controversies, the Brisbane Games were a success.

On October 26, 1983, the Australian Minister for Foreign Affairs announced that from then on, no South African teams would be allowed entry for competition in Australia. Further, Australian athletes would be discouraged from competing in South Africa, as would "third country" contacts, that is, involving Australian competition against South Africans in other countries. The government would seek to persuade Australian sports bodies to press for the expulsion of South Africans from international sports federations and competitions, and to put pressure on other governments to discourage South African participation in international sports competitions. In return, the Foreign Minister announced that prohibitions on entry into Australia of foreign cricket players who had competed in South Africa would be lifted. Finally, the Australian government announced that it did not support, nor did it interpret the Gleneagles Agreement to support, any such secondary boycotts against foreign nationals who might have participated in South African sports activity.[45]

In 1985 the Australian government condemned a proposed tour of South Africa by Australian cricketers, and offered assistance to individual players who would face legal action for breaking their contracts with the Australian Cricket Board to tour South Africa.[46] A court subsequently confirmed the validity of the contracts without applying the Gleneagles Agreement. The South African question helped an English cricket team on a tour of Australia in 1985. The English side had been strengthened by the renewed eligibility of team members who had been suspended for going to play in South Africa, whereas the Australian side was weakened because of the disqualification of standout players who refused to pledge that they would not compete in South Africa.

The scope and authority of the Gleneagles Agreement over athletes was tested in the courts after several English rugby players competed on a national team selected to tour South Africa in 1984. Their club had permitted them to tour South Africa. In response, a local governing council banned the club and its members from using a recreation ground for a period of 12 months. In *Wheeler v.*

---

45 1 AUS. INT'L L. NEWS, Jan. 1984, at 90.

46 TIMES (London), Apr. 19, 1985, at 7, col. 5; *id.* at 28, col. 1.

Leicester Council,[47] the House of Lords held that neither the Race Relations Act of 1976 nor the Gleneagles Agreement supported the local council's particular action in that case. Ignoring the Brisbane Code of Conduct, Lord Roskill wrote that "[t]he government policy recorded in the well-known Gleneagles Agreement . . . has never been given the force of law at the instance of any government, whatever its political complexion; and a person who acts otherwise than in accordance with the principles of that agreement commits no offence even though he may by his action earn the moral disapprobation of large numbers of his citizens."[48] Lord Templeman noted, and implied that it was acceptable, that although the government had signed the Gleneagles Agreement, it had left the decision to individuals whether to compete against South Africans. Governmental advice against participation was therefore without legal force in the United Kingdom, according to the opinion.

This same 1984 rugby tour jeopardized English participation in the 1986 Commonwealth Games, scheduled in the backyard (or front yard vis-á-vis Gleneagles) of Edinburgh, Scotland.[49] English participation came into question after the English Rugby Union decided to go ahead with the South African tour despite the government's advice and rather tardy, muted pleas against the trip by the English Commonwealth Games Council. The English Rugby Union arguably was not bound by the Gleneagles Agreement, the Brisbane Code of Conduct, nor for that matter, by the Commonwealth Games Council of England. Despite the brouhaha, the Commonwealth Games Federation ultimately agreed to allow the English to participate in the Games. The 1986 Games took place on schedule, although over a score of national teams withdrew to protest Prime Minister Thatcher's refusal to apply sanction against South Africa, a circumstance over which the English Commonwealth Games Council obviously had no control.

e. *Constitutional Problems in the United States*

In 1982 the Governor of New York attempted to cancel a rugby match between South African and American teams on the basis that a planned protest of the match would threaten the public welfare. In *Selfridge v. Carey*[50] a federal court enjoined the Governor's directive as a violation of First Amendment protections of freedom of expression under the United States Constitution. It is unclear, however, whether a prohibition of competition against South Africans would have been unconstitutional if the justification had been international human rights and sports law rather than simply the state's police powers.

---

[47] Wheeler v. Leicester Council, [1985] 2 All E.R. 106.

[48] *Id.* at 1109–10.

[49] *See* (Sydney) MORNING HERALD, Mar. 22, 1984, at 38, col. 3; CHRISTIAN SCI. MONITOR, May 21, 1984, at 7, col. 1.

[50] Selfridge v. Carey, 522 F. Supp. 693 (N.D.N.Y. 1981), *aff'd per curiam*, 660 F.2d 516 (2d Cir. 1982). *See generally* Comment, *Selfridge v. Carey: The First Amendment's Applicability to Sporting Events*, 56 ALB. L. REV. 937 (1982).

f. *Effectiveness of Boycotts and Their Validity for Human Rights Purposes*

Although a non-aggressive sanction such as a boycott may be patently more appealing than military alternatives, boycotts are often ineffective. The Supreme Court Council for Sport in Africa, which was largely responsible for the African boycott of the 1976 Games in Montreal, later repudiated its withdrawal. The Council reportedly concluded that the cause of Black Africa would have been better served by the participation of the African teams.[51] Sports boycott "as a tool for bringing about political change, has been effective only in the case of small and relatively defenseless countries."[52]

Primary boycotts to combat official racism may not work very well and may create problems, but they are generally valid under international law to vindicate a nearly universal consensus against official racism. That consensus is crystallized in many pronouncements of the global community and in the form of international custom. Indeed, under United Nations resolutions, states had an obligation to prevent South African athletes from competing on their soil. *Secondary* boycotts, however, are highly questionable. Thus, a state may abuse its powers by compelling a boycott of competition involving athletes from a state whose only involvement has been either to allow its athletes to compete against athletes from a targeted state or to refuse to take certain measures against that state. Boycotts of teams or of competition against individual athletes from a particular state are also questionable if the purpose is diplomatic or wholly political rather than truly human rights-oriented. The best test of a boycott's legality is whether it has been specified or sanctioned by recognized international authority.

2. Boycotts to Implement Geopolitical Strategy

Sports boycotts for geopolitical purposes are not generally protected by positive international law. They must therefore be analyzed on a case-by-case basis, according to the general rules and principles governing reprisals. The argument that all sports boycotts should be legal has some merit because they are basically peaceful. Indeed, until fairly recently sports boycotts might have been perfectly

---

[51] *See* remarks of Brendan O'Reilly, *quoted in* OLYMPIC REV., Mar. 1980, at 113. In his commentary on the controversy concerning the 1981 rugby matches between South African and New Zealand teams, one observer has written as follows:

> In the history of mankind this approach has seldom, if ever, been successful. Trade embargoes on oil have made South Africa a world leader in coal conversion; an arms ban has led to a self-sufficiency in arms. Boycotts, in the words of Chief Buthelesi, an ardent opponent of apartheid and leader of millions of Zulus, only hurts [sic] the blacks.

NEW ZEALAND TIMES, Jan. 27, 1985, at 8, col. 3.

[52] Cheffers, *The Foolishness of Boycott and Exclusion in the Olympic Movement*, OLYMPIC REV., Sept. 1979, at 512, 513. Generally, economic boycotts do not work well. G. HUFBAUER & J. SCHOTT, ECONOMIC SANCTIONS RECONSIDERED: HISTORY AND CURRENT POLICY (1985).

acceptable under the *Lotus dictum*.[53] They serve the interests of peace by sending a clear and prominent signal while avoiding a military threat or the sometimes inhumane effects of food and other trade embargoes. Moreover, sports boycotts are easy for governments to control.[54] On the other hand, boycotts may harm athletes and their careers, are seldom effective, and tend to harden diplomatic positions, while generating counterproductive retaliation. It must be remembered, also, that they patently, though rebuttably, violate Rule 1 of the Olympic Charter that "[a]ny person or organization belonging in any capacity whatsoever to the Olympic Movement is bound by the provisions of the Olympic Charter and shall abide by the decisions of the IOC." This rule is a cornerstone of the Olympic framework of international custom.

Retaliatory boycotts that do not respond to illegal acts, such as United States prohibition of travel by athletes to Cuba, are especially questionable. The customary rules are, however, of such generality that it is difficult to establish that boycotts for geopolitical reasons are invalid *per se*. Case-by-case analysis is unavoidable.

Let us suppose that a government imposes a boycott long after it has formally and repeatedly requested either termination of an ostensibly illegal act by another state or a peaceful resolution of a dispute under Article 2(3) of the United Nations Charter.[55] Let us also suppose that the boycott is necessary and proportional under the particular circumstances. Even so, it may be invalid if its purpose is neither to deter specific conduct nor to induce reparations from the offending state. Further, a boycott may be invalid if its purpose is unclear or if, in the language of the *Naulilaa* principles, it offends human experience and good faith. Thus, for example, the United States government's compulsion of a USOC boycott of the Moscow Games in 1980 was unacceptable under international law because its purpose was equivocal, amounting to little more than a bad faith effort to detract from the glitter and propaganda value of an adversary's hospitality and home advantage in competitions between United States and Soviet athletes. The Carter Administration acted in bad faith and unproductively in choosing to compel the 1980 boycott. By contrast, unilateral suspension of Argentinean-British soccer competition at the 1982 World Cup, had it occurred, would have been acceptable in the context of actual warfare between the two states.

---

[53] "[R]estrictions upon the independence of States cannot . . . be presumed." The Case of the S.S. "Lotus" (France v. Turkey), 1927 P.C.I.J., ser. A, No. 10.

[54] Note, *This Sporting Life*, 13 MELB. U. L. REV., I.264 (1981).

[55] "All Members shall settle their international disputes by peaceful means in such a manner that international peace and security, and justice, are not endangered." U.N. CHARTER art. 2(3).

C. THE BOYCOTT OF THE 1980 GAMES

Political conflicts threatened the Moscow Games well before the Soviet invasion of Afghanistan. As early as 1976, United States Senator Bill Bradley, former Olympic and New York Knicks basketball player, wrote a partly prophetic scenario in which "the President of the United States would call a boycott of the 1980 Olympic games just two weeks before they were to begin in Moscow, citing national security and difficulty with the Soviet Union as the reasons." By September 1979, several months before the invasion, the 1980 Games were "troubled" by a serious threat of boycotts in response to a variety of international conflicts. One such threat was that the United States would boycott the 1980 Games to protest Soviet treatment of political dissidents.[56]

Prophetic, too, were these words, spoken three years before the 1980 Games by Lord Killanin, President of the IOC: "I am watching Moscow very, very closely. But so much can depend on the relationships of the major powers at the time. The first Carter impact has been of going away from détente. That can create the atmosphere in which the Games [will] have to take place."[57] Lord Killanin's crystal ball proved to be clear. He added that the United States-Soviet rivalry worried him in another respect: "[T]here is no doubt at all that Moscow is anxious to run the Games extremely well and there is no doubt afterwards that the United States will want to show that they can do them better."[58] Thus, the Soviet invasion of Afghanistan may be seen, in the Bactrian cliché of that part of the world, as "the straw that broke the camel's back" and not as the sole cause of the President's call for a boycott of the 1980 Olympic Games.[59]

Against this gloomy political background, darkened by the Soviet invasion of Afghanistan, President Carter decided to compel a boycott of the 1980 Games. He did so by issuing a series of warnings[60] based on his executive power. He also took measures under the provisions of the Export Administration Act of 1979[61]

---

[56] Williams, *Moscow '80: Playing for Political Points*, SAT. REV., Sept. 1, 1979, at 12.

[57] *Quoted in* OLYMPIC REV., Sept. 1977, at 538.

[58] *Id.*

[59] To be sure, the United States Olympic Committee (USOC), not the President, made the formal decision against participation by the USOC, but the President compelled it. *See* De Frantz v. USOC, 492 F. Supp. 1181 (D.D.C. 1980) (upholding the statutory and constitutional rights of the USOC not to enter a United States team).

[60] President Carter on occasion seems to have assumed that he had the power, with or without a decision by the USOC, to order the boycott. For example, the President warned athletes on March 21, prior to the decision of the USOC, as follows: "I can't say at this moment what other nations will not go to the Summer Olympics in Moscow. Ours will not go. I say that not with any equivocation; the decision has been made." 16 WEEKLY COMP. OF PRES. DOCS. 518 (1980).

[61] Export Administration Act of 1979, Pub. L. No. 96-72, 93 Stat. 503 (1979) (codified at 50 U.S.C. §§ 2401–20 (2000)). On March 28, 1980, under the Export Administration Act of

and the International Emergency Economic Powers Act.[62] Both acts require an underlying economic transaction, and the latter requires presidential findings of an "unusual and extraordinary threat with respect to which a national emergency has been declared."[63] On March 28, 1980 President Carter exercised his powers by barring firms from exporting goods or extending payments to the Soviet Union.[64] The ban included a range of items from sophisticated communications systems to sports clothing, sports equipment and Coca Cola.

After the USOC withdrew from the 1980 Games in the face of President Carter's threats, other NATO-member governments announced their support of the boycott. In a last-ditch effort to compete in 1980, 18 European NOCs proposed a set of depoliticizing rules.[65] Each NOC would have been represented in the opening parade by only a name board and flag bearer. National flags or anthems would have been replaced on all occasions by the Olympic flag and hymn. There would have been no political speeches in the opening ceremony. If such arrangements could not be worked out, the NOCs were prepared to stay way from opening, closing and awards ceremonies. The NOCs proposed to arrive in Moscow just before competing and to leave immediately afterwards, remaining in the Olympic Village or training facilities during their time on Soviet soil. Uniforms would have carried only the badge of the NOC and an identification

---

1979, Pub. L. No. 96-72, 93 Stat. 503 (1979) (as codified at 50 U.S.C. § 2401 *et seq.* (2000), President Carter directed the Secretary of Commerce to enforce the Olympic boycott by taking the following measures:

1. To deny all pending validated license applications for goods and technology to be used in support of or in connection with the summer Olympic games in Moscow;

2. To revoke all outstanding export licenses for Olympic-related exports that have not already been shipped;

3. To impose validated license controls on all exports not now requiring validated licenses to be used in support of or in association with the summer Olympic games in Moscow. No such licenses shall be granted;

4. To prohibit other transactions and payments associated with all Olympic-related exports. Among other transactions, the order will bar NCB from making any further payments or exports under its contracts relating to the United States television rights for the Olympic games.

16 Weekly Comp. of Pres. Docs. 561 (1980).

62 International Emergency Economic Powers Act, Pub. L. No. 95-223, 91 Stat. 1626 (1977) (codified at 50 U.S.C. §§ 1701–06 (2000)).

63 *Id.*, 50 U.S.C. § 1701(b).

64 1980 Summer Olympics in Moscow, 16 Weekly Comp. Pres. Docs. 560, 561 (1980). A few days later, the government announced a validating licensing system covering all Olympics-related products within a "policy of the Department of Commerce to permit no such export which is significant in terms of its contribution to the success of or symbolism associated with the 1980 Moscow Summer Olympic Games," 45 Fed. Reg. 21, 612 (1980).

65 *See* N.Y. Times, May 4, 1980, § A1, at 1, col. 4; Or. Statesman (Salem), Apr. 3, 1980, § D, at 4, col. 5.

badge, without otherwise identifying nationalities. Further, team members would not have gone sightseeing, become involved in special youth camps organized for the Games, or become engaged in other tourist activities. The IOC responded in two ways. It amended its rules to provide for greater flexibility in the selection and display of flags and emblems at the Games[66] and allowed NOCs to decide whether to participate in Olympic ceremonies.[67] These conciliatory efforts failed, however, to avoid the NATO-oriented boycott of the 1980 Games in Moscow.

1. The Compelled Boycott as an Example of Foreign Policy

President Carter's call for a boycott of the 1980 Games apparently did not seek an unreasonable confrontation with the Soviets after they invaded Afghanistan, nor did he use that invasion simply as a pretext for doing what was inevitable. Instead, the President's action was simply ill-advised, in striking contrast to President Roosevelt's refusal to support a boycott of the 1936 Games in Berlin,[68] which resulted in the triumphs of the black superstar, Jesse Owens, and thus of non-Aryan aspirations. The 1980 boycott was a low point in foreign sports policy.

First, the delicate balance between détente and containment had become impaired by early 1980. President Carter's platform of highly selective initiatives in pursuit of human rights had sadly collapsed, leaving very little diplomatic, economic, or military base of strength for pursuing peace and resisting Soviet expansionism.

Second, the strength of the Soviet occupation of Afghanistan probably exceeded the capacity of the United States to respond effectively, short of unac-

---

[66] An amendment to Rule 24 providing that "[t]he flag and the emblem used by an NOC at the Olympic Games shall be submitted to and approved by the I.O.C. Executive Board," IOC Modifications to the Olympic Charter Adopted by the 82nd Sess. of the IOC at Lake Placid 2, has been interpreted as a means for each NOC "to use, during the Olympic ceremonies, the flag and anthem of its choice and thus assist athletes." OLYMPIC REV., May 1980, at 230.

[67] The IOC sympathetically considered the special request of the NOCs. OLYMPIC REV., May 1980, at 227. Several teams did not participate in ceremonies, and others participated by using Olympic rather than national flags. L.A. TIMES, July 21, 1980, § III, at 1, col. 1; Kahn, "The Sporting Scene—Circus in Moscow," NEW YORKER, Aug. 18, 1980, at 58, 59, 80.

[68] Historian William Shirer observed as follows:

> It fascinated me to see how easily Americans in the last quarter of the twentieth century knuckled under to presidential authority. President Franklin Roosevelt, apparently, did not dare to insist on a boycott of the 1936 Games in Germany, despite his hatred of the Nazis and a much greater hold on the country than Carter ever had. Ironically, he made no move in that direction even after Hitler, as we shall see, just prior to the Summer Games in Berlin, carried out a daring act of aggression, in violation of solemn treaties freely signed by Germany—an act that paved the way for the outbreak of another world war.

W. SHIRER, THE NIGHTMARE YEARS 1930–1940, II 20TH CENTURY JOURNEY: A MEMOIR OF A LIFE AND THE TIMES 230 (1984). On related developments, *see id.* at 231–34.

ceptable or unfeasible military measures. The Afghan invasion was one of those geopolitically unfortunate instances where virtually any response was apt to fail, at least in the short term.

Third, the boycott was somewhat disingenuous. A willingness to host Soviet athletes at the Lake Placid Winter Games earlier the same year, under the same political circumstances, did not square well with an unwillingness to allow United States athletes to compete on Soviet territory. Also, United States intervention, such as at the Bay of Pigs in Cuba, in the Dominican Republic[69] and in Cambodia,[70] had been similar in a number of important respects to the Soviet intervention in Afghanistan. As a result, the United States may not have had completely clean hands with which to respond to the Soviet invasion.

Fourth, President Carter seemed to exaggerate the utility of the boycott as a political sanction and thereby grossly misjudged the balance between its benefits and costs. This is largely because, in President Carter's judgment, the Afghan crisis was "the greatest threat to peace since the Second World War."[71] Moreover, the President apparently assumed, without adequate expertise at his disposal, that the boycott and other unilateral sanctions would soften the Soviets.[72]

---

69 *See* Nanda, *The United States' Action in the Dominican Crises: Impact on World Order*, 43 DEN. L.J. 439 (1966).

70 *See Symposium on United States Military Action in Cambodia*, 65 AM. J. INT'L L. 1–83 (1971).

71 80 DEP'T STATE BULL., Mar. 1980, at 33.

72 It is very difficult to identify exactly what sanctions the Carter Administration unilaterally imposed against the Soviet Union in response to the latter's invasion of Afghanistan. A review of the Weekly Presidential Documents from January through July 1980 reveals both indirect and direct measures. Indirect measures included the recall of the United States Ambassador to Moscow, a request to the Congress for a suspension of SALT II deliberations, delays in opening or allowing the opening of consulates of the United States and the Soviet Union, revival of selective service registration, a call for increased defense appropriations, accelerated development of rapid deployment forces and of the MX and cruise missile systems, a withdrawal of trade preferences for Afghanistan, and offers of military assistance to Yugoslavia and several Middle Eastern states. Direct measures included curtailment of federal licensing of a range of high technology and strategic items for export to the Soviet Union, an embargo on phosphate and grain shipments there, a ban on fishing by Soviet nationals within the 200-mile zone off United States coasts, and a curtailment of cultural, scientific, and other exchange programs between the two countries.

A State Department representative listed the following additional measures:

> [A]n increase of funds for the Voice of America and Radio Free Europe, the reduction of our personnel at the embassy in Kabul, the proscription on the issuance of visas for Soviet personnel to come to the United States, the suspension of negotiations on a general trade agreement with the Russians, laying groundwork for the United Nations General Assembly resolution denouncing the Soviet invasion, and demanding that the Soviets withdraw their troops . . ., increasing efforts to get out allies and other countries to restrict credit to the Soviet Union, and discouraging the Asian Development Bank and

Vice President Mondale and Secretary of State Vance also took extreme positions. In explaining the United States position before the IOC, Secretary of State Vance claimed that "[t]o hold the Olympics in any nation that is warring on another is to lend the Olympic mantle to that nation's actions."[73] Vice President Mondale went further: "History holds its breath," he said, "for what is at stake is no less than the future security of the civilized world."[74] Polite observers might well have responded to that comment by holding their breaths, too.

Fifth, had the Carter Administration been concerned about domestic political pressures in favor of a boycott in an election year, it could have relied on international sports law as a creditable defense to those pressures.

Lastly, and most importantly, President Carter may have discounted the genuine power in the long run of people whose liberties are endangered, of poorly equipped partisans to wage aggressive and effective insurgency. Appropriately, the Afghan team at the 1980 Games entered no shooting events, only events in hand-to-hand combat (boxing and wrestling).[75]

2. Evaluation of the Boycott

a. *Effectiveness*

The compelled boycott of the 1980 Olympic Games failed to accomplish either world order or national strategic objectives even though the Games did not enjoy full participation. The lack of clarity and purpose in the boycott contributed to the policy's ineffectiveness.[76] If one assumes that the object of the boycott was to nudge the Soviets out of Afghanistan and to deter them from further expansionism, rather than to stop the Games, the boycott was a futile gesture. The Soviets remained encamped in Afghanistan and undeterred from further expansionism by the sanctions imposed by the Carter Administration. Even without hindsight, the Soviet decision to stay in Afghanistan regardless of the boycott

---

> other international loan agencies from extending any more grants or loans to Afghanistan.

Shaplen, *Eye of the Storm—III*, NEW YORKER, June 16, 1980, at 44, 66.

[73] Remarks by Secretary of State Cyrus Vance before the International Olympic Committee (Feb. 9, 1980), 80 DEP'T STATE BULL., Mar. 1980, at 50.

[74] Moore, *The Decision: No Go on Moscow*, SPORTS ILLUS., Apr. 21, 1980, at 30, 32.

[75] Kahn, *The Sporting Scene—Circus in Moscow*, NEW YORKER, Aug. 18, 1980, at 58, 66, 67.

[76] *See supra* text accompanying notes 12–14. In sum, the President first premised the boycott in the presumed danger to United States athletes and spectators, 80 DEP'T STATE BULL., Jan. 1980, at Special-B, and, on another occasion, in the deterrence of future aggression and in the notion of sending the Soviets a "signal of world outrage." 80 DEPT. STATE BULL., Mar. 1980, at 51. The Secretary of State, however, viewed the boycott as retribution for the Soviet violation of what he claimed was an Olympic principle against contemporaneous involvement by a sovereign host in open warfare. 80 DEP'T STATE BULL., Mar. 1980, at 50.

should have been predictable, as was its unwillingness to appear as if the boycott affected it.

The boycott failed for several reasons. First, boycotts of sports competition seldom accomplish their purposes and are typically counterproductive.[77] As noted earlier,[78] even those boycotts that were directed against sports-minded South Africa for the almost universally accepted purpose of promoting human rights stimulated only gradual change. Jesse Owens expressed his opposition to a boycott of the Moscow Games shortly before he died. It is poignant to recall that his successes in the 1936 Berlin Olympics[79] were among the few contemporary affronts to Nazism.

Geopolitically inspired boycotts tend to have the unintended effect of hardening the positions of targeted states. Those states do not want to be viewed as yielding to foreign pressures. Despite the threat and imposition of boycotts by several states in support of Soviet dissidents, the Kremlin further restricted them.[80]

Second, since détente had begun to unravel in the late 1970s, the Kremlin became less sensitive to Western or even Third World criticism, and thus could have been expected to resist boycott pressures. Third, boycotts discourage exactly what should be encouraged: using sports rather than war to affirm nationalism. Finally, the compelled boycott of the 1980 Games was not apt to deter Soviet expansionism since no city in the Soviet Union was scheduled to host the Games in the near future. Thus, the boycott could not have been expected to provide much of an ongoing deterrent.

b. Political Cost

Besides being ineffective, the boycott was costly to the United States, its instigator. The IOC response was prompt and sharp.[81] In geopolitical terms the United States seemed to expend political energy and clout by insisting that its

---

[77] *See, e.g., supra* text accompanying notes 51–52.

[78] *See supra* text accompanying notes 13–14.

[79] *See* J. HOLMES, OLYMPIAD 1936: BLAZE OF GLORY FOR HITLER'S REICH (1971).

[80] Willis, *Arrests, Trials, Searches: Soviets Prepare for Olympics*, CHRISTIAN SCI. MONITOR, May 1, 1980, at 3, col. 3.

[81] Lord Killanin, President of the IOC, responded rather acidly as follows:

> I personally think it's unfortunate that the President of the United States, on sporting matters, was not fully informed on the facts. . . . This led to trouble . . . [the United States] did not understand how sport is organized in the world. . . . They did not understand how the national Olympic committees work or the working of the IOC. To my mind they had no knowledge of sport other than American football and baseball. If football and baseball had been in the Olympic Games, perhaps we would not have had a boycott.

N.Y. TIMES, July 19, 1980, at A3; N.Y. TIMES, July 21, 1980, at C7.

allies endorse the boycott against their better judgment. In addition, United States allies were confused about what the United States expected to accomplish by a joint boycott. A political cartoon portrayed Coach Carter at the chalkboard, talking his players through a complicated play called "Allied Master Plan for USSR, Iran, Olympics, etc." His players, each bearing the name of one of the United States allies, were all equipped for different sports. A British cricket player highlighted the players' confusion: "Now that I know *who* we're playing, I should like to know exactly *what* we're playing." Some thought that it was one thing for the United States to boycott the Olympics, but another to force the issue onto the playing field of the Western alliance. Indeed, if the boycott had been well advised, withdrawal of the United States team alone would have made the point sufficiently to the Soviets. In seeking the support of its allies, the United States government seemed to be searching for affirmation of a shaky policy. Instead, Allied leaders were pressed to advocate the boycott to their nationals without appearing to be servile to "those pushy Yankees." Even though the world scorned the Soviet invasion, national perceptions of subservience to the United States were costly.

c. *Justice and Wisdom*

Traditionally, the United States government has avoided trying to regulate athletics beyond the requirements of the Amateur Sports Act because it has recognized the harm to athletes that can be caused by unnecessary politics. The government has therefore been disinclined to interfere with the individual civil rights of athletes and to manipulate amateur athletics for political gain. In the instance of the 1980 boycott, it was therefore especially ironic that an Administration standing for the promotion of human rights compelled the boycott. Athletes from both boycotting and participating countries suffer unjustly from such actions.[82]

Finally, the boycott was unwise. Although hosting the Games was a triumph for the Soviet Union, as the President emphasized, the Moscow venue was a modest triumph for all who favored a liberalization of the Soviet Union by opening it up to what has been described as "the biggest cultural invasion of them all."[83] Had the United States not boycotted the Olympics, television would have dramatized the cultural invasion. Thus, the media could have accomplished much in the United States national interest by intelligent, on-the-scene commentary. Ironically, Soviet moderates appear to have been the chief sponsors of the invitation by Moscow to host the Games.[84] Perhaps most obviously but significantly, the boy-

---

[82] Eldridge, *Olympics: Big 'Losers' Even Before Flame Is Lit*, CHRISTIAN SCI. MONITOR, May 27, 1980, at 1, col. 1 ("Everybody comes out a loser in the Olympic boycott."); Eldridge, *Moscow Olympics: What They Are . . . What They Might Have Been*, CHRISTIAN SCI. MONITOR, July 17, 1980, at 12, col. 1.

[83] Williams, *Moscow '80: Playing for Political Points*, SAT. REV., Sept. 1, 1979, at 12, 15.

[84] *Id.*

cott was unwise in virtually ensuring the Soviet boycott of the 1984 Games in Los Angeles.[85] Before turning to the latter boycott, it will be useful to summarize the applicable legal constraints.

3. Legality of the Boycott

a. *International Law*

The validity of boycotts for geopolitical purposes alone is questionable within the process of international sports law. Under the customary law of the Charter, government, as an organization or institution belonging in any capacity to the Olympic Movement (for example, by virtue of national law or other acknowledgment of the authority of the Olympic Movement) "is bound by the provisions of the Olympic Charter."[86] The goal of the Olympic Movement, and, hence, the shared goal of international sports competition, is "to contribute to building a peaceful and better world by educating youth through sport practised without discrimination of any kind and in the Olympic spirit, which requires mutual understanding with a spirit of friendship, solidarity and fair play."[87]

Olympic boycotts for geopolitical reasons would seem to contradict at least the last three of these aims. Even the goals of the first aim may be violated to the extent that a government's call for a boycott inhibits athletes in their development. The Charter also prohibits discrimination on grounds of politics.[88] Similarly, governmentally compelled boycotts may offend the Rule that "[t]he Games are competitions between athletes in individual or team events and not between countries."[89] Of course, manipulation of the Games by host governments for propaganda ends may violate the same provision.

Other Rules obligate NOCs to be autonomous, to resist all political pressures, and to enforce the Rules and Bye-laws of the IOC.[90] Further, the Charter provides that "NOCs have the exclusive powers for the representation of their respective countries at the Olympic Games [and other international competitions patronized by the IOC]."[91] Because the Bye-laws define the term "representation" to cover a decision to participate,[92] violations of the Rules, such as yielding to political

---

[85] *See* text at notes 99–117, *infra*.

[86] OLYMPIC CHARTER, Rule 1.

[87] *Id.*, Fundamental Principle 6.

[88] OLYMPIC CHARTER, Rule 3. The term "discrimination" refers to practices against both countries and persons.

[89] *Id.*, Rule 9.

[90] *Id.*, Rule 31.

[91] *Id.*

[92] *Id.*, Bye-law to Rule 31.

pressures, expose NOCs to withdrawal of recognition and other rights.[93] Thus, the United States violated international sports custom in 1980 by: refusing to accept the authority of the IOC, placing the USOC in an unconscionably awkward position; and threatening legal action against the latter in the event of its non-compliance with the boycott. Finally, boycotts of the 1980 and 1984 Games may have violated the norms of East-West relations enshrined in the non-binding Helsinki Accords.[94]

b. Domestic Law

The boycott of the 1980 Games was questionable under domestic law, too. The Amateur Sports Act vests *exclusive* jurisdiction in the USOC in "all matters pertaining to the participation of the United States in the Olympic Games and in the Pan-American Games, including the representation in the games."[95] Arguably, the Act challenges the President's authority to interfere in such arrangements. Instead, the President must execute the law. That is his primary constitutional responsibility. President Carter's heavy hand on the USOC, however, was questionable. Not only the President[96] but his Attorney General and White House Counsel[97] clearly indicated that they intended to seek legal sanctions if the USOC or individual athletes refused to comply with the boycott. The obvious lack of authority for the White House to do this under the Amateur Sports Act may help explain why the Carter Administration elevated the issue to the national security level. Although *Regan v. Wald*,[98] a later United States Supreme Court decision, justified restrictions on the international movement of United States nationals, that case addressed the constitutionality of established, highly specific regulations to control transactions with Cuba, not ad hoc executive discretion.

D. THE BOYCOTT OF THE 1984 GAMES

The decision by the Soviet Union and its allies to boycott the 1984 Games in Los Angeles was a kind of mirror image of the boycott of the 1980 Games in Moscow. The visibility and sheer size of the Games proved once again that they could be "the biggest political football in human history."[99] The motivation for each boycott was confused and questionable, neither complied with international sports law, and neither was successful in achieving whatever objectives it may have had.

---

93 *Id.*

94 *See* text accompanying notes 20–22, *supra.*

95 Amateur Sports Act of 1978, Pub. L. No. 95-606, § 104(3), 92 Stat. 3045, 3046 (1978) (codified at 36 U.S.C. § 374(3) (Supp. IV 1980).

96 16 WEEKLY COMP. OF PRES. DOCS. 636 (1980).

97 Moore, *The Decision: No Go on Moscow*, SPORTS ILLUS., Apr. 21, 1980, at 30, 31.

98 Regan v. Wald, 104 S. Ct. 3026 (1984).

99 Triple-jumper Willie Banks, who had been prevented by the boycott from participating in the 1980 Games, *quoted in* WASH. POST, May 9, 1984, at D4, col. 4.

The seed for the Soviet boycott was planted in 1980. It grew noticeably as Soviet-United States relations continued to sour in the wake of the Korean airlines incident on September 1, 1983, in which Soviet jets downed a Korean commercial airliner over the Soviet Union.[100] Three developments were particularly damaging: the decision by Washington and New York airport authorities to deny landing rights to Foreign Minister Gromyko en route to the United Nations; a unanimous resolution adopted by the legislature of California, the host state of the 1984 Games, which asked the federal government to ban Soviet athletes from the 1984 Games; and the formation of a "Ban the Soviet Union" campaign of harassment, the apparent purpose of which was to discourage the Soviets from sending a team to Los Angeles.[101] Further problems developed. In early 1984, the United States government indicated that it had not yet decided how extensively it would limit the movements of Soviet journalists covering the Games. On March 1, the Department of State denied a visa to a Soviet Olympic attaché, reportedly on the basis of his affiliation with the KGB.[102] The Soviets denounced the visa rejection as a violation of Olympic practice. This gridlock in Soviet-United States relations did nothing to encourage participation by a Soviet team in the Los Angeles Games.

In response to Soviet criticisms of security and other preparations for the Games, the IOC moved expeditiously to avert another boycott. Within 15 days of a highly critical communiqué issued by the U.S.S.R. Olympic Committee, the IOC convened a meeting on April 24, 1984 among IOC officials, the President of the U.S.S.R. Olympic Committee, and the President of the Los Angeles Olympic Organizing Committee (LAOOC). Taking place "in an atmosphere of co-operation and good will," the meeting cleared up some misunderstandings and produced several decisions "aiming at the elimination of possible frictions due to insufficient communication." Most importantly, according to the President of the IOC, the latter "acquired a certainty that the main obstacles towards good collaboration had been eliminated. The LAOOC promised the Soviet NOC that, in the remaining 40 days preceding the closing date for final registrations, it would devote itself to the meeting of the latter's demands."[103]

Just two weeks later, however, the U.S.S.R. Olympic Committee announced that it would boycott the 1984 Games because of inadequate preparations by the LAOOC for the security of Soviet athletes. The announcement was made on May 7, just hours before the President of the IOC was to meet with President Reagan for confirmation of United States cooperation in ensuring the safety of Soviet athletes in Los Angeles.[104] The official response by the United States government was

---

[100] *See, e.g.*, Leich, *Destruction of Korean Airliner: Action by International Organizations*, 78 AM. J. INT'L L. 244 (1984).

[101] CHRISTIAN SCI. MONITOR, Oct. 6, 1983, at 1, col. 1.

[102] CHRISTIAN SCI. MONITOR, Apr. 10, 1984, at 1, col. 1.

[103] OLYMPIC REV., May 1984, at 319.

[104] CORRIERE DELLA SERA, May 9, 1984, at 1, col. 1.

low-keyed, and the LAOOC and the USOC expressed disappointment.[105] The USOC later called upon the Soviet NOC to enter into a bilateral, non-cancellation compact to insulate the Games from politics, with fines and banishment from competition as sanctions.[106] A resolution of European sports ministers, adopted unanimously, expressed their unreserved support for the Olympic Movement, without specifically mentioning the looming boycott of the Los Angeles Games.[107]

The President of the IOC responded to the Soviet announcement of a boycott by issuing a strongly worded statement that urged the Soviets to reconsider their decision not to send a team to Los Angeles, and confirmed that the Soviet decision "did not specify any new grievances not raised at the 24th April meeting."[108] Further efforts by the IOC to get the Soviets to reverse their decision were unavailing.[109] Some 13 other NOCs joined the Soviets in the boycott; at least one other NOC did not send a team to Los Angeles for a reason unrelated to the Soviet boycott.[110]

The stated justification for the boycott of the 1984 Games was as confused and questionable as that for the 1980 Games. Officially, the Soviets expressed concern about the lack of preparations for the athletes' security and the threat of terrorism against them.[111] They also condemned United States commercialization of the Games and the unhealthy physical environment in Los Angeles.[112] The latter two complaints cannot justify a boycott, but Soviet concern about the security

---

105 President Reagan responded by writing the IOC President as follows: "I have instructed agencies of the Federal Government to cooperate fully with Olympic and local officials to ensure the safety of all participants. . . . The U.S. is totally committed to upholding the charter and fulfilling its responsibilities as the host nation of the Games." 123 TIME, May 21, 1984, at 7, col. 2.

On the LAOOC and USOC responses, *see* INT'L HERALD TRIB., May 15, 1984, at 2, col. 4; Simon, *Beyond the Soviet Boycott: How to Save the Olympics*, INT'L HERALD TRIB., July 21–22, 1984, at 4, col. 3.

106 Simon, *id.*

107 CORRIERE DELLA SERA, May 17, 1984, at 25, cols. 3–4.

108 OLYMPIC REV., May 1984, at 319. In a speech at the 88th Session of the IOC, President Samaranch emphasized that "repeated verbal and written assurances" about security arrangements had been given to the boycotting NOCs. The President declined, however, to speculate on the motives for the boycott. OLYMPIC REV., Sept. 1984, at 597.

109 OLYMPIC REV., June 1984, at 419–20.

110 A total of 19 NOCs boycotted the Los Angeles Games. Fourteen boycotters led by the U.S.S.R. Olympic Committee are listed in OLYMPIC REV., June 1984, at 419. At least one other National Olympic Committee, that of Upper Volta (renamed Burkina Faso), boycotted the Games, but its motivation was to protest a tour of South Africa by a rugby team from the United Kingdom. INT'L HERALD TRIB., July 16, 1984, at 2, col. 7.

111 CORRIERE DELLA SERA, May 9, 1984, at 1, col. 1.

112 291 THE ECONOMIST, May 12, 1984, at 54, col. 2.

of their athletes was more serious. It is worth remembering that the United States initially justified its intent to compel a boycott of the 1980 Games on the same basis. In both cases the justification was quite likely disingenuous. Security precautions in both Moscow and Los Angeles were ample, and the Soviet decision was announced just two weeks after it had accepted good faith efforts to respond to its concerns about security and the threat of terrorism. Perhaps quite simply, "[t]he Russians know how to bear a grudge."[113] Several other motivations for the boycott were also plausible although no single one of them would seem to have been sufficient to explain the Soviet action. These motivations included irritation with United States authorities who had rejected a request for a visa by a Soviet sports official, a determination not to appear as if they had backed away from earlier threats, a fear of defections by Soviet athletes to the West, an opportunity to embarrass President Reagan during an election year, and a period of non-participation with the United States that began with the Soviet walkout from the nuclear arms-control talks in Geneva.[114] There was also speculation that the Soviets wished to avoid even minimal exposure by their television audience to western culture.[115]

Global reaction was so adverse to both boycotts as to help explain why the Soviet decision not to participate in the 1984 Games was the last major political boycott in the global sports arena.[116] Even a year later, athletes from the Soviet Union and other boycotting countries were barred from international competition. The International Amateur Swimming Federation (FINA) refused to waive its rules that made only the top eight Olympic water polo teams eligible for competition for the 1985 World Cup. Consequently, the top three teams in the last World Cup of water polo—from the Soviet Union, Hungary, and Cuba—were all barred from seeking a repeat performance in 1985.[117]

Although the Soviet boycott, unlike the United States boycott, was not explicitly tied to its adversary's foreign policy, the reasons given were no more persuasive nor conforming with the rules and general practice than those asserted by the United States to justify its compulsion of the 1980 boycott. Similarly, just as the United States had failed to achieve its objectives in compelling a boycott of the 1980 Games, so did the Soviet Union fail four years later. Both anti-Soviet

---

113 *Id.*, col. 1.

114 123 TIME, May 21, 1984, at 6, col. 2, and at 12.

115 "The Russians are staying away from this summer's Olympics because it is not in their interest that these should be a success—watched by more than 1 billion worldwide televiewers gawking into a rich Los Angeles, possibly with some sports at least sufficiently medically monitored to reveal how many east European athletes are stuffed to the eyeballs on drugs, and with impresarios waiting with cheque books to lure into rich exile some of their golden youth who would win fame at the games." 291 THE ECONOMIST, May 12, 1984, at 16, col. 1.

116 *See, e.g.*, OLYMPIC REV., Jan. 1985, at 18–19.

117 THE PRESS (Christchurch, N.Z.), Feb. 4, 1985, at 23, col. 3.

demonstrators and the already ample security preparations to protect Soviet athletes remained solidly in place. Once again, politics defeated some athletes and the public. Once again, the Games went ahead—record crowds attended the 1984 Games—and the world was grateful, but once again, a sports boycott served mostly to harm world-class athletes and the Olympic Movement. Fortunately, as became clear only years later, the era of retaliatory political boycotts was over.

E. AVOIDANCE OF BOYCOTTS

1. IOC Response

As a result of the 1980 and 1984 boycotts, the IOC met in extraordinary session to consider a proposal that would have imposed sanctions against boycotting NOCs. The Executive Board of the IOC specifically proposed to bar all NOCs that had participated in a boycott from appearing in a least two subsequent Games. On December 2, 1984, however, the IOC rejected the proposal, but adopted a Resolution without sanctions that, *inter alia*, "condemns the punishment of athletes which results from a decision not to participate in the Olympic Games."[118] That seemed to be enough at the time, but there was no assurance in 1984 that the idea of political boycotts would go away. Efforts needed to be made to deter boycotts in the future.

An amendment to the Olympic Charter that was adopted by the IOC in 1985 provided explicitly that the IOC must send invitations to all the NOCs to take part in the Olympic Games one year before the opening ceremony and, just as significantly, that the NOCs must reply within four months—that is, eight months before scheduled Games. These provisions were designed to prevent dramatic, last-minute grandstanding of the sort that imperiled the 1980 and 1984 Games.[119]

2. Single or Limited-Site Proposals

The dramatic boycotts of the 1980 and 1984 Games and nervousness about the 1988 Games in South Korea demonstrated the problems associated with a politically controversial site such as Moscow, Los Angeles, or Seoul. One response to this problem would be to limit the Games to either one or several politically uncontroversial sites. The usual nominee for a single, permanent site has been Greece, the chosen site for the 2004 Games, but its location on the margins of the Middle East has also been controversial. Another version of this proposal would locate the Games, presumably on a rotating basis, in five permanent sites, one on each of the five multiple-state continents. The IOC, working with other international sports organizations, would help establish and maintain first-class facilities at each of the sites, in return for which NOCs would commit themselves in advance to send participating teams regardless of political exigencies.[120]

---

[118] OLYMPIC REV., Jan. 1985, at 17.

[119] OLYMPIC REV., Aug. 1985, at 474.

[120] Simon, *supra* note 105, at col. 5.

These proposals received some support and commentary,[121] but the IOC and other international sports organizations seem to prefer the present system of constantly rotating sites for the Games, as a means of gaining broader visibility for the Olympic Movement and of developing facilities and athletic enthusiasm at each of the sites. Moreover, the broadcast market has become a paramount consideration in choosing venues for major international competition. The single or limited site proposal is attractive because of its simplicity, the appeal of Greece and its relatively middle position in east-west relations. On the other hand, the political future of a single country, Greece or any other, is uncertain, and no country or site is immune from politics. One might recall that in 1896, at the first Modern Games, a chauvinistic Crown Prince Constantine himself escorted a victorious Greek marathoner across the finish line.[122]

3. Non-Cancellation Compacts

The USOC responded to the 1984 boycott by suggesting that the NOCs of the two superpowers, at least, should enter into a non-cancellation compact.[123] Negotiations ensured between representatives of the U.S. and Soviet NOCs. In September 1985 they signed a memorandum of understanding that binds them to the principles of the Olympic Charter, commits them "to make efforts to insure that their teams participate in the Olympic Games," provides extensively for exchanges of sports personnel and information between the two countries, and pledges them "to work together to reach a mutual understanding of problems and concerns of common interest in sports in order to further develop the Olympic Movement in their countries." A more ambitious proposal would involve all NOCs, which would accept a binding obligation, in good faith, to resist all pressures for a boycott. Yet another proposal would transform this private compact into an international, non-cancellation treaty.[124] Signatories would agree, subject to negotiated sanctions, not to interfere in the conduct of international sports competition.

4. Comprehensive Proposals for Reform During the Boycott Era

Sir Roger Bannister, the great British runner, called the Olympics "one of the great leavening forces for good in the 20th century."[125] Whether that is so or not, national sports federations and authorities strongly condemned the political abuses of sports during the boycott era. For example, in 1977 a Final Report of

---

[121] Rich, *The Legal Regime for a Permanent Olympic Site*, 15 N.Y.U.J. INT'L L. & POL. 1 (1982).

[122] Williams, *Olympic Politics Past*, NEWSWEEK, Jan. 28, 1980, at 24.

[123] Simon, *supra* note 105, at col. 4.

[124] *See* Nissiotis, *The Olympic Games in the Past Present and Future*, OLYMPIC REV., Oct. 1984, at 759, 760.

[125] *Quoted in* Atkin, *Olympic Voices for Reform*, CHRIST. SCI. MONITOR, Feb. 12, 1980, at 18, col. 4.

the President's Commission on Olympic Sports "deplores the actions of governments which deny an athlete the right to take part in international competition, . . . [c]alls upon world sports leaders to take whatever steps are necessary to eliminate the misuse of the Games," and notes "with deep regret the declining ability of the nations of the world to separate sport from politics."[126] Ironically, the statement of the President's Commission fell on deaf ears. Just three years later the same President compelled the boycott of the Moscow Games. More specific constraints on the political abuse of sports were necessary.

In 1976, just before the African boycott of the Montreal Games, United States Senator Bill Bradley proposed sweeping reform of the Olympic Games, as follows:

1) the Olympics should be open to everyone including professionals so as to eliminate the recurrent disputes over the proper definition of amateurism;
2) team sports should be eliminated from the Olympics so that the participants do not feel that they represent their countries more than themselves and that they are competing for "national prestige rather than for the joy of collective fulfillment that a team's quest for excellence can uniquely provide;"
3) everyone in the Olympics should get a participant's medal and only gold medals should be awarded for breaking an Olympic record—thus athletes would compete against a standard rather than another athlete or another country;
4) the Olympics should be situated permanently in Greece, the country of their origin—the present system of host countries promotes the incursion of politics and creates financial woes; and
5) the Olympics should be more participant-oriented and everything should be aimed at providing the athlete with a unique experience.[127]

Other, less ambitious proposals have adopted one or more elements of the Bradley Plan.

In a 1984 Declaration in Mexico City the NOCs responded to the political problems that had beset the Olympic Movement by urging the IOC to take a number of steps. The IOC responded by ratifying the so-called Mexico Declaration, which established "that the opportunity to compete in the Olympic Games is the fundamental *right* of the athletes and therefore to guarantee this right is the fundamental *duty* of the NOCs and the other members of the Olympic Family, who should take all necessary steps to guarantee and facilitate this participation in con-

---

126 United States President's Commission, THE FINAL REPORT OF THE PRESIDENT'S COMMISSION ON OLYMPIC SPORTS, 1975–1977, at 1 (1977).

127 Bradley, *Five Ways to Reform the Olympics*, N.Y. TIMES, July 21, 1976, at 33, col. 1.

formity with the Olympic Charter." In awarding the Olympic Games to a specific city, the IOC should "take special account of such factors as the political, economic and geographical situation and even socio-cultural factors so as to ensure optimum conditions for the maximum participation by NOCs" and should establish "a mechanism of consultation and of participation in the decision with the NOCs prior to awarding the Games."[128]

5. United Nations Support

In 1982, even before the Soviet boycott of the Los Angeles Games, the IOC adopted a Draft Declaration relating to the Protection of the Olympic Games,[129] which IOC President Samaranch urged members of the United Nations to support under international law.[130] The IOC opted for a declaration rather than a convention as "a much less complex and difficult procedure."[131] The Declaration confirmed fundamental rules and principles of international sports law within the United Nations framework. The clear intent was not only to constrain governments more strongly, but to make explicit that the rules of the Olympic Charter constitute international law.[132] Of course, the IOC considered that it had to limit the applicability of the Declaration to the Olympic Movement, but the scope of its authority was nevertheless very broad.[133] The IOC selected the United Nations General Assembly rather than UNESCO or another specialized forum because it recognized that the subject matter of the Declaration is essentially political and not technical.[134]

F. CONCLUSION

> . . . so Olympia glitters and overshadows every other contest.[135]

An observer of modern international sports competition might reverse Pindar's lines: all other contests, military, political and economic, seem to have cast shadows over Olympia. Within the international sports arena, some of the glitter is of tarnished gold, some of the shadow ominous. International sports competition blends cultural ideals and politico-economic realities.

---

[128] Mexico Declaration, *supra* note 23.

[129] OLYMPIC REV., Aug.–Sept. 1982, at 481–82 (1982).

[130] Samaranch, *The Main Lines of the Program of the IOC*, OLYMPIC REV., Dec. 1984, at 962, 965.

[131] *Id.* at 482.

[132] *Id.*

[133] *Id.* at 483.

[134] *Id.* at 482.

[135] Pindar, quoted in ECONOMIDES, *Olympic Games: A return to Olympia*, 1 HELLENIC REV. INT'L REL. 168 (1980).

The Olympic Charter provides that the Olympic Games "are competitions between athletes in individual and team events and not between countries,"[136] but the Olympic motto—"faster, higher, stronger"[137]—captivates athletes and political leaders alike. The history of international sports competition is replete with political intervention. Boycotts and embargoes posed a particularly serious problem. The Canadian denial of visas to Taiwanese entrants in the Montreal Games, the African boycott of those Games, the boycotts of the Moscow and Los Angeles Games, and the boycotts of the Commonwealth Games in Edinburgh were particularly prominent instances of politics defeating athletes.

Boycotts against competitors and competitions to combat apartheid and other forms of official racism are generally acceptable under international law. International sports law would, of course, permit lifting the human rights veil to examine the validity of a claim. On the other hand, the validity under international law of boycotts for geopolitical purposes requires a more detailed, case-by-case analysis. Above all, the IOC, as a chosen instrument to supervise international sports law, can be expected to emphasize, as always, that competition in the field of sports belongs to athletes, not governments.

---

136 Olympic Charter, Rule 9.

137 Actually, "Citius, Altius, Fortius," Rule 6, *id.*

CHAPTER 12
GENERAL CHARACTERISTICS AND SHARED GOALS OF SPORTS COMPETITION

How strong is the process of international sports law? Can it be improved? Along what lines should more specific rules be formulated? To begin answering such questions, it may help to clarify the nature and purposes of sports activity. The strength of international sports law ultimately depends on its ability to confirm public expectations and perceptions about the general characteristics and shared goals of international sports competition. Rules of law should therefore be realistic and acceptable.

A. GENERAL CHARACTERISTICS OF SPORTS COMPETITION

> And unable to lay siege to each other Oran and Algiers meet, compete, and insult each other on the field of sports.
>
> —Albert Camus[1]

A fundamental problem in effectively defining public expectations and perceptions, however, is their diversity: "Sport does not speak with a single voice."[2] What, then, are its voices? At first sports competition might seem to be simply a form of conflict for its own sake. What is the point of the artificial conflict? The rewards for engaging in the artificial conflict seem to vary from one culture to another and from one athlete to another. For individuals the reward include individual pleasure, satisfaction, prestige among peers and larger communities, and perhaps remuneration and a profession. There may be bigger stakes for teams and nations. Some would describe sports activity as the leading folk religion, while others might agree with George Orwell that it is a war minus the shooting. Perhaps identity, forged in a "passionate feeling of togetherness and partisan

---

[1] A. Camus, Sports (The Minotaur), The Myth of Sisyphus and Other Essays 123 (Knopf ed. 1955).

[2] Lefort & Harvey, *What's in a game?*, UNESCO Courier, Apr. 1999, at 18, 19. As the authors observe:

> In some cases sport serves the establishment; in others it can be a seedbed for social activism. At one and the same time it plays a host of contradictory social roles at local, national and international level[s]. . . . It is not monolithic. It holds difference meanings for different social groups, partly depending on what they want to get out of it.

Id.

commitment is the core of spectator sports."[3] Perhaps the rewards of group identity best explain the partisan commitment to artificial conflict that might seem to be the essence of sports competition.

Conflict is not, however, the only nature and purpose of sports competition. Although it might seem that competition is a zero-sum game—what one side wins, the other loses—this metaphor is inaccurate.[4] Instead, athletic events often result in multiple rewards or mixed reward and loss for individual participants. There are the tangible, multiple rewards such as gold, silver, and bronze medals, but there are also the intangible rewards of personal satisfaction and camaraderie even for losers. Moreover, conflict on the playing field is not uninhibited. The technical rules that initiate the conflict also limit and control it.[5]

It is apparent, then, that sports activity involves more than simple, win-or-lose conflict. When we speak of "sports competition," we are actually referring to any of three complex types of social interaction, or combination of them: *cooperation, association or collaboration*, and *contest*.[6] *Cooperation*, with its elements of close identity—camaraderie, mutual benefit and a feeling of interdependency—emerges when values are extensively shared within a group or between groups. *Association or collaboration* involves less sharing of values among competitors but enough to encourage a continuing rapport between them. Like cooperation, association or collaboration among participants helps insure that the game will go on and that there will be future games, perhaps of increased popularity. The level of cooperation and association or collaboration between members of

---

[3] *See* Liotard, *The Agony and the Ecstasy*, UNESCO COURIER, Apr. 1999, at 28, 29. Specifically:

> Since the end of the second World War, sporting events have helped countries win international prominence and build up national identity. Every new state creates its own national sports teams. During the annual sporting calendar, patriotic feelings are regularly called on to support a team or a champion. Political and economic interests and the media can use the powerful symbol of sport to rally citizens, customers and spectators around a sense of national belonging.
>
> Sporting events help people [feel] that they belong to a community. To take part, you join one of the groups of spectators behind each of the two competing teams, and share the emotions of your fellow supporters. During the match, your sense of identity is mobilized on behalf of your national, village or neighbourhood team, whichever the case may be.

Id. at 29.

[4] *See, e.g.*, Lüschen, *Cooperation, Association, and Contest*, 14 J. CONFLICT RESOL. 21 (1970), a useful theoretical and empirical study of sports sociology.

[5] *See* Nieburg, *Agonistics—Rituals of Conflict*, 391 ANNALS 56 (1970). The philosopher Paul Weiss has defined sport as a "rule-governed bodily adventure." *See* P. WEISS, SPORT: A PHILOSOPHIC INQUIRY (1969).

[6] Lüschen, *supra* note 4, at 25, 26. Lüschen acknowledges his debt to Max Weber for the latter's distinction between *Vergemeinschaftung* and *Vergesellschaftung* (roughly, "community" and "association").

opposing athletes and teams depends on such external influences as the rules; the encouragement of sports organizations; the attitude of spectators; and symbolic identifications between the competition and schools, communities and nations. A *contest*, on the other hand, deliberately channels these same influences into an artificially initiated and controlled simulation of conflict with only minimal sharing of values among the participants. The purposes are excitement and victory. Whatever the type of social interaction on the playing field, an unavoidable consequence is inequality, for "the essence of sport is competition, and competition means making comparisons, setting up hierarchies and separating winners from losers."[7] The extent of this inequality, and the tolerance for it, seems to be the principal variable among the several types of social interaction.

What values do the social interaction of sports competition offer participants and the public? *Well-being* and *respect* seem foremost, if not obvious. In addition, there is a strong relationship between sports competition and *order*. The Dutch historian Johan Huizinga, in particular, has commented on the social role of play (or sports) in confirming the aesthetic and orderly qualities of rhythm and harmony.[8] Another value is *goodwill* among competitors as well as between spectators and "the other side." That is an aspiration of international sports organizations. Rule 2 of the Olympic Charter provides that the IOC "collaborates with the competent public or private organizations and authorities in the endeavor to place sport at the service of humanity [and] participates in actions to promote peace." Whether these prescriptions in any way constitute an accurate description of the effect of competition on humankind and international relations stirs endless debate. Although sports may be an orderly, aesthetically pleasing activity in itself, it is far from certain whether it actually contributes to *global* order or even in any real sense to international goodwill. To be sure, writers from Albert Camus to Agatha Christie[9] have suggested that sports competition at least provides an acceptable

---

7 Lefort & Harvey, *supra* note 2, at 19.

8 Inside the playground a special order reigns absolutely. Here we come across another, very positive

> feature of play: it creates order: it *is* order. Into an imperfect world, into the confusion of life, it brings a temporary, a limited perfection. Play demands order absolute and supreme. The least deviation from it "spoils the game," robs it of its character, and makes it worthless. The profound affinity between play and order may be why play has a tendency to be beautiful. The aesthetic impulse is perhaps identical with that impulse to create orderly form which animates play in all its aspects. The words we use to denote the elements of play belong mostly to aesthetics; they are terms with which we try to describe the workings of beauty: tension, poise, balance, contrast, variation, solution, resolution. Play is invested with the noblest qualities we perceive in things: rhythm and harmony.

J. Huizinga, Homo Ludens: A Study of the Play Elements in Culture, No. 7 (1950); *see also* B. Lowe, The Beauty of Sport (1977).

9 "You know, I don't like the sound of Vietnam *at all*. It's all very confusing, North Vietnam and South Vietnam and the Viet-Cong and the Viet—whatever the other thing is and

substitute for political violence, but we have little idea whether or to what extent sports competition helps deter international disputes or contributes materially to global order. Since *full* cooperation, association or collaboration between opponents on anything but the rules of the game would be self-defeating, athletic interaction by itself can have only a limited integrative function. Society, however, assigns a much larger role to sports and thereby amplifies its potential for good or bad. That is why such problems as corruption, drugs, violence, commercialization, and politics in the sports arena provoke enormous frustration and disenchantment with the Olympics and international competition.

Perhaps, then, sports competition is simply a microcosm of global society.[10] In the sports world, as in the larger world, individual motivation and capacity are correlated[11] and individual activity is becoming more and more specialized and technical.[12] Social trends sweep through the sports arena in often disturbing ways. For example, doping and gender equality have become significant issues in sports. Athletes and social history have always marched together. Although the Greek Olympic tradition was inspired by lofty ideals and was self-enforced for one thousand years, it nevertheless experienced its share of commercialism and violence and eventually disappeared under successive waves of religiosity and politics in the fourth century A.D.[13] Today doping, violence, and commercialization still haunt the sports arena.

---

all wanting each other and nobody wanting to stop. They won't go to Paris or wherever it is and sit around tables and talk sensibly. . . . I've been thinking it over and I thought it would be a very nice solution—couldn't you make a lot of football fields and then they could all go and fight each other there, but with less lethal weapons. Not that nasty palm burning stuff. You know. Just hit each other and punch each other and all that. They'd enjoy it, everyone would enjoy it and you could charge admission for people to go and see them do it. I do think, really, that we don't understand giving people the things they really want." A. CHRISTIE, PASSENGER FOR FRANKFURT 46 (Pocket Book ed. 1972).

10 "Rather than being a romantically inspired panacea for the world's ills or an escape from them, the plain truth is that sport is a reflection of the society, that it is human life in microcosm, that it has within it the maladies of the society, that some athletes do drink, that some athletes do take drugs, that there is racism in sport, that the sports establishment is quite capable of defying the public interest, and that in this contemporary civilization sport does invade sociology, economics, law and politics." Cosell, *Sports and Good-by to All That*, N.Y. TIMES, Apr. 5, 1971, at 33, col. 1.

11 Janeau, *Sport et Psychologie, in* 3 SPORT: REVUE BELGE DE L'ÉDUCATION PHYSIQUE, DES SPORTS ET DE LA VIE EN PLEIN AIR 194 (1970).

12 Noting a trend toward greater specialization, quantification and reliance on equipment, one writer commented that "play is changing everywhere from a complex, multi-dimensional activity which earlier helped man to relate to his social and cultural environment, to a simple but extremely specialized activity which affords him greater and greater control over a small and, in itself insignificant, area of experience." Csikszentmihalyi, *The Rigors of Play*, 208 THE NATION 210, 212 (1969).

13 *See, e.g.*, Paleologos, *Causes of the Decadence of the Ancient Games*, OLYMPIC REV., No. 48, at 475 (1971).

Some studies have concluded, however, that well-organized athletic competition is more noble, that it often rises above the social bogs and marshes to generate mutual contacts, confidences and lasting goodwill.[14] Athletes with record-breaking aspirations seem to value the interpersonal dimension and fellowship of sports.[15] Among the heroic instances of goodwill overcoming the compulsions of national prestige in Olympic competition was the crucial assistance given to Jesse Owens by his chief competitor in the broad jump during the racist 1936 Games in Nazi Berlin. Thus, sports activity, at its best, projects an indelible image of association and even cooperation that extends beyond the sports arena. Sport can aspire to be a symbol of human solidarity.

The question then becomes, how can we maximize the values of well-being, respect, order and goodwill in international sports? Clearly we need rules, principles and procedures to produce the optimal blends of social interaction involving cooperation, association or collaboration, and contest that will maximize those values for athletes, spectators, the general public and governments.[16] Some rules and procedures may be only technical—in the sense of governing only the more or less immediate conduct of the sports event, such as the length of the playing field, the suspension or exclusion of athletes for bad behavior, and so on. More comprehensive rules, principles and procedures, with which this book is primarily concerned, seek to discourage, manage or resolve larger conflict arising out of the planning, staging, or aftermath of an event. A proper formulation of this higher order of rules—a truly legal process—may depend on a further clarification of shared goals.

B. CLARIFICATION OF SHARED GOALS

> My worst suspicions about sport had been confirmed, it brings out the very worst in people. Football leads to violence and cricket to murder. God knows what ludo would do to a man.
>
> —Horace Rumpole[17]

---

[14] *See* Bouet, *The Function of Sport in Human Relations*, 1 INT'L REV. SPORT SOC. 137, 139 (1966).

[15] *See* G. LÜSCHEN, 2 DIE FREIZEIT DER ARBEITERSCHAFT UND IHRE BEZIEHUNG ZUM SPORT (1962), *noted in* Hammerich, *Critical Remarks Regarding the State of Sociological Research in the German Federal Republic*, 1 INT'L REV. SPORT SOC. 229, 236, n.51 (1966).

[16] *See, e.g.*, Heinilä, *Notes on the Inter-Group Conflicts in International Sport*, 1 INT'L REV. SPORT SOCI. 31, 33 (1966). This study, which is premised on an analytical distinction between "in-group" and "out-group" attitudes, is noteworthy to the international lawyer because of its rule-oriented plea for an "identification and clarification of the very concept of fair play," about which there is a surprising lack of consensus, and thereafter for a "common recognition of and a commitment to the clarified principles and norms by international authorities." *Id.* at 37.

[17] J. MORTIMER, RUMPOLE FOR THE DEFENCE 18 (Penguin ed. 1984).

It is essential to achieve some agreement on *shared* goals, not just individual or national goals, that are derived authentically from the general characteristics of sports competition. Otherwise, it is difficult if not impossible to develop an acceptable and efficient legal regime for producing the right blends of social interaction and thereby for maximizing desired values. A classic study of intergroup behavior in a summer sports camp illustrates not only the significance of shared goals, but the importance of relying on group experience to formulate them.[18] In this experiment, a camp was first fragmented into groups by kindling mutual antagonism. Then, in order to bridge the differences, several techniques were initially imposed on the campers, including mutual information gathering, intergroup leadership conferences and negotiation, the introduction of a common adversary (which proved temporarily productive), and limited mutual contacts and communication. The basic rules and procedures were clear, but *artificial*. Having achieved little success with the imposed structure, the experimenters created conditions for a more natural emergence of shared goals. They staged threats to the community and its basic needs, such as creating an imminent, camp-wide water shortage and stalling a truck en route to a vital food distribution point. The resulting collaboration among the two previously hostile groups developed intergroup and interpersonal ties. Once such harmony was achieved, it continued even without the presence of shared problems. A shared practice of collaborating or even cooperating to avoid disaster had become internalized.

Similarly, collaboration or cooperation in resolving common problems internationally often leads to broader patterns of cooperation among participating states.[19] This is the essence of functionalism in the process of world order. For example, functions defined by shared goals seem to have produced integration and a durable collaboration among decision-makers within the International Labor Organization (ILO). The ILO has thereby managed to harness the energies of its members despite frequent bickering between divergent interests. Through a dynamic process of interaction, "certain kinds of organizational tasks most intimately related to groups and national aspirations can be expected to result in integration *even though* the actors responsible for this development may not deliberately work toward such an end."[20] Thus, the mutual, ongoing pursuit of shared goals can help produce blends of social interaction that maximize the real-

---

[18] M. SHERIF, IN COMMON PREDICAMENT: SOCIAL PSYCHOLOGY OF INTERGROUP CONFLICT AND COOPERATION (1966).

[19] On problem-oriented approaches to global integration, *see, e.g.*, R. FALK, THIS ENDANGERED PLANET: PROSPECTS AND PROPOSALS FOR HUMAN SURVIVAL (1971); Lasswell, *International Lawyers and Scientists as Agents and Counter Agents of World Public Order*, 65 AM. J. INT'L L. 366 (1971). A classic exposition of functionalist theory is D. MITRANY, A WORKING PEACE SYSTEM (1966); Mitrany, *The Functional Approach in Historical Perspective*, 47 INT'L AFF. 532 (1971). An assumption that international cooperation in non-political activities leads to cooperation in political activities is discussed in 33 W. POL. Q., Sept. 1980, at 314, 329.

[20] E. HAAS, BEYOND THE NATION STATE: FUNCTIONALISM AND INTERNATIONAL ORGANIZATION 35 (1964).

ization of values regardless of the strength of *a priori* rules or elaborate procedures to achieve the goals. On this foundation, a strong legal regime may then develop.

The clearest, most widely accepted articulation of the shared goals of international sports competition is found in the Olympic Charter as follows: "to contribute to building a peaceful and better world by educating youth through sport practised without discrimination of any kind and in the Olympic spirit, which requires mutual understanding with a spirit of friendship, solidarity and fair play."[21] These goals have been formulated and refined after years of experience. Based on the nature and purpose of athletic competition as it has evolved throughout the 20th century, this formulation has proven to be a durable foundation for international sports law. The goals are functional. They are thus implemented far more often than they are ignored. Other instruments, including bilateral agreements, incorporated or supplemented them.[22] National legislation also incorporates these goals. The Amateur Sports Act of the United States (Appendix I) and China's Sports Law (Appendix II) are just two examples of such legislation.

C. POLITICAL CONSTRAINTS

> Magnanimity in politics is not seldom the truest wisdom; and a great empire and little minds go ill together.
>
> —Edmund Burke[23]

Too often, sovereigns ignore the "truest wisdom" of elevating shared goals above Machiavellian agendas. This tendency may bespeak little minds, but they cannot be ignored. The crucial problem is to devise a realistic way of encouraging magnanimity in politics, for politics and sports are inseparable.

Governments commonly justify political intervention in sports for such purposes as improving the physical condition of the population, safeguarding the public order, and enhancing national prestige.[24] These purposes might seem to

---

[21] OLYMPIC CHARTER, Fundamental Principle 6.

[22] *See, e.g.*, Agreement between the German Association of Gymnastics and Sports (DTSB) of East Germany and the Main Committee for Physical Culture and Sports of Poland, based on a 1967 treaty between the two countries. Treaty on Friendship, Cooperation and Mutual Assistance between the German Democratic Republic and the People's Republic of Poland, 6 I.L.M. 514 (1967), *ratification noted*, 6 I.L.M. 862 (1967). Article 2 of the agreement reads: "In this spirit, both sides will come out for a strict observation of the principles of mutual respect, recognition, and equal rights; they will oppose all forms of discrimination in international sports organizations."

[23] Burke, *Second Speech on Conciliation in America*, Mar. 22, 1775, *in* T.C. HANSARD, 18 PARLIAMENTARY HISTORY OF ENGLAND FROM THE EARLIEST PERIOD UNTIL 1803 (1806–20).

[24] J. MEYNAUD, SPORT ET POLITIQUE 126–27 (1966).

serve goals of well-being and order, for example, but too often political intervention degenerates into a *sovereign* contest, rather than an association or collaboration among *athletes*. Even if nationalistic fervor can be channeled onto the playing field rather than the battlefield, hostility may ironically flare up there, too. Sports competition sometimes heightens tension[25] as

> [t]he thousands of spectators, and sometimes the players as well, seem to behold a mighty contest between their 'country' and the 'enemy.' The national prestige is at stake; a victory is no longer the success of a team that could play better but becomes a national victory and is an occasion for national rejoicings, out of all proportion with reality. Such an attitude is not favorable to international understanding.[26]

Group identifications, encouraged by publicity and national stereotyping, can severely test the participants' loyalty—and especially the loyalty of spectators—to the purity of competition on the playing field.[27] Established patterns of political rivalry enhance the possibility of unprescribed conflict in sports. Resulting tension may range from unfavorable propaganda and diplomatic strain to open warfare.[28]

Governments sometimes exploit these tensions despite the rule of international custom that competition is "between athletes in individual and team events and not between countries."[29] It seems that athletes and governments alike want victory. For politicians, it produces a surge of national pride that they can easily and appealingly exploit to fortify their power and vindicate their systems. The mere presence of a national flag at an athletic event may generate tense rivalry.[30]

---

[25] *See* Wohl, *Conception and Range of Sport Sociology*, 1 INT'L REV. SPORT SOCI. 5 (1966). *See generally* OLYMPISM (J. Segrave & D. Chu eds., 1981). The author of a history of the politically charged 1936 Games in Berlin concludes that they "seem to have contributed more to international misunderstanding than to peace of the world and the furtherance of international sportsmanship." J. HOLMES, OLYMPIAD 1936, at 159 (1971).

[26] Jones, *Sport and International Understanding*, *in* REPORT OF THE UNESCO-CONGRESS "SPORT-WORK-CULTURE" IN HELSINKI IN 1959, at 163 (1959), *quoted in* Heinilä, *supra* note 16, at 33, n. 6.

[27] Heinilä, *supra* note 16, at 35.

[28] *See, e.g., Documents Concerning Conflict Between El Salvador and Honduras*, 8 I.L.M. 1079 (1969). These documents relate to the serious ensuing crisis between El Salvador and Honduras.

[29] OLYMPIC CHARTER, Rule 9 (2003). Also, Rule 2, *id.*, asserts that the IOC opposes any political abuse of sport.

[30] The use of Olympic and national flags on appropriate ceremonial occasions during the Games has proven to be controversial. According to one viewpoint, the use of national symbols designed to promote association unnecessarily promotes international rivalry and derogates from the individualized spirit of the competition. An opposing viewpoint maintains that their use serves to stimulate Olympic participants as well as the public in a collaborative enterprise.

Governments may deliberately flout international custom, for example, when a host government refuses to grant visas to foreign athletes whose government it does not recognize, as the "two Chinas" problem illustrated for so many years.[31]

Despite the political temptations, and the inclination to convert all sports competition into a contest, governments usually seek a measure of association or collaboration and cooperation. They do, however, need and expect rules, principles and procedures of international law to keep the game going on and to pursue larger goals. The process of international sports law has evolved from this need and expectation.

To summarize, sports competition involves several general characteristics that include a cluster of social values—particularly well-being, respect, order, and goodwill—and varying blends of cooperation, association or collaboration, and contest. The appropriate blend of interaction to maximize the social values depends on shared goals, which vary historically. To help achieve these goals, a distinctive process of international sports law is gradually evolving.

"Sport is something more than a mirror of the societies in which it is played. It is not a carbon copy of their inequalities and problems. It is a world in its own right, with its own life and its own contradictions."[32] In the real world, of course, expectations about the role of law in achieving the shared goals must then be tempered by an understanding of political and other constraints. Even in an emerging global civic society, national institutions still provide the best means of implementing international sports law. Intergovernmental cooperation will therefore remain essential in the evolving governmental, non-governmental and intergovernmental process of international sports law.

D. CONCLUSION

Although the contours of international sports law are still imprecise, it is best defined as a process. It is law in action, and it is a fast-developing field. At its core is a distinct body of institutions, rules and principles that influence and sanction both governmental and non-governmental behavior related to international sports competition. Historically, the various fibers of law have climbed a trellis of expectations within the Olympic Movement. This trellis of expectations now extends far beyond the Olympic Games and other high-profile events.

As issues emerge in sports—for example, those arising out of global marketing; media broadcasting; and the use of drugs, gene therapy and other performance-enhancing agents—so does the process of international sports law. The

---

[31] The "two Chinas" dispute was resolved by admitting the People's Republic of China and allowing the Taiwanese to participate under the designation of "Chinese Taipei Olympic Committee."

[32] Lefort & Harvey, *supra* note 2, at 19.

arrival of open competition, which blurred the distinction between "amateurs" and "professionals," has required a restructuring of the process.

What does the future hold? The scorecard for international sports law is modest but promising. To be sure, there are few provisions in international agreements that are immediately applicable to sports-related issues. Trends in judicial decisions are unclear and sometimes contradictory. It is not always clear which organizational rules are accepted as custom and which are not, in the absence of well-established secondary rules to make that determination. The process is, however, developing rapidly. For example, arbitration of international sports disputes, especially by the Court of Arbitration for Sport, already offers the potential of a coherent *lex sportiva*.

The interlocking rings of the Olympic emblem are a reminder of the peaceful and fraternal values which keep the Olympic torch ablaze in the human conscience and government councils. Quite likely, the Olympic Movement, interacting with athletes, governments, and international organizations, will continue to provide the framework for legal development. New issues will arise and new institutions and legal relationships will emerge. What seems certain is the growth of a process of international sports law—faster, higher, and stronger.

APPENDIX I
THE AMATEUR SPORTS ACT (UNITED STATES)

A. INTRODUCTION

The efficacy of international sports law relies heavily on cooperation and implementation by governments. Comprehensive legislation in the United States may be of particular interest because it was deliberately designed to fit into the Olympic framework.

The general law of the United States governing sport is extensive. It includes, for example, the federal Sherman[1] and Clayton[2] Acts prohibiting anti-trust activity; the Lanham Act[3] protecting trademarks; federal labor laws; federal and state tax laws; state common law rules concerning contract rights, agency relationships, and torts on the playing field; and various other authority.[4]

Against this background of the general law, the Amateur Sports Act[5] substantially governs the participation of United States nationals in international competition and staging of such competition in the United States. Because of the prevalence today of open competition, in which professionals and amateurs compete together, the "Amateur" Sports Act also governs "professional" athletes engaged in sports activity related to Olympic, Paralympic and Pan-American competition. The Act vests authority over eligibility and other requirements in separate national governing bodies (NGBs) for each sport. Provisions for mandatory arbitration and voluntary mediation of sports disputes have led to decisions applicable to amateur and professionals alike that are based on the Olympic Charter and the rules and decisions of IFs.

It is significant that the horse of international sports law has been pulling the cart of domestic practice in the United States. Usually in the United States legal

---

1 Sherman Act §§1, 2, 29 Stat. 209 (1890) (current version at 15 U.S.C. §§ 1, 2 (2000)).

2 Clayton Act, ch. 323, 38 Stat. 730 (1914) (current version at 15 U.S.C. §§ 12–27a (2000)).

3 Lanham Act, 60 Stat. 427 (1946) (current version at 15 U.S.C. §§ 1051–1127 (2000)).

4 *See generally* W. CHAMPION, JR., FUNDAMENTALS OF SPORTS LAW (1990 and Suppl. 1999); P. WEILER & G. ROBERTS, SPORTS AND THE LAW 1 (2d ed. 1998); R. YASSER, J. MCCURDY & C. GOPLERUD, SPORTS LAW: CASES & MATERIALS (5th ed. 2003).

5 The Ted Stevens Olympic and Amateur Sports Act, 92 Stat. 304 (current version at 36 U.S.C. §§ 220501–220529 (2000)) [hereinafter Amateur Sports Act or Act].

system, it is the other way around: domestic law shapes international practices. Sometimes the cart moves very slowly—as in professional baseball, a sport badly tainted by steroid use and doping but moving toward a program of testing and sanctions.[6]

In this process, non-governmental organizations (NGOs) have played a pivotal role in shaping and institutionalizing sports law in the United States as elsewhere. For example, courts in the United States normally deny standing to athletes who have failed to exhaust their internal administrative remedies within sports bodies. Even when they have done so, the courts have been reluctant to allow challenges to NGO decisions based on due process or equal protection claims. Indeed, it might be said that the central role of the IOC, the IFs, the CAS and other NGO institutions in sports is second only to the International Committee of the Red Cross, in its implementation of humanitarian law, as an NGO with substantial international legal personality.

Because of its complexity, the process of international sports law must continue to rely on evolving principles of paramountcy and cooperation among a mix of governmental and non-governmental institutions. Fortunately, rules and standards to overcome the complexity of dispute resolution are becoming more uniform and clear.

B. LEGISLATIVE HISTORY

The Amateur Sports Act[7] culminated a tenacious and often tense effort to create a modern and competent Olympic program in the United States. Its impetus was a coincidence of administrative *faux pas* that beset the United States team in the 1972 Munich Olympics. For example, a team doctor failed to note that a swimmer's drug list contained a stimulant which was on the IOC's prohibited list; as a result, the swimmer lost his gold medal. Two sprinters failed to qualify because their coach gave them a wrong time for their trials. Two medal winners were disqualified from all future competitions because they refused to face the American flag during the awards ceremony. The final blow was the unprecedented defeat of a United States men's basketball team by a team from the then Soviet Union amid controversial calls by the referees which were unsuccessfully, and, some maintained, incompetently appealed by U.S. officials.[8] In contrast, the Soviet team seemed to compete with competence and class.[9] Sportswriters pon-

---

[6] On the problem in the MLB, *see* Araton, *Players' Steroid Proposal Totally Lacking in Muscle*, N.Y. Times, Aug. 11, 2002, § 8 at 1.

[7] Act, *supra* note 5.

[8] The tales of the swimmer, the two sprinters, and the basketball defeat were repeated in Congress and elsewhere as evidence of the need for reform. *See, e.g.*, 120 Cong. Rec. 15,896 (1974) (remarks of Sen. Pearson). On some unruly applications of the Olympic Rules in Munich, *see* Nafziger, *On the Rules of the Games*, Olympic Rev., Sept.–Oct. 1973, at 449.

[9] The West Germans described the American delegation as the most arrogant and the worst

dered why this country was unable to field teams with the apparent depth and polish of the Soviet and East German teams.[10] These developments stirred public opinion and convinced authorities that the United States sports organization was buried in confusion and incompetence.

There were other problems, too. Critics charged that the United States Olympic Committee (USOC)[11] was an administrative "Tower of Babel" with a bloated committee structure, inadequate lines of authority, a great reluctance to change, and insufficient experience.[12] Only 30 percent of the team managers at Munich had had any Olympic experience.[13] Committee members were selected to satisfy internal politics and not on the basis of their merits.[14] USOC officials in general were said to be "hopelessly remote" from their respective sports and were "too casual and prestige-minded to be bothered with the legitimate concerns of athletes."[15]

On top of all this criticism, the National Collegiate Athletic Association (NCAA) withdrew from participation in the USOC, vowing not to return until the United States Congress had reformed the USOC's organizational structure.[16] The NCAA decision came amidst a turbulent campaign for the presidency of the USOC.[17] These internal problems alongside the unfortunate developments in Munich demonstrated that the USOC was in trouble.

---

led of all the delegations. The West German officials contrasted the Americans' behavior with the "gentility" of the Russians and East Germans. That appraisal may have had something to do with the fact that the Russians treated West German officials to a cocktail party complete with caviar, and also presented the officials with gifts. N.Y. TIMES, Sept. 2, 1972, at 10, col. 1.

10 Further prowess of Soviet and East German teams in the 1976 Olympics deepened concern about the status of amateur athletic performance by U.S. teams. *See, e.g.*, N.Y. TIMES, July 11, 1976, § 5, at 15, cols. 1, 2, 4, 6; N.Y. TIMES, July 30, at 16, col. 7; *How Russia Wins Olympics—Why U.S. Falls Behind*, 80 U.S. NEWS & WORLD REP., June 28, 1976, at 56–57.

11 The USOC, a non-governmental, national committee within the Olympic framework, was chartered by Congress in 1950 with the responsibility for U.S. participation in the Olympic and Pan-American Games. 36 U.S.C. §§ 220502, 220503 (2000). It is governed by its members through a House of Delegates. Members of the House of Delegates elect the majority of the Executive Board. The Board is charged with carrying out the "business, affairs and activities" of the USOC. The Administrative Committee oversees the day-to-day management of the USOC pursuant to the policy guidelines established by the Executive Board.

12 N.Y. TIMES, Nov. 5, 1972, § 5 at 4, col. 3.

13 *Id.*

14 N.Y. TIMES, Nov. 6, 1972, at 40, col. 1.

15 *Id.*

16 N.Y. TIMES, Oct. 27, 1972, at 47, col. 4; N.Y. TIMES, Oct. 28, 1972, at 24, col. 2.

17 Cornell University official Robert J. Kane opposed Phillip O. Krumm, a retired Wisconsin businessman. Krumm put together a coalition of independent National Governing Bodies to oppose candidates supported by the Amateur Athletic Union (AAU) and the National Collegiate Athletic Association (NCAA). Kane was backed by the NCAA. Krumm won the election. N.Y. TIMES, Dec. 6, 1972, at 57, col. 2; N.Y. TIMES, Nov. 7, 1972, at 41, col. 4.

Despite general agreement that something had to be done, there was disagreement on what, precisely. Congress repeatedly failed to pass legislation on the subject.[18] In 1975, President Ford appointed a study group, the President's Commission on Olympic Sports (PCOS), to examine the United States Olympic program, identify the problems, and recommend solutions.[19] During its deliberations a disappointing performance by U.S. athletes in the 1976 Games in Montreal underscored the perceived problems. The PCOS, not surprisingly, found the nation's amateur sports effort to be fragmented and uncoordinated.[20] Amateur sports organizations wasted valuable time, effort, and facilities by indulging in jurisdictional squabbles and by refusing to cooperate. These feuds harmed the athletes themselves. For example, athletes were torn between the desire to compete internationally and the threat that doing so might jeopardize their eligibility for interscholastic athletics when they returned.[21] The feuds encouraged cynicism among athletes caught in the middle and caution among potential corporate donors, who had difficulty determining which organization effectively represented a particular sport.[22]

The PCOS recommended, among other things, that Congress re-charter the USOC, giving it a vertical structure of representative organizations and athletes and, to quote, the following powers:

(1) A means to settle organizational disputes over the right to be the recognized national governing body (NGB) in a sport,

---

[18] The Amateur Athletic Act of 1974, S.3500, 93d Cong., 2d Sess. (1974), which failed in Congress, would have provided for an independent federal agency, the Amateur Sports Board, which would have implemented several legislative objectives designed to rectify the problems that were becoming acute during the 1970s. *See* Comment, *Administration of Amateur Athletics: The Time for an amateur Athlete's Bill of Rights Has Arrived*, 48 FORDHAM L. REV. 53, 66–67 (1979).

[19] N.Y. TIMES, June 20, 1975, at 15, col. 1. President Ford instructed the PCOS to find a way out of the "quagmire" of American amateur sport. *Id.*

[20] President's Commission on Olympic Sports, The Final Report 1 (1977) [hereinafter cited as PCOS Report].

[21] The PCOS noted a variety of instances where athletes were hurt as a result of jurisdictional squabbles. 1 PCOS Report, *id.* at 59–60.

[22] For examples of the attitudes of some athletes, *see* N.Y. TIMES, Nov. 18, 1972, at 46, col. 5; N.Y. TIMES, Aug. 11, 1974, § 5 at 1, col. 4. The PCOS Report noted the kind of incident that undermined the confidence of U.S. amateur athletes in their administrators. In 1973, the U.S. cycling team was stranded in Barcelona, Spain, for four days while airplane tickets for the trip home were being arranged. When help finally arrived, there was money for the airplane tickets but not for the hotel bill. The team was advised to "leave inconspicuously." 2 PCOS Report, *supra* note 20, at 41. A similar fate befell a U.S. biathlon team member stranded in Minsk, Russia. *Id.* at 17. The PCOS concluded that many businessmen who might want to contribute were unwilling because of jurisdictional disputes and perceived managerial incompetence. 1 PCOS Report, *supra* note 20, at 3–4.

(2) a means to induce all organizations with significant national programs in a sport to belong to the NGB so that their activities can be coordinated,
(3) a means to guarantee an athlete's right to compete,
(4) a means to finance amateur sports more effectively, and
(5) a central policy-making forum to identify U.S. sports problems and effect solutions.[23]

In response to the PCOS's recommendations and to a long history of failures to achieve a voluntary solution, Congress passed the Amateur Sports Act of 1978.[24] It has something old, something new, something borrowed, and, of course, something red, white, and blue. In 1998 it was substantially amended. This appendix will briefly review the structure and definitions section of the Act, as amended, and then analyze and evaluate substantive provisions in terms of the objects and purposes which the Act assigns to the USOC.

1. Structure of the Act

The Act is divided into two subchapters; the first concerning the USOC and the second concerning NGBs. The first subchapter provides definitions[25] and establishes the organization of the corporation;[26] purposes of the corporation;[27] membership details;[28] powers of the corporation;[29] intellectual property rights (including names, seals, emblems, and badges);[30] restrictions against engagement in profit, issuance of stock and political activites;[31] meeting places;[32] dispute resolution processes;[33] agency

[23] *Id.* at 2.

[24] Act, *supra* note 5.

[25] 36 U.S.C. § 220501.

[26] *Id.*, § 220502.

[27] *Id.*, § 220503.

[28] *Id.*, § 220504. The 1998 Amendments extended membership to Paralympic organizations and provided for USOC representation of all amateur sports organizations that conduct national programs or competition in at least two sports included in the program of the Olympic, Paralympic or Pan-American Games.

[29] *Id.*, § 220505. The 1998 Amendments, inter alia, conferred exclusive jurisdiction on federal courts in all court actions concerning USOC responsibilities under the Act. *Id.*

[30] *Id.*, § 220506. The 1998 Amendments extended trademark protection to the Paralympic and Pan-American Games, *id.*, § 220506(a), broadened the protected marks and slogans, and specifically permitted limited use of the word "Olympic" to identify some businesses in the area of the Olympic Peninsula in the state of Washington so long as the business is essentially localized. *Id.*, § 220506(d).

[31] *Id.*, § 220507.

[32] *Id.*, § 220508.

[33] *Id.*, § 220509.

requirements for service of process;[34] procedure for the annual report;[35] and the USOC's power to select athletes when not enough have qualified for an event under specific NGB rules.[36]

The second subchapter provides for recognition of NGBs,[37] eligibility requirements,[38] authority of NGBs,[39] general duties of NGBs,[40] granting sanctions for amateur athletic competitions,[41] restrictions on amateur athletic competitions,[42] complaints against NGBs,[43] application, notice and hearing requirements for replacing an incumbent NGB,[44] and arbitration of USOC determinations.[45]

Of particular significance, the Act stipulates the requirements for an amateur sports organization to become an NGB and the responsibilities and authority of the NGBs.[46] It also provides mechanisms for the resolution of complaints and the selection of a recognized NGB from among several competing organizations[47] and gives amateur sports organizations exclusive jurisdiction over "restricted competition," that is, competition limited to a specific class of amateur athletes. If a sports organization involved in restricted competition wishes to participate internationally, it must obtain a sanction, that is, approval.[48]

C. DEFINITIONS

In order to understand the Act one must have some grasp of who the players are and what positions they play. The USOC is given the authority to establish one NGB for each Olympic, Paralympic or Pan-American sport.[49] An NGB is an orga-

---

[34] *Id.*, § 220510. The 1998 Amendments required the USOC to designate an agent only in Colorado.

[35] *Id.*, § 220511.

[36] *Id.*, § 220512.

[37] *Id.*, § 220521.

[38] *Id.*, § 220522. The 1998 Amendments prohibited NGBs from establishing criteria that are more restrictive than those of corresponding IFs.

[39] *Id.*, § 220523.

[40] *Id.*, § 220524.

[41] *Id.*, § 220525.

[42] *Id.*, § 220526.

[43] *Id.*, § 220527.

[44] *Id.*, § 220528.

[45] *Id.*, § 220529.

[46] *Id.*, §§ 220521–25. The Act also spells out the requirements and procedures for formation of the USOC membership structure. *Id.*, § 220504.

[47] *Id.*, §§ 220521(c), (d), 220527, 220528, 220529.

[48] *Id.*, § 220526.

[49] *Id.*, § 220521(a).

nization recognized by the USOC according to detailed qualifications[50] and authorized to grant a certificate of approval or sanction.[51] A *sanction* must be obtained by any amateur sports organization or individual amateur athlete wishing to hold or participate in an international amateur athletic competition.[52]

It is important to understand that the definition of *amateur athletes* is a term of art under the statute. Amateur athletes are simply individuals who meet the eligibility standard established by the NGB for a particular sport.[53] Their sources of income, from sports or otherwise are immaterial. An *amateur sports organization* is a not-for-profit organization that sponsors or arranges *amateur athletic competition*,[54] that is, an event in which amateur athletes, as statutorily defined, compete.[55] *International amateur athletic competition* is any competition between athletes "representing the United States" and those from a foreign country.[56]

Generally, this definitional framework clarifies the scope of the Act. It underscores the two sets of relationships that the Act is primarily intended to govern: (1) relations between and among athletes eligible for international competition and the amateur sports organizations, the USOC and its authorized NGBs; and (2) relations between and among those organizations.

D. OBJECTS AND PURPOSES

Congress assigned 14 "objects and purposes" to the USOC. The remainder of this appendix will consider each of these by focusing on several questions: What was the intent of each objective, how well does the respective provision in the Act serve the objective, how has the USOC interpreted and acted upon the objective, and what problems remain, with consequences for amateur athletics and the development of international sports law?

1. National Goals

> The United States Olympic Committee shall "establish national goals for amateur athletic activities and encourage the attainment of those goals."[57]

---

[50] *Id.*, §§ 220501(b)(6), 220521–22.

[51] *Id.*, § 220501(b)(8).

[52] *Id.*, § 220523(a)(4), (7).

[53] *Id.*, § 220501(b)(1).

[54] *Id.*, § 220501(b)(3).

[55] *Id.*, § 220501(b)(2).

[56] *Id.*, § 220501(b)(5).

[57] *Id.*, § 220503(b)(1).

The apparent simplicity of this first objective belies the significant questions raised by its terms. What is meant by "amateur athletic *activities*?" How should the USOC "encourage the attainment" of the "national goals" it sets? For whom are these national goals to be established? Answers to these questions are important in order to understand not only this particular requirement but the Act as a whole.

Both the legislative history of the Act and ordinary canons of statutory construction suggest that it was designed to operate primarily by giving responsibility to the USOC for appointing NGBs to govern each sport and for coordinating competition in sports on the program of the Olympic, Paralympic or Pan-American Games. These sports therefore constitute "amateur athletic activities."[58] The definitions support this position. An amateur athletic competition is an event in which amateur athletes compete.[59] The Act defines "amateur athlete" as an athlete who meets the eligibility requirements established by an NGB,[60] which is defined simply as an amateur sports organization that is recognized by the corporation (USOC).[61] Inferentially, then, "amateur athletic activities" must refer to those sports that are featured on Olympic, Paralympic or Pan-American programs because the USOC is given the authority to appoint NGBs in those sports and the Act's definition of "amateur athlete" is tied to the existence of eligibility requirements established by particular NGBs.[62] It follows that the game of marbles is not an "amateur athletic activity" in the technical sense: A competitor in marbles is not an "amateur athlete" under the Act because the USOC cannot establish an NGB in an activity—marbles—that does not appear on the Olympic, Paralympic or Pan-American programs, and thus there is no NGB recognized by the USOC to establish eligibility requirements for competition in marbles. Without an "amateur athlete" there can be no "amateur athletic competition."

An opposing argument is that "national goals" for "amateur athletic activity" are not limited to Olympic, Paralympic or Pan-American sports. After all, to the lay person, the word "amateur athlete" has a plain, easily understood meaning: an athlete who does not earn his living from competition. More fundamentally, if the Act seeks to further athletic development in the United States, it follows that the encouragement of early training ought to extend to youngsters in non-Olympic, Paralympic or Pan-American sports. Moreover, other objects and purposes in the Act suggest that the USOC must make a broad commitment to provide opportunities in amateur athletics to the handicapped and others whose access to amateur

---

58 H.R. REP. NO. 1627, 95th Cong., 2d Sess., *reprinted in* 1978 U.S.C.C.A.N. 7478, 7482, 7486.

59 36 U.S.C. § 220501(b)(2).

60 *Id.*, § 220501(b)(1).

61 *Id.*, § 220501(b)(6).

62 *Id.*, §§ 220501(b)(1), 220521(a), (b).

sports is limited.[63] Those provisions strengthen a broad reading of the Act to encompass non-Olympic, Paralympic and Pan-American sports as well.

The USOC has, however, taken the position that it must work principally through its NGBs. It is unlikely to set comprehensive "national goals" for non-Olympic, Paralympic and Pan-American sports because it is not designed to work independently of its NGBs. It is, after all, a small administrative body, an organization of organizations.[64] The NGBs do the actual grass-roots work of organizing teams, instructing coaches and officials, preparing schedules, and developing young athletes. A major reason for this reliance on the NGBs can be found in the USOC's membership. The majority of the votes in the House of Delegates of the USOC is held by NGBs. Since these NGBs have their own responsibilities and problems, it is understandable that the USOC should be primarily concerned with Olympic, Paralympic and Pan-American sports.[65]

Nevertheless, the USOC membership structure has a place for national amateur sports organizations in sports not regularly included on the program of the Olympic, Paralympic or Pan-American Games but which are widely practiced in other countries. For an organization that is engaged in a non-Olympic, Paralympic or Pan-American sport to be accepted into this membership class, the sport must be eligible for inclusion in future Olympic, Paralympic or Pan-American Games. The USOC is therefore more interested in preparing an Olympic, Paralympic or Pan-American team than in otherwise organizing and controlling non-Olympic, Paralympic or Pan-American sports.

Of the wide variety of popular sports that are not in the Olympic, Paralympic or Pan-American Games, the first to be included by the USOC in this membership classification was Tae Kwon Do, through its organization, a division of the Amateur Athletic Union (AAU). The AAU, which had been the dominant influence in the USOC before the 1978 Act, thereby regained a vote in the USOC's House of Delegates.[66]

---

63 The Act suggests a broad scope in a number of sections, *e.g.*, at § 220503(6) (encouragement of physical fitness and public participation in amateur sport); § 220503(7) (development of amateur athletic programs); § 220503(10) (provision of technical information on training and equipment); § 220503(11) (encouragement of research in sports medicine); § 220503 (12) (encouragement of amateur athletics for women); § 220503(13) (assistance in creating athletic programs for the handicapped); and § 220503(14) (assistance to racial and ethnic minorities who are under-represented in certain amateur sports).

64 This structure is comparable to that of many other NOCs.

65 *But see infra* text accompanying notes 151–52, regarding the USOC's relationship with non-Olympic/Pan American sports competition where it affects principal functions and responsibilities of the USOC.

66 The AAU is one of the oldest members of the USOC and one of the strongest; it had been the NGB in a large number of sports. *See* 2 PCOS Report, *supra* note 20, at 27.

Besides defining the sports—Olympic, Paralympic and Pan-American—with which the USOC is to be primarily concerned, the Act adds another restriction. Section 220526(7) states that "amateur sports organizations" have exclusive jurisdiction over competition that is "restricted" to a specific class of amateur athletes competing within the United States, such as college students, Marines, or members of a downtown YWCA.[67] By contrast, international amateur athletic competition governed by the Act is considered "open" because it is not "restricted" to either a single class of athletes within a single country or to non-professionals. The USOC and its NGBs have authority over "open" competition and competition leading up to the Olympics, Paralympics or Pan-American Games but not over "restricted" competition within the United States.[68] Thus, for example, conflict between the College Football Association (CFA) and the National Collegiate Athletic Association (NCAA) was, for the USOC, *ultra vires* because North American-style football is not an Olympic, Paralympic or Pan-American sport, and the members of the two organizations represent institutions engaged in restricted competition among a single class of athletes, namely, college students.

2. Productive Working Relationships Among Sports Organizations

> The United States Olympic Committee shall "coordinate and develop amateur athletic activity in the United States, directly related to international amateur athletic competition, to foster productive working relationships among sports-related organizations."[69]

The intent of this objective is centered on the mandate to "coordinate and develop sport." To understand this phrase it is important to know what language was not included. The original phrase was "coordinate, develop, and direct." The Senate Commerce Committee removed the word "direct" at the insistence of the NCAA.[70] This change suggests that Congress did not want the USOC to have the authority to dictate to a sports organization how to conduct its activity in detail. The Act thus provides a less authoritative role for the USOC. The word "coordinate" implies communication and cooperation among independent groups, whereas the word "develop" implies a promotion of growth. An obvious element in the call to "coordinate and develop," but not to "direct," is that the USOC must be able to encourage amateur sports organizations to join the appropriate NGBs if it expects to develop or coordinate athletic activity.

---

[67] 36 U.S.C. § 220526(a).

[68] *See* S. Rep. No. 380, 93d Cong., 1st Sess. 2 (1973).

[69] 36 U.S.C. § 220503(2).

[70] Amateur Sports Act of 1978: Hearings on S.2727 before the Senate Committee on Commerce, Science and Transportation, 95th Cong., 1st Sess. 178–79 (1977) [hereinafter cited as Hearings].

An important factor in the USOC's working relationship with amateur sports organizations is a simple membership structure. Prior to the Act, the USOC had a complicated and curious nine-level membership structure.[71] Group A members were the NGBs. Group B members were other national organizations that convened national championships and had a substantial number of their athletes on Olympic or Pan-American teams, such as the NCAA. Assigned to Group C were national organizations that sponsored sports recognized only in the Pan-American Games. Group D consisted of representatives from the USOC fund-raising groups in each state. Group E included organizations carrying on regional competition, such as the Big Ten Conference. The last four groups, F through I, were made up of various patriotic groups, past presidents and officers of the USOC, representatives from the IOC and the Pan-American Sports Organization, and the current officers and directors. Conspicuously absent was any provision for representation by current athletes. This was especially noticeable in a sports organization which managed to find a place for 30 organizations of a "patriotic, educational, cultural, civic, or benevolent character."[72]

Despite the long list of membership categories, the appearance of a broadly based organization was a façade. Group A members, the NGBs, held two-thirds of the votes and could automatically receive extra votes if the number of NGB votes at a meeting slipped below two-thirds of the total. Within Group A membership, aquatics and track-and-field enjoyed twice the representation of all other sports combined because of the success, popularity, and relative importance in the Olympics of these sports.[73] On the lower membership rungs, the system took some particular twists. All members in Group E had the same number of votes, so that large national sports groups were encouraged to pile their subgroups into Group E.[74] Consequently, the small Alaskan AAU and the mammoth NCAA Big Ten Conference, for example, were Group E members of equal standing. The same problem existed in Group B. Similarly, the Catholic Youth Organization (CYO) had the same number of votes as the National Federation of State High School Associations (NFSHSA) despite the immense difference in size and scope between the two organizations. A voting structure that failed to balance properly the participation of amateur sports organizations in the United States and favored a relatively small group of NGBs was one of the chief problems confronting the drafters of the Act.

In its comparative simplicity, only one section of the Act directly addresses the membership structure of the USOC.[75] Fortunately, a lot is packed into that

---

71 2 PCOS Report, *supra* note 20, at 404–06.

72 *Id.* at 406. For example, the Daughters of the American Revolution could have been a Group F member of the USOC.

73 *Id.* at 407.

74 *Id.* at 406–07.

75 36 U.S.C. § 220504.

section. It requires the USOC to establish provisions in its constitution and bye-laws for the "reasonable representation" of (1) NGBs, (2) amateur athletes who are actively competing or have competed with the last ten years, (3) amateur sports organizations that conduct a national program or regular national amateur athletic competition in two or more sports on the program of the Olympic Games, the Paralympic Games, or the Pan-American Games at a level of proficiency appropriate for the selection of amateur athletes to represent the United States; and (4) individuals not affiliated with any sports group that represents the interests of the American public. The Act does not provide any specific guidance on the meaning of "reasonable representation." Despite this ambiguity, the USOC has amended its constitution to reform its membership structure.

Until the reforms of the USOC structure, major amateur sports organizations had less influence in their NGBs because of the latter's symbiotic relationships with the IFs that had granted them membership.[76] Before the Act's passage, the system had no principled procedure for selecting an NGB from competing organizations or for removing an NGB which no longer did the job.[77] As a very loose umbrella organization, the USOC was understandably reluctant to become involved in selecting and evaluating NGBs. Each NGB effectively possessed a sphere of influence or autonomy over decisions by the USOC concerning the NGB's sport. Thus, outside its sphere of influence, an NGB in hockey was likely to be unconcerned about the selection of an NGB in basketball: it was simply someone else's sport and problem.

Dissatisfaction with the representation provided by established NGBs led to acrimonious competition and proposals for reform. A primary target of that criticism was the AAU, which had been an NGB in eight different sports. Anxious to protect its accumulated jurisdiction, the AAU repeatedly told Congress that the AAU's position as an NGB was non-negotiable.[78] The AAU argued that Congress and the USOC should not even consider the question of selecting an appropriate NGB, since under the Olympic Charter only an IF could designate an NGB.[79]

---

[76] Address by Michael Scott, counsel to NCAA, Syracuse University (Sept. 19, 1980) [hereinafter cited as Scott address]:

> As private bodies, NGBs have historically been responsible to their respective parent international sport federations. Efforts over the years in this country to subject their often arbitrary conduct to judicial scrutiny have been singularly unsuccessful. Challenges to NGB conduct on a "due process" or "equal protection" theory have been unavailing . . . attempts to apply the anti-trust laws have normally foundered. . . . So, in effect, these NGBs have been permitted to operate over the years in this country as unregulated mini-monopolies, free to use their enormous power over athletes and others in their domain without regard for substantive or procedural fairness.

[77] 1 PCOS Report, *supra* note 20, at 47.

[78] *See, e.g.*, S. Rep. No. 753, 89th Cong., 1st Sess. 7 (1965).

[79] Olympic Charter, Bye-laws to Rule 24.

Understandably, the other unrecognized organizations saw the problem in a different light. The NCAA, in particular, would not accept the idea that an organization could have a very weak competitive program and still be an NGB.[80] This was most apparent in basketball where AAU-member basketball teams were of relatively minor importance. In response, the NCAA joined other organizations to form new federations in basketball, track, and wrestling to displace the AAU.[81] Much of the pain and confusion that let to the passage of the Act resulted from the struggles between NCAA-sponsored groups and the AAU to control a particular sport.[82]

The PCOS argued that the best way to make the NGBs a viable and credible part of the amateur sports structure would be to ensure that each NGB represents only one sport.[83] In other words, wrestlers should decide what is best for wrestlers, and gymnasts for gymnasts. The Congress accepted the recommendation of the PCOS, stipulating that an NGB must have the capacity to represent a sport abroad and the backing of the sport's participants at home.

---

80 The crux of the NCAA's argument can be demonstrated by comparing the financial commitment being made by the Wrestling Division of the AAU (WD-AAU) with that of NCAA members. The PCOS reported that the WD-AAU spent about $62,696 annually for "competition." 2 PCOS Report, *supra* note 20, at 293. In 1975, the NCAA-member host of the NCAA wrestling championships spent $93,054 on that event alone. *Id.* at 347. The NCAA's position was that its members, given the large financial commitments they had made in many Olympic and Pan-American sports, deserved highly placed representation in the NGBs that oversee these sports.

81 1 PCOS Report, *id.* at 47–48. One of the organizations, the United States Track and Field Federation, explained its opposition to AAU leadership in the following manner: "The AAU has no track facilities of its own, few meets of its own, few athletes who are not already recruited and trained through the school system, and almost no coaches except those involved with educational institutions. The AAU has just a piece of paper—its international franchise." 2 PCOS Report, *id.* at 227.

82 *Id.* at 400, 401. The Olympic House coalition agreement, the MacArthur arbitration decision, and the Kheel Commission were all unsuccessful attempts in the 1960s to reconcile the AAU and the NCAA and to deter jurisdictional struggles that might prevent U.S. athletes from competing. *See generally* Moore, *The Campaign for Athlete's Rights*, 445 ANNALS, Sept. 1979, at 59.

83 1 PCOS Report, *supra* note 20, at 2. The PCOS also recommended that an organization be able to have more than 20 percent of an NGB's votes in only one NGB. *Id.* at 135. This proposal, removed from the Act by the Senate Commerce Committee, was designed to prevent large multi-sport organizations from taking over a number of NGBs. Hearings, *supra* note 70, at 165 (statement of Sen. Stone). If Congress had included the provision, it would have enhanced the "single sport" concept by making it more difficult for one organization to corral effective control over a group of NGBs. The failure to approve this provision is not crucial to the success of the Act because there are many organizations which sponsor competition in more than one sport. For example, there are several members of the USOC that by definition must conduct competition in more than one Olympic or Pan-American sport. It is therefore unlikely that one organization could dominate a large number of NGBs.

The Act responded to the jurisdictional imbroglio and the related PCOS's recommendations by giving the USOC the authority to select NGBs based on detailed procedures and criteria. These criteria require the NGB to be responsive to the actual participants in, and only in, its particular sport. An NGB must belong to only one IF; be free from restraint and control by any larger parent organization; be open to membership by any individual or amateur sports organization active in the sport; and protect the opportunity of athletes, coaches, trainers, managers, or officials to participate. The NGB selected by the USOC must also include active athletes on its board of directors and grant them at least 20 percent of the board's votes; provide for direct representation on its board of directors for any amateur sports organization that conducts a national program of competition from which world-class athletes might be selected; and ensure that each organization's representation on the board reflects the "nature, scope, quality and strength" of that organization's program.[84]

In 1998 several amendments changed the administration and governance of the USOC by requiring the establishment of an Athletes Advisory Council "composed of, and elected by" amateur athletes as well as a National Governing Bodies' Council (NGB Council) "composed of representatives of national governing bodies and . . . paralympic sports organizations."[85] Additionally, amateur athletes must represent at least "20 percent of the membership and voting power held in the board of directors of the corporation and in the committees and entities of the corporation."[86] The Athletes Advisory Council, NGB Council and USOC must all concur on the qualifications of the athlete representatives described above. The USOC must approve any exceptions to the standard.[87]

Congress provided a grace period through 1980 for those organizations subject to displacement that were NGBs when the Act was passed. During this grace period the USOC could not enforce the new NGB criteria; afterward, the USOC could suspend or revoke recognition of any NGB that failed to bring itself into compliance. The USOC could also choose to grant a one-year extension if there were "clear and convincing" evidence that the NGB was unable to comply through no fault of its own. If, at the end of this extension, the NGB still had not met the criteria, the USOC revoked recognition of the NGB. After 1980 the Act introduced important changes in the affiliations and the organization structure of the NGBs,[88] primarily in sports that had been governed by committees of the AAU. The NGB in track and field, for example, had been the Athletics Division

---

84 36 U.S.C. § 220522(a)(11)(B).

85 *Id.*, § 220504(b)(1), (2)(A).

86 *Id.*, § 220504(b)(2)(B).

87 *Id.*, § 220522(a)(10).

88 *See also* text accompanying notes 72–85, *supra*, for a discussion of the new USOC structure in the House of Delegates.

of the AAU. In September 1979 that entity was reorganized to become independent of the AAU.

The membership of the new track-and-field NGB, The Athletics Congress of the U.S.A. (TAC) (since reorganized), is a good illustration of the positive results achieved under the Act. The members of the NCAA and the NFSHSA had organized the lion's share of the track-and-field teams in the United States.[89] Neither of these groups belonged to the AAU-sponsored NGB because, in their opinion, AAU membership did not provide sufficient representation.[90] Thanks to the Act, the board of directors to govern track and field became broadly based.[91] Thus, important groups that conducted track-and-field competitions at the high school, college and post-collegiate levels were represented, as they had not been before, in the decision-making structure of the new NGB.

With one major exception,[92] the structural reforms in sports previously administered by the AAU went smoothly.[93] New NGBs were formed out of the old AAU committee structure with remarkably little fuss. From the start, the Act's restructuring of USOC membership and NGB representation seemed to work well in accomplishing the objective of productive relationships among amateur athletic organizations in the United States.

3. Exclusive USOC Jurisdiction: Olympic, Paralympic and Pan-American Games

> The United States Olympic Committee shall "exercise exclusive jurisdiction, directly or through constituent members or committees, over (A) all matters pertaining to United States participation in the Olympic Games, the Paralympic Games, and the Pan-American Games, including representation of the United States in the games; (B) the organization of the Olympic Games, the Paralympic Games and the Pan-American Games when held in the United States."[94]

---

[89] In 1974, the NFSHSA reported that 96,189 high school athletes participated in track-and-field activities sponsored by it. In 1973, the NCAA reported that 20,579 college athletes participated in its members' track-and-field programs. 2 PCOS Report, *supra* note 20, at 231.

[90] Both the NCAA and the NFSHSA belonged to the U.S. Track and Field Federation, which was organized to unseat the Athletics Division of the AAU as the track-and-field NGB. *Id.* at 225–227.

[91] The Athletics Congress of the U.S.A., 1981 DIRECTORY 6, 21–23.

[92] The exception is the case of the wrestling NGB. *See infra* text accompanying notes 201–13.

[93] This is particularly noteworthy in respect to track and field and aquatics, traditionally the AAU's strongest sports. This harmony could only be ruptured if the NCAA and other organizations become dissatisfied with the openness of the reorganized NGBs.

[94] 36 U.S.C. § 220503(3).

How "exclusive" is the USOC's authority to control the participation of American athletes in Olympic, Paralympic and Pan-American Games? Although the Act does not explicitly define "exclusive jurisdiction," the range of specific tasks reserved for the USOC as a chosen instrument of Congress does suggest an extensive scope of authority. The USOC serves as the coordinating body for amateur athletic activity in the United States directly relating to international amateur athletic competition; represents the United States in its relations with the IOC and the Pan-American Sports Organization; and organizes, finances, and controls the United States teams in the Games.[95] It also recognizes eligible NGBs, and facilitates the resolution of conflicts arising in trials, the Games, or competitions preliminary to the Games.[96]

An NGB is authorized to sanction international competition in its sport between United States and foreign athletes, whether within or outside the Olympic, Paralympic or Pan-American Games.[97] Also, each NGB is authorized to be the official United States representative of its sport in its IF.[98] The NGBs also have the authority to recommend individual athletes to the USOC for participation in the Olympic and Pan-American Games and to select national teams for other competition.[99]

While the Act gives the USOC and its NGBs the authority to select Olympic, Paralympic and Pan-American teams, school and other authorities may effectively decide whether an athlete actually competes. Hence, a first chink appears in the armor of the USOC's "exclusive jurisdiction." For example, many state high school associations have been reluctant to allow student athletes to compete in non-school competition.[100] The effective jurisdiction of the USOC is arguably not "exclusive" if a gifted athlete's fear of being barred from high school competition after international competition could dissuade the athlete from entering even the Olympic trials.

Given such threats to individual athletes and the possibility of friction between amateur sports organizations and the USOC, a working cooperation, rather than insistence by the USOC on its "exclusive" prerogatives, offers a *modus vivendi*. A good example is a model eligibility rule recommended by the

---

95 *Id.*, § 220505(c).

96 *Id.*

97 *Id.*, § 220525(a)(1).

98 *Id.*, § 220523(a)(1).

99 *Id.*, § 220523(a)(6), (7).

100 Eleven states substantially restrict non-school participation during the school year and would probably not permit an athlete to participate in a USOC-sponsored development program. Telephone interview with Warren Brown, Assistant Director of NFSHSA (June 11, 1981).

NFSHSA for adoption by state high school athletic associations.[101] Although this rule generally prohibits a student from participating in organized non-school sports competition while a member of a high school team, it makes an exception for participation in an NGB-selected national team or a USOC-sponsored "Olympic Development Program." Thus, although its model rules are discretionary, one national amateur sports organization has chosen explicitly to cooperate with the USOC in order to protect athletes and to prevent conflict. In sum, the more the USOC has been able to inspire and retain the confidence of important non-NGB amateur sports organizations such as the NFSHSA and the NCAA, the more "exclusive" the USOC's jurisdiction has become.

Retaining the confidence of non-NGB amateur sports organizations will not by itself ensure exclusive jurisdiction for the USOC over the participation of U.S. nationals in the Games. When the United States hosts the Olympic, Paralympic or Pan-American Games, the Act grants the USOC exclusive jurisdiction over the organization of the Games.[102] In fact, the USOC's jurisdiction in this area is far from exclusive. As a practical matter, an OCOG and sometimes the host city itself or state government help organize and supervise the Games. The IOC also requires the USOC to share authority with the host city's OCOG.[103]

The federal government has also challenged the exclusiveness of USOC jurisdiction over amateur athletics. This should not be surprising since the federal government has been substantially involved in amateur sports for a long time. Indeed, the need and rationale for such involvement are clear. Conscientious execution of legislation designed to enhance the development of amateur athletics is commendable. The Act explicitly stipulates that the USOC must report every four years to Congress and the President.[104] The report must contain data and proposals concerning the participation of women, disabled individuals and racial and ethnic minorities.[105] Many facets of this policy have significant political implications even though the Act declares that "[t]he corporation shall be nonpolitical."[106] When the athletic

---

101 National Federation of State High School Associations, 1980–81 HANDBOOK 48–49.

102 36 U.S.C. § 220503(3).

103 OLYMPIC CHARTER, Rules 4, 35. The USOC had greater authority over the Los Angeles Olympics than it had had in the past. At the Lake Placid Winter Games, in 1980, the USOC served a "liaison and coordination" role but was never part of the "day-to-day planning and supervision of operations." The USOC had five representatives on the Los Angeles Olympic Organizing Committee (LAOOC) and 25 percent of the members of the LAOOC Board of Directors. The USOC therefore had substantial representation in the organization of the Los Angeles Games. USOC Report to the President of the United States for the Calendar Year 1980, at 617 (June 1, 1981) [hereinafter cited as USOC Report].

104 36 U.S.C. § 220511(a).

105 *Id.*

106 36 U.S.C. § 220507(b). Some language in this section inferentially supports the argument

interests of the USOC collide with the perceived national political interests, Congress and the President are likely to intervene, as in the instance of President Carter's compulsion of a boycott of the 1980 Olympic Games in Moscow.[107]

The USOC must file a report with the President and both Houses of Congress every four years.[108] The report must include information regarding the USOC's expenditures; the activities and accomplishments of the corporation; information concerning the participation of women, disabled individuals, and racial and ethnic minorities in amateur athletic activities; and a description of efforts made to encourage such participation.[109]

The compelled boycott of the 1980 Games appeared to raise serious legal questions under the Act by compromising its requirement that the USOC be non-political, that NGBs may withhold their sanction or approval of amateur athletic competition only for *sports*-related reasons (not political reasons), and that by analogy and implication the USOC must justify a boycott in terms of the Act's basic, non-political objectives.[110] "The inescapable import [of the Act] is that the USOC may not decline an invitation to participate in the Olympic Games for reasons that are politically motivated and not related to sport concerns."[111]

On the other hand, the USOC also has a national character. It is chartered by the Congress as a patriotic society.[112] The success or failure of the USOC's amateur athletes is typically greeted, respectively, with flag waving or national soul-searching. It would be hard for an organization so deeply anchored in the national psyche to ignore the lobbying efforts of the President and Congress. The USOC clearly can be in a very awkward, if not impossible, position.

The House of Delegates of the USOC agreed to the boycott by a two-to-one margin.[113] It had little choice under governmental compulsion. Several athletes

---

that the drafters did not intend to insulate the USOC from political pressure, but only intended to create the USOC as a nonpartisan organization in the American party system. "[T]he USOC as an organization . . . shall not support any candidates for office. . . ." Id. Nevertheless, the term "nonpolitical" carries much broader connotations; this section should be interpreted consistently with a strict reading of the rule of sports law that international sports competition be free of unacceptable political pressures.

[107] *See* Ch. 11, *supra* text accompanying notes 60–98.

[108] 36 U.S.C. § 220511(a).

[109] *Id.*, § 220511(a)(1)–(4).

[110] *Id.*, §§ 220524, 220507(b).

[111] Note, *infra* note 114, at 176.

[112] The USOC is chartered in Title 36 of the United States Code, which deals with "Patriotic Societies" recognized and incorporated by Congress.

[113] The vote was 1,604 to 798. The resolution explicitly states that it was based on the President's advice that "the National security of the country is threatened." De Frantz v. USOC, 492 F. Supp. 1181, at 1185 (D.D.C. 1980).

and one member of the executive board of the USOC promptly filed a civil action to enjoin it from barring the athletes' opportunity to compete in the Games. In *De Frantz v. USOC*,[114] a federal court held that under the rules of the IOC and the 1978 Act, the USOC not only had authority to decide against sending a team to the Moscow Games, but it could do so for reasons unrelated directly to sports considerations. In reaching this controversial decision, the court ruled that the Act did not provide individual athletes with a bill of rights that might include a right to complete.[115]

A pivotal issue before the court was whether the federal government's involvement in promoting the boycott was state action that could give rise to an actionable claim for infringement of the plaintiff's constitutional rights under the First, Fifth and Ninth Amendments to the United States Constitution. The court held that the government's involvement did not constitute state action. In a later case, *San Francisco Arts & Athletics, Inc. v. USOC & IOC*,[116] the United States Supreme Court held that action taken by the USOC to protect IOC symbols was non-governmental.

The *De Frantz* court considered two legal guidelines. The first concerned whether the state "has so far insinuated itself into a position of interdependence with [a private entity] that it must be recognized as a joint participant in the

---

[114] De Frantz v. USOC, 492 F. Supp. 1181 (D.D.C. 1980). *See* Note, *Political Abuse of Sport:* De Frantz v. United States Olympic Committee, 14 N.Y.U.J. INT'L L. & POL. 155 (1981). The plaintiffs stated three causes of action in their complaint: that the USOC violated the 1978 Act, that it engaged in unconstitutional state action, and that it violated its own constitution, by-laws and governing statute.

With respect to the statutory claim that the defendant violated the 1978 Act, the plaintiffs claimed as follows:

a. Defendant exercised a power it does not have—to decide that no United States amateur athletes shall participate in the 1980 Games.

b. Defendant breached a duty to organize, finance and control participation in the events and competitions of the Olympic Games by United States athletes.

c. Defendant denied to United States amateur athletes the opportunity to compete in these Games on a basis other than their athletic merit. . . .

d. Defendant yielded its exclusive jurisdiction over Olympic matters to the political leaders of the nation.

e. Defendant acted in a political manner.

f. Defendant yielded its autonomy and has succumbed to political and economic pressure.

492 F. Supp. at 1185.

[115] *Id.* at 1190–91. *Accord*, Michels v. United States Olympic Committee, 741 F.2d 155 (2d Cir. 1984) (an athlete suspended by an IF has no private cause of action under the Act to provide a hearing on validity of drug test results).

[116] San Francisco Arts & Athletes, Inc. v. USOC & IOC, 107 S. Ct. 2971 (1987).

challenged activity."[117] The court emphasized that the USOC received no federal funding. That is incorrect: Congress authorized financial support under the Act. The court also characterized the USOC as existing and operating independently of the federal government. This conclusion is also incorrect: Congress chartered the USOC and stipulated a substantial and influential intermingling between the USOC and the government. Also, without allowing the government to dominate the USOC, Congress nevertheless required the USOC to submit to it an annual report and accounting. To be sure, the two entities may not be involved in a "symbiotic relationship" of "joint participation"[118] in the governance of amateur athletics, but they must work with each other, within the framework of the Act. The Act requires governmental involvement.

The second guideline to define state action involved an inquiry whether "there is a sufficiently close nexus between the state and the challenged action of the regulated entity so that the action of the latter may be fairly treated as that of the state itself."[119] The plaintiffs argued "a novel theory," in the court's words,

> that the campaign of governmental persuasion, personally led by President Carter, crossed the line from "governmental recommendation," which plaintiffs find acceptable and presumably necessary to the operation of our form of government, into the area of "affirmative pressure that effectively places the government's prestige behind the challenged action," and thus results in state action.[120]

Citing two opinions,[121] the court disagreed, relying on language that would require plaintiffs "to show that the Government exercises some form of control over the actions of the private party."[122] The court concluded that the government exercised neither *de jure* nor *de facto* control over the USOC. In regard to factual compulsion, the court characterized the involvement of the federal government in the boycott decision as persuasion. As a matter of policy the court wrote that it could not

---

117 *De Frantz, supra* note 114, 492 F. Supp. at 1193 (*quoting* Burton v. Wilmington Parking Authority, 365 U.S. 715 (1961)). Curiously, the United States Supreme Court (majority opinion), *id.*, failed to mention *Burton*, as the dissenting opinion notes. San Francisco Arts & Athletes, Inc. v. USOC & IOC, 107 S. Ct. 2971, at 2991, n.12 (1987).

118 *De Frantz, supra* note 114, 492 F. Supp. 1181, 1193 (1980).

119 *Id.* (*quoting* Jackson v. Metropolitan Edison Co., 419 U.S. 345, 351 (1983)).

120 *Id.*, 492 F. Supp. at 1193.

121 Spark v. Catholic University of America, 510 F.2d 1277 (D.C. Cir. 1975); Paris v. NCAA, 506 F.2d 1028 (5th Cir. 1975).

122 *De Frantz, supra* note 114, 492 F. Supp. at 1197 (*quoting* Spark v. Catholic University of America, *id.*).

equate this with control. To do so in cases of this type would be to open the door and usher the courts into what we believe is largely a non-justiciable realm, where they would find themselves in the untenable position of determining whether a certain level, intensity, or type of "Presidential" or "Administration" or "political" pressure amounts to sufficient control over a private entity so as to invoke federal jurisdiction.[123]

The court then concluded that, even if the requisite state action had been shown, the plaintiffs had alleged no violation of a constitutionally protected right, such as liberty, self-expression, travel, or pursuit of a chosen occupation.[124] The court held that any possible right to compete was not absolute; the Act sought only to spare athletes from getting caught up in jurisdictional disputes between sports organizations. The court also held that whether a right to compete existed or not, the Act provided no private cause of action and that the plaintiff's argument would unreasonably expand the concept of due process and particularly the right to travel simply to cure one of life's disappointments. A final paragraph offered sympathy to the plaintiffs, but in a dubious analogy to military service, characterized the plaintiff's plight as one of the simple, harsh and "immutable" facts of life.[125]

While life's vicissitudes may be inevitable, the result reached by the court was not. First, the analogy between non-participation in the Olympics and military service is strained. More importantly, the President's threat of legal action for non-compliance with his boycott campaign went well beyond "persuasion" to *de facto* control. Finally, the President's actions, backed up by a resolution of Congress, which possesses the power to repeal the USOC Charter, arguably insinuated the government into a position of interdependence with the USOC that made it a joint participant in the boycott.[126]

De Frantz ignored a second issue of state action. Aside from direct governmental intervention, it is arguable that the USOC necessarily acted on behalf of,

---

[123] *Id.*, at 1194.

[124] Although the court's preliminary conclusion on state action seems incorrect, its determination that the plaintiffs had no constitutionally protected right to compete seems more reasonable. The USOC's boycott of the Moscow Olympics, while it was a bitter pill for the participants, did not preclude the athletes from engaging in other competition. In other words, even if the court had found a constitutionally protected "liberty" or "property" interest in competition, it is unlikely that the boycott was at a level of constitutional concern to create an actionable violation of due process or equal protection, although the decision almost certainly was inconsistent with international authority. *See* Board of Regents v. Roth, 408 U.S. 546 (1972). In *Roth*, the court held that "[i]t stretches the concept too far to suggest that a person is deprived of 'liberty' when he simply is not rehired in one job but remains free as before to seek another." *Id.* at 575. If the Court, the ultimate arbiter, was unwilling to recognize a liberty interest in *Roth* where the interest was employment, it is unlikely that it would hold that the USOC could not bar U.S. athletes from attending a single competition, even if the competition was the Olympics.

[125] *De Frantz, supra* note 114, 492 F. Supp. at 1195.

[126] *See Burton, supra* note 117, 365 U.S. at 725.

or in concert with the state, represented by public institutions which comprise the membership of such USOC constituent organizations as the NCAA and the NFSHSA. Courts have repeatedly found that the conduct of these organizations constitutes state action.[127]

The *De Frantz* opinion provides little useful guidance for determining the extent to which political intervention by the federal government would violate the USOC's exclusive jurisdiction and defeat the USOC's obligation to remain politically neutral under the Act and the IOC Charter.[128] The decision did not adequately explore either issue, and improperly relied on the following statement of the IOC Executive Board:

> [O]n April 23, 1980 the IOC Executive Board reviewed the actions of the USOC and concluded that they were not in violation of IOC Rule 24(C), which requires that NOC's "must be autonomous and must resist all pressures of any kind whatsoever, whether of a political, religious or economic nature." To the extent that plaintiffs are alleging that defendant has violated any provision of its Constitution and By-laws requiring it to be autonomous, *we adopt the conclusion of the IOC and find that this resolves any such allegations in favor of defendant.*[129]

In fact, the IOC publicly came to no such conclusion. Despite this statement, the IOC remained concerned about the possibility of a rule infraction; it decided on April 23, 1980, that "[t]he position of all National Olympic Committees which have declined the invitation to the Games of the XXIInd Olympiad will be reviewed after 24th May 1980."[130] The court decided *De Frantz* on May 16, 1980, at least eight days before the IOC was prepared to review the matter.[131]

---

[127] *See, e.g.*, Howard Univ. v. NCAA, 510 F.2d 213 (D.C. Cir. 1975); Wright v. Ark. Activities Assoc., 501 F.2d 25 (8th Cir. 1974); Assoc. Students, Inc. v. NCAA, 493 F.2d 1251 (9th Cir. 1974); Mitchell v. La. High School Assoc., 430 F.2d 1155 (5th Cir. 1970). These cases involved issues of racial discrimination. Williams v. Hamilton, 497 F. Supp. 641, 644 (D.N.H. 1980) stated the following reasons why state action had been found in NCAA activities: Fifty percent of the NCAA's members are state or federally supported, the vast majority of the NCAA's capital is provided by public schools, the public schools dominate policy-making, and the NCAA extensively regulates and supervises its member schools. It is arguable that some NGBs include and are dominated by public organizations such as the NCAA, the military, or state high school associations. These organizations provide the NGBs with membership and sanctioning fees. The NGBs in turn scrutinize and control the international amateur sports activities of these members. Consequently, the NGBs, like the NCAA, could be seen as state actors.

[128] *De Frantz, supra* note 114, 492 F. Supp. at 1192.

[129] *Id.* at 1192, n.23 (emphasis added).

[130] USOC Press Release, "In Conjunction with the Olympic Meetings." OLYMPIC REV., May 1980, at 228. May 24, 1980, was the deadline for the USOC to accept the invitation of the Moscow Olympic Organizing Committee to participate in the Summer Games. *De Frantz, supra* note 114, 492 F. Supp. at 1183.

[131] *De Frantz, supra* note 114, 492 F. Supp. at 1181. Although the court may have been anx-

As the President's political leverage demonstrates, the Act's grant to the USOC of "exclusive jurisdiction"[132] over amateur athletics is obviously qualified. When challenged by other sports organizations, the USOC is more likely to acquire effective authority by cultivating the confidence and goodwill of its members rather than relying on the "exclusive jurisdiction" conferred by the Act. The cooperative rather than legalistic stance of the USOC toward the NFSHSA is a good example of a productive relationship. In the face of *governmental* intervention, however, the USOC's inability to withstand political pressure is disconcerting. After *De Frantz*, it is more difficult to test the constitutionality of governmental restraints on the actual freedom of the USOC. The compelled boycott of the 1980 Games was a sad chapter in international sports history and a sad commentary on the capacity of the federal government to ignore the spirit and constraints of federal legislation, the interests and civil liberties of young athletes and the customary law against boycotts for geopolitical reasons contrary to the shared, participatory goals of international sports competition.

4. Competent Representation

> The United States Olympic Committee shall "obtain for the United States, directly or by delegation to the appropriate national governing body, the most competent amateur representation possible in each event of the Olympic Games, the Paralympic Games and the Pan-American Games."[133]

As a crucial note in the Act's clarion call to greater amateur athletic success, the phrase "most competent amateur representation possible" seems modest, even anti-climactic. The Act does not require the USOC to become *competitive* in all Olympic, Paralympic and Pan-American sports but merely *competent*—and only as competent as possible. While the phrase may not be inspiring, the tone of the requirement reflected the desire of the Congress to improve the U.S. position in international amateur athletics.[134] Congress assumed that if it cleared away the organizational problems and provided for better-structured support for athletic development, U.S. amateur athletes could achieve success without much

---

ious to announce its decision before the deadline for accepting the invitation to participate in the Olympic Games, its reliance on the IOC's Statement was premature and unjustified. No final review was ever specifically scheduled by the IOC.

[132] 36 U.S.C. § 220503(3).

[133] *Id.*, § 220503(4).

[134] The comments of Senator Long and Congressman Kemp in support of the proposed Amateur Athletic Act reflect the concern and wounded pride of many Americans. Senator Long was "sick and tired" of seeing "America beaten" and declared that such humiliation should not be visited on the "richest nation on earth." 120 CONG. REC. 22,459 (1974). Congressman Kemp argued that while people in this country may understand the reasons behind its amateur athletic shortcomings, these were unclear to our "Indonesian, Kenyan, or Venezuelan friends." 120 CONG. REC. 15,753 (1974).

governmental involvement or expense. Thus, although Congress provided some financial assistance, it refused to appropriate money to support the operating budget of the USOC,[135] and chose not to make the USOC an agency of the federal government.

5. Promotion of International Amateur Athletic Competition

> The United States Olympic Committee shall "promote and support amateur athletic activities involving the United States and foreign nations."[136]

The Act seeks to implement this objective by reforming the sanctioning process to provide detailed criteria, by establishing a means for avoiding conflicts between organizations, and by minimally correlating the amateur status requirements of each NGB with those of its IF. The USOC has responded to the Act's directive by establishing programs to assist post-collegiate and non-collegiate amateur athletes to continue their active involvement in sport.

a. *Sanctioning Process*

Amateur athletes may compete only in those international competitions sanctioned by an NGB. Before the Act, NGBs used their sanctioning power as a weapon to keep amateur athletes and sports organizations in line.[137] If an amateur athlete failed to secure a sanction from an NGB before participating in a competition, the NGB might have ruled the athlete ineligible for further competition. The NGB exercised complete, unreviewable discretion in denying, approving, or ignoring requests for sanctions.[138]

The Act seeks to prevent arbitrariness by specifying a procedure for requesting and issuing sanctions.[139] An amateur sports organization planning to hold an international competition in the United States must demonstrate to the appropriate NGB that the competition will comply with the Act's requirements. These requirements include payment to the NGB of any "reasonable and non-discriminatory" sanctioning fee as may be required, preparation of a financial report of similar events conducted by amateur sports organizations, and a showing that "appropriate measures" have been taken to protect the competitor's amateur status. The sponsor must also promise to validate records of the competition, comply with any specific amateur athletic requirements of the competition, employ

---

[135] H.R. Rep. No. 1627, 95th Cong., 2d Sess. 10–13, 18, 40–41, 44–48 (1978), *reprinted in* 1978 U.S.C.C.A.N. 7478, 7483–86, 7491, 7498–99, 7501–04.

[136] 36 U.S.C. § 220503(5).

[137] 1 PCOS Report, *supra* note 20, at 59–61.

[138] *Id.*, vol. 2, at 443.

[139] 36 U.S.C. § 220525.

qualified officials, and provide medical supervision to protect the safety of athletes and spectators. An amateur sports organization wishing to participate in competition outside of the United States must generally meet the same requirements, but provide the NGB with a report of its most recent foreign trip involving the sponsorship of amateur athletes instead of a financial report of similar events.

While the Act requires an amateur sports organization to submit information to show compliance with the Act, an NGB is free to consider additional information in deciding whether to grant a sanction. Unless "clear and convincing evidence" suggests that the proposed event would be detrimental to the "best interest" of the sports, the sanction must be granted.[140] The "best interest" standard is a flexible one. For example, after citing human rights violations, NGBs relied on this standard in implementing international sports law by refusing to sanction competition between United States and South African athletes during the apartheid era.[141]

Because of the Act, an NGB is more likely to be fair in exercising authority. First, an organization denied a sanction may appeal the decision to the USOC and, if still dissatisfied, to an arbitration board.[142] The burden of proof is on the NGB to justify its denial of a sanction by "clear and convincing" evidence that granting the sanction would be detrimental to the sport.[143] An NGB knows, therefore, that an unreasonable denial of a request for a sanction is likely to be reviewed and reversed. Second, an NGB is comprised of amateur sports organizations that will want sanctions for their events in the future. Thus, for political reasons, a member of an NGB is not likely to vote arbitrarily to deny a sanction to another member when it needs to secure a sanction for its own future competition. Finally, an NGB that arbitrarily refuses to grant sanctions may be replaced by another group: the Act explicitly provides for the replacement of NGBs which do not meet their duties, one of which is to review sanction requests with fairness.[144] For these three reasons, an NGB is likely to be evenhanded in its sanctioning process.

A basic question remains under the Act: Who, precisely, needs a sanction? An NGB has the authority to sanction "international amateur athletic competition"

---

[140] The operative phrase is "[i]f an (NGB) does *not determine* by clear and convincing evidence that holding or sponsoring an international amateur athletic competition would be detrimental to the best interest of the sport, the (NGB) shall promptly grant . . . a sanction." *Id.* (emphasis added).

[141] For example, the Wrestling Division of the AAU (WD-AAU) refused to allow Oregon State University wrestlers to compete against South African wrestlers. STATESMAN J. (Salem, OR), July 21, 1981, § d, at 1, col. 5.

[142] 36 U.S.C. §§ 220527(a)(1), 220529(a).

[143] *Id.*, § 220525(a)(2)(A).

[144] *Id.*, § 220528.

both inside and outside the country.[145] The Act defines "international amateur athletic competition" as "an amateur athletic competition between one or more athletes representing the United States, individually or as a team, and one or more athletes representing a foreign country."[146] Given the private character of the USOC and NGBs, what does it mean to "represent the United States?" The legislative history discloses that the phase is "not intended to be limited to athletes or teams known as 'national' teams of the United States."[147]

If the sanction requirement is not limited to designated national teams, how broad is its scope? Must a bush league team representing a tavern in Detroit secure a sanction in order to challenge a team across the border in Windsor, Ontario, to a basketball game? The legislative history discloses that the sanctioning requirement is not intended for normal high school and college competition with Mexican and Canadian teams.[148] There is, however, no similar *travaux* to protect other cross-border competition. Fortunately, common sense has prevailed. The Amateur Basketball Association of the USA (ABAUSA) quickly indicated that it would be foolish for it to punish athletes who engage without formal sanction in a basketball game with Mexican or Canadian teams.[149] The Act relies on the NGBs for this and other interpretations of the breadth of the sanction requirements: the USOC does not have the authority itself to grant sanctions although it does have the authority to review an NGB's sanctioning decision.[150]

Because the USOC may appoint NGBs only in Olympic, Paralympic and Pan-American sports, the Act contains no provision regulating the sanctioning process for non-Olympic, Paralympic or Pan-American sports. Thus, neither the USOC nor any of its NGBs has authority under the Act to review sanction decisions by groups governing non-Olympic, Paralympic or Pan-American sports.[151] The incapacity of the USOC and its NGBs to review sanction decisions by these groups poses a threat to the USOC and the Olympic Movement when another NOC (or government) threatens to retaliate against the USOC for its failure to police the activities of such groups. A good example was the threat of many Olympic Committees either to withdraw from the 1984 Los Angeles Games or to seek a relocation of the Games, in retaliation against competition in the United

---

145 *Id.*, § 220523(a)(4).

146 *Id.*, § 220501(b)(5).

147 H.R. Rep. No. 1627, 95th Cong., 2d Sess. 13, *reprinted in* 1978 U.S.C.C.A.N. 7478, 7487.

148 *Id.*

149 Telephone interview between Conrad Hutterli and Tom McGrath, Asst. Dir., ABAUSA (July 2, 1981).

150 36 U.S.C. §§ 220521(d), 220527(a), (b).

151 *Id.*, § 220521(a).

States between U.S. and South African rugby teams.[152] Although rugby is not an Olympic or Pan-American sport and is therefore beyond the USOC's competence to govern directly under the Act, the threat posed a serious crisis for the USOC in its dual capacity. As the host NOC for the 1984 Games, it was required to coordinate with the Los Angeles Organizing Committee in preparation for the Games, and as the protector of U.S. amateurs, the USOC was statutorily bound to protect the implicitly threatened eligibility of American athletes to participate in future international competition. Fortunately, the threat did not materialize. Despite such problems the sanctioning process required by the Act has worked well. By transforming the authority to grant a sanction from a weapon to defend an NGB's territory into a tool to protect amateur athletes, the Act made a major contribution.

b. Encouragement of Participation

The United States legislation to encourage participation is by no means unique. For example, French legislation enacted just before the 1984 Games[153] sought to generate widespread participation. The peculiar origins of the Act are, however, reflected in somewhat unique provisions.

Prior to the Act, NGBs sometimes authorized major competitions at awkward times. For example, while the AAU was the NGB in track and field, it scheduled a meet in China at the same time the NCAA planned to hold its conference championships in the United States.[154] This dilemma forced top college athletes to choose between competing for their schools and passing up an opportunity in China, or competing there and, most likely, losing their scholarships.[155] The Act attempted to avoid this situation through a scheduling provision that requires the NGB to "minimize" scheduling conflicts "through coordination with other amateur sports organizations."[156] Arguably, an NGB's authority under this provision extends beyond tendering its good offices to actually resolving scheduling conflicts whenever possible. At the very least, the language of the provision, couched in terms of a duty, seems capable of persuading amateur sports organizations to comply if they expect to elicit the necessary cooperation of an NGB.

The Act also enhances participation by preventing an NGB from establishing amateur status requirements that are more restrictive than those of the sport's

---

[152] Kilborn, *Storm brewing over South African Rugby team's U.S. tour*, CHRISTIAN SCI. MONITOR, Aug. 10, 1981, at 13, col. 1. On the importance to U.S. amateurs of staging the Games in Los Angeles, *see* Eldridge, *An Olympian peers at 1984 games and perceives 'winners' everywhere*, CHRISTIAN SCI. MONITOR, Aug. 10, 1981, at 16, col. 1.

[153] *See* DROIT DU SPORT (Dalloz ed., 1984).

[154] *Hearings, supra* note 70, at 179 (statement of Mr. Neinas).

[155] *Id.* at 179–82.

[156] 36 U.S.C. § 220524(2).

IF.[157] This provision is a response to the AAU's policy of establishing uniform amateur status requirements for all the many sports it governed.[158] The President's Commission had discovered that in many cases the AAU's standard was stricter than those of the IFs.[159] By requiring that rules on amateur status be no more restrictive than an IF's rules, the Act encourages participation by excluding fewer athletes and serving to make international sports law more uniform. American athletes now know they may take the same advantage of liberal eligibility standards as foreign athletes.

The first initiative was the USOC Olympic Job Opportunities Program, which sought to match athletes with employees who were sympathetic to the athletes' training schedule, enabling them to take time off with pay to train and compete.[160] An athlete might also obtain a career position that would continue even after the athlete retires from sport.[161] Similarly, the USOC encouraged state governments to give their employees time off with pay while the employees are engaged in international competition.[162] Several state governments agreed to this program. When the USOC was unable to persuade an employer to allow someone time off with pay to train and compete, the "broken time payment" program assisted the athlete. The program became less significant after the Olympic rules against remuneration of athletes were relaxed. Today the private sector is encouraged to support athlete-employees with financial support and other employment benefits, including flexible schedules to facilitate training.[163]

6. Physical Fitness and Public Participation

> The United States Olympic Committee shall "promote and encourage physical fitness and public participation in amateur athletic activities."[164]

The Act establishes the USOC as a chosen instrument not only for international amateur athletic competition but, to a degree, for purely domestic competition as well. Even if the phrase "amateur athletic activities" is interpreted to include only those in the Olympic, Paralympic or Pan-American programs, "physical fitness" clearly contemplates a much broader range of activity.

---

[157] *Id.*, § 220522(a)(14).

[158] 1 PCOS Report, *supra* note 20 at 85, 88–89.

[159] *Id.*

[160] N.Y. TIMES, Feb. 24, 1978, at 22, col. 4.

[161] *Id.*

[162] USOC Report, *supra* note 103, at 1–2.

[163] *See, e.g.* Boroshoe, *Can I take time off for Olympics?*, CHRISTIAN SCI. MONITOR, Mar. 8, 2004, at 14.

[164] 36 U.S.C. § 220503(6).

The USOC has implemented that goal partly by staging national Olympic Festivals. Its primary tools to achieve the goals of physical fitness and public participation, however, are the NGBs. Members of an NGB often comprise many constituencies. In swimming, for example, NGB members represent amateur swim clubs, high schools, colleges, YMCA/YWCA organizations, and city recreation programs.[165] Together, these programs provide a wide range of opportunities for participation related only indirectly to major international competition.

Of course, many of these programs are so competitive as to exclude less skilled or noncompetitive participants. If, because of the Act, competitive programs in Olympic/Pan-American sports come to claim a substantially greater share of available facilities, less skilled or non-competitive participants may end up with less than they had before the Act.[166] It is therefore imperative that the USOC concern itself with general physical fitness, with the public's need to participate in amateur sports, and with the concomitant turf problems of access to adequate facilities. The USOC and NGBs understand that encouragement of top competitors is not always synonymous with the encouragement of public participation.

7. Development of Amateur Athletic Programs

> The United States Olympic Committee shall "assist organizations and persons concerned with sports in the development of amateur athletic programs for amateur athletes."[167]

As already noted, the term "amateur athlete" refers to a person who meets the eligibility standards set by a USOC-recognized NGB. This means, technically, that the USOC's developmental responsibilities may be focused primarily on sports that appear on the program of the Olympic, Paralympic or Pan-American Games. Regardless of whether the term "amateur athlete" is defined in this way or more broadly, the key word in any development program is "money." How should the USOC raise and spend it?

The Act does not provide an ongoing commitment by the federal government to finance USOC activities. Instead, the Act adopted the viewpoint of the

---

[165] United States Swimming, *The Best the World Has to Offer* (no date) (brochure explaining the organization and nature of the aquatics NGB).

[166] For example, if more pool time is devoted to training and competition, there obviously is less time for non-competitive swimmers to use a pool for improving their physical fitness. For a view of a national program which was very successful in terms of developing elite athletes but was delinquent in providing athletic facilities for the masses, *cf.* commentary on Soviet athletics. N.Y. TIMES, July 11, 1976, § V, at 15, col. 2; Willis, *Moscow amasses medals but sport's not for masses*, CHRISTIAN SCI. MONITOR, Aug. 12, 1980, at 3, col. 1. *See also* Gabriel, *China Strains for Olympic Glory*, N.Y. TIMES MAG., Apr. 24, 1988, at 30.

[167] 36 U.S.C. § 220503(7).

President's Commission that private corporations would be willing to help if the USOC could be reworked into an organization to achieve it goals, inspire confidence, and become a more aggressive fund raiser.[168] The PCOS did, however, recommend that Congress authorize a "one time" appropriation of $83 million for general operating expenses.[169] These sums would have constituted a huge increase in the USOC's financial resources.[170] Congress, however, chiseled the recommended amount down to $16 million.[171] Even this money was not appropriated as expected; instead, the USOC received $4 million directly and $6 million as matching funds.[172] Public expenditures were thus restricted in amount and application; monies reaching the USOC were earmarked primarily to offset the costs of hosting Olympic competition in the United States.[173] Despite this initial lack of public funding, the USOC's fund-raising efforts have been successful. The

---

168 1 PCOS Report, *supra* note 20, at 3–4.

169 *Id.*

170 The USOC's projected revenue for the four years of the 1976 Olympiad was $12.6 million. *Id.*, vol. 2, at 422.

171 Act of Oct. 18, 1978, § 113, 36 U.S.C. § 384 (1978). The Act itself does not provide for any funding. A separate provision authorizing $16 million for the USOC was passed as part of a larger appropriation package. Pub. L. No. 95-492, 92 Stat. 1605 (codified at 36 U.S.C. § 384 (Supp. IV 1984)).

172 The original $16 million appropriation was to be released to the USOC in fiscal year 1980. In 1980 Congress did not include the $16 million in the budget. Senator Ted Stevens did manage to persuade the Congress to expend $4 million immediately and $6 million in matching funds to be disbursed by the Secretary of Commerce. Act of July 8, 1980, Pub. L. No. 96-304, § 203, 94 Stat. 898. According to the USOC, $4 million "was regarded as 'disaster funds'" to cover loans the USOC had taken out to finance U.S. preparation for the Moscow Olympics. *See* USOC Report, *supra* note 103, at 2, 3.

173 The United States government has been more willing to reimburse the USOC and related organizations for hosting international competition in this country than to provide federal funds for the broader development of amateur athletics. For example, the Department of Commerce was able to merge the Olympic Winter Games Authorization Act, which made federal money available for the Lake Placid Olympics, into a program administered by the Economic Development Administration, because Lake Placid is in a depressed area. The Department of Commerce was uncomfortable, however, with an appropriation to "finance the development and operation of programs to assist in the restructuring of amateur sports" because it has no similar program to which the appropriation could be tied. Letter from C.L. Haslam, Gen. Counsel of U.S. Dept. of Com., to Hon. Peter W. Rodino, Chairman of the House Committee on the Judiciary (June 20, 1978), *reprinted in* 1978 U.S.C.C.A.N. 7478, 7497–98. After the tremendous expense associated with the Munich, Montreal, and Lake Placid Olympics, city governments became reluctant to sponsor the Olympic Games. Galante, *The Olympic Games: Legal Hurdles and Lawsuits*, 4 L.A. Law., June 1981, at 19, 20, 28. A vocal minority of Congress for many years has been less willing to supply the money necessary to hold Olympic Games. *See, e.g.*, New York Times, Sept. 16, 1972, at 14, col. 3. *See also* N.Y. Times, Apr. 4, 1976, § v, at 2, col. 1. After Denver withdrew its bid to host the 1976 Winter Olympics, the USOC changed its procedures for determining potential U.S. Olympic sites. The new procedures require the potential host city to show that substantial funding and facilities already exist and that surveys show public support in the city. N.Y. Times, July 15, 1973, § V, at 1, col. 5.

financially profitable 1984 Games in Los Angeles provided a big boost.[174] Even before, the USOC had been successful in raising money: The USOC raised $12.6 million for the 1976 Olympiad,[175] and over $49 million for the 1980 Olympiad.[176] The USOC's budget for the 1984 (-88) Olympiad was $140 million. To be sure, this impressive fund-raising effort cannot be attributed solely to the passage of the Act: in 1977 alone, as the Act was being worked out, the USOC raised more money from corporations than it had over the entire previous Olympiad.[177]

Actually, the USOC and its membership had been courting corporate sponsorship for some time. For example, in 1974 the AAU swim committee persuaded Phillips Petroleum Company to sponsor the senior swimming program for the 1976 Olympiad.[178] As the 1980 Olympics approached, 50 corporations had bought the right to declare that their product was used or approved by the U.S. Olympic team, leading to the wry but un-prophetic observation that "[i]n 776 B.C. Greek Victors in the first Olympic games wore only a crown of laurel leaves. In 1980, when U.S. athletes march in Moscow, they'll be wearing Levi Strauss clothing, Timex watches, and Coppertone tans."[179]

Aside from the formal impetus from the Act, both Congress and the USOC have been helpful. Congress has encouraged the growth of amateur athletics through the Internal Revenue Code, which provides a qualified tax-exempt status to any entity organized to foster national or international amateur sports competition.

The USOC has also improved its use of money for programs of sports development. It is faced with the difficulty of incorporating external factors into its development plans. For example, academic institutions in the United States play a critical role in training young athletes.[180] This is at once an advantage and a potential problem. On one hand, almost every child is exposed to sports through gym classes and interscholastic competitions. On the other hand, schools often

---

174 *See* Ch. 1, *supra* text accompanying notes 40–41.

175 2 PCOS Report, *supra* note 20, at 422.

176 USOC, Financial statements and Supplemental Schedules for the Year and Four Year Period Ended December 31, 1980 and Auditor's Opinion (June 1, 1981) [hereinafter cited as 1980 Audit]. By 1981 the USOC's yearly revenue grew to $17.1 million. USOC, Financial Statements and Supplemental schedules for the Year and Four Year Period Ended December 31, 1981 and Auditor's Opinion 3 (June 1, 1982) [hereinafter cited as 1981 Audit].

177 N.Y. TIMES, Aug. 14, 1977, § V, at 4, col. 1.

178 N.Y. TIMES, Aug. 11, 1974, § V, at 5, col. 2.

179 WALL ST. J., Apr. 13, 1979, at 1, col. 1.

180 In 1971–72, the NCAA's 663 members had over 5,300 full-time coaches, $1.5 billion in facilities, and a total annual operating budget of $535 million, of which $154 million went for athletic scholarships. 2 PCOS Report, *supra* note 20, at 331. The scope of the NFSHSA is even more impressive. Over 20,000 high schools are members of the NFSHSA and their programs involved over three million athletes. *Id.* at 359.

have interests that diverge from those of the USOC. To an academic sports director many Olympic sports, unlike football, for example, are often regarded as "minor" or "non-revenue" sports.[181] When times are tough, these are typically the first to be cut from a school's athletic program.[182] To be effective in developing broadly based amateur athletic programs, the USOC must recognize and work with the schools.

The USOC's assistance for the development of world-class athletes had a checkered past prior to the Act. Instead of emphasizing under-developed programs, the USOC allocated development money on the basis of what amounted to a spoils system. The more successful and popular the sport, the more development money it received.[183] This left minor sports, which most needed the development programs, out in the cold. For example, in the 1976 Olympiad men's track and field received the most development money, $216,500; at the bottom of the appropriations list, synchronized swimming received only $17,060.[184]

After the Act, however, the USOC greatly improved its sports development program.[185] Indeed, the USOC has established an impressive fund-raising apparatus and a better method for funneling money to under-developed sports and a few established programs of sports development.

8. Conflict Resolution and Athletes' Rights

> The United States Olympic Committee shall "provide for the swift resolution of conflicts and disputes involving amateur athletes, national governing bod-

[181] The NCAA maintains that there is not a single college track-and-field program in the country which does not lose money. Hearings, *supra* note 70, at 160–61 (remarks of Mr. Byers). Football and ice hockey are the only sports which make much money; basketball breaks even. *Id.*

[182] *See generally* 1 PCOS Report, *supra* note 20, at 70.

[183] Six criteria were used to determine how much development money an NGB should receive. The criteria were medal production, world rank, participation (number of amateur athletes engaged in the sport), NGB activities (number of activities such as training clinics), team size (number of athletes on an Olympic team), and public interest (popularity of the sport in the U.S.). These criteria were weighted as follows:

Medal Production	15%
World Rank	27%
Participation	20%
NGB Activities	13%
Team Size	10%
Public Interest	15%

Id., vol. 2, at 423.

[184] *Id.* at 425.

[185] 2 PCOS Report, *supra* note 20, at 5, 76, 109, 201.

ies, and amateur sports organizations, and protect the opportunity of any amateur athlete, coach, trainer, manager, administrator, or official to participate in amateur athletic competition."[186]

The Act requires that the USOC,

> shall establish and maintain provisions [in its constitution and by-laws] for the swift and equitable resolution of disputes involving any of its members and relating to the opportunity of an amateur athlete, coach, trainer, manager, administrator, or official to participate in the Olympic Games, the Paralympic Games, the Pan-American Games, world championship competition, or other such protected competition as defined in the constitution and by-laws of the corporation.[187]

More directly, the Act specifies procedures for settling two common types of conflicts: (1) those arising when an amateur sports organization or an eligible person attempts to compel an NGB to comply with the organization and sanctioning criteria in the Act, and (2) those arising when an amateur sports organization seeks to replace an incumbent NGB.

a. *Complaint Mechanism: Enforcing Compliance with the Organizational Criteria*

The Act establishes certain criteria for establishment of an NGB.[188] If an NGB fails to satisfy the criteria, any person eligible to belong to it or an amateur sports organization may file a complaint with the USOC against the NGB.[189] A complainant may take this action only after having "exhausted all available remedies" within the NGB.[190] The USOC must waive this requirement, however, if the complainant can show by "clear and convincing" evidence that complying with it would result in "unnecessary delay."[191] Within 30 days after the filing date, the USOC must rule on whether the complainant's remedies within the NGB have been exhausted or, if not, whether unnecessary delay would result by insisting on an exhaustion of remedies.[192] If the USOC rules that the complainant is entitled to bring the complaint before the USOC, it must schedule a hearing within 90 days of the filing date.[193] After the hearing the USOC may either dismiss the

---

186 United States Olympic Committee, *The Olympic Games*, at 9 (1979); Atkin, *U.S. festival emerges as showcase for Olympic hopefuls*, CHRISTIAN SCI. MONITOR, July 31, 1981, at 14, col. 1; *id.*, Mar. 24, 1988, at 16, col. 4.

187 36 U.S.C. § 220509(a).

188 *Id.*, § 220522.

189 *Id.*, § 220527(a)(1).

190 *Id.*, § 220527(b)(1)(a).

191 *Id.*

192 *Id.*, § 220527(b)(2).

193 *Id.*, § 220527(c).

complaint, place the NGB on probation for up to 180 days, or revoke its recognition of the NGB.[194] If the NGB is placed on probation and fails to bring itself into compliance with the Act in the required time, the USOC must revoke recognition of the NGB unless the latter can show by clear and convincing evidence that it needs more time through no fault of its own.[195] Either party may appeal the USOC's decision to a regional office of the American Arbitration Association (AAA).[196] The demand for arbitration must be filed within 30 days of the USOC's decision. These procedures have the positive effect of curtailing formal complaints within the USOC; most complaints have been resolved amicably without arbitration.

b. *NGB Challenge Mechanism: Replacing an Incompetent NGB*

The challenge mechanism for replacing an existing NGB is similar to the complaint procedure except, of course, that an individual cannot file a challenge, and the relief sought by the challenging organization is generally its displacement of the existing NGB.[197] To succeed in its challenge,[198] an organization must first appear in a hearing to show by a preponderance of the evidence that it meets the criteria for recognition as an NGB. The challenger must also show either (1) that the current NGB does not meet those criteria, or (2) that the challenger will do a better job of meeting criteria and provides, or is capable of providing, a more effective national program of competition than the current NGB. Within 30 days after the hearing the USOC must decide whether to retain the existing NGB; revoke recognition of the existing NGB and declare a vacancy, recognizing neither party to a challenge; replace the existing NGB with the challenger; or place the existing NGB on probation.[199] The USOC has 61 days to recommend a new NGB to the appropriate IF; any party aggrieved by a USOC decision on a challenge has a right to arbitration if it files a demand within thirty days of the USOC's decision.[200]

While the complaint mechanism has worked quite smoothly, the challenge mechanism was seriously strained by a dispute between the United States Wrestling Federation (USWF) and the Wrestling Division of the AAU (WD-AAU). Both organizations wanted to represent amateur wrestling. Shortly before

---

194 *Id.*, § 220527(d)(2).

195 *Id.*, § 220527(d)(3).

196 *Id.*, § 220529(a).

197 *Id.*, § 220528(a).

198 The USOC does not, however, have to wait for a complaint or challenge before it takes action. On its own initiative the USOC may review the performance of an NGB. *Id.* § 220521(d). If the USOC is not satisfied, it may take whatever action it deems appropriate.

199 36 U.S.C. §§ 220528(f).

200 *Id.* § 220521(c), 220529(b).

the Act was passed in 1978, the USWF challenged the WD-AAU under the USOC Constitution. The Executive Board of the USOC, after a hearing, denied the USWF's application. The latter immediately filed a Demand for Arbitration. On September 7, 1978, the three arbitrators unanimously found that the USWF had successfully established its claim for recognition as the wrestling NGB and was therefore entitled to replace the WD-AAU as a Group A member of the USOC.[201] On September 23, 1978, the USOC legal counsel advised the Committee that while the arbitral award purported to establish the USWF as the recognized NGB, the International Wrestling Federation (FILA) still had to recognize the USWF before it could be seated as a Group A member of the USOC. That is a required step because the Olympic Charter specifies that national committees can recognize only members of appropriate IFs.[202] Therefore, the USOC President promptly wrote to FILA recommending "as strongly as we can" that FILA recognize the USWF as the NGB "as soon as possible."[203] On October 17, 1978, FILA replied that any application by the USWF for membership in FILA could only be determined by its Congress, which would not meet until 1980. The USOC President repeated his request that FILA take action before then.

The USWF, encouraged by this support from the USOC President, filed an application with FILA on December 5, 1978, that included an affidavit from the USOC Executive Director stating that the USOC recognized the USWF as the official NGB for wrestling. Four days after the USWF had filed its application to FILA, however, the Executive Board of the USOC repudiated its decision of September 23 by restoring its recognition of the WD-AAU.[204]

In response to the USOC's decision to let the matter rest until 1980, the USWF, which had already fought off a court challenge to the arbitration award,[205] brought an action against the USOC. The USWF sought an order compelling the USOC to recognize it as a Group A member. On April 19, 1979, the court held that the USWF had acquired the status of an NGB, contingent upon its recognition by FILA.[206] Thus, until then, the WD-AAU was required to give its "full recommendation and support" to USWF efforts to be recognized by FILA.

At its 1980 Congress FILA rejected the USWF's application for recognition. The USWF was not even allowed to present its case before FILA. Instead, the USOC presented the USWF's application to the FILA Congress, with a recommendation

---

201 *See* United States Wrestling Fed'n v. United States Olympic Committee, No. 13460-78, Findings of Fact, slip op. at 6 (Super. Ct. D.C., Apr. 19, 1979) ("Group A" refers to NGBs).

202 Olympic Charter, Bye-laws to Rule 24.

203 *See United States Wrestling Fed'n*, *supra* note 201, at 6.

204 *Id.* at 7.

205 For a reference to this decision, upholding it on other issues, *see* United States Wrestling Fed'n v. Wrestling Div. of the AAU, Inc., 604 F.2d 313, 315 (7th Cir. 1979).

206 *United States Wrestling Fed'n*, *supra* note 201, at 8–9.

that, sometime after the 1980 Games, the USWF should replace the WD-AAU.[207] FILA rejected the USOC's petition and amended its Constitution in order to eliminate a presumption that had existed in favor of any candidate supported by an NOC.[208]

At this point, Congress, in order to prevent the Act from being undermined, responded by passing the Bellmon rider to a bill appropriating money to the USOC.[209] This provision forbids the USOC to allocate any of the appropriation to an NGB when another amateur sports organization has been designated the NGB by binding arbitration, and prohibits any NGB so displaced from exercising its powers under the Act.

Later in 1980, the USWF brought an action in federal court against the WD-AAU and the USOC, as co-defendants, seeking a declaratory judgment that the Act, newly armed with the Bellmon rider, effectively prohibited the WD-AAU from acting as an NGB. In 1982, the court's opinion and order in favor of the plaintiff USWF[210] went well beyond the requested remedy. It permanently enjoined the defendant WD-AAU from exercising any of the powers of a national governing body, and required it to resign its membership in, and sever all relationships with, FILA. The court further ordered the defendant USOC to terminate its recognition of defendant WD-AAU as a Group A member and as the NGB for amateur wrestling in the United States. The WD-AAU's right to represent the United States in FILA and its right to exercise any other powers of an NGB, as set forth in the Act, were also terminated.[211] After that decision, the USOC withdrew its recognition of the WD-AAU and encouraged the formation of a new interim NGB for wrestling. It was essentially organized within the corporate framework of the USWF, but it contained features that would make the enterprise more palatable to the WD-AAU and FILA. The NGB was called "U.S.A. Wrestling."

The IOC, FILA, and the USOC then signed an agreement, as follows:

1. according to the United States law, the USOC has the supreme authority on all matters regarding sport;
2. according to the decision of its Executive Board, the USOC has expelled the AAU (wrestling division);

---

[207] *See* USOC Report, *supra* note 103, at 8–9.

[208] United States Wrestling Federation Statement of Position § VI (undated release explaining the USWF's position in the USWF—WD-AAU conflict). FILA did not respond to the author's request for information concerning its decision.

[209] Act of July 8, 1980, Pub. L. No. 96-304, § 203, 94 Stat. 898.

[210] United States Wrestling Fed'n v. Wrestling Div. of the AAU, Inc., 545 F. Supp. 1053 (N.D. Ohio 1982), *aff'd without opinion*, 711 F.2d 1060 (6th Cir. 1983).

[211] *Id.*

3. according to the decision taken by the District Court of the United States and the decision of the USOC, the AAU (wrestling division) is disbanded and has lost its rights to serve as the national governing body for representation of wrestling in its country and in other countries;
4. in the interest of the sport of wrestling in the United States, and of the athletes, and to assure good preparation for the Olympic Games, the FILA recognises the temporary Organisation called the "US Wrestling Association, Inc." (USWA), composed on an equal basis of members of the two groups which until now have governed wrestling in the United States. This Organisation is also recognised by the USOC, supreme authority in this matter;
5. the duties of the "USWA" will be to prepare the establishment of a new wrestling association by means of a democratic election, to be held before 31st December 1983, of members selected among the representatives of all structures of wrestling in the United States. This Organisation will prepare procedures for the elections and will prepare and submit draft statutes which will be adopted by all groups interested in wrestling in the United States;
6. meanwhile, the temporary organisation "USWA" will take over all the obligations and engagements of the previous federation regarding organisation as well as participation in national, continental, international and world championships;
7. in addition, functions of certain members from the previous federation (AAU—wrestling division) who are affiliated with FILA are maintained until the next FILA's elections.[212]

Although the wrestling controversy was triggered by a challenge under the USOC Constitution and not under the Act, its bitter and tortured proceedings are instructive. First, by flagrantly ignoring an arbitral award enforceable by treaty, FILA set an unfortunate precedent for other IFs. If this precedent had become more general in practice, an amateur sports organization challenging an NGB under the Act would no longer have been able to rely upon the Act to seek review before a disinterested arbitral body free from sports politics and less protective of the *status quo* than the USOC Executive Board is likely to be. Second, on the apparent assumption that the IFs would recognize any organization that the USOC recommended, the Act provides only that the latter must do so within 61 days after the new NGB has been selected. Prior to passage of the Bellmon rider, Congress had not provided for enforcement of either the USOC's determination or an arbitral award in the face of a contradictory decision by an IF not supported by international law.

---

212 OLYMPIC REV., Dec. 1982, at 721–22.

Even without the Bellmon rider, the wrestling dispute put a hammerlock on the USOC. On one hand, it is bound by the Act and its own constitution to honor the results of an arbitration by seating the prevailing party as a Class A member. On the other hand, it is obliged to follow IOC rules, which prohibit the USOC from recognizing an NGB that is not a member of an IF.[213] In such a situation, the USOC must depend upon the goodwill of the IF to defer to the reasonable provisions of the Act, the supremacy of an NOC's means for resolving such jurisdictional disputes, and, most importantly, the binding force of arbitral and judicial awards under positive international law.

The wrestling dispute brought one last problem to light: the sheer expense of the elaborate legal procedures for dispute settlement stipulated in the Act. The delays and expense of litigation, or even arbitration and its enforcement, discourages an amateur sports organization from seeking to complain against or challenge an NGB. These factors also encourage an incumbent NGB to delay a challenge process tactically in order to drain the resources of a challenger. To preserve the intent of the Act, the USOC has had to be careful to prevent the NGB challenge mechanism from becoming a test of financial strength instead of merit.

c. *Protecting the Opportunity of an Athlete to Compete: A Structural Approach*

The President's Commission recommended that Congress should enact an "athlete's bill of rights," to include a right to compete internationally.[214] Yielding to the vigorous opposition of the NCAA, Congress chose not to enact those rights but provided instead for an "opportunity . . . to participate in amateur athletic competition."[215] In contrast to the detailed provisions for resolving conflicts, an athlete's "opportunity" is poorly defined. Congress apparently believed that an athlete's opportunity to compete would be best secured by creating an accountable and responsible NGB structure with a well-oiled process for conflict resolution rather than by establishing a statutory bill of rights for athletes. Generally, Congress seems to have acted wisely. The statutory enactment of an athlete's bill of rights without including other reforms in the Act might not have readily resolved annoying details related to the principle of an athlete's opportunity to compete internationally. A bill of rights alone would have provided only a list of entitlements, perhaps enforceable in court but without a framework for developing a set of relationships that would promote harmony within United States amateur athletics. The Act's resolution of problems concerning membership in the USOC and the NGBs, establishment of responsible and accountable NGBs, and provision of a detailed mechanism for conflict resolution have already established an atmosphere in which an athlete is less likely to be the victim of a jurisdictional feud and in which an explicit bill of rights has been unnecessary.

---

213 Olympic Charter, Bye-laws to Rule 24.

214 1 PCOS Report, *supra* note 20, at 139–40.

215 36 U.S.C. § 220503(8). On the legislative history, *see* Hearings, *supra* note 70 at 149–61 (statement of Mr. Byers).

A loophole deliberately left in the Act could limit some of its protection of access to competition: restricted competition is beyond USOC competence. Despite their otherwise exclusive jurisdiction, the NGBs and the USOC have no statutory authority to prevent amateur sports organizations that are not NGBs, such as the NFSHSA and the NCAA, from denying an athlete the right to compete in restricted competition after participation in unrestricted international competition.[216] The NCAA argued in favor of this power on the ground that the expense and scope of its athletic programs justified the NCAA's authority to command the priority involvement of athletes.[217] For a variety of reasons, amateur sports organizations might choose to encourage participation in their restricted competitions to the exclusion of international competition. An academic institution may be legitimately concerned that too much classwork would be lost if an athlete should choose to participate in both interscholastic and international competition. High school competitors may be minors who need special supervision. Finally, academic institutions seek to protect young athletes from being exploited by unscrupulous promoters.[218] For these reasons some state high school associations have found it easier simply to proscribe student participation in non-school athletic programs during the school year.

Despite this loophole, it appears that Congress, wittingly or not, has avoided a situation in which amateur sports organizations are likely to use their jurisdiction over restricted competition as a tool to thwart an athlete's opportunities to compete. By encouraging responsible and broad-based NGBs, the Act created an atmosphere where the fears and concerns of the academic institutions are more likely to be heard and dealt with in a mutually satisfactory manner. An NGB that seeks to encourage college and high school participants, for the good of its own responsibilities for athletic development, will be disinclined to schedule major competitions during final exams or interscholastic seasons so as to pose conflicts[219] with academically oriented sports organizations; it is difficult for an NGB to ignore the special status of student athletes.[220]

---

[216] High school and college associations have exclusive jurisdiction over their "restricted competition." 36 U.S.C. § 220526(a). By its broad language, Congress ignored the recommendations of the President's Commission that would have explicitly limited the ability of an amateur sports organization to prevent an athlete from reentering its restricted competition after participating in unrestricted competition. 1 PCOS Report, *supra* note 20, at 139–40.

[217] *See generally* Hearings, *supra* note 70, at 182–86 (statement of Mr. Byers).

[218] These fears are expressed in the NFSHSA's explanation of its model rules for non-school participation. National Federation of State High School Associations, 1980–81 HANDBOOK 39–45 (1980).

[219] On the general problem of non-school competition, *see, e.g., supra* text accompanying notes 100–101. Hearings, *supra* note 70, at 179 (statement of Mr. Neinas).

[220] Three years before the Act, Houston McTear, then a promising high school student unable to travel without a chaperone, could not compete in the 1975 AAU National Championships because the AAU failed to send enough money for McTear's coach to accompany him. Neither McTear nor his high school could afford the travel expenses to the championships for the coach. The travel expense policy of the Athletic Division of the AAU failed to

Even though the Act itself contains no explicit bill of rights to protect athletes, the USOC has satisfied its international and statutory obligations by implementing a bill of rights in its own Constitution, enforceable against all USOC members including the NGBs. It forbids a member from denying an amateur athlete the opportunity to compete in "protected" competition. That term refers to international amateur athletic competition between foreign and United States athletes "representing" their respective countries.[221]

One of the Act's "objects and purposes" grants to the USOC exclusive jurisdiction over United States participation in Olympic, Paralympic and Pan-American competitions; another directs the USOC to "obtain for the United States . . . the most competent amateur representations in these games."[222] A construction of the Act to allow an amateur sports organization to prevent an athlete from returning to restricted competition after participating in Olympic, Paralympic or Pan-American Games could impinge upon the USOC's capacity to exercise its own exclusive jurisdiction to obtain the best representation possible at the Games. Thus, the USOC's Constitution is interpreted so as to confirm the USOC's power to enforce an opportunity to compete whenever an athlete is or has been participating in competition within the Olympic, Paralympic or Pan-American framework.

After the 1984 Winter Games, an only partially resolved issue of athletes' rights arose out of a decision by the USOC Alpine skiing director not to fill all the racer slots to which the United States team was entitled in Sarajevo. The issue pitted the USOC's bill of rights against the statutory requirement that the USOC seek to provide and, inferentially, allocate funding to encourage the most competent representation for the United States.[223] Then, in *Michels v. United States Olympic Committee*,[224] the Second Circuit Court of Appeals considered a claim by a weightlifter suspended by his IF because drug test results showed an impermissible level of drug-produced testosterone. The court held that the athlete had no private cause of action under the Act.

d. 1998 Amendments to Improve Dispute Resolution

The bitter dispute involving skater Tonya Harding[225] raised the issue of how to avoid or otherwise respond in a timely manner to legal action brought on the

---

anticipate that a 100-yard dash star might be a minor requiring a chaperone. N.Y. TIMES, June 20, 1975, at 16, col. 6.

221 36 U.S.C. § 220501(b)(5).

222 *Id.*, § 220503(3), (4).

223 CHRISTIAN SCI. MONITOR, Nov. 30, 1984, at 26, col. 3.

224 Michels v. United States Olympic Committee, 741 F.2d 155 (2d Cir. 1984). The 1998 Amendments codify the *Michels* bar to a private cause of action. 36 U.S.C. § 220505.

225 *See* Ch. 4, *supra* text accompanying notes 64–71.

very eve of major competition when it is too late for the appropriate NGB, NOC or IF to take effective action. Last-minute court filings invite abuse by athletes and sports organizations alike. Claimants can thereby delay or obfuscate an issue of eligibility for competition.[226] As a result, the flurry of arbitration and litigation at the 11th hour before major competitions is often more tactical that justice-seeking. Under time pressures, litigation often serves little more than an *in terrorem* or bullying function.

In response to this kind of ambush filing of litigation, the United States Congress amended the Amateur Sports Act in 1998.[227] Under the amendments, a court may generally not impose any injunction against the United States Olympic Committee within 21 days of the beginning of a major competition. The 1998 amendments thereby sought to deter ambush litigation and strengthened the law's encouragement of arbitration as a preferred means for resolving disputes in the arena of international competition.

The 1998 amendments apply to any members of the USOC and "relating to the opportunity of an amateur athlete, coach, trainer, manager, administrator, or official to participate in the Olympic Games, the Paralympic Games, the Pan-American Games, world championship competition, or other protected competition."[228] The prohibition of injunctive relief within the 21-day time frame is contingent upon the USOC providing a sworn statement to the effect that its by-laws do not provide for resolution of the dispute before the beginning of the Games.[229] No procedure addresses the issue of disputes that arise after the commencement of the Games.[230] As a result of the amendments, the USOC will likely require eligibility decisions to be made well before the 21-day limit so as to allow athletes ample time to challenge rejections of their eligibility.[231]

The 1998 amendments also clarified the type of award available to athletes when a dispute is resolved through arbitration by the American Arbitration Association. In opportunity-to-compete disputes, athletes, protected by "commercial rules," are entitled to money damages as opposed to only non-monetary relief,[232] as had been the interpretation prior to the 1998 amendments.[233]

---

226 *Id.*, text accompanying note 65.

227 Amateur Sports Act, *supra* note 5, at § 220509.

228 36 U.S.C. § 220509(a).

229 *Id.*

230 *Id.*

231 Benz, *The 1990 Amendments to the Amateur Sports Act*, 17 SPORTS LAW. 8 (1999).

232 36 U.S.C. § 220529(b)(2).

233 Benz, *supra* note 231, at 12.

The amendments also established the office of an ombudsman who, among other powers, may seek to mediate disputes.[234] This is a positive step even though disputes involving the eligibility of athletes are not easily mediated because the stakes are usually very high. The ombudsman also advises athletes regarding the Act, the constitution and by-laws of the USOC, and other organizations.[235] The ombudsman is required to report to the Athletes Advisory Council on a regular basis.[236] The Act then sets forth the hiring process for the Ombudsman, the procedure for filling a vacancy, and the grounds for termination.[237]

9. Development of Athletic Facilities

> The United States Olympic Committee shall "foster the development of amateur athletic facilities for use by amateur athletes and assist in making existing amateur athletic facilities available for use by amateur athletes."[238]

Access to training facilities is spread unevenly throughout society, to the advantage of students at educational institutions. Thus, a student athlete usually has greater access to equipment. A non-student unable to join an athletic club oriented to major competition may be left with either no training facilities or inadequate ones. The Act directs the USOC to remedy this problem.

The USOC has developed a successful national training center at Colorado Springs for athletes designated by NGBs and financially supported while at the center by the USOC. It has also developed smaller training units in other locations.

If the USOC is unable to establish new facilities for athletes, it must foster development, presumably by persuading its members who do have facilities, such as colleges and universities, to accommodate serious athletes for training purposes. Even if the USOC had the money to build training facilities for post-collegiate athletes throughout the United States, such an effort might be wasteful, given facilities built with public funds that may be idle for long stretches of time.

By utilizing advanced electronic processing systems for the benefit of the NGBs, the USOC fosters development by collecting information on the availability of training facilities in particular regions of the country. In this way, an amateur athlete can secure necessary information concerning access to training facilities.

---

[234] 36 U.S.C. § 220509(b)(1)(B).

[235] *Id.*, § 220509(b)(1)(A).

[236] *Id.*, § 220509(b)(1)(B), (C).

[237] *Id.*, § 220509(b)(2)(A), (B).

[238] *Id.*, § 220503(a)(9).

10–11. Research and Distribution of Information

> The United States Olympic Committee shall "provide and coordinate technical information on physical training, equipment design, coaching, and performance analysis" and "encourage and support research, development, and dissemination of information in the areas of sports medicine and sports safety."[239]

Prompted by the recommendation of the PCOS that a sports medicine program be established,[240] the USOC created the Sports Medicine Council to serve as a central depository for information and continuing education on sports medicine to amateur trainees.[241] The USOC owns a Mobile Fitness Van, which is equipped for cardiovascular testing of athletes at their own training facilities. In the first year of the USOC's sports medicine program, over 700 athletes from 17 different sports were tested by members of the Sports Medicine Council.[242]

The Council has developed a highly sophisticated sports medicine program in Colorado Springs.[243] Its name belies its active involvement in testing and training young athletes.[244] As a USOC official explained, "[f]or the first time, the USOC has decided to rely on scientific evaluation in training rather than simply on talent."[245] An example of the program that was already under way when the Act became law is the help American kayakers received. Computer analysis of European and U.S. teams revealed that the latter were emphasizing their strokes in the wrong place and as a consequence were working harder and achieving less than their European counterparts. A more efficient approach, drawing on the European experience, helped the kayakers to become more competitive.[246]

12–14. Encouragement of Women, the Disabled, and Minorities

> The United States Olympic Committee shall "encourage and provide assistance to amateur athletic activities for women; encourage and provide assistance to

---

239 36 U.S.C. § 220503(10), (11).

240 The PCOS recommended that the USOC establish a sports medicine program. 1 PCOS Report, *supra* note 20, at 13–25.

241 The Sports Medicine Council is authorized in the USOC by-laws. USOC CONST. By-laws, ch. XXVII, §§ 1, 2 (1981).

242 The program is designed to "maximize the individual skills, techniques, health, and physiological parameters of our athletes." *Id.*

243 N.Y. TIMES, Oct. 4, 1977, at 45, col. 1.

244 USOC Report, *supra* note 103, at 5.

245 N.Y. TIMES, Oct. 4, 1977, at 45, col. 1.

246 *Id.*

amateur athletic programs and competition for amateur athletes with disabilities, including, where feasible, the expansion of opportunities for meaningful participation by such amateur athletes in programs of athletic competition for able-bodied amateur athletes; and encourage and provide assistance to amateur athletes of racial and ethnic minorities for the purpose of eliciting the participation of those minorities in amateur athletic activities in which they are under-represented."[247]

The commitment to women athletes reflects the general attention to women's participation in all social activities. Since women in different sports face different specific problems, each individual NGB is required to initiate and execute its own program. The USOC's supervision or review of these programs has become vastly enlarged since the early days of the Act.

The 1998 amendments to the Act included several important changes to provisions regarding athletes with disabilities. The USOC has exclusive jurisdiction over the organization in the United States of the Paralympic Games, which take place quadrennially at the same venue and just after completion of the Games. The USOC also has the power to select the participants in the Games.[248] The USOC also represents the United States on the International Paralympic Committee and designates NGB for organization of athletes to participate in the Paralympic Games.[249] Where it is not feasible or in the best interest of the sport to designate an NGB, the USOC may recognize another amateur sport organization to govern the sport;[250] it, too, must meet the requirements of this Act.[251] A Paralympic sports organization is not limited to governing only one sport.[252] The USOC supports athletes with disabilities by underwriting their participation in such competitions as the Special Olympics.

Minorities remain under-represented in some sports, such as swimming, skiing and curling, which require expenditures at the world-class level beyond the capacity of most participants. The USOC offers assistance, but generally delegates to the NGBs its responsibility for developing programs to help promising young minority athletes to meet the expense of competing in those sports where they are under-represented. In recent World Figure Skating Championships, top women competitors on the United States team consistently have been members of minority groups.

---

247 36 U.S.C. § 220503(12)–(14).

248 *Id.*, § 220503(3)(B), (4).

249 *Id.*, §§ 220505(c)(2), 220522(b).

250 *Id.*, § 220522(b).

251 *Id.*, § 220522(b)(1).

252 *Id.*, § 220522(b)(2).

E. THE FUTURE OF AMATEUR SPORTS UNDER THE ACT

The Amateur Sports Act instituted a governing structure to strengthen the USOC, relying upon NGBs, one for each sport in the Olympic, Paralympic and Pan-American Games. Other organizations and individuals supplement the prescribed decision-making structure. Detailed provisions in the Act address a range of troublesome issues, from eligibility of individual athletes for international competition to organizational review, complaint and challenge procedures, subject to mediation and binding arbitration. Although the exigencies of major international competition and its roster of sports are paramount, the Act, directly or indirectly, influences a much broader range of physical education, public participation in sports, and athletic development in the United States.

Despite this favorable climate, two clouds remain on the horizon. First, USOC governance of participation by U.S. nationals in the Olympic, Paralympic and Pan-American Games, ostensibly within its "exclusive jurisdiction," is uncertain at times. Blatant governmental intrusion into the exclusive jurisdiction of the USOC is no longer much of a threat. Far more serious today, however, are the difficult problems associated with doping of and by athletes, especially involving the use of steroids and other performance-enhancing agents. Gene therapy appears as a gathering storm on the horizon. Such threats often transcend the regulatory capacity of the NGBs. The role of the World Anti-Doping Agency, the United Statcs Doping Agency, IFs, courts, and other decision-making bodies in meeting the threats must surely limit the exclusive jurisdiction of the USOC. Perhaps the Amateur Sports Act will need to be amended to take account of the need for greater organizational cooperation and a consequent modification of the exclusive jurisdiction of the USOC.

Another cloud, although somewhat wispy, casts shadows over the Act. It concerns the sources and proper allocation of funding for amateur athletics. There are a number of issues related to financial support of amateur athletics by private sources, the government, and the IOC's TOP program. For example, the Olympic Movement's unification of commercial sponsorships through TOP has diminished the USOC's capacity to raise funds for itself, although it has also led to a larger proportionate share of TOP revenue. There are also issues related to the proper allocation of funds between elite-and mass-development. Although the old tension between elitist and non-elitist objectives of the Act is minimal today, it may intensify if school programs atrophy and thereby prompt budding sandlot athletes to seek greater direct support from organizations within the USOC framework. Fortunately, the Act has had the effect of invigorating private support as a fairly dependable alternative for amateur sports organizations. If the financial cloud is not yet gold-lined, it nevertheless appears to be less ominous today.

Although athletes, sports organizations, and lawyers disagree on the efficacy of the Amateur Sports Act, it has generally met most of the original expectations for it. The Act has provided a comprehensive structure for promoting and coordinating amateur athletic activity in the United States and for enhancing participation by United States amateurs in international competition. It has effectively eliminated the jurisdictional feuds among amateur sports organizations that had seriously handicapped the performance of United States teams in international competition. In international sports the United States got its Act together to a remarkable degree. The federal legislation has furthered the basic goals and values of international sports law. Whether the Act will prove to be resilient and flexible enough to respond effectively to the constantly unfolding problems that beset international sports competition remains to be seen.

APPENDIX II
CHINA'S SPORTS LAW

China's Sports Law[1] is significant as a foundation for Beijing's staging of the 2008 Olympic Games. As China puts in place a market economy, the legislation also gives new meaning to the concept of Market-Leninism.[2] On one hand, the legislation confirms state control over sports. It essentially relies on standard political ideology, a regulatory structure, and administrative practice to address current issues. These issues include the best means to gain greater international prestige from the success of its athletes, to create a structure of effective sports associations and clubs, to provide a reliable central source of funding for sports, and to deter and punish such offenses as doping of athletes and bribery of sports personnel. On the other hand, the Sports Law also relies on non-governmental initiatives. In particular, it encourages the establishment of market-oriented sports associations to organize and fund sports activity and to impose sanctions for violations of their rules. The legislation also responds to the serious problem of doping and other issues that have beset the Chinese athletic program and Chinese participation in international competition.

The law's reliance on non-governmental mediation and arbitration to resolve disputes is a particularly interesting statement in the global debate about the rights of athletes. China's unwillingness to concede such rights by statute is no surprise. Neither tradition nor ideology favor the adjudication of individual rights. Ironically, the alternative of mediation and arbitration to resolve disputes in the sports arena has a distinctly modern ring. With the world-wide establishment of arbitration as a preferred means for resolving a broad range of issues in the international sports arena, China is really on the vanguard. Its skepticism about protecting the interests of athletes by routinely adjudicating their rights is shared by a growing number of legal systems.

What is missing in the law is, first, an identification of the interests of athletes, such as eligibility and due process, and, second, a recognition that adjudication can play a positive role by providing a remedy in exceptional cases involving the most serious breaches of fairness and justice. Although the Chinese legislation may not be an appropriate model for Europe and North America, it is, nevertheless, a reminder that western principles of individualism and personal autonomy should not be taken for granted. In particular, the Chinese approach

[1] ZHONGHUA RENMIN GONGHEGUO TIYU FA (THE SPORTS LAW OF THE PEOPLE'S REPUBLIC OF CHINA) (1995). [hereinafter Sports Law]. The NPC is China's principal legislative organ.

[2] A term borrowed from N. D. KRISTOF & S. WUDUNN, CHINA WAKES 440 (1994).

to resolving disputes involving athletes challenges European and North American assumptions about the merits of adjudication and may reinforce new directions in international sports law away from a reliance on adjudication.

This introduction to the law traces its origins, objects and purposes, and most important provisions. The first English translation of it appears in the annex. The legislation, though comprehensive, is rudimentary, reflecting its bureaucratic foundations. Its provisions claim only minimum authority over administrative discretion. They are more like policy declarations than concrete rules.[3] The flesh on the bones is a set of regulations that specifically implement the law, together with whatever regulations may be adopted by the State Council or the State Physical Culture General Administration (formerly known as the State Physical Culture and Sports Commission (SPCSC)).

The National People's Congress (NPC) enacted the Peoples Republic's first sports law in 1995.[4] Until then, Chinese sports had been governed by the SPCSC, based on three administrative rules adopted by the State Council and 523 regulations of the SPCSC, local sports commissions and other national and local administrations.[5] To understand the Chinese regime of sports law, a little background will be helpful.

I. HISTORICAL AND POLITICAL BACKGROUND

A. THE CONSTITUTIONAL AND IDEOLOGICAL PREMISES

The Chinese Constitution provides that "[t]he state develops physical culture and promote mass sports activities to improve the people's physical fitness."[6] It is not surprising, therefore, that over a third of the provisions in the Sports Law emphasize the traditional Maoist principle that sports should serve "the people."[7]

---

[3] Indeed, the declared objective of the law is simply to set forth general principles. Wang Junpu, *Result of Countless People's Hard Work*, PEOPLE'S DAILY (Overseas ed.), Sept. 27, 1995, at 5; Law & Rule Section, Law Division, SPCSC, YU TIYUFA YOUGUANDE JIGE ZHONGDIAN WENTI [SOME SIGNIFICANT ISSUES ABOUT THE SPORTS LAW] 8 (1995) (on file with the author). [hereinafter ISSUES].

[4] Strictly speaking, the Sports Law is modern China's second. The Nationalist government built China's first administrative structure for sports and adopted the National Sports Law of 1929. After the Maoist revolution of 1949, however, the new government of the People's Republic of China annulled the 1929 law together with all other laws enacted by the Nationalist government. RENPING JIANG & JUCHANG LIU, TIYU FAXUE (Sports Law Study) 33 (1994).

[5] ISSUES, *supra* note 3, at 4.

[6] CONSTITUTION OF THE PEOPLE'S REPUBLIC OF CHINA, art. 21 (1982).

[7] ISSUES, *supra* note 3, at 9; *see* Sports Law, art. 2 infra, Annex. Wang Shuwen, *Report of the Legal Commission of the NPC on the Deliberation of the Sports Law (Draft)*, *in* ZHONGHUA RENMIN GONGHEGUO TIYU FA (The PRC's Sports Law) 18 (1995) [hereinafter 1995 Sports Report].

"Sports for all" is a hallmark of the legislation, forged by Mao Zedong's understanding and resolution of modern Chinese history.[8]

Despite a long history of uniquely Chinese athletic competition,[9] Confucian tradition frowned on sport, particularly as a profession.[10] Only in the early 20th century did Chinese educational policy, on the initiative of foreign missionary schools, begin to encourage the development of athletic training as an antidote to China's persistent weakness.[11] The modern Chinese sports movement originated from this development. Mao's first published article, which appeared in 1917, was entitled "A Study of Physical Education"(Tiyu zhi Yanjiu). It was prompted by his concern about the effect of widespread poor health among the Chinese people.[12] While the Chinese word for physical culture ("Tiyu") embraces three activities—sports, physical education and exercise—Mao trumpeted the virtues of exercise above all.[13] This interpretation of physical culture shaped Mao's lifelong, revolutionary concept of mass sports—a healthy body and mind begets a strong nation. That maxim remains the official ideology. In 1952, after consolidating his victory in the Chinese Civil War, Mao called on the Chinese people to "promote physical culture and sports, and build up the people's health."[14] In the same year Chinese athletes competed in the Summer Games. Accordingly, the Chinese government established a program for mass sports called The National Physical

---

[8] Zou Sicheng, *China's Sports Poised for Reform*, BEIJING REV., July 15–22, 1995, at 8–10.

[9] Records of Chinese sports events go back about three thousand years. *See, e.g.*, Jiang & Liu, *supra* note 4, at 26–27. *See also, Sports in China Has Ancient History*, BEIJING REV., Feb. 3–10, 1986, at 32. *See also* Hessler, Great Sprint Forward, NEW YORKER, May 7, 2001, at 38, 39 (reporting that the Chinese language [presumably Mandarin] did not have a name for sports until the nineteenth century and that there are no traditional Chinese athletics in the Olympic Games, for example).

[10] R. C. WILCOX, SPORT IN THE GLOBAL VILLAGE 407 (1994). In Confucian thought, brains rule and brawn is ruled. Athletes were typically considered to be brawny. Thus, as late as the end of 1980s, when China began to commercialize sports, Chinese athletes rejected sports as a profession. Even those who had won world championships, such as gymnast Lou Yun, refused to become professionals. Trip Gabriel, *China Strains for Olympic Glory*, N.Y. TIMES., Apr. 24, 1988, (Magazine), at 30, 33. *See also* Y.L. FUNG, A SHORT HISTORY OF CHINESE PHILOSOPHY (1948).

[11] It was commonly thought that the poor health of the modern Chinese people, which was partly attributable to opium-smoking, contributed to China's tragic and humiliating sufferings in modern history. As a remedy, modern Chinese sports education began to appear in schools at the turn of the century. JIANG & LIU, *supra* note 4, at 30–32.

[12] *See* J. M. HOBERMAN, SPORTS AND POLITICAL IDEOLOGY 219–20 (1984). This article was republished recently by the SPCSC as a reminder of the importance and patriotic significance of mass sports. The achievements of Chinese athletes, especially those who participate in international competitions, are said to confirm the superiority of the socialist system and the physical health of the Chinese people. PEOPLE'S DAILY (Overseas ed.), Dec. 27, 1995, at 5; SPORTS LAW, art. 27, *infra*, Annex.

[13] HOBERMAN, *id.*, at 222–23.

[14] *Id.*

Training Program, based on the Soviet model and since upheld as a significant symbol of mass sports or mass exercise. In 1995 the SPCSC drafted and the State Council decreed the current National Fitness Program as an important means of implementing the Sports Law.

B. CHARACTERISTICS OF MAOIST AND EARLY POST-MAOIST SPORTS DIPLOMACY

During the Maoist era (1949–76), China's commitment to mass sports did not translate into victories at the Olympic Games or other international competitions. Unlike the former Soviet Union and its East European satellites, particularly East Germany, China did not use sports for national aggrandizement. Mao did not seem to recognize the role of mass sports in helping China achieve the status of a world power. Even her limited aspiration to leadership in the Third World did not translate into an assertion of international athletic prowess. Instead, Mao's sports policy was insular and reactionary. He wanted to use sports simply for nation-building. "Friendship first, competition second" was the national motto in international competition. The bright-eyed and rosy-cheeked waves of peasants and workers depicted in propaganda posters and postage stamps did not set any world records. Indeed, they could not even compete in the Olympic Games for several years after the P.R.C. withdrew its team in 1956 to protest the presence of Taiwan at the Melbourne Games that year. During the Cultural Revolution (1966–1976), "Maoist zealots considered sports a manifestation of bourgeois self-centeredness."[15] P.R.C. team rejoined the Olympic movement in 1979, but boycotted the Moscow Games the following year to protest Soviet intervention in Afghanistan.

"Ping-pong diplomacy," initiated by China in 1971 to improve its relations with the United States, was a brilliant exception to China's generally inept conduct of sports diplomacy during the Maoist and early post-Maoist era. During those years the exclusion of Taiwanese athletes from international competition seems to have been the name of the game.[16] Ping-pong's symbolism of initiative and response and of lively human exchange could not have been lost on Beijing. China's successful manipulation of this symbolism marked the end of a generally negative record of sports diplomacy in the time of Mao.

After Mao's death in 1976, Chinese sports began to change, but not very quickly. Deng Xiaoping's Four-Modernizations[17] did not include sports and

---

[15] Gabriel, *supra* note 10, at 34.

[16] The 1971 ping-pong initiative was followed by similar ventures, for example, "tennis diplomacy" between South Korea and China in 1984 as described in Chapter 10. Eventually, basketball diplomacy enabled P.R.C. athletes to compete in Taiwan. Diana Lin, *First mainland basketball teams visit*, FREE CHINA J., Mar. 2, 1993, at 4.

[17] *Viz*., agriculture, industry, defense, and science and technology. *See* RICHARD EVANS, DENG XIAOPING AND THE MAKING OF MODERN CHINA 204 (1993).

China's sports diplomacy was decidedly clumsy. Far from glorifying international competition in the Soviet-East European tradition, China's attention remained fixed on the problem of Taiwan and other perceived challenges to her sovereignty and national dignity.[18] Far from seeking to use sports to leverage better foreign relations, China magnified minor embarrassments into full-scale disruption of cultural exchange. The Hu Na case in 1983 is a poignant example.[19] After the United States had granted political asylum to Hu Na, China's top-seeded woman tennis player and its Female Athlete of the Year in 1981, Beijing reacted sharply. Claiming that the grant of asylum had been immoral and a "grave incident harming the relations between the two countries,"[20] the Chinese government temporarily suspended all bilateral cultural exchange programs.

In 1984, China launched a major sports program based on its new pragmatism. The backbone of this program has been a system of part-time sports schools, where young athletes train in the afternoon after finishing their classes.[21] It was during the same period of time that the government initiated work on a sports law.

II. LEGISLATIVE HISTORY

A. THE DRAFTING PROCESS[22]

In 1980, after yet another Chinese exercise to deny Taiwanese participation, this time in the Lake Placid Winter Games, Wang Meng, Minister of the SPCSC, proposed drafting the P.R.C's first sports law. Preparatory work started in September 1980, just after the conclusion of the politically charged Moscow Games, when the policy research section of the SPCSC began to collect foreign sports laws for reference and to outline legislation.

In June 1984 the SPCSC convened a special session attended by some 60 sports experts to articulate basic principles and a structure for the proposed legislation. Immediately after the 1984 Los Angeles Olympic Games, Peng Zhen, Chairman of the Standing Committee of the National People's Congress, instructed the SPCSC to accelerate the drafting process. Only in 1988, however, did the SPCSC organize a blue-ribbon leadership corps to supervise the actual drafting by a task force. The Chinese were so optimistic in 1988 that Xinhua, the national news agency, predicted that the law would be completed by the end of the year.[23] Instead, the process slowed down.

---

[18] *See* discussions in Chs. 10 and 11.

[19] *See* Ch. 9, *supra* text accompanying notes 36–45.

[20] N.Y. TIMES, Apr. 5, 1983, at A1.

[21] Gabriel, *supra* note 10, at 30, 36.

[22] *See generally* ISSUES, *supra* note 3, and Wang Junpu, *supra* note 3.

[23] XINHUA NEWS AGENCY (formerly, NEW CHINA NEWS AGENCY), June 10, 1988 [hereinafter XINHUA].

In 1989 the newly elected Minister of the SPCSC, Wu Shaozu, revived the drafting process. Meanwhile, members of the NPC and the National People's Political Consultative Conference (NPPCC) jumped on the bandwagon. Such leading legislators as Qian Zhenying, Vice Chairman of the NPPCC, and Zhao Dongwan, Chairman of the Education, Science, Culture & Health Committee of the NPC, urged adoption of a sports law. In March 1992, the task force submitted a draft of it to the State Council. That body was, however, preoccupied at the time with drafting economic legislation. It therefore took no action other than to voice its dissatisfaction with the draft. The following year the task force, prodded by Chinese sports authorities, prepared a revised draft that was finally submitted by the State Council to the NPC in May 1994. Thereafter, the NPC's Education, Science and Culture Committee and its Legal Affairs Committee, together with the Legal Affairs Bureau of the State Council and the SPCSC, jointly dispatched three research groups to several provinces for opinions on the draft. During more than 30 sessions these groups elicited comments on legislative proposals for the development of mass sports activities, the training and management of athletes, the development of a sports industry, and other topics. After further consultative sessions conducted by governmental agencies, provincial authorities and mass organizations, the NPC's powerful Standing Committee began a three-day review of the draft on June 23, 1995. All of those present voted in favor of adopting the law on August 28, 1995.

B. THE DOPING ISSUE: A SHOT IN THE ARM OF LEGISLATIVE DRAFTING

Several objects and purposes underlie the Sports Law. The original impetus for it was simply to codify and modernize the Maoist (and post-Maoist) concept of mass physical culture in order to improve China's standing in global sports. As the drafting process progressed, however, doping emerged as a prominent issue.[24] By the end of 1994, although Beijing still pointed a finger at foreign and capitalist origins of doping, it agreed that the problem had become a serious one for Chinese athletes and for China's reputation in the international sports arena.

This acknowledgment of reality represented a stunning reversal of Chinese policy. Until 1994 the Chinese government had officially opposed performance-enhancing drugs but had routinely denied the existence of a doping problem among Chinese athletes. As late as October, 1994, when initial, unconfirmed reports indicated that Chinese athletes had tested positive for doping during the Asian Games in Hiroshima, Japan, top officials from the SPCSC and the Ministry

---

[24] Wu Shaozu, *Guanyu Zhonghua Renmin Gongheguo Tiyu Fa (Caoan) de Shuoming [An explanation of the Sports Law of the People's Republic of China (Draft)] in* 1995 Sports Report, *supra* note 7, at 16. In submitting the draft law to the NPC, Wu Shaozu highlighted the doping issue and the importance of addressing it in the law. *Id.* The SPCSC issued Temporary Regulations Banning the Use of Stimulants in Sports in March 1995, prior to the adoption of the Sports Law, in order to quiet the shock waves of an emerging doping scandal. *China: Law Blunts Sports Doping*, SHANGHAI STAR, Sept. 1, 1995, at 1.

of Foreign Affairs still insisted that the accusation of doping among Chinese athletes was motivated by "jealousy and racism" on the part of Japanese and Western sports officials.[25] The problem, according to Beijing, was ideological. Doping was essentially a capitalist disease rooted in commercialization of sports activities and denial of mass participation in them. Thus, the doping problem that had plagued athletes from several socialist countries was simply a reflection of ideological revisionism, a corruption of Marxist ideology.[26] The Chinese, on the other hand, were proud of their friendly, ideologically correct engagement in sport for fun, health and friendly relations with other countries: "Friendship first, competition second." Hence, they were theoretically drug-free.

Theory, however, is not necessarily reality. As sports increasingly became a tool of foreign policy and as commercialization of the Chinese sports arena grew, rumors of doping inevitably spoiled the pristine image of rosy-cheeked Chinese athletes. These developments contributed to a disturbing problem of doping among a growing cadre of world-class competitors. Indeed, by 1994, evidence of doping among Chinese athletes had became rampant in the foreign press, even though random testing had turned up only isolated cases.[27] On November 29, 1994, the issue became unavoidable when the Olympic Council of Asia (OCA) officially notified the China Olympic Committee (COC) that 11 of her athletes, including seven swimmers, had tested positive for a banned muscle-building drug during the Hiroshima Games.[28] After a hearing, the OCA decided to withdraw all honors and medals that these athletes had won.[29] It was a major shock. For example, one of the accused, Lu Bin, the only athlete to break a swimming world record at the event, had garnered four gold and two silver medals at the Hiroshima Games.[30]

---

[25] Mufson, *China Leaps Backward; Swimmers' Positive Drug Tests Cast Pall*, WASH. POST, DEC. 6, 1994, at B2.

[26] HOBERMAN, *supra* note 12, at 223–25.

[27] Muttered accusations began in 1990, when the Chinese swept all the gold medals in swimming at the Beijing-hosted Asiad, but these accusations of doping were never published. The whispers continued in 1992 when Zhuang Yong broke the record in the women's 100-meter freestyle to win China's first-ever Olympic swimming gold, amidst observations about the Chinese women' s muscled physiques and deep voices. Whitten, *China's March to Swimming Dominance: Hard Work or Drugs?*, SWIMMING WORLD & JUNIOR SWIMMER, Jan. 1994, at 34. A U.S. swimming official openly accused them of using banned substances after they had set five world marks and won 12 gold medals. *The Scandal Could Hurt China's Olympic Hopes*, ASIA WK., Dec. 7, 1994, at 38; Montville, *Flora and Furor*, SPORTS ILLUS., Sept. 19, 1994, at 40–42. As the scandal became highly visible in 1993 and 1994, five Chinese swimmers tested positive for drugs. *The International Swimming Federation imposed sanctions*, CHRISTIAN SCI. MONITOR, Mar. 1, 1994, at 20; "Thirty-one Chinese athletes tested positive for banned drugs in 1994." N.Y. TIMES, July 28, 1995, at B8.

[28] Fachet, *Chinese Officials Express Shock at Drug Violations*, WASH. POST, Dec. 1, 1994, at B2.

[29] *Severe Punishment*, XINHUA *supra* note 23, Dec. 5, 1994.

[30] *Id.*

Another, Yang Aihua, a former gold medalist in Rome, was banned from competition for two years when excessive testosterone appeared during a random urine test at the Games.

The OCA's action was definitive. Only then did China finally acknowledge the reality of its problem. It could not muzzle the doping issue any more. The Chinese Sports Daily, which had never reported news of doping of Chinese athletes, finally did so.[31] Since then, the Chinese press has reported numerous doping incidents involving Chinese athletes.[32] A Doping Control Center opened in 1989 after approval by the IOC and began tests on athletes in 1990. Yang Tianle, a member of the Anti-Doping Commission of the COC and Director of the Doping Control Center, openly admitted that in 1993 24 athletes, some of them world-class, had tested positive and had been sanctioned accordingly.[33] Yang claimed that China had ranked second in Asia and tenth in the world in 1993 in the roster of athletes caught using drugs.[34]

Yang's admission revealed the failure, and perhaps corruption, of China's previously undisclosed anti-doping program. The China Olympic Committee (COC) asserted vehemently that it had started to take a tough line on drug-taking as early as 1989. In that year, the COC adopted the "three stricts" against doping—strict ban, strict testing and strict penalties—and established the China Doping Control Center.[35] In 1992 the COC established an anti-doping Commission.[36] Apparently, however, these efforts failed to deter some Chinese athletes from using performance-enhancing drugs. The refusal of governmental agencies to acknowledge the problem until it lurched out of control in 1994 may have been attributable to any or all of five possibilities: a fear of embarrassing Chinese athletes, an assumption that positive tests must have been mistaken,[37] efforts to regain control

---

[31] Fachet, *supra* note 28.

[32] For example, late in 1994, the International Amateur Athletic Federation (IAAF) formally notified the concerned Chinese federation that Han Qing, a woman field athlete, had failed a doping test. In 1995, two weightlifters, Li Dan and Wang Sheng, who had shared gold in the 54 kg class at the world championships in Istanbul, Turkey, were cited for doping. In November 1994 Li had set new world records for his class of 104.9kg and 106.4kg in the snatch.

[33] *Beijing to Continue to Take Its Firm Stand Against Drug Taking in Sports*, XINHUA NEWS AGENCY, Dec. 29, 1994. [hereinafter *Beijing to Continue*]. There does not appear to have been any such reports whatsoever in the Chinese press before the 1994 scandal.

[34] *Id.* China's official news agency, Xinhua, did not say which nation ranked first in the incidence of doping in Asia.

[35] XINHUA, *supra* note 23, Dec. 24, 1994.

[36] *Beijing to Continue, supra* note 33.

[37] On the eve of the 1994 scandal, the Chinese officials were still claiming that the positive tests were mistaken. For example, when people expressed surprise after Wang Junxia's record breaking performance as a long-distance runner, "[t]he Chinese authorities, deeply resentful of Western suspicions of drug use, insisted that the secret of Wang's success is simply that she

over the problem discreetly before it become too obvious, the inconsistency of drug-taking with ideological theory, or, worst of all, complicity in the doping by government sports officials.

The extent of the Chinese government's involvement in the doping of athletes is uncertain. Some Chinese athletes, coaches and officials of government-run sports institutes, where gifted youngsters are selected and groomed for competition, have admitted that steroid use was part of the training regimen in Chinese sports.[38] Moreover, international officials concluded that doping could have occurred only on the government's initiative and with its encouragement.[39] The COC, on the other hand, insisted that individual athletes had been entirely responsible for the problem.[40] He Zhenliang, former President of the COC and later Vice-President of the International Olympic Committee (IOC), blamed the problem on outside influences.[41] For him, doping was a world disease that had contaminated Chinese athletes.[42]

Whether the Chinese government was deeply involved or not in the doping of national athletes, two things became clear immediately after the shocking exposure of doping among world-class swimmers in 1994. First, the Chinese government had to take some action beyond a formal recognition of the problem and, second, the draft Sports Law would have to include express provisions against doping. China's reputation as a good sport and future sports power was on the line.[43] The COC, therefore, reacted quickly and firmly.[44] Within a week, Beijing

---

trains 180 miles each week and drinks a potion made from caterpillar fungus as well as a soup made from soft-shelled turtles." KRISTOF & WUDUNN, *supra* note 2, at 374 (1994).

38 It was reportedly common for promising young athletes, as young as 14 or 15 years of age, to start getting steroid injections at sports institutes. *See* BUS. WK., June 19, 1995, at 140. Two swimming coaches working in Thailand, Ren Chun Sheng and Tien Sac Tia, claimed that China had adopted an East German-style system that relied on the use of drug by athletes. Almond, *Olympic Sports Scene*, L.A. TIMES, Feb. 12, 1996, at S1.

39 Dr. Yoshio Kuroda, chairman of the OCA Medical Committee, asserted that young Chinese young athletes, having no knowledge of drugs, must have been instructed by experts with such knowledge. Dave Lindorff, *Does China Feed Its Athletes "Juice,"* BUS. WK., June 19, 1995, at 140. Prince Alexandre de Merode, the president of the IOC's Medical Commission, suspected that Chinese coaches and athletes had learned to use drugs from their former East German swimming coaches. *Former Germany Influenced Massive Doping*, JAPANESE ECONOMIC NEWSWIRE, Dec. 14, 1994, available in Lexis, Nexis Library, JEN File.

40 *Id.* Meanwhile, the COC, under pressure, was obliged to request all national sports associations to follow administrative rules strictly against the use of drugs, The COC also expressed its willingness to cooperate with international sports federations in their efforts to eliminate doping of athletes. *China Promises Severe Punishment for Doped Athletes*, MAINICHI DAILY NEWS, Dec. 5, 1994, at 1.

41 *Now the China Lifters Test Positive*, NEW STRAITS TIMES, Jan. 7, 1995, at 48.

42 *Id.*

43 *The Scandal Could Hurt China's Olympic Hopes, supra* note 27.

44 Fachet, *supra* note 28.

formed a committee to investigate and punish athletes who took drugs.[45] The COC also requested all sports associations to strengthen their rules against the use of drugs.[46] Investigations and sanctions against guilty athletes followed quickly and regularly.[47] In March 1995, the SPCSC confirmed its new attack on doping by adopting Temporary Regulations Banning the Use of Stimulants in Sport.[48] Under these rules, athletes taking performance-enhance drugs were to be punished. Their prizes were to be seized and their titles stripped from them. In addition, they were to be barred from competition for a certain period. The Sports Law confirmed the principles of these Temporary Regulations. In 2004 Premier Wen Jiabao signed a State Council decree, entitled "Anti-Doping Regulations," that replaced the Temporary Regulations.[49]

C. THE HUMAN RIGHTS ISSUE

Beijing aggressively sought to host the 2000 Olympic Games.[50] In 1993, however, the IOC selected Sydney over Beijing, by a narrow vote of 45–43.[51] The

---

[45] *Id.*

[46] *Id.*

[47] On Dec. 8, 1994 China barred seven swimmers from competition for two years for using banned drugs at the Asian Games, and also barred five coaches from the scandalous swimming squad from coaching for a year because of their involvement in the Hiroshima Games scandal in 1994. In the same year, China reported that a woman hurdler also faced a four-year ban for doping. Later, the Tianjin Track and Field Association suspended its coach, Bai Lin, because he had been the trainer of top Chinese discus thrower, Qiu Qiaoping, who had failed drug tests during the 1994 Asian Games. In 1995 Beijing officials investigated charges against the two women weightlifting world champions who had tested positive for banned substances. In the same year, canoeists Zhang Lei and Qiu Suoren were banned for two years by the Chinese Canoe Association, and cyclist Wang Yan was banned for six months by the Chinese Cycling Association. Shortly afterward, four more coaches were each banned for one year.

[48] It was reported that originally Chinese sports authorities were even considering criminal penalties to deter doping, but they did not do so. John Goodbody, *China Pledge to Jail Drug-Takers*, TIMES (London), Mar. 2, 1995. A spokesman for the SPCSC explained on Mar. 1, 1995 that no country jails athletes for taking performance-enhancing drugs. Since they typically do not threaten the safety of others, according to the SPCSC's theory, they have violated no law. *China Intensifies Doping Crackdown*, UPI, Mar 1, 1995, available at Lexis, Nexis Library, UPI File. Thus, although the Sports Law has banned listed drugs and therapies, it provides only for sanctions by sports associations and public security organs without stipulating any specific penalties. Sports Law, arts. 34 and 50, *infra*, Annex.

[49] *Tigong Shiyong Xingfengji Yanchengbudai Guowuyuan Banbu Fan Xingfenji Tiaoli (Supply or Use of Doping Agents Subject to Strict and Merciless Punishment, as the State Council Publishes "Anti-Doping Regulations.")*, XINMIN WANBAO, Feb. 3, 2004, at 12 [hereinafter Anti-Doping Regulations].

[50] *See* KRISTOF & WUDUNN, *supra* note 2, at 94. (recounting tragic consequences of Beijing's determination to put on a good face in its campaign to secure award of the Games.); Tyler, *Lure of Olympic Flame Defrosts China, Unevenly*, N.Y. TIMES, Sept. 19, 1993, at A4; Kristof, *The Yin and Yang of China's Bid for the Olympics*, INT'L HERALD TRIB., July 29, 1993, at 17.

[51] Mastrocola, *The Lord of the Rings: The role of Olympic Site Selection as a Weapon*

decisive issue, just four years after the Tiananmen Square-centered massacre, was human rights.[52] Ironically, the Chairman of the Beijing Olympics promotion was Chen Xitong, who as mayor had signed the martial decree that had led to the massacre.[53] Understandably, China's reaction to the IOC decision was one of profound disappointment, in view of the enormous prestige attached to the status of hosting the Games.[54] This experience, along with the revelations about the doping of athletes, seems to have accelerated the process of completing a sports law. Apparently, the idea was that, by enhancing China's performance in the global sports arena, the law would help eclipse memories of doping and human rights abuses and enlarge China's image as a global heavyweight. The law, however, avoids any articulation of rights for athletes or attention to disputes that might arise between them and their sports association. Human rights do not qualify for competition in the bold new program of Chinese sports.

III. SUMMARY OF THE SPORTS LAW

A. A BRIEF SUMMARY

Premised in the Constitution and Maoist ideological tradition, the Sports Law contains 56 articles in eight chapters. The chapter entitled "General Provisions" lays out basic state policies that confirm the state's commitment to sports as a means of enhancing public health and social development.[55] The next three chapters are devoted to community sports, school sports, and competitive sports.[56] The chapters on community sports and school sports follow closely Mao's ideas of nation-building and mass exercise, focusing on promotion of mass exercise by the state, communities and schools. The chapter on competitive sports, on the other hand, focuses on the organization of competitions, dispute resolution, and a general declaration against doping corruption and gambling. Chapters 5 and 6 concern the role of sports associations and support of sports activities respectively. Besides noting the leading role of the COC in the development and advancement of the Olympics, Chapter 5 assigns the sports associations a more active role in administering sports. The apparent intent is to vest future substantial authority in nongovernmental associations of athletes. Chapter 6 requires central and local

---

Against Human Rights Abuses: China's Bid for the 2000 Olympics, 15 B.C. THIRD WORLD L.J. 141 (1995); Hersh, *IOC Brass Say Chinese Boycott Unlikely*, CHICAGO TRIB., Jan. 4, 1996, at 1.

52 *Id.*

53 KRISTOF & WUDUNN, *supra* note 2, at 162 (citing media account). In a further twist of irony, he was soon dismissed from powerful posts as a Member of the Politburo of the CPC Central Committee and Mayor of Beijing. Citing numerous serious corruption charges, the authorities also put him under criminal investigation. PEOPLE'S DAILY (Overseas ed.), Apr. 27, 1995, at 1.

54 On the prestige of hosting the Games, *see* Ch. 10.

55 Ch. 1, arts. 1–16, the Sports Law, *infra*, Annex.

56 Ch. 2, 3, 4, the Sports Law, *infra*, Annex.

governments to allocate necessary financial sources for sports activities whenever possible and to increase investment when economically feasible. Chapter 7, on legal liabilities, lists general principles dealing with sports-related misdemeanors and crimes such as gambling on sports and drug-taking. The law generally subjects these misdemeanors and crimes to administrative sanctions and criminal investigation, but falls short of setting forth specific penalties for them. Given the special status of the armed forces in China, Chapter 8 provides the Central Military Commission with general authorization to regulate sports activities inside the armed forces.[57] Several provisions of the law merit special attention beyond this brief summary.

B. MASS SPORTS TRAINING

The Sports Law, still conforming to an essentially Maoist-socialist model, provides that the state shall continue to implement the National Fitness Program.[58] The legislation adopts several reforms that an earlier program had recommended: allocating more money for mass sports, training more sports instructors, opening all state-owned sports grounds and facilities to the public, and prohibiting them to be used for any other purpose.[59] Local governments must take measures to implement the program accordingly.[60]

Mass exercise in itself requires only modest funding. The people themselves pay for most of the necessary training to develop basic techniques of such exercises as morning drills, basic tai chi, and simplified wu shu (martial arts).[61] The Sports Law, however, provides technical support of mass exercise in four ways: (1) a ranking system for community sports instructors who are to be paid according to their technical rankings;[62] (2) the construction and maintenance of play-

---

[57] Ch. 8, the Sports Law, *infra*, Annex.

[58] The current program was unveiled just before the NPC's adoption of the Sports Law.

[59] Zou Sicheng, *supra* note 8, at 8–10.

[60] Already, Beijing has undertaken to train 1,000 instructors and 10,000 activists to promote mass sports, to conduct physical examinations for 100,000 adults annually, and to encourage one million residents to exercise daily. Shanghai has already opened all of its sports facilities to the public and is determined to achieve, by the end of this century, such goals of mass sports as encouraging families to own at least one piece of sports equipment; providing exercise sites for communities; and providing daily, on-premises exercise to all students. Several provinces are moving in a similar direction, as required by the State. *Id.; see also* PEOPLE'S DAILY (Overseas ed.), Dec. 22, 1995, at 10; Dec. 29, 1995, at 10.

[61] According to an official report, about one third of the Chinese population regularly participates in varied physical exercises, probably because they are deemed to enhance longevity. Every morning, it is very common for people, regardless of age or sex, to visit nearby parks and playgrounds for exercise. Training courses for physical exercise often attract many people. Zou Sicheng, *Olympic Spirit Spreading in China*, BEIJING REV., Sept. 20–26, 1993, at 22.

[62] Sports Law, art. 11, *infra*, Annex.

grounds for mass sports;[63] (3) special encouragement of students, the elderly and the mentally and physically disabled; and (4) a requirement that schools hold annual games and boost mass sports activities by releasing students for sports activities.[64] These provisions are designed to overcome the underutilization and backwardness of sports facilities and playgrounds.

Ironically, just as the Sports Law and a reinvigoration of governmental commitments to mass sports have emerged, China's market-driven population has become hard pressed to find time for the exercise regimen prescribed by the National Fitness Program.[65] As a result, China perceives that it can gain less from organizing mass sports and more from a Soviet-style emphasis on professional training as a means to global prowess in the sports and political arenas. That is where the money has been going anyway.

C. COMMERCIALIZATION

An important feature of the Chinese Sports Law is that it legalizes and codifies the commercialization of sports as "[a] core of sports reform."[66] Within an otherwise Maoist-socialist framework, the law seeks to establish a modern, Western-style organizational structure, in the hope of creating a profitable sports industry.[67] Although the new commercialization of sports in China cannot yet be compared with Western systems, the legislation nevertheless provides the flexibility to undertake substantial reforms in that direction.[68]

1. Sports Sponsorship

Before the end of the Cultural Revolution, all sports funding was from governmental sources.[69] No sports sponsorships by public or private sources existed.[70] Beginning in 1977, however, China gradually allowed for such sponsorship, first

---

63 Several provisions instruct that land-use plans for any urban area must provide for adequate playgrounds to be used for sports only. Sports Law, art. 41–48, *infra*, Annex.

64 Sports Law, arts. 19, 20, *infra*, Annex.

65 According to Chinese newspapers accounts, young people consider that regular exercise, as prescribed by the National Fitness Program, is a luxury for retired people, rather than for young people busy making money. Unfortunately, too, much sports equipment remains a luxury for ordinary working people.

66 ISSUES, *supra* note 3, at 7, 11. The proclaimed purpose of establishing a sizable sports industry is to overcome the shortage of sports funds necessary for improving the prowess of Chinese athletes. *Id.*, at 19; PEOPLE'S DAILY (Overseas ed.), Dec. 27, 1995, at 6.

67 The reforms that were initiated primarily to overcome the shortage of sports funding have evolved more in the direction of commercialization, which the State now promotes. Zou Sicheng, *supra* note 8, at 8; ISSUES, *supra* note 3, at 18–19.

68 ISSUES, *supra* note 3, at 11.

69 J. RIORDAN, SPORTS, POLITICS AND COMMUNISM 5 (1991).

70 Zou Sicheng, *supra* note 8, at 9.

from public work-units, then from private enterprises as well. Sports sponsorships have caught on quickly as a marketing tool among both foreign and major Chinese companies.[71] They now spend millions of dollars annually on sponsorships,[72] each costing between $1,000 and $100,000.[73] Nowadays, whether hosting a tennis match in Beijing, a soccer tournament in Chengdu, or a regional athletic event such as the Asian Games, China's sports stadiums are festooned with the names and logos of products ranging from Marlboro and Salem cigarettes to M&M candies.[74] Citizens are declared to have a right to invest in sports.[75] The Sports Law encourages these developments but does not provide any effective regulatory guidance.

2. Club System

China's emerging sports structure relies on a new club system whose impetus has been the need to equip athletes with necessary funding for their facilities, training, and material incentives.[76] The China Soccer Association initiated the club system and a professional league, with the establishment in 1992 of the "Sichuan Nande Soccer Club" in Chengdu.[77] Gamely selling shares in an untested market, Sichuan Nande and other clubs achieved surprising success. Soccer and soccer profits boomed in a little more than a year.[78] The sport soon replaced table tennis in popularity, as reflected in both match attendance and television viewing.[79] The

---

[71] Lam, *Into the Big League*, CHINESE BUS. REV., Nov. 1994, at 41.

[72] *Id.* Cleveland-based International Management Group (IMG), one of the pioneer agents of sports sponsorship in China, estimated that sponsorship money channeled to the PRC in 1994 was at least 200 percent above the previous year. The company predicted similar growth for 1995. *Id.*

[73] Lam, *supra* note 71, at 43.

[74] *Id.*

[75] Sports Law, arts. 3, 42, *infra*, Annex. In explaining this provision, Minister Wu assured the NPC as it reviewed the draft Sports Law that such investment tallied with state practice elsewhere. Wu Shaozu, *supra* note 25. The SPCSC, in a document distributed nation-wide to promote the Sports Law, confirmed that this reform put the development of China's sports system on the right track. ISSUES, *supra* note 3, at 22.

[76] China had been frustrated for many years in its efforts, without a market mechanism, to develop soccer as a major sport of obvious international importance. Tian Bo, *Reform to Turn Round Soccer*, BEIJING REV., Sept. 6–13, 1993, at 31–33.

[77] Lou Linwei, *Reforms in Soccer*, BEIJING REV., Dec. 28, 1992–Jan 3, 1993, at 36. The Nande Soccer Club is jointly sponsored by the Nande Economic Group, a well-known private enterprise, the Sichuan Provincial Sports Commission and the Information Research Institute of the State Sports Commission. The club is an economic entity with legal status and independent accounting. It has a registered capital of 10 million yuan (about $1.2 million), and allocates 500,000 yuan (about $60,000) each year for training, competition and awards, staff salaries, and bonuses. This amount does not include any income from the club's commercial activities.

[78] *Id.*

[79] Lam, *supra* note 71, at 41.

Marlboro Soccer League alone managed to raise more than a million dollars, which was then distributed among all teams in the new league.[80] Club soccer has led to interest in commercialized club systems for other major sports such as basketball, volleyball, swimming and table tennis.[81] The Sports Law recognizes the club system as a revenue-saving alternative to the traditional state monopoly.[82]

3. New Functions for Sports Associations

Before the Sports Law, China's sports associations were essentially administrative units within state sports organs. Limitations on the use of their funding greatly restrained their work.[83] Under the law, sports associations, in effect, are granted more managerial responsibilities and independence, including the power to raise funds from private sources, and the capacity to earn a profit by organizing their own commercial events.[84] Specific rules will be necessary to implement this grant of authority to the associations. The law stipulates only that they shall function, each according to its own rules. They are thus left to make their own rules in accordance with the law and under SPCSC guidance.[85]

D. PRIVILEGES AND RESPONSIBILITIES

The Sports Law reaffirms long-existing special privileges for athletes. These include a ranking system,[86] which, on the former Soviet model, grants allowances and bonuses according to ranking, and ensures college enrollment and job security.[87] These privileges, along with strengthened recruitment efforts,[88] are intended to improve China's future athletic performance.

The legislation strictly prohibits the use of banned drugs and therapies in sports activities, as well as gambling on sports events.[89] Governmental drug-testing

---

[80] *Id.* at 43.

[81] Beginning in 1995, shortly before enactment of the Sports Law, the SPCSC began to aggressively promote a comprehensive commercialization of sports. Zou Sicheng, *supra* note 8, at 9.

[82] Sports Law, art. 3, *infra*, Annex.

[83] ISSUES, *supra* note 3, at 7, 9.

[84] Wu Shaozu, *supra* note 24, at 15; ISSUES, *supra* note 3, at 11, 18.

[85] Sports Law, art. 36, *infra*, Annex; ISSUES, *supra* note 3, at 11.

[86] Sports Law, art. 30, *infra*, Annex.

[87] *Id.*, art. 28.

[88] Experienced scouts now routinely seek out young children whose physiques indicate athletic potential. The most promising children are then sent to special sports schools, usually away from home, for full-time or all but full-time training. Sometimes, the chosen few live with their coaches. KRISTOF & WUDUNN, *supra* note 2, at 374–75.

[89] Sports Law, art. 34, *infra*, Annex.

institutions are required to conduct the necessary tests according to the rules and procedures of the IOC and international federations.[90] Sports associations are vested with the authority to apply sanctions against doping and gambling.[91] This decentralized approach is somewhat less rigorous than had been expected, though state officials will be subjected to administrative sanctions if doping occurs within their ambit of supervision.[92] Other prohibited conduct—such as gambling, fraud, bribery and corruption, destruction of state sports property, embezzlement, and violation of public order during sports activities—not only will be subject to administrative sanctions but will incur criminal liability under the Sports Law.[93]

E. DISPUTE RESOLUTION

Article 33 of the Sports Law makes clear that " [a]ny disputes arising in competitive sports shall be subject to mediation and arbitration by organs established for sports arbitration. Rules governing the establishment of organs for sports arbitration and the scope of their mandates shall be adopted by the State Council."[94] This provision for non-adjudicative dispute resolution is both a reiteration of traditional Chinese methods and an up-to-date reliance on special arbitration organs to do the job. Presumably, sports associations would conduct the mediation. The Chinese have confirmed that non-governmental, that is, private organizations would be responsible for arbitrating disputes.[95] One possible conflict-of-interest problem is, of course, that if such NGOs are the sports associations themselves or are closely related to them, the same bodies that apply sanctions would arbitrate disputes brought by or against them.

IV. IMPLEMENTATION OF THE LAW

A. THE 1996 AND 2008 OLYMPIC GAMES

The first test of the law was the 1996 Olympic Games in Atlanta. Although too little time had lapsed since adoption of the law to judge its effect on the caliber of athletic performance, it can be said that the law had no effect on China's public relations. Instead, China missed an opportunity to improve its post-Tiananmen Square image. It sent a large delegation to the Atlanta Games, led by senior sports officials, including Minister Wu Shaozu and Deputy Minister Yuan

---

90 *Id.*

91 Sports Law, art. 50, *infra*, Annex.

92 *Id.* The Sports Law does not, however, spell out what kind of administrative sanctions may be imposed.

93 The Sports Law, arts. 49, 51, 52, and 53, *infra*, Annex. The SPCSC expected that more than fifty laws and regulations will be eventually implement the Sports Law. Jiang & Liu, *supra* note 4, at 14. *See also* text at note 99, *infra*.

94 Sports Law, art. 33, *infra*, Annex.

95 SHANGHAI STAR, Sept. 1, 1995.

Weimin of the SPCSC. During the Games and immediately afterward, the officials blamed the Atlanta Organizing Committee for poor administration, anti-Chinese bias among judges, the absence of good Chinese food, a faulty bus system, and anti-Chinese comments by television commentators.[96] What makes the Chinese complaints ring somewhat hollow is that as early as 1993, they had warned the United States that they might lodge a protest at a later date in "revenge"[97] for Beijing's failure to secure an invitation from the IOC to host the 2000 Games. However true the deficiencies and insults in Atlanta may have been, the Chinese government certainly did not win any medals for its comments, nor did it help to improve its international image by these comments. Instead, the Chinese government encouraged continuing skepticism about its sensitivity to the etiquette of sports diplomacy and diplomatic sportsmanship.

Since the Atlanta Games the Chinese government and Chinese NOC have skillfully conducted a public-relations campaign to elicit support for Beijing's successful bid to host the 2008 Olympic Games and overcome China's reputation for doping and corruption of referees. The result has been China's new role as a leader in global sports.

B. REGULATIONS

The legislation is just the beginning of China's efforts to regulate athletic activity. The SPCSC has drafted regulations governing sports arbitration, the construction and maintenance of sports facilities, the protection of athletic trademarks, and the management of commercial sports. The declared goal of the SPCSC is a full-fledged legal regime for sports.[98]

C. DOPING, CORRUPTION OF REFEREES AND VIOLENCE

Since enactment of the Sports Law, the Chinese sports program has been tainted by several doping controversies that have required the withdrawal of Chinese athletes from international competition, sanctions against athletes, and stricter regulatory implementation of the law.[99] The Anti-Doping Regulations of

---

96 *Asian "Big 3" Complain, Others shine in Atlanta*, Japan Economic Newswire, Aug. 5, 1996, available in Lexis, Nexis Library, JEN File.

97 In a television interview broadcast in Australia last week, a Chinese Olympic official, Zhang Baifa, said that if Beijing were passed over, "We could, frankly, boycott their Atlanta Games in 1996." And he added, "If our bid fails, we could write to Congress to protest about their interference and justify our revenge." Riding, *With Politics Again at Center Stage, the I.O.C. Must Choose a Site for 2000*, N.Y. TIMES, Sept. 20, 1993, at B9.

98 Wei Qun, *Zhongguo Tiyu zhi "Sihua," (The Four Modernizations of Chinese Sports)*, PEOPLE'S DAILY (Overseas ed.) Jan. 5, 1996, at 10.

99 *See* State Physical Culture General Administration & China Olympic Committee, CHINA ANTI-DOPING AFTER TEN YEARS (1990–99) (2002), *reported in* Guojia Tiyu Zongju he Zhongguo Aoweihui Fabiao "Zhongguo Fan Xingfengji Shinian" (State Physical Culture General Administration and COC Publishes "China Anti-Doping After Ten Years"), *available on internet at* china.com.cn; *see also* Ch. 7, *supra* note 33.

2004[100] are designed to strengthen Temporary Regulations published in 1995.

The Chinese football (soccer) program has also been rocked by a series of scandals involving bribery of referees ("black whistles"), particularly in 2001,[101] and acts of spectator violence ("hooliganism") in the stadium.[102] Strong measures have been taken to apply administrative and criminal sanctions against those responsible, including entire teams.[103]

V. CONCLUSION

The theme of China's Sports Law is one of organization. It is an old theme, one might say a Maoist theme. What the law does, primarily, is to modernize and codify well-established rules and procedures within an established framework of bureaucratic control. But the law is innovative in providing for sports associations and clubs as well as sanctions against doping and other threats to fair play. The P.R.C.'s first sports law is thus a hybrid of the old and the new.

Fundamentally, the Chinese have clung to a Maoist interpretation of the role of physical culture in society and a heavy reliance on administrative discretion to govern sports activity. Much of the law therefore reads like a restatement of superseded Soviet or East German practice. The legislative style is dated and the provisions are state-centered. Vaguely expressed responsibilities, prohibitions and sanctions provide very little actual check on administrative discretion. Even in its innovative provisions for more or less private sports associations, the law confines their activities to "appropriate roles,"[104] which are to be defined, presumably, by the State.

It is noteworthy that the Sports Law rejects any recognition of the rights of athletes, except to provide financial, educational and other privileges and incentives to them. In this important respect, China has chosen to participate in a global trend toward avoiding the courtroom in disputes involving the interests of athletes. Specifically, Article 33 of the Sports Law prescribes mediation and arbitration by special, presumably non-governmental organs to be established for the purpose. In taking this traditional and yet progressive approach, China may better avoid the risks and complexity of dispute avoidance and resolution that so beset the sports arena in other countries. On the other hand, China's apparent unwillingness to adjudicate the rights of individual athletes denies them an appropriate remedy for

---

[100] *See* Anti-Doping Regulations, *supra* note 49.

[101] *See Soccer Nightmare*, SHANGHAI STAR, Jan. 17, 2002, at 1.

[102] *See* Xiao Yu, *Soccer Hooliganism Plays Havoc*, CHINA DAILY, July 24, 2000, at 7.

[103] *See Soccer Team Punished for Riot*, CHINA DAILY, Mar. 29, 2002, at 3; *Soccer Nightmare, supra* note 101.

[104] Sports Law, arts. 37, 39, *infra*, Annex.

the most serious breaches of fairness and justice that more informal methods of dispute resolution do not always rectify.

The law is progressive in restructuring Chinese sports and creating sports incentives through sponsorships and other market mechanisms, a product of China's Market-Leninism. It is also a product of our times. China seeks to deter the problems of doping, bribery and violence, as well as the more traditional practice of gambling on sports activities. It also seeks to establish a comprehensive structure of sports sponsorships and clubs. The growing commercialization of Chinese sports and the new access of Chinese athletes to worldly temptations justify these fresh approaches to national sports management. China also appreciates the role of sports in overcoming tarnished images of its government and in bidding for greater leadership in global affairs. In sum, the law encourages a large-scale, on-going program of sports development that China hopes will serve her larger interests. The runup to the 2008 Olympic Games will be a test of the efficacy of the Sports Law. China has truly entered the modern sports arena under a banner of many colors.

ANNEX

SPORTS LAW OF THE PEOPLE'S REPUBLIC OF CHINA

(Adopted by the Fifteenth Session of the Standing Committee of the Eighth National People's Congress on August 29, 1995)

Table of Contents:

Chapter 1 General Provisions

Article 1. This law is formulated in accordance with the Constitution for the purpose of promoting the cause of sports, enhancing the health of the people, raising the level of sports activities, and accelerating the construction of socialist material and spiritual civilization.

Article 2. The State shall promote the cause of sports, carry out mass sports activities, and enhance the health of the whole nation. All efforts concerning the cause of sports shall be based upon the promotion of body-building activities throughout the nation, shall combine the popularization of sports with the improvement of standards, and shall accelerate the coordinated development of various sports activities.

Article 3. The State shall ensure that sports facilitate economic development, the development of the national defense, and social development. The cause of sports shall be included in national economic and social development programs.

The State shall promote the reform of the system of sports management. The State shall encourage enterprises and institutions, social organizations and citizens to establish and support the cause of sports.

Article 4. The administrative organ responsible for sports within the State Council shall administer nation-wide efforts concerning sports. The other ministries of the State Council shall administer this work within their respective areas of authority.

The administrative agencies responsible for sports within all local people's governments above the county level or the agencies authorized by the people's government at the same level shall administer local efforts concerning sports within their administrative competence.

Article 5. The State shall provide special support for sports activities of young people so as to improve their physical and mental health.

Article 6. The State shall promote the cause of sports in the regions where minority nationalities reside, and train athletic talent among minority nationalities.

Article 7. The State shall promote physical education and sports science research, apply advanced and practical findings from sports science and technology, and base the development of the cause of sports on science and technology.

Article 8. The State shall award work units and individuals for their contributions to sports.

Article 9. The State shall encourage international sports exchanges. International sports exchanges shall uphold the principles of independence, equality and mutual benefits, and reciprocal respects. They shall also safeguard state sovereignty and dignity and abide by the international agreements that the People's Republic of China has concluded or entered into.

Chapter 2 Community (Social) Sports

Article 10. The State shall encourage citizens to participate in community sports activities to enhance their health.

Community sports activities shall be amateur, voluntary, small-scale and diverse, suitable to local conditions, and in line with science and mores.

Article 11. The State shall carry out a program for the health of the whole nation, implement sports exercise standards, and monitor the health of the people.

The State shall maintain a technical ranking system for community sports instructors. Community sports instructors shall direct community sports activities.

Article 12. All local governments shall provide necessary conditions for citizens to participate in community sports activities, and support and assist the development of mass sports activities.

In cities, grass-root organizations of communities such as residential committees shall be given free rein in organizing residents to conduct their sports activities.

In rural areas, village committees and other grass-root cultural and sports organizations shall be given free rein in developing sports activities suitable to the special conditions there.

Article 13. State organs, enterprises and institutions shall carry out a variety of sports activities and hold mass sports contests.

Article 14. Trade unions and other social organizations shall organize sports activities in accordance with their distinctive functions.

Article 15. The State shall encourage and support the development, processing and promotion of traditional national and folk sports.

Article 16. The entire society shall ensure and encourage participation by the elderly and handicapped in sports activities. The people's government at all levels shall adopt measures to provide facilities for the elderly and handicapped to participate in sports activities.

Chapter 3 School Sports

Article 17. Administrative organs responsible for education and schools administrations shall make physical education a part of schooling, in order to cultivate students morally, intellectually, and physically.

Article 18. Schools shall offer physical education courses and include physical education as a required course that every student shall take and pass.

Schools shall provide conditions to organize mentally and physically handicapped students for sports activities suitable to their capabilities.

Article 19. Schools shall implement national physical exercise standards and shall ensure that each student will have time for sports activities at school.

Article 20. Schools shall organize various extracurricular sports activities, carry out extracurricular training and athletic contests, and hold school games each academic year according to their respective capabilities.

Article 21. In accordance with relevant regulations of the State, schools shall employ qualified sports instructors and provide them with extra benefits related to their particular employment.

Article 22. In accordance with standards set by the educational organ of the State Council, schools shall provide playgrounds, facilities and equipment.

School playgrounds must be used for sports activities only. They shall not be used for any other purpose.

Article 23. Schools shall set up a system to monitor the health of students. Administrative organs responsible for education, sports and health shall strengthen supervision of the health of students.[1]

Chapter 4 Competitive Sports

Article 24. The State shall accelerate the development of competitive sports and encourage athletes to improve their level of technical competence, so as to achieve excellence in athletic contests and win honors for the nation.

Article 25. The State shall encourage and support the promotion of amateur sports training to prepare a reserve of outstanding sports talent.

Article 26. The athletes and athletic teams selected for major national and international games shall be based on merit, to be determined by fair competition. The administrative organ responsible for sports within the State Council shall establish detailed rules.

Article 27. Athletes must be strictly trained and administered in a scientific and moral way. Athletes must be educated about morality and discipline as well as patriotism, collectivism, and socialism.

Article 28. The State shall provide top athletes with preferential treatment in employment and enrollment in schools.

Article 29. Each national association of an individual sport shall administer the registration of its athletes. Registered athletes may participate in athletic contests and may transfer between sports teams in accordance with regulations established by the administrative organ responsible for sports within the State Council.

Article 30. The State shall maintain a technical ranking system for athletes and a technical ranking system for umpires and coaches.

Article 31. The State shall administer athletic contests in accordance with the status and characteristics of the particular contest.

National Games that include all sports events shall be administered by the administrative organ responsible for sports within the State Council alone or together with concerned organizations.

---

[1] These organs are, respectively, the State Education Commission, the SPCSC, and the Ministry of Health in the central government, and their counterparts at local levels.

National Games in each sport shall be administered by the respective national association for each sport.

Administrative rules for comprehensive athletic contests at the local level and for athletic contests for each individual sport shall be established by local governments.

Article 32. The State shall maintain a system of examining and approving national records of athletic contests. National records shall be affirmed by the administrative organ responsible for sports within the State Council.

Article 33. Any disputes arising in competitive sports shall be subject to mediation and arbitration by a sports arbitration body.

Rules governing the establishment of a sports arbitration body and the scope of its mandate shall be adopted by the State Council.

Article 34. Athletic contests shall follow the principle of fair competition. Organizers, athletes, coaches and umpires shall abide by sports morality and shall be forbidden from resorting to deception or engaging in improper practices for selfish ends.[2]

The use of banned drugs and therapies shall be strictly forbidden. The testing institute for banned drugs shall conduct strict tests for banned drugs and therapies.

All work-units and individuals shall be strictly forbidden to engage in gambling on athletic contests.

Article 35. The names, emblems, flags, lucky symbols and other trademarks designed for major Games held inside China shall be protected according to relevant state regulations.

Chapter 5 Sports Associations

Article 36. The State shall encourage and support sport associations in organizing and carrying out sports activities according to their own rules and in advancing the development of the cause of sports.

Article 37. Sports associations at all levels are mass sports organizations for linking and uniting athletes and other people involved in the cause of sports. Sports associations shall play their appropriate roles in promoting sports.

---

[2] This provision, together with Article 51, serves as the basis for claims of bribery or corruption.

Article 38. The China Olympic Committee is an organization which is primarily responsible for developing and advancing the Olympic Movement. It represents China in international Olympic affairs.

Article 39. Associations of sports science are mass academic organizations of workers engaged in sports science and technology. These associations shall play their appropriate roles in promoting sports science and technology.

Article 40. Sports associations for individual sports shall be responsible for popularizing and improving their respective individual sports, and for representing China in related international sport federations.

Chapter 6 Supporting Conditions

Article 41. All people's governments above the county level shall include an expenditure for the cause of sports and a fund for development of the sports infrastructure in their respective financial budgets, as well as investment plans for construction of the infrastructure, and shall gradually increase investment in sports to the extent that the national economy allows.

Article 42. The State shall encourage enterprises, institutions and social organizations to raise funds by themselves for the promotion of the cause of sports, and encourage organizations and individuals to help finance and sponsor the cause of sports.

Article 43. The concerned organs of the State shall strengthen the management and supervision of sports funds. No organization or individual shall be allowed to divert or embezzle any part of these funds.

Article 44. All local people's governments above the county level shall strengthen and supervise commercial sports, such as body-building and athletic contests, in according with State regulations.

Article 45. All local people's governments above the county level, in accordance with the State regulation concerning land-use distribution for urban public sports facilities, shall include urban public sports facilities in plans for urban construction and in the general plan for land use, and allocate these facilities rationally and in a uniform manner.

City administrations shall include sports facilities in their urban construction plans as part of their arrangements for zoning enterprises, schools, streets and residential areas.

Administrations of towns, minority towns, and townships shall gradually build and improve sports facilities consistent with their levels of economic development.

Article 46. Public sports facilities shall be kept open so as to facilitate the masses in their enjoyment of sports activities, and shall provide preferential treatment to students, the elderly and handicapped, in order to expand the use of these sports facilities.

No organization or individual shall be allowed to wrongfully appropriate or damage public sports equipment and facilities. Permission must be obtained from organs responsible for sports administration and construction planning if sports facilities need to be temporarily taken under special circumstances, but these facilities shall be timely returned for normal use. Before a playground may be transformed into any other use according to urban zoning plans, a new playground shall be built on newly selected land as a substitute, in accordance with pertinent State regulations.

Article 47. Sports equipment and appliances for national and international athletic contests shall be inspected and approved by the institutions appointed by the administrative organ responsible for sports within the State Council.

Article 48. The State shall promote specialized physical education and establish various sports colleges or sports departments in ordinary colleges, in order to train professionals in fields of sports, sports-related training, teaching, scientific research, management, and mass sports activities.

The State shall encourage enterprises, institutions, social organizations and citizens to conduct specialized physical education in accordance with law.

Chapter 7 Legal Liabilities

Article 49. Violations of sports etiquette and rules in athletic contests, such as fraud and deception, shall be punished by sports associations in accordance with their respective rules; administrative sanctions shall be applied in accordance with the law to State employees who are directly responsible for violations.

Article 50. Those who use banned drugs and therapies in sports activities shall be sanctioned by sports associations in accordance with their respective rules, as well as by public security organs in accordance with the Provisions for Sanctions to Maintain Public Order.

Article 51. Public security organs assisted by administrative organs responsible for sports shall stop those who illegally engage in wagers on athletic contests, and the public security organs shall punish them in accordance with the Provisions for Sanctions to Maintain Public Order.

During athletic contests, those who bribe, defraud, or organize gambling activity of a criminal nature shall be investigated for criminal liability in accordance with the law.

Article 52. Those who wrongfully appropriate or damage public sports equipment and facilities shall be ordered by administrative organs responsible for sports to correct their wrongdoing within a specific time. They shall also bear civil liability in accordance with the law.

Such behavior, insofar as it violates the Provisions for Sanctions to Maintain Public Order, shall be sanctioned accordingly; if the behavior constitutes a crime, it shall be investigated for criminal liability in accordance with the law.

Article 53. During athletic events, those who pick quarrels, make trouble, or disturb public order shall be criticized, educated and prohibited; if they violate the rules for the management of public order, they shall be sanctioned by public security organs in accordance with the Provisions for Sanctions to Maintain Public Order; if they commit crimes, they shall be investigated for criminal liability in accordance with the law.

Article 54. Those who violate state financial and accounting regulations, or divert or embezzle sports funds shall be ordered to return the diverted or embezzled funds by their supervising organs. Those in a managerial position who are directly responsible and others who are also directly responsible, shall be subject to administrative sanctions in accordance with the law. If their violations constitute crimes, they shall be investigated for criminal liability in accordance with the law.

Chapter 8 Supplementary Provisions

Article 55. Detailed rules for carrying out sports activities inside the armed forces shall be established by the Central Military Commission in accordance with this law.

Article 56. This law shall take effect on October 1, 1995.

TABLE OF CASES

INDEX